DICTATORS, DEMOCRACY, AND AMERICAN PUBLIC CULTURE

D1529127

DICTATORS, DEMOCRACY, AND AMERICAN PUBLIC CULTURE

ENVISIONING THE TOTALITARIAN ENEMY, 1920s-1950s

BENJAMIN L. ALPERS

The University of North Carolina Press   Chapel Hill & London

Manufactured in the United States of America
Set in Charter and Champion types
by Tseng Information Systems, Inc.

Chapter 6 appeared previously in slightly different form in
Benjamin L. Alpers, "This Is the Army: Imagining a Democratic
Military in World War II," *Journal of American History* 85, no. 1
(June 1998): 129–63; reprinted with permission.

The paper in this book meets the guidelines for permanence
and durability of the Committee on Production Guidelines for
Book Longevity of the Council on Library Resources.

Library of Congress Cataloging-in-Publication Data
Alpers, Benjamin Leontief, 1965–
Dictators, democracy, and American public culture :
envisioning the totalitarian enemy, 1920s–1950s /
Benjamin L. Alpers.
    p. cm. — (Cultural studies of the United States)
Includes bibliographical references and index.
ISBN 0-8078-2750-9 (cloth : alk. paper)
ISBN 0-8078-5416-6 (pbk. : alk. paper)
1. Dictatorship.   2. Democracy.   3. Mass media—
United States—Influence.   4. Public opinion—
United States.   I. Title.   II. Series.
JC495.A46   2003
321.9—dc21
2002009193

cloth 07 06 05 04 03   5 4 3 2 1
paper 07 06 05 04 03   5 4 3 2 1

To Karin Schutjer,

Noah Schutjer Alpers, and

Mira Schutjer Alpers

CONTENTS

ACKNOWLEDGMENTS

I am deeply indebted to the many people who have helped this project reach completion: to Daniel Rodgers, my graduate adviser, and the rest of my doctoral committee, Richard Challener, Arno Mayer, and Alan Brinkley; to Gary Gerstle, without whom I would never have become a twentieth-century historian; to Joan Rubin, Bill Jordan, Tony Grafton, and Karen Merrill, who each taught me much about what it means to be a historian and a scholar; to Phil Katz, Kevin Downing, Darryl Peterkin, John Earle, Leslie Tuttle, and many other fellow graduate students whose intellect, wit, and fellowship will always be with me; to Jennifer Delton, Andrew Cohen, and Rebecca Plante, with whom I shared many ideas and hope to continue to do so; to David Nord and my other editors and readers at the *Journal of American History,* in which Chapter 6 appeared in slightly different form; to Don B. Morlan and Abbott Gleason for bibliographic insights; to Randy Lewis, who, in the final stages of this project, has been an indispensable reader and an even better friend.

Thanks must also go to the many librarians and archivists who have made my research possible: Rosemary Hanes and the other librarians at the Motion Picture Section of the Library of Congress; the staff of the National Archives' Motion Picture, Sound, and Video Branch; Robert Denham of the Studebaker National Museum in South Bend, Indiana; Elizabeth Carroll-Horrocks of the American Philosophical Society Library; the librarians at Houghton Library at Harvard University; the wonderful staff of Princeton's Firestone Library; and the many librarians at the Universities of Missouri and Oklahoma.

I am grateful for the material generosity of the Woodrow Wilson National Fellowship Foundation (which, through the Mellon Fellowships in the Humanities, the Princeton Wilson Fellows, and Princeton's Mellon post-enrollment dissertation fellowships, funded my work for four and one-half academic years and two summers), the Eisenhower World Affairs Institute, and Princeton University.

I wish to thank all of those who have made the University of Oklahoma's Honors College such an extraordinary place in which to work: to Steve Gillon for laying the groundwork for a wonderful scholarly environment and to all my colleagues and former colleagues at the Honors College for making that environment a reality. I also deeply appreciate the encouragement of my many colleagues in history and in film and video studies at the University of Oklahoma.

Finally, thanks go to my family. To my parents, Paul and Svetlana Alpers, who have both been avid, if not unbiased, readers of this manuscript. Their emotional support, even in periods of difficulty for them, has helped sustain me. Each has taught me more than I consciously know about what it means to be an intellectual. To my late grandfather, Wassily Leontief, who knew and worked with many of the people who appear in this book, and to my grandmother, Estelle Leontief. To my brother Nick Alpers, my sister-in-law Kati Sipp, and my niece Lina. Finally, my love and thanks go to my wife Karin Schutjer, my son Noah Schutjer Alpers, and my daughter Mira Schutjer Alpers. They make my life a wonderful adventure, and it is to them that I dedicate this book.

INTRODUCTION

This book is the history of a conventional wisdom. For much of the twentieth century, Americans understood democracy, and their own political identity as Americans, largely in opposition to modern dictatorship. Americans couched many of their fiercest political struggles in the language of opposition to dictatorship, whether engaging in the Popular Front's campaigns against fascism or the second Red Scare's campaigns against communism, whether arguing against Jim Crow laws as akin to Nazi racial policies or opposing the civil rights movement as a tyrannical imposition of centralized authority, whether fighting against Hitler in World War II or against Saddam Hussein in the Gulf War. Even President Bill Clinton, in his largely unremarkable second inaugural address, boldly claimed for his first administration the ultimate foreign policy success: "For the first time in all of history, more people on this planet live under democracy than under dictatorship."

Despite their central role in our political culture, American understandings of dictatorship have received surprisingly little scholarly attention. Like much conventional wisdom, the place of dictatorship in American political culture has become naturalized: dictatorship simply *is* democracy's opposite, though all would probably acknowledge that there have been heated battles over what counts as a dictatorship and what we should consider a democracy. However, there is nothing necessary about the peculiar and central role that dictatorship has played in the political life of this country. In the late twentieth century Americans treated dictatorship and democracy as the only two political options available to a society, as Clinton's claim suggests. Yet for most of the history of Western political thought, dictatorship and democracy were regarded as only two of many possible forms of political organization—among them, tyranny, aristocracy, and monarchy. Although dictatorship and democracy were certainly distinct from one another, they were not complete opposites. In the political thought of the ancient world, dictatorship was a temporary measure that could be adopted by any polity in times of emergency, especially war. This classical notion was invoked even in the United States to justify the policies of President Abraham Lincoln during the Civil War and President Woodrow Wilson during World War I. Some nineteenth- and early-twentieth-century political theory suggested yet another relationship between dictatorship and democracy. Marxist social democrats embraced the notion of a dictatorship of the proletariat as not only compatible with true democracy, but also a necessary step toward achieving it.

Throughout the twentieth century, American understandings of dictatorship were rooted in interpretations of events abroad, especially in Europe. Of course, many non-European nations have had dictatorships, and these have been of tremendous concern to U.S. observers. However, the regimes of Europe have been the models for American imaginings of dictatorship for a variety of reasons. First, Europe has been the crucible of modern political ideologies. The French Revolution in many ways pioneered modern dictatorship. More recently, Italian Fascism, German Nazism, and Soviet Communism—each a product of Europe—have dominated American understandings of the phenomenon and have underlaid many dictatorships elsewhere in the world. Second, Europe has always loomed larger than other regions in the self-understandings of American elites, whose forebears tended to come from Europe. Although Europe has often been considered to be a cultural exemplar, politically the Old World has often been seen not as a model, but as a warning, a sign of what could happen to the United States if it were somehow to stumble. The modern European dictatorships easily fit into this line of thought in ways that non-European dictatorships never have. Americans have variously feared that the nation might descend the path taken by Germany in 1933 or Russia in 1917; few if any Americans worried in the 1930s that the United States would become like Japan or, more recently, Iraq. These non-European regimes are understood as utterly Other, their danger entirely external (though, as with Japanese Americans during World War II, fear of that danger has led many Americans to deny others their rights as U.S. citizens).

In part as a result of the importance of events overseas, American views of dictatorship exhibit another common quality of conventional wisdom: they have been defined largely by a series of conversations among a heterogeneous set of cultural elites. By labeling something a "conventional wisdom," we acknowledge its constructed or *conventional* quality. And when we talk of conventional wisdom, at least in its current usage, we are usually referring to the conventions of the political elite. A comparatively small group of men and women has been in a position to interpret events abroad to American mass audiences and suggest an answer to the question of dictatorship. This group has included, among others, professors, policymakers, speechwriters, presidents, filmmakers, novelists, and business leaders. In this work I refer to these people collectively as "cultural producers." I use the phrase not to reduce the various and complicated social roles of the people grouped under this term, but to indicate a social space that was shared by these individuals and denied to others. The production of works about dictatorship in American public culture was limited to a fairly select group of people. Whether by virtue of having special access to one of the mass media (screenwriters or novelists), of having expert status (German refugee scholars, political scientists, or U.S. government officials), or of having both (foreign correspondents), these cultural producers have enjoyed bully pulpits from which to instruct the broader public about dictatorship. Their perspectives were not unquestioned but they were, in the Gramscian sense, hegemonic. They have profoundly shaped American political culture in the mid-to-late twentieth century. They have defined what views were "mainstream" and what views were "extreme."

The history of this conventional wisdom begins in the 1920s. The press praised Mussolini for single-handedly bringing order to Italy's political life. Many saw a similar quality in Stalin's first Five-Year Plan. In the early years of the Great Depression, dictatorship was an important political fantasy for a heterogeneous group of Americans. Although most Americans were not attracted to dictatorship, for some it seemed necessary in light of the socio-economic crisis, either as a permanent, more efficient solution to the problems of modern life or, in the classical sense, as a temporary measure to put democracy back on course. *Barron's,* the conservative business weekly, hoped in February 1933 that the newly elected and yet-to-be-inaugurated Franklin Delano Roosevelt might act as a "semi-dictator" to save America from social chaos. Liberal filmmaker Walter Wanger produced *Gabriel over the White House* (1933), a political fantasy in which a president solves the country's problems by becoming a divinely inspired dictator. The Communist Party (CP), in its ideologically militant "Third Period," declared that capitalist, bourgeois democracy was already doomed and that the only real political choice was between a communist dictatorship of the proletariat and a fascist dictatorship of the bourgeoisie.

By the second half of the 1930s this had changed. Dictatorship became the evil against which nearly everyone in American political life struggled. Congress of Industrial Organizations (CIO) leader John L. Lewis declared in 1936 that the greatest question facing American workers was "whether the working population of this country shall have the voice in determining their destiny or whether they shall serve as indentured servants for a financial and economic dictatorship that would shamelessly exploit our resources."[1] The Popular Front strategy, adopted by many liberals, radicals, and the Communist Party, sought to organize all political effort around the struggle between democracy and fascism. Although it is today correctly remembered as a document entirely honored in the breach, the Soviet Union's Constitution of 1936 formally recognized political and civil liberties and thus enabled Communists and the much larger group of those generally sympathetic to Russia to argue that the Soviet Union itself was well on its way to embracing democracy. Their opponents on the anti-Stalinist left and liberal anticommunists argued that the USSR was a dictatorship as brutal as Nazi Germany. Toward the end of the decade, the Roosevelt administration, interested in nudging the country toward intervention in Europe, backed what Leo Ribuffo has called the "Brown Scare," raising fears that America was threatened by a Nazi "fifth column." Anti-interventionists, on the other hand, argued that U.S. involvement in the European war might lead to dictatorship. Republicans saw signs of dictatorship in FDR's 1940 quest for a third term and donned buttons that read, "Third Reich. Third International. Third Term."[2] In an interventionist tract, published just before the collapse of the Nazi-Soviet Pact, William Dow Boutwell, head of the Division of Radio, Publications, and Education in the U.S. Office of Education, captured the situation effectively:

> American leaders are united in their distaste for totalitarian governments. Like President Coolidge's minister who was "against sin," they are, with almost no exception, "against totalitarianism." Yet each finds a different "sin" in dictatorship. The men who want wider freedom for corporate business fear totalitarian "collectivism." Writers, poets, artists are against dictators because dictators restrict freedom of expression. To labor leaders the liquidation of unions is the greatest threat. Religious leaders make the issue a holy war. Educator, farmer, scientist, merchant—each finds his central faith and interest imperiled, his own ox gored. They are all against totalitarian rule.[3]

Boutwell's statement captures another aspect of the growing conventional wisdom about dictatorship: by the late 1930s the word "totalitarian" and its substantive sibling "totalitarianism" were regularly applied to the European dictatorships.

Understanding the idea of totalitarianism as a product—and an important component—of 1930s U.S. political culture forces us to reconsider that political culture. To a great extent, our understandings of the political culture of the thirties have been products of a scholarly continuation of many political battles of that tumultuous decade. The era has been a favorite hunting ground for those in search of a usable past. The Popular Front (understood either as a movement led by the Communist Party or as a broad-based coalition of the left), the anti-Stalinist left, noninterventionists, liberal anticommunists, and New Dealers, among others, have each had their acolytes and their detractors among historians. Most recently, the CIO, usually as an object of celebration, has found itself in the center of many understandings of 1930s political culture. These studies have clearly illumined the battle lines in American politics during the decade of depression. Taken together, such studies contribute to a rich understanding of the complexity of those political battles. Indeed, with the exception of World War II, the Great Depression is probably the most studied and debated period in the last century of the American past.

For historians, one of the attractions of the period has been the fascinating and complicated state of American politics. With world economic and political crises calling into question some of the most basic aspects of U.S. social, political, and economic life, it is not surprising that American writers and thinkers, as well as the public at large, adopted a wide range of political views. It is common to describe politics as a spectrum, ranging from left to right. This terminology, derived originally from the way in which parties were seated in the constituent assembly during the French Revolution, is significant, both because it is the way that most modern Western political actors have understood their own politics and because it allows us to draw some admittedly rough comparisons between the politics of our own time and the politics of the past. But if we cannot avoid talking in terms of a left-right spectrum, we should acknowledge the limitations of this model. Politics takes place in many dimensions and cannot be reduced to a single one. Often, people's own descriptions of their politics owe more to the rhetorical requirements of the day than to an unchanging political spectrum: today, politicians avoid the word "liberal" like the plague; in the 1930s few wanted the label "conservative." Moreover, unlike an optical spectrum, which naturally divides into a series of separate colors, we can, and often must, group political actors in a variety of ways. With all these caveats in mind, I will try to provide a roadmap of American politics in the 1930s and early 1940s from left to right.

The American left of the 1930s was large and heterogeneous. Those located on the left in this book believed that modern capitalism was in one way or another fundamentally flawed and urged a radical transformation of American society to distribute goods more democratically. There were many ideological splits within this left. Among the most salient of these divisions—both in later decades and for the purposes of this study—was the division between the Communist Party and its sympathizers on the one hand and the anti-Stalinist left on the other. Although small and deeply opposed to coalition politics at the start of the depression, the CP grew to become the most influential left-wing party in the middle of the decade when it adopted the Popular Front strategy of encouraging most left-of-center parties to band together to oppose fascism. The Popular Front tent ended up encompassing a diverse set of groups and individuals (some more liberal than leftist), drawn together by antifascist, antiracist, and pro-labor politics and a sincere, if misguided, belief that the Soviet Union stood in the forefront of such efforts around the world.

The non-Stalinist (or anti-Stalinist) left was smaller, but even more variegated. Its ranks included Marxist-Leninists who contended that Stalin had betrayed the Russian Revolution: Trotskyists and quasi-Trotskyists, among them many intellectuals associated with the *Partisan Review* in the late 1930s and the 1940s; Lovestoneites, who were associated with the Bukharinite critique of Stalinism; and a variety of independent Marxist thinkers. Many, like the young Sidney Hook, left, or were expelled from, the CP during the ideological warfare of the 1920s and early 1930s and later drifted in and out of various groups on the sectarian left. The non-Stalinist left also included individuals and groups from other radical traditions, including the old Socialist Party, then led by Norman Thomas. Although much less visible than the Popular Front, anti-Stalinist leftists were intellectually very important in the development of the American critique of dictatorship. Many, though by no means all, of them moved steadily rightward over the course of the 1930s and 1940s.

Liberalism stood at the center of the nation's politics in the 1930s, though it was itself undergoing change. Franklin Roosevelt might stand as a perfect symbol for American liberalism during this decade. First and foremost a political experimentalist, FDR would try a variety of approaches, often simultaneously, to solve the problems facing America in depression and war. While liberals tended to embrace the notion of a vigorous federal government, their other commitments were extraordinarily various. Although some shared the belief that U.S. social and economic life needed to be fundamentally transformed to meet the challenges of the modern world, liberals were generally gradualists. They tended to place a lot of hope in the New Deal and Roosevelt's leadership. Those pushing for radical change often allied themselves with the Popular Front or other parts of the left; I have identified them as "left liberals" in this book. Other liberals—like Dorothy Thompson, who was both one of the leading antifascist voices in the American media and a Republican whose support for FDR wavered on a number of occasions—welcomed an aggressive federal response to the worldwide economic and political crises but were suspicious of fundamental transformations in American capitalism and democracy; I have designated such people "moderate liberals."

Finally, there was the beleaguered American right. If support for FDR defined 1930s liberalism, opposition to him largely characterized 1930s conservatism. Anti–New Dealers included much of the southern wing of the Democratic Party, as well as a large portion of the Republican Party, especially its conservative wing, which was strongest in the Midwest. If most of America loved FDR, his enemies hated him. Indeed, for much of the right, FDR himself became a symbol of dictatorship. Some of the most prominent voices on the right, such as former president Herbert Hoover, were most concerned about federal intervention in the economic marketplace. Others, like many white Southern Democrats, worried about the demands for racial justice emanating from the left. Further to the right lay a variety of individuals and groups often accused (fairly or unfairly) of representing the beginnings of American fascism, including various proponents of reactionary populism, most famously Huey Long and Father Coughlin; fundamentalist leaders of the old Christian right like Reverend Gerald Winrod; and even a small number of self-identified fascists, such as Lawrence Dennis.

By the middle of the decade, a political division very important for this study began to cut across this rough spectrum: the rift over intervention in the growing European crisis. With the start of the Spanish Civil War in 1936, the invasion of Czechoslovakia in 1938, and the invasion of Poland in 1939, Americans faced the question of whether, and how, to intervene in Europe. Although history has tended to associate the interventionist position with liberals and the left and the noninterventionist (or isolationist, as interventionists were apt to call it) position with the right, in fact the division was more complicated. Although many of the most prominent noninterventionists, such as *Chicago Tribune* publisher Colonel Robert McCormick, were conservatives, boisterous opponents of intervention also included noted liberals like United Mine Workers president John L. Lewis. And following the Nazi-Soviet Pact in the summer of 1939, the Communist Party, and those who chose to go along with it, abruptly switched from strong support for intervention in Europe to equally strong opposition, only to change course yet again when Germany invaded the USSR in June 1941.

Historians have done much to illuminate this complicated world of 1930s U.S. politics. But, despite its richness, the historiography has suffered from its reliance on the political divisions of that decade. Much that distinguished the political culture of the Great Depression cut across the political fault lines of the era. Drawing attention to these commonalities should in no way suggest that the differences between competing groups were any less real. Rather, such a focus can provide a valuable new understanding of the dynamics of the period. One of the reasons we write history is to rethink the past in ways that those who lived at the time could not have understood it. This is roughly how Richard Hofstadter, still one of the greatest students of American political culture, came to understand his own work. As he put it in a preface to *The American Political Tradition* written twenty years after the book's 1948 original publication: "I had been looking at certain characters in American political history not only somewhat from the political left but also from outside the tradition itself, and that from this external angle of vision the differences that seemed very sharp and decisive to those who dwelt altogether within it had begun to lose their distinctness, and that men on different sides of a number of questions appeared as having more in common, in the end, than one originally imagined."[4]

Although it is well established that the word "totalitarianism" was widely used in the United States by the late 1930s, thinking of the concept as a product of the thirties still strikes most historians as odd.[5] This is in large measure due to the extraordinary cultural power that the term, and its equation of communism with Nazism, accrued during the Cold War. To a certain extent, totalitarianism seems out of place in the Age of Roosevelt precisely because the concept seems so at home in the era of the Truman Doctrine. It is easy to reduce the popularity of the word "totalitarianism" during the 1930s to a kind of dramatic foreshadowing, a gun appearing in Act I that is doomed to go off in Act III. Such an explanation, however, is unsatisfying historically. Rather than dealing with the idea of totalitarianism in the age of the Popular Front, it replaces explanation with teleology. But historians are not wrong to regard the wide use of the term in the 1930s as an anomaly, for the notion of totalitarianism seems, in many ways, fundamentally at odds with 1930s political culture as we usually understand it.

The thirties are correctly remembered as a decade in which populism flourished in many forms. On the left, Upton Sinclair's End Poverty in California (EPIC) campaign, the rise of the CIO, and the growth of the Popular Front all represented different forms of populism. Father Coughlin and Huey Long were but the most famous heirs to the right-wing strain of American populism. In between were all sorts of liberal versions, from Roosevelt's rhetorical attack on "economic royalists" to the political fantasies of film director Frank Capra. The American populist tradition divides the world into "us" and "them." It typically imagines the great, virtuous mass of hardworking people arrayed against a small group of distant elites, bankers, bureaucrats, and the like.[6] At first glance, the populism of the 1930s easily fit this mold. Coughlin railed against Jewish bankers, Capra's Jefferson Smith battled corrupt U.S. senators, and the CIO's John L. Lewis railed against the "money trust" of Wall Street.

All of this seems very different from the Cold War fears of totalitarianism. The postwar critique of totalitarianism, at least as it developed among intellectuals in the United States such as Hannah Arendt, had at its core a critique of mass culture. Far from extolling the people, these intellectuals most often saw them, at least in their modern-day form, as the greatest potential source of political danger. Rootless, dispossessed of even folk culture, often fanatical, the modern masses were imagined not as sturdy preservers of individualism but as a "lonely crowd" that threatened American democracy.[7] Like populism's celebration of the people, such fears of the people had deep roots in American political culture. In the 1920s, for example, Walter Lippmann and a host of social scientists suggested that the vast majority of people in a modern society were incapable of rational political action.[8] But among American thinkers in the 1930s, we tend to associate such views with dissenters who felt out of step with the times, such as the anti-Stalinist left-wing critics identified with the *Partisan Review*.

Despite their celebration of the people, many Americans we connect with populism in the 1930s harbored fears of the masses. Usually, cultural producers tried to distinguish between the people, on the one hand, and the crowd on the other. But the distinction often proved hard to make, and as the decade wore on fear of the crowd often began to trump faith in the people. Frank Capra's social trilogy—*Mr. Deeds Goes to Town* (1936), *Mr. Smith Goes to Washington* (1939), and *Meet John Doe* (1941)—is usually seen as a locus classicus of the centrist variety of 1930s populism. But though honoring Deeds, Smith, and Doe as everyman heroes, these films see the biggest threat to the protagonists' success not in the scheming, corrupt elites but in the great mass of the people. This is especially true of the latter two productions. Senator Jefferson Smith (James Stewart), an idealistic political novice, is opposed in his plan to build a boys' summer camp by his state's corrupt senior senator Harrison Paine (Claude Raines). Paine and his political machine represent classic populist enemies: elites scheming against the interests of honest citizens like Smith and the boys of his home state. But Smith's darkest moment comes when thousands of his constituents, successfully rallied by the Paine machine, send letters to the floor of the U.S. Senate urging Smith to give up his plan. Although Smith represents average people, the people themselves are easily turned against him and become his most intractable opponents. Only when Paine, struck by a sudden bout of conscience, first attempts suicide and then confesses his corruption to the Senate is Smith able to get his project approved.

Doe's indictment of the people is even more direct. Long John Willoughby (Gary Cooper), a minor-league baseball player turned hobo, is hired by a newspaper to play the role of "John Doe," in whose name columnist Ann Mitchell (Barbara Stanwyck) has been writing homey, populist truths. Willoughby/Doe is soon catapulted to radio stardom with the help of scripts written by Mitchell. Suspicious of posing as an authentic voice of the masses, Willoughby almost quits until he experiences firsthand how much strength ordinary people have gained from his messages. But Willoughby soon becomes an unknowing tool of the newspaper's publisher, D. B. Norton (Edward Arnold), who hopes to lead a quasi-fascist American political movement built on popular support for John Doe. When Willoughby discovers the plot, Norton easily turns the people against Doe by passing out flyers attacking him at a John Doe rally. As in *Smith* (and so many other Capra films), it takes an attempted suicide (in this case by Willoughby himself) to bring the people to their senses at the film's conclusion—regarded then and since as the least convincing part of the movie. As in *Smith,* populism and "the people" triumph in *Doe.* However, in both films the people are easily manipulated and prove to be the greatest threat to the hero's (and populism's) success.

Versions of late 1930s populism to the left of Capra also viewed the people in decidedly ambivalent ways. Orson Welles, for instance, was extremely active in the Popular Front theater, leading a series of Federal Theatre Project productions before striking out on his own by establishing the Mercury Theatre, which in turn migrated from the stage to radio and eventually to Hollywood. Welles was deeply concerned with democratizing the theater, creating stage and radio productions of classic plays and novels that would both engage current events and speak to the broadest possible audience. He also shared Capra's fascination with the media's ability to manipulate popular opinion. But even more than Capra, Welles had trouble imagining that the people could resist such manipulation. His famous "Blackshirt" stage presentation of Shakespeare's *Julius Caesar* as an antifascist allegory portrayed the public as incapable of resisting propaganda. The 1938 *War of the Worlds* radio broadcast, the most famous production of Welles's Mercury Theatre before *Citizen Kane,* displayed his skill at revealing to the public the ease with which it could be duped. Although Welles hoped to educate the audience about this manipulation, he was never able to portray—on stage, over the air, or on screen—such an unmanipulated public. Whereas the people were always Welles's imagined audience, his plays and films portrayed only the crowd.[9]

In Welles's case, and arguably in Capra's as well, the catalyst for this growing suspicion of the crowd was antifascism. American antifascism, which dated back to the 1920s, was particularly strong on the left. Nevertheless, a variety of Americans unconnected to the left, such as Dorothy Thompson, began to embrace it in the 1930s. In the early thirties some American observers, especially those on the left, came to regard fascism as a movement that simply represented the interests of an old, failing elite. In fact, in both Italy and Germany a traditionally conservative head of state (King Victor Emmanuel II in Italy and President Paul von Hinderburg in Germany) had invited the future fascist dictator to head the government. Such a view nicely dovetailed with that of Americans who admired Mussolini: for both fascism was a top-down affair.

But over the course of the 1930s, this portrayal of fascism came to be less and less tenable for many Americans. The absence of any strong domestic opposition in Germany and Italy and the new regimes' apparent ability to build mass support for huge and costly state projects—most spectacularly, wars of conquest—persuaded more and more U.S. observers that these regimes were based not in the singular authority of a dictator and his henchmen but rather in the often irrational desires of the masses. The move away from a cautious optimism about dictatorship in the early 1930s to the nearly universal condemnation of the phenomenon late in the decade was accompanied by a shift from dictator-centered to crowd-centered explanations of modern dictatorship. Such reasoning was relatively comfortable for many conservative critics, who could draw on a well-developed antimodernist critique of mass culture and who tended to focus on Soviet Communism, which they had long considered to be a mass movement. Similarly, critics connected with the small, anti-Stalinist left developed a scathing analysis of mass culture that became a substantial part of their indictment of Stalinism, fascism, and capitalism alike.

For liberals and leftists associated with the Popular Front, however, understanding fascism as essentially a mass phenomenon was intellectually and ideologically more difficult. The Popular Front eagerly embraced mass culture. It placed great hope in the ability of mass media such as film, popular theater, radio, and magazines to function, in Michael Denning's phrase, as a "cultural front" in the struggle against fascism. Whereas "Third Period" Communism had talked incessantly of "the proletariat," the Popular Front tended to speak of "the people." For Orson Welles, Max Lerner, Lewis Mumford, Richard Wright, and many others on the American left, understanding fascism as essentially a mass movement raised many thorny questions. These questions were not new; mass culture and mass political movements had frequently been viewed with suspicion by those who considered themselves to be fervent democrats. But the rising danger of fascism and changes in American understandings of it helped these questions metastasize in the late 1930s.

It is in this context that the rise of the term "totalitarianism" in the late 1930s can best be understood. "Totalitarian" and "totalitarianism" came to be associated both with the equation of communism and fascism and with the crowd-based understandings of the regimes in question. Although the first of these two meanings obviously divided American observers, many of whom felt that communism and fascism were polar opposites, the second was attractive across the political spectrum. When the Committee for Cultural Freedom, a group of anti-Stalinist American intellectuals from both left and right, denounced in its 1939 founding manifesto both Nazi Germany and Soviet Russia as examples of totalitarianism, *Nation* editor Freda Kirchwey, who was generally sympathetic to the Soviet Union, responded not by attacking the notion of totalitarianism, but rather by arguing that the term ought to be reserved for fascist states alone.

World War II changed this conversation in several key ways. With the signing of the Nazi-Soviet Pact in August 1939 and the USSR's invasion of Finland the following winter, the notion that Nazism and Stalinism were essentially alike gained much ground in the United States. By the time Germany attacked the Soviet Union in June 1941, totalitarianism had come to be used almost invariably to link dictatorships of the left and the right. Whereas interventionists had invoked the notion of totalitarianism before the summer of 1941, following the invasion of the Soviet Union and the U.S. decision to extend Lend-Lease to the USSR, noninterventionists began to use the term to criticize a war in which the United States would side with Russia. Once America entered the war in December 1941, the word "totalitarianism" began to lose its currency, except among those most critical of the U.S. alliance with the Soviet Union.

Another change in American views of dictatorship also took place during the war years. For rather different reasons, depictions of both Nazi Germany and Soviet Russia began to distinguish between each country's people and its leadership. Although the sense of Nazism and communism as mass regimes never disappeared, wartime understandings tended to emphasize the importance of small leadership groups in crafting and maintaining these regimes.

The idea of totalitarianism would come back into vogue with the end of the war, the collapse of the U.S.-Soviet alliance, and the coming of the Cold War. But American understandings of totalitarianism were subtly altered during World War II. This book concludes with an attempt to place three of the most significant and popular accounts of totalitarianism from early in the Cold War—Arthur M. Schlesinger Jr.'s *Vital Center* (1949), George Orwell's *Nineteen Eighty-Four* (1949), and Hannah Arendt's *Origins of Totalitarianism* (1951)—in the context of the decades-long public discussion of dictatorship that had been taking place in the United States. Each of these books became crucially important in American political culture. Each is most often seen as a product of the Cold War, as a starting point, not an ending point, for a consideration of the idea of totalitarianism in American public culture. Yet we misunderstand Schlesinger, Orwell, and Arendt if we do not take full measure of the grounding of their ideas in understandings of modern dictatorship that began two decades earlier. By placing this analysis at the end of my study, I am suggesting that there are real continuities in American political culture between the late 1930s and the late 1940s that historians have often overlooked. In emphasizing these continuities, I am in no way disputing that there were also real differences. However, just as historians have shown the many ways in which Popular Front culture continued long after the collapse of the Popular Front, I believe that the roots of Cold War political culture go deeper into America's past than we often suppose.

In this book I examine not only works of social theory, political speeches, and serious journalism, but also novels, plays, radio dramas, and motion pictures. The late Warren Susman famously argued that the 1930s should be seen not as the Age of Roosevelt, but rather as the Age of Mickey Mouse. It was, of course, both. Conventional wisdoms are formed both by highbrow texts, such as works of political theory, and by low-brow ones, such as movies. There is always some interconnection between these realms, but during the period considered in this study, these connections are particularly deep and important. Academics attempting to analyze the behavior of the European dictatorships frequently had to rely on journalists and the popular works of recent exiles for up-to-date accounts of conditions in Italy, Germany, and the Soviet Union. In the politically serious cultural worlds of the 1930s and 1940s, playwrights, novelists, moviemakers, and journalists read the works of intellectuals to inform their representations of dictatorship. Thus, a book like Gregor Ziemer's *Education for Death* (1941), a relatively serious study of Nazi educational and child-rearing practices, was abridged in the *Reader's Digest* and later turned into a hit motion picture, *Hitler's Children* (1943). In short, the images and understandings of dictatorship that journalists, politicians, moviemakers, and academics created informed each other and, together, represent a single—albeit complicated and multifaceted—discussion of dictatorship in American culture.

1 THE ROMANCE OF A DICTATOR
DICTATORSHIP IN AMERICAN PUBLIC CULTURE, 1920s-1935

In the summer of 1927, Studebaker introduced a new car. Originally called the Model EU Standard Six, the smaller cousin of the Big Six Commander and President models was soon given a name that would fit in with the rest of the line: the Dictator. There were, of course, some political problems connected with the name "Dictator." A number of the European monarchies to which Studebaker exported the car were wary of the moniker. Diplomatically, the company marketed its Standard Six as the "Director" in these countries. In the United States, however, the name appears initially to have caused no problems. In its introductory year alone, Studebaker produced over forty thousand Dictators, which the company advertised—one assumes with no pun intended—as "a brilliant example of excess power."[1] The Dictator continued as the bottom of Studebaker's standard sedan line, its sales seemingly affected only by the arrival of the Great Depression in 1929. Yet after 1937, the name "Dictator" was abruptly dropped by the company. No internal records of the reasons for this decision exist, but a name that had been commercially worth keeping in the United States despite European protest had suddenly become unusable.

With decades of hindsight, the decision to drop the name appears only natural. As one history of the Studebaker Corporation puts it, "no one could have predicted in the peaceful days of 1927, however, that a madman would arise in Europe to give dictators a bad name forever." Such an account sidesteps a more interesting history. Studebaker Dictators were named not out of political naïveté, but out of political-cultural calculation. When the first of these cars rolled off the assembly line in South Bend, Indiana, Americans would have thought of only one person when they heard the word "Dictator": Benito Mussolini. In the five years since he had assumed power, Mussolini had already vividly indicated to the world that Italian Fascism was not entirely "peaceful." Studebaker executives, like other Americans, would have read in newspapers and magazines about the brutalities of the Italian regime, such as the 1924 murder of socialist politician Giacomo Matteotti, which received much negative coverage in the U.S. press.[2] But also like many other citizens, the decision markers at Studebaker continued to see in Mussolini, as in the figure of the dictator generally, a positive icon, an image that could inspire and, not incidentally, sell cars.

Since the mid-1930s, dictators and dictatorship have been the absolute Other of democracy in U.S. political culture; thus their place in American political cultural life immediately before that time is, in retrospect, surprising. From the time of Il Duce's "March on Rome" in October 1922 until well into the 1930s dictatorship played a less significant role in U.S. political culture than it later would, but that role was also more multifaceted and ambivalent. Dictatorship and especially the figure of the dictator himself evoked positive as well as negative fantasies. Many of these fantasies were only quasi-political. Like the members of the British royal family after World War II, Mussolini was enormously attractive to many Americans who had no wish for his form of government. Just as the success of brand names such as "Burger King" and "Royal Crown Cola" does not indicate that the country is teeming with monarchists, so the attraction of Studebaker's Dictator to American consumers in the 1920s and 1930s cannot, by itself, be taken as evidence of a desire for dictatorship. But the car's popularity does suggest that the dictator was a powerfully attractive figure at the time.

A smaller number of Americans in the 1920s and early 1930s saw dictatorship as an attractive political system. On the American left, the Communist Party (CP) of the United States and its predecessors, the Workers Party of America and the Workers (Communist) Party, were deeply committed to the Russian model of a conspiratorial party seeking to create a dictatorship of the proletariat through revolutionary action.[3] Many reform-minded liberals in the 1920s, including Charles Beard, Horace M. Kallen, and Herbert Croly, briefly regarded Italian Fascism as a possible solution to problems of modern society. On the right, especially prior to the advent of the New Deal, Mussolini's apparent restoration of order to Italy made a number of American conservatives sympathetic to the idea of dictatorship. The coming of the Great Depression, which suggested the possibility of total social collapse in the United States, increased the attractiveness of the dictatorial model.[4]

Rather than viewing Studebaker's 1937 decision to stop producing Dictators as the company's belated recognition of its own political naïveté, we should see it as marking the end of an era in American political culture, a period in which the figure of the dictator lent itself to a variety of uses that became increasingly untenable as the 1930s progressed. Understanding the political culture in which a car called the "Dictator" could flourish in the United States is important for at least two reasons. First, it provides a crucial reminder that the later place of dictatorship in American political culture was and is a highly contingent one, far from the automatic result of a "madman" arising in Europe. Second, the changes that took place in American views of dictatorship over the course of the 1930s were subtle and complicated; they involved much more than simply the nearly universal condemnation of the phenomenon. Those writing and thinking about European dictatorship before the mid-1930s most often focused on the dictator himself, frequently as a romantic or even eroticized figure. At the very least, he was the author of his regime and the principal source of its program. By the late 1930s, Americans had begun to see the European dictatorships in less personalistic terms: Nazism in Germany, Fascism in Italy, and Communism in Russia were presented less often as the creation of heroic, or horrific, individuals who molded society to their will and more often as the result of peculiar changes in mass psychology.

This chapter explores the ambivalent place of dictatorship in American political culture in the 1920s and early 1930s, starting with the enormous popularity of Mussolini in the United States during his first decade in power. His celebrity inspired the idea that a dictator might solve the problem of the crowd. This notion gained greater domestic importance as social conditions worsened during the depression. For a brief period between the end of 1932 and the beginning of 1933 a small but varied group of influential citizens began to call for some variation of dictatorship in the United States. However, the nation's romance with the dictator soon faded with the arrival of the New Deal at home and the rise of Hitler in Germany. But even as dictatorship became nearly universally unpopular in America, the problems of social disorder that a dictator had seemed to solve continued. Many Americans searched for alternative authority figures, men (and it was almost always *men*) who could provide the benefits of a dictator without the drawbacks. If dictatorship represented an extraordinary authority, then the most feasible alternative was the most ordinary authority imaginable in American society during the 1930s—the patriarchal domination of husband and father within the bounds of the nuclear family.

A Brilliant Example of Excess Power: The Dictator before 1932

From his 1922 March on Rome through the early 1930s Benito Mussolini received an uncommonly favorable reception from many elements of American society. The press devoted much space to his praise, with the

Saturday Evening Post leading the way. Italian Americans found a new sense of national identity and pride through his rise to power.[5] Business leaders looked to his example first as a way of dealing with labor problems and, with the advent of the depression, as a way of ordering the economy along nonsocialist lines. A number of progressive thinkers flirted with the idea that Fascism might have something to teach Americans interested in reorienting society. Toward the end of his life, even Samuel Gompers, president of the American Federation of Labor (AFL), saw Italian Fascism as a model of labor-management reconciliation. Despite his claim that he opposed dictatorship on principle, Gompers went out of his way to celebrate Mussolini as "a man whose dominating purpose is to get something done; to do rather than theorize; to build a working, producing civilization instead of a disorganized, theorizing aggregation of conflicting groups." Many Americans, of course, bitterly opposed Il Duce and his regime, among them, most, but by no means all, intellectuals; most of the labor movement, including the AFL following Gompers's death in 1924; the Italians in exile from Fascism; and the multifaceted American left. Moreover, events in Italy occasionally produced some oscillation in support for Mussolini even among those more favorably disposed toward him. But the predominant view of Italy's new political course was positive and remained so until 1935. As biographer Emil Ludwig told Il Duce during one of many interviews in 1933, "Curiously enough, in the course of my travels I have found you more popular in America than anywhere else."[6]

Two aspects of Mussolini's popularity stand out. First, much of his initial appeal to the business community, the mainstream press, and the conservative elements of the labor movement was that he had apparently solved the problem of social unrest. The specter of communism haunted U.S. business and government leaders following World War I. In the immediate aftermath of the October Revolution, fearful Americans tended to see Bolshevism not as a form of dictatorship but as a form of anarchy.[7] Many elites feared social unrest at home and abroad. U.S. reaction to the Russian Revolution, which bolstered earlier images of bomb-throwing radicals, sowed the seeds of the 1919 Red Scare, which led to the deportation of many suspected radicals and eventually to the imposition of strict immigration restrictions the first ever levied on Europeans.

Fear of the crowd and of social disorder extended well beyond the antiradicalism of U.S. elites. Responding to a widely perceived explosion of mass individualism, many cultural producers from across the political spectrum expressed concern that democracy in a modern society might shatter necessary bonds of social solidarity or lead to total anomie.[8] A 1928 U.S.

Army training manual, widely used by the War Department, denounced democracy for harboring a "communistic" attitude toward property and for generally leading to "mobocracy." Democracy, the manual warned, resulted "in demagogism, license, agitation, discontent, anarchy."[9] In *Public Opinion* (1922) and *The Phantom Public* (1925), liberal (formerly socialist) social critic Walter Lippmann warned that irrational, mass thinking might make modern democracy impossible. The classic silent film *The Crowd* (1928) elaborated what was by then a cultural cliché: the destruction of the American individual by the social and economic realities of the modern city. The film's hero goes from a small town to New York City to make his fortune. But the more he pursues individual success and happiness, the less satisfied and individuated he becomes.

As American cultural producers questioned the ability of democracy to function in a modern society, Mussolini strode onto the political scene. The war that the United States had fought to make the world safe for democracy seemed to have done little good for countries like Italy, where the collapse of the regime seemed imminent from the end of the war to Mussolini's March on Rome. Americans regarded Italy as both a font of culture and a repository of social and political disorder; this latter view fueled, and was fueled by, American nativism. So relieved was the U.S. press at Mussolini's seizure of power in 1922 that few journalists bothered to report his hostility to democracy. Most of them also overlooked his radical past. What was important was that he had declared war on social chaos and seemed to have won. Mussolini appeared to have tamed the crowd single-handedly.

The second significant aspect of his popularity in America was its extremely personal nature. Although his anticommunism was an initial attraction, Il Duce's acclaim was due more to persona than ideology. In taming the crowd, he appeared to rise above it. For many Americans as well as many Italians, he became an almost heroic figure. Mussolini presented himself as physically powerful and tremendously masculine. He enjoyed being photographed bare-chested, engaged in athletic activities. In the first installment of his serialized autobiography in the *Saturday Evening Post,* he is pictured in suit and hat powerfully striding along a beach. Mussolini's most famous action was also imagined physically: his seizure of power was a *march* on Rome. In fact, as some commentators eventually began to point out, he did not join his Blackshirts in their parade into the capital, preferring to stay in Milan. Nevertheless, with or without proper disclaimer, a favorite image in American publications was of Il Duce leading marching columns of *fascisti,* flanked by his deputies, the Quadrumviri. All of this athleticism and pseudoathleticism, although designed primarily for Italian consumption, appealed to the United States, which was busily glorifying the physical achievements of its own Tildens, Ruths, and Lindberghs. Comparing Mussolini to a pugilist, Clarence Streit summed him up in one word: "Punch." In keeping with the image of his physicality and his Latin background, otherwise staid press organs mentioned his sexual prowess admiringly. "Switzerland," wrote *Fortune* magazine of Mussolini's two-year self-appointed exile there, "was full of Russian Anarchists, some of the most appealing being blond-maned women who admitted Benito Mussolini to their confidence and their beds. With Russian intuition they surmised before he surmised it himself that they were sleeping with a great revolutionist."[10]

This political capability intuited erotically by *Fortune*'s "blond-maned" Russians was the final, and most important, ingredient of Mussolini's heroic persona. More than anything else, he was a man of iron will who could get any job done if he set his mind to it. Such an individual, leading a country known in the United States largely for social chaos, was a wonder indeed. Born in the humblest of circumstances, Mussolini rose to political power through his own skill and persistence. His Blackshirts violently beat back the forces of social disorder—the socialists and communists. His attitudes and policies toward women—"Woman must play a passive part," he told Emil Ludwig—ensured that the nuclear family would be strengthened. The historic Lateran Accords of 1929 between Mussolini's government and the Vatican both gave the Italian state recognition that had been denied it since the Risorgimento and added a sense of religious commitment to Il Duce's many other virtues. His agricultural and industrial programs—the most spectacular of which was the draining of the Pontine Marshes—also garnered a fair bit of attention. But perhaps most amazing of all was his command of the crowd. The masses that seemed so threatening and disorderly after the war, and whose cousins in the United States had put fear in the hearts of business leaders during the Red Summer of 1919, hung on Mussolini's every word. The image of him deftly playing crowds of incredible size was perhaps the most powerful icon of fascism in American public culture. *Fortune*'s special issue on Italian fascism in July 1934 featured large images of enormous crowds being addressed by Mussolini, photographed from above; in one spread, they form a frame for the story's text. These throngs—huge, active but ordered and at the beck and call of their leader's superior intellect—were the anarchist/communist striking mobs of 1919 defanged. By the late 1920s Mussolini had become an authentic American hero. In 1927 the *Literary Digest* conducted an editorial survey on the theme, "Is There a Dearth of Great Men?" To refute the suggestion, newspapers mentioned Mussolini more frequently than anyone else, followed in order by Lenin, Thomas Edison, Marconi, Orville Wright, Henry Ford, and George Bernard Shaw.[11]

As Mussolini's prestige rose in the United States, the American image of the Soviet Union changed as well. U.S. observers began to regard the Soviet system less as a cousin of anarchy and more as a form of dictatorship. Following the death of Lenin, Joseph Stalin began slowly to compete with Mussolini for America's attention. With Stalin's consolidation of power in the late 1920s and the beginning of his Five-Year Plans in 1928, the new Russia, which many Americans had viewed as a site of social chaos, was slowly reimagined as a great social experiment. A steady stream of U.S. visitors—including delegations of labor representatives, public health workers, and, perhaps most significantly, engineers called in to work on the numerous Soviet industrial projects—began to report back on the amazing accomplishments of the Soviet state. Even accounts critical of the state of personal liberties in the Soviet Union admitted that its economic and social achievements held many lessons for the United States. At the center of this great experiment was Stalin himself. American engineers who met with the general secretary noted his frankness, leadership, sincerity, and concentration.[12]

In some ways Stalin was totally unlike Mussolini. In marked contrast to the Italian leader, Stalin kept himself aloof from the foreign press. Although he would occasionally greet delegations of U.S. visitors, it was nearly impossible to obtain an interview with him. When Eugene Lyons, after living for some time in Moscow as a foreign correspondent, finally had his long-promised conversation with the Soviet ruler in 1931, he received congratulatory telegrams literally from around the world. Stalin's attitude toward the foreign press contributed to his general image as considerably more private than Mussolini.[13] Often stiff in public and by all accounts an uninspiring orator, Stalin did not command crowds the way that Mussolini, and later Hitler, did.

On the other hand, Stalin, like Mussolini before him, developed a reputation as someone who would stop at nothing to achieve what he set out to do. He, too, was from humble origins. And in the manner of Il Duce, political skill brought him into power and then enabled him to set about remaking his country. By the early 1930s Stalin, despite his dour personality, was being extravagantly celebrated in the Soviet Union; Russia's man of steel developed what Nikita Krushchev would later famously denounce as a "cult of personality."

Stalin's great personal will and power were featured even in otherwise negative accounts of the Soviet leader, such as those published in the Lit-

erary Digest in the late 1920s and early 1930s. Reporting in 1929 on a series of articles by a former associate of Stalin's that had appeared in a French journal, the *Literary Digest* portrayed Stalin as a superhuman ascetic: "This strange mysterious dominator of Soviet Russia, whom nobody seems to know, is pitilessly pictured by his former secretary as a man in whom all human desire is reduced to a minimum with the exception of his insatiable thirst for power. He lives like an anchorite in two small rooms in the Kremlin, which under the Czarist régime were occupied by servants of the palace and it is declared that he hardly ever indulges in any amusements, never dissipates and steals no money from the Government."[14]

In a generally hostile seven-part biography of Stalin entitled "The Red Czar," which ran in *Collier's* from 12 December 1931 to 23 January 1932, Essad Bey expressed amazement at the achievements of the Five-Year Plan, which "in the grandeur of its scope and the high-handed manner of its execution . . . is profoundly Asiatic, stupendous in its ingenious primitiveness and entirely in keeping with the nature of the new generation of rulers." Stalin was the sole reason for its success: "Stalin's great gifts as a ruler are best proved by the magic power with which he has directed the imagination and will of a vast nation towards one common goal."[15]

Less antagonistic accounts presented a similar picture. In the pages of *Foreign Affairs,* Paul Scheffer, a German newspaper reporter, began by noting Stalin's incompetence at controlling crowds from a balcony, only to argue that his strength was his ability to exert a more permanent sort of authority: "He had at his disposal, in a way no one else could have, an immense acquaintance with the 150 million inhabitants of Old Russia. . . . The hypnosis of crowds and the frenzy of words of the first year, then the inspired and inspiring civil crusade against the remnants of Tsardom and its allies, must some day come to an end. It would then be a question of governing people no longer hypnotized, of using ways and means for forcing the masses together independently of such ephemeral throngs." Scheffer contended that, despite initial appearances, Stalin resembled Il Duce: "With or without allies [in the Politburo], Stalin is Mount Everest. He is the dictator of dictators. Only he prefers not to look the part. He is not Mussolini. Yet he has one trait in common with Mussolini—an extraordinary suppleness and pliancy—and he demonstrates it under a more difficult test." Scheffer concluded that the greatest danger facing the Soviet system was that it had become so dependent on Stalin himself that it might collapse after his death.[16]

Reporting, from Moscow, for the *Nation* on the sixteenth Communist Party congress in 1930, Louis Fischer gave an extremely positive description of Stalin's personal qualities: "He is . . . the Soviet Union's most striking personality. He outranks all other Russian statesmen in courage, will power, maneuvering talents, political organizing ability and primitive tenacity. If he lacks the intellectual attainments of a Trotsky or a Bukharin his very directness, force, and even crudeness appeal to a party whose membership has changed radically since 1924." Fischer's politics, however, led him to distrust the cult of personality developing around the Soviet leader. He suggested that Stalin might end it in good dictatorial fashion:

> A good friend might also advise Stalin to put a stop to the orgy of personal glorification of Stalin which has been permitted to sweep the country. This is Stalin's achilles heel. From being the modest retiring leader whom few saw or heard—the silent power behind the "throne"—he has in recent months stepped forth into the brightest limelight and seems to enjoy it. He has become the object of thickly smeared praise, fawning adulation, and tasteless obeisance. . . . If Stalin is not responsible for this performance he at least tolerates it. He could stop it by pressing a button.[17]

Although he soon joined Mussolini as an archetypal dictator, Stalin did not become nearly so popular with the American public. His reluctance to talk to the press made him a more distant figure. Although some engineers and intellectuals were attracted to the Soviet experiment, most Americans remained deeply hostile to communism. Nativist, patriotic, and Christian associations, ranging from the American Legion and the Ku Klux Klan to the U.S. Chamber of Commerce and countless church groups, railed against communism, as did the American Federation of Labor, which under both Gompers and his successor William Green was committed to anticommunism. Even Robert M. LaFollete set out to exclude all communist participation from his 1924 Progressive campaign. For its part, the CP seemed to be battling itself into political oblivion. In 1923 it had emerged from its underground period with 15,000 members. Following years of factional infighting, the party was reduced to 9,300 members by 1929. By 1930, due to more factionalism, that number had dropped to 7,545.[18] Although the party doubled its membership by 1933, it did little to attract broad interest before 1934. Mired in its "Third Period" sectarianism, the CP could garner little sympathy even from others on the left, whom it denounced as social fascists.

Out of the images of Mussolini, and after him Stalin, general notions about the figure of the dictator formed. He was a Great Man, one who was able to lift himself to prominence despite humble beginnings. Almost single-handedly he remade his country into a newly ordered form. He represented power, intelligence, and will. Whether vibrantly, sometimes erotically athletic like Mussolini or stern and ascetic like Stalin, his relationship to his people was personal and emotional. He gave his undivided effort to the molding of his nation. In return, his nation gave him its unquestioning love and obedience. The American advertising copy for English journalist George Slocombe's 1931 novel, *Romance of a Dictator,* perfectly captures this public fascination with mythicized European current events: "THIS NOVEL IS SENSATIONAL NEWS. It is headline stuff because George Slocombe, famous foreign correspondent, knows his Mussolini, his Stalin, his Hitler, as few men today have known them. In the medium of an exciting novel, he has taken his readers past the guards and sentries into the presence of the greatest romantic figure of the post-war age. The small beginnings, the growing vision, the achievement, the passion and the disaster, together with that curious and portentous episode of his recall are described in biting, racy prose."[19]

American cultural producers connected their understandings of the new regimes in Europe to the personalities of the dictators. "The most important single fact with regard to any government under [a dictator's] control," wrote Robert C. Brooks in his 1935 study, *Deliver Us from Dictators!,* "is the character of the dictator himself." Even the regimes' detractors often stated their case in terms of cutting the Great Man down to size, although such authors often had a tough time getting their views aired. In 1932 George Seldes wrote *Sawdust Caesar,* the earliest major American book attacking Fascism. No American publisher would touch it until 1936, after Mussolini's fall from glory in the United States.[20]

A Dictatorial Moment in U.S. Political Culture, 1932–1933

In the 1920s the new dictatorships were a European phenomenon. Studebaker's decision to name its Standard Six "Dictator" in 1927 reflects the many positive connotations that attached to the term: power, effectiveness, modernity, control, erotic appeal. With the stock market crash of 1929, however, the relationship of American public culture to the dictator began to change. By 1932 the United States no longer seemed so unlike Europe. It was involved in the same economic crisis as the Old World. Its government seemed incapable of solving the problems associated with the depression. Dissatisfaction with the two old parties appeared to be reinvigorating the Socialist Party, which had not been a serious player in national politics since World War I. In the spring and summer of 1932 fifteen thousand veterans of that war, calling themselves the Bonus Expeditionary Force

(BEF), marched on Washington, D.C., camped in and around various federal buildings, and demanded advance payments of their war bonuses. When Congress failed to pass a bill authorizing the payments, President Herbert Hoover ordered Army Chief of Staff General Douglas MacArthur to clear the veterans out of the city. Remarkably, the two hundred cavalrymen and three hundred foot soldiers managed to complete their task without causing a single fatality, although many were injured. The saga of the BEF reminded the public that the war had failed to achieve world peace and prosperity and reinforced the sense that Washington was gradually losing its remaining control over the country's political and economic situation.

Around the time that the BEF marchers descended on the capital, a number of liberal and left-liberal periodicals began to suggest that the United States might soon resemble Europe in a particularly unpleasant way. "More significant than all the maneuverings of the professional politicians, it seems to me," wrote Paul Y. Anderson in the *Nation,* "is the obvious purpose of certain interests, under cover of the present emergency, to set up some kind of political and economic dictatorship." Citing a "campaign of propaganda and slander against Congress" as the first stage of this campaign, Anderson singled out Federal Reserve official and sometime Democratic presidential hopeful Owen D. Young's proposal for greater presidential powers and Republican Senator Dave Reed's call for an "American Mussolini" as the most obvious examples of the trend.[21] In a later article entitled "Wanted: A Mussolini," Anderson repeated the charge that "certain powerful interests" wanted to establish a dictatorship, this time mentioning two meetings—the first, called by Young, of bankers and industrialists in New York, the second in Chicago—to explore the possibilities. The article, which also railed against the banality of the major party conventions, may have left the reader wondering who was calling for an American Duce: "Heretofore each major crisis in American history has produced leaders of sufficient intelligence to understand it and ample courage to cope with it. The modern American tragedy is that times which call for men seem to produce only vermin."

In fact, one of the political conventions whose banality Anderson decried produced a remarkable leader. Franklin Roosevelt's first electoral victory was the last time an American president-elect had to wait until March to be inaugurated. The country's deteriorating economy and the many questions surrounding Roosevelt heightened the usual anticipation that occurred during the four months between the election and the inauguration of a new president. Thus the election by no means put an end to fears of, or hopes for, dictatorship. In December 1932 the moderately conservative *North*

American Review printed literary scholar Fredericka Blanker's interview with Mussolini that openly packaged him as a model for the United States. Under the title "What a Real Dictator Would Do" was the subhead, "For those many people who have bewailed the lack of a 'strong man' to solve our problems, here is Benito Mussolini's prescription." The interview itself emphasized the role of the corporative state and the increase of spirituality in Italian life under fascism.[22]

The *Nation*'s Paul Anderson might have thought that his worst fears were coming true had he read the 13 February 1933 issue of *Barron's*. The editorial section of this conservative business journal converted the anticipation surrounding Roosevelt into the hope that FDR himself might be an American Mussolini:

> It is doubtful whether another President-elect in the history of this country has plunged so vigorously or with such an air of joyfulness into preliminaries to his inauguration as has Mr. Roosevelt. He has the knack of taking up back-breaking problems like war debts, farm relief, utility regulation, tariff adjustment, budget balancing, and revival of industry as though he knew how to render their solution an exhilarating sport. . . . His capacity to digest [the many suggestions for depression relief] we unconsciously assume. And that is the sort of man we have all been anxiously scanning the horizon for, whether we are quite ready to admit it or not. Sometimes openly and at other times secretly, we have been longing to see the superman emerge. The question whether Mr. Roosevelt properly belongs in that category is not now answerable; the point is that for the moment he acts like one. Perhaps that is why more or less furtive suggestions of more or less dictatorship after March 4 continue to crop up here and there from time to time. Of course we all realize that dictatorships and even semi-dictatorships in peace time are quite contrary to the spirit of American institutions and all that. And yet—well, a genial and lighthearted dictator might be a relief from the pompous futility of such a Congress as we have recently had. . . . So we return repeatedly to the thought that a mild species of dictatorship will help us over the roughest spots in the road ahead. Only, let our semi-dictator smile upon us as he semi-dictates.[23]

Two aspects of this appeal are noteworthy. First, it is clear from the title ("Semi-Dictatorship?"), from the many modifying "semi-s" in the text itself, and from the suddenly reticent tone in its conclusion that the editors of *Barron's* were worried about openly calling for dictatorship. Second, however, the description makes Roosevelt sound extremely dictatorial. The language is full of metaphors of his physical ability. Roosevelt, plunging into the country's problems with vigor, "renders their solution an exhilarating sport." His mind is also incredible, digesting the very complicated proposals for ending the depression with the greatest ease. And the American people have complete faith in his ability to succeed; they simply "unconsciously assume" it. Finally, whether they admit it or not, this "superman" is what the nation has been waiting for.

On 4 March 1933 Franklin D. Roosevelt took the oath of office and delivered one of the more celebrated inaugural addresses in U.S. history. His first inaugural address is usually remembered for the declaration, early in the speech, that "the only thing we have to fear is fear itself." But much of what followed struck a different and, to the twenty-first-century reader, more disturbing tone. "We must," the new president told the crowd, "move as a trained and loyal army willing to sacrifice for the good of a common discipline, because without such discipline no progress is made, no leadership becomes effective. We are, I know, ready and willing to submit our lives and property to such discipline, because it makes possible a leadership which aims at a greater good. . . . Larger purposes will bind us all as a sacred obligation with a unity of duty hitherto evoked only in time of war." FDR argued that such a program could be undertaken within the confines of the U.S. system of government provided that Congress was willing to join him in decisive action. But if Capitol Hill did not take such action, he warned, "I shall not evade the clear course of duty that will then confront me. I shall ask the Congress for the one remaining instrument to meet the crisis—broad Executive power that would be given to me if we were in fact invaded by a foreign foe." The speech concluded with a declaration of commitment to democracy and another invocation of strong executive power, mystically linked to the will of the people: "We do not distrust the future of essential democracy. The people of the United States have not failed. In their need they have registered a mandate that they want direct, vigorous action. They have asked for discipline and direction under leadership. They have made me the present instrument of their wishes. In the spirit of the gift I take it."[24]

The crowd attending the swearing-in reacted favorably to FDR's calls for greater power. Eleanor Roosevelt later remembered finding the occasion a "little terrifying . . . because when Franklin got to that part of his speech when he said it might become necessary for him to assume powers ordinarily granted to a president in war time, he received his biggest demonstration." The spectators were not alone in their approval of Roosevelt's calls for concentrated power, as the next morning newspapers featured headlines that announced, "FOR DICTATORSHIP IF NECESSARY." In fact, the press almost universally noted the new president's calls for greater power and just as universally had nothing detrimental to say about them.[25]

As it turned out, Congress responded promptly to the programs proposed by FDR. The inaugural address had been a political masterstroke. Roosevelt had convinced press and public that he would, if necessary, seize dictatorial powers without ever having to say so directly. Many Americans had longed for such discipline and leadership, as well as congressional acquiescence that made the actual seizure of such authority moot. Never again would Roosevelt even hint that he desired to be a dictator. By the end of the first one hundred days, there seems to have been no one clamoring for dictatorship. Indeed, given the changing attitude of the political culture in the later 1930s, FDR had to spend most of his remaining time in office scrupulously denying that there was anything dictatorial about his administration.

The moment in which some voices called for "semi-dictatorship" was short. However, during the fall and winter of 1932 and the spring of 1933, the idea that America might need some kind of dictator appeared in a wide variety of places, including a pair of unusual Hollywood films. The first of these was *Mussolini Speaks* (Columbia, 1933), a feature-length documentary lauding the dictator's accomplishments. Opening just a week after FDR's inauguration, the film nicely captures the positive U.S. view of Il Duce at a time when many Americans viewed his policies as possible models for their own ailing country. *Mussolini Speaks* credits studio head Jack Cohn for "editing and compiling," although most of the footage appears to have been taken from Italian newsreels. "Describing and narrating" the hodgepodge of scenes is Fox Movietone's chief commentator Lowell Thomas, whose voice and face would have been extremely familiar and reassuring to audiences of that era. At the start of the film, the Fascist anthem "Giovinezza" (Youth) blares over the soundtrack and a plaque on the screen announces: "THIS PICTURE IS DEDICATED TO A MAN OF THE PEOPLE WHOSE DEEDS FOR HIS PEOPLE WILL EVER BE AN INSPIRATION TO MANKIND." As this title fades out, a bigger one fills the screen: "BENITO MUSSOLINI." The general tone of Thomas's introduction is open-mindedness in the presence of a great man: "Whether we agree with a man's policy or not doesn't matter. We are interested in a man if he makes himself a leader. If he molds history. If he's a man of achievement. And if he has that rare gift: Personal Magnetism."

Mussolini Speaks spends little time on the creed of Fascism or even the nature of Mussolini's policies. Instead, it spotlights Il Duce himself and his purported attainments. The first half focuses on his early background and the rise of Fascism in Italy. Omitting any references to Fascist brutality, the film describes how Mussolini led his Blackshirts against "the dark forces that were disrupting Italy." In doing so, he called upon "strength, laughter, and courage of youth," made more effective by "a gospel of discipline." The film shows, and Thomas emphasizes in voice-over, that "crowds hail him with wild acclaim," as Mussolini—"a man of tireless energy" who "works incessantly"—sets about remaking Italy. The entire second half of the film is taken up with footage of a long speech by Mussolini in Naples describing the achievements of his regime. Both visually and narratively, this scene repeatedly emphasizes two points. First, through shots of Mussolini speaking and countershots of the reactions of the throng below, the documentary celebrates his enormous control over the crowd. Second, whenever Mussolini recounts a success of his regime, the crowd goes wild and the film cuts to newsreel footage of what he has just described.

Mussolini Speaks presents an extraordinarily positive image of the Italian dictator, a leader who is solely responsible for returning order and prosperity to his country. Italy's problems of unemployment and crime, ailing cities and farms, and general social disarray—all of which plagued the United States in 1932—are on the mend. Although the new American president is not mentioned by name, the narration emphasizes a deliciously Rooseveltian moment. At a pause in the speech, Thomas alerts the viewer as to what is coming: "And now Mussolini is going to say something with a punch. He's going to say we have nothing to fear." The dictator speaks in Italian, and Thomas follows with a translation: "We have nothing to fear."

During its initial run at New York's Palace Theatre, *Mussolini Speaks* enjoyed both critical and popular success.[26] The film's advertising copy included an explicit reference to a popular longing for dictatorship in the United States: "A lot of us have been asking for a dictator. His name is not Mussolini or Stalin or Hitler. It is Roosevelt." On 13 March 1933 the *New York Times* gave the film an enthusiastic review. Declaring that Thomas's narration "represent[ed] something of a triumph for this sort of off-screen commentary," the *Times* praised both the leader's mastery of playing the crowd and the film's effectiveness in showing "how Mussolini has kept his promises to his people." Indeed, "even those in the audience who are not Italians cannot resist a surge of patriotic feeling." The documentary was so successful that Fox Studios began to plan a movie, entitled *The March of Two Worlds,* that would feature "Benito Mussolini as a dramatic character."[27]

The March of Two Worlds was never made. As *Mussolini Speaks* spread across the country and began to play in second-run theaters as the back half of double bills featuring such forgotten B movies as *Parole Girl* and *Girl Missing,* interest in the documentary tailed off dramatically. Nevertheless, there appears to have been no effort to protest its showing. Critics continued to recommend the film, but audiences stopped showing up. "Only Italians and a few teachers came out to see it," the owner of Brown's Theatre in Nashwauk, Minnesota, commented. "Box-office took a nose-dive the second night."[28]

A second major motion picture sympathetic to dictatorship premiered in April 1933. Entitled *Gabriel over the White House* (Cosmopolitan, 1933) and starring Walter Huston, this drama openly advocated dictatorship, not for some foreign country, but for the United States.[29] As the film begins, America is on the verge of economic and social collapse, with unemployment at a record high. Nevertheless, the newly elected chief executive, Jud Hammond (Huston), insists on conducting business as usual. The calm emanating from the White House is shattered when President Hammond crashes his car while speeding to a public engagement. When Hammond suffers a brain injury and lapses into a coma, his doctors declare him "beyond human help." But the president receives help from a higher source: the Archangel Gabriel awakens him from his coma, and Hammond emerges a changed man.

Apparently with Gabriel's help — the film never shows the angel, who is represented by the trumpet theme of the finale to Brahm's First Symphony, but characters in the film continually attest to his presence — President Hammond becomes grim, determined, and radical. He refuses to call out the army to disperse the one-million-strong throng of unemployed workers who are marching on Washington, D.C. Instead, he addresses them and proposes the creation of an "Army of Construction" to provide jobs and help rebuild the economy. When the cabinet and Congress resist his plan, Hammond dismisses his cabinet and tries to convince Congress to dismiss itself. "Mr. President," a senator complains, "this is a dictatorship! . . . The United States is a democracy! We are not yet ready to give up the government of our fathers!" "You have given it up," Hammond replies. "You've turned your backs. You've closed your ears to the appeals of the people. You've been traitors to the concepts of democracy upon which this government was founded. I believe in democracy as Washington, Jefferson, and Lincoln believed in democracy. And if what I plan to do in the name of the people makes me a dictator, then it's a dictatorship based on Jefferson's definition of democracy: a government of the greatest good for the greatest number." Faced with the threat of martial law if the president's demands are not met, Congress reluctantly goes along. Newspapers declare that Hammond is now a dictator. Armed with dictatorial powers, he proceeds to solve the problems of unemployment, organized crime, and

the international arms race. Having completed his holy mission by bring-
ing economic security to the country and peace to the world, President
Hammond briefly returns to his old self, then dies, as the audience hears
Gabriel's trumpet theme for the last time.

Gabriel over the White House had been created by a politically surprising group of people. The film was rather faithfully adapted from a novel
of the same name written by a prominent member of the British Liberal
Party, Thomas F. Tweed. Producer Walter Wanger, a liberal Democrat in a
profession dominated by much more conservative men, and William Randolph Hearst, who owned Cosmopolitan Pictures and funded the film, col-
laborated with writer Carey Wilson on the screenplay, which they completed in the fall of 1932. The film was an entirely self-conscious call for an
American dictatorship. Hearst almost certainly saw the movie as a tribute to
Franklin Roosevelt, whom he had backed for the presidency in 1932.[30] The
pre-accident insistence of President Hammond that the government need
do nothing new to solve the economic crisis and his folksy invocations of
the pioneer spirit were just as clearly modeled on President Herbert Hoover.

The film's radical message, its depiction of political mobs, and its implied
denigration of the outgoing Republican president raised hackles at Metro-
Goldwyn-Mayer (MGM), which distributed the film, and at the Hays Office,
which was in the process of gaining the enormous power it would wield for
the next three decades. Indeed, a battle over the film had erupted from the
moment the Hays Office received the script in January 1933. Hays censor
James Wingate was deeply disturbed by what he saw. Fearing that the film
would decrease faith in constitutional government and perhaps even encourage communists and other radicals, Wingate showed the script to Will
Hays, who was equally troubled. A Republican and former cabinet member
under Warren G. Harding, Hays was sensitive to the film's apparent attacks
on President Hoover and scenes showing Hammond, prior to the accident,
engaging in cronyism. The Hays Office demanded changes in the movie and
the filmmakers complied. When Louis B. Mayer previewed the film in early
March, he interpreted it, correctly, as an attack on Republican presidents
Harding and Hoover and was furious. *Gabriel* was sent back to the Hays
Office, which demanded more changes. Despite the two sets of changes,
however, the essence of the film was unaltered.[31]

When MGM finally released *Gabriel* in April, it was a hit at the box office
but encountered mixed reviews. In fact, it was one of the six most popular movies that month. Critic Mordaunt Hall, who responded favorably, reported in the *New York Times* that "the film, though materially changed
[from the book] and softened, is still inflated with propaganda which found

favor with many in the Capitol [Theatre] audience." No reviewer ignored its political content and possible political effect. By and large, the more high-brow liberal journals, such as the *Nation* and *Commonweal,* expressed fearful disapproval of the film's message. *Time* characterized it as a projection of the fantasies of William Randolph Hearst, although the magazine had, in an earlier review of Tweed's even more dictatorial novel, seemed more open to *Gabriel*'s politics.[32]

Gabriel over the White House hit the theaters just as the period of dictatorial longings and fears was coming to an end. From the start of the 1932 presidential race through the spring of 1933, a small, but heterogeneous group of Americans seemed ready to consider the possibility of dictatorship. The country's disastrous social and economic situation, the futility of the Hoover administration's final months, the apparently astounding performance of the European dictatorships, and powerful admirers of Mussolini and his corporative state all converged to create a political moment in which America's admiration for the dictator in foreign lands briefly became hopes for, and fears of, his arrival on its own shores.[33]

Two aspects of this dictatorial moment are worth emphasizing. First, American understandings of dictatorship, both positive and negative, were largely based on the image of the dictator himself. Paul Anderson's pieces in the *Nation, Barron's* dreams about a dictatorial Roosevelt, and the films *Mussolini Speaks* and *Gabriel over the White House* all understood the dictator in terms of his personality and power, not some supervening ideology. Even appeals for America to draw on fascist or Stalinist planning were overwhelmingly phrased in pragmatic terms, a rhetoric that fit in nicely with the image of the dictator as the ultimate "Doer."[34]

Second, those who openly supported dictatorship rarely engaged in explicitly antidemocratic rhetoric.[35] Jud Hammond's speech about dictatorship and democracy is the clearest example of the argument for their compatibility, but such reasoning was at least implicit in all calls for a dictatorship or semidictatorship of the period. Most of these calls argued directly or obliquely for a temporary dictatorship. Although we now think of dictatorship as permanent in intent, this was much less an assumption of 1930s political culture. The dictators of the ancient world, after whom Mussolini supposedly modeled himself, had been temporarily appointed; a permanent dictator was no dictator at all—he was a tyrant. Many liberals sympathized with the Soviet Union in the early 1930s but admitted that it was a dictatorship; they came up with a whole series of reasons why its dictatorial character did not make it inimical to democracy, from the theoretically majoritarian claim of a "dictatorship of the proletariat" to the equally theoretical idea that such a dictatorship would wither away. Even fierce opponents of the contemporary European dictatorships often went out of their way to point out that what they objected to was not dictatorship per se but the permanent, contemporary European form of dictatorship.[36]

This distinction between bad dictators who destroyed democracy and good ones who could save it appeared in the work of one of America's best-known antifascist journalists, Dorothy Thompson. This moderate Republican and frequent supporter (as well as critic) of FDR was one of the most consistent antifascist voices in America during the 1930s. With regular columns appearing in the *Ladies' Home Journal* and the conservative *New York Herald Tribune,* Thompson's opinions reached audiences that other fervent antifascists, writing for more liberal publications, might miss. Although her hostility to Adolf Hitler was long-standing—she first encountered, and was disturbed by, the Nazis while reporting in Germany during the late 1920s—her views about dictatorship and democracy developed over the years. In 1932, before the National Socialists came to power, she published *I Saw Hitler!,* which was structured as a primer to the German political crisis. Despite her adamant opposition to Hitler, Thompson in this slender, copiously illustrated volume, went out of her way to distinguish his notion of dictatorship from the more salutary variety offered by more traditional German conservatives as a way out of Germany's crisis. In a glowing portrait of Chancellor Heinrich Brüning, Thompson wrote, "He is a democrat who has suspended democracy to save the Republic. He is a dictator who abhors dictatorship."[37]

One important exception to this rhetoric of dictatorship for the sake of democracy could be found in the Communist Party. During the Comintern's Third Period (1928–35), the CP insisted that "bourgeois democracy" was merely a front for fascism and that social democracy was in fact "social fascism." As the Comintern's Eleventh Party Plenum explained, capitalism was dying and the only two political alternatives were bourgeois dictatorship—that is, fascism—or proletarian dictatorship. In the Third Period, the CP thus made a point of denouncing not only Roosevelt and the New Deal, but also the Socialist Party, which had experienced a brief return to prominence in the 1932 elections, and other Americans on the left, including some would-be fellow travelers. Not surprisingly, the Third Period line helped limit the appeal of communism even in the early years of the depression.[38]

After the spring of 1933, calls for dictatorship or semidictatorship in the United States were rare except on the political fringes. Nevertheless, as late as March 1934 a study comparing the attitudes of 360 unemployed engineers with those of 300 of their employed colleagues showed that 34 percent of the employed group and 19 percent of the unemployed group "agreed" or "strongly agreed" with the statement, "What we need in this country is a good strong dictator."[39]

Roosevelt, Hitler, and the End of the Romance

As the Roosevelt administration began to govern, a number of factors favored antidictatorial feelings among the U.S. public. First, after the appeals for greater authority in his first inaugural address, Roosevelt, while claiming more powers for the office of the presidency than had any previous peacetime leader, avoided rhetorically assuming the mantle of a dictator. Though he deftly and subtly played the dictatorial card against congressional repudiation at his first inauguration, thereafter he couched all his pronouncements in the more conventional language of U.S. political culture. Even in the inaugural address, he had been careful never to utter the words "dictator" or "dictatorship." As a skilled political innovator who was also a brilliant politician, Roosevelt tried to explain his actions, particularly the more original ones, as belonging strictly within the tradition of American government; unlike the fictional President Hammond, FDR did not attempt to claim that one of those traditions was dictatorship. Liberals who, like *Gabriel*'s producer Walter Wanger, might have been attracted to dictatorial rhetoric in early 1933, quickly abandoned it in favor of the democratic populist language of the New Deal.

As could be expected, the president's political opponents kept alive the notion that he had dictatorial ambitions. Indeed, the leitmotiv of Roosevelt as dictator became more and more common in criticisms of his policies throughout the 1930s. Over the course of his twelve years in office, he answered these accusations in a variety of ways. His public responses are a potent indication of the relationship between dictatorship and democracy in American public culture.

During his first term, FDR often relied on arguments based on national character to rebut charges of dictatorship. He tended to assert that simply by virtue of being an American president, he was no dictator. If U.S. political culture was inherently democratic, nothing that the president did, even to increase the powers of the federal executive, could change that fact. No matter how much authority he exerted, the American people could be secure that he was not a dictator. Roosevelt always stressed that his programs, especially the controversial National Recovery Administration (NRA), followed "the democratic procedure of our Government itself."[40]

The notion that American culture was inherently democratic was by no means Roosevelt's invention. The concept of democracy as a "way of life" had been a major theme in the massive final report of President Hoover's Research Committee on Social Trends, completed in 1932 and published in 1933. A few years later Hamilton Fish Armstrong, an informal adviser to FDR on foreign policy, echoed these sentiments in his popular book on dictatorship, *"We or They"* (1937). Armstrong described "the gulf between" two utterly different "conceptions of life": the American, dominated by "reason and intellect," and the disturbing modern European conception, based on the unreason of fascism and syndicalism.[41]

The inevitability of American democracy, though often expressed, was at best half believed. In the mid- and late 1930s American political culture was marked by the constant specter of dictatorship. Americans from across the political spectrum regularly accused their opponents either of desiring dictatorship or of being the dupes of those who did. We often regard this ploy as typical of the post–World War II anticommunist right, but in the thirties it was as frequently employed by the antifascist left.[42] As dictatorship came to be seen as the result of social chaos rather than as its solution, raising its danger became a rhetorical means to express a wide variety of domestic social fears.

A second major source of the decline of dictatorial rhetoric following the spring of 1933 was the disenchantment of American business with the Italian economic model. Much conservative business support for a dictator or a "semi-dictator" had been related to the idea of establishing a corporative state in the United States. In a time rife with labor unrest, the prospect of the federal government stepping in to ensure peace between labor and capital was attractive to many business leaders. The last gasp of support for Mussolini's solution to the problems of labor and management may have been the publication of *Fortune* magazine's special issue on the fascist state in July 1934. Business approval of government intervention in capital-labor relations had begun to wear off as the business community began to actually experience it under the NRA; it discovered that such an arrangement, at least in its American incarnation, meant state involvement in business, not self-government by wealth. The attractions of the corporative state probably delayed negative reaction to the NRA, but when dissatisfaction with FDR's industrial policies grew, the political meaning of the corporative state and Italian Fascism changed completely. After 1935, business journals began to equate fascism with communism, denouncing both the Italian system and the NRA as "state socialism." At exactly the same moment liberal supporters of Roosevelt began to deny the similarity between the NRA and fascism.[43]

The calls for dictatorship that had arisen from some business quarters during 1932 and early 1933 became an embarrassment. On 10 October 1934 Arthur Krok, Washington correspondent for the *New York Times,* addressed the New York Board of Trade and a national radio audience on the relationship of business and government. Although agreeing with some complaints about the New Deal, Krok was quick to nip in the bud any potential self-righteousness on the part of the assembled business leaders: "These are some of your grievances against government, and you have every right—indeed a duty—to proclaim and insist upon their redress. But the government has some counts against you. You have forgotten your demands in March, 1933, that the President assume dictatorial powers and regiment everything in national life to prevent collapse."[44]

But the most important factor in dictatorship's declining reputation in America after 1933 was the arrival of a new dictator in a major European country. The rise of Adolf Hitler and National Socialism in Germany created an almost immediate negative response in the United States. Unlike Italy, whose main problem was seen as a lack of discipline and a predominance of social disorder, the image of Germany, heavily reinforced if not created in World War I, was of a barbaric, ordered nation with a thirst for blood and conquest. Although stories of German war atrocities printed by the Wilson administration's Committee on Public Information had come under fire by the 1930s, saber rattling in Germany was far more threatening to most Americans than Italy's bellicosity during the first decade of Mussolini's rule.

From the start, Hitler's regime was simply more brutal than Mussolini's. The targets of Hitler's repression—most notably Jews, labor, and any Christian group unwilling to yield absolutely to his demands—had more powerful and more eloquent constituencies in the United States in 1933 than did the principal groups repressed by Mussolini—communists (who, of course, were also a Nazi target), Italian freemasons, and the Mafia. Mussolini was no friend of labor, but Samuel Gompers's favorable impression of him had initially cut into labor's opposition to Italian Fascism. Moreover, American labor was becoming stronger and more vocal in 1933 than at any time since 1919. Whereas Italian Americans felt great pride in the rise of Il Duce and remained surprisingly devoted to him until Italy joined Germany's invasion of France in 1940, German Americans, having experienced virulent anti-German nativism during World War I, were quick to show their allegiance to the United States. So fierce was the U.S. opposition to the new regime that, by 1935, to avoid further inflaming American detractors, Nazi authorities sought to suppress the Friends of the New Germany, the largest U.S. group supporting the Nazi government. Even before official discouragement began, the organization had only ten thousand members, 60 percent of whom were German citizens. For the balance of the decade, the Friends and its successor, the German American Bund, remained a thorn in the Third Reich's side, more often generating propaganda for American anti-Nazis than gaining public support for Hitler's regime.[45]

Many interest groups in America were prepared to wage an information campaign against the Nazis. Among the first to organize was the Jewish community. In the summer of 1933, *The Romance of a People*, a dramatic pageant designed to heighten awareness of the plight of Jews throughout history and to raise money for the resettlement of German Jews in Palestine premiered at the Chicago World's Fair. It later played in New York, Philadelphia, Cleveland, and Detroit. The vibrant Yiddish film industry, which, unlike Hollywood, was unconcerned with keeping the German film market open to its productions, created a series of strongly anti-Nazi films, the best known of which was *Der Vandernder Yid* (*The Wandering Jew*, Jewish American Film Arts, 1933).[46] On 7 March 1934 the American Jewish Congress sponsored a mass anti-Nazi rally at New York's Madison Square Garden. Addressing the thousands of people who packed the building were the state's German-born senator, Robert F. Wagner; Republican mayor of New York City, Fiorella LaGuardia; the secretary of state under Woodrow Wilson, Bainbridge Colby; former governor and Democratic presidential candidate Al Smith; AFL vice president Matthew Woll; Senator Millard Tydings of Maryland; historian Mary Beard; and many others. In May 1934, barely a year after *Mussolini Speaks* had enjoyed a successful run in New York, the Nazi propaganda film epic *S.A.-Mann Brand* was unable to open on Broadway due to the vociferous protests organized by Jewish groups.[47]

Labor's response was nearly as resolute. The AFL aggressively denounced the Nazi regime, conducting a mock trial of Adolf Hitler in Madison Square Garden in March 1934. The entire spectrum of American Protestantism joined the struggle, as well. The spring of 1933 had been marked by Hitler's attempts to impose "German Christianity," a doctrine that put the semi-official German Protestant church entirely in the service of National Socialism. Much of the clergy, historically apolitical and very pliable to state direction, balked at such an extreme change in doctrine and control. A battle ensued between the regime and the church. Both the liberal and conservative wings of American Protestantism unequivocally opposed the actions of the Third Reich in the religious realm—the liberals because they felt that the new German Christianity was a reversion to tribalism and the conservatives because Hitler's vision of the church denied its absolute transcendence and self-sovereignty.[48]

The notion, suggested by some historians, that Americans were indifferent to, or even supported, Hitler when he first assumed power is incorrect.[49] Nevertheless, words of protest did not easily translate into practical anti-Nazi actions. Indeed, the response of a number of U.S. cultural producers to Nazi Germany in the early 1930s helped feed the idea, exploited by interventionists in the years leading up to Pearl Harbor, that a sizable minority of Americans harbored strong sympathies for Adolf Hitler. One of the people most frequently associated with such feelings was newspaper tycoon William Randolph Hearst, an early supporter of FDR, who, after 1934, became one of the president's most irrationally ardent critics. On a visit to Germany in 1934, Hearst, according to the German press, said kind words about the new Germany and was photographed with Alfred Rosenberg and other prominent Nazis. The result back home was a storm of protest. Hearst immediately insisted that he had been misquoted. Later in the trip, he arranged a meeting with Hitler in Berlin, at which he apparently urged the Führer to end discrimination against the Jews. The newspaper magnate managed to convince himself that he had begun to change Hitler's mind on antisemitism and, until Kristallnacht about four years later, insisted that the German leader would change his ways, even while being highly critical of many Nazi policies. Hearst's direct praise of Hitler was reserved for the dictator's anticommunism, which, in Hearst's estimation, allowed his regime to remain popular, despite its "very obvious and very serious mistakes."[50]

The occasional positive statement about Hitler that did appear in the American press almost never went unqualified. As late as August 1934, the moderately conservative *Collier's* magazine printed an article by Nazi press official and Harvard graduate Ernst "Putzi" Hanfstaengl that sung the Führer's praises. By that time, however, Hanfstaengl had long been embroiled in a headline-catching debate over whether or not he would be invited to attend his Harvard class reunion. Putzi Hanfstaengl—by now a household name—was generally portrayed in the press as a clown and as Hitler's toady. *Time* published the occasional amusing human interest story about the Führer, but the piece would invariably appear next to an article about some atrocity of his regime. For instance, a 1 January 1934 story recounting Hitler's kindness to a German resident of Pennsylvania (the Führer had paid his passage to Germany and found him a job in Munich) was immediately preceded by stories about Nazi eugenics and the show trial for those wrongfully accused of burning the Reichstag. A week later, the magazine printed comments of the former Pennsylvanian praising the Nazis, as well as an amusing story of Hitler helping a hitchhiker in the Bavarian Alps, all of which was preceded by a brutal tale of "legal Naziism": a Kosher butcher was put on trial and forced to give up his business because of Nazi racial policies.[51] Such puff pieces about the Nazi leader when juxtaposed with the horrors of the Third Reich only made him appear all the more grotesque.

Some of the more conservative periodicals did join Hearst in greeting Hitler's rise with an anti-Bolshevik sigh of relief and expressions of hope that he would revive social stability in Germany. Roberta Sigel's study of the coverage of Nazi Germany by the *Saturday Evening Post, Collier's,* and *American Magazine* found that these moderately conservative publications largely ignored the regime during its first two years. Their limited interest was driven entirely by fears that another war might break out in Europe and by the occasional, tragically misplaced, hope that Hitler, by providing stability, might prevent such a conflict. As coverage increased in 1935, it also became more negative toward Hitler. Although the German dictator largely escaped criticism in the pages of these three popular magazines during the first half of the 1930s, he received nothing like the praise that Mussolini still garnered in some American publications. In less conservative periodicals and in those more concerned with overseas news, Hitler's domestic policies were almost universally censured.[52]

Soon after the Nazi Machtergreifung (seizure of power), publicly voicing approval of Nazism quickly banished one to the fringes of American politics. On those fringes there *were* unequivocal supporters of Hitler's policies, the most notorious being Gerald Winrod, an antisemitic minister from Kansas whose fundamentalist newspaper the *Defender* had a large national circulation. But there were far more purported advocates of Hitler than actual backers. Once people stated positive views about his regime, it tended to mark them for life. Often one did not even have to hold such views for the damage to be done; suggesting that a political opponent harbored Nazi sympathies became a major way to secure the delegitimation of various U.S. political actors throughout the 1930s.[53]

This is not to say that every influential voice was anti-Nazi. Many Americans on the right doubtless harbored sympathies for the Third Reich that went unexpressed. Moreover, there were numerous people whose rhetoric, could be described as, for lack of a better term, anti–anti-Nazi. Whether out of anticommunist convictions, unspoken pro-Nazism, antisemitism, or a genuine desire to find a disinterested center, many responded to outright anti-Nazism with calls for political calm. Thus when Cornelius Vanderbilt attempted to release *Hitler's Reign of Terror* (Jewel, 1934), a collection of footage supposedly spirited out of Germany to illustrate the horrors of the new regime, the Steuben Society of America, a fifteen-year-old German American organization, urged that the film be banned. The society's board argued that *Reign of Terror* would create divisiveness in the United States and uncalled-for bitterness between German Americans and other citizens. The society declared that it did not endorse Nazi racial theories, which it called a "European excrescence," but pointedly remained neutral in the battle between pro- and anti-Nazi opinion within the German community, arguing against "extremists on both sides."[54]

That vocal pro-Nazi extremists were few in number and lacked powerful spokespeople did not prevent anti–anti-Nazis from imagining a vigorous argument between the regime's extreme supporters and detractors. By and large, those who counseled against criticizing the new German regime did so on the ground that Nazism was essentially a local phenomenon that was none of America's business. Such a view did not suggest that the United States could learn from the German leader. Hitler was so widely disliked that Mussolini, by presenting himself to the world as a bulwark against German designs on Austria, was able to parley the Führer's rise to power into another wave of popularity in the United States. Indeed, some early anti-Nazi writings in America went out of their way to distinguish between Nazism and Italian Fascism.[55] Despite the continuing acceptance of Mussolini, the figure of the dictator in American political culture had lost much of its luster with Hitler's rise to power.

The early anti-Nazi publicists faced a daunting task. Because Americans had envisioned dictators as supermen, much effort had to be expended to cut Hitler and his fellow Nazi leaders down to size. Dorothy Thompson's *I Saw Hitler!* (1932) is one of the best examples of this antidictatorial rhetoric: "It took just about [fifty seconds] to measure the startling insignificance of this man who has set the world agog. He is formless, almost faceless, a man whose countenance is a caricature, a man whose framework seems cartilaginous, without bones. He is inconsequent and voluble, ill-poised, insecure. He is the very prototype of the Little Man."[56]

Other authors stressed the pathology of the Nazi leadership, including their rumored sexual deviance. "Of Hitler's make-up," wrote Matthew Josephson in a 1933 anti-Nazi pamphlet, "we know that besides having the familiar Napoleonic obsession, and a species of paranoia (which after long, uneasy drifting, and failure, vents itself in anti-Semitism), he shows pronounced evidence of sadism." Josephson, a former assistant editor of the *New Republic* and later a well-known biographer, was even harsher in his evaluation of Gestapo founder Hermann Göring ("a dangerously violent lunatic and morphine addict [who] would now be reduced to driveling idiocy if deprived of his drug for a single week"), SA leader Ernst Röhm ("a notorious homosexual"), and Propaganda Minister Josef Goebbels ("a cripple with a persecution complex"). Josephson stressed that these cases were "the very reverse of accidental" as "the leading spirits of the 'Third Reich' are literally honeycombed with insanity, perversion, venereal disease and the drug habit." Similar references to their perversity abound in early anti-Nazi writings.[57] Such accounts presented the Nazi leadership as the polar opposite of the mental, sexual, and physical vigor of the positively imagined dictator.

The combination of negative reactions to the New Deal from the very people who had been most in favor of a "semi-dictatorship" as FDR stood ready to become president and the rise of Nazism in Germany helped end the calls for an American dictator from within the mainstream of public culture. For a brief time dictatorship had seemed to bear the promise of reunifying a society in danger of being torn apart; now it represented a potentially dangerous phenomenon that could exacerbate the social crisis. It was no accident that the Communist Party's large growth in membership and importance took place only after it made opposition to fascism and the defense of democracy the centerpiece of its rhetoric beginning in 1935.

Too Many Fathers: The Patriarch as a Substitute for the Dictator

If American public culture began to see the dictator as flawed, there re-mained the sense that some authoritative figure had to be established — or reestablished — to restore social order. In the first half of the 1930s, crit-ics of dictatorship often advanced alternative images of effective authority. The problem of dictatorship was still largely viewed in terms of a crisis of leadership. As in *Gabriel over the White House,* the president of the United States was often seen as being in the best position to assert such control. In *Gabriel,* President Hammond gained power by becoming a dictator; how-ever, the authority of FDR and later fictional presidents in the early 1930s was constructed in contrast to the figure of the dictator.

Although after his inaugural FDR avoided the rhetoric of dictatorship and strenuously denied any intention of establishing one, he managed to co-opt one of the phenomenon's central appeals. The hope, once associated with the dictator, that a single, charismatic man might arise to unite the Ameri-can people appeared to be fulfilled in the person of FDR. The charismatic as-pect of Roosevelt's presidency became most apparent in the "Fireside Chat" radio broadcasts that he began shortly after entering office. Today, as a mat-ter of course, the president speaks to the nation regularly to explain matters of policy. In 1933 such use of radio was new to the American presidency. Taking full advantage of the medium, FDR broadcast forty speeches be-tween the spring of 1933 and the spring of 1935.[58] The Fireside Chats served not only to convince the public of the efficacy of New Deal programs, but also to forge a personal and emotional bond between Roosevelt and millions of Americans. FDR stood in marked contrast to his two immediate predecessors: it would have been hard to imagine the distant Calvin Coolidge or the managerial Herbert Hoover entering the nation's living rooms to chat with the American public about the issues of the day.

One fundamental difference between the charismatic image projected by President Roosevelt and the dictatorial model embodied in Mussolini and the fictional Jud Hammond involved the leader's relationship to family. Mussolini, although married, received much more attention in America for his abilities as a seducer, his many extramarital affairs, and his large sexual appetite than for his role as a family man. In the original cut of *Gabriel over the White House,* Jud Hammond also engaged in a premarital tryst. Although the affair was removed from the film following Will Hays's objections, President Hammond remained unmarried.[59] Hammond's bachelor status is remarkable given the strong Hollywood convention of giving the film's hero a love interest; in *Gabriel,* the romantic subplot is transferred to supporting characters.

The sexual life of the dictator underscored two significant attributes of his image in American public culture. First, it called attention to the dictator's powerful masculinity and physicality. Women were attracted to him because of these traits; he courted them because no one woman could satisfy his desires. Second, it placed him outside the constraints of societal norms. The dictator could thus act truly independently and heroically. Stalin represented a different, monastic model of abnormal sexuality; despite his marriage, he was said to spend *all* of his time working and was not bound by the normal responsibilities of family life. The supposedly sexually perverse Hitler represented a grotesque version of the same pattern.

The dominant American perception of FDR was markedly different. Roosevelt's public image was quite consciously familial. Although she would become a highly controversial political figure, Eleanor Roosevelt was very much in the public view from the start of the New Deal. And despite a marriage that we now know was often distant and stormy, the Roosevelts developed a parental relationship with many Americans. Workers saw Franklin and Eleanor Roosevelt as personally responsible for improving their lives over the course of the 1930s. Many of them addressed appeals to "father" and "mother" Roosevelt when hard times hit.[60] Unlike the figure of the dictator, FDR was not beyond the social norms and human bonds that defined the lives of most Americans. Indeed, his position within those bonds helped citizens imagine that this man from a privileged background with extraordinary political powers was very much like them and truly understood their problems.

To grasp the importance of this familial twist on charismatic authority, it is necessary to consider the general role that evocations of the family played in 1930s political culture. For most American families, the depression made it impossible to survive on one income. As high-paying jobs disappeared, women—who then, as now, received substantially less compensation for comparable work—began to replace men in the workforce. The result was a serious disruption of family life. Working-class men experienced a loss of authority within the household as their positions as breadwinners deteriorated. This loss of authority seems to have had significant psychological effects on men. In part as a result of these economic and social trends, the thirties was the one great period of liberal reform in American history that was not accompanied by a resurgence of feminism. Indeed, the New Deal contained a kind of official backlash, as the Roosevelt administration sought to remove women from the workforce and replace them with men. As one slogan aimed at women put it, "Don't take a job from a man!"[61] For many people, rebuilding American society thus involved rebuilding the "traditional" family: getting men back to work and women back to the home.

This emphasis on family was at least as important for the New Deal's critics as it was for its supporters. Herbert Hoover, who after 1932 became one of the most prominent conservative opponents of the New Deal, suggested that the newly activist state threatened the family, which formed the basis of American society: "The objective of American life must be to upbuild and protect the family and the home, whether farmer, worker, or business man. That is the unit of American life. It is the moral and spiritual as well as the economic unit. With its independence and security come the spiritual blessings of the nation. The fundamental protection of these homes is the spirit as well as the letter of the Bill of Rights, with the supports from the framework of the Constitution." The move to reconstruct American families coexisted somewhat uncomfortably with national pride in women's progress during the first three decades of the twentieth century. New Deal images of women attempted to capture this sense of their public attainment, while expressing the desire that they play traditional roles. The murals and plays produced in the 1930s under federal auspices showed the functions of women and men to be complimentary but definitely unalike; they emphasized the need for men and women to work together in reconstructing American life but in clearly distinct ways.[62]

The tension between pride in women's progress and a desire to return women to the home affected American responses to the European dictatorships. Many U.S. commentators argued that Nazi and Fascist efforts to restrict women to a purely domestic existence were among the most atavistic and brutal aspects of these regimes. Numerous writers, male and female, devoted articles and chapters of popular books on dictatorship to denouncing the women's policies of Mussolini and Hitler. Authors frequently compared the proud achievements of women in the United States and Weimar Germany to the extremely constricted roles that Fascism and Nazism offered them.[63] But ambivalence could appear even in such criticism. A 1934 advertisement for *Woman's Home Companion* features a well-dressed, youngish woman giving a speech. Next to her, in large print, the ad proclaims, "Mr. Hitler would not approve." In smaller print, the copy continues: "But he'd have a tough time restricting *her* to the kitchen and nursery. She has learned the thrill of a good scrap in an election campaign or on the tennis court. She knows the deep satisfaction that comes with the leisure to engage in the arts, social welfare, sports—all the thousand and one new influences that have made her life richer, broader. The modern American woman is going ahead, not back." The ad goes on to praise the *Companion* for allowing her to have more leisure time by making housekeeping easier. It concludes, "A WOMAN CAN DO MORE THAN MANAGE A HOME—PROVIDED SHE DOES *THAT* WELL."[64]

The dream of defeating dictatorship through patriarchal authority backed by supportive women was present in a number of American films, most notably *Gabriel* producer Walter Wanger's next political project, *The President Vanishes* (Paramount, 1934). *The President Vanishes* was the only major Hollywood production from the first half of the 1930s to deal with the subject of fascism in America. Although explicitly critical of fascism, the film argues that only strong, personal leadership backed by the family can prevent social chaos. As it opens, America is threatened by a series of shadowy political cabals. Behind closed doors a group of economically and politically powerful men including a lobbyist, a steel magnate, a banker, a newspaper owner, a retired judge ("friend of the people, especially the right people"), and an oil man/philanthropist are conspiring to involve America in another European war. A war, the conspirators think, would be the best way to improve business. Rather than trying to pay off legislators to promote their scheme, they decide to enlist the support of the American people in order to make a vote against war politically impossible. They thus launch a campaign built around the slogan "Save America's Honor." In case this plan does not work, the oil magnate is also funding a second political conspiracy: a fascist, paramilitary organization called the Greyshirts led by Lincoln Lee (Edward Ellis). Meanwhile, in the streets of U.S. cities, communists are holding rallies, accusing capitalists, correctly as it turns out, of plotting war, and brawling with the Greyshirts. How can order and democracy be restored in this environment of disorder and political conspiracy?

The answer provided by *The President Vanishes* is to be found in yet another conspiracy, this one devised by the benign, peace-loving President Craig Stanley (Arthur Byron). The president vanishes. The nation is convinced that he has been kidnapped, possibly by the Greyshirts, and everyone's attention is diverted from war to the effort to find President Stanley. Along the way, we see the all-male Greyshirts meet in secret and greet each other with a modified Nazi salute and the cry "Unity!" Lincoln Lee proves to be evil, clever, and truly, if insanely, dedicated to his cause. "I'm not following ambitions," he tells the secretary of war, who questions him about the kidnapping, "I'm pursuing destiny. A petty politician like yourself wouldn't understand that." At the end of the film, Lee is dead and President Stanley reappears as a national hero, able to go on radio and easily persuade the nation to stay out of war. Stanley, it turns out, planned his own disappearance to "bring the people back to their senses." The final scene reveals the members of the presidential conspiracy: in addition to the president, they include Mrs. Stanley, her personal secretary Alma, the president's personal secretary Brownell, his secret service guard Moffett, and his grocery delivery boy Val.

The film thus revolves around three conspiratorial groups: the war profiteers, Lee's Greyshirts, and the presidential plotters (the communists fade into the background after the movie's first few reels). The members of the first two groups are all corrupt adult men. Both factions with some success manipulate the symbols of American politics: the slogans of the war profiteers, Lincoln Lee's very name, and his salute of "Unity!" The two are also structurally linked: one of the war profiteers is funding Lee's activities, and both groups advocate order through violence.

The third group of conspirators differs in a number of important ways from the first two. The presidential plotters are committed to peace and a nonviolent return to domestic order. Moreover, here men, women, and children work together. The group includes one actual family unit, the president and first lady, but functions, at the film's end, as an extended political family, the other members being in effect their children (President and Mrs. Stanley are much older than their fellow conspirators). The presidential conspiracy is undertaken by a cooperative family unit, a trope that was central to New Deal artistic and theatrical representations of manhood and womanhood.[65]

Through the war profiteers and the Greyshirts, *The President Vanishes* imagines both the creation of social disorder and its eventual resolution in dictatorship. Dictatorship becomes a threat because the people, absent from the screen except in crowds and gangs, are gullible and easily aroused to violent, irrational political action. The only way out is virtuous, but extreme, behavior by someone above the people, namely the president. What guarantees his virtue is the family—a most undictatorial institution—which stands behind President Stanley, but to which his political opponents, like his cinematic predecessor Jud Hammond, are notably unconnected. *The President Vanishes,* despite Stanley's extraconstitutional means to save American democracy from itself, was seen by some viewers as a powerful statement against fascism.[66]

In this film, the leader's wife exists solely to assist her husband. Mrs. Stanley appears not to have any job outside of her role as helpmate. Obviously, outside of Hollywood the 1930s were a difficult time for this model of the American family. The first lady was one of an increasingly small number of American women who could define themselves entirely by their husband's career—though it is to the great credit of Eleanor Roosevelt (and to the annoyance of her critics) that she did not choose to do so.

Both the dictatorial and familial modes of personal male leadership appealed to the cultural concerns about gender roles, but they did not go far in solving them. There is even some evidence to suggest that "father" Roosevelt may have contributed to the problem of masculinity: a Chicago worker reported that his wife rejected him on the grounds that "F.D.R. is the head of the household since he gives me the money."[67] A single, symbolic father might be insufficient to solve America's social problems. A more general reconstitution of masculinity and the family thus might be necessary to save democracy from social chaos. The real alternative to dictatorship might not be a single, national family, but many nuclear ones. Of course, the argument that love and marriage would solve the political problems of the world was tailor-made for the movies.

Hollywood's first attempt to address German politics in the 1930s, *Little Man, What Now?* (Universal, 1934), centered on the contrast between familial order and social chaos. *Little Man,* based on German writer Hans Fallada's best-selling novel of the same name, was the first of three movies directed by Frank Borzage that dealt ever more explicitly with the reasons for the Nazi Machtergreifung in Germany.[68] But given Hollywood politics of 1934, the film had to couch its argument carefully. *Little Man* makes no direct mention of the Nazis, nor is the social crisis confronting Germany ever resolved on screen. Borzage allowed the viewer to fill in these details.

Politics, rarely wholly visible, lurks off-screen as the negation of the picture-book Germany of *Little Man.*

Fallada's novel was in many ways the perfect vehicle for an early Hollywood exploration of German politics that would avoid offending Nazi authorities, would capture public interest at home, and, rather than highlighting events in Germany per se, could claim to address universal themes of social hardship and love conquering all.[69] The book was an immediate popular success when it appeared in Germany in 1932, although it received an extremely mixed critical reception. The novel explores the fortunes of Hans Pinneberg and his wife Lämmchen, a typical petit bourgeois couple during the depression of the early 1930s. Although Fallada surveys the entire German political scene, including one major Nazi character and numerous cameo appearances by other Nazis, communists, and socialists, his message is apolitical. *Little Man* suggests that through love and the self-respect born of it, men and women might be able to weather any storm. German readers were drawn to this combination of social realism and sentimentality; the book remained a best-seller through the Nazi period and well into the 1960s, when sales abated until the 1980s. Although initially hostile to the book, the Nazis ultimately deemed it acceptable.[70] Even before *Little Man* arrived in the United States, it had proven to be tremendously politically malleable.

A year after its publication *Little Man,* made its English-language appearance in the United States, where it was nearly as successful as in its native Germany. It was the Book-of-the-Month Club selection for May 1933 and by the end of the year had become the number ten best-seller among works of fiction in 1933. As in Germany, the political press was most critical of Fallada's sentimentalism. *"Little Man, What Now?,"* wrote Granville Hicks in the *Nation,* "is a good enough book for those who can afford the luxury of pity." However, other reviewers praised the novel and even saw realism in its sentimentality.[71]

Little Man was as safe a basis for a film about life in Germany as Hollywood was likely to find. It also suited the style of Frank Borzage, a director who had built his reputation in the late 1920s and early 1930s as one of Hollywood's great sentimentalists.[72] On-screen, *Little Man* was transformed from an apolitical work, which celebrated perseverance despite the chaotic public life of late Weimar Germany, to an antipolitical work, which saw love and domesticity as the route to escape from that life. Indeed, though it remained true to the novel in most respects, the alterations that the film introduced, including most spectacularly its ending, drew much starker contrasts between the Pinnebergs' life and the life of sociopolitical involvement.

From its opening sequence, *Little Man* contrasts the stable bonds of matrimony with the chaotic bonds of mass political action. Whereas the novel begins with the young couple going to see a gynecologist, who tells Lämmchen that she is pregnant, the movie considers some political matters before the actual visit. The film starts with an establishing shot of a very German city, complete with gothic-lettered signs in German.[73] It is raining and a communist speaker extols a small crowd on the virtues of absolute equality. Hans Pinneberg (Douglass Montgomery) and Lämmchen (Margaret Sullavan) enter a nearby building where their doctor has his office. Inside, they encounter a working-class man and his wife who accuse Hans of being a "bourgeois" because the Pinnebergs get to see the doctor before the working-class couple. Although Hans insists that, unlike the worker, he has an appointment, the man grumbles that he is leaving for a place where "people are more equal"; he drags his nearly silent, and clearly unhappy, wife along with him. From the window of the doctor's office, we see the speaker being pulled away by police. "It's better to accept one's place, isn't it?" muses Hans while surveying the scene in the street below. "Nothing very wrong can happen to the peaceful man."

The great body of the film follows the novel. The Pinnebergs encounter hardship from the start. Hans's first employer is a malevolent man who runs his business from his home and desperately wants to marry his daughter off to one of his workers, who all must at least pretend to be single to keep their jobs. Unfortunately for Hans, his boss discovers his marital status and fires him. The Pinnebergs decide to move to Hans's hometown of Berlin, but life in his mother's house quickly proves impossible for the couple. Mia Pinneberg (Catherine Doucet) is rude and impatient. She also lives a life of total decadence. Hans and Lämmchen finally leave after a male guest at one of Mia's parties grabs Lämmchen and Hans picks up a knife to defend her. Although no violence ensues, the couple moves into the upper floor of the simple house of Herr Puttbreese (Christian Rubb), an old, unmarried furniture maker.

In Berlin, we again encounter the working-class couple from the gynecologist's office. In a city park, the man and his wife discuss their search for housing:

MAN: Perhaps we'll find a friend of our beliefs to house us.
WIFE: Wouldn't it be better to find work?
MAN: Am I not doing great work now?
WIFE (sounding unconvinced): Yes, of course. But aren't you hungry? I am!

The man manages to convince Lämmchen, whom he discovers feeding pigeons, that he and his wife are more worthy of her bread than the birds. Feeling sorry for the couple, Lämmchen gives the man Hans's lunch, which she is holding for him while she waits for his lunch hour to arrive at his new job. Upon hearing of this later, Hans announces how "superior" he feels to people like the working-class couple. "Still," he notes, "without my job, I'd be right with them." Soon, however, Hans is fired. He searches for his friend Heilbutt (G. P. Huntley Jr.), a former coworker who had quit earlier, in the hope of getting another job.

Here, the film departs significantly from the novel. In the book, Heilbutt—in both film and novel a nudist—has begun to produce pornography for a living. Though unable to stomach working in that business, Hans is willing to accept Heilbutt's offer of cheaper lodging in a cabin that he owns outside of town. After the Pinnebergs' child is born, Hans becomes progressively downtrodden as he is less and less able to support his offspring. Finally, on a trip into Berlin, Hans, dressed in tattered and dirty clothing, is hassled by a police officer. Seeing his reflection in a storefront mirror, Hans realizes that he has fallen so low that his mere presence is offensive. Depressed, he returns home to find Lämmchen still totally supportive of him. In the end, the novel suggests that her support will enable Hans to persevere.

The film's message is both explicitly antipolitical and more upbeat. Hans discovers that Heilbutt has moved to Holland to open a business. Depressed, he goes to the park and once again bumps into the man from the doctor's office, this time without his wife.

> MAN: Coming, Comrade . . . to the meeting? There's a message in it for you. A message from a great leader. . . . He'll show you why you shouldn't need any money to send your wife to the hospital.
> HANS: Where's your wife?
> MAN: She died. Died in my own hands. They killed her.
> HANS: Who?
> MAN: They . . . they . . . the one's we're against!
> HANS: It would have been better for her if you'd waited to see [the doctor]!

Nevertheless, in his one political act in the film, Hans decides to go to the meeting, which is being held outside. As Hans and the man arrive, police are breaking up the crowd. Hans, knocked to the ground by one of the officers, rises to find two cobblestones in his hands. Heroic music plays on the soundtrack, but Hans, recoiling in horror at the possibility of political violence, drops the stones and runs home.

Encountering Puttbreese outside the house, Hans tells the old man that he can never face Lämmchen again, so embarrassed is he by his behavior in the park. But when the landlord tells him that his son has just been born, Hans rushes inside to see his wife and child. The mere sight of the child renews his hope, which is encouraged by his wife. "Isn't he small and helpless?" Lämmchen says. "Life can't be any bigger than he is 'cause he is life, isn't he? And we created him, didn't we? We created life, so why should we be afraid of it?" At this moment, Heilbutt bounds into the room and invites Hans to join him in Holland, where he is now an employer. Hans gladly accepts as the movie ends.

In the film *Little Man,* Germany—on the verge of Nazi dictatorship—is torn by economic ruin and political strife. One of the most prominent signs of this collapse is the destruction of home life, as evidenced by the communist and his wife. By understanding his family's condition politically, the political agitator dooms his wife to death and himself to hunger and degradation. The movie repeatedly suggests that if he merely took responsibility for his own life, he would be able to survive and perhaps prosper. This stark antipolitical stance is absent from the book, in which Lämmchen at one point decides that both she and Hans must vote communist in the next election, although Hans indicates that he "should like to" but "can't quite make up [his] mind."[74] In the film, Hans remains frankly and vocally opposed to any political action except in the moment of emotional stress when he is knocked to the ground by the police officer. But as he had a similar reaction when the guest grabbed Lämmchen at Mia Pinneberg's party, his snatching up the cobblestones is evidently brute instinct, not rational choice.

In the Germany of the film, boundaries of public and private are confused in ways that create disorder. The house/office of Hans's first employer is destructive of both his domestic and labor relationships. Mia Pinneberg's extremely public house becomes an impossible place for Hans and Lämmchen to live in; although we are never really made privy to Mia's social world, what we see of it indicates that it gives little weight to the sanctity of marital vows. Only the completely domestic space of the Pinnebergs' upstairs apartment provides a truly separate realm in which Hans can escape the disordered world outside. By cultivating such a space and retaining faith that the sanctuary of their marriage can outlast the world around them, the Pinnebergs are able to leave the chaos of Germany.

In *Little Man,* there is apparently no way to save Germany itself; the film's notion of survival is escape—to the family order and from the country. Those left behind must put their hopes in a "great leader" while their lives and families continue to deteriorate. In this important way, the film does not really present the return to family as a solution to political problems. The coming Nazi dictatorship is never mentioned, but the 1934 audience would have seen intimations of Hitler's rise to power in the political activity that forms the backdrop for the Pinnebergs' lives. Dictatorship *will* come to Germany; Pinneberg can only hope to escape. *Little Man* thus combines a deep political cynicism with the simple-minded hope that, as Hans puts it early in the movie, "Nothing very wrong can happen to the peaceful man"—so long, that is, as he puts his trust in a woman.

If *Little Man*'s equation of the breakdown of family with the rise of social chaos and the arrival of dictatorship represents a fairly significant theme in early 1930s public culture, Hans's ability to solve these problems simply by deciding to support his family is pure Hollywood. The embattled family of the 1930s was not so clearly a haven from the dangerously masculine world of politics for those whose notions of love and gender relations were more complicated than Borzage's soft-focus romances. Sinclair Lewis's novel *It Can't Happen Here* (1935), one of the decade's most meaningful attempts to envision the dangers of dictatorship to the United States, suggests that individual masculine authority backed by the love of a woman might be the best response to such a threat. But in Lewis's novel that authority is less secure, and the love less traditional and more ambivalent, than in Borzage's film.[75]

Lewis, winner of the 1930 Nobel Prize for Literature, had built his reputation as a sharp critic of American society in such novels as *Babbitt* (1922) and *Arrowsmith* (1925). But, ever suspicious of politics, he had kept a distance from European events in the thirties. This disassociation from politics abroad became more difficult for Lewis as his second wife, journalist Dorothy Thompson, became increasingly concerned with them. Beginning in 1932, when a visit to Germany led to the writing of *I Saw Hitler!*, Thompson's career began to revolve around reaching an understanding of Adolf Hitler. Throughout this time, Lewis remained vocally uninterested in the phenomenon of Nazism. When asked in New York for his opinion on German politics following Thompson's expulsion from Nazi Germany in August 1934, Lewis testily answered, "Miss Thompson is the political expert. I am not." In letters to friends, he referred contemptuously to the entire subject of Nazi Germany as "This Situation," or simply "It," and reportedly commented in 1932 that, if he ever divorced Thompson, he would name Hitler as a corespondent.[76]

It Can't Happen Here would almost certainly never have been written had it not been for Lewis's marriage to Thompson. Lewis set his story in 1936 in the small Vermont town of Fort Beulah. The protagonist is Doremus Jessup, a sixty-year-old newspaper editor and cynical observer of the follies of his country and community. Doremus is married to Emma, a homebody who is the absolute picture of domesticity. But he is having a torrid affair with the younger Lorinda Pike, the independent widow of a Unitarian minister who runs a boardinghouse in town. Lorinda is an activist in the community, "constantly poking into things that were none of her business."[77]

As the book opens, the presidential campaign of Senator Berzelius "Buzz" Windrip is only beginning to show signs of success. Windrip, a populist demagogue with fascist overtones, is backed up by a rogues' gallery of cronies, most notable of whom is the effeminate Lee Sarason, who appears to be the brains behind the candidate. The early chapters begin with quotations from *Zero Hour—Over the Top,* the fictional *Mein Kampf* of Lewis's American dictator. Windrip also has his corps of Brownshirts— actually *white* shirts so that the senator can disclaim any connection to the Nazis, fascists, and their *colored* shirts—called "Minute Men." By focusing much of its attention on Windrip and his deputy Sarason, Lewis has made the figure of the dictator himself a principal part of his analysis of a prospective American dictatorship.

Despite the gathering storm, the community leaders of Fort Beulah do nothing. Most fear for their careers should Windrip prevail. Doremus, ever the cynic, is deeply opposed to Windrip but believes that America will deserve what it gets if it elects him. Windrip wins the race and begins to destroy American democracy. Within a week of his inauguration, the Minute Men have seized Congress and Windrip has become a dictator. That summer the president abolishes all other political parties and declares that the country is a corporative state. Henceforth, his followers become known as "Corpos." Meanwhile, the Corpos begin to take over Fort Beulah. After Doremus publishes an anti-Windrip editorial, he is arrested and is forced to write a pro-Windrip recantation.

Windrip's oppression worsens. Following a raid on his office, Doremus tries unsuccessfully to escape to Canada with his family. Returning to Fort Beulah, he and Lorinda join the resistance, the New Underground (NU). Doremus is arrested and beaten for distributing anti-Corpo pamphlets. Finally, he is sentenced to a long term in a concentration camp. Meanwhile, Sarason replaces Windrip in a coup. Another former Windrip follower, Colonel Dewey Haik overthrows Sarason. Lorinda arranges for Doremus's escape to Canada, where the NU is now based. The lovers have a final meeting before Doremus's departure. At the close of the book, the future of the United States is still very much in doubt.

It Can't Happen Here effectively presents the dangers that fascism could pose to the United States. Although, as critics noted at the time, events in the novel follow those in Nazi Germany a tad too closely, there was enough of Huey Long in Buzz Windrip to make him a convincing, if not exactly realistic, candidate for dictator of the United States.[78] But Lewis, always a better social critic than proponent of social action, failed to suggest an adequate response to the threat of dictatorship. Although the book is a critique of a fascist dictator, it has nothing good to say about the political left either. Throughout the novel Communists and Socialists are involved in the NU, yet they are hopelessly dogmatic and seem more interested in arguing among themselves and labeling Senator Trowbridge, the NU's leader, a "social fascist" than in contributing constructively to the Windrip opposition. In Lewis's narration and in the thoughts and speeches of his alter ego Doremus Jessup, as well as in some of Windrip's remarks, Windrip and his movement are as frequently compared to Stalin and Communism as they are to the other European dictators and their respective movements.[79] Nor is Lewis above sounding nativist notes in his portrayal of the book's ethnic characters, such as the heavy-set Shad Ledue, Doremus's shiftless hired man of French Canadian extraction who becomes a Corpo leader in Fort Beulah.

Nevertheless, for many readers on the left, the book's clearly antifascist stance overwhelmed the cynicism toward other political groups. To Lewis's great discomfort, communists, socialists, and liberals of a more left-leaning bent than the author himself responded favorably to *It Can't Happen Here*. In November 1935 Malcolm Cowley, Genevieve Taggard, and Henry Hart invited Lewis to a New York dinner in his honor and an informal discussion of the novel sponsored by the radical League of American Writers. Feeling that he was being set up by the Communist Party, Lewis arrived prepared to shock. After a variety of speakers, including Carl Van Doren, praised his novel, Horace Gregory remembers Lewis standing and announcing: "Boys, I love you all, and a writer loves to have his latest book praised. But let me tell you, it isn't a very good book—I've done better books—and furthermore, I don't believe any of you have *read* the book; if you had, you would have seen that I was telling all of you to go to hell. Now, boys, lets join arms; let's all of us stand up and sing 'Stand Up, Stand Up for Jesus.'" As Cowley and Gregory hurried from the room, the remaining guests nervously rose and joined in the hymn.[80]

One of the great weaknesses of *It Can't Happen Here* is that, at one time or another, it seems to tell *everyone* to go to hell. The author's deep suspicions of politics reveal themselves throughout the novel. Doremus Jessup, whom Lewis himself played in one of the many theatrical productions of *It Can't Happen Here,* is a reluctant member of the New Underground. Doremus's great strength, his Yankee individualism and refusal to compromise his independence, is hardly an asset in any collective struggle. In the novel's final line, Lewis leaves the reader with the hope that "still Doremus goes on in the red sunset, for a Doremus Jessup can never die."[81] But the book never satisfactorily resolves the paradoxes of Doremus's indefatigability. He "cannot die" because he is such an individualist. But this individualism will always prevent him from working for a world in which there can truly be a place for such a person. Despite its final note of optimism, *It Can't Happen Here* reveals an America in which Babbittry may result in a dictatorship that leaves little hope of anything but individual escape. Even this individual escape is complicated by Lewis's fear of the relationships between gender, sexuality, and politics.

As in Borzage's *Little Man,* issues of family and masculinity pervade the view of mass politics in *It Can't Happen Here.* The Corpos are sexually questionable. Lee Sarason, Windrip's right-hand man, "had [no wife], nor was [he] likely to." At various points, Sarason is arrested on "unspecified charges" in the basement of a D.C. boys' club before police recognize him, is said to be living with "several handsome young M.M. officers," and, when he is finally killed, is wearing violet silk pajamas. Windrip, though married, is the product of overmothering: "I got my [cultivated taste] from my Mother as I did everything that some people have been so good to admire in me." To a 1930s reading public exposed to popular Freudianism, the subtext of such a passage would have been clear. Later a character refers to Windrip "and his boyfriend Hitler." The Minutemen and their effeminately named leader, Effingham Swan, also engage in homoerotic activities.[82]

Also as in the film *Little Man,* mass politics in *It Can't Happen Here* is a realm of imperfectly masculine men. But the open homophobia of Lewis's novel and the implied sexual perversions of its characters are closer to contemporary stories about the Nazis than to Borzage's communist failed father. And unlike Fallada's and Borzage's faith in the feminine world of the domestic sphere, *It Can't Happen Here* is deeply suspicious of women and the family. As Barbara Melosh points out, at the beginning of the novel a speech by Mrs. Adelaide Tarr Gimmitch to the Fort Beulah Rotary Club on Ladies' Night presents traditional women as a force for political conservatism and, more specifically, the curtailment of personal liberties. Mrs. Gimmitch argues for discipline for America, praising the German and Italian regimes for instilling duty and strength in their people and for making their boys warlike and virtuous and their girls maternal.[83]

Doremus's wife is more quietly emasculating. "A parochial Tory, an orthodox Episcopalian, and completely innocent of any humor," Emma Jessup maternally calls her husband "Dormouse." Doremus complains of the "sympathetic and extremely feminized atmosphere of his home." But such an atmosphere also prevents the Buzz Windrips of the world from developing: Sarason creates Windrip's oratorical style, "while other Senators were encouraged by their secretaries and wives . . . to expand from village back-slapping to noble, rotund, Ciceronian gestures." Indeed, "no potential dictator ought ever to have a visible wife, and none ever has had, except Napoleon."[84]

Melosh suggests that It Can't Happen Here presents a world in which men with women are emasculated and infantilized while men without women, as nearly all the Corpo leaders are, are fascists and candidates for sexual perversion. For Doremus, one possible escape from this dilemma is his affair with Lorinda Pike. As his modern-minded, eighteen-year-old daughter Sissy tells him (not knowing that Doremus and Lorinda are already involved): "If you're going to fight [Windrip's followers], you've got to get some pep back in you—you've got to take off the lace mitts and put on the brass knuckles—and I got kind of a hunch Lorinda might do that for you, and only her." But the Lorindas of the world are hardly safe. Lewis suggests that there is something untoward about her activism: when Lorinda first appears, scolding Mrs. Gimmitch during the Rotary speech, "her eyes filled with embarrassing fury." Later she finds herself becoming domesticated in her affair with Doremus and ultimately chooses her politics over her man. At the novel's end, Lewis describes her as "this defeminized radical woman." Doremus ends up isolated and out of the country. Although his relationship with Lorinda works in the short run, it is unstable and illicit. He has the support of a woman in an atmosphere that does not emasculate him, but he must live a lie to keep it up. Moreover, Doremus, as Lewis, is deeply ambivalent about the qualities of Lorinda that distinguish her from Emma, qualities that cannot, in any case, survive in Lorinda so long as she stays in the relationship. Like so much else in Doremus's life, his affair with Lorinda is the site of temporizing and indecision. Doremus is supposed to be the model of the heroic, independent man, but his vacillation makes him unconvincing. The most decisive male character in the novel is the utterly evil Lee Sarason, who is free from the need for female companionship and the various dilemmas that both domestic and independent women pose for Lewis.[85]

In the context of Hollywood movies, the family and patriarchal authority, whether symbolically embodied by a democratic leader or experienced by "little men" as individuals, could function well as a source of order in a world of social chaos. In the more complex cultural work of Lewis's novel and in the actual realm of American politics, patriarchal authority was not nearly as effective in restoring social order and holding fears of dictatorship at bay. Sinclair Lewis was unable to imagine a return to social order in *It Can't Happen Here*. And FDR as symbolic father could as easily make working-class fathers feel less authority in a time of crisis as he could make them feel that social order had been restored.

The place of women in these visions of patriarchal leadership also provided grounds for objection. Indeed, some American women saw such patriarchs not as an alternative to dictatorship, but as another version of the same dangerous phenomenon. Gertrude Stein most famously presented this critique in *Everybody's Autobiography* (1937):

> There is too much fathering going on just now and there is no doubt about it fathers are depressing. Everybody nowadays is a father, there is father Mussolini and father Hitler and father Roosevelt and father Stalin and father Lewis and father Blum and father Franco is just commencing now and there are ever so many more ready to be one. Fathers are depressing. England is the only country now that has not got one and so they are more cheerful there than anywhere. It is a long time now that they have not had any fathering and so their cheerfulness is increasing.[86]

Stein was, of course, in the extraordinary position of having, by her lights at least, constructed for herself a world without fathers. She was unabashed about her rejection of male authority; dictators provided perfect grist for her mill. Hollywood and others saw in dictatorship a kind of masculine authority that was illicit or dangerous when not bounded by the moral guidance of a family unit; Stein saw in it simply a reinscription of a familiar masculine authority. The kind of authority represented by the dictators was, for Stein, evil in and of itself, not merely because it was not tempered by a family.

But as unusual as Stein's argument might seem, it was not unique. In a remarkable editorial, the *Woman's Home Companion* also turned the critique of the European dictators into a critique of masculinity. Although the *Companion* prided itself on involving readers in politics, its editors had never before addressed the issue of dictatorship.[87] In May 1935, however, the magazine printed as its lead editorial a small piece entitled "Men Who Never Grew Up." Citing the work of Dr. Elizabeth Chester, a London psychologist, the editors argued that the real problem of "the current craze for dictatorships" was that "too many of the world's leaders today are men who never grew up." Referring to vanity, self-importance, and pomposity as classic traits of boyhood, they suggested that even a man who is "intellectually a brilliant politician" may "be emotionally only ten or fifteen years old." "Boys love to wear uniforms," it is pointed out, "to parade, to make a show of physical force, to bully and boast, to be ever ready for a fight. In the normal boy this phase passes. But in all too many it lasts all through life. And when the people raise to power a man who has never made the psychological adjustment, they put into his hands great armies and navies and all the paraphernalia of war as terrible toys for his ghastly play." Although admitting that "such analysis may be pressed too far," the editors felt that its ultimate confirmation was to be found in the women's policies of the dictatorial regimes: "Boys have contempt for girls. Dictators have *contempt* for women. . . . The 'acceptance of masculine superiority' is a dangerous sign of our times."

The editors of the *Companion* thus also understood dictatorship as representing a failure of masculinity. Like Stein, their critique was not directed at men, but at women, who were suffering under "masculine superiority." Unlike Stein, however, the *Companion* was not in a position to argue for a world entirely devoid of masculine authority. On the one hand, the magazine was deeply committed to the involvement of its readers in politics and public life, but on the other hand, it consisted largely of recipes, homemaking tips, and advertisements for items of use in the home. As might be expected, the editors suggested that the solution to the problem of "men who never grew up" rested mainly on improving motherhood: "The responsibility falls especially on women, for as Dr. Chester says, 'Those nations with educated mothers—educated, I mean, in child welfare, dietetics, hygiene, above all psychology—will train citizens to a mature and courageous technique of living.'" Ultimately, then, the *Companion*'s argument was as similar to that of *Little Man, What Now?* as it was to Stein's. Dictators were produced by rifts in the social fabric. Improved family life offered the best opportunity to mend such rifts.

This chapter has surveyed the celebrations and critiques of the dictator through the early 1930s. Mussolini and to a lesser extent Stalin provided the real-world models for the romanticized figure of the dictator in American public culture: a superhuman leader, not bound by normal morality, who would tirelessly use his will to forge national unity and a new society. In the second half of 1932 and the first half of 1933, the dictator, for some Americans, seemed to embody a model of authority that could solve the problems of a country overwhelmed by the Great Depression. Although Mussolini remained a popular figure until 1935, the dictatorial model of authority became less and less acceptable to American cultural producers following Hitler's rise to power in 1933.

But the social and economic crises remained. FDR's self-presentation, films such as *The President Vanishes* and *Little Man, What Now?,* and Sinclair Lewis's *It Can't Happen Here* all attempted to provide alternative models of authority that might respond to these crises. In *Little Man* and *It Can't Happen Here,* social chaos is connected to the rise of dictators. Yet in neither case is this connection made as tightly as it would be made later in the decade. *Little Man* provided no hope for Germany; individual escape—a totally personal solution—was the only path to the film's Hollywood ending. *It Can't Happen Here,* while indicting American society and political life, still focused on personalities to explain the rise of dictatorship in the United States and the character of that dictatorship once it was in power. The novel also offered its protagonist little but personal escape. Having briefly seen dictatorship as an effective solution to social chaos, Americans came to see it as a false hope and the potential cause of further social breakdown. But in both positive and negative accounts, dictatorship took hold both as a reaction to social chaos and as the result of the rise of an extraordinary man, the dictator himself. Later in the 1930s, an entirely different sense of the relationship between social crisis, the dictator, and dictatorship would become dominant in American political culture.

THE TOTALITARIAN STATE
MODERN DICTATORSHIP AS A NEW FORM OF GOVERNMENT, 1920s–1935

Despite the attractions of the dictator, most Americans were hostile to fascism and communism throughout the 1920s and 1930s. In the 1920s fascism and communism were usually seen as polar opposites, a perception that reflected the way most supporters of these two systems understood their relationship. The fiercest anticommunists were often among the strongest admirers of Italian Fascism. And the staunchest antifascists were the Communists who, during their "Third Period" in the late twenties and early thirties, used "fascism" as a term of abuse for every political view to their right, including democratic socialism. In the 1920s even those who shared an antipathy to both systems tended to see them as quite separate threats. "Democracy is challenged today on two sides," wrote Felix Adler, leader of the Ethical Culture movement, in 1926, "by the Soviet minority which rules Russia, and by the Italian dictator."[1]

Shortly after the Nazis came to power, however, American magazines and newspapers began periodically to suggest that Hitler's and Stalin's governments were similar. Hitler's Röhm Purge (often called the "Blood Purge" or the "Night of the Long Knives") and Stalin's Kirov Purge, both of which occurred in 1934, provided early occasions for such comparisons, even by liberal organs like the *New Republic,* the *Nation,* and *Common Sense.* But these comparisons were either personal—Hitler and Stalin were said to be alike—or were critiques of dictatorship per se.[2]

The nature of these comparisons reflect the absence of a conceptual vocabulary that could encompass dictatorships of both left and right. In the early 1930s some liberals such as Horace Kallen and conservatives like Herbert Hoover linked Nazism, Fascism, and Stalinism through these regimes' fundamental opposition to a number of political values that Americans held dear.[3] But what term could describe what these regimes stood *for?* "Dictatorship," which Kallen and others used, lacked specificity, especially as the present regimes seemed fundamentally different from earlier models of that form of government. "Collectivism" became more and more popular among conservatives and skeptical, cautious liberals like Walter Lippmann; indeed, by the second half of the decade it was Hoover's term of choice for the European dictatorships. But "collectivism" tended also to be used to malign the New Deal. Although this was an attraction of the term for those on the American right, for most U.S. observers of the European regimes in the 1930s, collectivism must have seemed too obviously and narrowly political to comfortably serve as an analytic category. By the end of the decade another descriptor of dictatorships of both the left and the right had emerged: "totalitarian."

Comprehending the evolution of the idea of the totalitarian state—and later totalitarianism—in the nation's political, social scientific, and popular discourse during the 1930s is crucial to understanding American political culture in the mid- and late twentieth century. Yet it is a story about which too little is known.[4] The history of the term "totalitarianism" is, in a sense, the victim of the concept's successes and failures. In popular discourse, the word "totalitarianism" became a commonplace by the end of the thirties. Although it lost its currency during World War II, it quickly regained its popularity and has played an important role in the way Americans talk about the world ever since. In U.S. social science, the term played an increasingly important role in the 1930s, faded during the war, and then became a central concept in Cold War analyses of modern politics, especially of communism. Since the 1960s, social scientists have been bitterly divided over the term: generally for the right, totalitarianism remains an indispensable analytic category; for the left, it is an ideological fabrication of the Cold War that has little if any analytic value. But the history of the term has been of scant interest to either its supporters or its detractors. For those who use the term, totalitarianism suggests a phenomenon to be discovered, not a concept to be forged. For most of those who find little value in the theory, the political valence of totalitarianism seems so obvious as to render the particulars of its history almost irrelevant. But whether or not one finds the term analytically useful, it is necessary to get a better handle on the way it entered American discourse, for totalitarianism came to sit at the center of dominant understandings of the political Other, and, through these understandings, of political self-understandings as well.

For all their ideological usefulness during the Cold War, the terms "totalitarian state" and "totalitarianism" are very much products of the interwar period. They rose to prominence in America during the 1930s. Totalitarianism was an ideologically practical concept for Cold Warriors after World War II precisely because of its status in American discourse before the war. Without a thorough understanding of that status, any account of its rise to greater salience in the late 1940s will tend to fall back on a callow functionalism, explaining its place in Cold War discourse as purely a result of political convenience.[5] Moreover, its rise in the earlier period tells us something important about American political culture during the Great Depression; no past is merely prologue.

This chapter recounts the early history of the word "totalitarian" in American discourse, from its arrival in the 1920s through the beginnings of its use as a way of conceptually linking dictatorships of the left with those of the right in the mid-1930s. This history, while far from unknown, is somewhat obscure. Whatever its ultimate empirical value, totalitarianism achieved its status in American political culture without anyone producing a paradigmatic theoretical or analytical account of it. Emerging from Italian debates about the nature of fascism, "totalitarian" made its way by the early 1930s to the United States, where it began to appear regularly in anti-Nazi writings during the years immediately following Hitler's assumption of power. At first, Germany was singled out as the only example of a totalitarian state. By the middle of the decade, however, American writers had begun to use "totalitarian" to conceptually link the German regime, and other dictatorships of the right, with the Soviet Union. But without a well-established conceptual foundation, "totalitarian" in 1930s America functioned more as a negative buzzword than as a clear political category.

"Totalitarian" first appeared as a term of abuse that opponents hurled at Mussolini as he was consolidating his power. Arguing, in May 1923, against Il Duce's proposed new electoral law to eliminate opposition to fascism, antifascist journalist and politician Giovanni Amendola coined the term "totalitarian system [*sistema totalitaria*]" to describe the emerging political order and to contrast it with older "majoritarian" and "minoritarian" systems of government. Apparently, this was the first time that "totalitarian" was ever used. Amendola applied it very narrowly to suggest a breach of standard electoral procedures. The word soon spread among the Italian opposition, although its precise meaning was often far from clear. By late 1923 the use of "totalitarian" among Italian anti-Fascist activists had become, in the words of Abbott Gleason, "general, if strikingly inconsistent."[6]

By 1925 Mussolini had adopted the term as a positive description of his rule. At first, he used it to indicate the revolutionary vitality of his new regime, its commitment to transform society totally and violently; in June 1925 he spoke of "our fierce totalitarian will [*la nostra feroce volontà totali-*

taria]." But soon he and his supporters revised its meaning. As the regime eliminated effective opposition, a sense of stability became more important than revolutionary vitality. As Il Duce moved to consolidate his power by placating traditional nationalists and distancing himself from the squadristi (Fascist militias), "totalitarian" came to mean not revolutionary ferocity but rather the state's desire to absorb all aspects of life into itself. This sense of the word was most clearly developed by political philosopher Giovanni Gentile. Schooled in the Hegelian tradition, Gentile had become by the twenties an extreme statist who denied any place for individual liberty against the will of the national community. After 1925 Gentile used "totalitarian" in reference to his boundless conception of the claims of the state, although its precise definition often remained vague. Soon, the "totalitarian state [*lo stato totalitario*]" became one of Mussolini's favorite phrases to describe the system he had created.[7]

While the term "totalitarian" was getting its start in Italy, a parallel political discussion was developing among conservative German thinkers. German conservatives believed that the chaos of the 1920s represented the general failure of liberal democracy and its conception of the state. In response to this perceived crisis, right-wing political philosophers, most notably Carl Schmitt, began to use the term "total [*total*]" to describe their rival conception of the state. Although Schmitt's "total state [*totaler Staat*]" bore an intellectual relationship to the Italians' "totalitarian state," it was also distinctly different. A Hegelian like Gentile, Schmitt saw a dialectic historical development in which the powerful "executive" state of the ancien régime was replaced by the minimal liberal state, which would in turn be replaced by a synthesis of the two that would fuse state and society—the "total state." If society won this battle, the result would be a "quantitatively total state," essentially an enormous welfare state that would indoctrinate the masses in a powerful ideology designed to support it. If, however, as Schmitt hoped, the state came out on top, the result would be the "qualitatively total state." But even the latter type of regime more closely resembled traditional authoritarianism than the total absorption of all elements of society in the state envisioned by Gentile.[8]

Schmitt's view of the "total state" was extremely influential in Germany during the years marking the end of the Weimar Republic and the beginning of the Third Reich. Although Schmitt had not been a Nazi, he initially was an enthusiastic collaborator when Hitler came to power. The idea of the *totaler Staat* in Nazi Germany probably reached its political apogee in Joseph Goebbels's declaration on 7 November 1933 that the goal of the National Socialist revolution was "the total state [*der totale Staat*], the assumption of the collective public life and the enlistment [*Indienst-nahme*] of all public and private relations." Despite Goebbels's endorsement, many other Nazi leaders were suspicious of a formulation that placed so much emphasis on the state as such. In a January 1934 article in the *Völkischer Beobachter*, party ideologue Alfred Rosenberg urged all Nazis to abandon the phrase. The term never again had resonance in official Nazi pronouncements. Hitler himself preferred to view the state as merely a means to an end, serving an instrumental function for the party. Nor did the term capture one of the essential qualities of National Socialism: its racialized sense of German nationhood. This aversion to the terminology of the *totaler Staat* on Hitler's part intensified during the 1930s as he increasingly sought to present Nazism as a unique achievement. As the *totaler Staat* had, in German political theory, become deeply implicated in assessments of the regime that stressed the similarities between Nazism and Italian Fascism—and even between Nazism and Soviet Communism—the term lost out. Throughout his years in power, Hitler rarely used the phrase and then only on occasions where it made strategic sense to emphasize his indebtedness to Mussolini and Italian Fascism, as in a rather sycophantic letter of 1940 to the Italian dictator. In general, he preferred to refer to the *völkischer Staat* or the *autoritärer Staat*.[9]

Although the totalitarian state had established itself as a meaningful concept in European political debates of the 1920s and 1930s, the idea was exceedingly protean. Coined to suggest a contrast with the majoritarian electoral systems, "totalitarian," in the Italian context, came alternately to refer either to the forcefulness (or fanaticism) of the Fascists' political faith or to the total dominance of the state over the individual in the new Italy. In Germany, Schmitt gave the name *totaler Staat* to two distinct, prospective phenomena, neither of which was quite the same thing as any of the Italian versions.

The Italian discussions of the *stato totalitario* and the German discussions of the *totaler Staat* involved a style of political thought far removed from American political science, let alone popular discourse about politics in the United States. Both the Italian and German conversations partook of a philosophical idealism that had long since lost favor in America. Although in the late nineteenth and early twentieth centuries American academics had built their studies of politics around an idealism descended from Hegel, by the 1920s this style of thought was nearly absent in the United States. Indeed, American political scientists attached a great deal of suspicion to the word "State," often emphasizing its foreignness by capitalizing it.[10] Political scientist Carl Friedrich, born and trained in Germany before immigrating to the United States in the 1920s and after World War II one of the foremost analysts of totalitarianism, explicitly renounced the concept of the state in his first English-language monograph, *Constitutional Government and Politics* (1937).[11]

In the United States, both the variability of meanings assigned to the term "totalitarian state" and the remoteness of the idea from mainstream America help explain the relative absence of the concept even from discussions of Italian Fascism through the early 1930s. The word "totalitarian" made its way into English in 1926 in a translation of an Italian anti-Fascist tract, Luigi Sturzo's *Italy and Fascismo*. But despite its centrality for both friends and foes of Mussolini in Italy, the term was almost never used in America—in either antifascist or pro-Mussolini writings about Italian Fascism—before 1933. When "totalitarian" did appear, it was in the writings of Italians, such as Giovanni Gentile's article on the philosophical basis of Fascism for *Foreign Affairs* in 1928, or in American commentaries that placed it in quotation marks, with an apology by the author for its foreignness. Occasionally, presumably to avoid what might have been seen as an awkward neologism, American authors would describe the Fascist state as "total."[12]

Rather than focus on the totalitarian state, U.S. accounts of Mussolini's regime tended to center on one or more of the other ways in which he described it. Alongside the *stato totalitario* stood the *stato autoritario* and the *stato corporativo*.[13] It was this last term, translated into English as the "corporate state" or occasionally "corporative state," that those who wrote about Italy for American audiences in the 1920s and early 1930s emphasized and that seemed most to capture the attention of U.S. observers of Fascist Italy.[14] Like the totalitarian state, the corporative state was often vaguely defined even by its Italian fascist proponents. Nevertheless, the notion of the corporative state impressed many U.S. business leaders, liberal opinion makers, and even the more conservative elements of the labor movement, as it promised to provide both class harmony and a more substantial safety net—for capital if not for labor—than the potentially hazardous free market. As a characterization of the essence of Fascism, the corporative state thus addressed the interest-group issues that informed most American political understandings. Although idealist notes could be sounded by official Italian Fascist representatives regarding the theory of the corporative state, most at issue for Americans was the ideal relationship between labor and management, the position of the government vis à vis the two groups, and the possibility of greater government management of the economy.[15] Unlike the abstractions of Italian neo-idealism, these issues were very much on the minds of most Americans in the 1920s. They were addressed by President

Hoover's notion of "associationalism." And their importance grew immeasurably with the arrival of the Great Depression.

Only with Hitler's rise to power in Germany in 1933 did the term "totalitarian state" begin to appear frequently in American public discourse, though many, if not most, discussions of the European dictatorships did not yet use the term and the phrase was often of peripheral interest in those that did. In July 1933 the *Christian Century* cited the totalitarian state as the driving force behind Hitler's attacks on German Protestant churches during his first months in power. In December *Newsweek* emphasized its significance in the title of an article: "Totalitarian State Finally Achieved by Hitler." Elmer Rice's *Judgment Day* (1934), considered the first major American anti-Nazi play, tells the story of a show trial in a fictional southeastern European country ruled by a Nazi-like regime. Early in the first act, one of the judges warns Conrad, the dissident defendant, to respect the new order: "See that you do not forget that we have the good fortune here to be living in a totalitarian state."[16]

The growing importance of the term can be seen in its many appearances in *Nazism: An Assault on Civilization,* a collection of popular essays dramatizing the Nazi threat written by twenty-one journalists, academics, and public figures ranging from former Democratic presidential candidate Al Smith to European correspondent Emil Lengyel. Published in March 1934, the book went through three printings the next year. Six of the contributors referred to the new German regime as "totalitarian": James Waterman Wise, a journalist and Jewish community leader who coedited the collection; Dorothy Thompson; Stanley High, *Christian Science Monitor* correspondent in Germany, Russia, and elsewhere in Europe until 1933; Werner Hegemann, a German expatriate historian and economist who had been at the New School for Social Research since fleeing the Third Reich; Ludwig Lore, a German writer and labor activist before his escape to America; and John Haynes Holmes, pastor of the Community Church of New York.[17]

That the term "totalitarian" first gained prominence in America as a negative depiction of the Nazi state seems a bit paradoxical. Despite its vital role in Italian debates on fascism since the 1920s, the idea of the totalitarian state had never made it into common parlance in U.S. discussions of Italy. At the time that American magazines, plays, and books were popularizing the term as a distinctive attribute of Nazism, the Nazis themselves were backing away from the totalitarian state (or its German cognate *der totale Staat*) as a description of National Socialism. And nothing had happened to change the most probable reason for the earlier lack of attention to the concept by American writers: its foreignness and philosophical obscurity.

But in a number of ways, the very foreignness and obscurity of the "totalitarian state" must have recommended it to American anti-Nazi publicists in the years immediately after Hitler's rise to power. Such a term could alert the public to the novelty and danger of Nazism. In 1933 many Americans still were favorably disposed to Mussolini. Anti-Nazi writers would have wanted to efficiently convey the notion that Hitler's New Order was fundamentally different from any system that would be acceptable to the United States and certainly worse than Fascist Italy. The "totalitarian state" would naturally suggest itself to writers providing early anti-Nazi accounts of Hitler's regime. The foreign correspondents and antifascist European refugee intellectuals who presented Americans with their first views of the Third Reich would have been well exposed to the idea of the totalitarian state through its use in European political debates. Indeed, Hitler's German opponents were much more enamored of that description of the Nazi state than was the Führer himself.[18]

The term was particularly significant to Protestant opponents of Hitler's plans to create a new "German Christianity" that would put Protestant Churches entirely in the service of the state. Indeed, it was first in connection with Hitler's attempt to dominate the German churches that the concept of the totalitarian state became conspicuous in American public culture. In the early months of the Nazi regime, Hitler's goal of Gleichschaltung—the "coordination" of all political, economic, and social power—was widely reported, and criticized, in the U.S. press.[19] The Nazis quickly applied the doctrine of Gleichschaltung to the Evangelical Churches of Germany. Although Pastor Niemöller, Karl Barth, and a number of other Protestant clergymen opposed this move and formed a group known as the Confessional Church, most German Protestant leaders eventually agreed to join the German Christianity movement, which formally endorsed Nazi doctrines on race and politics.

These events deeply troubled many American Protestants. The concern was not merely humanitarian sympathy. At a time when pacifism was a major cause for many liberal Protestants in the United States, the ability of the state to order citizens to violate their religious convictions was a potential problem even for American believers.[20] The *Christian Century,* the most esteemed mainline ecumenical Protestant journal, expressed concern over two aspects of the German situation. The first and most obvious was Hitler's attempt to dominate Germany's spiritual life. But equally disturbing was the relatively low level of protest by German Protestant leaders, a silence that the *Christian Century* attributed, probably correctly, to the traditional otherworldly attitude of the German Evangelical Churches. To

American Protestant heirs of the social gospel, the German Lutheran re-treat from social and political involvement was generally alarming. In light of their apparent acquiescence to Hitler's desires for "German Christianity," the German churches' otherworldliness became a powerful negative object lesson for Protestants everywhere.[21]

For months, in editorials and articles, the *Christian Century* discussed the crisis of the German churches without ever invoking the totalitarian state. Then, in a 28 June 1933 article attacking both the Nazis and their "Barthian" opponents, Reinhold Niebuhr labeled the German system "totalitarian" and attributed it to the Führer himself: "Nothing can, for the time being, hin-der Hitler in developing his 'totalitarian' state, a state which exercises au-thority over every type of human association and assumes direct control of all organizations whether athletic, artistic, commercial, religious or merely social."[22]

The object of Niebuhr's attack was not new to the journal. His argument that Nazism desired a new level of state involvement in previously private aspects of life had been made before in the *Christian Century*.[23] By using the phrase "totalitarian state," Niebuhr did not so much contribute a novel idea as give a name to an aspect of the Nazi regime that had already been rebuked in the journal. Although more precise in his formulation than most other Americans who used the term in the early 1930s, Niebuhr's definition of the totalitarian state was clearly related to some of its most important European meanings and captured the essence of what would quickly be-come its most common American usage: a state that claimed competence in all aspects of life. The antithesis of the totalitarian state was thus the liberal state.

Over the next several months, the totalitarian state was repeatedly cen-sured in the *Christian Century*. Not all of the articles about the crisis in German Protestantism invoked the totalitarian state, but even those that did not do so raised the issue of the dangerously expanding scope of the German state.[24] The totalitarian state became an important concept for the *Christian Century* because it seemed to characterize exactly that as-pect of Nazism that the journal's editors and many of its contributors found most disturbing. Like many other American commentators, the editors were apparently also convinced that the term was favored by the Nazis them-selves.[25]

Shortly after it appeared in the *Christian Century,* the "totalitarian state" began to surface in the secular press. Whereas the *Christian Century* found that the concept matched its concerns about the Nazi regime, the secu-lar press took longer to adopt it, invoked it less frequently, and used it to suggest more generally Hitler's pernicious ambitions to expand the scope of the state. In July 1934 *Time* magazine covered a speech by Franz von Papen, a non-Nazi and, at the time, Hitler's vice chancellor, that offered "the first candid and sweeping criticism of Nazi policies voiced by any German statesmen since Hitler came to power." *Time* presented the speech as a political crisis for the Third Reich. In dramatizing its point, *Time* used the term "totalitarian state" to indicate the extent of the state's involvement in the lives of its citizens. In its characteristic purple prose, the magazine described von Papen as "raking the Brownshirts' vaunted 'Totalitarian State' from stem to stern . . . flaying its muzzling of the Press, its meddling with religion, its encouragement of fanaticism."[26]

In 1933 and 1934, when journalists and anti-Nazi polemicists in America spoke of the totalitarian state, they did so in reference to Nazi Germany exclusively. Although U.S. observers saw similarities between the government of Germany and those of Italy, the Soviet Union, and various other countries around the world (including the United States under the New Deal), the term "totalitarian" tended to be reserved for the Third Reich. Whereas the *Christian Century* accused Russia and Italy, along with Germany, of abandoning limits on the state, only the Nazis were said to advocate a totalitarian state. Simeon Strunsky, writing about lessons to be learned from the regimes of Mussolini, Stalin, and Hitler in the *New York Times Magazine* in January 1934, referred to "Mussolini's Corporative State and Hitler's Totalitarian State." Although he reserved the word "totalitarian" for the Nazis, Strunsky felt that Hitler, Mussolini, and Stalin were rather similar; emphasizing dictatorship itself, he noted that all three leaders advocated "the Autocratic State."[27]

Others alluded to Germany's purportedly unique, "totalitarian" nature to point out genuine differences between Hitler and Mussolini. In his introduction to *Nazism: An Assault on Civilization* (1934), James Waterman Wise distinguished Nazi Germany from Fascist Italy, with which it shared an "economic motivation." In Wise's view, Nazism was not simply a variety of fascism, for "differences in degree, if they are great enough, become differences in kind." Unlike fascism, Nazism was

> in essence the regression of an entire nation to sub-civilization level. The extent of this regression may be gauged from its insistence on race as the determinant of the state, and its sequent expulsion or extermination of all who do not belong to the racial majority; from its attitude toward women and the inferior status it assigns them; from its scarcely veiled glorification of war as the goal of national life and as the norm of

international relations; from its intellectual regimentation and its ruth-less suppression of political, religious, and even scientific freedom—in, sum from the totalitarian state envisaged by Hitler and executed by his government.[28]

A number of things are worth noting about the way in which secu-lar writers referred to the totalitarian state in addressing American mass audiences of the early 1930s. They used the term rather loosely. Although most applied the concept in connection with the growth of the state into new areas of social life, few if any of these observers made clear what they meant by "totalitarian." They identified the term, at least implicitly, as the Nazis'—or Hitler's—own conception. This identification may have justified their failure to clarify the meaning of the "totalitarian state." The phrase was applied almost exclusively to Nazism, even by authors who saw similarities between the German, Italian, and Russian regimes. Finally, the totalitarian state was usually cited as only one aspect of Hitler's Third Reich. In the texts surveyed, only James Waterman Wise used "totalitar-ian state" to characterize the entire Nazi regime. Indeed, it was possible to discuss, and indict, Nazism without ever mentioning the totalitarian state.

In the American academy, too, writing about the totalitarian state began in earnest after Hitler assumed power. His regime was responsible for the immigration of a large number of German scholars to the United States, as the Nazis purged German universities of Jews and political opponents. Though Mussolini's rise had also led to the arrival of some anti-Fascist Ital-ian academics in America, German refugee scholars had a much greater impact for a variety of reasons. First, anti-Fascism, particularly in the 1920s, was a contested political view among American academics. Unlike Hitler, Mussolini had prominent and vocal admirers among U.S. scholars. Most of them opposed Fascism, yet Harvard philosopher George Santayana, Yale English professor William Lyon Phelps, and Columbia's Shepard B. Clouch, Herbert W. Schneider, and Carlton J. H. Hayes all wrote admiringly about Fascism at one time or another. Although the Italian regime was guilty of abridging academic freedom, the public book burnings, mass dismissals of "non-Aryan" faculty, and other open, brutal assaults on Germany's univer-sities went far beyond anything Mussolini had done and made the Nazi regime especially repugnant to American academics. This greater brutality also accounted for the much larger number of German refugee scholars. Over the course of the 1930s more Italian political exiles entered the Ameri-can academy, but relatively few of them had come to the United States in the 1920s.[29]

Moreover, due in part to historical links between American academics and Germany, German refugee scholars rose to positions of far greater prominence than did their Italian colleagues. Although a figure like Gaetano Salvemini, an Italian anti-Fascist historian who spent time in the United States in the 1920s and left Italy to take a post at Harvard in 1933, was widely respected in anti-Fascist circles, he never achieved the level of fame or cultural importance in America that Paul Tillich, Erich Fromm, or Hannah Arendt would eventually attain. One institution proved especially significant for German refugee scholars: the University in Exile—soon renamed the Graduate Faculty of Political and Social Science—established by Alvin Johnson at the New School for Social Research in 1933. The Graduate Faculty, which had twelve members in 1933 and twenty-six by 1941, became a home for German sociology, a field that had been maligned by the Nazis, as most of its prominent members were Jewish. The New School not only provided an institutional base but also, with its new journal *Social Research,* gave an intellectual bully pulpit to the refugee scholars. Unlike its uptown compatriot, the Institut für Sozialforschung, better known as the Frankfurt School, housed at Columbia, which worked in isolation from American academics and published almost exclusively in its own German-language journal *Zeitschrift für Sozialforschung,* the University in Exile reached out to American academics. The first volume of *Social Research* (1934) published the first academic article printed in America that was devoted entirely to analyzing the totalitarian state.[30] The German scholars at the New School and elsewhere, who felt totally comfortable in the intellectual world of the Hegelian state, helped bring the state back as an important category in American social science, if not in analyses of the United States, certainly in examinations of the European situation.

Nevertheless, American social scientists still must have felt uncomfortable with the category of the totalitarian state. Although most academic uses of the term involved Nazi Germany, social scientists often acknowledged that the "totalitarian state" was an Italian coinage. Even after Hitler took over the Reich, they used the term gingerly and inconsistently. Often the totalitarian state was mentioned briefly in more general analyses of the Italian and German regimes. Most authors kept the term in quotation marks or avoided defining it; some even implied that it had no clear definition.[31] Such uses were but a small step away from journalists' vague deployment of the term as an epithet for Nazism.

A small number of American social thinkers, who found the term analytically useful, sought to be more precise about its meaning. They did not, however, arrive at any general agreement. Max Lerner suggested that the totalitarian state was the corporative state, that is, a state organized around government-supervised organizations of the major economic groups in society. Sidney B. Fay at Harvard asserted that "the establishment of the 'Totalitarian State' . . . means that the Nazi revolution must go uncompromisingly forward until it embraces the totality of the German people in every phase of activity." Yale's Carl Loewenstein stated that totalitarian systems are those that denigrate the rights of the individual. Drawing explicitly on Carl Schmitt while quietly eliminating the idealist conception of the state, Arthur Steiner of the University of California at Los Angeles maintained that "the theory of totalitarianism" was "that there is no limit to the legitimate objects and subjects of eventual public jurisdiction."[32] The diverse meanings given to "totalitarian"—a corporative state, revolutionary fervor, the denigration of individual rights, growth in the area seen as subject to public control—reflect the wide range of ideas that had been attached to the term in Europe. Yet the divergent European meanings, and the similarly disparate American ones, appear not to have been remarked upon by American writers in this period. "Totalitarian" seems to have slipped into American social scientific discourse with neither agreement nor acknowledgement of disagreement on its meaning.

The extent of this disagreement can be seen most clearly in attempts to use the term nonpejoratively. Certain meanings attached to the concept of the totalitarian state, most notably an open or even fanatical hostility to all individual liberties, were obviously negative in the eyes of most American thinkers. But other meanings were more ambiguous. Seeing "no limit to the legitimate objects and subjects of eventual public jurisdiction" (Steiner's definition), was not necessarily a bad thing, especially in light of the failures of the classical liberal conception of the state in the midst of the Great Depression. Although Steiner did not suggest that the achievement of a totalitarian state might be good for a democracy, other American intellectuals with similar conceptions of the totalitarian state did. In a short book entitled *Crisis Government* (1934), New York University law professor Lindsay Rogers analyzed democratic and dictatorial responses to the world economic crisis. Rogers, an anticommunist and antifascist liberal, offered a ringing endorsement of the New Deal and suggested that President Roosevelt had managed to extend the purview of government action without destroying representative institutions: "Indeed, without a dictatorship we have more of a totalitarian state than can be found anywhere save Russia; but our state has not abandoned egalitarian and libertarian ideals, and, if we so choose, we can without violence limit its range. . . . Mr. Roosevelt has demonstrated that you can have all the advantages of a dictatorship and not abandon democracy."[33]

Further to the left, Alfred Bingham, coeditor of the journal *Common Sense,* associated the totalitarian state—in his view, an exclusively German phenomenon—with the Italian corporative state and indicated that both might be unintentional, but positive, first steps toward true socialism. Similarly, the *Christian Century* briefly flirted with "Christian totalitarianism" as a response to the German "totalitarian state" that the journal had repeatedly attacked. Starting in December 1933, it published a series of editorials suggesting that, although Christianity could live side by side with other "sovereignties," it had to claim for itself power in all aspects of life, thus it had to be "totalitarian." The journal's call for a totalitarian religion appealed both to old ideas of the social gospel and to the need for a vigorous offensive against the encroachment of the state. By February 1934, however, the *Christian Century* had dropped the notion of Christian totalitarianism, in part because it sounded perilously close to a call for a totalitarian *church,* which would have been an odd plea for an American Protestant publication to make in the 1930s. Indeed, the final editorial calling for totalitarian Christianity explicitly noted that a totalitarian church would be just as bad as a totalitarian state.[34]

These positive appropriations of "totalitarian" were certainly unusual, but they also appear not to have been particularly shocking to readers in the early 1930s.[35] Reviewers of Rogers's *Crisis Government,* for instance, praised the book and said nothing about the author's suggestion that the New Deal was a democratic example of the totalitarian state.[36] But both the attempts to formulate a concept of the totalitarian state that encompassed democratic as well as authoritarian regimes and the *Christian Century*'s appeals for totalitarian Christianity quickly faded. Although not clearly defined, "totalitarian" had already begun to accumulate overwhelmingly negative connotations in American discourse. By the second half of the 1930s, only Roosevelt's most bitter enemies would have dreamed of referring to the New Deal as totalitarian.

Although the negative associations of the term "totalitarian" would become a permanent feature of the concept in America, its exclusive application to Nazi Germany began to decline. In fact, by the end of the 1930s most American authors tended to use "totalitarianism" to refer to dictatorships of both the right and the left. Although arguments over the concept in Europe essentially concerned the nature of fascism, early European proponents and opponents of the totalitarian state occasionally included the

Soviet Union as an example of the phenomenon.[37] In America, the various meanings that began to accrue to the totalitarian state—hostility to individual liberties, the omnipotence and omnipresence of government in all aspects of social life, the desire to coordinate independent social institutions with the will of a single revolutionary party, even the vague whiff of foreignness that accompanied the term itself—happened to coincide with many concerns of the growing number of American journalists and intellectuals who drew comparisons between Nazism and Stalinism.[38]

The association of the term "totalitarian" with the equation of left- and right-wing dictatorships was a slow process in American political culture. Essentially a number of separate, but related, transformations took place in the way American writers used the term. First and most obviously, the totalitarian state was no longer presented as a uniquely German political phenomenon. Second, many Americans comparing dictatorships of the left and the right began to see them not as different systems with similar characteristics, but rather as essentially similar systems. Finally, then, the totalitarian state went from being *one aspect* of Nazi rule to the *essence* of all the regimes to which it was applied. These transformations can be found in the writings of one of the first American authors to use the term "totalitarian" to link the Soviet and German regimes: Duke University economist Calvin B. Hoover. A specialist in comparative economic systems, Hoover went to the Soviet Union in the late 1920s and became an expert on the Soviet economy. Late in 1932 he visited Germany, where he witnessed the Nazi accession to power, then returned to the Soviet Union. Seeing similarities in the turn of events he witnessed in the two countries, he drafted a series of articles for the *Virginia Quarterly* that compared the German, Soviet, and Italian regimes. The first, entitled "Dictators and Democracies," appeared in April 1934.

Hoover set out to address the following question: "Are the dictatorships in Russia, Italy, and Germany so similar in nature that it is legitimate to lump them together under any term such as Caesarism?" Applying the concept of the totalitarian state to all three regimes allowed a moderately liberal comparative economist like Hoover to highlight similarities between them that were usually obscured by their quite different doctrines. After denying any common elements in the circumstances or methods by which they came into power, Hoover turned to the nature of the old regimes in Germany, Italy, and Russia and the characteristics of those that had replaced them. In all three cases, the old "systems of law and of economics were founded upon individualism, that is to say, upon the principle of economic liberalism, in the German meaning of the term." And in each case, the old regime lacked dynamism and had lost confidence in itself. These old regimes were thus replaced by dynamic, "totalitarian states." The new, totalitarian states claimed to serve the group interest while "the individual is completely stripped of protection against acts of force by agents of the state." Their stress on the cult of force also made all of the totalitarian states prone to expansion and war.[39]

Nonetheless, Hoover insisted that differences remained between the regimes in Italy, Germany, and Russia:

> The three totalitarian states have certain basic characteristics in common. They are alike in their contempt for democracy, liberalism, pacifism, and parliamentary methods, in their admiration of force, and in their reliance upon direct action. These similarities do not, however, warrant the conclusion that if parliamentary institutions were to be destroyed, it would be a matter of indifference as to which type of dictatorship succeeded them. It would make a tremendous difference to individuals who are living in the countries which still retain parliamentarianism, which type of dictatorship came to power.

Nor did Hoover feel that greater state involvement in the economy was necessarily totalitarian. Indeed, for parliamentary regimes to survive, they needed to become more dynamic in their efforts to control the economy and defeat depression. He was optimistic that the level of discipline and cohesion necessary for constructive economic control could be gained without resorting to a totalitarian state: "It may be objected that only in a totalitarian state could such conditions obtain, but we cannot assume this is so. There is no reason why those who believe in the maintenance of parliamentary, democratic, and liberal institutions should not prove as effective in organization and propaganda as the advocates of a Communist or Fascist dictatorship."[40]

In 1937 "Dictators and Democracies" was revised and reprinted in a short volume of Hoover's essays that bore the same name. It is worth glancing ahead to this later version of the 1934 essay, as Hoover's revisions to the text reflect the changes that were to take place in American ideas of the totalitarian state and highlight some of the essential elements of Hoover's thinking in 1934. In the 1937 collection, Hoover greatly narrowed the differences between the regimes and denied the possibility for great state economic involvement outside of totalitarian regimes. He retained the above-quoted passage on the differences between the regimes but suggested in a new section that "no unbridgeable gulf any longer separates the National Socialist and Soviet ideologies." Indeed, the entirety of a July 1936 article by Hoover entitled "The Dictators March," which also appeared first in the *Virginia Quarterly* and then in *Dictators and Democracies,* argues that these systems were in the process of converging. No longer did Hoover think that the kind of regime that took over would "be a matter of tremendous difference to individuals" living in a country whose democratic institutions fell: "The only significant distinction which remains is that in Russia the totalitarian state arose as a means of establishing economic collectivism. In Italy and in Germany, on the other hand, the totalitarian state was established for its own sake, but leads inevitably to economic collectivism. This difference is of moment, however, only to the student of historical evolution."[41]

The optimistic section of the 1934 essay on the possibility of parliamentary regimes attaining more discipline and cohesion to control the economy was completely altered in its 1937 printing. Rather, Hoover now asserted: "The difficulty is, of course, that these conditions may be attainable only under a totalitarian state system, or that a parliamentary government so organized might become in fact a totalitarian state." In 1937 he concluded that parliamentary regimes had to survive not by seizing economic authority similar to that of the totalitarian states but by managing the economy "without the necessity for the exercise of such a degree of power by government over the economy that a totalitarian system would become almost inevitable."[42]

These changes highlight the ways in which Hoover's pre-1936 uses of the totalitarian state to link regimes of left and right differed from those of the later period. Though in 1934 he drew on the idea of the totalitarian state to suggest similarities between Soviet Communism and German National Socialism, these similarities did not overwhelm differences he perceived between them. The totalitarian state was but one aspect—albeit the most important aspect—of these regimes, which remained in other ways distinct. The stated ideologies of the various dictatorial regimes were still significant, in his analysis. Nor did he initially extend the idea of the totalitarian state to encompass all economic planning schemes, as he, and many other intellectuals, would later do. Moreover, in 1934 Hoover was nearly alone among American academics in using the term to link Communism, Fascism, and Nazism. By the end of the decade, he would have much company.

In the first half of the 1930s, American writers had only begun to use the concept of the totalitarian state to link dictatorships of the left and right. By the end of the decade, however, the idea of totalitarianism had begun to play a central role in linking these regimes. Yet this growing significance of the term was not accompanied by an evolving precision in its use. No real theoretical discussion of the meaning of the "totalitarian state" took place in America in the early 1930s. Indeed, few even bothered to define "totalitarian." No single writer emerged as the authority on the subject. There was no canonical account of the totalitarian state. Nonetheless, through a slow process of osmosis, a network of associations began to form around these terms. Despite some attempts to use the word neutrally or even positively, "totalitarian" quickly accumulated entirely negative connotations in the United States. The "totalitarian state" came to be associated with foreign political ideas, the expansion of state authority, and the degradation of individual liberties. Though "totalitarian" was principally used as a journalistic epithet for Nazism, the vagueness and foreignness of the term could function as a way of drawing attention to the peculiar evils of Nazism. As it came more and more to be used not to distinguish Nazism, but rather to suggest first common features and later the essential equivalence of dictatorships of the right and left, its imprecision took on a further purpose. The "totalitarian state" and "totalitarianism" became canvases on which American thinkers could project a whole series of loosely related fears about the nature of certain foreign regimes and the fate of American democracy. Rather than providing a clear conceptual grounding for comparisons between fascism and communism, the terms functioned for most of the 1930s as buzzwords, powerful expressions whose precise meaning was never clear.

In the second half of the decade, the concepts of the totalitarian state and totalitarianism would become sites for an important aspect of 1930s American political culture often overlooked by historians: a growing fear of certain kinds of mass politics. This fear was most pronounced on the political right and was famously exhibited by the editors of the *Partisan Review* and others on the anti-Stalinist left. But even some individuals associated with the Popular Front left would begin to express these concerns. By the end of the thirties the European dictatorships would become, for many Americans, negative object lessons in the effects of modern mass politics. For many, including Calvin Hoover, "totalitarianism" came to stand for all of these lessons. But in the early 1930s, most American analyses of these regimes still focused on their leaders. Most discussions of the totalitarian state were brief or confined to fairly specialized writings of economists and other social scientists. As attention shifted from the persons of the European dictators to the political systems they represented, "totalitarianism" would grow in importance in American political discourse.

3 THE DISAPPEARING DICTATOR
DECLINING REGARD FOR DICTATORS AMID GROWING FEARS OF DICTATORSHIP, 1936–1941

When sociologists Robert and Helen Lynd returned to Muncie, Indiana, in the mid-1930s, a decade after their work that had led to the already classic study *Middletown* (1929), they found *Middletown in Transition,* as the Lynds titled the 1937 sequel to their original book. One of the transitions that appeared to be taking place had to do with attitudes toward dictatorship. In a chapter entitled, "Middletown Faces Both Ways," the Lynds report that on the eve of the 1936 elections there existed deep antifascist, anticommunist, and generally antidictatorial sentiments among all residents of Muncie, including the business class. A business leader supporting Alfred Landon confidently proclaimed, "We go into the closing days of the campaign determined to achieve our goal of true American government . . . as opposed to radicalism, waste, and dictatorial powers."[1]

Yet, though all the residents of Middletown seemed to oppose dictatorship, there was great fear that it might take root there. In 1936 numerous editorials in local papers decried the dangers of fascism and suggested "BUT IT COULD HAPPEN HERE." Rather than rejecting this fear as ill-founded, the Lynds ominously suggested that the business class—the only group in Middletown to build true class solidarity, according to the Lynds—at least secretly desired a dictatorship. The Lynds made their case based on the business community's strenuous objections to the New Deal, its impatience with the status quo, and its strong anticommunism, which was greater than its antifascism. Most significantly, two newspaper editorials called for dictatorship. The Lynds mention, but do not attach weight to, the fact that these editorials appeared in 1931 and 1932.[2]

In the mid-1930s American attitudes toward dictatorship underwent a transition. As the Lynds' evidence suggests, dictatorship was nearly universally unpopular in the United States by 1936. Despite this fact, fears that dictatorship would soon arise in America were, if anything, growing. The

Lynds' ability to find fascism brewing in Muncie, Indiana, in 1936 despite much evidence to the contrary is a good example of this apprehension. Along with the growth in the fear of dictatorship, important changes were taking place in the nature of that fear. If in the early 1930s Americans were fearful, or hopeful, of a single man asserting himself and ruling the country by his will, in the last half of the decade they dethroned the dictator from his central role in the image of dictatorship.

Events in the mid-1930s—both overseas and at home—made the dangers of dictatorship more vivid for Americans. Italy's invasion of Ethiopia in 1935 received a generally unfavorable reaction in the U.S. press, prompted the first large mobilization of the African American community on a purely foreign policy issue, and ended Mussolini's popularity in the United States. Before the Nazi takeover, Germany had been elected to host both the Winter and Summer Olympic Games of 1936. Afterward, some Olympic officials in Germany and elsewhere feared that the new regime's hostility to modern sports would impel it to cancel the games. Instead, the Nazis decided to seize upon the games as a propaganda opportunity of the first order. By 1934 the International Olympic Committee faced a different challenge: a worldwide movement to boycott the Olympics in Germany and schedule alternate games for the summer of 1936 in Barcelona, Spain. In the United States, the games became a focus of the anti-Nazi drive that had emerged even before 1933 and had steadily gained momentum since then, building on a base of Jewish, labor, and liberal Protestant and Catholic opinion. A 23 March 1935 poll by the American Institute of Public Opinion (AIPO) indicated that 43 percent of Americans favored shunning the upcoming games in Garmisch-Partenkirchen and Berlin. Avery Brundage, president of the U.S. Olympic Committee and the most vocal American voice for participation, eventually won out. The U.S. decision to send teams to both Winter and Summer Olympics in Nazi Germany took much of the wind out of the boycott movement. The Olympic Games, garnering extensive coverage in the U.S. press, gave the American people an extended glimpse into Nazi Germany, albeit groomed for international consumption.[3]

Even if the boycott had succeeded, the rival Barcelona games would have failed. By the summer of 1936, Spain had erupted in civil war. Conservative rebels led by Francisco Franco were attempting to overthrow the legitimate government of the Spanish Republic, which had grown more left-wing and anticlerical over the previous few years. Soon Italy and Germany were aiding the rebels, while the Soviet Union provided supplies to the Loyalists. The war aroused passions and debates in the United States. The resurgent Communist Party (CP), newly embarked on its Popular Front strategy, tried to galvanize assistance for the Loyalists. The American Catholic hierarchy, on the other hand, organized support for Franco's rebels. Proponents for both sides presented arguments that would appeal to large segments of the American public: pro-Loyalists argued to uphold democracy and governmental legitimacy and even to oppose Catholicism; those in favor of Franco appealed to Catholicism, traditional values, and anticommunism. Both sides railed against outside influence in Spain (while, of course, trying to raise just such backing from the United States). By its conclusion in 1939, the Spanish conflict gripped America. It seemed to presage the expected clash between fascism and communism throughout Europe; although such a war did come, it would be delayed for two years by the Nazi-Soviet Pact. Though most Americans refused to support either side at the start of the Spanish Civil War, by 1939 a large majority favored the Loyalists.[4]

While events overseas provided Americans with examples of dictatorship, concerns about such a prospect at home continued. Whatever desires for an American dictator that may have existed in 1932 had long since disappeared. The rhetoric of dictatorship that FDR had used so effectively at the start of his first term had been dropped almost immediately. What remained, however, were fears of dictatorship fed and conditioned by White House efforts to restructure the federal government and by the sometimes jarring encounters, experienced by people across the country, with the growing bureaucracy in Washington and its alphabet soup of agencies. The Roosevelt administration scrupulously avoided describing its actions as expanding the powers of the president per se, while its opponents warned of a dictatorship. In general, the administration and its friends won the war. Even in 1940, when FDR sought an unprecedented third term, Republican attempts to exploit the fear of dictatorship in campaign materials—one button read "Third Reich, Third International, Third Term"—were only marginally successful.[5]

Some administration battles were lost to the rhetoric of impending dictatorship, most notably FDR's plan to restructure the federal judiciary, which was defeated by Congress in 1937. White House opponents warned of the dangers posed by "court packing" to the U.S. Constitution and ominously suggested that dictatorship might be just around the corner. Dorothy Thompson, who had publicly supported Roosevelt's reelection in 1936, testified at length before the Senate Judiciary Committee against the president's restructuring of the federal judiciary; much of her testimony revolved around parallels she saw between Germany on the eve of Hitler's rise to power and the United States. Arguing against FDR, North Carolina's conservative Democratic senator Josiah W. Bailey claimed that the independence of the Supreme Court had both protected the South from the evils of "the social equality of the Negro" and prevented the sort of persecution that Jews faced in Nazi Germany from ever arising in America. Many Americans believed that FDR's plan to restructure the judiciary was driven by a desire to increase his power.[6]

Poll numbers from 1936 on show a fairly strong belief, particularly among Republicans, that Roosevelt's policies might lead to dictatorship: in 1936, 45 percent of Americans surveyed thought so; the number among Republicans was 83 percent. One-third of those responding to an April 1938 poll believed that "the United States will have a dictator in our lifetime." Virtually nobody thought that this putative trend toward dictatorship was a good thing. In May 1937 only 3 percent of those asked if they would "like to see a dictatorship established in this country" answered yes.[7]

Although the prospect of dictatorship was on people's minds, their notions of what it was they were afraid of were evolving. The poll numbers given above are, at best, an imperfect snapshot of popular sentiment. What exactly did Americans fear? For many on the right, FDR's personal power was the issue. Whereas in 1932 a variety of citizens, especially in the business community, all but called for a dictatorial presidency—and in 1933 Roosevelt himself echoed these desires in his first inaugural address—in the mid-1930s suggestions of such concentrated power were a real problem for the administration. In the early 1930s, it had looked to many Americans as if Mussolini's style of heroic, personalistic leadership might be able to solve the economic and social disorder that faced the nation. But the experience of Ethiopia and Spain and events in Germany and the Soviet Union in the intervening years had cast a negative light on dictatorial regimes by 1936. This made the charge of dictatorship—or prospective dictatorship—extremely dire. Roosevelt himself constantly tried to shift attention to other concentrations of power, as in his attacks on the Supreme Court or "economic royalists." But even as his growing power and desire for a third term set off fears of dictatorship, the very meaning of the word and the image of the dictator were shifting away from the heroic Mussolini model.

Except for FDR opponents engaged in short-term political hyperbole, Americans in the second half of the 1930s had more occasion to stress the differences between the United States and the European dictatorships than to imagine similarities. Obviously, it was crucial for liberals and those on the left who were generally enthusiastic about Roosevelt to deflect accusations that the president was a would-be dictator. The middle years of the decade saw the emergence of a new, left-liberal coalition organized mainly around the issue of antifascism. Although its domestic roots were arguably deeper, the Popular Front received much of its organizational impetus from the Communist Party following a major change in direction by the Comintern in 1935. From 1936 to 1939 the CP adopted a new policy toward other parties of the left and center, like the Socialists and pro-FDR Democrats. Rather than calling them "social fascists," the CP announced that it would work with them in a "popular front" to defeat fascism. Despite the new tone, the CP was still committed to a class analysis that would lead them to understand fascism in terms other than the power of the leader. But the Popular Front nonetheless drew sharp distinctions, in a way that Third Period Communists never had, between bourgeois democracy and dictatorship. Thus, the CP endorsed FDR in 1936 as the best strategy for defeating fascism in America; Alf Landon, on the other hand, was labeled a fascist. As U.S. intervention in Europe became an important issue for the Popular Front, liberals and leftists were even more committed to convincing a broad public that Nazi Germany and Fascist Italy were completely unlike, and necessarily threatened, the United States. As the title of one best-seller from early 1941 put it, *You Can't Do Business with Hitler.*

Most Americans outside the Popular Front also drew sharp contrasts between democracy and dictatorship. For foreign correspondents in Germany, Spain, Italy, and Russia, the experience of conditions in these countries made communicating the great differences between life in the United States and life in the dictatorships of paramount importance. For most noninterventionists, the very foreignness of these regimes—their distance both physically and ideologically from the United States—made involvement with them both unnecessary and potentially harmful. Even for those who hoped to convince the American public that Roosevelt wanted a dictatorship, emphasizing the huge dissimilarity between dictatorship itself and American democracy could be a useful strategy, particularly given the president's personal popularity.

Although in the late 1930s dictatorship was almost universally seen as being diametrically opposed to American democracy, the fear remained that America might be on that road. Depending on their politics, many Americans felt that dictatorship was possible if Landon (or Roosevelt) won in 1936, if the president (or the Supreme Court) was allowed too much power, or if the United States did (or did not) intervene in the war in Europe.

Along with these growing apprehensions, a great shift took place in American discourse on European dictatorships and the European dictators themselves. The dominant image of dictatorship early in the decade had been that of the heroic—or horrific—man who single-handedly tamed—or oppressed—the unruly masses beneath him and restored honor and pride, or at least power, to his nation. As the archetype of this model, Mussolini was a traditional hero to many Americans, a traditional tyrant to others; either way, his personality was at the center of most understandings of his regime. His willingness to submit to countless interviews with the U.S. press underscored his charisma and contributed to American understandings of Fascism. Even *Fortune* magazine's attempt to study the Fascist state time and time again relied on Il Duce to explain events in Italy.

In the late 1930s, not only did dictatorship become an almost entirely negative concept in American political culture, but also the dictator himself became less important in explaining dictatorship. Observers of all political stripes focused more on the social situation in countries under dictatorship and less on the dictator's personality. Even in the case of Roosevelt's attempted court packing—which would appear to be a simple case of a leader trying to increase his own power—a number of witnesses testifying before the Senate Judiciary Committee against the plan, including Dorothy Thompson, suggested that public opinion, not any desire on the part of the president, was responsible for the danger that the plan posed to democracy.[8]

In the mid-1930s commentators often causally unmoored the dictator from his regime. Not everyone in the early 1930s had explained Italian Fascism, Soviet Communism, and German Nazism by appealing to the personalities of the respective dictators; some anticommunist explanations of the Soviet Union, Marxist understandings of the new German and Italian regimes, and even prophetic fantasies of certain premillennialist Protestants, saw the dictators as mere representatives of deeper forces. But the dominant understandings of Italy and Germany, and even the Soviet Union under Stalin, were dependent on a personalized explanation of dictatorship. In the late 1930s, this was much less the case; moreover, the positive, heroic mode of this explanation had almost completely disappeared.

Although it is always tricky to talk of dogs that do not bark, the case of Franco is a telling example. The evolving American debate over Spain emphasized the warring camps themselves, not the personalities of their leaders. Pro-Loyalist publicists argued that the civil war was a struggle between the heroic Spanish people and the forces of fascism, which combined old Spanish elites and bloodthirsty foreign powers. Those supporting Franco's rebels made many of the same appeals that apologists for Mussolini had offered in the 1920s and early 1930s: the restoration of law and order, the destruction of international communism, and so forth. But though perfectly placed to assume Mussolini's heroic mantle as dictatorial state builder, Franco was never as elevated by the conservative American writers who favored the rebellion. Franco himself was rarely the center of attention; when he was, he appeared not as a firm-handed dictator who would restore order, but rather as the true bearer of democracy.[9] The anxieties that had led to much of the earlier support for Mussolini—fear of communism, anarchy, and mob rule in general—remained. But over the course of the late 1930s dictatorship came to represent, even for most American conservatives, not the solution to these problems, but the very embodiment of them. Heroic restorers of order could no longer be dictators.

One striking manifestation of this new view of dictatorship was the emerging vision of the dictator as buffoon or madman. Humorous representations of dictators were, of course, already common. Back in 1933, the Marx Brothers had made *Duck Soup* (Paramount), in which the parliamentary leaders of the small European nation of Freedonia turn to Rufus T. Firefly (Groucho Marx) to save the nation from economic disaster. Firefly's sole qualification for this task appears to be the affection that the wealthiest and most influential woman in the country (Margaret Dumont) has for the unlikely leader. Firefly, of course, has no interest in her. On taking the reigns of power, he runs the country much as one would expect. He insults important guests at his inaugural celebration. He sings about the quite unserious plans he has for Freedonia:

> The last guy nearly ruined the place,
> He didn't know what to do with it.
> If you think this country's messed up now,
> Just wait till I get through with it!

He eventually leads the nation into war against neighboring Sylvania just for the hell of it. All of this he does with impunity; after all, he is the dictator. Rufus T. Firefly shares one important characteristic with Benito Mussolini in *Mussolini Speaks* and President Jud Hammond in *Gabriel over the White House:* when he wants to do something he easily gets it done. *Duck Soup* works because its implicit view of dictatorship grants the dictator absolute authority, thus creating a wonderful stage for the Marx Brothers' crazy form of farce.

In the years leading up to Pearl Harbor, American cultural producers frequently belittled the authority of the real European dictators. Countless newspaper and magazine articles engaged in this project. In 1939 Hollywood studios finally allowed the many antifascist directors, stars, and screenwriters to express their politics on screen. The only films before Pearl Harbor to actually feature fictional representations of the European dictators themselves turned Hitler and Mussolini into slapstick comics.[10] Although it seems odd in retrospect, this increasing depiction of the dictators in a comic mode occurred as Hitler replaced Mussolini as the archetypal dictator. The obvious growth in Hitler's importance in European diplomacy, the end of hopes that Mussolini would act as a counterweight to him, the imposition of antisemitic laws in Italy, and the growing brutality of the Nazi regime all contributed to Hitler's rise to the center of attention. As the ecumenical Protestant weekly, the *Christian Century,* observed in June 1940, "Any dictator on screen or in fiction now means Hitler."[11] Today, Mussolini, to the extent that he retains any cultural significance in America, is remembered as something of a clown. Hitler, on the other hand, is usually treated with deadly seriousness. World War II and, above all, the Holocaust have made humorous representations of Hitler understandably difficult for many Americans to watch. At the time, however, a comedic response to Hitler made much sense.

Unlike Mussolini, Hitler was never a darling of the American press. Il Duce enjoyed endlessly talking about himself to reporters, who reciprocated by printing numerous uncritical accounts of his rise to power that helped cement the earlier American view of him as a heroic individualist. Hitler was much more secretive. He rarely granted interviews and produced no tailor-made autobiographies for the U.S. press. Even the official, expurgated 1933 American edition of *Mein Kampf,* which toned down the book's antisemitism, presented enough of Hitler's worldview to disturb its readers; by the end of the decade, competing, unabridged editions had been published in the United States with more or less explicit anti-Nazi intent.[12] The Führer's secrecy about his personal life led to much speculation about everything from his lineage to his sexuality.

In the late 1930s a dark, comic portrait of Hitler both challenged notions of dictatorial greatness and suggested that the Nazi leader could not be dealt with through normal diplomacy. His appearance, so different from the image of the Aryan superman that he promoted, was a source of ridicule. The conservative, noninterventionist *Chicago Tribune* suggested that "the best explanation for Hitler's power is Germany's weakness for a freak mustache."[13] Consciously playing off the title of Hans Fallada's famous book, American commentators presented Hitler as a "Little Man." *Time* magazine used this theme to describe his famed oratorical prowess: "With the 'Little Man' ever in mind, Realmleader Hitler, the 'Apotheosis of the Little Man,' hammers away coarsely, repeating his points over & over again for hours at a stretch until his more cultivated radio listeners are ready to scream."[14]

Hitler's sexuality was also the subject of humor. His bachelor status made him somewhat suspicious, notably in his pleas for the German family: "After all," wrote the *Boston Herald*, "a bald-headed barber touting a hair tonic is no less convincing than bachelor Hitler blandly advocating marriage for everybody else." Leni Riefenstahl, attempting to dismiss rumors that she was Hitler's mistress, announced, to the glee of the American press, that Hitler "could not love except platonically." *Reader's Digest,* excerpting the popular book *Inside Europe* by John Gunther, European correspondent of the *Chicago Daily News,* went out of its way to include his view of Hitler's sexuality: "Hitler is totally uninterested in women. He thinks of them as housewives and mothers." Gunther also noted his less-than-masculine behavior: "Hitler dams emotions to the bursting point, then is apt to break out in feminine tears."[15] Rumors of Hermann Göring's purported homosexuality were so widespread that the Hollywood Anti-Nazi League's newspaper *Hollywood NOW* could expect its readers to find amusing a Mother Goose cartoon showing a fat Göring watering a patch of Hitler-faced flowers with the caption:

Goering, Goering—oh so daring
How does your garden grow?
With little pansies here and there
And fairies, all in a row.[16]

Moreover, Hitler's competence and sanity were constantly questioned. His mind was characterized in a variety of disparaging ways: John Gunther called it, "limited, vulgar, narrow, suspicious"; *Time* described it as an "architect's mind . . . enormously isolated and emotional, lik[ing] simplicity." A cartoon in the *Dallas Journal* showed him shouting at a confused chicken to lay more eggs. *Americana* printed a cartoon entitled "The Latest Thing from the Bughouse": the "Napoleon Dept." of a mental institution is being changed to the "Hitler Dept.," as a number of Napoleon and Mussolini look-alikes look on while brown-shirted, mustachioed Führers march within. *Time* suggested that Hitler's behavior was so duplicitous that he might have a "split personality." A 1941 *Collier's* review of a book entitled *My New Order,* a collection of speeches and writings of Adolf Hitler, considered what life would be like if America were under a Nazi government. *Collier's* asserted that Nazism was little more than a projection of the Führer's addled mind: "We would be ruled by little rascals with ingrown inferiority complexes and a yen to take out their perpetual peeves on the rest of the human race."[17]

In the mid-1930s this image of Hitler could coexist with the older image of Mussolini. Thus, *Time,* even after Il Duce's enormously unpopular invasion of Ethiopia, occasionally gave him glowing notices. A July 1936 *Time* cover story on the Italian dictator sounds like much earlier accounts: "A scant 14 years ago, the Kingdom of Italy was as confused, irresolute and radical-ridden as are France and Spain today. The years have dignified and tempered Benito Mussolini, as he has dignified and tempered the Italian people." But as any hope of his acting as a counterweight to Hitler disappeared, Mussolini's importance and positive image faded. In 1938, when under pressure from Germany he enacted antisemitic legislation, the American press began to raise questions about his mental health.[18] The jokes, cartoons, and quotations in *Gagging the Dictators,* a 1938 compendium of humor about Mussolini, Stalin, Hitler, and the Japanese, make the Italian dictator look as ridiculous as his German partner.

Of course, satirizing Hitler, Mussolini, and Stalin was a two-edged sword. On the one hand, such humor debunked the older, heroic view of dictators. The perception of Nazi Germany, Fascist Italy, and Soviet Russia as worlds in which normal logic did not apply reinforced the differences between life in America and life in the European dictatorships. On the other hand, the danger always existed that such humor would make light of the problem. Thus, the Catholic *Commonweal* and the Protestant *Christian Century* were particularly critical of such comedic understandings of dictatorship. Quoting Shakespeare, the *Christian Century* wrote, in a review of the new complete edition of *Mein Kampf,* "If it is madness, yet there's method in it."[19] And Roderick MacEachen in *Commonweal* suggested poetically that Cardinal George Mundelein's (actually false) charge that Hitler had been "a paper-hanger, and a poor one at that" should not lull the public into complacency:

Heil, the conquering hero comes
   (And "cleaning-house" begins),
He plasters swastiks on the walls,
   And thus another nation wins.

His Eminence mistook his skill
   (He spoke no doubt in haste),
For who before has conquered worlds
   With paper, brush and paste?[20]

In fact, joking about the sanity and competence of Hitler and the other dictators most often took place in a context that fully acknowledged the horrors of their regimes. Both *Commonweal* and *Christian Century,* however, were committed to treating Nazism as a coherent system of thought that directly challenged religion's place in society. Such a view was weakened if Hitler was seen as a madman rather than an evil, but rational, actor.

For dedicated interventionists, the portrayal of Hitler as a madman posed another problem. An insane Hitler made negotiating futile. And if Nazism were simply a projection of one man's madness, why even think about war? Hitler's purported insanity was only half an argument for American involvement in a coming European war. A noninterventionist reader wrote the *Commonweal* that if, as the British were insisting, Hitler really were clinically insane, the German people would be innocent and would thus not deserve war. More likely, the correspondent noted, Hitler was no different from other undemocratic leaders, distasteful but not beyond the pale of diplomacy. Even if he could not be dealt with, assassination would surely be enough. As late as October 1941, H. R. Knickerbocker declared in *American Magazine* that someone should just kill Hitler: "He is Germany, he is the Nazi party, its authority, its brains, and its boss. There is nobody behind the throne."[21] This view was reinforced by the notion that the European dictators actually had little popular support. Some American journalists believed that Hitler would not last simply because the German people would come to their senses and get rid of him.[22]

The single most famous comic portrayal of Hitler, Charlie Chaplin's *The Great Dictator* (United Artists, 1940), suggests that merely replacing the madman behind the microphone with a voice of compassion might solve the problem of Nazism. Following *Modern Times* (United Artists, 1936), Chaplin decided that he wanted to make a movie satirizing Hitler. The physical similarity of Hitler and Chaplin had often been noted, frequently for comic affect.[23] But Hollywood studios were loath to allow direct criticism of Nazi Germany in the mid-1930s, despite pressure from Chaplin and other Hollywood progressives. With the closing of European markets, Hollywood eased its rules against antifascist films, but problems remained for Chaplin's idea. Chaplin's films had always made more money in Europe than in America, so the closure of the Italian and German markets was a mixed blessing for his project. Moreover, American audiences might not accept a satire of Nazism, especially after the invasion of Poland in September 1939. Reports circulated late that month that Chaplin had delayed filming. In fact, shooting began late in 1939 and was completed in March 1940. The release of the film in October was accompanied by a massive publicity campaign, arguing for the appropriateness of a Chaplin movie on Hitler. The film was a huge success in the United States. It played for fifteen weeks in New York, earned more than any other Chaplin movie, and was the third highest money-making film of the ten-year period from 1933 to 1942. It was also the only pre–Pearl Harbor Hollywood feature to present a fictional portrayal of Adolf Hitler as a major character.[24]

Chaplin plays two roles in the movie: a Jewish barber (essentially a talking version of his "Little Tramp" character) and the dictator of Tomania, Adenoid Hynkel. The film opens with the barber fighting a heroic, losing battle for Tomania in World War I, establishing both the folly of war and the barber's patriotism. The rest of the movie alternates between scenes of oppression and hope in the ghetto where the barber lives and scenes of dictatorial idiocy in Hynkel's palace. Hynkel—known as "the Phooey"—is a megalomaniac who has built a little world in which even Rodin's *Thinker* is recast to salute him. In spare moments, he dashes into a side room where a sculptor and painter work on his portrait. The Phooey is a cynical, self-interested man whose life is entirely removed from that of his people, whom he sees only as objects to be manipulated. But even in the artificial world of the palace, he is unable to make his fantasy a reality. When he dreams of world domination while playing with a globe, the globe bursts like a balloon. Aids frequently barge in to tell of wonderful new Tomanian inventions, such as a bullet-proof vest, which invariably fail when a poor scientist attempts to demonstrate them to Hynkel. In the ghetto, normal life is constantly interrupted by Hynkel's storm troopers. Hannah, a World War I orphan and the barber's love interest, imagines that "life could be wonderful if people could be left alone." But the ghetto appears to provide little hope of this. At various points, both Hannah and the barber engage in small acts of resistance, but they can do little more but delay the ever-greater encroachment of Hynkel's men.

At the end of the film, Hynkel invades the neighboring country of Ostrich and attacks the Jews with renewed vigor. Half by design, half by chance, the barber finds himself confused with the dictator; Hynkel is thus arrested, and the barber is called upon to address "his" victorious soldiers, the conquered people of Ostrich, and a radio audience of millions. Minister of Propaganda Garbitsch opens the ceremony with a short, brutal statement of fascism: "Today, democracy, liberty and equality are words to fool the people. No nation can progress with such ideas. They stand in the way of action. Therefore, we frankly abolish them." After declaring that all shall serve the state and only Aryans shall be citizens, he introduces the people of Ostrich to their new dictator. Reluctantly, the barber dressed as Hynkel takes the stand. In a six-minute speech, the barber pleads with the assembled citizens and soldiers to turn away from greed and cynicism. We have allowed knowledge to overcome feeling, he says, cleverness to triumph over kindness, machines to dominate over people. He declares that power rests with the people. He shouts, "Soldiers, in the name of democracy, let us unite!"; the crowd cheers, and Hannah listening on the radio sits up and takes notice. In a shot suggesting a brighter future, Hannah and her adoptive family stand bathed in sunlight in front of their country hiding place as hills and vineyards stretch out behind them. Hannah says, "Listen." The film ends as orchestral music suggesting salvation and resolution plays in the background.

The Great Dictator touches on most of the comic themes associated with Hitler. The small, mustached Chaplin embodied all that was physically funny about the Nazi leader. In a number of mock-German outbursts, Hynkel displays Hitler's legendary temper. The Phooey's self-importance matches that of the Führer. The ease with which the barber and Hynkel are switched emphasizes the extent to which Hynkel is a "Little Man." Hynkel's sexuality is called into question when he asks a huge, matronly woman to dance with him at a ball. Hynkel refuses to lead and tries to get the woman to dip him. Failing this, he abruptly breaks off the dance.

But although the film presents a compelling portrait of the horrors and idiocies of the German dictatorship, it fails to plausibly suggest how it got there or how to get rid of it. Originally, Chaplin had wanted to end the film with the barber waking up in a concentration camp, the heroic speech having been a dream.[25] There are a number of reasons why he might have backed down from such an ending. First, it might simply have been too bleak a conclusion, particularly if Chaplin wanted to touch a large audience used to Hollywood's happy endings. Second, such an ending might indicate too forcefully that there was no internal solution to the problems of dictatorship. With the United States still officially neutral and noninterventionists on the lookout for "war propaganda," Chaplin had to be careful of openly calling for American intervention.

As released, the ending is the weakest part of the film. Even the more favorable reviews of *The Great Dictator* tended to criticize its conclusion.[26] The movie's final sequence left important plot lines unresolved: Does the assembled crowd actually believe the barber is Hynkel? Do the soldiers unite and overthrow the real Phooey? Moreover, its filmically unconventional, long, uninterrupted speech by the barber made it difficult to watch, especially for audiences accustomed to the much faster pace of most Hollywood movies.[27]

Perhaps the biggest problem with the film's ending is its confusing political message. At the time of its release, the question of whether America should become involved in the European conflict was already gripping the nation. No film about Nazism could avoid being seen in light of the debate over intervention. Indeed, accusing Chaplin of engaging in pro-war propaganda, the newly formed, noninterventionist Senate Subcommittee on War Propaganda called him to testify about the film in the fall of 1941. However, the conclusion of *The Great Dictator* seems to suggest that American involvement in Europe might be unnecessary. Though it does leave the ultimate fate of the characters up in the air, the closing music and final shot strongly imply that, with the barber's speech, a revolution has taken place. Chaplin's final message appeals to noble ideals that could be seen as the antithesis of fascism: humanism, charity, sympathy, and so forth. But if such a speech could solve the problem, if a mere suggestion could break the spell, intervention would be entirely unnecessary.

The Great Dictator intimates that the media themselves create dictatorial power, that whoever stands behind the microphone might be able to instantly control millions. In the movie, the world of Hynkel and the world of the barber seem totally disconnected. The only things linking them are the radio and the loudspeaker. In one famous early sequence, an ss man chases the barber while Hynkel delivers a furious speech in nonsense German over loudspeakers placed throughout the ghetto. Both the ss man, who is presumably a true believer in the Phooey, and the barber, who despises him, move in perfect time to the rhythm of the speech. Only such an understanding of the absolute power of the mass-reproduced voice really makes sense of the film's concluding moments. Otherwise, why should thousands of troops loyal to Hynkel's ideology, and presumably millions of listeners with similar beliefs, be moved by the barber's plea? As shown in the next chapter, the notion that the media themselves explained the phenomenon of modern dictatorship had become widespread by the end of the 1930s.

Not surprisingly, among the most positive reviews of the film were those of two very different noninterventionist publications, the conservative *Catholic World* and the cp's house organ, the *Daily Worker*. The former preferred to conceive of the struggle against fascism as a spiritual rather than a physical war: "More devastating than any bomb invented, his caricature of tyrants will outlive their tyranny." The *Daily Worker* was operating under the suddenly noninterventionist line taken by the cp after the Nazi-Soviet Pact. Since the summer of 1939, the party had been maintaining the difficult position that the war against fascism was best served by urging the United States to stay out of the conflict, which was imperialist and thus could not be truly antifascist. Although this change in stand more or less shattered the Popular Front, a small group of party members and sympathizers put forward this left-noninterventionist approach in the years between the invasion of Poland and the invasion of Russia. The growing tide of liberal anticommunism hardened the pacifism of CP members and these remaining fellow travelers.[28] The *Daily Worker*'s reviewer, David Platt, praised Chaplin's film as a "tremendous contribution to peace" with nothing for the "Roosevelts and Churchills and little Hitlers in industry." Though Chaplin probably did not intend to create a film that adopted the current CP line, the film could easily be read as an argument for internal revolution and an end to war as a solution to the problem of Germany.[29]

If *The Great Dictator* suggested that the power of the dictator was almost entirely a function of his relationship to the instruments of mass communication, one of the most famous antifascist radio plays of the 1930s truly made the dictator disappear: Archibald MacLeish's *The Fall of the City,* a half-hour experimental piece, originally broadcast in April 1937. MacLeish, a prominent poet who would later direct one of the first propaganda agencies set up by FDR during World War II, was both politically committed and interested in expanding the horizons of radio drama. Produced in an armory, *The Fall of the City* featured a cast that included Orson Welles, Burgess Meredith, and over two hundred drama students as a crowd of citizens. Music for the production was the work of Bernard Herrmann, future composer for such film scores as *Citizen Kane, Cape Fear, Taxi Driver,* and most of the great Hitchcock movies of the postwar period. *The Fall of the City,* which helped launch the career of the young Welles, was a critical and popular success.[30]

An allegorical drama in verse, the production begins with a dead woman speaking a cryptic prophecy to the citizens and leaders of the city from her tomb:

The city of masterless men
Will take a master.
There will be shouting then:
Blood after!

Soon word arrives that a conqueror, who has enslaved many other countries, is heading toward the city. A succession of speakers propose different courses of action: an orator preaches resistance through pacifism, priests urge the citizens to return to their gods, a general encourages the people to fight. But the citizens listen to none of them, making instead an argument for dictatorship:

The city is doomed!
There's no holding it!

Let the conqueror have it! It's his!
The age is his! It's his century!
Our institutions are obsolete.
He marches a mile while we sit in a meeting. . . .
The age demands a made-up mind.
The conquerors mind is decided on everything. . . .
He's one man: we are but thousands!
Who can defend us from one man!

The conqueror appears, clad in armor. But when he lifts his visor, the armor is empty. The announcer, played by Welles, informs us:

There's no one at all there: there's only the metal:
The barrel of metal: the bundle of armor. It's empty!
The push of a stiff pole at the nipple would topple it.

But the people ignore the fact that there is no conqueror:

They don't see or they won't see. They are silent. . . .
The people invent their oppressors: they wish to believe in them.
They wish to be free of their freedom: released from their liberty.

As the empty armor raises its arm in a salute, the people shout with happiness:

The city of masterless men has found a master!
The city has fallen!
The city has fallen!

The play ends; the prophecy's "blood after" is left to the imagination of the audience.[31]

In neither Chaplin's film nor MacLeish's radio play can the power of the dictator be explained in terms of his personal qualities. Indeed, in *The Fall of the City,* the dictator has entirely disappeared. He is simply a projection of the desire of the citizens to be dominated. This picture is grimmer than that of *The Great Dictator.* Chaplin's film suggests that mass communications themselves create the necessary preconditions for dictatorship. The crowds of Tomania, Ostrich, and presumably the rest of the world appear totally malleable; they will follow whatever the loudspeaker says, whether it be war or of peace. In contrast, MacLeish's citizens refuse to listen to those who address them. They appear to have a deep commitment to enslaving themselves. Both the film and the radio play are effective critiques of dictatorial authority. They clearly reject the early 1930s view of the dictator as the author of his own power, although MacLeish puts that belief in the mouths of his mistaken citizens. Yet once the dictator has disappeared, what explains the rise of dictatorship? Neither Chaplin nor MacLeish provides a satisfactory answer. Why should people listen to anything they are told or, alternatively, desire their own oppression? For many American cultural producers of the late 1930s, the answer lay in explaining a social actor that played a central, but ultimately inscrutable, role in both MacLeish's and Chaplin's narratives: a new kind of crowd.

THE AUDIENCE ITSELF IS THE DRAMA DICTATORSHIP AND THE REGIMENTED CROWD, 1936–1941

In May 1937, three years after its special issue on the Italian Fascist state, *Fortune* printed an extensive assessment of the Nazi regime. In 1934 the magazine had focused on Mussolini—his life, personality, and philosophy. Il Duce, it wrote, had personally forged the fascist state and remained its guiding light. But Hitler appeared in the 1937 analysis only as an object. "There have been reports . . . that Hitler's mind is cracking under the strain," *Fortune* reported. "But inasmuch as Hitler's supreme value is symbolic, these reports have little relevance to the future of Nazism. Hitler doesn't have to do the work of the ordinary executive; all he has to do is remain alive, a palpable god for the Germans to revere. . . . As a matter of fact, he has never done much actual State work other than sign State papers." The backbone of the Nazi state, the magazine argued with explicit apologies to Hans Fallada, were the Pinnebergs of Germany. The "Little Men" who "felt on the outside of things during the Social Democratic days now have a sense of political participation, and they love it."[1]

As in 1934, a huge crowd was the dominant visual image of the 1937 article. The earlier issue featured a photograph of a crowd taken from high above, with a large picture of Il Duce superimposed over it. In 1937 the lead photograph showed columns of ss men arrayed at Nuremberg. Photographed from behind and only slightly above head level, the troops face a speaker who is so distant as to be invisible. The earlier image, like the earlier article, revealed the dictator's great personal control over crowds. In 1937 the crowd remained, but its function had changed. As the caption for the photograph of ss troops stated, "THE AUDIENCE ITSELF IS THE DRAMA."[2]

The change in *Fortune*'s view of the European dictatorships—from a product of the mind of the dictator to a great mass regime in which the dictator was of crucial, but symbolic, importance—is but one instance of a marked shift in the understanding of American cultural producers. In January 1941 psychologist Hadley Cantril of Princeton University warned: "If the democratic opponents of Nazism oversimplify its causes, overemphasize the importance of the single man who happens to lead it, fail to appreciate the reasons why disgruntled people turned to it, their analysis will be dangerously, perhaps suicidally, superficial."[3]

This chapter will explore these new ideas about the European dictatorships in the half decade leading up to Pearl Harbor. These views shared one major feature with both older right anticommunist perspectives and older left analyses of fascism: a tendency to explain these regimes by looking not at personalities, but at social forces. But whereas often the former imagined communism as social breakdown and anarchy and the latter regarded fascism as the simple tyranny of a minority class, the newer images of fascism and communism emphasized the ordered, regimented, uniform crowd.

The crowd that had created such fear in 1919 was a quite different social object. It represented disarray and the breakdown of social ties. Its behavior was instinctive and necessarily disorderly. Many observers felt that some suspect European nationalities had never left a more primitive state of human development. The problems caused by this crowd could be solved by the imposition of greater social order. Indeed, just such a process had attracted many Americans to Mussolini in the 1920s. For those who saw capitalism as the root cause of social disorder, the Soviet experiment embodied many hopes. The Great Depression initially reinforced these desires, on both the right and the left, for greater social order.

In the middle and late 1930s, however, many American cultural producers began to lose faith in social order as a good in itself, particularly when that order was under the direction of the state. Domestically, FDR's efforts to create a more ordered economy through the National Recovery Administration (NRA), limits on wages and hours, and regulated collective bargaining made many question the value of order for its own sake. In 1934 the president had to repeatedly refute the accusation that the New Deal constituted a form of regimentation.[4] In his second term, his attempts to reorganize the federal judiciary and executive branch met with vocal opposition from all of his usual political foes and many of his friends. Roosevelt's stated purpose in offering these measures was to make the federal government more efficient, more ordered; his opponents accused him of dictatorship. Overseas, the search for order had produced more dire results. The Nazi Gleichschaltung of churches and independent organizations, the Soviet show trials, and the Italian invasion of Ethiopia contributed to a growing sense among many Americans from across the political spectrum that order could be a dangerous thing.

As the fears of regimented order grew, however, the object of these fears changed. Early in the decade, the dictators themselves—Mussolini, Hitler, and Stalin—or even Roosevelt were held largely responsible for creating dangerous forms of order. In the later 1930s cultural producers more frequently blamed the people for desiring regimentation. In their separate testimony against FDR's prospective 1937 reorganization of the federal judiciary, Dorothy Thompson, Princeton University president H. W. Dodds, and Yale law professor Edwin Borchard all suggested that the proposal was ill-conceived not so much because the president desired to increase his own power but because the American people themselves might threaten democracy if the plan were to pass.[5] Lowell Thomas, who had praised Mussolini in his voice-over commentary to *Mussolini Speaks* for single-handedly restoring order to Italy, coauthored a book in 1940 warning against such dictatorships, which were caused not by dictators, but by the people's desire for order: "It can and does happen in Germany because a people sold their liberty for the promise of security and order. Hitler did not originally grab power in Germany, the people gave it to him by their votes."[6]

From the 1910s through the early 1930s, American cultural producers frequently invoked mechanical images to describe a healthy society. In the 1910s Woodrow Wilson likened liberty itself to a well-functioning machine.[7] In the 1920s engineers became great heroes: Frederick W. Taylor and Henry Ford seemed to hold the answers to the problems of industry; Herbert Hoover could solve the ills of society. Even after Hoover's failure, radical social critic Stuart Chase, though not entirely untroubled by machines, also adopted mechanical language to portray modern society. The main question, according to Chase, was how to harness the machine: "The machine promises more freedom than primitive nature peoples [*sic*] or the most stable of handicraft communities ever dreamed of. The price of that freedom is control of the mechanism: the mechanism of steel and the mechanism of gold."[8]

As the idea of a rigidly ordered society began to seem more threatening, it quickly lost its popularity. In fact, many came to see mechanized society itself as the problem. With his study *Technics and Civilization* (1934), Lewis Mumford emerged as the premier American critic of the general mechanization of modern life. Mumford argued that the ideal of making life conform to a mechanical order, promoted over the centuries by monastic Christianity, the scientific revolution, and capitalism, threatened to turn individuals into mere automatons.[9] His critique of mechanization was unusual in its thoroughgoing indictment of modernity, but less radical fears of mechanization became common in the late 1930s.

Mechanization seemed most deadly in Spain. The Spanish Civil War evoked passions among, and deeply divided, the American public. As Allen Guttmann has pointed out, both sides in the conflict presented the war as a battle of machines versus people. In U.S. representations, the dominant image was of warplanes—usually German warplanes—bombarding civilians. Newsreels, films such as *Blockade* (United Artists, 1938), and fictional accounts of the war by such luminaries as Ernest Hemingway all presented this image. The only significant American novelist to take General Franco's side, the Baroness de Zglinitzki (née Helen Nicholson), also dramatized the opposition between machines and men; she merely substituted Franco's troops for Loyalist civilians and "the machine guns of Russia" for German tanks and planes. This new war of machine versus humanity was brutally ordered: warplanes flew in precise "V" formation, tanks advanced in a uniform line. But this order created greater disorder and destruction, at least to noncombatant civilians, than any previous kind of warfare. The description of bombers from Archibald MacLeish's 1938 verse play about the coming European war, *Air Raid,* which was broadcast on CBS, provides a good example of this rhetoric:

> They swing like steel in a groove:
> They move like tools not men:
> You'd say there were no men:
> You'd say they had no will but the
> Will of motor on metal.[10]

The machine did not have entirely adverse connotations in late 1930s America. The 1939 World's Fair featured a number of corporations celebrating the future mechanization of American life to the delight of crowds. Nevertheless, as a political metaphor, the machine and mechanization, which Woodrow Wilson had presented as a model of freedom in the 1910s, had become negatively charged in American political culture.[11]

Just as the bomber squadron—powerful, ordered, cruel, devoid of free will—was the dominant representation of dictatorial forces in European conflicts, so the similarly endowed regimented crowd—standing or goose-stepping—became the prevailing image of the European dictatorships at peace. This was particularly true in Hollywood. The coming of war to Europe closed much of the lucrative foreign market to U.S. films, while making the British market more significant. As the concern about the European regimes and war grew, first in the White House, then nationwide, the studio heads cautiously allowed their producers and directors to make movies critical of the dictatorships. But even this window of opportunity for antifascist projects closed somewhat in mid-1940. With Hitler's invasion of France, studios, projecting a European market that might be dominated by the Nazis, began to slow the production of anti-Nazi films.[12] Nevertheless, the Hollywood films that first tackled the subject from 1939 to 1941 were an important source for images of dictatorship, both because of their broad circulation and because the industry's internal politics dictated that these films be fairly bland and inoffensive. In their need to please politically disparate cultural producers, these films are a valuable record of a minimal definition of dictatorship. Hollywood's prewar films about dictatorship reveal both the importance of the regimented crowd and the ways in which it differed from, and was similar to, earlier throngs.

The most striking aspect of the regimented crowd was its fervent order. Aggregations in earlier Hollywood movies, even the ones that were politically motivated (e.g., the communists in *Little Man, What Now?*), were disorderly, chaotic gatherings. But in films of the half decade before Pearl Harbor, crowds engaged in fanatical, but *ordered* behavior: chanting and saluting in unison, parading in quasi-military fashion. In *Confessions of a Nazi Spy* (Warner Brothers, 1939), a drama loosely based on real events involving Nazi conspirators in the United States, the second sequence begins at a German American Bund meeting where a speaker addresses a uniformed crowd. As he concludes ("We Germans must make the United States *unser Amerika,* our America!"), the participants rise and repeatedly shout "Sieg Heil!" with arms outstretched in the Nazi salute. In *The Man I Married* (Fox, 1940), the protagonist's final descent into Nazism is marked cinematically by his enthusiastic "Heil"-ing at a large mass meeting in Berlin. D. B. Norton (Edward Arnold), the would-be dictator behind the John Doe movement in *Meet John Doe* (Warner Brothers, 1941), Frank Capra's study of fascism in America, has a precision motorcycle corps that wears black ss-like uniforms. We see the corps drilling even before Norton makes his first appearance on-screen. In *Ninotchka* (MGM, 1939), the title character's (Greta Garbo) return to her native land is signified by a close-up of marching feet in a state-sponsored parade. The film cuts to a medium, high-angle shot of the marchers, including Ninotchka, dressed identically; many of them carry identical portraits of Stalin.

The creation of the new crowd was imagined as a moment of mechanization, not a moment of chaos. In *The Mortal Storm* (MGM, 1940), Frank Borzage's film about the effects of the Nazi Machtergreifung on a small university town in Bavaria, the first visual representation of the arrival of Nazism is the formation of such a crowd. Martin (Jimmy Stewart), the anti-Nazi hero, agrees to go to the tavern with his friend Freia (Margaret Sullavan) to meet her boyfriend Fritz (Robert Young) and a number of other young men, all of whom are fervent Nazis. The tavern sequence begins with a large gathering of patrons singing a German drinking song. The revelers are seated in groups at tables and at the bar; each group looks at its own members. The singing is an activity for both small units of friends and the tavern as a whole; it is emotional and messy, with some voices a little off-key. Sometime after Freia and Martin arrive—and have an abortive discussion about Fritz's desire that Martin join the Nazi Party—a man rises and calls for someone to suggest another song. A Brownshirt jumps on a platform and calls for "a glorious song of the new Germany." Everyone— except Martin, Freia, and an elderly man in the front of the room—rises and sings the "Horst Wessel Song" while giving the Hitler salute.[13] As at the start of the sequence, the camera pans the crowd. This time, however, all face the front, all stare dispassionately and sing rhythmically. Each face that the camera dwells on is male. The song stops when the elderly man's refusal to join in is noted. Martin alone defends his right not to sing, but at the end of the sequence the old man is beaten up outside the tavern.

The transformation at the tavern features many typical elements of the regimented crowd as symbol of dictatorship in late 1930s America. The patrons, who are highly individuated and animated while singing the drinking song become more or less identical automatons while chanting the Nazi Party song. Individual will thus surrenders to a greater, mechanical group will. Those who take part in the "patriotic" song do so willingly and with robotic commitment; the man who refuses to sing receives a beating. Unlike earlier images of forced regimentation, the regimented crowd forms voluntarily. Its actions, however, become compulsory for anyone drawn into its midst.

In this way, the regimented crowd, for all its differences from the chaotic crowd, retained one of the most meaningful features of its predecessor: it sowed disorder. The internal order of the regimented crowd simply made it more efficient in its ability to disrupt normal social bonds around it. In *The Mortal Storm,* the performance of the "Horst Wessel Song" eliminates all intermediate social groupings, as each automated individual orients himself or herself only to the symbol of the new state. Just as the order of German bomber squadrons enabled them to destroy Spanish towns more efficiently, so the order of the regimented crowd made it more effective in exacting vengeance on its enemies.

The party and its activities become the site of sexual desire and pleasure for the regimented man. Sometimes this aspect of the crowd is represented by a "loose" and, in terms of Hollywood morality, forbidden woman. Erich

(Francis Lederer), the protagonist in *The Man I Married,* is drawn to the Nazis through his attraction to Frieda (Anna Sten), a blonde party member. His decision to abandon his wife Carol (Joan Bennett) for Frieda and raise his American son Ricky in the New Germany are part and parcel of his decision to become a Nazi.[14]

More often, however, the sexual desire of crowd members is thoroughly displaced. Despite the occasional seductive party woman—a character who would play a greater role in the post–World War II anticommunist imagination—the regimented crowd, like the older chaotic crowd, was a generally male place. As the Nazi Fritz continually insists to his fiancée Freia in *The Mortal Storm,* politics is for men, not women. In the final sequence of *Meet John Doe,* two choruses of people, one in favor of dictatorship and one opposed to it appear on-screen: those opposed—the people of Millville—include men and women of different heights and appearances; those in favor—would-be dictator D. B. Norton and his supporters—are all men, identically dressed and of similar size and looks.

Left to themselves, the men of the regimented crowd often express their sexuality in homoerotic or masturbatory ways. The brutal, mechanized war takes place off-stage in *There Shall Be No Night* (1940), the hit Broadway play on the Russian invasion of Finland by Robert Sherwood, author of *The Petrified Forest* (1935) and soon-to-be speechwriter for FDR. However, the presence of reporters who had been in Spain and Poland allows the audience to hear what such warfare is like. When one character says that Helsinki might hold out for a long time, Dave, a reporter, expresses concern: "I wouldn't like to be here when that happens. I saw [the German battleships] at Danzig when they were battering Westerplatte. I could see the Nazis, watching their own barrage. They were deriving a sexual thrill from that display of devastating power."[15]

Displaced male sexuality had, of course, played a role in chaotic crowds as well. The libidinal energy expended by the usually male members of older mobs was energy not spent in the controlled environment of marriage. *Little Man, What Now?* provides clear examples of this economy: the communist loses his wife in childbirth because he is too busy agitating to wait for her to receive proper medical care, and, in a climactic moment, Pinneberg finds two bricks in his hands during a riot and realizes that his position is totally incompatible with being a father. But the new regimented crowd displaced male sexuality much more efficiently. Whereas in old crowds displaced sexuality led simply to chaos, which, if unchecked, threatened to breed further disorder, in the regimented crowd it resulted in purposeful destructive action. Rather than representing a mere lack of moral order, the budding Nazis' affairs with seductive party women drew them into a New Order. And the masturbatory shelling of Danzig was part of a Blitzkrieg that was as decisive, efficient, and controlled as it was destructive.

The old crowd was an entirely male place. Although the new crowd also tended to be male in its Hollywood manifestation, women who did become involved had their sexuality transformed as well. Sometimes, as in *Ninotchka,* the regimented crowd made women into asexual or mannish creatures, humorously unsuited to their "normal" roles as objects of male desire. In the case of the seductive female Nazis of *The Man I Married* and *Confessions of a Nazi Spy,* women's sexuality, once "properly" confined to the private sphere of home and family, was made public and used to ensnare men in the very different order of the regimented crowd.

Finally, the regimented crowd, as represented in film and other media, differed from the older mob in its seemingly limitless extent, both spatially and temporally. Although certain conditions, ideologies, and people no doubt favored the formation of, or even actively fomented, the older kind of group, individual crowds were a limited phenomenon. Social psychologists understood that the physical presence of a crowd was crucial to the formation of the "crowd mind." This meant that such mobs could be stopped by fairly crude methods of social control. Individual throngs could be dispersed; those who fomented mob action could be deported. But the regimented crowd could not be handled so easily. The existence of a formal, organized purpose, manifested in the dictatorial state itself, allowed individuals to maintain a crowd mind even when they were alone. That this purpose was destructive and possibly incoherent little affected its ability to ensnare. After they leave their rallies and meetings, the Nazis of *Confessions of a Nazi Spy, The Man I Married,* and *The Mortal Storm* are still possessed by the logic of the regimented crowd. As the *Fortune* article of May 1937 noted, everyone in Nazi Germany felt that they were working for a higher cause.

Modern communications technology, particularly the radio, allowed crowds to be called into existence even when people were not physically gathered together and even when the speaker was at a great distance. In *The Man I Married,* all activity in Berlin stops as everyone listens to a radio address by Hitler. Radio could create a crowd that was difficult to locate, let alone disperse. As Hadley Cantril, head of the Princeton Radio Project, one of the first long-term attempts to understand the sociology of the relatively young medium, noted in 1940: "By its very nature radio is the medium par excellence for informing all segments of a population of current happenings, for arousing in them a common sense of fear or joy and for inciting them to similar reactions directed toward a single objective. . . . The radio audience consists essentially of thousands of small, congregate groups united in time and experiencing a common stimulus—altogether making possible the largest grouping of people ever known."[16]

Its very regimentation also made the new crowd more difficult to disperse. When the Nazi spies are put on trial in Confessions of a Nazi Spy, the prosecutor shows the jury a flow chart of the "vast machine" in which the spies were but "little cogs." This "machine" extended around the world; it included not only the Nazi government in Berlin, but also accomplices in such unlikely places as a small village in Scotland. Such charts had been popular among anticommunists and other conspiracy theorists since at least the 1920s. But by the 1930s, they became all the more plausible with the growth of organized crime. The word "mob" had taken on a new meaning with the rise of Al Capone and other crime barons in the late 1920s. J. Edgar Hoover's Federal Bureau of Investigation (FBI), having made its reputation battling these enemies of society, constructed a view of the Nazis and communists that was similar to popular notions of organized crime: a vast, secret network running a racket that, in this case, was political rather than financial. Indeed, in Confessions it is the heroic G-man Renard (Edward G. Robinson) who draws up the flow chart that later appears in court.

Thus, although not entirely new, the regimented crowd was more structured, focused, and permanent than the older crowd. Whether invading another country, spying, marching, or singing, it worked with mechanical efficiency. Yet in other ways, it was similar to the previous group. Its members lost their individuality, becoming mere expressions of the crowd mind. Though internally ordered, the regimented crowd was destructive of normal social bonds and created chaos around it. It channeled the sexuality of its members away from the domestic sphere and into violent activities. Perhaps most importantly, as in the case of the earlier chaotic crowd, the group that elites most feared would form the regimented crowd was the great mass of humanity—common people, workers, radio listeners, consumers. Unlike some other accounts of the rise of dictatorship, the regimented crowd was a majority, not a minority, movement. It was thus both primitive—in its violence and its refusal to submit to "civilized" moral principle—and modern—in its organization, its reliance on advanced technology, and its mechanical behavior. In 1940 psychiatrist Edward Strecker of the University of Pennsylvania captured this duality in his description of what he called the "mass-man": "The mass-man of our day is a combination of Neanderthal man and robot, seemingly differing from the former in that there is little, if any, promise of evolution; from the latter in that he has learned to gather en masse and use the impact of violence. The crowd-man need not be observed in mobs. There are not many facets to the crowd-mind, and some of them may be examined in a single specimen. . . . He is not only commonplace, but he makes a gospel out of being commonplace."[17]

The new crowd required new solutions. Imposing order had been sufficient to quell the chaotic mob, but order was part of the problem with the new crowd. Therefore, writings and images of the crowd changed their focus from order to individuality. Of course, individualism had been contrasted with communism and other "foreign" systems of government for decades before the new regimented crowd was fully imagined.[18] But with the increased prominence of the regimented crowd, preserving individual identity—especially individual male identity—became a crucial task in the fight against dictatorship.[19] This concern for individualism—as well as the anxieties about all that might beset it—became a crucial component of the ways in which American cultural producers understood democracy from the late 1930s on.

Of course, what was believed necessary to preserve individuals was largely determined by what was thought to threaten their existence. The most obvious explanation for the rise of the regimented crowd was based on nationality. As Hamilton Fish Armstrong, editor of *Foreign Affairs* and an informal adviser to FDR, had suggested in *"We or They"* (1937), Europe was simply different from America.[20] This was, in a sense, an updated version of the rationale Wilson used during his first term to keep the United States out of World War I. In its milder version, common among moderately conservative publications such as the *Saturday Evening Post,* Europe was stuck in its ways. Even in the fall and early winter of 1938, the *Post* continued to see the whole continent as a political morass that demanded neutrality as the only sensible response.[21] The more extreme version of this argument linked the European dictatorships not to the world of European politics, but to the character of individual Europeans. Part of the American Legion's struggle against communism—and, at least rhetorically, fascism—was a call to cut European immigration quotas by 90 percent.[22]

Mere national identity, however, had limited support as an explanation of the rise of dictatorship. Although plenty of anti-immigrant sentiment existed in the late 1930s, those groups most interested in anti-Nazi activity, from the Popular Front organizations to the National Conference of Christians and Jews, were also deeply involved in building tolerance and reducing nativist sentiment. National identity–based accounts of people's political behavior could easily be equated with Nazism. Occasionally, the point was made explicitly. In *The Man I Married,* which provides no reason other than lust for Erich's turn to Nazism, his own racialist account— that his German blood convinces him to become a Nazi—is clearly dismissed. In the film's climax, his anti-Nazi father reveals to Erich and his Nazi lover Frieda that Erich's deceased mother was a Jew, thus destroying Erich's sexual relationship, his party membership, and his explanation of them both.

For most Americans, especially those not on the political right, nationality alone did not explain the rise of the regimented crowd and the European dictatorships. For different reasons, and in different ways, they saw in Europe a pattern that might be repeated in the United States. What linked almost all of these visions was a sense that modernity itself had created the conditions necessary to elevate the regimented crowd. For some, the key factor was a deteriorating economy that had left masses of people out of work and largely without hope. For others, economic difficulty was less crucial than ways in which modernity changed people psychologically, driving them, in Erich Fromm's celebrated phrase, to seek an escape from freedom. Still other cultural producers focused on the growth of the mass media, which were, of course, essential to the functioning of the regimented crowd. Although most views drew on all of these factors, let us consider— in turn—explanations that stressed socioeconomics, psychology, and the media. These understandings were connected as intimately with the ways in which their proponents regarded democracy as with how they interpreted dictatorship.

After offering a number of other reasons for the rise of dictatorship, President Roosevelt himself emerged as the foremost proponent of the socioeconomic explanation. It was necessary for him to address two very different concerns about dictatorship. Toward the end of the 1930s, he had to convince an often reluctant Congress and public to endorse his internationalist stance on foreign policy. This process consisted largely of convincing his audience of the importance of events in Europe, notably the growing power of Nazi Germany, to the United States. Beginning with the 1936 presidential race, the struggle between dictatorship and democracy, abroad and at home, played a prominent role in Roosevelt's public statements and speeches. FDR repeatedly argued that, whether it wanted to or not, America would have to participate in the struggle for democracy. By 1940 his task had become even more onerous: preparing Americans for the real possibility of war.

But the president was also involved in a very different discussion about dictatorship. Political opponents ceaselessly accused him of being a dictator himself. His attempted reorganization of the federal executive and judiciary in 1937 and his efforts to purge the Democratic Party of anti–New Dealers in 1938 led to charges that he was preserving democracy as it had been preserved in Russia, Italy, and Germany. His responses to these accusations were never entirely successful and often fanned their flames.[23] One of his stock rejoinders was to point out his own majority support at the polls. Dictatorship as it often appeared in FDR's public statements was a system of government in which minorities ruled; democracy was a system of majority rule. Roosevelt's electoral victories thus proved that he was not a dictator.[24] This claim could be an effective ploy against a Republican minority willing, at times, to accuse FDR of virtually anything to turn the public against him. Ultimately, the argument that majority support constituted democratic government was just a tautological defense of his administration: since he had been elected president, Roosevelt could not be a dictator.

The contention that his very election was a hedge against dictatorship had never stood alone in FDR's speeches. During his first administration, he emphasized the impossibility of such a form of government ever taking root in America in his broader attempt to build support for, and confidence in, New Deal experimentation.[25] Roosevelt's early efforts to allay the public's fear of dictatorship at home failed to a great extent, as numerous polls of the mid-1930s suggest.[26] In both 1936 and 1940 the Republican Party tried, with some success, to capitalize on that fear. Therefore, in the late 1930s Roosevelt began to argue that his policies were not only guaranteed not to lead to dictatorship but were, in fact, necessary to prevent it.

By the late 1930s the dominant image of Nazi Germany was that of a state with almost robotic, regimented public support. This made Roosevelt's dichotomy between majoritarian democracy and minority-driven autocracy even less satisfying. Starting no later than 1938, FDR began to suggest that majority backing might be an important characteristic of the modern dictatorship. In January 1938, while explaining American history as a struggle between "the minority of education and of wealth" and those who would make government "more responsive to the public will," he introduced a new element: "There is an ancient strategy, recently used, whereby those who would exploit or dominate a people, seek to delude their victims into fighting their battles for them. And in these days of organized nation-wide publicity, the strategy for undermining a government move against minority abuses is to make this appear to be an attack upon the exploited majority itself."[27] Initially, he made this warning in passing, more as an attack on his political opponents than as an analysis of the causes of dictatorship.

Over the course of 1938 and continuing at least until the end of the 1940 campaign, however, Roosevelt's explanation of dictatorship began to center on this majority support and the reasons for its growth. In his public statements, dictatorship became a Faustian bargain into which an entire people entered when they had lost hope and were overcome by fear. In this view, would-be oligarchs were but the beneficiaries of what was predominantly a popular movement: "Democracy has disappeared in several other great nations—not because the people of those nations disliked democracy, but because they had grown tired of unemployment and insecurity, of seeing their children hungry while they sat helpless in the face of government confusion and government weakness through lack of leadership in government. Finally, in desperation, they chose to sacrifice liberty in the hope of getting something better to eat."[28]

If the government did not meet their needs, the people would turn to more effective, dictatorial systems of government. Fascism and communism, Roosevelt often seemed to imply, did work in simple economic terms, but at too great a cost. These systems created a "regimented people" without personal liberties. They would get their bread and jobs but would become "pawns molded and enslaved by a machine."[29] According to FDR, Roosevelt Democrats or liberals distinguished themselves by recognizing "that the new conditions throughout the world call for new remedies." Conservatives failed to recognize the new conditions.[30]

Although the contrast between democratic majoritarianism and authoritarian minority rule did not disappear from his speeches, the new emphasis on dictatorship as an entire people's response to failed democracy suggested that conservative accusations that FDR was dictatorial were, in addition to being hysterical, a direct danger.[31] The real roots of dictatorship, the president maintained, were economic depression and a loss of faith in democracy. A return to the conservative policies of the 1920s might result not only in a further plunge into recession, but also in the rise of a real American dictator, supported by a fearful and hopeless populace. Thus the expansion of the federal government into new aspects of American life was not a threat to democracy, but rather its only possible means of survival under the same "new conditions" that created dictators abroad. Emphasis on the socioeconomic roots of the regimented crowd allowed Roosevelt to package liberal social programs in a manner that might well have appealed to certain elite fears of the masses.

Although locating the causes of dictatorship in economic hardship was politically useful, it was also inadequate. For all its experimentation, the

New Deal had not pulled the United States out of the depression, yet public support for dictatorship—as opposed to fear of its imminent arrival—was much smaller in the middle and late 1930s than it had been in 1932. Moreover, the European dictatorships seemed to retain their domestic popularity despite their decidedly mixed effects on quality of life.

A variety of thinkers began to view dictatorship not simply as the result of a rational, calculated response to new economic conditions, but as the product of a more complicated, new social psychology. The most intellectually significant, and in many ways the most radical, of these new approaches was Erich Fromm's *Escape from Freedom* (1941). Until 1938, Fromm was a member of the Institut für Sozialforschung, more popularly known as the Frankfurt School. At the time of Hitler's rise to power, the Institut had relocated en masse to New York but continued to operate much as it had in Germany: its members published almost exclusively in German until 1939 and made little attempt to become part of the American intellectual scene, unlike their compatriots at the New School for Social Research. Although the Frankfurt School had long had some contact with American academia, its intellectual impact in its new home was minimal, not least because its dominant mode of thought—an idiosyncratic brand of Marxism—did not fit easily into U.S. academic circles at the time.[32]

Fromm was one of the first scholars of the Frankfurt School to gain a wide readership in the United States. The reasons why seem fairly clear. To begin with, *Escape from Freedom* was one of the first major works by a member of the Frankfurt School to be published in English. Moreover, it was an extremely readable text. Finally, Fromm's central theoretical concerns were more in line with those of American thinkers than were the current interests of many of his Frankfurt School colleagues. Indeed, his differences with those colleagues led Fromm to sever his ties with the Frankfurt School in 1938; by their measure, his version of Freudianism was too unorthodox, his understanding of modernity insufficiently gloomy.[33]

Happily for Fromm, his own intellectual style was better suited to the reading public of his adopted country than it had been to the Frankfurt School. Freudianism had made a great impact on American thought. By the late 1930s and early 1940s, Freudian ideas had permeated all of the social sciences and had done so without the theoretical orthodoxy that pervaded the Frankfurt School. The place of psychoanalysis in Fromm's thought made *Escape from Freedom* both more understandable and more attractive to American social scientists. What one scholar has called his "combination of skepticism, humanism, and eclecticism," which had tended to offend Europeans, struck a chord in America. His frequent citation of influential American thinkers such as Ralph Waldo Emerson, Henry David Thoreau, and John Dewey no doubt helped as well.[34]

In *Escape from Freedom,* Fromm masterfully combined the concepts of Sigmund Freud, Karl Marx, and Max Weber to explain what he called "the totalitarian flight from freedom." Fromm declared that it was a dangerous illusion to believe "that men like Hitler had gained power over the vast apparatus of the state through nothing but cunning and trickery, that they and their satellites ruled merely by sheer force; that the whole population was only the will-less objects of betrayal and terror." Instead, people have an "innate wish for submission," a wish that is aggravated in times of social stress and alienation. During the Reformation, Fromm argued, Lutheranism and Calvinism provided such a dogma of submission—blended with hatred and resentment—to a rising middle class that felt the traditional social bonds of the medieval world collapsing around it. The birth of liberal freedom in the modern world was a mixed blessing. The new, capitalist economy ground people increasingly into automatons, who were, in turn, less likely to assert their individuality and more likely to submit. Modern advertising, newspapers, and electoral politics all added to this sense of alienation and automation. This proliferation of authorities led people to develop "pseudo-selves," mouthing received opinion without ever thinking critically. The "pseudo-self" emerged not because people were told to think the wrong things, but simply because they were told—and were willing to be told—what to think. All of this led to the attraction of the regimented crowd. Fromm, quoting Hitler's *Mein Kampf* as an "excellent description" of Nazism, sounded a tone similar to *Fortune*'s 1937 article on Nazi Germany:

> The mass meeting is necessary if only for the reason that in it the individual, who is becoming an adherent of a new movement feels lonely and is easily seized with the fear of being alone, receives for the first time the pictures of a greater community. . . . If he steps for the first time out of his small workshop or out of the big enterprise, in which he feels very small, into the mass meeting and is now surrounded by thousands and thousands of people with the same conviction . . . he himself succumbs to the magic influence of what we call mass suggestion.[35]

Fromm's use of psychoanalysis made his book popular among more intellectually flexible American Freudians.[36] His willingness to extend his critique of fascism to a critique of capitalism and liberal democracy appealed to more independent-minded members of the American left.[37] Nevertheless, certain elements of the book, notably its harsh treatment of Protestantism as a psychological precursor of fascism, limited its attraction. Moreover, the solutions it proposed were frankly utopian, imagining a world in which individuals could gain a sense of truly positive freedom by comprehending both their individuality and their relatedness to others.

Among many American liberals and Popular Front radicals, a less nuanced psychological explanation for the rise of the regimented crowd took hold. These cultural producers rejected the socioeconomic explanation offered by Roosevelt and others because fascism simply did not deliver the material goods that, based on that view, accounted for its mass appeal. Nevertheless, unlike Fromm, supporters of a more straightforward psychological interpretation, clung to a view of social psychology that continued to distinguish between rational and irrational actions. Both liberals and more orthodox Marxists tended to explain political behavior in terms of rational actions. As long as fascism was seen as a movement of a small oligarchy of big capitalists, it could be so explained. But as mass support for the European dictatorships continued through the 1930s, another explanation was needed. For the great mass of people in Nazi Germany, the move to fascism was irrational; reasons for the regimented crowd thus lay in abnormal social psychology. "In its large outlines," wrote Lewis Mumford in *Men Must Act* (1939),

> the economic interpretation [of history] clarifies the motive of men: unfortunately it cannot explain why men will work more cheerfully for a starvation wage, under the impression that they are serving their fatherland, than they did for a living wage, when they thought only of keeping their families alive. No one can doubt that, at least temporarily, this has happened in Germany. And it is precisely what is irrational in this situation, what cannot be explained in terms of pecuniary gain or rational self-interest, that constitutes the strength of fascism.[38]

Ironically, Mumford was led by the radical nature of his material critique of modernity as a whole to explain fascism—a term he, like some other members of the anti-Stalinist left, used to describe not only the regimes of Italy and Germany, but also of the Soviet Union—in terms of an irrational psychological reaction. Mumford believed that *all* modern society, fascist and capitalist, was regimented. Fromm, too, saw in capitalism the reduction of individual will, but he distinguished between the masochistic submission to another's will under fascism and the creation of the pseudo-self under capitalism. Perhaps because of his conviction that the logic of capitalism lay at the heart of mechanization, Mumford did not see fascism as a further stage in regimentation. Instead, what distinguished fascism from capitalism was not its regimentation, but its return to primitive, brutal violence or "barbarism." Fascism was, according to Mumford in *Faith for Living* (1940), a psychological response to regimentation that unfortunately did not challenge regimentation itself: "In short: these victims of the machine will confirm their slavery in order to recover, at second hand, at least the illusion of freedom. This is, I believe, the psychological basis of fascism. Out of frustration come its grand aggressions: out of an inhuman mechanical discipline comes its more primitive assertion of humanity." Mumford concluded that the ultimate inability of liberalism to understand fascism before war descended on Europe was precisely because liberals could not understand any motivation except for rational self-interest, because they could not grasp that the sources of fascism "are in the human soul, not in economics."[39]

Stopping somewhat short of Mumford's interest in the irrational, Max Lerner sought to retain economics as the central explanatory factor in politics, while adding psychology to explain the regimented crowd. In *It Is Later Than You Think* (1938), which attempted to construct an antifascist, left liberalism, Lerner argued that in concentrating entirely on class, Marxists had forgotten the irrational element in politics and had thus lost the working classes of countries like Germany and Italy to fascism. He continued to give fascism a bourgeois class base, but he did not see it as an inevitable, final stage of capitalism in which the bourgeoisie resorted to dictatorship. Instead, the development of fascism was a contingent event, built as much on psychological strain as on economic crisis. And though fascism was orchestrated by industrialists, its attraction was universal, appealing to the basest instincts of all people: "There is a little bit of the fascist in every one of us, and a good deal in some of us." Ultimately, Lerner embraced psychological explanations of fascism only tentatively. Though he argued that Marxists should pay more attention to irrational causes of behavior, he considered "the cult of the irrational flowing from the discoveries of Austrian psychoanalysts" to be one of the bases of fascism. Although the left had to acknowledge the irrational roots of fascism, according to Lerner, the ideal democratic order would be a rational one; there was no need for the "faith for living" proposed by Mumford.[40]

Unlike Fromm, who came from an intellectual community in which a rhetoric of total, revolutionary transformation was highly valued, both Lerner and Mumford—at least in his two books on fascism—wrote in a left-liberal mode that emphasized the practical. Neither scholar suggested that the path leading out of the crisis of the late 1930s required a total sea change in consciousness: Lerner urged the extension of democracy, whereas Mumford—who had previously sounded more radical notes—suggested that the primary need in the war against fascism was "the need to save the institutions of a free civilization, the institutions of democracy, founded on a profound respect for the personality of all men, and for a power, not ourselves, that makes for righteousness."[41] Psychological perspectives such as those of Lerner and Mumford, which relied on the irrational, suggested that the nature of movements like fascism severely limited one's ability to understand them.

The crudest psychological accounts of the regimented crowd, which included those offered by Hollywood, indicated even more conservative responses to the threat, an even greater failure of interpretation, and, perhaps most significantly, a certain level of prophylaxis. In film after film, Nazis and communists were represented as more or less insane. That there was a method to their madness, that they were regimented, made them more dangerous but no less mad. *Confessions of a Nazi Spy* made this connection between fascism and madness explicit. In the epilogue, having smashed a Nazi spy ring, G-man Edward Renard (Edward G. Robinson) and the attorney that successfully prosecuted the Nazis (Henry O'Neill) talk over a cup of coffee:

RENARD: Funny thing working on a case like this for so long. It's
   something like spending a great deal of time in a madhouse. You see
   these Nazis operating here and you think of all those in Germany
   and you can't help feeling somehow that they're, well absolutely
   insane.
ATTORNEY: As a matter of fact, you begin to doubt your own sanity.
RENARD: True. We see what's happening in Europe. We know what
   they're trying to do here, and it all seems so unreal, fantastic, well
   . . . like an absurd nightmare. Absurd. But when you think of its
   potential menace, it's terrifying.
ATTORNEY: I don't think, Renard, that kind of people are going to
   have much luck in this country. It's true, we're a careless, easy-
   going, optimistic nation. But when our basic liberties become
   threatened, we wake up!

The sequence concludes with a conversation between two other diner patrons about the Nazi trials. "This ain't Europe," one of them says triumphantly. "Thank God for such people," comments Renard. By making Nazism a question of sanity and more or less assuming the sanity of Americans, *Confessions* was able to portray dictatorship as an exclusively European phenomenon without quite blaming it on Europeanness. Ultimately, it is Americans' ability to see the insanity—their ability to laugh at the dictators—that is both the mark of their sanity and the key to their triumph over dictatorship.[42]

All of these understandings—from Roosevelt's socioeconomic explanation to Fromm's Freudianism, from Mumford's theory of irrationality to Hollywood's accounts of madness—saw the regimented crowd starting in the failure of the individual to feel secure materially or psychologically. The people who joined this group relinquished their individuality for some less valuable currency—mere sustenance, the fulfillment of a sadomasochistic urge, the call of baser instincts, or simple madness. Individuals could stay out of the crowd so long as they felt comfortable as individuals in society. The promoters of each of these views hoped that their works would educate the reader or viewer and, directly or indirectly, contribute to this process of individuation in their audience.

In addition to socioeconomic and psychological explanations, a third alternative called into question this entire educational process: that is, the very creation of a mass media audience might lead to the formation of the regimented crowd. Anxiety about the new media's ability to turn their audiences into dangerous crowds had a long history in the United States. Control of the mass media and manipulation of those media through propaganda were obvious characteristics of the modern dictatorships. Foreign correspondents, who were among the first to inform U.S. audiences about these regimes, were also among the first to feel the effect of this control. Once dictatorship was seen as flowing up from the regimented crowd, not simply down from the dictator, cultural producers began to suggest that the techniques of mass persuasion themselves might lead to dictatorship, as mere participation in the mass audience might destroy individual thinking. As Max Lerner argued in 1935, "'We think with our blood,' says Hitler, and there seems to be something a bit alien and shocking about the irrationalism that underlies such a statement. But actually that is the basic premise of all the techniques of mass communication that we have ourselves been using. The most damning blow the dictatorships have struck at democracy has been the compliment they have paid us in taking over (and perfecting) our most prized techniques of persuasion and our underlying contempt for the credulity of the masses."[43] German émigré Emil Lederer suggested that, "in the case of an 'abstract' crowd (radio or press crowd) the leader frequently discovers that he makes an appeal to the masses of which he has not been aware."[44]

Of course, the strongest version of this argument—the simple equation of the mass audience with the regimented crowd—was not put forward by the producers of works for a mass audience. Even Lerner suggested that an "economic and political convulsion" was necessary for the media to take on this role. Nevertheless, the producers of mass media products, who often had a healthy regard for their own influence, were faced with a dilemma. In instructing the public on the dangers of fascism, how were they to get around the real possibility that the instruction itself was part of the problem? And how, when communicating through the mass media, could cultural producers debunk the media without losing their own authority? These questions were never satisfactorily answered. However, the media clearly felt an ambivalence about itself in the half decade before Pearl Harbor.

A major feature of fictional representations of the regimented crowd was the presence of an observing character whom the audience knew was not taken in by the crowd. In Robert Sherwood's *There Shall Be No Night,* such characters carry the story, as the audience gets only secondhand, critical reportage of regimented crowds. In all of the movies cited above, the most important crowd scenes contain such characters. In *Confessions of a Nazi Spy,* one woman at the German American Bund meeting does not take part in the shouting and saluting; after the gathering, she criticizes the Bund to her German American friends—"aren't we all supposed to be Americans in America?" In *Ninotchka,* the title character, on her return to Russia, participates in the parade halfheartedly. At the Nazi rally in *The Man I Married,* Carol, Erich's American wife, sits impassively as Erich and others "Heil" enthusiastically. In *The Mortal Storm,* the anti-Nazi Martin and his friend Freia stare at each other with fear and incomprehension as the tavern patrons mechanically sing the "Horst Wessel Song."[45]

Such observers served a key function—particularly in cinematic images of Nazism. Obviously, they provided a character with which the audience could sympathize in what might otherwise be an unsympathetic, hopeless image. More importantly, by serving as dramatic and visual objects of identification, these figures guarded against the more deadly prospect that the audience itself would be drawn into the crowd. In other words, the theatrical crowd could become the regimented political crowd. The fear of a film's effects on its audience, which had always underlay—and belied—industry claims that movies were merely entertainment, was increased by the studios' self-conscious decision to inform its public about the dictatorships.[46] The observing character gave filmmakers a comforting way out of this conundrum.

At least one filmmaker, however, grappled with the relationship between the media and the formation of the regimented crowd more directly. Frank

Capra enjoyed certain advantages that most directors lacked in the late 1930s. Having won Academy Awards for *It Happened One Night* (Columbia, 1934; Best Picture, Best Director), *Mr. Deeds Goes to Town* (Columbia, 1936; Best Director), and *You Can't Take It with You* (Columbia, 1938; Best Picture, Best Director), Capra wielded enormous power in Hollywood. In 1938 *Time* magazine gave him a cover story and the *Saturday Evening Post* profiled him. His decision to join the Screen Directors Guild (SDG) in 1938 turned the tide in the union's recognition battle with the studios, although it also contributed to the SDG's status as the most conservative Hollywood union. When asked years later whether he had feared being blacklisted following his decision to join the union, Capra replied, "Fuck, *I* didn't get worried about being blacklisted. How could they blacklist me? I'd blacklist *them*."[47] The creation of Frank Capra Productions, an independent film production unit, in October 1939 gave the director even more ability to operate outside of the direct pressures of the studio system. The first production of the new company was *Meet John Doe* (Warner Brothers, 1941), the only major Hollywood film in the five years leading up to Pearl Harbor that treated the fascist threat to America in purely domestic terms.

Despite the special status that allowed him to make politically controversial films such as *Meet John Doe* and the earlier *Mr. Smith Goes to Washington* (Columbia, 1939), Capra was an odd antifascist messenger. Although many, including Capra himself, have attempted to package him as a New Dealer, populist, or early crusader against Hitler, Joseph McBride argues convincingly that Capra was a conservative Republican who voted for his party in every election from 1920 until the end of his life. Capra's politics were not sophisticated. By and large, he voted his pocketbook, which from early on was rather substantial. Nevertheless, like many American conservatives, he occasionally had kind words for both Mussolini and Franco before general war came to Europe. But even in the 1930s, Capra was rarely seen as a conservative. As he almost never discussed politics, people looked to his films for his political views, a process encouraged by the director's egocentric insistence that his films were his and his alone. What they found in Capra's social problem films could be seen to suggest that he held just about any political view. In fact, the ambiguous politics of his movies were the result of production and writing teams that included a wide array of political opinion, from left liberals such as Joseph Sistrom and mainstream liberals like Sidney Buchman and Robert Riskin to the increasingly important right-wing screenwriter Myles Connolly.[48]

But if the political ambivalence of so many of Capra's films came in part from the disparate views of his screenwriters, Capra himself seems to have harbored ambivalent attitudes toward his own position as a mass cultural producer. On the one hand, throughout his career he desired to claim full authorship for his movies and to increase directorial authority within the motion picture industry. Starting with *Mr. Deeds,* Capra's was always "the Name Above the Title," which in turn became the title of his notoriously inaccurate autobiography.[49] As president of the Screen Directors Guild in the late thirties, Capra fought for increased directorial authority for his fellow directors. In February 1939 he threatened a directors' strike if his demands were not met for official recognition of the guild and for a guarantee that directors be given sufficient preparation time before shooting began on a film. The producers quickly acquiesced.[50] His decision to set up Frank Capra Productions was part of this drive for independence.

On the other hand, despite all of his calls for independence and claims of sole authorship of his films, Capra was a highly conventional director. Some have noted the irony of how little his films escaped the Hollywood production system and style.[51] As much as he desired power and recognition "above the title," Capra described his success and style in ways that effaced his own authorship. "A director's touch," he wrote in November 1939, "is the extent to which his personality has been imparted to a picture. Obviously, a picture that pretends to show human beings in a natural and engaging light should not be tinged with too apparent a personality behind the scenes. My own fond hope is that my pictures reflect not myself, but life; that what people enjoy in my work is the presentation of personalities in whom they can recognize something of themselves."[52] On another occasion, Capra characterized himself as one of those directors who "strive to make their actors the dominating factor, effacing themselves and their technique in the interests of the characters portrayed on the screen. This school . . . constantly strives to make the audience forget it is seeing that amazing combination of art and the mechanical age—the motion picture."[53]

This ambivalence about authority was pronounced in Capra's attitude toward his films' social messages. In connection with a 1941 appearance on the radio show *I'm an American!*—a Justice Department–sponsored program on NBC that presented "distinguished naturalized citizens" discussing their adoptive country—Capra was sent a series of written questions. In response to a question about the role of film in the struggle for democracy, he replied: "Personally, I refuse to believe the American public needs educating in democracy. I have a profound faith in the American people. It's the leaders who need the educating. The people are way ahead of them." Nevertheless, in his social films, especially *Mr. Smith Goes to Washington* and *Meet John Doe,* Capra tried to offer just such an education to the American people. Indeed, he was well aware of his competition. Shortly before making *Meet John Doe,* he told journalist Geoffrey Hellman: "I never cease to thrill at an audience seeing a picture. For two hours you've got 'em. Hitler can't keep 'em that long. You eventually reach even more people than Roosevelt does on the radio." Only a year after telling the Justice Department's questioner that the American people needed no lessons in democracy, Capra was creating the best-known series of U.S. propaganda films, *Why We Fight* (Army Pictorial Service, 1942–45).[54]

His social films also reveal his ambivalence about the media's role in promoting democracy. Although much has been written about his "social trilogy"—*Mr. Deeds Goes to Town, Mr. Smith Goes to Washington,* and *Meet John Doe*—little attention has been given to the role of the media in these films, despite the fact that the mass media, particularly the press, are central to each of them.[55] Neither *Deeds* nor *Smith* present a regimented crowd, but both shed light on how media create a regimented crowd in *Doe.*[56] In *Deeds* and *Smith,* the press is almost totally responsible for the creation of public opinion. It is capable of distorting the truth yet convincing readers that they have received a true representation of the way things are. Although both films, notably *Smith,* hold out the possibility that the press can behave responsibly, explaining complicated truths, exposing frauds, and supporting the public good, there is no guarantee that it will, nor that those elements on the side of the truth will prevail. When, in *Smith,* Senator Jefferson Smith (James Stewart) attempts a filibuster to save his political career from being ruined by the evil political machine of Boss Jim Taylor (Edward Arnold), radio personality H. V. Kaltenborn, playing himself, explains what the senator is doing to an implied radio audience and the actual film audience. While Smith's own newspaper, *Boys' Stuff,* attempts to defend him, Taylor's machine turns all other media in his home state against him. Although Smith prevails on the floor of the Senate, he does so despite the fact that public opinion has been turned against him at home, as represented by the thousands of letters that his opponent, Taylor stooge Senator Joseph Paine (Claude Rains), brings to the Senate floor.

In *Meet John Doe,* the power of the press is more pervasive. Like Capra's ideal motion picture, the press in *Doe* actually makes the people believe that they are seeing themselves; the results of this recognition are frightening. When the sinister, dictatorial D. B. Norton (Edward Arnold) buys the *Bulletin,* he decides to streamline his staff, dismissing, among others, feisty columnist Ann Mitchell (Barbara Stanwyck). To fire off a final shot, Mitchell writes a story in which she claims to have received a letter from one John Doe, a man who will, to protest the injustices of the world and "slimy politics," throw himself from the top of City Hall on Christmas Eve. When the piece is a huge success, Norton decides to keep Mitchell on to ghostwrite a column for "John Doe" entitled "I Protest." The paper searches for someone to play John Doe and finds Long John Willoughby (Gary Cooper), a down-and-out baseball pitcher with a bad arm. Mitchell, using her father's diary for material, writes radio speeches for John Doe. The speeches, which extol a love-thy-neighbor ethic more or less standard in Capra films, are a hit. John Doe makes the cover of *Time*. Tired of all the attention, John Willoughby tries to run away, only to discover that he is a big hero in small-town America. So much have the great mass of people seen themselves in John Doe, that the residents of Millville have spontaneously formed a "John Doe Club" to carry out "his" principles.

The devotion of the little people keeps Willoughby in his John Doe role. But D. B. Norton has other plans. Believing that "what the American people need is an iron hand," he urges the establishment of more John Doe Clubs, hoping to convert them into a third-party movement for his own presidential candidacy. Neither Willoughby nor Mitchell are aware of this scheme, whose secrecy is made easier to keep by Willoughby's practice of never reading his speeches before delivering them in order to make them sound more sincere. Unbeknownst to him, he is to announce Norton's political intentions when he addresses the assembled delegates of a national John Doe Convention in New York City. The *Bulletin*'s cynical but good-hearted editor, Harry Connell (James Gleason), gets wind of Norton's plan and warns Willoughby, who furiously marches into a meeting of Norton and his industrialist followers to announce that he will tell the convention the truth. As John Doe starts to address the crowd, standing under umbrellas in Yankee Stadium in the pouring rain, Norton's motorcycle troops cut off the public address system. Silenced, Willoughby stands in desperation as the troops pass out copies of the *Bulletin* revealing that John Doe is a fraud. The troopers start shouting insults at the speaker, epithets that the crowd then picks up and repeats. The crowd, shot by Capra from above as a uniform sea of umbrellas, shouts down Doe and forces him to leave the stage.

Willoughby decides that the only way to prove his sincerity is to actually jump from City Hall on Christmas Eve. He goes to the roof, where he is met by most of the film's other characters: Ann Mitchell, who hopes to stop him from jumping; Norton and his henchmen, who hope to convince him that he cannot stop their plans no matter what; and the members of the Millville John Doe Club, who just hope for a miracle. From this point on, Capra filmed a number of endings, none of which seemed to work.[57] In the version eventually released, Mitchell and the members of the Millville

John Doe Club convince Willoughby not to jump. "We just lost our head and acted like a mob," explains Burt Hansen, a Millville soda jerk. Other members chime in that they are not alone: a lot of John Doe Club members have, since the convention, independently decided to continue the movement. John Doe walks away from the roof with his supporters. In the film's final line, editor Henry Connell turns to Norton and, pointing at the Millville John Does, says: "There you are Norton, the people. Try and lick that!"

Like a movie, the title character of *Meet John Doe* is an "amazing combination of art and the mechanical age." He is conceived by Ann Mitchell, ghostwritten by her deceased father, played by John Willoughby, sustained by the urgings of Millville citizens, and broadcast, published, and eventually manipulated by D. B. Norton. Like Capra's ideal film, as well, the people see themselves in John Doe. However, in identifying with Doe, they open themselves up for manipulation and become a regimented crowd. This happens despite the fact that Capra, and all of the movie's main characters, are convinced of the worthiness of the ideals espoused by the John Doe Clubs. What exactly causes the regimented crowd to form? How does Capra propose preventing its formation?

Despite Hansen's protestations on the rooftop, the film seems to indicate that the John Doe movement reaches its crisis point not when the crowd turns on Doe, but when that undifferentiated crowd is formed. *Meet John Doe* continuously tries to distinguish between the dangers inherent in such a movement and the noble sentiments of its members. Ultimately the distinguishing characteristic is not sincerity—after all, the Millville club is formed when John himself is only in it for the money. Instead, the film commends the spontaneity and independence of the Millville club and those other clubs that, we are told, persist despite the convention debacle.

The film depicts John Doe activities at the local, community level, as laudable, whereas at the national level, they are sinister. The national organization is entirely the product of the mass media. Its roots are in John Doe's newspaper columns and radio broadcasts; its growth is organized by Norton's publishing empire. It is the very existence of this larger organization, the film suggests, that creates the regimented crowd. The only time that the John Doe movement appears in an unambiguously positive light is when John meets personally with the Millville club. Mass media presentations of John Doe are, at best, ambivalent, at worst, frightening. The radio broadcasts and newspaper columns in *Meet John Doe* always distort their subject, at the very least, putting words into Willoughby's mouth. Like the crowds in Hollywood representations of Nazi rallies, the throng at the John Doe Convention is undifferentiated and willing to follow anything that the public address system shouts at it. Willoughby's discovery of Norton's intentions and his resolution to tell the truth are significant only because the conventioneers would do anything that John Doe tells them, even endorse Norton for president. As he learns when the public address system is turned off, however, Willoughby is already at the mercy of mass media that he does not control. But despite the fact that Norton can manipulate the crowd to turn on Willoughby, the destruction of the national John Doe movement—its disappearance from the media—ultimately creates the space for the spontaneous local John Doe movement to form again. The people need John Doe—not a media representation of him; in the end, they receive him.[58]

Unfortunately the film's conclusion is rather incoherent, which probably accounts for low audience ratings at the time as well as a now long tradition of negative critical response. Given his decision not to jump, little changes in the final scene. Despite editor Connell's closing line, Norton still controls powerful radio and press operations. John Doe would appear to have no way to get his message out to the country, both because he has no media access and because the mass media themselves are at the root of the regimented crowd.

The film explicitly rejects the possibility of trying to live without the mass media. Willoughby has a sidekick, the Colonel (Walter Brennan), who tries to do just that. A much more committed hobo, the Colonel has only contempt for the media and all who pay attention to it. "I don't read no paper, and I don't listen to no radio, neither!" he proudly tells a reporter early in the film. Though he is never taken in by Norton, the Colonel is incapable of being a functioning member of society. Unlike Willoughby, who responds to human kindness and the feeling of community offered, at different times, by Ann Mitchell and the Millville residents, the Colonel is able to maintain his independence only by regarding them as helpless dupes, or "Heelots." As both Mitchell and the Millville John Doe Club point out at the end, they do need John Doe. The film suggests that the people have good instincts, but they are easily tricked. The positive aspect of the John Doe movement is its spontaneous eruption in small towns like Millville. Nevertheless, Capra will not trust people to love their neighbors without John Doe telling them to do so.

Charles Maland has suggested that *Meet John Doe* is, at least in part, an exploration of Capra's own ambivalence about leadership. Like Doe, Capra catapulted to fame and garnered a *Time* cover. He also was unsure about his role as a leading voice of democracy. Doe's attitude toward his own authority mirrors Capra's sense of himself as an artist: Doe expresses his independence from those who seek to control him, yet he can assert that he is simply responding to and embodying the feelings of the people; Capra always claimed absolute authority over his pictures while asserting that he was merely presenting his audience with an image of itself. Recognizing that the ending was unsatisfactory, Capra throughout his life maintained that audience preference alone decided how the film should end. Preview audiences did, in fact, object to other endings that Capra tried. The director went so far as to claim that the idea for the film's actual ending was provided by a fan letter signed simply "John Doe."[59]

In *Meet John Doe,* Capra's attempt at the end of the film to resolve these contradictions merely reinforced them. Unable to conclude the plot in a way that preserved the ideals of the John Doe movement and John Doe's authority while eliminating the dangers inherent in mass-mediated politics, Capra instead offered an impossible solution: John Doe, himself a fiction, personally joins the American people, who are symbolized by the Millville John Doe Club, while all turn their backs on the evil media tycoon, D. B. Norton. From a purely cinematic perspective, Capra did wonders with the final sequence: judiciously mixing soft focus, his signature close-ups of actors' faces, and the like to create a moving set piece. But that is an odd way to conclude a film that critiques media creation of popular symbols.

Although he tried to grapple with the relationship between the media, democracy, and the creation of the regimented crowd, Capra ultimately succeeded only in embodying the fears about the media's role in that crowd's formation. Audiences were upset that the conventioneers turned on John Doe. Capra's reply to such criticism was that he was simply presenting a realistic view of humanity.[60] Ultimately, the people in *Meet John Doe* are incapable of independently developing the strong individualism that would prevent them from joining the regimented crowd. Capra's view saw a popular audience whose vulnerability to media suggestion created the need for more education from the media, which in turn reinscribed the initial danger. Neither Capra nor anyone else in Hollywood who shared these fears was able to resolve this dilemma on-screen.

In hindsight, the arrival of a homegrown dictatorship in the United States during the late 1930s seems to have been highly unlikely. Although Roosevelt, Fromm, Capra, and others tried to imaginatively construct what might cause one to arise, the danger never materialized. But the problems that these cultural producers saw as the fundamental roots of dictatorship—material poverty, the social psychology of modernity and freedom, the growing importance of the mass media—were very real and thus provided some ground for concern. The dangers of the regimented crowd at home did not appear to be simply the stuff of clever politics, social theory, and dystopian Hollywood fantasy.

Perhaps the clearest materialization of these dangers occurred on 30 October 1938, when Orson Welles's Mercury Theatre on the Air presented an adaptation of H. G. Wells's novel, *The War of the Worlds* (1898). The story of the ensuing panic and subsequent apologies of the apparently surprised Welles are among the more familiar cultural events of the period. Today the broadcast is usually remembered as a humorous cultural oddity revealing the naïveté of the radio audience.[61] Over fifty years later, it is easy to forget the serious intent of the broadcast, the extent of public reaction, and the gravity with which that reaction was understood.

The best contemporary studies indicated that more than one million people were frightened or disturbed by the broadcast, which, in a series of special bulletins interrupting a musical program, seemed to indicate that Martians were invading the United States. Many listeners ran into the streets to arouse the neighborhood, attempted to flee by car, or telephoned police and other authorities in horror. For weeks afterward, newspapers across the country printed reports of local reactions to the broadcast.[62] Most significantly for our purposes, the entire event was connected to the debate about the causes of the regimented crowd. The broadcast embodied one of Welles's central concerns: spreading democracy by limiting the hold that mass media had on its public. Hadley Cantril, funded by the federal government to study the panic, started from the premise that the panic itself was an indication of the dangers of dictatorship in the United States. The similarities and differences between Welles's and Cantril's analysis of the problem addressed by their two very different productions help illuminate the ways in which the prevailing material, psychological, and media-related understandings of the origins of the regimented crowd were applied in practice.

Orson Welles was deeply concerned with both the deterioration of democracy around the world and the possibly damaging effects of mass media authority. In the summer of 1937, at the age of twenty-two, he had founded the Mercury Theatre with political intent; in the pages of the *Daily Worker*, Welles and his collaborator, John Houseman, announced that their new troupe would be "another step . . . toward a real People's Theatre in America."[63] Among the Mercury's first productions was a celebrated version of Shakespeare's *Julius Caesar* as an antifascist statement, complete with modern dress and sets and uniforms based on the Nuremberg rallies. Welles subtitled the production, *Death of a Dictator.* It had also been adapted for the radio, using voice-over narration by radio news announcer H. V. Kaltenborn to add a greater sense of immediacy to the broadcast.[64] The fall of 1938 had been full of portentous news from Europe, as the Munich Crisis brought the continent to the brink of war. Americans were at the mercy of their radios for the latest news, which often came in the form of special bulletins interrupting regularly scheduled broadcasts; at least one such bulletin during the Munich Crisis had interrupted a Mercury Theatre broadcast. These events heightened the urgency of Welles's and the Mercury's antifascist messages.

Despite Welles's claims to the contrary, the script for *War of the Worlds* appears to have been the work of Howard Koch, a young writer who had just joined the Mercury troupe. However, like all Mercury radio shows, *War of the Worlds* was a collaborative affair. Inspired in part by MacLeish's *Air Raid*, which used similar techniques, Houseman instructed Koch to dramatize the novel in the form of news bulletins. Welles's chief contribution was directing the piece. Finding the script "corny" at rehearsal, he encouraged further use of the device of program interruptions.[65]

The broadcast took place as part of the regularly scheduled weekly, hour-long Mercury Theatre on the Air program on CBS. It opened at 8:00 P.M. with the normal theme music and a prologue read by Orson Welles, which closely followed Wells's novel but moved the action to America in 1939. Thereafter, until a station identification about halfway through the program, the format of *War of the Worlds* was highly unusual. What appeared to be a broadcast of big-band music from the Park Plaza in New York was interrupted by a series of news bulletins, first about unusual explosions on the planet Mars, then about a strange object landing in Grovers Mill, New Jersey, and finally about the beginnings of a Martian invasion. The bulletins included studio reporters, on-the-scene correspondents, and a variety of experts (a Princeton University astronomer, a military officer, a government official). While this drama was being aired, CBS phones began to ring uncontrollably as confused police departments and panicked citizens called to find out what was going on. At the insistence of the police, following the station identification at 8:42 P.M., listeners were reminded that they were tuning in to the Mercury Theatre's adaptation of *War of the Worlds*.[66] The second half of the broadcast was more conventional. It took the form of a series of diary entries by Princeton astronomer Professor Pierson (Orson Welles), which spanned a number of days or weeks. At the start of these entries, Pierson is on the run from the man-eating Martians; in the final entry, the Martians have suddenly dropped dead from the common-cold virus. The broadcast concluded with a closing speech by Orson Welles as himself.

In the furor that followed, Welles expressed amazement than anyone could have believed the broadcast. He cited a number of factors to support this view: the production was said to occur in 1939, one year in the future; it took place at the regular time for Mercury Theatre; throughout the program the audience was reminded that it was listening to a play; and the place of Martians within "the American idiom" was one of fantasy. In a television interview years later, however, Welles admitted: "Radio in those days, before the tube and the transistor, wasn't just a noise in somebody's pocket—it was a voice of authority. Too much so. At least, I thought so. . . . [I felt that] it was time for someone to take the starch . . . out of some of that authority: hence my broadcast."[67]

What the Mercury Theatre had hoped to accomplish with *War of the Worlds* becomes more obvious on closer examination of the radio play. The most unusual aspect of the first section is its news bulletin format, which made the reports of the Martian invasion seem to be actual news. Welles's broadcast appealed to audience expectations in interesting ways. From the start, the apparent news bulletins were accompanied by expert commentary by such figures as Professor Pierson. But the experts in *War of the Worlds* are most notable for the fact that they are almost always incorrect.[68] Pierson rules out any suggestion that there might be something dangerous happening on Mars. Even after he and the radio announcer travel from Princeton to Grovers Mill to view the object that has fallen from the sky, the astronomer is the last character on the scene to realize that the object is not a meteorite. Long after the Martians have made their first appearance and killed their first victims, an announcer informs the listening public that a Professor Indellkoffer, speaking to the California Astronomical Society, expressed the opinion that the explosions on Mars were just volcanic activity. Immediately before being routed by the Martians, the captain of the New Jersey State Militia declares that "all cause for alarm, if such cause ever existed, is now entirely unjustified."

Of course, the ultimate authority that the Mercury Theatre hoped to prove false was radio itself. In his final speech, Welles as himself assured listeners that the broadcast had "no further significance than as [a] holiday offering" but then undermined his own disclaimer by adding:

> Starting now, we couldn't soap all your windows and steal all your garden gates, by tomorrow night . . . so we did the next best thing. We

annihilated the world before your very ears, and utterly destroyed the Columbia Broadcasting System. You will be relieved, I hope, to learn that we didn't mean it, and that both institutions are still open for business. So good-bye everybody, and remember, please, for the next day or so, the terrible lesson you learned tonight. That grinning, glowing, globular invader of your living-room is an inhabitant of the pumpkin patch, and if your doorbell rings and nobody's there, that was no Martian . . . it's Hollowe'en.[69]

Radio, as Welles proved, can do far more than soap windows. Although he dressed the moral of his broadcast in holiday language, the greater message he hoped to convey was a general skepticism about what the radio told its listeners.

War of the Worlds thus addressed the same issues of media and audience psychology that Capra would grapple with in *Meet John Doe*. But, unlike Capra, Welles appeared to have a formula for keeping the individualism of his audience on safe ground: make the audience question the medium itself. Two aspects of Welles's personality made him more likely to adopt such a solution than Capra. First, Welles was a more comfortable democrat. Capra was never quite able to overcome his suspicions of the people, as the formation of the crowd in *Meet John Doe* demonstrated. Second, Welles was even more confident of his own genius and delighted in self-consciously inserting his own personality into his works. In contrast, Capra's commitment to permitting the audience to see itself or forget that it was watching a movie was part and parcel of his evident concerns about the sort of hyperidentification that could create the regimented crowd. For Capra, unquestioned audience belief in the realism of his movies was as much a sign of their success as it was a potential danger; for Welles, the desire of an audience to believe what it was told was nothing but a social danger, an accidental, rather than an essential, aspect of mass media consumption that had to be eliminated.[70] However, as Michael Denning has noted, even Welles could never fully imagine an audience that would actually resist the media. On-stage, on-screen, and on the air, the crowds in Welles's productions never evinced such resistance.[71]

In the long run, the *War of the Worlds* and its aftermath probably did create greater audience skepticism. But the panic that occurred during the broadcast indicated that its immediate impact was, at least on a large minority of the listening audience, quite different. Within a week, Cantril and his research team were interviewing people who had heard the broadcast and recording their reactions. Soon they received federal funding for the project, and two years later Cantril published *The Invasion from Mars,* his study of the panic that is still a canonical work in the field of communications.

Cantril thought that the *War of the Worlds* broadcast and ensuing panic were worthy of study not just because of the scale of the event, but because they presented a rare opportunity to gain "insight into the psychology of the common man and, more especially, the psychology of the man of our times." Most significantly, he felt that the panic was an indication of how easily the United States might fall victim to dictatorial propaganda.[72] Obviously, the panicked reactions of the audience on 30 October 1938 did not create a regimented crowd; however, the audience's willingness to believe what the broadcast appeared to be telling it could be the first necessary ingredient for such a crowd to form.

Viewing the panic as fundamentally a result of "errors in judgment," Cantril devoted the bulk of his study to investigating why the audience had made them. Why had listeners not checked other radio stations? Why had even those who looked outside concluded, upon seeing nothing, that the Martians simply had not arrived at their houses yet? Cantril hypothesized that some people lacked the critical ability or skepticism needed to disbelieve what the radio was telling them. Among the factors he identified as important in determining an individual's response to the broadcast were formal education, social and economic stability, and listening situation (i.e., whether the person had tuned in to the broadcast from the start or had been told by panicked friends to tune in in the middle of the program). People who were less educated or who found themselves in extremely unstable social and economic situations, such as unemployment, were more likely to believe the broadcast's tale of disaster.[73]

Cantril also noted that the recent Munich Crisis and surrounding war scare contributed to a general climate that was "painfully serious and distressingly confused." After weeks of dire warnings about events in Europe that, because of their complexity, much of the American public only dimly understood, many in the *War of the Worlds* audience did not attempt to impose independent standards of judgment.[74] Instead, these listeners deferred to the authority of the radio. This was particularly true of people who were experiencing social stress at the time of the broadcast. Cantril concluded that this psychology lay at the heart of modern dictatorship: "It is not the radio, the movies, the press or 'propaganda' which, in themselves, really create wars and panics. It is the discrepancy between the whole superstructure of economic, social, and political practices and beliefs, and the basic and derived needs of individuals that creates wars, panics or mass movements of any kind. And human needs can only be curbed by the deliberate and forceful cultivation of ignorance, intolerance, and abstention. Such practices all adherents to democracy abhor." Given this understanding of the causes of the panic, Cantril's solutions to the underlying problem were fairly straightforward. In the long run, greater economic stability would lower the level of "frustration and anxiety" that make people so susceptible to suggestion. In the short run, greater education might allow even those in desperate economic circumstances to retain their critical abilities.[75]

Cantril's explanation of the rise of dictatorship was therefore socioeconomic, but it varied greatly from FDR's discussions along these lines. Like Roosevelt, Cantril saw economic hardship as the major contributing factor to the rise of dictatorship. The president imagined that people who had lost hope of achieving economic stability under democracy would more or less rationally choose to give up their individuality in exchange for well-being. But in Cantril's view, people made no such Hobson's choice. Instead, socioeconomic hardship made them less rational and thus vulnerable to manipulation, even if unintentional, by the new medium of radio.

Cantril's study largely ignored what was almost certainly the most important variable in the cause of the *War of the Worlds* panic: the broadcast itself. Cantril stated that the news bulletin format was largely responsible for confusing listeners, especially those who may have tuned in late and missed the opening theme music and Welles's prologue. But though he acknowledged the many ways in which the broadcast appealed to audience expectations of realism, he never suggested that Welles had done this to fool his audience. Cantril went so far as to call the Mercury Theatre, which had built its reputation on daring dramas of social significance, an "innocent little group of actors" and to characterize the *War of the Worlds* as an "incredible, old-fashioned story appropriate for Hollowe'en."[76]

Why did Cantril give the Mercury Theatre's intentions short shrift? In part, this failure to address the troupe's role in causing the panic is yet another manifestation of the focus on audiences in explaining dictatorship. Whereas Cantril closely examined the lives and listening situations of those who panicked, he dealt with the text of the broadcast only in passing, despite the fact that he reproduced the full text of the radio play as the first chapter of his book. In part, this failure to analyze the play itself can be explained by the purpose of Cantril's project. He wanted to understand why some listeners panicked and others did not. Hearing the broadcast was thus a common factor and of relatively little explanatory value. Cantril's focus on the socioeconomic status of his listeners determined the conclusions he reached. In his view, the Welles broadcast did not so much create a dangerous situation as indicate that the preconditions for an even more serious crisis existed.

Both Welles and Cantril sought a solution to the potential dangers of dictatorship in the creation and protection of individual conscience. Both hoped for greater skepticism in the radio audience. And both saw the dangers that the modern world held for the individual: for Welles, the fact of the mass media, received without sophistication, was the source of the danger; for Cantril, the nature of the mass media only exacerbated the problems created by the socioeconomic deprivations that a modern economy could cause its people. Yet they disagreed both about how to develop skepticism and what the nature of that skepticism should be. For Cantril, people should be skeptical about *false* things, such as the news reports in *War of the Worlds*. Therefore, he was most interested in creating the conditions necessary for people to achieve well-grounded standards of judgment. These conditions were to be located in external facts about people's lives: socioeconomic stability and formal education, goods that could be provided by the state, not the media. In Cantril's account, the *War of the Worlds* broadcast was primarily a warning to democracy. He never suggested that the Mercury Theatre contributed to audience skepticism or that it had such a purpose in mind. Welles, however, intended the broadcast as precisely such a contribution. Like Fromm, he had a more radical vision of individualism: it was suspicious of all conformity to received opinion, even when that opinion seemed more sensible than an invasion from Mars. Welles's skepticism had more to do with autonomy than with firmly grounded standards of judgment. Skepticism was to be valued in and of itself, not simply as a means to an end.

All of these explanations of the rise of the regimented crowd shared a number of characteristics. Each saw the problem arising structurally from some aspect of modern life: the economic hardship of masses of people, the social psychology of modernity, the influence of the mass media, and so forth. For one or more of these reasons, individuality was threatened with a new menace: the regimented crowd. These interpretations regarded the modern European dictatorships analogically as societies that had encountered the same structural problems and had failed to deal with them. Some course of action was needed to create, or at least protect, individuality among the American public: state-sponsored social programs (Roosevelt and Cantril), media-produced changes in social psychology (Welles and, to some extent, Capra), or even changes—material and psychological—brought about by social revolution (Fromm and Lerner).

None of these visions reached fruition. Franklin Roosevelt successfully defended his social programs, but they only partially alleviated the economic hardship that, in different ways, both he and Hadley Cantril saw as the root of the dictatorial danger. Erich Fromm's dream of a radical transformation of society remained unfulfilled, as did the more modest hopes of Max Lerner. Although the *War of the Worlds* panic became a cautionary tale about putting too much faith in the mass media, the desire of Orson Welles for a more skeptical public was largely unrealized, even within his productions. And Frank Capra never did resolve his ambivalence about the relationship of the media and the crowd.

For, even as Cantril studied the panic, FDR defended himself against charges of dictatorship, and Capra produced the only Hollywood film of the half decade before Pearl Harbor to explore the dangers of a homegrown dictatorship, the focus of many Americans' fears shifted from social conditions at home to dangers from abroad. As war broke out in Europe and the United States began edging toward involvement, the European dictatorships became ever more significant as a direct threat, rather than as merely cautionary tales. This threat could be viewed in strictly military terms, or it could be seen through the nativist lenses of many noninterventionist groups. But increasingly the dominant view of the European dictatorships, particularly among interventionists, was as an ideological threat, one that grew with each Axis victory.

5 DICTATOR ISMS AND OUR DEMOCRACY THE RISE OF TOTALITARIANISM, 1936–1941

"The most important single fact with regard to any government under [a dictator's] control is the character of the dictator himself," wrote political scientist Robert C. Brooks back in 1935.[1] But by the mid-1930s the "dictator himself" began to seem less important than did the structure of dictatorial regimes. As the last chapter explored, in the half decade before Pearl Harbor some American cultural producers understood dictatorship in terms of the emergence of a new, regimented crowd, produced by certain new conditions. *Which* new conditions were significant, however, was widely debated. Yet it was generally agreed that the regimented crowd was created by a failure of people to maintain their own individuality. Whether destroyed by economic conditions, the mass media, the social psychology of capitalism, or even a lack of education, individuation gave way to a mass mind. The European dictatorships thus presented a warning to the United States by analogy: We, too, suffer from the economic and social strains of modernity that struck Weimar Germany; it *could* happen here.

The European dictatorships presented a more direct danger as well. In Spain, Austria, and Ethiopia, they seemed bent on spreading their rule by force of arms. Through magazines, newspapers, and short-wave radio broadcasts, their doctrines reached all the way to the United States. These doctrines could be seen as essential to the construction of the regimented crowd and dictatorship. It is hard to imagine a view of dictatorship more diametrically opposed to Brooks's view than that appearing in the 1940 pamphlet *Dictator Isms and Our Democracy* by Gertrude Quitman and William H. Allen of the Institute for Public Service, an old New York–based Progressive organization dedicated to reforming education and fighting urban corruption:

[German soldiers] have not just been fighting for Hitler. They make wars, as their home folks make sacrifices, for isms. . . . We can reduce the danger from dictator isms by recognizing that they are ideas and feelings, not leaders or dictators. . . .

Fascism's *duce,* leader, has an aggressive chin and plays the violin; but those are no part of fascism.

Nazism's *fuehrer,* leader, is a bachelor, has a make believe mustache, consults astrology and was once a paper hanger; but those are no part of nazism.

Communism's *comrade,* leader, is oriental, suspicious and vindictive; but those qualities are no inherent part of communism.

. . . Therefore, to keep our minds on *impersonal dictator isms,* let us shut out *foreign personalities and peculiarities.*[2]

This chapter will examine dictatorship in terms of isms and the rise of "totalitarianism" as an all-encompassing term to link these seemingly disparate doctrines. Although most American cultural producers maintained some sense that communism and fascism were different from each other, ism talk became a way of emphasizing those elements that seemed most similar. At the same time, writing of isms tended to highlight, by contra-distinction, that aspect of U.S. political culture with which many American cultural producers were most comfortable, pluralism, while casting a suspicious glance at any potential mass movement. As the term "totali-tarianism" emerged to link the various isms, academic discussion of the totalitarian state significantly shifted to a consideration of totalitarianism, which, though a good deal more sophisticated, bore a close resemblance to the popular discourse about isms and totalitarianism. The chapter also will briefly consider the key role that the term "totalitarianism" played for both interventionists and noninterventionists between the start of World War II in Europe in September 1939 and the bombing of Pearl Harbor over two years later.

By the end of the 1930s the use of "totalitarianism" to link dictatorships of both left and right had become common coin in the United States.[3] Of course, to speak of "dictator isms" was already to link two apparently dia-metrically opposed belief systems: communism and fascism. Starting in the mid-1930s, a number of events took place that made it easier to equate these disparate regimes. In 1934 the Nazi Blood Purge and the Soviet Kirov Purge created an opportunity for Americans to analogize Nazism and Soviet Communism, although they did not use the term "totalitarian" to link them. In the second half of the decade, the Soviet Union, Nazi Germany, and Fascist Italy continued to behave in ways that many Americans saw as simi-larly brutal. From 1936 to 1938 the Soviet Union prosecuted a large number of Old Bolsheviks in three show trials that captured the world's attention. Convicted of plotting to overthrow the regime they helped found, Lev Kamenev, Gregory Zinoviev, Nikolai Bukharin, and others were sentenced to death following long, often bizarre, confessions. Although some, including U.S. ambassador Joseph Davies, sided with Stalin's government in the matter, the trials produced another, more widespread round of newspaper and magazine articles emphasizing the similarity between the USSR and Nazi Germany.[4]

The clearest difference between the fascist regimes and the Soviet government, in the opinion of many American observers, was their foreign policy. Stalin's goal of socialism in one country and his commitment to collective security made the Soviet Union, despite its internationalist heritage, seem less bent on expansion than Italy and Germany. The fascist states, for their part, had begun or become involved in a number of aggressive military actions: Italy invaded Ethiopia (1934), Germany seized Austria and the Sudetenland (1938), and both took part in the Spanish Civil War (1936–39). Although Soviet involvement in Spain made some newspaper journalists abandon their view of the USSR as a status quo power, the final difference between the two kinds of regimes seemed to be erased when the Nazi-Soviet Pact was signed in the summer of 1939.[5] That pact merely confirmed what many American cultural producers had been arguing for a number of years.

In the second half of the 1930s, most Americans who linked dictatorships of the left and the right did so with some ambivalence. On the one hand, the thought that these two systems were exactly the same did not have a wide following among U.S. cultural producers, although certain people— largely among the anti-Stalinist left, moderate anticommunist intellectuals, various elements of the right, and some more liberal religious groups—did regard the USSR and Nazi Germany as identical throughout the late 1930s.[6] On the other hand, many more commentators portrayed them as distinct, but equally dangerous and nefarious. It was easy to identify similar evils caused by both regimes. It took a good deal more abstraction, however, to claim that fascism and communism were simply one and the same, given the evident hostility between the two systems.

Antifascism and anticommunism were both powerful forces in American society in the 1930s. With some notable exceptions, antifascists saw communism as, at worst, the much lesser of two evils and, at best, a major force for good in the struggle against fascism. Although generally less openly enthusiastic about fascism, many anticommunists viewed it in a not dissimilar light. Particularly before the Nazi-Soviet Pact there were major differences in the way many Americans regarded the two regimes, although just what these differences were varied.

As the Communist Party (CP) began to adopt the Popular Front strategy after 1935, many American liberals began to feel that the Soviet Union stood firmly on the side of democracy in the battle against fascism. These feelings seemed to be confirmed by a number of events on the world scene. The new Soviet Constitution of 1936, which claimed to guarantee a variety of civil liberties, was naively hailed by many as marking a profound change in the way the USSR was governed. The war in Spain similarly reinforced the impression that communism was now on the right side of the struggle for the world.[7] Popular Front liberals were not uncritical of communism.[8] However, many felt that the Soviet Union had changed over the 1930s and that a country that was once a dictatorship was exploring new kinds of democracy. Other liberals remained skeptical. Whether critical of a dictatorship of the proletariat, the apparent regimentation of the CP, or the way in which the Soviet Union was actually governed, writers like Alfred Bingham, Charles Beard, and John Dewey kept their distance from the Popular Front and subscribed to various flavors of anticommunism.[9]

Events toward the end of the decade, most notably the show trials and the Nazi-Soviet Pact, soured many liberals on the Soviet Union. Running from 1936 to 1938, the Moscow trials divided U.S. intellectuals. Many Americans, including some anticommunists like former secretary of war Newton Baker, accepted the trials at face value and congratulated the Soviet Union for uncovering a massive fascist plot. But others saw the trials as a sign that the Soviet Union's journey from dictatorship to democracy would simply take some time; still others utterly condemned the USSR for staging them. Most Popular Front liberals, however, continued to support the Soviet Union on the grounds that the battle against fascism required unity above all else.[10] Not surprisingly, the Nazi-Soviet Pact, which shattered the premise of a unified force against fascism, broke the back of the Popular Front.

Nevertheless, for many liberals, even those who had mistrusted the Popular Front from the start, the Soviet Union represented a sort of lost dream. After the collapse of the Popular Front, liberals still invoked the hopes that had once been associated with the USSR. When, in a February 1940 speech, FDR chided delegates to the American Youth Conference for objecting to his criticism of the recent Soviet invasion of Finland, he expressed his past aspirations for the Soviet Union even as he condemned it as "a dictatorship as absolute as any other dictatorship in the world."[11]

Even American movies that criticized the regime and its supporters tended to present them in a less than totally negative light. Although Hollywood would later be falsely accused of producing films supportive of communism in the 1930s, major movies of the half decade before Pearl Harbor were actually an unlikely place to find sympathy for the Soviet Union. The conservative, anticommunist Hays Office was constantly on the lookout for anything that might remotely constitute communist propaganda. The studio heads and most producers were fearful of labor activism and were themselves committed anticommunists. Members of the heterogeneous Hollywood left, organized around such Popular Front groups as the Hollywood Anti-Nazi League, were much more in agreement about the industry's labor situation and fascism than about communism.[12] Each of these factors contributed to Hollywood's relative silence on Soviet matters in the late 1930s.[13] The lack of a Soviet market for American movies eased the process of squelching what Soviet-related projects did almost see the light of day.[14] Nevertheless, prior to the U.S. alliance with the Soviet Union and U.S. involvement in World War II, Hollywood made a series of films that portrayed Soviet Communism in a less negative way than its representations of Nazism in, for example, *Confessions of a Nazi Spy* (Warner Brothers, 1939) and *The Mortal Storm* (MGM, 1940). The first significant pre–Pearl Harbor movie about Soviet Russia was *Ninotchka* (MGM, 1939), a highly successful star vehicle for Greta Garbo. *Ninotchka* spawned two lesser efforts: *Comrade X* (MGM, 1940) and *He Stayed for Breakfast* (MGM, 1940). All three films concerned a communist softened into western, capitalistic ways by falling in love with a noncommunist.[15] No studio made an equivalent movie about a Nazi softened into normalcy.

Ninotchka provides an interesting snapshot of apolitical ambivalence toward the Soviet Union in late 1930s America. The title character, played by Greta Garbo, is a tough, cold, work-obsessed, Soviet-style new woman, who has been sent as an envoy to Paris.[16] There she falls in love with Leon D'Algout (Melvyn Douglas), the lawyer of an expatriate Russian countess. Douglas transforms Garbo from a cold comrade into a warm woman. Angered by their relationship, the countess arranges to have Ninotchka sent back to Russia. Once she returns to her dreary Muscovite existence, Leon cannot visit her because of his involvement with white Russian expatriates. Ninotchka receives his letters, but their contents are censored. Finally, through some trickery involving the original three commissars, he manages to get her assigned to Turkey, where they reunite and she defects.

Certainly, the picture that *Ninotchka* presents of life in Soviet Russia is grim: total censorship of outside information, regimented support of the regime, cramped living conditions, rationed food, fear of spying neighbors. When the three commissars in Paris search for the special envoy, whom they do not even know is a woman, they initially walk toward a bearded man. "He looks like a comrade," one of them suggests. Before they reach him, however, he raises his arm to another man and says "Heil Hitler!" But *Ninotchka* does not present communism as the utterly monstrous belief system that Hollywood always suggested Nazism was. Even the disenchanted protagonist is able to give an impassioned speech about the horrors of life in tsarist Russia.

More importantly, Ninotchka's failure to be a "normal" woman, around which the central romantic plot develops, is connected to her excessive rationality. She is emotionless and overly interested in statistics and engineering. When Leon follows her to the Eiffel Tower for romance, she is only interested in the number of steps to the top. The Soviet state, as represented by the figure of Ninotchka, is genuinely concerned with the great mass of its people. But it is so interested in their statistical well-being that it has forgotten their emotional needs and has become cold, oppressive, inhuman. Pre–Pearl Harbor Hollywood Nazis could be calculating as well. But their calculations tended to be based on a crazed irrationalism (*The Man I Married*—Fox, 1940) or a crude desire for conquest (*Confessions of a Nazi Spy*). Despite its clearly anti-Soviet message—and despite the fact that it had to run the gauntlet of Joseph Breen's watchful minions at the Hays Office—*Ninotchka* retains a sense that, in its conception, the October Revolution was not entirely evil. Such notions are not present in any Hollywood film about Nazism.

Americans on the political right, of course, drew very different distinctions between fascism and communism, with communism emerging as the greater of the two evils. Some conservatives could find a little solace in the anticommunism of the fascist states, as well as their less total rejection of religion. But over the course of the 1930s, most American conservatives who were not truly on the political fringe backed away from the earlier view of fascism as a necessary evil. Instead, groups such as the American Legion tended to halfheartedly denounce fascism, while claiming that it did not pose the same danger that communism did: Communism was an international movement whose plans for world revolution included the United States; Italian Fascism and German Nazism were preeminently national and thus, by definition, did not concern themselves with America. Unlike their communist counterparts, argued some conservatives, at least fascists spoke honestly about their invidious plans and ideas.[17]

In the 1930s the anticommunist image of communism and the antifascist image of fascism began to converge. American anticommunists had long pictured communism as a vast conspiracy of front organizations, teachers, intellectuals, entertainers, and the like, all of whom seemed fairly innocent but were poisoning the nation from within. Anticommunist books and pamphlets often consisted largely of endless lists of suspect organizations and individuals.[18] This image was a fairly old one in American anticommunism, reaching back at least to the 1920s.[19] As a view of the ways in which powers outside America hoped to bore into the nation, it was not dissimilar to the antimasonry and anti-Catholicism that stretched back well into the nineteenth century. By the late 1930s it had been adopted by antifascists. The film *Confessions of a Nazi Spy,* in which a spiderweb chart of Nazi activity is displayed in the climactic courtroom sequence, shows this image in its purest form, perhaps because it was made with major assistance from the primarily anticommunist Federal Bureau of Investigation (FBI). The Dies Committee, the predecessor of the House Committee on Un-American Activities, treated both communism and fascism this way, although it was always more concerned with communism.

Communism lent itself to this grand conspiratorial view more easily than fascism. The clearly universal claims of the Comintern, the dominant role of Moscow in it, and the open ties of the CP to it made the notion of a single, united communist threat more plausible, despite the existence of a small but vibrant anti-Stalinist left. The fractious American far right, which included Silver Shirts, White Shirts, the German American Bund, the Knights of the White Camellia, and a variety of smaller groups, did not so easily fit a single organizational chart whose top position was in Berlin. But although these groups did not share a leader or an organization, they seemed to share a philosophy whose most significant exponent was Adolf Hitler.

By the late 1930s many American cultural producers subscribed to the view that fascism—or, more specifically, Nazism—was an international movement of fanatic cobelievers and their unwitting dupes. Even if Nazi armies could not directly threaten the United States, Hitlerite thinking already did. In 1937 Dorothy Thompson, one of America's most prominent antifascist journalists, focused one of her regular radio broadcasts on Hitler's call to people of German descent around the world to rally around the New Germany. "German Nazism," argued Thompson, echoing Hitler's pronouncement, "is a world philosophy." When the antisemitic, Hitler-admiring, but thoroughly homegrown and independent Protestant fundamentalist minister Gerald Winrod of Kansas ran for the U.S. Senate in 1938, his opponents were quick to link him to a worldwide Nazi movement. On the eve of America's entry into World War II, FDR, presumably wanting to convert rather than alienate noninterventionists, tended to speak of them as the unwitting dupes of these forces.[20] Such warnings had a profound effect on public opinion. A July 1940 Elmo Roper poll for *Fortune* magazine revealed that 71 percent of the Americans surveyed believed that the Nazis had already begun to organize a fifth column in the United States.[21]

In February 1939 the German American Bund held a rally celebrating Washington's Birthday in Madison Square Garden. The gathering, complete with uniformed storm troopers and swastika banners, galvanized many of the concerns about Nazism spreading from Germany to the United States. The previous year Hitler's government had disassociated itself from the Bund, calling it "too radical," perhaps realizing that the small but loud group was more likely to attract attention and breed antifascism than to convert Americans to the cause of Nazism. The Third Reich's fears, in fact, proved correct. In a much-publicized gesture, Dorothy Thompson herself attended the celebration and was ejected for laughing at the speakers. In the wake of the rally, periodicals from the *Saturday Evening Post* on the right to the *Nation* on the left devoted stories to the rising tide of Nazism in the United States.[22]

Two points in the coverage stand out. First, although the German American Bund was explicitly an organization of and for Americans of German extraction, nobody argued that German Americans, or any other ethnic group, were responsible for the Nazi threat. Perhaps because of continued regret about the campaign waged against "hyphenated Americans" before and during World War I, cultural producers went out of their way to emphasize that a majority of German Americans totally opposed the Bund.[23] Second, articles that denounced the Bund and other American fascist movements tended to condemn communism in the same breath. Although the ideologies of fascism and communism were completely different, the movements could be presented as more or less the same. In an article entitled "Star-Spangled Fascists," Stanley High, writing in the extremely popular and moderately conservative *Saturday Evening Post,* put it this way:

> [A future unified American fascist movement] will include some sincere citizens and, with them, as unlovely an assortment of aliens, bigots and malcontents as any that ever abused the privileges of a democracy. The only comparable collection is that of the Communists. That partly accounts for the rivalry between them. The passwords differ, but the area of operations is virtually the same. Both work on the lunatic fringe. Between them, they have organized it, groomed it and promised it the kingdom. In better-tempered times, that would hardly alarm anybody. Today, however, the lunatic fringe is no laughing matter. In too many places its capers have proved to be the stuff out of which history is made.[24]

Newsweek made a similar argument, conceptually linking "Bunders and Reds" throughout its coverage of the Bund rally. Rather than using the term "lunatic fringe," however, *Newsweek* referred to "totalitarian ideas of all varieties," "totalitarianism," and, in the article's title, "America's 'Isms.'"

The word "ism" had been used as a pejorative term for a political ideology for more than a century, but in the late 1930s its use appears to have reached a high-water mark in the United States.[25] Indeed, "ism" became one of the terms most commonly used to link the dictatorships of the left and right and to describe the danger they posed to American democracy. Numerous books and pamphlets from across the political spectrum purported to explain the various isms to the general reading public. Some claimed to be neutral surveys of the isms; others were polemical tracts warning Americans of the danger of isms.[26] From these works emerged a fairly standard laundry list of the isms: communism, Marxism, fascism, socialism, and Nazism were almost universally mentioned, possibly because each was often in the public eye and each had vocal proponents on the world scene; capitalism, democracy, and liberalism also appeared regularly, with the caveat that they were different from the other isms; more esoteric isms—fabianism, Christian socialism, and anarchism—occasionally showed up in the more encyclopedic lists; Americanism could be found in the right-wing National Americanism Commission of the American Legion's *ISMS*, which argued that other isms were simply "alien"; finally, syncretic isms such as collectivism and totalitarianism frequently made an appearance. Beyond these works on isms per se, many more books and pamphlets compared one or more of these systems with the "American Way," democracy, or "Americanism."[27]

Writings on isms tended to link various ideologies while simultaneously acknowledging their differences. What communism shared with fascism, for instance, was an ideological rigidity. Isms were said to have extreme and inflexible views of the world. American critics of the isms could use their disagreement to emphasize the wrongheadedness of their rigidity. "Fifty million isms must be wrong," began *Dorothy Thompson's Political Guide* (1938). "On the face of it, some of them *must* be! Capitalism, Socialism, Communism, Naziism, Fascism, Collectivism, Nationalism, Internationalism, Totalitarianism—the words are not all in the dictionary, but they are in every newspaper that we pick up. Ideologies! Words! Faiths! Creeds!" In three pages, Thompson explained all the various crises of the day based on the existence of these warring isms: they had created the regimented crowd ("for the sake of these words . . . men wear black shirts or brown, put red ties around their necks, . . . desert their parents, parade, shout, make camps"); had brought war to Ethiopia, Spain, and China; had made millions homeless; and had destroyed countries and systems of government. She admitted, however, that one of the isms that she had listed was not at fault: "It is hard to call Capitalism one of the isms, because Capitalism is not a creed at all. Capitalism was not 'invented' by any sociologist or philosopher. Capitalists never called themselves that. The word was invented by socialists to describe what they hated."[28]

According to Thompson, even the real isms were not what they seemed, for "the Communists and Fascists are engaged in a sham struggle of ideas. The actual forms of government under which Fascists and Communists live are almost identical." Their real enemy was what she called "Liberalism," which she associated with capitalism. Liberalism, in her view, was deeply woven into the founding documents of the United States. Thompson's Liberal (the term is always capitalized) is actually more of a pluralist than a classical liberal, one who is committed to individual freedom but is willing to let government play an increased role in society so long as everyone's interests are considered. "The Liberal," wrote Thompson, "is the great mediator."[29]

In their pamphlet *Dictator Isms and Our Democracy*, Quitman and Allen also explained the European crisis in terms of isms. After establishing that "war-making, crusading isms," not the dictators themselves, were responsible for the war in Europe and the threat to democracy, the authors similarly equated isms of the left and right. They imagined three U.S. cities that were taken over by a fascist, a Nazi, and a communist dictator respectively. "The central fact about each dictator is that he was *drafted* by his city. He did not conquer and enslave by force." Four years later, these cities were identical. They had lost the same freedoms: free press, free reading, free libraries, free radio, free assembly, free movies, free speech, political parties, scientific inquiry, free labor, free courts, and so forth.[30]

Like Thompson, Quitman and Allen regarded the various isms as similar despite the fact that Nazism, communism, and fascism professed different beliefs. The effect of these isms was much more dictated by the rigid and totalizing implementation of the beliefs than by the beliefs themselves, which after a short time no longer made any difference. Unlike Thompson, who somewhat anti-intellectually equated isms with dangerous theorizing and liberalism with human nature, Quitman and Allen warned that even if communism, Nazism, and fascism somehow disappeared off the face of the earth, America would not be entirely safe. Sounding a little like Lewis Mumford, they observed that human nature itself creates isms. The "eternal vigilance" that they urged on their American audience as the price of liberty thus included vigilance against not only foreign ideologies, but also potential new dictator isms of American provenance. Every freedom lost in their three imaginary cities, Quitman and Allen asserted, had already been lost somewhere in America. U.S. political parties were not democratic. American "hearts and minds" often failed to be as well. The U.S. economy was frequently undemocratic. "We invented actual totalitarianism in great corporations, like the great steel and oil trusts, before Europeans invented and popularized the word totalitarian for politics," declared the authors. "No nation can be democratic in government whose industry is run by hosts of dictators."[31]

But the radical democracy hinted at in *Dictator Isms* was unusual. Both the Popular Front and the anti-Stalinist left generally avoided speaking of isms as a single entity, for their members subscribed to one ism or another and believed that the specific content of the various creeds dubbed "isms" was crucial. On the right, the American Legion's *ISMS* was much more about communism than anything else. Indeed, the isms under consideration were referred to as *alien* isms, which the legion contrasted with "Americanism."[32] By and large talk of isms was aimed at broadly promoting the American status quo, usually by emphasizing its assumed pluralism.

The increased attention to isms helps explain the concurrent extraordinary growth in the use of the word "totalitarianism" by cultural producers in the late 1930s. Early in the decade, Americans most frequently associated the totalitarian state with Nazi Germany. As U.S. opinion soured on Italian Fascism in the mid-1930s, the Italian regime was often added to the list of totalitarian states. On 22 March 1936 the *New York Times* ran a small box announcing, "'Totalitarian' Idea Spreads." Associating "totalitarian state" entirely with right-wing regimes—Germany, Italy, and Paraguay are mentioned—the paper rather unhelpfully suggested that, "while interpretations of 'totalitarian State' differ as much as definitions of democracy, the underlying idea goes back to the Latin 'totus,' meaning all."

The *Times*'s confusion was understandable. "Totalitarian" meant different things to different people; only rarely did a writer bother to clarify what he or she meant by the term. By the mid-1930s "totalitarian" carried with it a series of common associations. Most significantly, totalitarian states were believed to force themselves into all aspects of social life and to be willing to use brutal means to remake society in their image. As late as 1938, the *Times* attempted to reject the word outright. On 6 June an editorial, entitled "Nickel Word Needed," declared that the word "totalitarian" was unnecessary: "What this country needs is a good five-cent word to replace such fifty-cent alien importations as 'totalitarian'. . . . Our forefathers had a word for it. They called it tyranny and let it go at that." But the paper's call for plain speaking ignored one of the most important associations that "totalitarian" had taken on in American public culture: the totalitarian state was widely treated as a *new* phenomenon. The regimes characterized as totalitarian, whether Nazi Germany alone, all dictatorships of the right, or fascism and communism together, were almost invariably considered to represent a form of government that had never before existed.

By the mid-1930s the terms "totalitarian state" and "totalitarianism" began ever more frequently to refer to both the right- and left-wing European dictatorships. In America, the use of "totalitarian state" to apply to both communism and fascism dated back at least to April 1934, when Calvin Hoover's essay on "Dictators and Democracies" appeared in the *Virginia Quarterly*.[33] At the time, before either Hitler's Blood Purge or Stalin's Kirov Purge, Hoover's notion that Nazi Germany and Soviet Russia, though sworn enemies, were actually very much alike was unusual in the United States. As the decade progressed, however, many more Americans of diverse political views reached the same conclusion. "Totalitarian" became one of a number of terms that American cultural producers used to link communism and fascism.

Among these cultural producers were the leftist writers who reconstituted the *Partisan Review* (*PR*) in 1937. Originally an organ of the CP-affiliated John Reed Clubs, the *PR* broke decisively with the Communist Party to reemerge as an independent publication with strong Trotskyist leanings. From its first issue, the new *PR* announced that the movement it had abandoned was totalitarian. "Formerly associated with the Communist Party," the *PR*'s editors—F. W. Dupee, Dwight Macdonald, Mary McCarthy, George L. K. Morris, William Phillips, and Philip Rahv—noted in the "Editorial Statement" that opened the December 1937 issue: "*Partisan Review* strove from the first against its drive to equate the interest of literature with those of factional politics. Our appearance on an independent basis signifies our conviction that the totalitarian trend is inherent in that movement and that it can no longer be combated from within."

Although the *PR* was a highbrow magazine read initially by a small sectarian audience, the articles that appeared in its pages were among the most intellectually serious assessments of totalitarianism written in the 1930s. More importantly, some of the meanings that *PR* writers attached to the term became key components of broader understandings of totalitarianism in American public culture. The editors of the *PR* did not oppose the Communist Party because it insisted that art and artistic criticism be political; indeed, in their opening editorial statement they declared that "any magazine . . . which aspires to a place in the vanguard of literature today will be revolutionary in tendency." Rather, they objected to the communists' insistence on a unified party line. The antonym of the "totalitarian trend" of the CP was "independence" of those involved in the *PR*—independence not *from* politics but *as* artists and writers.

In its use of "totalitarian," the *PR*'s editorial statement both reflected and enhanced certain tendencies that were already evident in American usage. Earlier in the decade, the *Christian Century* had taken the term from its usual position modifying "state" and tried to write of "totalitarian Christianity" in a positive sense: Christianity had to be totalitarian in that it must involve itself in all aspects of life. Even in the first half of the 1930s, however, most American cultural producers who referred to the totalitarian state did so to emphasize not only the state's claim of omnicompetence, but also its desire for the "coordination" (to use the standard English translation of the Nazi's "Gleichschaltung") of all aspects of society. By labeling the CP "totalitarian," the *PR* editors were not indicating that the party desired a totalitarian state—although they doubtless would have argued that it did—but that the movement itself was totalitarian: like a totalitarian state, it sought to coordinate all aspects of life, thus robbing artists and critics of their necessary independence.

Over the next few years, writers for the *Partisan Review* developed their critiques of totalitarianism. The term always included both dictatorships of the left and the right. Despite decrying sectarianism, the editors of the new *PR* were mostly interested in engaging in factional left-wing politics. As a result, the Soviet Union and the CP received more attention than fascism. And, perhaps because it was a literary magazine, articles appearing in the *PR* overwhelmingly linked the term "totalitarian" to restrictions on cultural freedom.[34]

At about the same time as the *PR*'s declaration of independence, the more liberal elements of the Christian press—*Commonweal* and the *Christian Century*—were using the term "totalitarianism" to link fascism and communism. In the January 1937 editorial "Communism and Fascism Are Not Opposites," the Protestant *Christian Century* praised *Commonweal*'s endorsement of Father Wilfrid Parsons's statement that "the issue today is not between fascism and communism; it is between democracy and all forms of totalitarianism, including communism."[35] Although later that year, Samuel McCrea Cavert again suggested in the *Christian Century* that "by its very nature Christianity is totalitarian," his view now contradicted the magazine's own affirmation of totalitarianism as the opposite of democracy. By 1939 the conservative *Catholic World* began regularly using the term to link and denounce fascism and communism and to emphasize their hostility to the individual. "Pius XI," wrote Gerald Vann in the April 1939 issue, "condemned alike the crimes of anti-semitism and the crimes of financial oligarchy, the errors of totalitarianism whether of Left or of Right; and the truth to which incessantly he referred in his teaching was that what is of the greatest value on earth is the human person, whose end is God."[36]

On the secular right, writers for the *American Mercury* also adopted the term. Although they used it to link dictatorships of the left and the right, like their counterparts at the *Partisan Review,* they came to use "totalitarian" to denounce more than simply communist and fascist states. As for the *PR*'s leftist essayists, as well, the notion of a rigid party line and the punishment of independent thought was central to more general applications of "totalitarian." The similarity between the left-wing *Partisan Review* and the right-wing *American Mercury* was not entirely accidental. Like the *PR,* the *Mercury* featured many writers who were former Communists or fellow travelers, such as Max Eastman, Eugene Lyons, and William Henry Chamberlin. Of course, the *Mercury*'s targets were somewhat different. In April 1939 Lyons denounced "Our Totalitarian 'Liberals'":

> Once the basic virtue of the liberal approach to public affairs was its application of independent reason to all problems and to the claims of all contending parties. Small trace of that approach can be discovered in the fashionable liberalism which flourishes today in Hollywood and on college campuses, in certain penthouses and editorial offices. It is blindly sectarian, and as intolerant as the most intractable Calvinism. Its faithful scream "Heretic! Fascist! Reactionary!" at the first faint sign of non-conformist thinking on the sacred subjects. Certain ideas are respectable—others *verboten*. . . .
>
> The transformation of American liberalism into another variation on current lunacy makes it that much more important for those who have not been swept into the maelstrom to oppose—as The American Mercury intends to do—all totalitarian ways and totalitarian thinking, whether homegrown or imported, no matter how beguiling the colors and labels.[37]

Of course, "totalitarianism" was not the only term available to link left and right dictatorships. It is worth considering why it began to attain more cultural purchase than competitors such as "dictatorship" itself, "fascism," or "collectivism." Two aspects of the meaning of "totalitarianism" could simply not be captured by "dictatorship." First, dictatorship was an old political concept; it alone could not suggest the novelty that so many saw in the Italian, German, and Soviet regimes. Second, the idea of dictatorship drew attention to the person of the dictator himself, who became less important to understandings of fascism and communism in the second half of the 1930s. "Dictatorial liberals" could not be used as Eugene Lyons used "totalitarian liberals"; the intolerance that Lyons saw in American liberalism was not based on any single authority figure.

"Collectivism" was also frequently used to link fascism and communism, but its appeal was limited to the political center and right.[38] In some ways, "collectivism" would seem to have had a number of advantages over "totalitarianism." To begin with, the meaning of "collectivism" was more immediately clear than that of "totalitarianism." "Collectivism" always signified the opposite of individualism or liberalism. It was a conception of society that was fundamentally different from that of many Americans. Whereas an individualist or liberal society regarded the individual as the basic social unit, a collectivist society subordinated the individual to itself. Not only was this meaning clear, but it would seem to correspond to one of the central anxieties in much American thought about dictatorship: the dangers that the regimented crowd posed to individuality. However, unlike totalitarianism, which was an entirely negative term in the United States, many Americans on the left actively and openly supported collectivism. Many in the Popular Front argued that modern economic conditions required some compromise between collectivism and individualism.[39] And the sworn enemies of totalitarianism who wrote for the *Partisan Review* would not have been so quick to denounce collectivism.

Like "collectivism," "fascism" was occasionally used to describe not just the German and Italian regimes, but also the Soviet one. Lewis Mumford was the most notable exponent of this use of "fascism," but he was not alone. Austrian-born economist Peter Drucker included the Soviet Union among the "totalitarian fascist" regimes.[40] In American public culture, however, "fascism" had come to be applied specifically to groups to the right of center. Despite the writings of Mumford and Drucker, calling the Soviet Union fascist would have seemed bizarre to most Americans, even those hostile to Soviet Communism.

"Totalitarianism" had other advantages over competing terms. In the late 1930s it retained some of the meanings it had collected in the early 1930s and added others. "Totalitarianism" was a more wholly negative term than "collectivism." The root "total" itself suggested the impossibility of political compromise.[41] Collectivism was usually presented as a rational, if wrongheaded, philosophy of the relation of the individual to society or state.

Totalitarianism, on the other hand, like the more general term "ism" suggested irrationality. Indeed, the use of "totalitarianism," while retaining the sense of an all-powerful state that lay at the heart of the term "totalitarian state," could be little more than an emphatic evocation of "ism." What made isms bad was their tendency to totalize, to demand of their faithful an absolute, militant devotion that led them, whether dressed in brown, black, or red, to silence or kill all who disagreed. "Totalitarianism" retained its older definition: the belief in or existence of a totalitarian state.[42] But the word also came to mean a more general, organized intolerance of dissenting opinion. Totalitarianism was more a faith than a philosophy. Although considered a universal phenomenon, it retained the whiff of foreignness associated with the totalitarian state. Though totalitarianism could take hold in the United States, the virus had to be transplanted from without. "The enemy of democracy and civilization is not any country," wrote Max Eastman in January 1940, "but the totalitarian state of mind. And that state of mind is most successfully introduced into the United States by the adherents of and fellow travelers of Stalin."[43]

One of the unusual strengths of the term "totalitarian" and its cognates was that people from across the political spectrum could feel comfortable denouncing it. Its relative vagueness may actually have made it a more accurate reflection of Americans' diverse fears about communism and fascism. Its association with the destruction of individuality and dissent made it particularly attractive to writers and artists in an era when free speech seemed seriously threatened around the world. Thus, when in May 1939 Sidney Hook assembled a large group of public intellectuals under the banner of the Committee for Cultural Freedom to denounce these trends, totalitarianism was the natural term to unite them.[44] Hook's committee had over eighty members, including other leftists such as Norman Thomas, a variety of liberals like Dorothy Thompson and Elmer Davis, and conservatives such as Max Eastman and Eugene Lyons. "The tide of totalitarianism is rising throughout the world," began the Manifesto of the Committee for Cultural Freedom. "It is washing away cultural and creative freedom along with all other expressions of independent human reason. Never before in modern times has the integrity of the writer, the artist, the scientist, and the scholar been threatened so seriously. The existence of this danger and the urgent need for common defensive action inspire the undersigned in issuing this statement. Under varying labels and colors but with an unvarying hatred for the free mind, the totalitarian idea is already enthroned in Germany, Italy, Russia, Japan, and Spain."[45]

Many members of the Committee for Cultural Freedom, like Hook himself, had once been Communists. Indeed, former CP members were among the most avid, and creative, users of "totalitarianism" in the half decade before Pearl Harbor. The long series of expulsions and schisms that had wracked first Socialist, then Communist, Parties around the world, had left in its wake a succession of movements and parties that lay some claim to the legacy of revolutionary Marxism, and in some cases Marxism-Leninism, but that had hostile or at the very least deeply ambivalent attitudes toward the USSR. In the United States, and around the world, these sectarian leftist groups tended to be tiny in membership and, by most conventional measures, politically insignificant. But in part because they usually consisted of a party intelligentsia without an actual party, they produced a steady stream of densely argued essays, pamphlets, and tracts, many of which were designed to distinguish their hopes for the world of the future from the reality of Soviet Communism. By the end of the 1930s, nearly all of these groups had found their way to the concept of totalitarianism as a way of linking the Soviet regime with the fascist dictatorships.[46] For many in the Marxist-Leninist wing of the sectarian left—those, that is, who still laid claim to the legacy of the October Revolution—it would take the August 1939 Nazi-Soviet Pact to lead them to embrace this view. These included the Lovestoneites—followers of Jay Lovestone, who had been expelled from the CP in the 1920s for supporting Nikolai Bukharin. Even though they preferred the term "bureaucratic collectivism" to "totalitarianism," Max Shachtman's heterodox Trotskyist Workers Party (WP) would eventually become the most famous of these factions, in part because a number of influential intellectuals, including James Burnham and Dwight Macdonald, passed through its ranks.[47]

The term "totalitarianism" had such wide currency in part because it was so flexible. It *suggested* a rigid creed, a force at work in the world, and so forth. But, with a meaning much less set than that of a word like "collectivism," "totalitarian" and "totalitarianism" left it up to the individual author to specify exactly what was similar and essentially wrong about fascism and communism. William Dow Boutwell of the U.S. Office of Education, writing in *America Prepares for Tomorrow* (1941), an interventionist tract published just before the collapse of the Nazi-Soviet Pact, captured perfectly the strengths and weaknesses of the term "totalitarianism":

American leaders are united in their distaste for totalitarian governments. Like President Coolidge's minister who was "against sin," they are, with almost no exception, "against totalitarianism." Yet each finds a different "sin" in dictatorship. The men who want wider freedom for corporate business fear totalitarian "collectivism." Writers, poets, artists are against dictators because dictators restrict freedom of expression. To labor leaders the liquidation of unions is the greatest threat. Religious leaders make the issue a holy war. Educator, farmer, scientist, merchant—each finds his central faith and interest imperiled, his own ox gored. They are all against totalitarian rule.[48]

If one great strength of "totalitarianism" was that it could easily refer to that which nobody liked, the term's vagueness could also be a weakness. Those sympathetic to the Popular Front, who would have disagreed with equating the Russian and German regimes, treated the term as if it had little intrinsic meaning. Reviewing Walter Lippmann's *Good Society* (1937), Max Lerner complained that "Lippmann has . . . extended the sphere of his aversions and antipathies until he labels anything he does not like as 'totalitarian.'" Rather than simply denying that the Soviet Union was totalitarian, *Nation* editor Freda Kirchwey suggested that Hook's Committee for Cultural Freedom was making a strategic error: "The only important feature of the present manifesto is its emphasis on Russian totalitarianism. . . . Now [this] is an arguable position, but it lies in the field of political strategy and should be debated as such." Though admitting that the CP's methods left much to be desired, Kirchwey maintained that the party's goals were noble and that it was a terrible mistake to split the left.[49]

The Popular Front was not alone in avoiding the term. Many others who continued to feel that the differences between communism and fascism were more than incidental, or merely of historical interest, generally avoided "totalitarian" and its cognates, or used it with its older referent to Fascism and Nazism. On the right, the *Chicago Tribune* and much of the rest of the conservative noninterventionist press, although extremely critical of Hitler as well as Stalin, shunned the term "totalitarianism" throughout the period leading up to Pearl Harbor.[50] On the left, Erich Fromm continued to use "totalitarian" exclusively in reference to the dictatorships of the right.

Although the many cultural producers who used "totalitarianism" as an antonym to "democracy" had very different ideas about what democracy itself meant, the general growth in the use of "totalitarian" and its cognates in American public culture during the late 1930s often implied a particular, relatively narrow, view of the meaning of democracy. Like the enumeration of isms, the many different objections that one could raise to totalitarianism mentioned by William Dow Boutwell had the collective effect of setting up pluralism as its direct opposite. Boutwell himself made this argument. Although people disagreed about what democracy meant, he admitted, nonetheless democracy was what America must fight for. Rather than defining democracy by first principles, Boutwell then set out to compare American democracy as it existed with the totalitarian systems. Through the help of charts and diagrams, he graphically made his point. In a democratic society the individual and the family were the most important units. But all other elements of society—local, state, national, and international public, private, and nonprofit organizations—had a role to play as well. In totalitarian societies, by contrast, nothing was important except the national, public sector—the state. In any society conflicts and disagreements would arise time and time again. Democracies, unlike totalitarian systems, could deal with these disagreements because they "institutionalize conflict."[51]

The view of democracy that totalitarianism suggested by contradistinction tended to be limited and rather negative. Across the political spectrum, those who used the term "totalitarianism" suggested that it was the intellectually autonomous individual whom it endangered. Some writers, most notably those for the *Partisan Review,* felt that revolution was necessary to create a social order that regularly produced such individuals. But, as noted in the previous chapter, the goal of maintaining individual autonomy was more frequently associated with less revolutionary designs; democracy did not have to be created but merely preserved. For many, the preservation of democracy involved the protection of a large, entirely private sphere of individual and family action. Political conflict was desirable, but only in carefully institutionalized ways. Defending American democracy meant preserving the institutions of democracy: the family, two-party electoral politics, and so forth.

When describing the many kinds of behavior prohibited in the European dictatorships, accounts of totalitarianism tended to center on expressive individualistic acts—creating art, writing fiction, pursuing science, choosing one's faith—rather than collective action—political agitation, union organizing. It is no accident that the single most widely circulated statement against totalitarianism before Pearl Harbor, the Manifesto of the Committee for Cultural Freedom, concerned itself entirely with "creative and intellectual freedom." Rather than telling readers of the *Political Guide*—described in its text as "the intelligent Woman's Guide to Isms"—how to get involved politically, Dorothy Thompson concludes the slim volume with a call for women to have more children and be better parents. The triumph of the term "totalitarianism" did much to support these conservative views of democracy.[52]

The use of "totalitarianism" also grew among academics. On 17 November 1939 the American Philosophical Society held a "Symposium on the

Totalitarian State" in Philadelphia. The following day the American Academy of Political and Social Science, also located in Philadelphia, hosted a meeting on "The Roots of Totalitarianism." Together, these two gatherings heard from nine scholars from the United States and Europe; economist Mauritz Bonn of the London School of Economics addressed them both. That these meetings were held testifies to the growth in popularity of a term, "totalitarianism," that remained, at best, ill-defined. "Of all the catchwords of the day," Harvard philosopher Ralph Barton Perry began his comments to the American Academy of Political and Social Science, "totalitarianism is the most difficult to define. A catchword is difficult to define at best, since its meaning is largely emotional. But communism can at least be defined in terms of Marxism, and democracy has both a long history and a classic formulation in the political philosophy of the seventeenth and eighteenth centuries. Totalitarianism has no history and no orthodoxy." Addressing the American Philosophical Society, economic historian Herbert Heaton made much the same point: "A definition of totalitarianism would have been a useful hitching post for this discussion. Unfortunately that invaluable reference work, the *Encyclopedia of the Social Sciences,* does not help us, for it jumps from Torts over Tory Party to Totemism." The papers at the conference did not, in Heaton's opinion, give a "unified definition"; they did, however, "with unqualified unanimity give us a uniform bad opinion."[53]

Scholarly writing on the "totalitarian state" and "totalitarianism" was similar to more journalistic uses of the words in other ways. Although Erich Fromm continued to use the term only in connection with fascism, in scholarly literature "totalitarianism" came to generally include fascism and communism as a matter of course: "Nobody will deny," Austrian-born English economist Mauritz Bonn told the American Academy of Political and Social Science, "that Russia, Germany, and Italy are totalitarian states."[54] Indeed, the word became a touchstone for intellectuals who wished to link the two systems. With the signing of the Nazi-Soviet Pact in the summer of 1939 and the invasion of Poland in September, this linkage took on a greater importance. But as both Heaton and Perry noted in November of that year, scholars had not settled on a single definition of the term. That there was no paradigmatic theory of totalitarianism in the United States in the late 1930s was almost certainly more of a problem for scholars than for journalists.

But there were clearly discernible trends in the way in which scholars used "totalitarian" and its cognates. Most obviously, as in the popular press, a discussion of the totalitarian state, a feature of some new regimes, by 1939 had become, to a great extent, a conversation about totalitarianism, which at the very least implied a philosophy and at times an active force in the world. Part and parcel of this terminological change was a change in emphasis in the scholarship from a focus on the kinds of claims that a state made on society to considerations more akin to the concerns about the regimented crowd that we saw in the last chapter.

In the early 1930s, what scholarly discussions there were of the totalitarian state had centered on the relationship between state and society. Scholars described as totalitarian, states that claimed the right to involve themselves in aspects of society that had previously been regarded as private, notably religious and economic life. Often, but not always, a certain brutality was suggested by the description "totalitarian." *How* the state interfered in previously private aspects of life varied from regime to regime and, according to some observers, from dictator to dictator. Even Calvin Hoover, the Duke economist who was one of the first to apply the term "totalitarian state" to dictatorships of both right and left, wrote in 1934 that, despite all of the similarities between communist and fascist regimes, it would make a great deal of difference for any given individual what kind of dictatorship he or she lived under. A communist regime, bent on establishing a proletarian state, would oppress those who did not belong to the working class. A fascist state, set up to defend industry against that working class, would oppress primarily the proletariat.[55]

The late thirties saw a great change in the way American cultural producers viewed the European dictatorships. Scholars, too, began to view dictatorship less in terms of the intent of the dictator, or even of a regime's stated political philosophy, and more in terms of the general structure of political belief under dictatorship. The first signs of this change are visible in Calvin Hoover's 1936 essays. By 1936 Hoover had abandoned most of the distinctions he had made between the regimes in 1934, explaining both the economic behavior of totalitarian states and the frequency with which they resorted to terror in terms of the logic of a totalitarian state per se. The only real effect of the proletarian character of communism was that officials in the USSR tended to have working-class backgrounds.[56]

At the two Philadelphia conferences of November 1939, talk of the totalitarian state as a force acting on an essentially independent society in Italy, Germany, and Russia was largely replaced by talk of totalitarianism as a structure of belief shared by those living in these regimes, particularly the masses. Although ideology was important, the speakers emphasized that the content of that ideology was irrelevant. "Totalitarian ideology boasts of its dynamic character," Fritz Morstein Marx pointed out. "It is long on suggestive phraseology and short on concrete commitments. Thus it has acquired an elasticity of content which may stun the opponent." Robert Mac-

Iver told the American Academy's gathering that "the ideologies may be utterly different, utterly opposed, as have been those of Germany and of Russia, but they are enlisted in the service of the same totalitarian creed." Mauritz Bonn noted that although communism and fascism had "no common principles underlying their attitude to economics," these conceptions were unimportant in understanding the behavior of the regimes. In fact, as the Soviet economic system "almost inevitably" began to resemble the Nazi system, in a short time "the economics of all totalitarian States can be described in a few words."[57]

But whereas the specific content of the regimes' ideologies was insignificant, the structural importance of ideology was one of the central factors linking the totalitarian regimes. Totalitarianism demanded that everyone in the society accept the dominant creed.[58] "There can be no freedom from faith, there can be no exemption from the postulates of the secular religion," claimed Fritz Marx.[59] Summarizing the novelties of "dictatorial totalitarianism," Carlton J. H. Hayes noted first: "It is really totalitarian. . . . It leaves no room for the free play of individual wills and recognizes no utility in free inquiry. On the contrary it has a passion for making everyone conform to the will and thought of the governing party and the dictator." Robert MacIver made the same point more succinctly: "Totalitarianism will not allow difference to be different."[60]

According to most of the papers presented at the two conferences, this structure was the work of the masses, made weary of freedom by the social and economic dislocations of the times.[61] This was Hayes's second novelty of dictatorial totalitarianism: "It is frankly for and by the half-educated and half-propertied lower middle class and upper proletariat. It springs from and returns to the great median of what are truly the masses, and everyone above or below who is not sycophantic is suspect and liable to liquidation." Although Bonn, in his comments on "The Economic Roots of Totalitarianism," sought to distinguish between the specific circumstances under which totalitarianism arose in Italy, Russia, and Germany, in each case the masses demanded it in response to hardship. In Russia, the largely agrarian masses' desire for land "made them acclaim a totalitarian government as provider of those eagerly sought after benefits"; in Italy, the roots were more "psychologically tinged," as the great mass of the petit bourgeoisie resented the rise of a new middle class of skilled workmen; in Germany, a mass feeling "of malaise, of covetousness, frustration, and dissatisfaction forms the main root of nazism." Even Fritz Marx, who carefully described totalitarian politics in terms of a manipulative party acting on the rest of the population, toward the end of his paper on "Totalitarian Politics" turned to an image of the masses: "Even if we discount propagandistic pretense, there remains the spectacle of millions chanting the militant hymns of a militant faith, people like ourselves, people to whom our liberty is a sham and to whom their serfdom is liberty."[62]

These societies shared another important attribute: they were structured like armies. "All differences between the military and other walks of life are gradually abolished," argued Hans Kohn, "until the totality of life is subordinated to the set of values of the army, and farmers and teachers, industrialists and scholars are turned into soldiers of the régime." In his discussion of "The Relation of Totalitarianism to International Trade and Finance," C. R. Whittlesey claimed that "the best guide we yet have as to the nature of significance of totalitarian policies in international economic relations is the pattern of a modern state at war." Bonn agreed: "Totalitarianism is social militarism."[63]

A certain dynamism and expansionism accompanied the militarist and pseudoreligious strains in totalitarianism. Just as it would brook no opposition at home, totalitarianism almost had to expand. The totalitarian state might set "a new international standard" in the "physical plant" of the nation-state, argued Fritz Marx. "Other countries might find themselves under compulsion to meet the standard." "Totalitarianism has an almost irresistible allure," Hayes claimed. "It moves people—by reason of the emotional and essentially religious spirit which its leading apostles have infused into it." And Kohn, surveying the totalitarian philosophy of war, found the logic of expansion at its heart: "[The totalitarian army] draws its very inspiration from the totalitarian vision according to which each individual war is nothing but a step towards imposing the new way of life upon the whole of mankind."[64]

These discussions obviously bore a close resemblance to those on the regimented crowd surveyed in the last chapter. Nevertheless, notable differences existed between these academic studies of European totalitarianism and contemporary works that puzzled over the potential for dictatorship in the United States. First, although the participants in the meetings of the American Philosophical Society and the American Academy offered similar descriptions of the social and psychological preconditions of dictatorship, these were not their focus. Except for Bonn's rather historically minded paper on the economic roots of totalitarianism, none of the presenters dwelled on the conditions that created totalitarianism. Instead, their concern was the operation of these systems once they had been established. In the opinion of most of the presenters, the way these systems operated was itself a threat to other nations.

Second, totalitarianism was often represented as a force in and of itself. Earlier in the decade, "totalitarianism" had tended to denote the condition of having a totalitarian state.[65] By 1939, as demonstrated in the statements quoted above, American scholars often spoke of totalitarianism as an actor, a tendency that would increase over the next decade. Throughout his discussion of the new dictatorships, Hayes spoke of "dictatorial totalitarianism" *doing* things. In one way this change made sense. Political scientists and historians often referred to communism and fascism as actors. However, as Ralph Barton Perry pointed out, unlike communism and fascism, totalitarianism was not a doctrine. Indeed, *nobody* called himself or herself a "totalitarianist" or a "totalitarian." This made totalitarianism a particularly odd force in the world.[66] A kind of belief rather than a particular belief, totalitarianism, according to the scholars gathered in Philadelphia, was distinguished not by a single program or philosophy but rather by particular attitudes toward its programs and toward opposing programs.

Although a good deal more rarefied than the popular discussions of isms and totalitarianism, academic colloquies reached similar conclusions about the nature of the challenge posed by totalitarianism. One major difference was a more open hostility among academics to mass politics. It is worth noting that in the 1930s Carlton Hayes was not alone among U.S. political scientists and historians in his suspicions of the political abilities of the average person. Carl Friedrich, an eminent theorist of totalitarianism after World War II, in his first American monograph, *Constitutional Government and Politics* (1937), also suggested that popular sovereignty could become dangerous:

In theory and in practice modern democracy has been haunted by the spectre of direct popular action as an alternative to all kinds of representative schemes. The potential manipulation of mass psychology with a view to destroying any and all constitutional restraints in the name of His Majesty the People has taken concrete form in recurrent dictatorial regimes. . . . All political power is subject to abuse, no matter what the legal form of its exercise. But concentrated power is very much more easily abused than divided power. Direct popular action, while not concentrated power under a constitutional set-up, is its nearest kin. . . . Direct popular action in its several forms serves to strengthen the democratic element of the mixture. If the dose is too strong, it will destroy the balance. That it provides "real democracy," as the German propaganda minister would try to make us believe, is a Utopian dream or a sorry sham.

Like the less scholarly Boutwell, Friedrich endorsed the American political system: it divides power, encourages citizens to use voting as their chief form of political expression, and encourages them to think about their own interests, rather than some grand political philosophy, when entering the voting booth.[67]

Before the summer of 1939, linking dictatorships of the left and right under the term "totalitarianism" was most common among the true skeptics of the apparent conflicts between communists and fascists.[68] This almost certainly encompassed a large percentage of the American public.[69] Among cultural producers, it included people from across the political spectrum — such as Eugene Lyons on the right, Dorothy Thompson in the center, and Sydney Hook on the left. As Europe drifted toward war in the late 1930s, the term "totalitarianism" was not particularly associated with interventionism or noninterventionism. Dorothy Thompson was staunchly in favor of U.S. intervention in Europe from before the war started; Dwight Macdonald opposed U.S. involvement in the conflict.[70] Many leading interventionists, especially those aligned with the Popular Front, envisioned a war against fascism in which the USSR and Communism would play a positive role. On the other hand, some prominent noninterventionists, most notably Charles Lindbergh, saw Hitler as much the lesser evil in Europe.

The sense of a world divided between representative democracies and varieties of totalitarianism was heightened immeasurably by the signing of the Nazi-Soviet nonaggression pact in the summer of 1939 and the subsequent start of World War II. Although the events of August and September 1939 broke the back of the Popular Front and significantly—if temporarily—upset the view that Spain was a prelude to the coming European conflict, they confirmed much in the image of totalitarianism: the linkage of dictatorships of left and right and the basically warlike nature of both. As the hostilities began, two new books spread this equation of Nazism and communism: ex-Nazi Herman Rauschning's *The Revolution of Nihilism* (1939) and former Soviet secret service agent Walter Krivitsky's *In Stalin's Secret Service* (1939; published serially in the *Saturday Evening Post* in the spring and appearing in book form in the fall). Both volumes argued that Soviet Communism and German Nazism were essentially the same. Both were successful and provided useful quotations for many scholars, writers, and journalists. From September 1939 until the Nazi invasion of the Soviet Union on 22 June 1941, arguments about totalitarianism became strongly associated with the interventionist position as embodied in such organizations as the Committee to Defend America.[71] *Time* magazine's military correspondent, Fletcher Pratt, suggested in 1941 that American involvement in

World War II was inevitable, the result of the "inextinguishable conflict" between democracy and totalitarianism.[72]

Though the Nazi-Soviet Pact made it plausible to describe the war as a battle between totalitarianism and democracy, the prospect of entering the war still worried many Americans concerned about totalitarianism. One of the most frequently mentioned aspects of totalitarianism was its essential military nature. Totalitarianism regimented society, turning entire nations into armies. At the least this meant that the totalitarian states would be formidable opponents. But they might be so formidable that only through militarizing U.S. society—by making America itself totalitarian—could they be defeated. A few cultural producers who mentioned this possibility viewed it as only a temporary measure. Most notably the young John F. Kennedy, hedging his father's bets with the publication of his cautiously interventionist senior thesis *Why England Slept* in 1940, argued that, before Munich, England had failed to realize

> that if it hoped to compete successfully with a dictatorship on an equal plane, it would have to renounce temporarily its democratic privileges. All of its energies would have to be molded in one direction, just as all the energies of Germany had been molded since 1933. It meant voluntary totalitarianism, because, after all, the essence of a totalitarian state is that the national purpose will not permit group interest to interfere with its fulfillment. But there was nothing in 1936 or in 1937 that caused the people to feel that the situation warranted allowing themselves to be regimented.[73]

But the argument that military action in Europe, even directed against totalitarianism, might involve adopting totalitarian methods in the United States was more easily used to oppose intervention. "We cannot regiment America (and how!) through another war," leading Republican noninterventionist Senator Arthur Vandenberg wrote to Alton Roberts in September 1939, "and ever get individual liberty and freedom of action back again. We shall be ourselves a *totalitarian state,* to all intents and purposes, within ten minutes after we enter this war as a protest *against* totalitarian states. And we shall remain one forever."[74]

In the early days of World War II the Roosevelt administration was not among those calling for a war against totalitarianism. From the start of the war, FDR appears to have been more concerned about Germany than Russia and dubious about the stability of the Nazi-Soviet alliance. His decision not to include Russia under the Neutrality Act when it attacked Poland in

September 1939 seems to have been driven by a desire not to drive Stalin further into Hitler's camp. Following the invasion of Finland, the Soviet Union was treated more stringently.[75] But the invasion of Finland—which took place during the "phony war" in the West and thus drew public attention almost entirely to the USSR—signified the low-water mark of U.S.-Soviet relations from 1939 to 1941. Despite strong anti-Soviet feelings in the State Department, one of the goals of the administration remained driving a wedge between Hitler and Stalin; the war was rarely presented by Roosevelt himself as being about totalitarianism.

As relations between the United States and the USSR improved in 1940, the administration's strategy seemed to pay off. In January 1941 Sumner Welles passed on to Soviet ambassador Constantine Oumansky intelligence warning of a planned Nazi attack on the Soviet Union. By that spring, it had become official White House policy to avoid mentioning Japan and Russia in connection with other "aggressive dictatorships"; words like "Nazism" and "Hitlerite" generally replaced "dictatorship" and "totalitarian" in administration speeches.[76]

For the administration, the Nazi invasion of the Soviet Union in June 1941 vindicated its efforts. But the invasion proved to be an enormous thorn in the side of the many interventionists who had, since September 1939, been arguing for a war against totalitarianism. Some shifted ground, adopting more pragmatic and less ideological defenses of intervention. Some, like the liberal Catholic editors of *Commonweal,* whose devotion to intervention was entirely dependent on struggling against totalitarianism, lashed out at these changes of heart. A *Commonweal* editorial of 17 October 1941 blasted Secretary of the Navy Frank Knox for calling for "the defeat of the totalitarian powers": "What constitutes such a defeat? What are totalitarian powers? The 'defeat' in any sense at all has been clearly repudiated by the administration in regard to the great totalitarian power of Russia. How much are we worrying about 'totalitarian'?"[77]

Noninterventionists had a field day with the shifting position of Russia in the war. Speaking over CBS radio two days after the invasion of the Soviet Union, Republican senator Robert Taft led the way:

The complete absurdity of going to war even to spread our highest ideals is certainly revealed by the present situation in Europe. In the alleged battle between the totalitarian states and the democracies, we now find Communist Russia transformed into a democracy. In some way the illusion was created in the newspapers and radio and movies by skilled propaganda that Greece and China and Brazil and other friendly nations were democracies, although they were governed without question by dictators. But how can anyone swallow the idea that Russia is battling for democratic principles?[78]

Although the White House had generally avoided explaining the war as a battle of democracy versus totalitarianism, this idea had gained currency over the first two years of the war. After June 1941, such a view became difficult to maintain. The Nazi invasion of the Soviet Union remade World War II; it could no longer be a war against totalitarianism.

In part through skillful management of public opinion by the administration, the hopes of Taft and other noninterventionists that a war pitting communism and democracy against fascism would be unattractive to the American public proved false. Although as late as November 1941, 63 percent of the American public surveyed in an American Institute of Public Opinion poll objected to going to war with Germany, already by August 1941 people had seemed willing to sacrifice if the nation did become involved.[79] Ultimately, the attack on Pearl Harbor sealed the fate of opposition to intervention in the war.

But Senator Taft was right in one important respect: the view of the European dictatorships as examples of the same phenomenon—totalitarianism—could not be part of the official understanding of why America fought. For those who were still willing to subscribe to a revamped version of Popular Front rhetoric, the war made perfect sense. But different ways of understanding the European dictatorships, their relationship to each other, and the dangers they posed to the United States had to be used to explain the world war into which America was thrust in December 1941 and to mobilize Americans to wage that war effectively.

6
THIS IS THE ARMY
THE PROBLEM OF THE MILITARY IN A DEMOCRACY, 1941–1945

In the years leading up to U.S. involvement in World War II, American cultural producers from filmmakers to political theorists had crafted an image of totalitarianism in which the military played two crucial, related roles. First, it provided the dominant model for all aspects of the new totalitarian order, or at least one important metaphor for American commentators: totalitarianism regimented society. Second, totalitarianism was often seen as necessarily militaristic. American cultural producers argued both that the totalitarian state had to conquer any and all democratic nations to survive internationally and that it had to wage war frequently to survive at home.

To protect American democracy from these threats, interest in citizenship education, which had declined in part because of the many restrictions placed on immigration in the 1920s, increased. Educating the citizenry—even native-born Americans—in the ways of democracy, many felt, was a crucial, nonmilitary response to the world crisis. In the late 1930s the National Education Association (NEA) inaugurated the Educational Policies Commission, a Washington-based group that devoted much of its time to pondering the role of education in democracy and the ways in which American educators could improve citizenship and save the nation's democratic "way of life" from foreign and domestic foes.[1] Following intense lobbying from educational groups, Congress passed a resolution declaring the third Sunday in May national "I Am an American Day."[2] Citizenship education often stressed the essentially peaceful and voluntary nature of American life, attributes that were the exact opposite of the militarism and regimentation of the European dictatorships. Indeed, mere participation in a war could threaten to turn a democracy into a totalitarian state. A decade of revisionist accounts of World War I and strong anti-interventionist sentiments in the late thirties fueled this idea. A 1938 publication by the NEA's

Educational Policies Commission put the case strongly: "It has been wisely said that there will never be a war between a democracy and an autocracy because the moment war begins, the former will lose its democratic characteristics. Violence, whatever its forms, its agents, or its motives, makes for material destruction, intellectual regimentation, and spiritual and physical impoverishment."[3]

As the country prepared for and eventually entered World War II, these understandings of the European dictatorships were a two-edged sword. On the one hand, long before Pearl Harbor the American public had clear ideas about the difference between life under dictatorship and life in a democracy, ideas that could—and did—form the basis of domestic propaganda and official statements of national purpose, such as the Atlantic Charter, the Four Freedoms, and the Declaration of the United Nations. Although convincing Americans "Why We Fight" would be an arduous task, an image of the enemy had already been well established before December 1941. The war that came to America did not pit democracy against totalitarianism, as the latter term was generally understood in the late 1930s. After the German invasion of Russia in June 1941, the Soviet Union became Nazi Germany's most powerful enemy. The United Nations fighting against the Axis powers thus included one of the countries most often mentioned as an example of totalitarianism.[4] Nevertheless, the dominant elements of the image of totalitarianism remained central to American understandings of the Axis powers: in his first Fireside Chat of 1942, the president declared that the United Nations were "committed to the destruction of the militarism of Japan and Germany."[5]

But this image of the enemy also presented enormous problems for the American war effort. For though it provided a clear appreciation of the conflict ahead, it suggested that the very act of engaging in that conflict might be dangerous to America. Was it possible for a democracy to go to war against a dictatorship and remain democratic? How could one organize a war effort and avoid the twin pitfalls of militarism and regimentation? This question was most pressing with regard to the military itself. The armed forces were both the most regimented aspect of any society and the institution most immediately responsible for militarism. How could a modern military be democratic?

This chapter explores a number of official and unofficial answers given to that question during World War II. The simplest solutions—an appeal to U.S. military history or the insistence that America only fought because it had been attacked—were frequently invoked but could not by themselves overcome the more general fears about the place of the military in a democracy. In response to the anxieties about militarism and regimentation, anxieties that existed in the military as well as in society at large, those writing for and about the troops developed more sophisticated ways of suggesting how the American military could be compatible with democracy. In training and morale materials for soldiers and in representations of soldiers created primarily for civilian audiences, the military was presented so as to emphasize the continuing individuality and autonomy of each American serviceman. By describing the most regimented elements of military service as analogous to civilian life, by highlighting the moral autonomy of men even in a military situation, by attempting to train Americans to fight for empirical, rational reasons, and by basing authority within the military on putatively objective data, the United States set out to construct a military suitable for a democracy.

The nation's primary propaganda agency was the Office of War Information (OWI). Formed on 13 June 1942, the OWI replaced a myriad of agencies and individuals who had been responsible for disseminating information during the six months since Pearl Harbor.[6] Established under the direction of journalist and popular radio commentator Elmer Davis, the OWI took over almost all domestic and foreign information tasks. In the course of its work, the agency had deep internal disagreements over what sort of propaganda effort to pursue in America.[7] By the time its 1944 budget was under consideration in Congress, Republican anger at the OWI virtually eliminated its domestic functions.

For the purposes of this study, the most important branch of the OWI was the Bureau of Motion Pictures (BMP), previously part of the Office of Government Reports.[8] Directed by Lowell Mellett, a presidential aide who had been in charge of media relations, and Nelson Poynter, a Mellett friend initially unknown in Hollywood, the BMP served as the federal government's point of contact with the motion picture industry. Severely restricted in actual authority, the BMP reviewed all Hollywood films, passing judgment on their war-related content, and attempted to elicit the voluntary cooperation of the Hollywood studios. In the summer of 1942, it published a *Government Information Manual for the Motion Picture Industry*. Although it had limited impact on film production, the manual was, in the words of Clayton Koppes and Gregory Black, "a comprehensive statement of OWI's vision of America, the war, and the world."[9]

While the Office of War Information explained the conflict to civilians, the Information and Education Division of the U.S. Army designed morale and training programs for the members of the armed forces. The division also set out to study its own effectiveness, for which purpose a Research

Branch was created. Staffed by an impressive corps of social scientists, the division's Research Branch conducted a series of surveys of Americans in uniform that began the day after Pearl Harbor and continued for the duration of the war. It also published *What the Soldier Thinks,* a periodical for officers that presented the survey's findings. Later, these results were compiled in the four-volume *Studies in Social Psychology in World War II.*[10] Together with the OWI, the Information and Education Division was the agency most responsible for providing solutions to the problem of a military in a democracy.

War had, of course, come to America many times before. Indeed, during this war, one of the standard modes of understanding the U.S. military was historical: World War II was represented on screen and over the air as simply the latest in a long series of American struggles for political independence. Even the Civil War was frequently invoked, with both sides representing the fight for freedom.[11] An old view that taking up arms itself was ennobling, expressing the depths of society's willingness to sacrifice for democracy and vital for forging masculinity, found echoes in the World War II period but never fully took hold.

Portraying war as a good in and of itself was much less possible in World War II than it had been in World War I. Even during World War I, romantic visions of war had belonged largely to an older generation.[12] American experience with modern warfare in World War I, the rise of revisionist accounts of that war in the early 1930s, and perhaps most importantly public culture's assessment of the new totalitarian enemy had made warfare at best an unfortunate necessity. By the time war came again to America, the revisionist accounts of the Great War and their accompanying negative representation of warfare had lost their authority. War was again necessary, but a new, positive image of the military had to be forged, one that distinguished the U.S. military from enemy forces.

One simple way to do this was to insist that, unlike Nazi Germany, America was an essentially peaceful, unregimented society that had been forced to defend itself. Pearl Harbor became the key element of this story; in many ways it remains so to this day. Despite the fact that it occurred over a year after the start of military conscription and months after the United States had begun to provide nations fighting the Axis forces with munitions and other material aid, and despite national polls from as far back as May 1940 showing that most Americans expected direct U.S. involvement in the war, the Japanese attack on 7 December 1941 almost immediately became the climax of a narrative in which a slumbering nation was suddenly awakened to the need to go to war.[13] This story soon became a staple of

Hollywood war movies, such as *Wake Island* (Paramount, 1942). In fact, this narrative of sudden, unexpected violence forcing America to participate in World War II predated the actual, if belated, assault on that Sunday morning in Hawaii; *Arise My Love* (Paramount, 1940) had told a similar tale.[14]

But the general acceptance of the peaceful nature of the United States did not fully resolve the problem of how a democracy could wage a modern war—a war against a system grounded in militarism and regimentation—without becoming militaristic and regimented itself. Before Pearl Harbor, many Americans believed that the nation might lose its democratic character merely by participating in the war. Once America had entered the war, fears about the antidemocratic effects of U.S. participation usually related to the postwar world.[15] Which particular aspects of the war effort were said to be deadly to democracy once the conflict was over varied greatly. For many, it was peacetime military training. In late 1944 and early 1945, a national debate erupted over universal military training for men (with or without some equivalent for women), an idea supported by, among others, the American Legion, Eleanor Roosevelt, and General George C. Marshall. Not surprisingly, many opponents of the scheme, including representatives of labor, church, educational groups, and a variety of political leaders, raised concerns that postwar conscription would make America like the very countries it was fighting. "The disciples of defeatism, the isolationists, and the crowd that wants to regiment Americans," Senator Edwin C. Johnson (D-Colo.) declared in December 1944, "are now whooping it up for compulsory military training. They would teach Americans to rattle sabers and to cook and to brush their teeth, and learn democracy from screwball masters; and they would launch a new worldwide armament race. That sounds like Adolph [*sic*] Hitler to me." "Militarism breeds militarism," warned Senator Claude Pepper (D-Fla.) in an article for the November 1944 issue of *Parents' Magazine*. Dr. Charles A. Ellwood, a professor emeritus of sociology at Duke University, suggested in September 1944 that such training had laid the groundwork for the Bolshevik Revolution in Russia and was the surest way to produce violent class warfare in the United States. "Military discipline provides excellent training for citizenship in a totalitarian society," argued the liberal *Christian Century* in an 18 October 1944 editorial. "Compulsory military training means militarism," asserted Dr. John Haynes Holmes, pastor of the Community Church in New York. "Militarism, sooner or later, means totalitarianism."[16]

For those who welcomed military training, other aspects of the war effort appeared threatening were they to continue after the Axis defeat. In a speech before families of soldiers from Freeport, New York, on 5 December

1942, Roane Waring, national commander of the American Legion, warned against wartime "regimentation" after American victory:

> We have to fight fire with fire. We have to regiment, too, for unified defense. But we don't want any wartime regimentation carried over into peacetime! . . . Our total war effort must not be permitted to become the cloak of advancement for new-fangled social reforms and the spread of freak ideologies, the chief purpose of which is to uproot those most cherished possessions of ours—individual initiative and private enterprise. . . . Let's not beat the armies of the Axis only to succumb to their poisonous "isms." We have to guard against having permanently with us after this war a government by regimentation.[17]

Although differing profoundly over which aspects of the wartime state were most dangerous, American cultural producers from across the political spectrum were thus willing to suggest, even during the conflict, that the war effort itself held the seeds of totalitarianism.

Anxieties about the political effect of a nation engaging in modern warfare extended to the military itself. On the eve of U.S. involvement in World War II, the War Department began an unprecedented series of projects in military psychology. From developing "scientific" ways to screen out those most likely to become "psychiatric casualties" to conducting numerous studies on the morale of the troops, social scientists helped shape the American armed forces and the War Department's understanding of them.[18] In May 1945 Lieutenant Colonel Roy R. Grinker and Major John P. Spiegel, both psychiatrists in the U.S. Army Air Force Medical Corps, published *Men under Stress,* the most thorough study of the psychological effects of combat produced during the war. In a concluding chapter on "General Social Implications," Grinker and Spiegel considered what masses of returning combat veterans would mean for postwar America. Arguing that combat experience produced large numbers of "angry, regressed, anxiety ridden, dependent men," they suggested that veterans represented a potentially huge social problem: "A far cry from the self-reliant American . . . [the combat veteran] offers little hope that his resocialization will be easy. To anticipate that in the normal process of events he will fit himself into his old routines, and not bother the nation with a new veteran problem, is indulging in naive and wistful optimism. Because he is so unhappy, so full of intense longings, so inadequate to satisfy himself through his own activity, he will be driven to seek a solution somewhere. Where will he find it?"[19]

The answer, the authors feared, might well be in a fascist organization. They then described the mechanisms of group identification and transference of the "frustration of masculine independence and authority" to hatred of the group's enemy that "enable individuals belonging to fascist groups to function so effectively in peace or war, and which make them, after their defeat, such a severe problem to societies oriented toward more democratic policies." What made this threat most acute was that these mechanisms were quite familiar to their subjects:

> It comes with something of a shock to realize that these are also the mechanisms which apply to the American combat soldier, both in psychological health and in the illness which overtakes him. In order to become an effective soldier, he must learn to adapt himself to a completely undemocratic group, which required of him submission and fixation in a dependent position. The fascist enemy, which is in essence a military group, cannot be dominated or held in check by a democratic society unless that society to some extent regresses to the level of the former. The first step in that regression is the formation of a large and effective military group. Whether or not this is also the last step in the regression, whether or not, after a victory, the remainder of the democratic world can proceed along its accustomed path and retain the personal dignity of the individual, cannot easily be foreseen at the present time.[20]

The men described by Grinker and Spiegel should, by now, be familiar. Overly dependent, imperfectly masculine, and violently aggressive, they bear a strong resemblance to the members of the regimented crowd that formed an essential component of prewar views of totalitarianism. But these were Americans, not Germans or Russians. And their transformation had been effected neither by the failure of the socioeconomic system nor by some process of modernization, but by the success of the American war effort.[21]

Grinker and Spiegel feared that the military experience could have profound, negative effects on postwar society. One way to hold such fears at bay was to attempt to make military life seem fundamentally similar to normal, civilian life. The war could be seen as but a radical change in circumstances, demanding a redirection of the skills and efforts of every American, but allowing even those men drafted into the armed forces to continue revised versions of their civilian lives. At the movies, sometime pacifist *Sergeant York* (Warner Brothers, 1941) could use his turkey-calling technique to get German machine gunners to peak up from their nests, thus allowing him to shoot them as if they were turkeys back in Tennessee. In World War II the entire U.S. military classification system was designed, whenever possible, to place men in jobs similar to their civilian occupations. Although the other two components used in classification—physical fitness and intellectual capacity—were measured using fairly rough scales—four different physical classifications and five different mental ones—the army had a list of eight hundred numbered Military Occupation Specialties. The system assumed that the more similar a man's military job was to his civilian job, the higher his morale would be. One result of this system, however, was that those who had no useful civilian trade, usually the young, less educated, or socially disadvantaged, were assigned to jobs with no civilian equivalent, which generally meant they became fighting men. This more or less built low morale into U.S. fighting units.[22]

The U.S. Army explained even those aspects of the military experience that draftees found most jarring as just like civilian life. In 1940 it produced *The Soldier's Handbook,* a book-length manual designed to acquaint draftees with army life.[23] "You are now a member of the Army of the United States," the handbook begins. "That Army is made up of free citizens chosen from among a free people. . . . Making good as a soldier is no different from making good in civil life." Whenever an unusual aspect of army life is introduced, the handbook describes it as exactly like that aspect of civilian life with which one might expect it to be contrasted and which the army in totalitarian societies seemed to undo. The section on "The Responsibilities of Group Life" provides a good example. The first two paragraphs address the least military social group—the family:

1. Before you joined the Army you were a member of a family of closely related individuals who had many things in common. The members of your family shared the same dining room, the same bathroom, and the same amusements around the house. All worked together, read the same newspaper, and were largely dependent upon each other for comforts, pleasures, and a living.
2. You learned that to get along with other members of your family you must have consideration for them, do your part of the work, and share things with the rest of the household. That was your golden rule and the primary law of family relationship and citizenship.

Only in the third, and final, paragraph of the section does the army enter the picture. Other than its scale, according to the handbook, life in the army is exactly like life in the family: "You have the same obligations in the Army but instead of the small family group you are one of a much larger group." And far from creating an experience that potentially challenged civil life, group life in the army complemented life outside of it. "A soldier who has learned to respect the rights of his comrades," this section concluded, "has made a big step forward in his training as a soldier and as a citizen."[24]

The handbook described that aspect of military life that was most authoritarian—military discipline—through a series of home-front metaphors:

> The average civilian or recruit coming into the Army often misunderstands the meaning of the words *military discipline*. He thinks of them as being connected with punishments or reprimands which may result from the violation of some military law or regulation. Actually, discipline should not be something new to you for you have been disciplined all of your life. You were disciplined at home and in your school when you were taught obedience to your parents and teachers, and respect for the rights of others. On your baseball or other athletic team you were disciplining yourself when you turned down the chance to be a star performer in order that the team might win; you were acquiring discipline in the shop, or other business, when your loyalty to your employer and your fellow employees was greater than your desire to secure your own advancement. All of this was merely the spirit of team play; that is, you were putting the interests of the "team" above your own in order that the "team" might win.[25]

The final metaphor—the army as a team—dominates the rest of the section on military discipline.[26]

Indeed, the idea of a team became one of the most significant ways in which American cultural producers assimilated the army experience to civilian life. "The American standard of discipline," General Marshall declared, "[is] cheerful and understanding subordination of the individual to the good of the team."[27] "I'm not just a foot-slogger with a rifle in this new army," Infantry declares in Stephen Vincent Benét's radio script "Your Army" (written in 1942; broadcast nationally during the first half of 1944), "I'm a member of a combat team, trained like a football squad and with plenty of razzle-dazzle stuff and the Rose Bowl stuff of modern war."[28] As once adversarial characters played by Brian Donlevy and Albert Dekker in *Wake Island* await the inevitable Japanese onslaught as the last surviving Americans on an island base under attack, they share memories of their football-playing days at Notre Dame and Virginia Military Institute.

The attractions of the army as a team are obvious. American team sports, particularly football, are organized and regulated forms of violence; as such, they are full of martial metaphors. Perhaps the most important aspect of sports is the relationship between team and individual success. Ultimately, the team's success is the measure of attainment. Yet each player has his or her own specialized tasks that fit both individual skills and the needs of the team. And within a given role, each player can individually excel and be recognized for excelling.

The preservation of a space for individuality and individual attainment even on the front lines played a crucial role in the representation of the U.S. military during World War II. It also was a key element in pre–Pearl Harbor ideas about democracy and totalitarianism. Totalitarianism was the antithesis of democracy precisely because it eradicated the individual. The ability of modern warfare to similarly reduce the individual to an expendable cog in a fighting machine was thus of grave concern. Paul Fussell notes that wartime journalists, conscious of the troops' experience of this tendency of modern warfare and their desire to maintain their prewar identities, frequently emphasized the names of—and minute biographical details about—the soldiers who appeared in their stories.[29] However, Fussell fails to note the ideological dimension of such reportage. The primary audience for most reporting from the front was, after all, not the troops but those who remained at home. For this latter group, assurance that their sons, brothers, and friends remained identifiable individuals, changed perhaps, but not fundamentally, from their prewar selves, was an important part of the image of the American war effort as democratic.[30]

Modern warfare allowed only limited opportunities for individual heroics. The advantage of metaphors such as the army as a team was that they acknowledged individuality while suggesting that individual attainment only gained meaning in relation to the group. In the motion picture *This Is the Army* (Warner Brothers, 1943), the army appears as a male chorus. The film presents a fictionalized version of the creation of Irving Berlin's two military Broadway shows, the World War I era *Yip Yip Yaphank!* and World War II's *This Is the Army,* both performed on Broadway by actual soldiers. George Murphy plays a dancer drafted to serve in World War I. Wishing to use his talents to help win the war, he convinces skeptical officers that if the men put a show together, it will help morale both among the troops and on the home front. The show is assembled collectively, with the players each contributing their own theatrical or musical skills. After a wildly successful Broadway run, an order arrives midperformance that the troops have to ship out to France. Murphy's character decides to end the finale (in which the troops sing of marching off to war) by marching the troops out of the theater and into waiting trucks rather than simply marching offstage. The audience immediately understands what is happening and roars with approval. In France, the company loses some of its soldiers and Murphy loses a leg; all, however, are glad that they fought. As war approaches again in the 1930s, Murphy's son (Ronald Reagan) is drafted and assembles a similar show that provides the climax of the film. Once again, the troops march into the orchestra and off to battle. The World War II review features a huge chorus of uniformed men.

This Is the Army also made explicit something already implicit in the team metaphor and in World War II combat movies: all put the nonmilitary audience in the position of the fan. The existence of an on-screen audience in the film emphasized this relationship. This may have played into the studio's decision to alter the musical's finale: "Dressed Up to Kill." Deeming that the piece was "not symbolic of the humane manner in which the United States has waged war,"[31] Warner Brothers altered the lyrics so that the soldier-chorus, posing with lowered bayonets, sang instead that they were "Dressed Up to Win." The studio's concern appears odd in retrospect because movies regularly showed the army killing "Japs" and, slightly less frequently, Nazis. What was troubling about "Dressed Up to Kill" was its expression of desire on the part of both the army and the audience for which these particular troops had been assembled. It was more morally comforting to root for victory than for slaughter. Killing as an end in itself might have sounded suspiciously like the American image of the enemy.

The collective star of *This Is the Army* was particularly pleasing to the Office of War Information. An OWI analyst praised the picture for "the representation [it] gives of the American soldier, the unnamed soldier, of whom there are hundreds in the cast. The composite soldier is, against the competition of those of his comrades who do individual stunts, and against the competition of Hollywood actors in blazing technicolor, the star of the show. And that is how it should be."[32] Even in praising the collective, the OWI spoke in the singular: the film's star was not the collectivity of the army but the "unnamed . . . composite soldier" for which the army was but a synecdoche. *This Is the Army* could nicely fit the left-liberal OWI's often self-contradictory attitude toward the American military and the movies' depiction of it. The armed chorus both acknowledged the collective nature of modern war yet, in the words of the OWI, could represent a form of democratic individualism.

However, the mere structure of a metaphoric group, whether a team or (more infrequently) a chorus, was not expected to convey the retention of individuality in a war fought by collectives. One of the most prevalent and important ways in which American cultural producers figured individuality in the World War II military was through the convention of the multiethnic and multisectional group. In films, books, and radio scripts, battalions and bomber crews inevitably featured a man with a Slavic name from the Midwest, an Italian or a Jew from Brooklyn, a New England WASP, a southerner, and so forth.[33] Although reaching its apogee during the war, the multiethnic combat group can be seen in some prewar movies as well. *The Fighting 69th* (1940) and *Sergeant York* both include such groupings, despite the fact that the action takes place in World War I, in which most American combat units were organized by home state and some were even assembled by ethnic group.[34] During World War II the multiethnic and multisectional unit became one of the central representations of the military.[35]

The multiethnic combat unit was a powerful symbol because it represented the negation of American understandings of the enemy's military. The totalitarian military, like totalitarian society, demanded that its members be absolutely alike. In the case of Germany and Japan (and to a lesser extent Italy), this similarity was understood in America to be figured in terms of racial purity. The USSR, the other country that U.S. public culture had widely understood to be totalitarian before mid-1941, notably did not figure its unity this way. The ability to accept and even celebrate ethnic diversity thus nicely distinguished between a wartime "us" that included the Soviet Union and a "them" that included the other European dictatorships and Japan. Marked by differences in mannerisms, accents, last names, and memories of home, the members of the multiethnic combat unit were in no danger of being reduced to identical automatons similar to the Nazi soldiers, goose-stepping through an occupied city or rallying at Nuremberg.[36]

As an attribute of the troops viewed collectively, diversity was a crucial symbol. But the position of the multiethnic combat unit in World War II–era representations of the U.S. military was possible only because what we would today call "ethnicity" mattered less as an individual attribute of Americans of European descent than it had ever mattered before. Many Americans still harbored strong antisemitic, anti-Irish, anti-Polish, or anti-Italian feelings. But the long process of assimilating ethnic whites into once WASP-dominated American culture was well under way by the time of Pearl Harbor. After two decades of immigration restrictions, there were far fewer white ethnic Americans whose linguistic and cultural differences clearly marked them as outside the cultural mainstream. The category of "race," once as easily applied in America to Jews as to blacks, had begun to fade as a way of differentiating among European Americans, perhaps because of Nazi racial ideology.[37] During the war years the Japanese provided an absolute racial Other against whom all Americans—with the notable exception of Japanese Americans—could be portrayed as standing united.[38] Only after the war would works such as Arthur Laurents's play *Home of the Brave* (1946) and Norman Mailer's novel *The Naked and the Dead* (1948) demonstrate to a larger American audience that some irresolvable interethnic tensions pervaded the U.S. military.

Much liberal opinion, including that of most social scientists, had come to see the process of assimilation as crucial for American democracy, especially once the nonimportance of ethnic distinctions had become a major way of distinguishing America from its foes. Popular representations of the military always suggested that ethnic hostilities among Americans had no basis in fact and could lead only to division and defeat. Perhaps because they assumed that ethnicity and region of origin—the key differences between troops in Hollywood's multiethnic battalions—were, prima facie, attributes of no real consequence, the social scientists who conducted the extensive surveys of Americans in uniform for the Research Branch of the army's Information and Education Division shied away from analyzing the troops along ethnic or sectional lines; the variable they studied most thoroughly was educational differences.[39] American social scientists, outside the military as well as within, were more drawn to the issue of the color line than to questions of white ethnicity.[40]

When they did address white interethnic conflict, Americans suggested that its main cause was the fallacious belief that significant differences existed between white Americans of different ethnic backgrounds. *Weapon of War* (1944), an animated short produced for the *Army-Navy Screen Magazine,* the newsreel portion of military movie programs, warns its audience of soldiers and sailors about "the most ingenious weapon" created by the Nazis: "race hatred" and "religion hatred." In the cartoon, these appear as a bottle of poisoned liquid. The Nazis first try it on the German people in peacetime. The liquid from the bottle is poured onto a figure in a test tube: "If his right arm goes up, he was certified as a member of the great master race." The cartoon next shows the magic bottle conquering Europe. Small silhouettes run around confused as large ghostly figures intone "This race. That race. This race. That race." Finally, the weapon of war is taken to the United States, a country, the cartoon points out, of 61 different nationalities and 259 different religious creeds: "Here, they thought, were jealousies and prejudices to play upon. [On screen, fragments on a map of the United States start flashing different shades.] Here was the perfect set up for their plan: divide and conquer." From atop a stage, a dark silhouette hawks the poisoned liquid packaged as a patent medicine: Dr. Hitler's Blood Tonic. "Is your system sluggish?" the salesman intones. "Try the world's most famous purge. Take home a bottle. Are you highstrung and irritable? Do you stay up at nights and worry about Armenians? Peruvians? Scandinavians? and Greeks? Try a bottle and you'll lick any feriner in town." The speaker goes on to mention Poles, Mexicans, Negroes, Chinese, Catholics, Presbyterians, Jews, Baptists, and other groups against which his audience might feel anger. During this harangue, viewers on-screen look quizzical, but the audience watching the cartoon is assured of the illogic of the salesman's message because, other than the fact that some are dressed as soldiers, some as sailors, and some as civilians, the stylized audience on-screen consists of identical white figures. When the spokesman for Dr. Hitler's Blood Tonic suggests that "you and you and you are much better than you and you and you," all the figures he indicates are identical. The film ends when the salesman fails to sell the tonic to the American troops: his audience gives him an enormous Bronx cheer as "Columbia the Gem of the Ocean" swells over the soundtrack.[41]

Ethnic markers provided a perfect way of representing the continued individuality of the men in an American combat unit and of indicating that the national unity forged by the United States was pluralistic and thus fundamentally different from that created in Nazi Germany. But this vision was clouded by the continued racial segregation of the U.S. military. Hollywood films and other wartime representations often attempted the basically impossible task of suggesting that African Americans were full members of the country's pluralistic armed forces, while avoiding criticism of the military's segregation policies, and catering to an audience that was uncomfortable with the idea of integration of the military or American society at large. World War II combat films sometimes include a black enlisted man among their multiethnic battalions, but these characters invariably die, often more horribly than their white cohorts.[42] *This Is the Army* neatly embodies this ambivalence toward black troops in a different way. On the one hand, it features a sequence celebrating the black soldiers: the musical number "That's What the Well-Dressed Man in Harlem Will Wear" includes heavyweight boxing champion Joe Louis, who on enlisting in the army had instantly been made into an icon of the "Negro soldier." On the other hand, the sequence is a now embarrassing piece of latter-day minstrelsy, performed in front of a set featuring huge sambolike figures. And *This Is the Army*, like the army itself, was wholly segregated: the black soldiers only appear in this one sequence, and except for a short exchange between George Murphy and Joe Louis and a brief shot of the black performers running offstage after their number, blacks and whites are never on-screen at the same time. Race, unlike white ethnicity, was of great interest to Research Branch social scientists, who devoted much effort to studying the role of the color line in the U.S. military.[43] The Research Branch could, perhaps, assume interethnic peace in the ranks; no such assumption was possible across the color line.

It was more difficult still to represent in a military setting what was perhaps the most crucial element of prewar and wartime notions of individual autonomy: voluntarism. If totalitarianism was understood as arising when members of a society gave up their free will for blind obedience to a leader or a rigid system, democracy was possible only when people's political decisions were the result of rational, free choice. When in 1944 President Roosevelt suggested in his State of the Union speech that the time had come for civilian conscription of war workers, the leading argument of the diverse and ultimately successful opposition to the plan was that this would be a fundamental violation of democratic principles and a violation of the very principles for which the United States fought.[44]

Even the liberal Office of War Information made a point of emphasizing the voluntaristic aspects of the American war effort. In a 1942 addendum to its manual for the motion picture industry, the Bureau of Motion Pictures urged filmmakers to celebrate "The Children's Army" in an effort to "enlist America's youth in the war effort." After describing the ways in which children could contribute to America's prosecution of the war, the memo used two of its eleven pages to distinguish the U.S. youth effort from that of the Axis: "The contrast between our program of youth mobilization and the Axis system of regimentation and enslavement tells the story of what this war is about—of what we are fighting for and against." The crucial difference was voluntarism: "The Axis makes use of children, too. Not on a voluntary basis, to be sure, for nothing in Axis countries is done on a voluntary basis." In fact, the forced mobilization of youth, either to work as slave labor or to be trained as slave masters, was the primary way that the Nazi system reproduced itself.[45]

But the U.S. military would not seem to have been a social space that allowed for much voluntarism. Men were, after all, drafted into the armed forces and assigned specific tasks. The movies could invent opportunities for characters to make the decision to fight voluntarily. Sergeant York considers himself a conscientious objector and is given the choice by his commanding officer to fight or to go home; after much contemplation of the Bible and the Tennessee mountains, he decides to go to Europe. In *Lucky Jordan* (Paramount, 1942), a gangster (Alan Ladd) successfully dodges the draft only to undergo a personal conversion. When Nazi agents beat up an old woman who has befriended him, Lucky gives up the life of crime, helps round up the Nazi spies, and joins the army. As the title character in

Mr. Lucky (RKO, 1943), Joe Adams (Cary Grant) is a crooked gambler whose plans to escape to Cuba are interrupted when he receives a 1A draft card. Then, while playing craps, he wins the 4F draft card of a deceased immigrant. Having assumed this new identity, Adams receives a letter from the dead man's mother in Greece and asks a Greek Orthodox priest to translate it. The letter, which tells of the horrors of the Nazi invasion of Greece, causes Adams to undergo a conversion experience. He donates the proceeds from his gambling operation to war relief and joins the merchant marine.[46] Lucky Jordan and Mr. Lucky could decide for themselves to join the service; most American men were not so lucky.

Even in the armed forces, voluntarism thus had an important rhetorical role to play. Military discipline and military courtesy were presented to entering troops as expressions of an individual soldier's desire. "Discipline has never been a popular word with Americans," admitted the War Department pamphlet *Army Life* (1944), "because it has been thought of in connection with punishment and restriction. Actually, discipline suggests a disciple—a *willing* follower. It is *willingness* that separates the soldier who follows from the soldier who must be driven. Order in the Army can only be established and maintained by discipline. Did you ever think what might happen if we did not possess the habits of discipline? We'd have an armed mob . . . not an army."[47]

One of the most interesting examples of the rhetoric of voluntarism in the armed forces comes from an unusual source: the Private Snafu films. These twenty-six cartoon shorts were produced for the Army Signal Corps by the Warner Brothers animation unit. Usually appearing as the final segment of the *Army-Navy Screen Magazine,* Private Snafu was very popular with the troops.[48] The cartoons were of high quality—other than being in black and white, they were very similar to other Warner Brothers cartoons in visual style—and well written. The creator of the series and one of its chief writers was Theodor Geisel, who later became better known to millions around the world as "Dr. Seuss."[49] The popularity of the cartoons was no doubt enhanced by their mildly risqué content: Snafu's name itself was an obscene, army slang acronym ("Situation Normal, All Fucked Up"), and the backgrounds of some frames featured seminude pinups posted on the walls of characters' barracks. Snafu films were light entertainment whose success derived both from their obvious quality as cartoons and from the special opportunities for identification they would have offered their military audiences. Though only a cartoon, Snafu could move closer to the real, unsanitized army experience than most movies, which featured considerably more expurgated visions of raunchy male army culture.

But more important than its entertainment value, the series played a significant role as propaganda. Private Snafu, as his name suggested, was constantly getting into trouble. In each cartoon, he would make a different mistake—telling army secrets to civilians while on leave and to his girlfriend in a letter, spreading rumors at his base, failing to take precautions against getting malaria—and in each instance, he would end up regretting his blunder. First and foremost, the Snafu series was about the consequences of ignoring military discipline. But conspicuously absent from the films was the military disciplinary system itself. Snafu would pay for his mistakes not by punishment but by risking, or more often losing, his life and the lives of his comrades. Snafu's final regrets were sometimes expressed from the afterlife.[50]

In *Censored* (1944), Snafu attempts to sneak a note revealing his unit's next mission to his girlfriend, Sally Lou, back home in America. Twice, the army censor apprehends the note and redacts it. Finally, the "technical fairy," a tiny, but coarse and hairy man dressed in a Tinkerbell outfit, materializes and offers to deliver the note in code. The plan works, Sally Lou—shown, as are many women in the Snafu series, almost nude—tells her mother over the telephone that the unit is headed to Bingo Bango Island. The Japanese, naturally, are bugging her phone line. Snafu and his unit arrive at Bingo Bango only to be blown to smithereens by awaiting Japanese forces. Luckily, the whole second half of the cartoon turns out to be a dream. Snafu gets his letter back from the technical fairy, who appears actually to exist, and rips it up. "Like I always said," concludes Snafu, "every man his own censor." *Censored* is typical of the series, both in its celebration of army life—civilian life, and particularly women in civilian life, are hazardous—and in its voluntaristic notion of army discipline. Ultimately, the army's censor can be bypassed, but the result is death. The film's message, as Snafu indicates, is that each man in the army must individually accept the responsibilities of censorship.

In addition to its emphasis on voluntarism, the Snafu series also embodied another central theme in World War II–era representations of the U.S. military and its own self-understanding: the importance of knowledge of the truth. The plots of the films revolve around the use and misuse of key pieces of military information, some true and some false, from methods of malaria prevention to rumormongering. Even before the war, the public's ability to grasp the truth was a key component of some important American theories of democracy. Hadley Cantril's analysis of Orson Welles' *War of the Worlds* broadcast concluded that the audience members who panicked did so because they had failed to be skeptical of what was obviously untrue.

Democracy could be protected against the threat presented by such panics, as well as by many modern social movements, only by ensuring that everyone in the society had sufficient emotional and material security to be able to distinguish between empirical truth and empirical falsehood.

In his first Fireside Chat of 1942, President Roosevelt began by asking his radio audience to "take out and spread before you a map of the whole earth, and to follow me in the references which I shall make to the world-encircling battle lines of this war." This was but one of many times that Americans would be asked to look at a map during the war. In newspapers, magazines, and films of the period, the map, illuminated by expert commentary, was a principal way of presenting the facts of this global war. Indeed, most geographic references in Roosevelt's speech were not to specific, obscure locales. Rather, they occurred in Rabelaisian lists of places: "Look at your map. Look at the vast area of China, with its millions of fighting men. Look at the vast area of Russia, with its powerful armies and proven military might. Look at the islands of Britain, Australia, New Zealand, the Dutch Indies, India, the Near East and the continent of Africa. . . . Look too at North America, Central America, and South America." FDR's point was that, far from being removed by great oceans from the geographic center of conflict, the United States, along with the rest of the world, was at the heart of the action. But the president also made a more general observation that evening, one that would be echoed throughout the war:

> Your government has unmistakable confidence in your ability to hear the worst, without flinching or losing heart. You must, in turn, have complete confidence that your government is keeping nothing from you except information that will help the enemy in his attempt to destroy us. In a democracy there is always a solemn pact of truth between government and the people; but there must also always be a full use of discretion — and that word "discretion" applies to the critics of government as well.
>
> This is war. The American people want to know, and will be told, the general trend of how the war is going. But they do not wish to help the enemy any more than our fighting forces do; and they will pay little attention to the rumormongers and the poison-peddlers in our midst.[51]

This Fireside Chat explicitly dealt with one of the ways in which truth became a major theme of wartime representations of American democracy, while implicitly acknowledging the other: on the one hand, the government's ability and duty to trust the public with the truth even in wartime was an essential part of democracy; on the other hand, the possession and use of that part of the truth that was not public served as justification for the seemingly undemocratic military hierarchy. The theme of acknowledging the truth was widely echoed. Describing the purpose of the government information program at the beginning of its *Manual for the Motion Picture Industry,* the OWI emphasized the importance of government truth telling:

> The Government of the United States has an unwavering faith in the sincerity of purpose and integrity of the American people. The American people, on the whole, are not susceptible to the Strategy of Lies. They prefer the truth as the vehicle of understanding. The government believes that truth in the end is the only medium to bring about the proper understanding of democracy, the one important ingredient that can help make democracy work. Axis propagandists have failed. They have not told the truth, and their peoples are now beginning to see through the sham. If we are to keep faith with the American people, we must not resort to any devious information tactics. We must meet lies with a frontal attack—with the weapon of truth.[52]

The authors saw the chief obstacles to truth in much the same way that Cantril had. Only "from the ignorant, the frustrated, and the poverty-stricken" could fascism marshal support. In October 1942 Byron Price, U.S. director of censorship, similarly endorsed wartime truth telling. "In a democracy," he told a *New York Times* radio forum, "the public is entitled to essential information. It is entitled to know about the tough realities of the war. And it must not be subjected to such a blackout of news as now pervades totalitarian countries."[53]

Needless to say, how much truth was the right amount of truth was widely debated in government circles. Almost from the beginning, OWI's Elmer Davis pressed for more complete disclosure of American setbacks. Davis tried to allow newspapers to publish photographs of dead U.S. servicemen, but the White House and the Office of Censorship resisted. Despite the nearly universal rhetoric of withholding information only to keep secrets from the enemy, opponents of greater openness often censored evidence of U.S. defeats for a different reason: to keep up home-front morale. Indeed, in the same Fireside Chat in which Roosevelt declared that the "government has unmistakable confidence in your ability to hear the worst, without flinching or losing heart," he deliberately underreported the amount of damage caused at Pearl Harbor.[54]

The government also saw knowledge of the facts as essential to the morale of U.S. troops in a war against fanatical belief systems. Thus, in the process of forming a strategy to keep up military morale, key figures stressed the importance of conveying the truth. In March 1941 Secretary of War Henry Stimson, addressing a conference of army public relations officers in Washington, D.C., argued:

> The success of the army depends upon its morale. . . . Nothing can undermine this morale . . . so rapidly as the feeling that they are being deceived; that they are not being given the real facts about their progress and the progress of the cause which they are preparing to defend. This is true even in the case of the army of a free people. . . . Therefore, the army of such a country does not need to be bolstered up by false propaganda. What they want is to be sure of the fair truth; and, if they feel they are getting that, they will carry through to the end. Therefore, it is vital that both the army and the people behind it must know the real basic facts, free from any false exaggerations either one way or the other.[55]

A later memo from the War Department's Information and Education Division, which laid out the objectives of the morale program, emphasized the need to foster both a "belief in the cause for which we fight" and a "resentment, based on knowledge of the facts, against our enemies who have made it necessary to fight."[56]

The earliest attempt to put a morale program into action was the Army Orientation Course, a series of lectures and pamphlets on the war presented to new troops. Begun in 1940, this original effort proved to be a failure. The use of didactic lectures, which General Marshall felt were poorly delivered, was precisely the wrong way to reach soldiers, especially those who were exhausted from the rigors of basic training. The pamphlets faired little better. By the summer of 1941 Marshall began to consider alternatives.[57]

Frank McCarthy, a young aide to Marshall, brought to the general's attention two articles that had appeared in the *Atlantic* that spring: Stewart Alsop's "Wanted: A Faith to Fight For" (May 1941) and Cleveland Amory's response, "What We Fight For" (June 1941). Alsop, a self-described former "Marxist Liberal," called for the creation of a new American faith to rival those of Russia and Germany (still allies at this point against whom Alsop expected the nation to fight) and to replace (at least among what Alsop admitted was a small group of left liberals) liberal Marxism. Amory, an army friend of McCarthy's, disagreed. America needs nothing more than it has, he argued. What it had was not a "faith," for "it cannot be expressed by any one word—least of all by any one word with an 'ism' on the end of it." Instead, the nation had "a very simple and undramatic idea . . . that plain, ordinary people, free people . . . can work out for themselves a better government than has ever been worked out for any people in any country." Inspired by these articles, McCarthy, who had worked in Hollywood as a technical adviser, suggested to Marshall that films, made by someone from the entertainment industry, could present ideas such as Amory's to the troops more effectively than had the lectures and pamphlets of the Army Orientation Course. Marshall, a great movie fan, quickly warmed to the idea. From this germ was born the *Why We Fight* series.[58]

Shortly after Pearl Harbor, Frank Capra was named to head the Film Production Section of the Army Signal Corps Special Services. In his autobiography, *The Name above the Title* (1971), and in a famous 1984 television interview about *Why We Fight* with Bill Moyers, Capra told a heroic story of the inspiration for his wartime films. Suspicious of propaganda and unversed in documentary filmmaking, he was shown Leni Riefenstahl's *Triumph of the Will* to acquaint him with the opposition's propaganda skills. Capra was devastated by the film: "I could see that the kids of Germany would go anyplace and die for this guy. The power of the film itself showed that they knew what they were doing. They understood propaganda and they knew how to reach the mind. So how do I tell the kid down the street — the American kid riding his bike — what he's got in front of him? How do I reach him? The thought hit me, 'Well how did it reach me? *They* told me.'"[59] So Capra decided to build his films around images from enemy propaganda. After a heroic fight against Army Signal Corps brass, all of whom were against using the footage, little man Capra managed to bring his vision to the screen. Or so the story goes.

In fact, the idea of using enemy propaganda footage did not originate with Capra. Long before he screened *Triumph of the Will* at the Museum of Modern Art, *The March of Time* had concluded its feature-length *The Ramparts We Watch* (1940) with the German propaganda film *Feuerstaufe (Baptism by Fire)* to convince audiences of the brutality of the Nazi war machine. While Capra was planning the *Why We Fight* series, Samuel Spewack was assembling for the owi the documentary *A World At War* (1942), which also featured enemy footage. Capra's version of viewing *Triumph of the Will* also failed to mention that his reaction was shared by Edgar Peterson and Anatole Litvak, both of whom had joined Capra's unit and watched *Triumph* and other German films with him.[60]

All of this is worth noting because the *Why We Fight* series should not be seen as the sole product of an auteur who imposed his vision over or against the desires of others. Rather, the films were typical of the War Department's morale effort and became that effort's centerpiece. As Joseph McBride argues in his biography of Capra, the seven *Why We Fight* films — *Prelude to War* (1942), *The Nazis Strike* (1943), *Divide and Conquer* (1943), *The Battle of Britain* (1943), *The Battle of Russia* (1943), *The Battle of China* (1944), and

War Comes to America (1945)—along with the many other films produced by Capra's unit—including *The Negro Soldier* (1944) and the infamous *Know Your Enemy—Japan* (1945)—were collaborative ventures. Capra did make his mark early in his unit's history by personally purging anyone he suspected of communist sympathies. But far more accurate than his postwar assessments of his own importance was his statement during the war that "everybody from top to bottom deserves equal credit for anything we've done." Indeed, in addition to his filmmaking skills, Capra's greatest personal contribution to his unit's success was the vagueness of his own politics. Capra was more than willing to accept guidance from the War Department on the films' content. As Charles Maland has observed, "If we do discover some of Capra's social vision in the *Why We Fight Series* it is probably because his vision coincided with and followed American policy and not vice versa."[61]

Although both *Prelude to War* and *The Battle of Russia* were released (unsuccessfully) to the general public, the *Why We Fight* series was intended for U.S. servicemen. The films were built around the notion that factual knowledge about the war was the best basis for troop morale. As the War Department Research Division's book-length study of the effect of these films on the troops put it, the "two basic assumptions" of *Why We Fight* were "1. That a sizable segment of the draftee population lacked knowledge concerning the national and international events that resulted in America's entry in the war. 2. That a knowledge of these events would in some measure lead men to accept more willingly the transformation from civilian to Army life and their duties as soldiers."[62]

The *Why We Fight* films emphasize that they are presenting facts in a number of ways. Dates are flashed on-screen and emphasized by voice-over narration. "Remember that date, September 18th, 1931," the narrator intones in *Prelude to War* as the date graphically emerges from a map of Manchuria stabbed by an animated Japanese bayonet, "as well as we remember December 7th, 1941, for on that date in 1931, the war we are now fighting began." Quotations from famous figures—from Jesus to Hitler—are simultaneously spoken and printed on-screen, often with page references. Events mentioned are graphically displayed in the form of actual newspaper headlines. At other times, pictures of combat accompany the mention of specific battles. Occasionally, as in the case of the German invasion of France in *Divide and Conquer,* military experts appear on-screen to explain strategy and tactics. Captured German, Japanese, and, to a lesser extent, Italian footage is presented to indicate the true nature of the enemy regimes by showing the Axis nations presumably as they wanted themselves to be represented.[63] Film originally intended to produce an emotional response on the part of enemy audiences was thus shown in the *Why We Fight* series as a factual portrait of the enemy regime; the film still elicits an emotional response, but it has become a response to fact. Much of *War Comes to America* consists of animated renditions of public opinion polls and votes in Congress, both empirical representations of the general will. And throughout the series there are animated maps, with arrows indicating the directions of military movements and enemy ambitions.

Obviously any propaganda must persuade its audience that it is the truth. But the insistence of the U.S. military in World War II—both in the texts it produced and elsewhere, in public and private self-presentations—that the morale of its troops must be rooted in factual knowledge had ideological significance. First, a strategy of facts could be, and was, explicitly contrasted with the Nazis' by then famous strategy of the "Big Lie." But second, beyond such a contrast, the notion that men could be motivated to fight based purely on a knowledge of the facts expressed a hope that this modern, total war, a war caused by nations organized and motivated by isms, could be prosecuted without planting the seeds of any dangerous ism in the minds of American troops. Democracy demanded that the behavior of citizens, even citizen soldiers, be rationally informed and individually considered. By constructing *Why We Fight* around empirical facts, Marshall, Capra, and others involved in its production tried to embody this principle.

For all of its emphasis on the knowledge of facts, *Why We Fight* was ultimately more factitious than factual. Much of the footage was, quite simply, not what it claimed to be. Following a cinematic tradition established long before by newsreels, the *Why We Fight* series included footage from Hollywood features passed off as actual battle footage, staged scenes of life in the Axis countries, and captured footage taken entirely out of context.[64] For Marshall, Capra, and other supporters of the project, the films provided, in an exciting fashion, the empirical foundation on which military audiences could rationally improve their morale.[65] But others believed that the films were dangerous. In a letter to FDR, Lowell Mellett of the Bureau of Motion Pictures angrily denounced *Prelude to War:* "I feel that it is a bad picture in some respects . . . possibly even a dangerous picture. . . . One of the most skillful jobs of moviemaking I ever have seen, the picture makes a terrific attack on the emotions. . . . Engendering nervous hysteria in the Army or in the civil population might help to win the war, although I doubt it. It won't help in the business of making a saner world after the armistice."[66] Capra defended the film's style, maintaining that it was simply the most effective way to package fact.

In 1944 Brigadier General Frederick Osborn complained to Capra that *The Battle of China* incorporated many sequences that were "not actually pictures of historical events, but scenes taken from entertainment or other film to produce the desired effect." Capra admitted that many of the films contained such footage but argued that its usage was only a matter of style and was necessary to the job at hand: "I know there are people in the War Department who claim we have put too much 'emotion' in these films. They may be right. A dry recitation of facts might have been a 'safer' way to present them. But my experiences with audiences has [sic] long ago taught me that if you want facts to stick, you must present them in an interesting manner. A teacher who can excite and stimulate the imagination will in the long run, impart more lasting knowledge in his students."[67]

Both Capra and his critics underestimated the films' audience.[68] The Research Branch's study of the *Why We Fight* series revealed that the troops, by and large, had a very favorable response to the productions.[69] But many viewers in the test audiences commented on the films' one-sidedness, repeated use of the same "fake" or "untrue" footage, "exaggeration" and "unrealistic" presentation, and the impossibility of obtaining some of the shots the films purported to show, especially scenes of Hitler plotting with his inner circle and close-ups of combat. Most importantly, although the films did impart greater factual information about the war, this information had little effect on "opinion items of a more general nature" and no effect whatsoever on morale or combat motivation. Indeed, the Research Branch concluded that *Prelude to War* might actually have decreased combat motivation. One of the more significant, if still rather small, general opinion changes that viewing *Prelude to War* seemed to produce was an increase in troop assessment of Axis military strength. The same study revealed a negative correlation between the soldiers' assessment of Axis strength and their own desire to fight.[70]

The Research Branch concluded that the central fault with the army's orientation strategy was the assumption that increased factual knowledge would produce changes in opinion that would then motivate the troops. Writing four years after the war, the Research Branch suggested that people may not be as rationally motivated as the orientation program assumed:

It is possible that the lack of effects may be due simply to the fact that the attitudes and motivations investigated in these studies cannot be appreciably affected by an information program which relies upon "letting the facts speak for themselves." It may be that such a program will prove effective with only a small segment of the population whose attitudes are primarily determined by rational considerations. For most other individuals, motivations and attitudes may generally be acquired through nonrational channels and may be highly resistant to rational considerations.[71]

Such an assessment of the possibilities for popular rationality, which appeared in the third volume of the Research Branch's study, absent any dire warnings about the political consequences of such widespread irrationality, suggests a profoundly different sense of social psychology and its relationship to democracy than that held by the architects of the army's information program, the authors of *Men under Stress,* and many others who considered the same issues during the war.

The experience of the war itself no doubt contributed to this difference. At the time of Pearl Harbor, the only Americans who had encountered battle recently enough to be the subjects of a study on combat morale were those who had fought as volunteers in the Spanish Civil War. In 1943 John Dollard, a professor of anthropology at Yale University and a prominent consultant to the Research Branch, completed a study of such veterans—of the Abraham Lincoln Brigade—for Yale's Institute of Human Relations.[72] Entitled *Fear in Battle,* Dollard's study reported that the most critical factor for morale was "a belief in war aims," cited by 73 percent of the respondents as one of "the most important things that help a man overcome fear in battle" ("leadership," mentioned by 49 percent of the survey subjects, came in a distant second). Dollard concluded that knowledge of military objectives could be something of a cure-all on the battlefield: "War aims, say our informants, must be concrete, personal, intimate. The soldier must have the war aims within his skin, operating as personal motive to fight. It is not enough that statesmen know the cause is just. The soldier must know it and feel it. . . . Identification with cause is like a joker in a deck of cards. It can substitute for any other card. The man who has it can better bear inferior matériel, temporary defeat, weariness, or fear." Hatred of the enemy could also improve morale, but only if this hatred was directed at the enemy's mission, not his person: "Our informants are firm in the opinion that the long-term hatred excited by the symbols and agents of the Fascist cause is far more important" than the momentary anger felt toward the particular enemy soldiers who killed a comrade.[73]

But Dollard noted that members of the Abraham Lincoln Brigade fought as volunteers for openly ideological reasons. This potentially made them quite different from conscripted soldiers fighting to defend their country following a military attack. Furthermore, he argued, some causes "permit identification throughout society as a whole" more easily than others: the "Four Freedoms" may have less immediate appeal than "Asia for Asiatics." Despite these caveats, Dollard still believed that knowledge of one's own cause was the single biggest contributor to battlefield morale and that hatred of the enemy, though an important factor, must be directed toward the enemy's ideals.[74]

Dollard's reservations were more on target than he may have realized. Frontline reporters continually suggested that American troops were motivated more by local hatreds and loyalties than by hatred of a grand Axis cause or devotion to United Nations war aims. "It makes the dogfaces sick to read articles by people who say, 'It isn't actually the Germans, it's the Nazis,'" commented Bill Mauldin. "Our army has seen few actual *Nazis,* except when they threw in special ss divisions. We have seen the Germans — the youth and the men and the husbands and the fathers of Germany, and we know them for a ruthless, cold, cruel, and powerful enemy." As far as knowledge of the United Nations cause was concerned, Mauldin declared that "friendship and spirit is a lot more genuine and sincere and valuable than all the 'war aims' and indoctrination in the world."[75]

The Research Branch's studies of U.S. troops in World War II similarly indicated a lack of "proper" orientation. Fewer than a tenth of the men surveyed in August 1942 had a "consistent, favorable, intellectual orientation to the war."[76] In the summer of 1943 the Research Branch evaluated troops' knowledge of the Four Freedoms. Partially incorporated in the Atlantic Charter and much repeated by President Roosevelt from early 1942, the Four Freedoms — freedom of speech, freedom of religion, freedom from want, and freedom from fear — were often touted by government information campaigns as the essence of United Nations war aims. Yet over a third of a 3,000-man sample had never heard of the Four Freedoms and only 13 percent could name three or four of them.[77] The Research Branch concluded paradoxically: "The general picture in this volume of men preoccupied with minimizing their discomforts, acquiring higher rank or pay, securing safe jobs which would offer training useful in civilian life, displaying aggressions against the Army in many different ways, and in getting out of the Army as fast as possible does not suggest a particularly inspired work performance in the American Army. But Americans fought brilliantly and tenaciously when they had to, usually aided . . . by superior materiel."[78]

Despite the mounting negative assessments by its own Research Branch during the war, the army's Information and Education Division continued its orientation program. The notion that widely disseminating facts about the war could motivate troops to fight for rational reasons was powerful enough to last until the United Nations achieved victory. But while the military and civilian information agencies suggested that the truthful presentation of most facts about the war was both evidence of America's democratic nature and the foundation for preserving democracy in wartime, other facts were carefully withheld. Public pronouncements of openness would invariably include an exception for information that might be of use to the enemy, although the scope of such information was the source of much behind-the-scenes, interagency wrangling.

Restricted knowledge, as well as public knowledge, played a crucial role in the official effort to create and represent a democratic military. Empirical truth was widely regarded as the safest—sometimes the only safe—basis for social solidarity in a democracy. By rationally arriving at the same conclusion based on thorough knowledge of important facts, the argument went, individuals in a democracy could engage in massive collective undertakings such as a modern war without falling victim to isms that threatened their very rationality and individuality. But empirical truth could also justify hierarchy in a democracy. As facts properly understood could yield objectively correct decisions, a greater knowledge of facts and how to understand them could make even the rigid command structure of an army make democratic sense. And the general notion that given empirical truths indicated a single, correct course of action provided the government, which possessed a near monopoly of crucial facts in wartime, with apparently apolitical, almost scientific justification for the centralization of such command structures.

The hierarchical aspect of the official significance placed on facts can be seen in the rhetoric surrounding government censorship policy. Part and parcel of the importance of facts was the clear distinction between facts and opinions. Describing the limited scope of his task in October 1942, censorship director Byron Price noted that U.S. censorship "deals only with information, and does not invade the realm of editorial or other opinion. Every request made by Censorship has been confined to some topic of factual information." To Price, this distinction happily allowed for both sensible wartime limits on information and the full operation of the First Amendment: "The Government's requests are unquestionably a restraint upon normal operations, but I don't think it can be argued that they are a restraint upon any right bestowed by the Constitution. In a broad sense, the freedom guaranteed by the First Amendment has been accepted as a freedom to criticize, to protest, to petition, to speak opinions freely; but not as a right to play fast and loose with facts. In the realm of opinion and criticism, it is highly essential that there be no arbitrary action by the Government."[79] As with ethnic pluralism, the official face of wartime political pluralism was oddly limited. On the one hand, a central component of American democracy was that "opinion" could be freely expressed even in wartime and that the government promised no "arbitrary action" in the realm of opinion. On the other hand, no such promise was forthcoming in the ultimately more significant realm of fact. What made such a distinction more or less palatable was the idea that facts, properly understood, pointed to unexceptionable conclusions. Despite Price's evident concern to express the limits of U.S. censorship, he did not present the question of when someone was or was not "play[ing] fast and loose with facts" as a complicated one.

The organizational structure of the wartime military was similarly built around an unusually rigid obedience to empirical facts. In addition to being designed to place men in jobs most similar to their civilian occupation, the extremely articulated U.S. system of military manpower allocation—in which eight hundred Military Occupational Specialties were specified—was designed to centralize allocation decisions and to make those decisions on as "scientific" a basis as possible. Compared to the German military, U.S. classifications were thus more specific, more reliant on quantifiable measures (as opposed to the professional opinion of examining physicians and psychologists), and, once made, much more difficult for field commanders who were actually in charge of the troops to alter.[80]

Differences in officer evaluation procedures also reveal the greater importance of producing and analyzing empirical facts in the U.S. Army's management procedures. German officers were evaluated by their superiors once every two years, at which time the officers responded in writing to questions on a five-page form. In contrast, the U.S. Army required an Officer Evaluation Report to be filed every six months. This sixteen-page document contained eighty questions, answered, with an electrographic pencil, according to five different point systems. The form was then reviewed by the evaluating officer's superior, thus doubling the paperwork. Finally, the results were reduced to a single five-digit number. The army insisted that officers fill out these forms even on the battlefield. One infantry officer recalled being awakened by a runner and requested to fill out an Officer Evaluation Report at midnight while sheltering in a shattered German bunker on the Siegfried Line in February 1945.[81]

Not only was the military organized by empirical knowledge, but also the official Field Service Regulations on military leadership sought to ground commanders' authority on knowledge. Here the comparison with Germany is particularly instructive: presumably because the official German manual on military leadership used during the war, *Truppenführung* (1936), was a direct lineal descendent of earlier manuals that were themselves the foundation of modern military doctrine, the American manual, *Field Service Regulations* (1941), had long passages that were identical to the German regulations. In summarizing the differences between the two on the nature of leadership, Martin Van Creveld notes that, unlike the German manual, the American regulations suggest that superior knowledge is the most important attribute of a commander. The sections of the two manuals dealing with military decision-making differ as well: the German manual emphasizes creative, independent decision-making, calling war a "free creative activity resting on scientific foundations," and warns that "it is impossible to exhaustively lay down the art of war in regulations"; the American manual puts much less emphasis on independent thought and goes into much greater detail on all points. In short, the U.S. Army's view of war stressed doctrine and planning over individual initiative.[82]

It is ironic that the German military put more faith in creative individual decision-making than the U.S. forces. Van Creveld makes little attempt to explain the American army's insistence on knowledge and doctrine as the bases of leadership and command, but he does suggest that it might have to do with "the fact that scientific management was first developed and widely applied in the United States."[83] Yet by World War II scientific management was widely known, and if anything more widely used, in the planned economies of Europe, including Nazi Germany. Apart from the military, the United States engaged in much less scientific management of human resources than did other countries that participated in the war.

The U.S. military's management style was based much more on contemporary democratic theory than on a general American predilection for scientific management. The home front could be, and was, managed in a more roundabout way: for instance, massive public spending to support the war effort created jobs, and people moved to where the jobs were. Unlike Great Britain, Canada, Australia, New Zealand, China, the USSR, Germany, Italy, and Japan, the United States never attempted to organize home-front manpower through civilian conscription, although the Roosevelt administration fought hard for Congress to approve such a plan.[84] But a modern army necessarily requires a more coordinated effort. Just as the U.S. military's fact-based orientation method attempted to create rational collective action, its scientistic, overquantified method of management attempted to rationalize command. Military leadership necessarily asks men to do what isms are said to demand of their believers: to be willing to kill and be killed for the cause. Like totalitarian states, the armed forces necessarily regimented their members. In its public commitment to empiricism and rationality, the U.S. military hoped to capture the difference between the military of a democracy and that of a totalitarian society.

The notion that the Japanese and German militaries were fundamentally different and less rational than the U.S. armed forces was frequently repeated during the war. John Dower has explored the ways in which the Japanese and their fighting forces were represented as barbaric, subhuman, deranged, immature, and homogenous.[85] But the German military was also characterized as essentially ideological and irrational. *Divide and Conquer* (1943), the *Why We Fight* film that deals with the war in Europe up through the fall of France, is notable in this regard. The title concept, which was central to wartime understandings of Nazism, describes not only Nazi ideology, but also Nazi diplomacy, military strategy, and battlefield tactics. Hitler "divides and conquers" by sending mixed diplomatic signals. Nazi strategy "divides and conquers" by picking off one country at a time. And Nazi tactics "divide and conquer" by splitting the forces defending France with arrow-shaped lines of attack. *Divide and Conquer* suggests that Nazism and all of its efforts can be explained by a single, rigid, brutal principle.[86]

In contrast to this image of the German military, American command was structured so as to be deeply empirical in its approach, which was reflected in descriptions of the U.S. war machine. In *How the Army Fights* (1943), written for the general public, Reserve Captain Lowell Limpus describes a hypothetical command decision that flows down the chain of command from the War Department General Staff to field commanders. At each level the decision is made in a similar way: "Every man went about making his own estimate of the situation in the same way. He secured all the *information* available, endeavored to convert it into *military intelligence,* and embodied the latter in his *plan of action,* which he then sought to carry out by issuing *orders.*"[87]

Limpus's presentation of military decision-making was in keeping with the army's own self-image. The U.S. military during World War II attempted to base its actions on rational, empirically based decisions. From the classification of inductees to the orientation of troops, from the evaluation of officers to the making of command decisions, military planners and publicists gave facts and their "scientific" analyses center stage. They did so, at least in part, because they regarded empirical knowledge and rationality as the only acceptable reasons for collective action in a democracy and the only way in which such action might not threaten to warp the psychologies of participants in the direction of totalitarianism.

In the half century since the conflict, much that appeared rational and scientific to those in charge of the war effort now looks at worst vicious and at best sadly mistaken. Anthropological understandings of the Japanese fostered an image of an entire people as infantile, ruthless, and barbaric that has yet to work its way entirely out of American public culture. Military psychologists began to disqualify from service homosexual inductees and volunteers as "sexual psychopaths," likely to become "psychological casualties" of war. The complicated military classification scheme disproportionately ended up putting those least educated and most socially disadvantaged on the front lines. And the morale effort, unprecedented in its scope, ultimately contributed little, if anything, to American victory.

7 HERE IS GERMANY
UNDERSTANDING THE
NAZI ENEMY, 1941–1945

America entered World War II at a time when the precise nature of the enemy was more in question than it had been during the first two years of the conflict. With the invasion of Poland first by Nazi Germany and then by Soviet Russia in September 1939, the war appeared, to many Americans, to pit the forces of democracy against those of modern dictatorship. In the winter of 1939–40, as Germany fought a "phony war" on its Western front, the chief villain in the American press was the Soviet Union, which had invaded "little Finland." With the assault on Holland, Belgium, and France in the spring of 1940, Germany again seized center stage. But until the collapse of the Nazi-Soviet Pact with Germany's sudden push over the Soviet border in June 1941, World War II seemed to feature liberal democracy against an unusual alliance of far right and far left regimes, regimes that many Americans collectively labeled "totalitarian."

Although the demise of the Nazi-Soviet Pact came as no surprise to the Roosevelt administration, it appeared to fundamentally alter the nature of the war and the drive for U.S. intervention. Russia was a formidable new military enemy for the Germans, stirring in FDR the hope that American troops might never have to be committed to ground war on the European continent.[1] But ideologically, Russia's involvement in the war against Germany created problems in the democracies. For two years, interventionists had urged Washington to enter a war pitting totalitarianism, in both its left and right manifestations, against democracy. Now, to the initial delight of many noninterventionists, the struggle had become less clear ideologically.

The new face of World War II did match an earlier vision of world conflict: a war pitting fascism against a Popular Front coalition of liberalism, socialism, and communism. Indeed, before the summer of 1939 this was the war that many interventionists had expected, a conflict prefigured tragically in Spain. But this metanarrative was severely damaged by the first two years of the war. The Nazi-Soviet Pact brought a very different war to Europe. As Communist Party members in America turned to noninterventionism and the Popular Front collapsed, the voices urging America's entry into a great war against fascism disappeared along with the rationale for such a war. The growth in popular sentiment for involvement in the European war occurred during a period in which the sufferings of Finland garnered as much attention as the retreat at Dunkirk.

Expecting the collapse of the Nazi-Soviet Pact, the White House had been careful not to invoke the word "totalitarianism" in public statements during the first two years of the war. This strategy effectively obviated any need to shift rhetorical ground with the pact's demise, but it did not provide a positive answer to questions about the nature of the conflict. The Four Freedoms and the Atlantic Charter provided positive statements of what the United Nations were fighting for, but exactly what they fought against proved more complicated. One obvious way of explaining the war in Europe was carefully avoided by U.S. officials. The lingering bad taste left by the World War I–era campaign against "hyphenated Americanism"—as well as FDR's own reliance on the political support of many white ethnic groups—led the White House to shun representations of the European war as a battle against German-ness. Officially, at least, World War II was an ideological, not a national conflict.

But how were Americans to understand the ideological enemy? Ideas of totalitarianism, which did not go away, could not adequately distinguish the nation's enemies from its allies. To some observers, the word "fascism" seemed an appropriate way to distinguish the German, Italian, and Japanese systems from their opponents (although it is worth bearing in mind that a number of thinkers, most notably Lewis Mumford, had labeled the Soviet Union "fascist" in the late 1930s). But the notion of fascism as the enemy had lingering Popular Front associations that often aroused suspicion among American conservatives. Moreover, the nature of fascism itself was far from undisputed. In 1943 psychologist A. H. Maslow described the problem in one of the earliest papers written on a phenomenon that would become an academic industry after the war—the authoritarian personality: "In this war it is difficult to differentiate our friends from our enemies. The usual criteria that have been used in the past fail us now. But even so, our press and our leaders come back to them again for lack of something better. A fascist cannot be defined by his geographical location, his nominal national citizenship, the language he speaks, his religion, his skin color or other racial characteristics, his economic class, or even his social caste."[2]

Maslow was not being entirely honest with his readers. Whether he liked it or not, American public culture understood the war in the Pacific along many of the lines that Maslow claimed could not be used to distinguish friend from foe. As John Dower has exhaustively documented, American cultural producers often presented the Japanese enemy in racial terms.[3] Even those who rejected these racialized portrayals explained the Japanese enemy in terms of rigid notions of "national character." Unlike race, a national character might eventually change. But like race, the putatively peculiar national characteristics of the Japanese made them both totally unlike Americans and, almost inherently, a dangerous force in the world.[4] Dower and others who have studied American images of the Japanese foe tend to treat wartime representations of the Nazis as a control group: because U.S. cultural producers were willing to treat the Germans in a fairly subtle way—distinguishing between Nazis and good Germans, never presenting Germans as totally subhuman—their representation of the Japanese seems all the more horrible. Comparatively little attention has been paid to Maslow's problem of identifying the ideological enemy, an issue debated in countless magazine articles and books and thematized in dozens of movies and plays during the war.[5]

Some of this silence is due to the representations themselves. Compared with its images of the Japanese, America's characterizations of Germany during World War II seem, even today, relatively fair. The targets of most cartoons and many motion pictures attacking the German enemy were not ideal-typical Germans, but identifiable individuals: Adolf Hitler, Hermann Göring, Joseph Goebbels, Reinhard Heydrich. Even when a particular Nazi was not singled out for attack, the enemies were identified not simply as Germans but as Nazis, in marked contrast to their Japanese allies. The horror that Americans experience today when faced with U.S. images of the Japanese—and U.S. treatment of Japanese Americans—is simply missing from the experience of viewing American representations of Nazis. From the vantage point of the twenty-first century, American representations of Germany during World War II also compare favorably to portraits of that country during World War I. Then, in the guise of the "Hun," Germans met with racial and cultural stereotypes similar to those with which the Japanese were burdened during World War II. For instance, both World War I Germans and World War II Japanese appeared in cartoons as murderous apes.

Although U.S. wartime understandings of the German enemy are less alarming today, they are no less historically important than are wartime understandings of the Japanese. Indeed, views of the Germans during the war played, and continue to play, a much more central role in the ways in which Americans understood and understand the relationship between dictatorship and democracy. By dint of their perceived otherness, the Japanese posed a threat that was entirely external. Americans could not become Japanese; Japanese (as the internment camps for Japanese Americans suggested) could not become American. Nazis were less unlike Americans. Though numerous commentators—predominantly noninterventionists—argued in the years leading up to the war that America and Europe were completely unalike, many other cultural producers saw in the rise of the European dictatorships events that could be repeated in the United States. Whereas all sorts of Americans could be pictured as fifth columnists for Germany, only Japanese and Japanese Americans were imagined as a fifth column for Japan.[6] The fact that Hollywood's on-screen Nazis, unlike its Japanese characters, retained marks of humanity suggested that the difference between Nazis and good Germans (in the unironic, wartime sense)— and by extension between Nazis and good Americans—was uncomfortably small.[7]

Whereas Americans tended to understand the Japanese enemy in terms of its total otherness, comprehending the Nazi menace proved more complicated. Was the problem Germany as a whole or merely a clique of Nazis? Was Nazism just a form of fancy dress for a nation that, under Frederick the Great, Bismarck, and Kaiser Wilhelm II, had long been bent on conducting aggressive wars against its neighbors? Was the key to Germany's behavior to be found in a peculiar philosophical tradition starting, perhaps, with Luther and running through Fichte, Hegel, and Nietzsche to Spengler and Rosenberg? Or had the nation succumbed to an evil to which any nation might fall? If a small clique was responsible for Germany's behavior, did it have roots deeper than the Nazi Party: a Pan-Germanist conspiracy stretching back fifty years, the evil plottings of the unchanging General Staff of the German military, or an alliance of industrialists and Junkers? Or was such a conspiracy a less local phenomenon, related perhaps to the last stand of capitalism? And if a clique was responsible, were the rest of the German people slaves, yearning to breathe free, or stooges, duped into expressing irrational enthusiasm for their Nazi masters?

Different analyses of Nazi Germany that appeared in the United States during the war gave positive answers to each of these questions. On these answers hinged a number of crucial problems facing the country. As soon as America entered the conflict, journalists, academics, and politicians began to discuss the need to devise a postwar settlement that, unlike the Versailles Treaty, would prevent Nazism, or anything like Nazism, from again triumphing in Germany. Obviously the starting point for such a settlement had to be an understanding of who or what was responsible for Nazism. Moreover, assuming that this arrangement would require U.S. involvement in Europe after the war, it would have to be sold to the American public during the war, lest war weariness lead Americans to desire another "return to normalcy" built on international disengagement. Finally, U.S. participation in the war was itself transforming American government and society. Cultural producers hotly debated whether these changes—from the draft to rather timid forms of economic planning to increased female participation in the workforce—should be continued after the war or quickly discarded as unfit for a democracy at peace. As it had during the 1930s, dictatorship, now epitomized by Nazism, seemed to many observers to offer a critical negative lesson for thinking about postwar America. Once again, the nature of this lesson depended largely on what one believed to be the cause of Nazism. This chapter will explore the various ways in which American cultural producers represented and understood Nazism and the consequences these understandings had for the United States.

For over a decade, American public culture had considered the etiology of dictatorship. The war with Germany, Italy, and Japan, however, changed the conditions under which this issue was considered as well as the consequences of such a consideration. The problems that the new alliance with the Soviet Union created for understanding totalitarianism was only the most obvious change. During the social and economic crises of the 1930s, U.S. analysts had briefly hoped, then more universally feared, that dictatorship might offer a more efficient way to unite modern society and organize its economy. As the decade progressed, their estimates of the social costs of modern dictatorship became increasingly dire. And cultural producers more and more frequently located the roots of dictatorship in the masses themselves. With the return of economic recession early in FDR's second term, a number of commentators expressed the fear that a regimented unity might replace the anomie of the depression. In the late 1930s the evils of the European dictatorships were of interest not only as an argument for intervention in Europe, but also because of the horrific glimpses they might provide of America's future. Indeed, noninterventionists themselves raised the specter of totalitarianism, based on the organizational requirements of modern warfare, to argue against U.S. intervention.

American entry into the war profoundly altered the relationship between the United States and the European dictatorships. War production had boosted the U.S. economy, and Pearl Harbor seemed to forge a new unity in the nation. As indicated in the last chapter, this unity presented its own ideological difficulties. Nevertheless, the war ended the economic and social crises of the 1930s, at least temporarily. Dictatorship had seemed frighteningly effective in peace and in the first two years of war, as the German Blitz ripped through Poland, Scandinavia, and Western Europe. By the time of Pearl Harbor, the Battle of Britain had begun to make the Nazi military machine look less invincible. Less than a year after the United States entered the conflict, the Nazi failure to take Stalingrad provided further evidence that Germany could be beaten. U.S. military victories—first in the Pacific in mid-1942 and then in North Africa and Europe in 1943—suggested that democracy could be proficient in modern warfare. For all but a small number of pacifists such as Dwight Macdonald, the war experience, or at least elements of it, indicated that democracy was ultimately more effective than dictatorship in uniting and organizing a modern society.

Officially, the contest in Europe was to be a war against Nazism, not the German people. Roosevelt made this clear well before Pearl Harbor when, on 27 May 1941, he proclaimed "an unlimited national emergency" during a Fireside Chat. The president gave a rich and frightening picture of the Nazi menace. An important part of this image was the notion that many Germans and Italians were as much victims of Nazism and Fascism as the peoples of conquered Europe: "We do not forget the silenced peoples. The masters of Germany have marked these silenced peoples and their children's children for slavery—those, at least, who have not been assassinated or escaped to free soil. But those people—spiritually unconquered: Austrians, Czechs, Poles, Norwegians, Dutch, Belgians, Frenchmen, Greeks, Southern Slavs—yes, even those Italians and Germans who themselves have been enslaved—will prove to be a powerful force in the final disruption of the Nazi system."[8]

The distinction between Nazis and Germans made good political sense and was consistent with the most powerful pre–Pearl Harbor ideas about dictatorship, which had downplayed national characteristics in favor of socioeconomic and, more notably, psychological explanations for the rise of Nazism, Fascism, and Soviet Communism. Such a transnational view was a key component of much interventionism before the Japanese attack, suggesting that the war in Europe was not a local matter. In 1943 playwright Robert Sherwood, by then the head of the Overseas Branch of the Office of War Information (OWI), sought to mount a production of his 1940 play, *There Shall Be No Night,* in London.[9] Although the drama originally concerned the Russian invasion of Finland, Sherwood changed the setting to Greece during the Nazi invasion. The original equation of Nazism and Communism obviously had to be dropped, along with those speeches most clearly designed to spur the audience to support intervention in Europe, which was simply not an issue for the English in the middle of the war. The characters' names and the location of the action were also altered. But *There Shall Be No Night* could easily be adapted to the new circumstances; national characteristics were only important to the play insofar as they provided local color to humanize the Finnish/Greek victims.[10]

For many commentators, particularly those on the left, the claim that World War II was ideological in nature and international in scope was of great importance. The war offered the possibility of transforming not only Europe, but also America, eliminating isolationism at home and fascism or militarism both overseas and in the United States. If the fight was allowed to degenerate into a mere conflict of nations, however, hatreds could spread at home and a resolution could be reached that would leave Germany defeated militarily but relatively unaltered politically.

The *Government Information Manual for the Motion Picture Industry* produced in mid-1942 by the left-liberal Bureau of Motion Pictures (BMP) of the OWI describes the enemy as fundamentally ideological. "The enemy is not just Hitler, Mussolini, the Japanese war lords," it asserts. "The enemy is much bigger and older than the Nazi and Fascist parties. The enemy is militarism—the doctrine of force—the age-old idea that people cannot co-inhabit the earth unless a few men dominate all others." The *Manual* warns against believing that the war will be won with the destruction of Hitler, Mussolini, and the Japanese warlords, for "it is conceivable that the enemy, by means of a spurious 'revolt' against present leadership, might seek to dupe us into a 'peace treaty' which would not be worth the ink with which it was written."[11]

Although the enemy was not just the leadership, neither was it all Germans, Italians, and Japanese. Indeed, in their study of the OWI in Hollywood, Clayton Koppes and Gregory Black suggest that the BMP was most interested in persuading the studios to present the need for unconditional surrender while demonstrating that some Germans were victims as well.[12] "The power, cruelty and complete cynicism of the enemy should be pictured," the *Manual for the Motion Picture Industry* advised filmmakers, "but it is dangerous to portray *all* Germans, *all* Italians, and *all* Japanese as bestial barbarians." Instead, echoing pre–Pearl Harbor views of the regimented crowd and totalitarianism, a belief system was ultimately responsible: "[This war] is the result of a deliberate plot by which a relatively small faction seeks to exploit the peoples and monopolize the resources of the entire earth. Those who subscribe to this doctrine have only contempt for the individual. Under their system, the individual is a cog in a military machine, a cipher in an economic despotism; the individual is a slave." According to the *Manual,* this enemy, bigger than the Nazis and smaller than the German people, was not limited to enemy nations. For, through the existence of the fifth column, "composed of native sympathizers no less than enemy agents," the enemy "attacks from within as well as from without." This attack was aimed not merely at U.S. war production, but at the minds of Americans.[13]

In a fact sheet entitled "Footprints of the Trojan Horse" written later in 1942, the OWI elaborated on the danger posed by the fifth column. Sounding familiar notes, "Footprints" describes who was likely to fall victim to Axis lies: "The lies spread by the enemy are generally coated with a thin veneer of truth. They are made to seem near enough to the truth to sound plausible to people whose state of mind is already one of doubt and suspicion. Our ability to resist the Axis poison, therefore, depends on our state of mind. A positive, resolute state of mind, bulwarked by the truth is the best immunization to the poison." Much as Hadley Cantril indicated in his examination of the *War of the Worlds* panic, the OWI suggested that psychological stability allowed one to distinguish truth from falsehood and resist dictatorial impulses. The great difference between the two analyses, however, is in the OWI's emphasis on avoiding skepticism. For Cantril, writing before Pearl Harbor, psychologically and emotional stable people could distinguish truth from falsehood and thus could call on properly grounded skepticism to dismiss a radio broadcast suggesting that the impossible was in fact occurring. For the OWI, engaged in a government propaganda effort during the war, "doubt and suspicion" were part of the problem. "Footsteps of the Trojan Horse" told filmmakers to urge Americans to "question all word-of-mouth information," but only "until it has been verified by government spokesmen." In wartime, the government understandably felt that it should be the final arbiter of truth.[14]

The *Manual for the Motion Picture Industry* suggested that the central strategy of the Nazis embodied the antithesis of wartime American unity: divide and conquer (always capitalized in the *Manual*). Although both the OWI and Roosevelt himself presented "divide and conquer" as an Axis strategy, the term became associated specifically with Nazism.[15] The BMP devoted another fact sheet, "'They' Got the Blame," to the divide-and-conquer principle. Scapegoating was as old as history, argued the fact sheet, citing Roman persecutions of the Christians, English persecution of the Puritans, nineteenth-century U.S. persecution of the Irish, persecution of African Americans "after the Civil War," and constant persecution of the Jews. In most of these cases, a small group out for its own political advantage blamed a minority for the nation's problems. This, too, was the origin of Nazism. The party fed on the disunity in Germany after World War I: "Post-war Germany was chaotic, a land of misery and despair. The people, seeking a way out, seeking a panacea for their troubles, were divided into numerous bitterly-squabbling factions. The situation was ideal for the rise of Hitler and the National Socialist Party. The program they sold the masses was the Rebirth of Germany. Their real program was Divide and Conquer." According to "'They' Got the Blame," Nazi scapegoating was entirely tactical. Even antisemitism was just a means of gaining political power:

> Hitler and the Nazis won support of the foremost party, the Social Democrats, by parading the scapegoat of Communism. They won the support of the unthinking, impoverished masses by bringing forth the scapegoat of the Jews, labeling them Communists or usurious bankers as it served their purpose. They set the Protestant Church against the Catholic Church (again a minority) and smashed both. The people awoke to find the Nazis in complete power, to find their liberties suppressed, to find themselves launched on a frenzied atavistic struggle for world power. The Nazi divide-and-conquer pattern now assumed world-wide proportions.[16]

From the standpoint of the U.S. government, the description of Nazism as an embodiment of the divide-and-conquer principle sent the perfect message: the defeat of Nazism depended first and foremost on unity. Indeed, Frank Capra's motion picture unit and the Army Signal Corps, both more conservative than the BMP, prominently incorporated the idea of divide and conquer into their productions. The third *Why We Fight* film, which focused on the early years of the war in Europe, was entitled *Divide and Conquer* (1943) and applied the notion of divide and conquer to Nazi diplomacy, military strategy, and military tactics. Divide and conquer also lay at the center of *Weapon of War* (1944), the animated short produced for the *Army-Navy Screen Magazine* that concluded with the snake-oil salesmen failing to sell Dr. Hitler's Blood Tonic to Americans: the Nazis first try their poisonous bottle of hate on the German people and then take the show on the road.

A similar tale is told in *Don't Be a Sucker* (1945), a three-reel, Army Signal Corps production. While the film's protagonist Mike is introduced, a voice-over tells the audience how lucky he is: not only is he young, healthy, and employed, but "he's got a big country, called America." America is presented in a montage of occupations, religions, races, and ethnic groups as the voice-over praises the country for containing "all kinds of people, people from different countries, different religions, different colored skins, free people." But, warns the narrator, there are people who are trying to take this away from Mike. Mike wanders into a town square where a speaker is denouncing "Negroes" and people with foreign accents. At first Mike is interested, to the horror of an accented stranger who approaches him. Suddenly, when the speaker argues against Freemasons, Mike becomes shocked: he is a Mason; the speaker is talking about *him*.

The accented stranger tells Mike that he had heard such talk in Germany, where he was a professor when the Nazis rose to power. The rest of the film consists mainly of flashbacks to Germany, framed by a similar, Nazi speaker. Erich (a Catholic), Anton (a Jew), and Heinrich (a Freemason) are all attacked and "split off against each other." Hans, an unemployed metal worker, is so thrilled to discover that he is a member of the "Master Race" that he does not notice when the Nazis fail to improve the economy, take away his freedoms, and send him off to die in Normandy. The accented stranger makes it clear, however, that it was the Nazi leaders, not Hans, who achieved power, however much Hans may have felt superior. The film then details the horrors of Nazi Germany. Nazism "could have been stopped if those people had stood together," the stranger explains to Mike. "If they had protected each other they could have withstood the Nazi threat." The stranger warns that this must not happen in the United States, where "we all belong to minority groups. I was born in Hungary. You are a Mason. These are minorities. And then you belong to other minority groups, too. You are a farmer. You have blue eyes. You go to a Methodist Church." The film ends on this note of pluralism, extolling the viewer to think of "us," not "we" or "they."

One aspect of the divide-and-conquer strategy emphasized by U.S. accounts of fascism in wartime was the destruction of the family. Like the depression, the war threatened patriarchal family structures. Unemployment was no longer a problem, but the draft removed an enormous percentage of young men. Families were postponed. Women joined the workforce in greater numbers. These changes were due to wartime expediency; the nightmare fantasy that the family might be permanently destroyed had great resonance. Although frequently appearing as an incidental theme, the Nazi desire to destroy the family features most prominently in *Hitler's Children* (RKO, 1943) and *Tomorrow the World* (play: 1943; film: United Artists, 1944).

Hitler's Children—a low-budget ($200,000) exploitation picture that became a "sleeper" hit in 1943 ($3.5 million gross)—was loosely based on Gregor Ziemer's spectacular account of youth in Nazi Germany, *Education for Death* (1941). Ziemer, a native Michigander and former rector of the American Colony School in Berlin, had been able to make a tour of Nazi "educational" institutions. His book described assorted horros from forced sterilization to young girls bearing children out of wedlock for the state, from bloody-minded rallies around bonfires for Hitlerjugend to euthanasia of "feeble-minded" children. Ziemer's study received a wider audience when a condensed version appeared in the *Reader's Digest* in February 1942.

A number of things about the book had to be changed for it to become a hit movie. Gregor Ziemer became "Nicky" Nicholls (Kent Smith), still the director of the American Colony School and the film's voice-over narrator. As the book was basically an analysis of conditions in Germany, Hollywood added a plot to Ziemer's narrative. Naturally, it was a love story. Anna Müller (Bonita Granville), a student at the American Colony School in 1933, has become Nicky's assistant by 1939, when most of the movie's action takes place. Karl Bruner (Tim Holt), attired in a variety of Nazi uniforms throughout the film, attends a Volksschule in 1933 and has become a lieutenant in the Gestapo by 1938. Karl, despite the teachings of the Nazi Party which he fervently believes, harbors a lifelong infatuation with Anna. Anna, a free spirit, despises everything about Karl's worldview. Their growing romance only makes sense structurally: in a Hollywood movie, the male and female leads ought to fall in love.

The regime demands more and more of Anna, and her resistance leads to greater and greater repression, despite Karl's attempts to soften the blows. First she is forced to leave the school to work in a women's labor camp; her refusal to study Geopolitik and take a more active part in the Nazi state results in her incarceration as an inmate of the camp; her consistent espousal of "dangerous political ideas" threatens further punishment. Only when Karl discovers that she is slated for sterilization does he help her escape. She hides in a Catholic cathedral but is captured by the Gestapo. Forced to attend her whipping prior to the promised sterilization, Karl intercedes and is himself captured. Finally, at a show trial where he is expected to recant, he instead delivers a message of freedom to his radio audience and is dramatically shot along with Anna. In essence, the plot of *Hitler's Children* does little more than provide a conventional excuse to expose the horrors of Nazism. Nicky's search for Anna, the film's major subplot, creates the need for his tour of Nazi institutions.

There was one final change from the book: to the delight of the Office of War Information, *Hitler's Children* was full of "good Germans," people who, despite the horrors of the regime, dreamed of and worked for freedom as best they could.[17] Thus, in a monument to the growing acceptance of Catholicism in America, a German bishop is given the opportunity both to give a sermon against the regime as Anna hides in his cathedral and to lecture a Gestapo officer on the inalienable rights of man. Nicky's closest German friend is the "brilliant, courageous" journalist Franz Ehrhardt. Franz is too fearful of the regime to help Nicky much at first. But, invigorated by Karl's closing speech, he pulls the plug on an official loudspeaker after the trial comes to its bloody end. One is not a Nazi simply because one is German. The film makes this point even more explicitly by its representation of Anna and Karl's nationalities. Anna was born in Germany to German parents. Having spent most of her early life in America as a naturalized citizen, she has been sent to Germany to live with her grandparents and attend school because of her parents' honest love for their homeland (they are, we are assured, anti-Nazi). Karl, on the other hand, was born in America; we are not told how he ends up in Germany. But for both Karl and Anna, nationality is a question of choice, not blood.

The focus of *Hitler's Children,* however, is the threat of Nazism to the family. What unites all of the horrors exposed in the film is that each atrocity is an attempt by the state to undo the structure of normal family life. The women's labor camp where Anna works is largely devoted to impregnating single Aryan women so they will have children for the state. In an incident taken directly from *Education for Death,* Nicky meets a woman in the camp named Magda. Asked by Nicky/Ziemer whether she would prefer to have a home and a man to care for her, Magda responds: "We are having children for the State, and for Adolf Hitler who personifies the State. Is that not much nobler, much grander, and much more glorious than having a home and husband?"[18] Nicky also visits a Frauenklinik, where women who are not deemed physically fit or who express "dangerous" political views are sterilized.

Nazism interferes as well in parenting within households. When Nicky goes to the home of his friend Franz Ehrhardt, Franz tells him that they cannot speak inside, as both of his young sons might report anything they say to the boys' troop leader. Later both sons—much blonder than the dark-haired Franz—leave the house in uniform scowling at their father. Franz draws Nicky's attention down the street, where a female official is questioning a janitor's wife and her children. The official asks the children a number of questions to confirm that they are sufficiently indoctrinated and tells the mother that she ought to have more children. The children pass the test; the mother looks downtrodden.

Finally, Nazism interferes with the progress of romantic love. Anna and Karl can never consummate their love. The one opportunity they have occurs when Karl, wanting to save Anna from sterilization, suggests that he impregnate her. Anna, despite proclaiming her love for Karl, quickly says that that would be wrong. All space for normal, heterosocial interaction has been eliminated. The only mixed-gender space permitted outside of the American Colony School is a dance at the women's labor camp for the express purpose of producing out-of-wedlock babies for the Reich. Otherwise, women and men appear only in homosocial groups and usually in military formation.

Whereas the Nazis destroy the German family in *Hitler's Children,* one of Hitler's children threatens an American family in *Tomorrow the World.*[19] In *Tomorrow the World,* the family serves as both a microcosm of the Nazi threat and a metaphor for a world in which former Nazis must one day be reincorporated. A Broadway hit, the James Gow/Arnaud d'Usseau production is perhaps best remembered for launching the career of child star Skip Homeier. On both stage and screen, Homeier played Emil Bruckner, a German child who in 1942 has come to live in the slightly unconventional household of Professor Michael Frame, a scientist at a midwestern university working on a secret government project. Emil is the orphaned son of Michael's sister and Karl Bruckner, a Nobel Prize–winning German scientist, philosopher, and anti-Nazi who was killed while in Nazi custody and whose portrait hangs in Michael's living room. Michael, a widower, lives with his eight-year-old daughter Pat and his unmarried sister Jessie, who shares responsibility for the domestic chores with Frieda, their German émigré maid. At the start of the play, we discover that, over Jessie's objections, Michael has secured passage for young Emil to come to the United States. Before Emil arrives, Michael and Leona Richards, a Jewish schoolteacher with whom he is having an affair, decide to get married. The marriage is great news to Pat, who is in Leona's class and adores her, but bad news to Jessie, who feels that it would leave her without a purpose in the household.

The complexities of the Frame household are worth explaining because we first see it as happy if highly unconventional. In the play's first real action, the decision of Leona and Michael to marry, the home suddenly appears about to become more conventional and, we imagine, more stable. But then twelve-year-old Emil enters the scene, changing into a Hitlerjugend uniform shortly after his arrival. Emil has been well indoctrinated in Nazism. He repeats the official lies about his heroic father and slashes the portrait of him with his dagger. He clicks his heels and says "Heil Hitler!" He argues with Leona because she is Jewish.

After a few days, his behavior becomes more subtle. He spreads lies about Leona at school, where he also picks fights with the other children. Playing on her feelings of being left out of the household as a result of her brother's marriage, he befriends Jessie and wins her over despite her initial suspicion of Germans as a people. And he has fantasies about spying on Michael: he searches through Michael's desk and tries to enlist the help of a German American janitor in Michael's building. When Pat catches him spying, he nearly kills her by tossing her down the cellar stairs.

Only Frieda, a classic good German, has the sense to realize how dangerous Emil is from the start. Leona, not surprisingly, catches on quickly as well. "We've got to see this thing more clearly," she tells Michael in the second act. "We've considered him a child, more or less like other children. Being rational people, we've treated him as if he were a normal human being. And he isn't. Oh, I grant you he's changing—outwardly. He's given up clicking the heels and heiling Hitler. But inwardly, he hasn't changed at all. He's just become more cunning, more shrewd. As far as he's concerned, we're still the enemy. So, he's got to split us up. He's got to turn us against each other. Divide and conquer!"[20] Michael laughs at the cliché and accuses Leona of exaggerating. But, of course, she turns out to be correct. Michael first thinks that he only needs to get rid of Emil's uniform and expose him to Karl Bruckner's banned writings. However, though praising his father's book to Michael, Emil does not believe its humanistic message.

Only when Emil tries to kill Pat do Michael and Jessie, who had become Emil's confidante and ally, realize the threat that Emil poses to their household. Jessie admits that the boy fooled her and reconciles herself to Michael's marriage. Michael decides to turn Emil over to the authorities, but Leona argues that they should keep him: "We can't turn our backs. We can't put him behind bars, nor simply wipe him out. You can call it pride, if you want, but I won't admit failure like that, and I won't let you. . . . And it's not just our problem. There are twelve million other children just like him in Germany. They can't all be put behind bars. They can't all be exterminated."[21] Michael refuses to listen. When Emil, who had fled, is captured and Michael lectures him on the coming defeat of his "Master Race," doubt enters Emil's mind. The mere fact of his defeat, apparently, makes Emil question all that the Nazis taught him. He recalls their torturing him and declares that his father was a hero. Michael decides to keep Emil. In the play's final moment, paternal authority is fully reestablished: as Michael secretly watches from the hallway, Emil, alone in the living room, painstakingly places the now repaired portrait of Karl Bruckner back on the mantelpiece.

Both *Hitler's Children* and *Tomorrow the World* depict divide-and-conquer methods that center on the family. But who *are* the Nazis and why do they do this? *Hitler's Children* simply suggests that the Nazi masterminds are "barbarians," as Nicky repeatedly calls them; how they became that way or how they might be changed is never revealed. *Tomorrow the World* ultimately suggests that Emil himself is a victim. Despite his nearly successful attempt to divide and conquer his adoptive family, Emil is only a severely damaged child. He and the twelve million other children in Nazi Germany will have to be repaired, the play suggests. Who Emil's torturers were and why they tortured him is never explored. The divide-and-conquer understanding of Nazism put a strategy—social division—at the heart of the analysis and shifted attention away from the question of who exactly cultivated this strategy.

The postwar army short *Don't Be a Sucker* had a decided advantage over earlier efforts in this regard. Produced in the immediate aftermath of the war in Europe, it could define the beneficiaries of Nazism narrowly, suggesting that only the Nazi leaders were fully responsible; most of their supporters were merely "suckers." Obviously a small leadership cadre can be individually punished. But what should be done with the suckers? Conveniently in the army film, these suckers—the characters who accept the Nazi faith—all die. During the war, cultural producers who sought to portray Nazism were in more of a quandary, as blaming the Nazi leadership alone might play into the hands of those who argued for a negotiated peace. If it was dangerous to suggest either that the Nazi leadership was the problem or that the German people as a whole were responsible, who exactly was doing the dividing and conquering? The suggestion by the Bureau of Motion Pictures that, following the rise of Nazism, "the people awoke to find the Nazis in complete power, to find their liberties suppressed, to find themselves launched on a frenzied atavistic struggle for world power," seems vague at best. What could it possibly mean to "awake . . . to find [oneself] launched on a frenzied atavistic struggle for world power"? If many Germans were good, if many apparent perpetrators were primarily victims, who were the real villains and what drove them to villainy?

Neither the Office of War Information nor Hollywood was particularly interested in answering these questions. The themes of Nazi hatred of difference, the need for democratic unity against the divide-and-conquer strategy, and the more specific notion that Nazism attacked society at the level of the family, appealed across the political spectrum and were relatively uncontroversial. To dig deeper into the cause of Nazism, to inquire about what made one become not just a sucker but an out-and-out Nazi or about what had made Nazism take hold where and when it had, was to enter a heated debate in wartime America. Due to its understanding of moviegoers, the political leanings of its leaders, and the Hollywood Production Code, the motion picture industry was, by and large, averse to political controversy. Some films exploring the roots of Nazism were made during the war. The extraordinarily didactic *Keeper of the Flame* (MGM, 1942), which was scripted by Donald Ogden Stewart, the former head of the industry's largest Popular Front organization, the Hollywood Anti-Nazi League, explored the dangers of fascism in America by grafting a class analysis onto more typical themes of the dangers it posed to the family. By and large, however, Hollywood's explorations of Nazism avoided explaining its roots. For its part, the OWI had relatively little leverage in Hollywood and, especially for its domestic activities, less and less political capital in the U.S. Congress. The OWI's Bureau of Motion Pictures had its hands full simply trying to get pictures produced that even partly presented the enemy in ideological terms.[22]

In the print media, on the other hand, controversy raged over the essence of Nazism. Through early 1942, "totalitarianism" was still occasionally used as an analytic category in discussions of the political and social systems of the Axis powers.[23] But the term continued to be used more frequently to include Soviet communism.[24] The adjective "totalitarian"—and occasionally the older, weaker sense of "totalitarianism" as "the belief in having a totalitarian state"—was still applied to Nazism even by those who wished to draw a sharp contrast between the Axis systems of government and Soviet communism.[25] But for those who wanted to make that distinction, it could not be the central organizing category.

Of the other plausible ideological terms used to distinguish friend from foe, one of the most important and most contested was "fascism."[26] Before 1939 the fight against fascism per se was most promoted by the left, particularly the Communist Party (CP) and others associated with the Popular Front. Although the CP returned to an antifascist line following the collapse of the Nazi-Soviet Pact, fascism played a less exclusive role in the party's understanding of the war than might have been expected. Communists did use "fascism" as a description of the enemy, as well as an all-purpose term of abuse. The founding convention of the Communist Political Association (CPA), which officially replaced the CP in May 1944, passed a resolution denouncing the "Hoover-Taft-Vandenberg-Dewey machine" as part of a cabal attempting to "use the elections to prolong the war, to bring about a compromise peace with Nazism-fascism and to establish a pro-fascist government within the United States." But influenced both by the Soviet government's nationalistic understanding of the war between Russia and Germany and by the frequent vilification of Germany in the United States, communist publications often denounced the German people themselves, not just the Nazis, the ruling class, or Hitler.[27]

For others on the left, fascism remained central to understanding the enemy. Independent left-wing journalist George Seldes, in his *Facts and Fascism* (1943), argued that the war was fundamentally a struggle of democracy against fascism.[28] Seldes had published the first book-length American attack on Mussolini, *Sawdust Caesar* (1936); had been the correspondent for the left-liberal *New York Post* in Spain during the civil war; and since 1940 had edited the privately published *In Fact,* a weekly newsletter that specialized in critically analyzing the press.[29] *Facts and Fascism* maintained that although the United Nations were defeating fascism abroad, America was in danger of losing to fascism at home. Seldes equated fascism with "reaction." For him, American fascists were not just Wiliam Dudley Pelley's Silver Shirts and the Ku Klux Klan, which he considered to be the "lunatic fringes of Fascism," but a much broader group of wealthy and powerful Americans who opposed the struggle for a more democratic country:

> The real Fascists of America are never named in the commercial press. It will not even hint at the fact that there are many powerful elements working against a greater democracy, against an America without discrimination based on race, color and creed, an America where never again will one third of the people be without sufficient food, clothing and shelter, where never again will there be 12,000,000 unemployed and many more millions working for semi-starvation wages while the DuPont, Ford, Hearst, Mellon and Rockefeller Empires move into the billions of dollars. I call these elements Fascist. You may not like names and labels but technically as well as journalistically and morally they are correct.[30]

One of Seldes's heroes in *Facts and Fascism* was Vice President Henry Wallace.[31] Wallace was one of the most prominent left-liberal commentators on fascism and, due largely to his position as vice president, drew much fire from conservatives for his views. Though accused of doing so, Wallace did not join Seldes in identifying fascism merely with the views of wealthy Americans. Nor did he use the term as regularly as many others on the left to describe the enemy. Indeed, in his famous "Century of the Common Man" speech, delivered on 8 May 1942, Wallace did not use "fascism" once.[32]

Wallace provided what amounted to half of a class analysis of fascism. He identified a great, "millennial" struggle, a "people's revolution" that had slowly, over the course of history, gained more and more power for the "common man." According to the vice president, when Nazism and similar movements succeeded, they did so largely due to the backing of the wealthy, who were fearful of the people grabbing too much political and economic power. But the dynamism of these movements came not from their financial backers, but from a force of absolute evil: "Satan now is trying to lead the common man of the whole world back into slavery and darkness. For the stark truth is that the violence preached by the Nazis is the devil's own religion of darkness."[33]

Two years later, when asked by the *New York Times* to answer the questions, "Who is a fascist? How many fascists have we? How dangerous are they?," Wallace responded with a similar analysis. "A Fascist," he said, "is one whose lust for money or power is combined with such an intensity of intolerance toward those of other races, parties, classes, religions, cultures, regions or nations as to make him ruthless in his use of deceit or violence to attain his ends." For Wallace, the fascist's hatred was not a mere strategy but, along with greed, was the essence of fascism. This was in keeping with the vice president's almost eschatological view of Nazism. Again, his explicitly religious understanding of the enemy's evil was grafted onto his deep commitment to economic democracy. The result was a class analysis of fascism that stopped short. Though "very often big business gives unwitting aid to fascism," there was no particular class base to fascism: "It may be encountered in Wall Street, Main Street or Tobacco Road." His two suggestions to improve the future chances of democracy against fascism were, first, to increase the production and distribution of economic goods and, second, to "vivify with the greatest intensity the spiritual processes which are both the foundation and the very essence of democracy."[34]

Although antifascism's roots were on the left, at least one more conservative writer developed an alternative analysis of fascism that received much notice during the war. In his book *As We Go Marching* (1944), John T. Flynn joined Seldes in contending that the fight against fascism at home might be more difficult than the war against it in Europe. Flynn, a former columnist for the *New Republic,* had made his fame as an anti-Roosevelt polemicist: his campaign book, *Country Squire in the White House,* was a best-seller in 1940. *As We Go Marching* traces the development of fascism in Italy and Germany and, in the final third of the book, considers its potential threat in the United States. Flynn, too, saw fascism as a misguided way of organizing capitalism. According to him, fascism had eight main attributes: (1) a government with unrestrained powers (which he sometimes calls "totalitarianism"); (2) a dictator with unlimited powers, responsible to a party elite; (3) an economic system with private owners carrying out production and distribution under the auspices of a government plan; (4) economic planning controlled by "great government bureaus" whose pronouncements had the force of law; (5) through planning, a "socialization of investment" that "regiments" the uses of private capital and integrates government and private finance; (6) government maintenance of an adequate purchasing power by a permanent system of borrowing and spending; (7) permanent militarism to provide employment and drive production for industries entirely supported by public spending; and (8) imperialism to provide a cause that could justify the great sacrifices people made under fascism.[35]

Flynn's view of fascism thus resembled left critiques of fascism in many ways. But his understanding of the cause of fascism was significantly different from that of Seldes or Wallace. Flynn believed that fascism resulted not from the failures inherent in capitalism but from the abandonment of the free enterprise system and the growth of government management of the economy. Like Italy and Germany, the United States ran up a large public deficit in the 1930s; for Flynn, deficit spending was one of the pillars of fascism, letting in government control of investment through the backdoor. John Maynard Keynes appears, not surprisingly, as an important bête noire in Flynn's story. The growth of trusts, monopolies, and labor unions, according to Flynn, further interfered with free enterprise and encouraged governments to experiment with planning. He also expressed suspicion about the growing militarism that accompanied U.S. participation in World War II, as well as the growth of "internationalism," which he claimed was a mask for imperialism. Although Flynn readily admitted that free enterprise had its inequities—and that he had no solutions to offer—he found its shortcomings far preferable to the dangers posed by fascism.[36]

Flynn's hostility to deficit spending, planning in general, and New Dealers in particular earned him a positive reception from American conservatives. The *Saturday Evening Post* cited his book in an editorial attacking Wallace's views on fascism. And John Land devoted a long article to *As We Go Marching* in the *American Mercury*. In his glowing review, Land emphasized Flynn's attacks on the policy of "tax and tax, borrow and borrow, spend and spend" and his suggestion that the creation of trade unions was a root cause of fascism.[37]

Flynn's book was savaged by the left. Malcolm Cowley, writing in the *New Republic,* accused Flynn of playing games with the concept of fascism: "When Mr. Flynn calls [the New Deal] fascism, on the strength of economic parallels that he discovers or invents, he is saying in effect that wolves and chairs both have four legs and therefore chairs should be exterminated." Cowley argued that it was ridiculous to consider deficit spending as more essential to fascism than official race hatred and suppression of freedom of speech. Most seriously, Cowley accused Flynn of, perhaps unwittingly, aiding the real fascists in America:

> There is something more involved at this point than a dispute about logic or language. What Mr. Flynn fails to says [sic] is that there are hordes of people in this country who are fascists in the exact or institutional sense of the word. They are the people who hate Jews and foreigners, who want to parade the streets in colored shirts, who hope for an American dictator to set things straight and who say in their hearts that Hitler had the right idea. They crowded by thousands into America First, to the great discomfort of Mr. Flynn, who is not in the least a fascist, but who nevertheless continued to act as a spokesman for that organization until Pearl Harbor. . . . My quarrel with Mr. Flynn is that, in this book, he is helping to create the confusion in which they flourish.[38]

Whatever confusion existed in America over the term "fascism," however, was not created by John Flynn. Its "proper" meaning was a matter of much wartime debate, a debate that Flynn can reasonably be said to have lost. The analyses of fascism by Seldes and others on the left during the war remained important to the postwar left. Wallace's notion that hatred was essential to fascism also had many postwar sequels. Flynn's book was largely forgotten, in large measure because his treatment of communism, fascism, and their relationship to each other ultimately failed to appeal to either the left or the right. Flynn, while absolutely anticommunist, draws a strong distinction between communism and fascism throughout *As We Go Marching,* a fact that no doubt led him to use fascism—as opposed to totalitarianism—as his primary analytic category. Fascism, writes Flynn, is a method of organizing capitalism; communism opposes capitalism. At one point he ridicules those who suggested that communism threatened the United States: "It must stand as a strange commentary on our times that almost all of the criticism leveled at the current course of government in America has been on the theory that it was surrendering to communism and moving in the direction of Moscow. Nothing could be further from the truth."[39]

By disassociating fascism and communism while condemning both, Flynn cut across political lines. The equation of communism and fascism was central to the dominant understanding of totalitarianism before the war and remained, throughout the war, a part of that understanding, particularly for those on the right. None of his reviewers mentioned his distinction between communism and fascism. Paul Hutchinson, in a positive review in the *Christian Century,* asserted that Flynn was writing about "why modern states go totalitarian." In his *American Mercury* review, Land similarly projected his own views onto Flynn. Although Land took Flynn to task for not coming up with a more satisfying solution for "conservatives" who "now stand in one of history's darker valleys, threatened by landslides of totalitarian fascism or totalitarian communism," he never suggested that Flynn had a fundamental disagreement with him over the nature of the problem.[40]

All sides of these debates shared one important belief with the other views already expressed in this chapter: the war was first and foremost a battle of ideas, not nations. America was fighting Nazis, not Germans. And the fact that Nazism began in Germany said much less about that country than about more universal political, economic, or psychological phenomena. But many commentators rejected the notion that the United States was not at war with the German people. Frontline observers like journalist Bill Mauldin mocked the idea that the country was fighting Nazis, not Germans. But many others suggested that fighting the Germans qua Germans was not only a practical necessity of modern warfare but also the only way to defeat the ideological enemy. Such views became stronger in America over the course of the war.

The idea that the German people as a whole were responsible for Nazism was most often associated with Sir Robert Vansittart, sometime British permanent undersecretary of state for foreign affairs and author of one of the most famous wartime philippics against the German people, *Black Record* (1941). Vansittart's book, bizarrely dedicated to Dorothy Thompson whose ideas about Germany were quite different from his, collected seven of the author's radio talks contending that Nazism was but the latest proof that Germany had not changed since the days of Tacitus, who said that Germans would sooner get things done by blood than by sweat.

During the war "Vansittartism" came to be used pejoratively in American public culture to refer to the view that measures such as mass exterminations of the German people might be necessary to ensure world peace—a perspective, it should be noted, that virtually everyone, including Vansittart, rejected. Along with the related and equally unattested notion that Germans were racially—as opposed to merely culturally, historically, or philosophically—inclined to militarism, Vansittartism frequently appeared as a straw man in books and articles arguing for a strong distinction between Germans on the whole and Nazis.[41]

But if Vansittartism in this sense was largely chimerical, many believed that the German nation as a whole—or some large and long-existing portion of it—bore responsibility for Nazism. The prevalence of such views is to be expected. In wartime, particularly in a modern war, it has been much easier to think negatively of the entire enemy nation than to imagine that it, too, is a victim of an ideology that is the real enemy. In World War I, the Committee on Public Information's pamphlets celebrating German liberalism had much less effect than their better-remembered attacks on "Kultur" and Prussianism.

In World War II, notions of German collective guilt were usually aired in discussions of what to do with Germany after the war, for if Germany as a whole were responsible for Nazism, even unconditional surrender might not ensure the permanent eradication of that system. At their crudest, arguments for German guilt consisted of little more than collections of incriminating quotations from German historical figures. The outstanding example of this genre was W. W. Coole and M. F. Potter's *Thus Speaks Germany* (1941), a collection of these quotations originally published in England for the American edition of which Hamilton Fish Armstrong, long a believer in the essentially European roots of Nazism, wrote an introduction. Less-involved examples of denouncing Germany by selective quotation appeared in American magazines. Of course, this game could be played to the opposite effect as well: Harlan R. Crippen assembled a collection of quotations from liberal and humanitarian Germans entitled, *Germany: A Self-Portrait* (1944).[42]

By and large, however, those who maintained that Germans were collectively responsible for Nazism had more sophisticated arguments; they went beyond simple quotation to suggest philosophical traditions or psychological facts that predisposed the German nation to Nazism. Among the most important of these efforts was Columbia University psychiatrist Richard M. Brickner's *Is Germany Incurable?* (1943). Brickner's book received ringing endorsements from anthropologist Margaret Mead and psychiatrist Edward Strecker, both of whom provided introductions to it. The *Atlantic Monthly* gave Brickner two articles in which to summarize his views. And the *Saturday Review* assembled a panel of prominent writers and thinkers—including Erich Fromm, Bertrand Russell, and Nobel Prize–winning author Sigrid Undset—to debate the merits of the book. The panel discussion, in turn, led to a seven-month debate in the magazine's Letters to the Editor section labeled "The Incurable Controversy."[43]

Brickner's answer to his title question was no, but the aptness of the question itself was the center of the controversy. The theory expounded in *Is Germany Incurable?* was that, as a nation, Germany displayed all the traits that, were they encountered in an individual patient, would lead a psychiatrist to a diagnosis of paranoia. The paranoid is megalomaniacal and possesses "grandiose mystic notions of the cosmos" that contribute to a belief in a "personal divine mission." A paranoid develops a "persecution complex," believing that "they" have it in for him and cause all the world's problems. And the paranoid's belief system, though totally fantastic, obeys its own form of rationality: "Grant the paranoid's warped premises and it is all utterly logical." Nazism and its leaders were, according to Brickner, only symptoms of this paranoia. To bolster this claim, he noted that other fascistic systems were not paranoid. The grandiose schemes of Italian fascism, for example, were purely cynical. Japan might be paranoid, but "we lack sufficient sociological and psychological knowledge of Japanese culture to make scientifically sound deductions." As his assertions about Japan suggested, Brickner's analysis constantly stressed that he was writing as an expert, with clinical care. "Paranoia," he noted in both his book and his *Atlantic* article, "is not used here as an epithet, but as a responsible medical diagnosis."[44]

But it was a diagnosis that allowed Brickner to hedge his bets. To begin with, as he readily admitted, little was known about paranoia in 1943 other than its symptoms. Its cause had not yet been identified. Nor was the cure for paranoia clear: "Contemporary psychotherapy can offer nothing but institutionalization to persons whose thinking is completely and continuously dominated by paranoia."[45] Brickner's expertise thus gave him ample room for speculation.

The object of his analysis was similarly vague. "The German group— as a collective force, not necessarily as individuals—both 'feels' paranoid and displays a remarkable number of classical paranoid symptoms," wrote Brickner. But who, then, in Germany was paranoid? Not the whole German nation, for "the present situation is far too serious for us to expand the huge web of fantasy already spun around the Germans both by themselves and by others." Instead, once again, Brickner sounded a scientific note: "In speaking of the group called Germany, we are not speaking of some mystic whole, but of an organized congeries of individuals, sharing a common language and common traditions, who have been reared in a common, particular way, technically called a 'culture,' so that they develop common, particular manners, morals, tastes in food, dress, and other departments of life."[46] Brickner's patient was thus German culture, which he characterized in *Is Germany Incurable?* with a series of quotations and anecdotes not unlike those in *Thus Speaks Germany*. Indeed, Brickner cites *Thus Speaks* more frequently than any other text.

His recommended form of therapy depended, in a sense, on the weakness of his portrait of a paranoid Germany. Although totally paranoid patients are incurable, those who occasionally show signs of nonparanoid behavior—so-called clear areas of their personality—can be encouraged out of their paranoia by careful psychotherapy, Brickner told his readers. German culture had such clear areas: "The indubitable existence of such a group within Germany is one reason—besides the demands of fairness and accuracy—why this book has insisted all along that calling Germany a paranoid-tending group does not outlaw the belief that a great many Germans have little or nothing to do with the national paranoid trend. Anybody who knows anything of Germans should not need demonstration that there are millions of non-paranoid countrymen of Lessing and Goethe as well as millions of paranoid countrymen of Wagner and Vater Jahn."[47] Brickner stopped short of claiming to know how to exploit such clear areas when the patient was a nation. But he concluded *Is Germany Incurable?* with a strong claim that clinical psychiatry must play an important part in any postwar reconstruction of Germany.

Brickner's book received much acclaim, especially from other American clinical psychiatrists.[48] Not surprisingly, anti-Nazi Germans in exile in America tended to object to his argument, presumably because they did not like being reduced to a "clear area" in an otherwise paranoid culture.[49] Of the *Saturday Review*'s largely foreign-born panel, only Norwegian novelist Sigrid Undset wholeheartedly praised Brickner, claiming that his picture of Germany matched her personal experiences of Germans. Russian- and German-trained psychiatrist Gregory Zilboorg blasted Brickner's use of psychiatry, his blinkered view of German culture, and his failure to follow his own warning about expanding the "huge web of fantasy already spun around the Germans." Frank Kingdon attacked Brickner for practicing "pseudo-science." Bertrand Russell more or less ignored the book and explored the theme of reeducating the Germans.

But Erich Fromm gave the most interesting analysis of the book. While acknowledging the value of using psychiatry or psychoanalysis—the latter being his preference—to arrive at an understanding of Nazism, Fromm joined Kingdon and Zilboorg in attacking Brickner's diagnosis by selective quotation. In addition, he warned that the use of psychiatry to explain Nazism presented a twofold danger: first, that psychiatric concepts might be used as rationalizations for political slogans, and second, that they might "become a substitute for the valid ethical concepts; that they tend to weaken the sense for moral values by calling something a psychiatric term when it should be called plain evil."[50]

Although more noticed than others, *Is Germany Incurable?* was only one of many books and articles that tried to give an intellectual gloss to the idea that German-ness was responsible for Nazism. Predictably, more of these publications began to appear as the problem of German reconstruction loomed. In *The Hidden Enemy: The German Threat to Post-War Peace* (1943), Heinz Pol contended that behind Nazism—and, in fact, the entire modern history of Germany—was Pan-Germanism, a philosophy and a movement founded in the nineteenth century that had come to dominate the major institutions of German life before the rise of Hitler and would continue to do so after the war unless the United Nations undertook a "great purge" following victory over Germany. Not only the Nazis but also many prominent anti-Nazi refugees such as Herman Rauschning and Otto Strasser were doing the bidding of Pan-Germanism.[51] Emil Ludwig, himself a German refugee, also warned against trusting anti-Nazi Germans in *How to Treat the Germans* (1943). Sigrid Schultz's *Germany Will Try It Again* (1944) argued that since 1918 Germany had been plotting another attempt at world conquest and that, if the victors over Nazi Germany in the present war were not careful, Germany would continue to do so. "Never again must we be deluded into misplacing responsibility for German aggression," Louis Nizer warned in his *What to Do with Germany* (1944). "It is not the leader of the day . . . who wages war against mankind. It is the German people. Conditioned by centuries of false indoctrination . . . the German people have ever been arch-conspirators against civilization."[52] For each of these books there were dozens of magazine articles framing similar arguments.[53]

Brickner stood out from the other theorists of collective German guilt largely by his special claims to expertise. The psychiatric and anthropological approach that he brought to data, which consisted largely of a standard set of incriminating quotations, put his work in a genre of national character studies that gained popularity among social scientists during the war.[54] Presenting the problem of Germany as psychiatric had two other advantages. First, social psychology was a major component of prewar understandings of the regimented crowd. The discipline remained important during the war, as discussions of the psychological dimension of Nazism and the wisdom of attempting to reconstruct Germany psychologically appeared frequently in American magazines.[55] Brickner's theories fit neatly into this discourse. Finally, his arguments had just enough of a sense of contingency and universalism to be compatible with a more transnational, ideological understanding of the war. He devoted one chapter of *Is Germany Incurable?* to what he called the "Paranoid International," suggesting that, in principle, the paranoia from which Germany suffered could strike any nation.

Assertions that the Germans bore a collective guilt or that there were deep connections between German national characteristics and Nazism played least well among those who saw the war in nonnational terms. Although it ran a few articles on the opposite side of the issue, the left-liberal *New Republic* was vociferous in its insistence that the war was not about German-ness. Dorothy Thompson, who despite Vansittart's book dedication, had always believed that Nazism could strike anywhere, addressed the issue of German reconstruction in a lengthy article for *Life* magazine in December 1943.[56] Thompson began the essay by attacking what she called the "Conspiracy Interpretations of History," a rubric she attached to Brickner's psychological theorizing, "Vansittartist" notions of Prussian militarism, left-wing ideas of a "capitalist plot," conservative theories of communist destabilization, and liberal fixations on the failures of Versailles to explain the rise of Nazism. Comparing these theories to antisemitic fears of a Jewish conspiracy, Thompson offered instead a close view of Germany's recent history, especially as it affected the psychology of the generation then forty to fifty years old. After describing the impact of war and social breakdown on Germans of this generation, she considered the contention that this was a necessarily German experience. "It may be said," she argued, "that all this could not have happened in any other nation. It is my opinion that it could happen to any people if the continuity of all their traditions were so drastically broken by the convergence of many circumstances. . . . But the question is not pertinent. It did happen. The Germans are the people to whom all this happened."[57]

In the analyses of the causes of Nazism that appeared in books from *Thus Speaks Germany* to *Is Germany Incurable?* as well as in magazine articles, there was not much middle ground between those arguing for the essentially German character of Nazism and those who insisted that Nazism only happened to have happened in Germany. But in less analytic wartime representations of Nazism, the two contrasting explanations often mixed. Hollywood movies, Broadway plays, and popular books could simultaneously present Nazism as an international ideological menace—which could find itself at home even in countries now democratic—and something deeply connected to Germany or, more generally, Europe.

American public culture in World War II tended to present white ethnicity in the general population as politically insignificant: the country was made up of the descendants of immigrants from many lands whose "funny" last names and favorite foods made them no less American nor significantly different from other Americans. But the line between colorful but politically insignificant ethnicity and dangerous foreignness could be thin and porous. One of the most celebrated horror movies of the war years, producer Val Lewton's *Cat People* (RKO, 1942), was built around just this tension. Oliver (Kent Smith), a WASPish American, meets and quickly falls in love with Irina (Simone Simon), a recent immigrant from Serbia. Unfortunately for their love, and eventually their marriage, Irina is obsessed with a legend about her village. When Serbia was under foreign rule and Serbs were forced to be slaves, her village had begun to practice witchcraft. After King John of Serbia liberated the country and restored Christianity, some of the witches escaped and returned to the village. Now, it is said, the female descendants of these evil villagers are cursed: whenever sexually aroused or even angered, they turn into huge, man-eating panthers.

At first Oliver is amused by this story and encourages Irina not to take the legend seriously. But when she refuses to consummate their marriage, he becomes annoyed. What had appeared to be a colorful tale of the old country now seems to be a serious psychological problem. At Oliver's insistence, Irina goes into therapy. The audience, however, begins to feel that Irina might really be a very different sort of creature from Americans like Oliver and her therapist. By the end of the film, Irina is dead, apparently killed while in the form of a cat. *Cat People* never shows Irina in cat form— most likely for budgetary reasons—but this absence adds to the effectiveness of the horror. Irina as a panther is something utterly unimaginable and foreign to the film's American characters. Oliver is entirely prepared to deal with ethnicity; he, and everyone else for that matter, are unprepared to deal with real otherness.

Although not as menacing and mysterious as "cat people"—the war demanded that, eventually, we understand Nazism—German characters could possess something of Irina's otherness. *Tomorrow the World* carefully presents good Germans in the form of Frieda, the Frames's maid, and Emil's heroic, martyred, humanitarian father. Nevertheless, at the end of the play we find out that Fred, the German American janitor whom Emil tried to enlist as a Nazi spy is, in fact, a fifth columnist. The drama explains Emil's Nazism as a reaction to the torture he received at the hands of Nazi authorities. Fred's Nazism has a more mysterious root. The play suggests that it has something to do with his frustration with being a janitor. But we find out about his Nazism from Frieda, the good German, who obliquely describes seeing Fred at a German American Bund meeting she accidentally attended at the urging of a cousin whom she does not like very much.[58] Fred's politics and Frieda's account of the Bund suggest not only that there are American Nazis but that these Nazis are Germans. The good Frieda is on the surface much more German than the more outwardly Americanized, but actually Nazi, Fred. Nevertheless, every Nazi in the play is German. *Tomorrow the World* demonstrates that all Germans are not Nazis, suggests strongly that outward German-ness has little to do with Nazism, and yet ultimately implies that, for some, there is a connection between their German identity and evil politics. What this connection is, however, the play never explores.

John Roy Carlson's exposé of American fascism, *Under Cover* (1943), displays a similar attitude toward foreignness. Carlson's sprawling book was the number-one nonfiction best-seller of 1943. In *Under Cover,* the author, an ethnic Armenian immigrant and freelance journalist, describes the four years he spent exploring "the Nazi underworld of America." Carlson proudly announces in his preface that he refused to edit his manuscript, which would be immediately obvious to any reader. Rambling for more than five-hundred pages, the book is largely a chronological account of endless meetings of innumerable radical right-wing organizations; it is difficult to imagine reading it from start to finish. Carlson carefully drops the names of key participants as he describes their plans for destroying American democracy and paints vivid portraits of conspiratorial gatherings. He provides five indexes, including one, entitled "Geographical Fever Index," listing places mentioned in the book. Along the way, Carlson touches on many familiar themes: Nazis win converts by penetrating the home. Movements are built around "the mob" and the mass meeting. Leaders use antisemitism and race hatred as a strategy to gain converts. Nazism is a psychological problem, a "state of mind."

One of the most pervasive issues in *Under Cover* is foreignness. Carlson, writing as an immigrant himself, points out in the preface that neither democracy nor fascism has anything to do with ethnicity: "One need only recall that Major Vidkun Quisling was a 'pure-blooded' Norwegian, and Pierre Laval was a 'pure-blooded' Frenchman from the heart of Auvergne, to realize that 'Democracy' like 'fascism' is a state of mind, not of physical boundaries or hallowed ancestry."[59] True to his word, Carlson fills his account with fascists from a wide variety of backgrounds. His Nazi underworld is a funhouse mirror of the multiethnic combat battalion: Americans of all backgrounds joining to subvert democracy.

But the author's own background forms a frame for the book and suggests the difference between mere ethnicity and frightening foreignness. Carlson begins by describing his upbringing and explaining why he undertook an investigation of American Nazism. Born in Greece, he and his family endured successive invasions and forced flights. It is a typical immigrant story; Carlson's family came to America to escape the horrors of the Old World. Yet these horrors followed him to New York, where he witnessed the assassination of the Armenian archbishop Leon Tourian. "It was nearly impossible for me to conceive," writes Carlson, "that this frightful murder had occurred in my adopted America." It was this event that led him to attempt to uncover America's Nazis.[60]

From the start, then, Carlson portrays Nazism as an Old World evil that threatens the New World. Although a "state of mind" to which blue-blooded WASPs also fall victim, Nazism is easily transmitted from overseas to ethnic Americans. The author's subjects, full of ethnic hate even for one another, suggest the dangers inherent in a nation of immigrants. Carlson himself was a figure of great ethnic ambivalence: writing under an American-sounding pseudonym, he both proudly referred to his Armenian roots and explained how he carefully crafted an Italian persona, "George Pagnanelli," for his undercover activities by living in New York's Little Italy. "I came from a land of oppression, of fear and age-long hatreds," he writes on the final page. "I dread seeing this country, my adopted homeland, swept by those same ancient winds of bitterness and prejudice. I felt the first cold gusts of those winds as I drifted through the shadowy alleys of America's fascist underworld and determined to do my part to check it."[61] Although he celebrates his own ethnicity and declares that Nazism has no physical or genealogical base, Carlson pictured American fascism as emanating from the Old World. Despite the fact that America has many of the same horrors as Europe, his experience with the American Nazi underworld led him to reinforce, rather than question, the Old World/New World dichotomy.

The films produced by Frank Capra's unit, including the *Why We Fight* series, also mix notions of foreignness into a generally ideological and universalist understanding of the nature of the war. The quite vicious *Know Your Enemy—Japan* (1945) is a classic example of racialized images of the Japanese. But the Germans as portrayed by Capra's production group also come across as dangerous by dint of their nationality. The first *Why We Fight* film, *Prelude to War* (1942) introduces the series' central, Lincolnesque metaphor (borrowed from Henry Wallace): the world was half slave, half free; the war was a struggle to the death between the slave world and the free world. In *Prelude,* the national attributes of the Axis countries seem irrelevant. Time and again, visually and in its voice-over narration, we are told that Italian Fascism, German Nazism, and the Japanese social and political systems amount to exactly the same things: slavery and militarism.

But when Capra's propaganda pictures focus on the Germans, as when they did on the Japanese, the message changes in significant ways. "In our first film," announces the opening title card of the second film of the series, *The Nazis Strike* (1943), "we saw that this is a war between a *free* world and a *slave* world. . . . Now we are going to see how the Nazis struck." The second title, however, changes the tone: "German ambitions for world conquest go back a long way." As Wagnerian leitmotivs and the "Wacht am Rhein" play in the background, a series of quotations from Bismarck, Kaiser Wilhelm II, and Hitler flash on-screen. The film cuts to footage of a Nuremberg rally and, in the first words spoken, the voice-over emphasizes the point of the preceding quotations: "The symbols and the leaders change but Germany's maniacal urge to impose its will on others continues from generation to generation." Throughout *The Nazis Strike,* it is never clear whether the villain is Nazism or an eternal Germany, a country for which, we are told, treaties have "always" been something to ignore.

After describing Nazi racial doctrine, the film inserts a disclaimer about German Americans: "Some people we know of German descent think this is a lot of hogwash." Pictures of Admiral Nimitz, Senator Robert Wagner, Wendell Willkie, and others flash on the screen. Yet, immediately after this interlude, we are told that, "in the Sudetenland, [Hitler] found some stooges who fell for this bunk." A similar contrast is made in the final *Why We Fight* film, *War Comes to America* (1945). Early in the movie, there is praise for the contributions of various ethnic groups, including Germans, to the building of the American nation. Later, in an attempt to emphasize the proximity of the Nazi threat, the film discusses the menace of Germans in South America who "live as they do in Germany." Again, as in *The Nazis Strike,* something about German culture appears to predispose Germans to evil. This aspect of German-ness is not racial, but it can exert a mysterious pull, even for those outside of Germany.

At war's end Capra's unit released *Here Is Germany* (1945), a production that embraced a national understanding of the causes of the conflict. By far the unit's most thorough examination of the problem of Germany, the film retains much of its power today. Originally written and produced, but never released, in 1942 as *Know Your Enemy: Germany,* the final version—produced for U.S. occupation troops immediately following the fall of Germany—was released in October 1945. *Know Your Enemy: Germany* had been written by Bruno Frank and directed by Ernst Lubitsch, himself a German Jew. It told the story of the rise of German militarism through three generations of a symbolic German named "Karl Schmidt." Perhaps because it too clearly blamed the German people, *Know Your Enemy: Germany* was not released.[62]

After years of reworking at the hands of a half-dozen people, including William L. Shirer, John Huston, and Anatole Litvak, Karl Schmidt and his history of German militarism were relegated to a lesser role. Nevertheless, in *Here Is Germany* the causes of the recently concluded war are entirely local: Nazism is explained wholly in terms of German culture. The film's final director, Gottfried Rheinhard, another German Jewish émigré, focused on the problem of German reconstruction and the need for a "hard" settlement at the end of the war.[63] Although in wartime or after the conflict the notion that Americans, too, might fall victim to Nazism could be used to "sell" the war or warn against intolerance, the otherness of Germany was a more viable theme for a film on reconstruction.

From the start, *Here Is Germany* depicts a country that is a nightmarish conundrum. As lovely symphonic music plays and a traveloguelike montage is presented, a voice-over speaks of a nation that was "beautiful, historic, prosperous, modern." We are told that the Germans are "a clean and tidy people, an educated, musical people, an industrious people." As the camera shifts to an apparently typical small town, the voice-over reaches a climax: "These people look alright: a mailman, a farmer, a cop. They all look pretty much like folks back home. . . . They certainly look like the kind of people we can understand—OR CAN WE?" A montage of contrasts begins: peaceful Germany followed by scenes of Nazi military parades; Germans attending church, yet participating in religious persecutions; gentle Germans contrasted with shots of piles of dead bodies in liberated concentration camps.[64] "These are some of the reasons," the voice-over continues, "why the German farmer, and the German mailman, and the German cop can't be quite like the people back home. Why we've got to look a little deeper into the German character." This is the problem of Germany: "A clean industrious people fond of music, fond of children, fond of tyranny, fond of aggression, fond of gas chambers."

The voice-over assures us that Hitler's answer to the question of German character—German blood—is incorrect, for "many of our friends and neighbors had that blood" and, indeed, so did many great Americans. What makes both Americans and Germans is not blood but "tradition." However, "tradition" in *Here Is Germany* is totally rigid. As contrasting pictures of a smiling GI with shots of grim-faced Nazis appear, the voice-over declares that, according to the American tradition, "no American" can believe in government not of the people, by the people, and for the people. The film then tells the story of the generations of Karl Schmidts to illustrate that Germans, too, are bound by their traditions. The conclusion provides a clear message: the only response to the German tradition is to eradicate it utterly. "We control all of Germany today," the voice-over announces. "We arrive at Germany not as liberators, but as conquerors. We will stay as long as necessary until Karl Schmidt realizes he is responsible. He must rid himself of his history and tradition. Only then can Germany join the peaceful nations of the world."

Despite the best efforts of the Office of War Information and others who sought to promote a war against the Nazis and not the German people, polls over the course of the conflict began to indicate growing public agreement with those who blamed the German people themselves. In December 1939, 66.6 percent of the Americans surveyed believed that Germans were "essentially peace-loving and kindly" but unfortunately misled by their rulers. From February 1942 to May 1946 the National Opinion Research Center conducted an ongoing poll that repeatedly asked Americans to indicate which of three views they agreed with: (1) "The German people will always want to go to war and make themselves as powerful as possible," (2) "The German people may not like war, but they have shown that they are too easily led into war by powerful leaders," or (3) "The German people do not like war. If they could have the same chance as people in other countries, they would become good citizens of the world." In February 1942, 42 percent of the respondents still agreed with the third point of view. This number steadily declined until it hit a low of 19 percent in July 1945. Whereas only 21 percent felt that the Germans were essentially warlike in 1942, by mid-1945 the first option received a narrow plurality of responses (39 percent). After the summer of 1945, hatred of the German people steadily subsided.[65]

The course of the war influenced much of the change in opinion. It was easier to believe in a more abstract Nazi enemy when U.S. troops had yet to encounter Germans in the field in any large number. During the first year of America's involvement, most of its forces that saw conflict were in the Pacific. Although they engaged German troops in North Africa beginning in November 1942, Americans did not see action in Europe until mid-1943, with the invasion of Italy. As Bill Mauldin eloquently reported, war-torn Europe was unlike anything the GIs had ever seen, or could imagine seeing, in America. Frontline accounts and letters home conveyed a sense that America and Europe were quite different. Some observers at home expressed disappointment that the behavior of U.S. troops in Europe indicated that they had not embraced true "international-mindedness."[66] But the actual experience of the war in Europe, an experience that touched nearly every family in the United States, could hardly have been expected not to contribute to a sense that America was unlike Europe, especially Germany.

8 THE BATTLE OF RUSSIA THE RUSSIAN PEOPLE, COMMUNISM, AND TOTALITARIANISM, 1941–1945

Of all the United Nations fighting alongside the United States against the Axis powers, the Soviet Union was the country least likely to arouse American sympathy.[1] Since 1917, Russia had been the home country of communism. Consequently, the USSR had been a symbol of hope for many Americans, particularly in the 1930s, and a focal point of fear for many more. For the first months of World War II, the Soviet Union had been an aggressor. As Germany waged the "Phony War" to its west in the winter of 1939–40, the Soviet invasion of Finland grabbed the headlines in the U.S. press. When the American Communist Party's line swung with the changes in Soviet foreign policy during 1939, numerous liberals who, in the Popular Front period, had developed sympathy for Communism and Russia began to view them in a less favorable light. Across the political spectrum, many Americans began to consider Nazism and Communism to be two examples of a single phenomenon: totalitarianism. Between long-standing anticommunist Russophobia, liberal feelings of betrayal by the Communist Party (CP), and sympathy for "little Finland," American opinion of the Soviet Union on the eve of Germany's surprise attack on Russia was extremely negative.[2]

Whereas the notion that Germans as a people were essentially dangerous and unlike Americans grew ever more central to U.S. understanding of the Nazi enemy, the idea of a natural affinity between Americans and the Russian people played a preeminent role in representations of the USSR in American public culture from the start of Russo-German hostilities. On the day of the invasion, 22 June 1941, Winston Churchill, in a speech heard by millions in the United States on NBC, and widely reported and praised in papers across the country the next day, put forth an argument for supporting Russia that in many ways set the tone for U.S. representations of the Soviet Union over the next four years. "No one has been a more consistent opponent of Communism than I have for the last twenty-five years," proclaimed the British prime minister. "I will unsay no words that I have spoken about it. But all of this fades away before the spectacle which is now unfolding. The past with its crimes, its follies and its tragedies flashes away." Turning to the present, Churchill's rhetorical gaze moved from the Soviet form of government to the Russian people:

> I see Russian soldiers standing on the threshold of their native land guarding the fields which their fathers have tilled from time immemorial. I see them guarding their homes, where mothers and wives pray. Ah, yes, for there are times when all pray for the safety of their loved ones, for the return of the bread winner, of the champion, of the protector. I see the 10,000 villages in Russia where the means of existence is wrung so hardly from the soil, but where there are still primordial human joys, where maidens laugh and children play. I see advancing upon all this the invidious onslaught of the Nazi war machine, with its clanging, heel-clicking, dandified Prussian officers, its crafty expert agents, fresh from the cutting and cowing down of a dozen countries.

"There are those who will say we are now allied with communism," the liberal *New York Post* editorialized the following day. "Our answer is the Prime Minister's speech."[3]

Most American cultural producers understood Germany as primarily an ideological enemy, whereas they tended to regard the U.S. alliance with Russia as basically an affiliation of nations, not ideologies. The "Russian people" (a term often used to refer to all the peoples of the Soviet Union) and the Red Army itself stood at the heart of wartime images of the Soviet ally. Some commentators looked beyond the Russian nation to suggest that Americans ought to respect—or even learn from—the Soviet social, political, or economic system. But arguments that there was, or should be, an ideological affinity between the United States and the USSR were strongly disputed by many who formally supported the U.S. military alliance with the Soviet Union. The vast majority of American cultural producers condemned Nazism; some of them also condemned the German nation. In contrast, there was nearly unanimous praise for the Russian nation, but much less approval—and a good share of condemnation—of Soviet Communism.

This chapter explores the place of, and relationship between, the Russian nation and Soviet Communism in U.S. wartime representations of the Soviet Union. It first describes the groups of American cultural producers who tended to celebrate the Russian people themselves. It then examines some examples of wartime representations of the Russian ally and the different ways in which filmmakers and writers used sympathy for the Russian people as a starting point for discussions of the Soviet Union. Finally, the chapter returns to the wartime employment of "totalitarianism"—a term that continued to link fascism and communism—and its relationship to these views of Russia. Mainly invoked by those most hostile to the Soviet-American alliance, ideas of totalitarianism were themselves altered by the experience of that alliance.

Anticommunism continued to run deep both among the American people and within the halls of power in Washington. Even after the United States entered the war, conservative Democratic congressman Martin Dies investigated and red-baited supposed American Communists and their sympathizers. Some formerly noninterventionist congressmen and the powerful Hearst and McCormick-Patterson newspaper chains urged that America concentrate on "Japan First" and took every possible occasion to find capitulation to communism in the president's attempts to aid Russia and defeat Hitler.[4]

The most ideologically committed anticommunists, like Martin Dies, could not be expected to support America's alliance with Russia no matter how that coalition was framed. But a much broader spectrum of the American public and cultural producers was both strongly anticommunist and generally supportive of the U.S.-Soviet alliance in the war against Hitler. On the right, both the *Catholic World* and the *American Mercury* grudgingly embraced a position in favor of assisting the Russian war effort while maintaining rabid anticommunism. Deeply anticommunist business groups such as the National Chamber of Commerce welcomed the possibility that closer ties to the Soviet Union would open up huge markets for American goods. Hollywood studio heads were interested in publicly "doing their bit" to help the cause, in part to recapture the lucrative European markets. Although their antifascist credentials varied, anticommunism was strong among the movie moguls. Those writing for moderate and moderately conservative publications such as the *New York Times, Newsweek,* the *Saturday Evening Post* (for much of the war), and Henry Luce's powerful *Time, Life,* and *Fortune* magazines, as well as independent writers such as Dorothy Thompson and Walter Lippmann, were, by Pearl Harbor, both fiercely anticommunist and ardently supportive of a major U.S. role in the war in Europe.

The moderate and liberal wings of American Protestantism and Catholicism—whose views were presented in such journals as the Protestant *Christian Century* and *Christianity and Crisis* and the Catholic *Commonweal*—maintained a general antipathy to communism while endorsing the war against Nazi Germany, whose attitude toward religion was at least as disturbing to them as that of the USSR.[5] To the left of center, the CP's endorsement of the Nazi-Soviet Pact had increased the ranks of liberal and socialist anti-Stalinism. The *Nation* and the *New Republic,* though committed to the war against fascism in Europe, frequently printed articles critical of Soviet Communism.[6] Notable in this regard was Kenneth Crawford, who wrote the *New Republic*'s "TRB" column from 1940 to 1943.

Members of all of these groups disparaged the American Communist Party. For the most part, this criticism took the form of ridicule rather than vilification. The CP was still reeling from its party-line changes over the Nazi-Soviet Pact; despite the U.S.-Soviet alliance, it was not until the end of the war, after a vigorous membership drive for the officially less militant Communist Political Association (CPA), which briefly replaced the CP from May 1944 to July 1945, that the Communist movement restored its national membership to over seventy thousand, the total it had enjoyed at its peak on the eve of the Nazi-Soviet Pact. During the war, many viewed the CP as little more than a mouthpiece for Soviet foreign policy, more politically irrelevant than dangerous. "In the U.S.," opined conservative anticommunist William Henry Chamberlin in February 1942, "Communism has been a nuisance rather than a menace." Kenneth Crawford wrote in June 1942 of "the irritating connivers who run the Communist Party of the United States and continue to bask in reflected Russian glory." The party's July 1943 decision to endorse Jersey City mayor Frank Hague, a notoriously red-baiting machine politician whose perfect track record in backing Roosevelt's war policy won him the CP's change of heart, was widely mocked in the press, as was Earl Browder's January 1944 decision to disband the CP and replace it with the CPA. In November 1944 left liberal Max Lerner acknowledged that "the American people have been troubled by . . . the blundering seesawing of Communist Party politics here." And even Vice President Henry Wallace, who believed that the United States could learn much from the Soviet system of government, noted in his diary that "a typical American Communist is the contentious sort of individual that would probably be shot in Russia without ceremony."[7]

Despite their shared commitment to active U.S. support for the Russian war effort and to anticommunism at home, significant political differences remained among these cultural producers. There was a broad consensus that the war should transform the world. At the very least, Axis militarism would be wiped from the face of the earth. But what would the post-Axis world look like? Would the remaining powers fill the vacuum and reconstruct states in their own image? Would the world, even the Soviet Union, become more like the United States? Or would the transformation change all nations, including the United States? Should Americans accept communism as a form of government for the Soviet Union? Or did the Soviet regime, in the long run, represent an international danger and a morally unacceptable limitation on the freedoms of the heroic Russian people? How, following a decade of depression and who knew how many years of war, would American political and economic life best be organized to ensure peace and prosperity? These questions sparked much controversy; the meaning of the Soviet experience and America's relationship to it lay at their heart. "What we have learned about Russia," Lerner wrote in a special section of the *New Republic* on the Soviet Union in November 1941, "is less important for us than what we can learn from Russia. We are primarily interested not in Russia but in America. What we require is not, as many have contended, a revaluation of Marxism and the Russian Revolution in the light of recent events, but a revaluation of democracy. And to that our assessment of the Russian experience can contribute."[8]

The emphasis on the heroic struggle of the Russian people and army per se neatly evaded these questions. All but the most rabidly anticommunist noninterventionists could agree that the struggle of the Russians to expel their German invader deserved American sympathy. Within a month of 22 June 1941, when German troops streamed across the Soviet frontier, nearly three-quarters of the American people expressed a preference for the Russians in their war against Germany.[9] Invoking the Russian people themselves was a safe place to start any argument in favor of sending aid to the Soviet Union. Thus, Vera Micheles Dean began the Foreign Policy Association's twenty-five-cent "Headline Book" on the Soviet Union, *Russia at War: Twenty Key Questions and Answers* (1942), with the question, "What Are the Russian People Like?" This starting place allowed Dean to create greater sympathy for the nation's Soviet ally. It also let her explain the October Revolution and the USSR's system of government—subjects of later questions in the book—primarily in terms of local events and conditions, not universal ideological conflicts.[10]

In the early days of U.S. involvement, with a premium on rhetorics of wartime unity and no guarantee that Russia would not fall to the German armies, even those fearful of the political effects of a strong Soviet Union in the postwar world almost ritualistically expressed support for the struggle of the Russian people before engaging in criticism of Stalin and the Soviet state.[11] Of course, those who maintained that the Soviet regime was, or was becoming, acceptable to the United States—as well as those who suggested that both the United States and the USSR could contribute to a richer, postwar brand of democracy—could draw more directly on sympathy for the struggle of the Russian people by arguing that this struggle had a positive political dimension.

The U.S. government, which naturally sought the broadest possible support for its policies, relied heavily on invocations of the Russian people. Official representation of the wartime allies frequently centered on people, not states: the Britons and Chinese, for example, who, along with the Russians, were seen as bearing the brunt of Axis aggression, were often invoked by FDR. But this emphasis on the people of the United Nations was especially pointed in official discussions of Russia. Even the left-liberal Bureau of Motion Pictures (BMP) of the Office of War Information (OWI) in the 1942 *Government Information Manual for the Motion Picture Industry* began its discussion of Russia with the disclaimer: "Yes, we Americans reject Communism. *But we do not reject our Russian ally.*" The *Manual* urged movie studios to dramatize heroic individuals from the United Nations: "We have not seen the Russian farmer destroying his fields and his home before the enemy advance. . . . But we can see them, dramatically and heroically through the medium of film." Portraying the people of the various United Nations as exactly like Americans was an obvious and much-used propaganda strategy. "We can see them as people," the *Manual* stated, "as one of us. . . . This is a war for the anonymous individual and his inalienable rights. We want to know this anonymous individual, because he and we are one and the same."[12]

American celebrations of the Russian people and army were aided by changes in official Soviet discourse that had begun before the war. Competing with, if never entirely replacing, proletarian imagery, mythologized celebrations of the prerevolutionary Russian past—which previously had been celebrated only for Stenka Razin and other plausibly revolutionary figures—and strictly nationalist rhetoric became commonplace in the Soviet Union. The fiction of Aleksei Tolstoi celebrated Russian blood and soil. Sergei Eisenstein's film *Alexander Nevsky* (1938) showed Russia heroically fending off German invaders while turning a prerevolutionary Russian prince into a hero for a new age. Alexander Suvarov and other prerevolutionary leaders had medals named after them. The Russian Orthodox Church, once ruthlessly attacked, was cautiously cultivated. The word "motherland" [*rodina*] once absent from Soviet rhetoric, returned to common usage. The causes of these changes do not concern us here. For Americans choosing to celebrate the heroic struggle of the Russian people, however, they provided a wealth of Soviet-produced texts and images from which to draw. Ironically, the Soviet state had created precisely the sort of images from which Frank Capra's unit could assemble a film on Russia that entirely avoided considering Soviet Communism.

The Battle of Russia (1943), also known during production as *The People's War in Russia,* was the fourth movie in the *Why We Fight* series and the only film produced by Capra's unit to focus on the Soviet Union.[13] John Sanford was Capra's original choice to write the screenplay. However, Capra, who was irrationally fearful that "Communist propaganda" might appear in his unit's films, was apparently unaware that Sanford was a CP member. Although Sanford's preliminary scripts about Russia avoided political controversy, this was not good enough for Capra and army superiors. On discovering that Sanford was a Communist a few days after selecting him for the project, Capra promptly fired him, disingenuously claiming that he did so only because of pressure from Congress and the army.[14]

That the official army orientation film about Russia could not say anything kind about communism had been clear even to the blacklisted Sanford. "The idea that I would have sneaked in a line saying that 'Karl Marx was a great fellow' . . . is one of the most ridiculous things I've ever heard," he told an interviewer in 1986.[15] All who were involved in the project appear to have agreed that *The Battle of Russia* would center on the heroic Russian people. Comprised mostly of Soviet footage brilliantly edited by a team under the supervision of Anatole Litvak, *The Battle of Russia* remains one of the more powerful of the *Why We Fight* series. The film presented the Russo-German war as part of a centuries-old tradition of Russians repelling invaders from the west. *The Battle of Russia* opens with a series of quotations on title cards praising the Russian people and army:

> History knows no greater display of courage than that shown by the people of Soviet Russia.
> —Henry L. Stimson, Secretary of Defense

> We and our allies owe and acknowledge an everlasting debt of gratitude to the armies and people of the Soviet Union.
> —Frank Knox, Secretary of the Navy

> The gallantry and aggressive fighting spirit of the Russian soldiers command the American Army's admiration.
> —George C. Marshall, Chief of Staff, U.S. Army

Similar statements from Ernest King, commander in chief of the U.S. Navy, and General Douglas MacArthur follow. After these tributes, the film quickly runs through seven centuries of Russian history, from the Russians' heroic expulsion of the Teutonic Knights from their territory under the command of Alexander Nevsky through their defeat of the Swedes at the Battle of Poltava, their victory over Napoleon, and World War I. These events situate the Red Army in a long tradition of popular resistance to invasion.

Why was Russia so frequently invaded? In answer to this question, *The Battle of Russia* presents magnificent montages first of the country's rich land and resources and then of its people, "people of every race, color, and creed." We are shown both the ethnic and occupational diversity of the Soviet Union. Luckily for the defense of Russia, the land and people are inseparably bound. In what was the single most common wartime cliché about the Russians, the narrator assures us that "regardless of what they do or where they live, they all have one thing in common: love of their soil."

The film then describes the first years of the war. The first prints of *The Battle of Russia* included the explanation of the Nazi-Soviet Pact that had been offered in the earlier *Why We Fight* film, *The Nazis Strike* (1943): the Soviets signed the pact only to buy time to prepare for the inevitable German invasion. Many later prints, however, do not mention the pact.[16] As Germany conquered countries to Russia's west, *The Battle of Russia* informs the viewer, the Russian nation prepared; montages show Russians working in industry and engaged in military training. When the Germans finally invade, the Russians are ready. *The Battle of Russia* spends a few minutes describing the superior strategy of the Russian generals, a strategy that involved planned retreats and relied on Russia's huge size. But the biggest difference, the narrator tells us, was not strategic: "There was another item the Germans overlooked: they overlooked people. Generals may win campaigns; people win wars." The remaining two-thirds of the film focuses on the heroic resistance and sacrifices of the Russian people and armed forces. Villagers are shown executing the "scorched earth" policy of destroying all before the path of the invading Germans. People attend church to pray for success. Soldiers take the new Red Army oath, pledging to fight the German invaders to the death. In Leningrad and Stalingrad, civilians and soldiers alike fight off the Nazi siege. In Leningrad, they even pause to enjoy that most Russian of arts, the ballet. "There are no invincible armies against the determined will of free and united people," a title card observes at one point. "We are United Nations," a chorus sings to the upbeat theme from the third movement of Tchaikovsky's *Sixth Symphony* as the film ends.

The Battle of Russia was one of only two *Why We Fight* films released to the public during the war—the other was *Prelude to War* (1942). It garnered generally positive notices and an Academy Award nomination in 1943. Although elsewhere he indicated that he had mixed feelings about the film, James Agee called *The Battle of Russia* "the best and most important war film ever assembled in this country" next to *Birth of a Nation*. Even the Russians were impressed by it. With the addition of an introduction by Stalin himself, the film was shown to Soviet audiences and was praised by the leading Russian montage theorist, Vsevelod Pudovkin, for its editing.[17]

But *The Battle of Russia* is most interesting not for the ways in which it stood out from among the other American wartime films about Russia but for its many similarities to them. Like Capra and his army superiors, Hollywood studio owners had long been anticommunist. Nevertheless, as it was very interested in putting itself at the front and center of the war effort, the industry produced a series of films that celebrated the Soviet Union as an ally. Most of the studios made at least one film about Russia. The majority were produced in 1943, including MGM's musical *Song of Russia,* United Artists' *Three Russian Girls,* Samuel Goldwyn's *The North Star,* and Columbia's *Boy from Stalingrad.* The following year RKO released *Days of Glory,* and in 1945 Columbia produced *Counter-Attack.*[18] With the notable exception of *Mission to Moscow* (Warner Brothers, 1943), all of these films focused on the military struggle of the Russian people against the German invaders and ignored, as much as possible, the political life of the Soviet Union. Although Hollywood would probably have been able to come up with this strategy without the OWI's help, the wartime Russian films essentially followed the suggestions of the BMP *Manual:* they presented a case for the American-Soviet alliance by building sympathy for the Russian people.

The North Star originated when Harry Hopkins asked Lillian Hellman to write a documentary about the Russian struggle. The project slowly evolved into a small dramatic film, scripted by Hellman, to be shot in a "semi-documentary" style. Over the author's objections, however, *The North Star* eventually ballooned into a lavish Hollywood production, with songs by Aaron Copland and Ira Gershwin, neither of whom performed to the best of his abilities.[19]

The action in *The North Star* takes place in June 1941. Living in the small Ukrainian village of North Star is a cast of characters who are the Russian equivalent of the American multiethnic battalion, although here, as in other Hollywood films about Russia, the diversity is figured in terms of occupation, age, and gender, not ethnicity and place of birth.[20] Dr. Kurin (Walter Huston) is an internationally famous pathologist. Damian (Farley Granger) has just finished high school and has won a scholarship to attend the State University in Kiev. His brother Kolya (Dana Andrews) is a Soviet Air Force pilot. Marina (Anne Baxter), Damian's love interest, also hopes to study at the university. Clavdia (Jane Withers) is a simple, sweet, but unattractive girl with a romantic imagination. Karp (Walter Brennan) is an old farmer who dishes out wisdom and recalls how the villagers fought for their soil back in 1914.

The film begins on 21 June 1941, the day before the Nazis strike. The village works and celebrates together. Family life is vigorous, in implicit contrast both to Nazi destruction of the family and to the older view of similarly destroyed families in the Soviet Union. Like most Hollywood Russians from the war years, the villagers of North Star are prone to break into song. By the end of the next day, the entire village is drawn into the war. As soon as news of the German invasion reaches North Star, the villagers divide themselves into two groups. One leaves the town to fight as partisans with arms supplied by an official command post that we never see. The other group stays to execute the scorched earth policy. All are sworn into service with an oath similar to the one that new soldiers take in *The Battle of Russia*.

The Nazis provide a contrast to their Russian victims. Whereas the Russian airmen fight with grim determination, the one Nazi aviator we see smiles viciously as he fires. Two Nazi doctors arrive to provide a counterpoint for Kurin: Dr. von Harden (Erich von Stroheim, who had been playing evil Germans in Hollywood since 1917) and Dr. Richter (Martin Kosleck). Both participate in the film's major Nazi atrocity: bleeding the village children to death to provide plasma for the German wounded. Dr. Richter, an ardent Nazi, enjoys the task; Dr. von Harden, an older man, does it with regret and teases Richter for his enthusiasm. In a classic Hellman touch, when Dr. Kurin eventually shoots them both, he expresses much greater disgust at men like von Harden, who "do the work of fascists while they pretend they are much better than the men for whom they work," a confrontation that particularly pleased OWI reviewers.[21]

But the heroic Russians in *The North Star* have only the most rudimentary political sentiments. Occasionally younger characters make vague references to the fact that "ours is a new world." Youth is repeatedly thematized: "We're the younger generation / And the future of the nation," a group of young people merrily sing. This emphasis on youth is a politically shrewd touch, as the audience could view Russian youth as representing either the New Russia that so many on the left looked to in the 1930s or the newer postrevolutionary Russia that many anticommunist wartime supporters of the Soviet Union claimed was emerging. *The North Star* itself gives us no particular sense of the beliefs of this younger generation. Its Russians, young and old, frequently express allegiance both to their country and to the land. Scenes of the villagers working and celebrating together and a few references to North Star's collective farm quietly suggest the USSR's economic system. But neither Russians nor Germans make any positive or negative assessments of these aspects of village life. In the film's final speech, Marina expresses hope for the future, but her words steer clear of the politically specific: "Wars don't leave people as they were. . . . We'll make this the last war. We'll make a free world for all men. The earth belongs to us, the people, if we fight for it. And we will fight for it." In the end, *The North Star* puts its hope in the transformative power of the heroic struggle of the Russian people themselves.

Days of Glory (1944) follows much the same pattern. Featuring Gregory Peck in his first screen role, the film is a more standard combat picture about a band of Russian partisans who manage to divert German forces just long enough for the Red Army to counterattack. Although successful, all the partisans die fighting. Even more clearly than in *The North Star,* the group of characters around which the action in *Days of Glory* centers is a Russian version of the multiethnic battalion, although once again the group's diversity is not figured ethnically. As if to emphasize the importance of this group, the film opens with an extraordinarily inelegant voice-over narration introducing the film's cast and the characters they portray: Vladimir (Peck), a soldier and the group's leader; Semyon (Lowell Gilmore), a Russian-born former teacher at Oxford; Yelena (Maria Palmer), "a girl from the factories turned soldier"; Sasha (Alan Reed), "the amiable drunk"; Fedor (Hugo Haas), "the sentimental blacksmith"; Dmitri (Igor Dolgoruki), "a farmer"; Petrov (Edward Durst), "the silent one"; sixteen-year-old Mitya (Glenn Vernon), "the brave volunteer"; Olga (Dena Penn), "the little mother"; and Nina (Tamara Toumanova, herself a ballerina), "a dancer from Moscow."

The band of partisans live in an abandoned monastery in Nazi-occupied Russia. Even in these circumstances, Russian cultural life continues. Olga cooks recognizably Russian foods like borscht and kasha. Semyon, the group's intellectual, enjoys reading literary manuscripts saved from the nearby museum at Leo Tolstoy's former estate, Yasnaya Polyana. All enjoy singing—with the possible exception of the lovesick Yelena. Family, or what is left of it in the wake of the Nazi onslaught, continues in the relationship of the orphaned Olga and her brother Mitya. The film is full of subtle signs of religious life. Nina, the dancer, who is found lost in the woods, wears a large cross around her neck and nobody seems to care. The partisans give one of their fallen comrades an audible, but off-screen, Russian Orthodox funeral. And icons are visible on the walls of the partisans' hiding place, although the film never makes clear whether these are left over from the monastery. Once again, there is a Red Army oath-taking scene, although this time it has a tragic twist: latecomer Nina is given the oath in the film's final moments as a German tank overruns the last survivors of the partisan band.

Although the partisans in *Days of Glory* and the villagers in *The North Star* form their own Russian versions of the multiethnic group, the fact that their diversity is not figured ethnically deserves further consideration. One explanation might be the simple lack of ethnic and sectional stereotypes for the various peoples of the Soviet Union. In wartime magazine articles and books, Soviet ethnic diversity was frequently mentioned, sometimes accompanied by pictures of the many peoples of the USSR.[22] And *The Battle of Russia* contains a montage of these peoples. But there was no easy way to present, for example, an Uzbek fighting alongside Great Russians and have that character be meaningful to Hollywood audiences. Americans would not have recognized Uzbek accents, food, or costumes—the standard Hollywood ethnic markers. More significantly, the shared ethnicity of the diverse groups of characters in *The North Star* and *Days of Glory* suggests that the Russian people, to which the characters individually belong and whom they collectively represent, themselves are members of a higher pluralistic collective: the United Nations. Like the ethnicity of the American characters in the World War II combat picture, the Russian-ness of Hollywood's Russians is largely a matter of style: their clothes, their food, their songs. If they vary in any significant way from Americans, it is that their Russian-ness makes them more willing to work together selflessly. Although different from the behavior of most Americans—or even many Hollywood American characters—such unity and self-sacrifice were American wartime ideals. In no way did the behavior of Hollywood's Russians indicate that their values were threatening or even enigmatic. Like the Southern WASP and the Brooklyn Italian, they were well qualified to be a part of the multiethnic army that was the United Nations.

Song of Russia, MGM's musical take on the Russian genre, more directly thematizes the relationship of Russia to America.[23] American conductor John Meredith (Robert Taylor) goes on tour in Russia in 1941. Drawn to the country by his love for the music of Tchaikovsky, John immediately falls in love with Russia itself and with a young Russian pianist, Nadya Stepanova (Susan Peters). Nadya takes John out on the town in Moscow, which boasts restaurants and supper clubs in which performers sing of their love of Russia and of the arrival of Coca-Cola and jazz from America. After Nadya orders them a huge meal of Russian dishes, John proclaims that the country is not as he imagined it: "I always thought Russians were sad—melancholy people. You know, sitting around brooding about their souls. This is such a surprise." Nadya, too, is a surprise; she is almost like an American girl, John tells her. Nadya, however, turns out to retain one characteristic of prewar Hollywood Russian women. Though less doctrinaire than the title character at the start of *Ninotchka,* Nadya shares a tendency to be overly rational. After spending days together with John, she declares their love to be "unrealistic" because their cultures are too different and announces her intention to return alone to her little village of Tchaikowskoye.

John follows Nadya to her village, ostensibly to conduct there. Tchaikow-skoye is a typical Hollywood Russian village with a twist. As in the stereo-typical village, the inhabitants joyfully help to work the land and are ex-tremely proud of their farm.[24] Family life is vibrant: one character refers to his children as "the finest crop of all." And all the villagers receive mili-tary training so that they can defend the country if attacked. Tchaikow-skoye is special because, despite being a tiny village, it contains an impres-sive music school, thus institutionalizing the standard Hollywood Russian love for music. After some hesitation on her part, John convinces Nadya to marry him. They are wed in a Russian Orthodox ceremony.

Nadya joins John on tour. On 21 June 1941 she plays for a national radio audience in Sevastopol. But her triumph is short, for war comes the next day. In an address to the nation on the invasion, Stalin draws on themes that are nationalistic rather than revolutionary. Somewhat prematurely, given America's neutrality in the summer of 1941, he emphasizes the im-portance of the American alliance: "In this war of liberation, we shall not be alone. We shall have loyal allies in the peoples of Europe and America. Our war for the freedom of our country will merge with the struggle of the peoples of Europe and America for their independence for democratic liberties and against enslavement by Hitler's fascist armies." A montage of Russians listening to their leader indicates that the nation is willing to fight.

Among those moved to action is Nadya. She insists on returning to her village to take part in the war. Hank Kiggins (Robert Benchley), John's cyni-cal personal secretary, has been suspicious of the marriage all along. When he comes to speak to Nadya about her leaving for Tchaikowskoye, she tells him that she knows he will call her a fool. At first Hank does so. He says that the smart thing to do would be to return to America with him and John. But then he changes his tone. "Nadya, I—uh—wanted to say that—uh—I come from a small town too," Hank begins. "A little place up in New England called Lexington. A lot of fools—like you—fought for that once—died for it right there on the village green. Some day you'll see my town—you and John. I'm sure of it. It'll still be there because back home we have a lot of fools like you." Nadya thanks Hank effusively and heads off to her village.

John cannot stand being separated from his new bride. He gets a special pass to the front and, against unbelievable odds, finds his way to her. Tchaikowskoye is destroyed, but Nadya is in the woods preparing to fight as a partisan. A leader of the village, Boris, tells her to go to America with John and spread news of the fighting Russian nation. The scene dissolves to Nadya and John performing at an American Russian Relief concert as Boris speaks the film's final words: "No matter where your duty takes you and no matter how far away you and John may be, we will feel you fighting side by side with us. All soldiers in the same army. Fighting to bring a new life to our children. For that great day of victory when the whole world will ring with a new song of freedom. For you will be bringing our great countries closer together in this fight for all humanity."

In *Song of Russia,* both the Russian and American characters incorrectly assume that their countries are too different for a close relationship, represented by Nadya and John's love affair. It turns out, however, that most of the apparent differences between America and Russia are mythical or cosmetic. The Russians are a churchgoing, family-oriented people who enjoy nightclubs and care about their hometowns. Hank's comparison of Lexington and Tchaikowskoye neatly manages to efface both the American and Russian revolutionary traditions. The Russian Revolution is nowhere in sight, and the American Revolution is reduced by analogy to a defensive war. At the end of the movie, the coming of war provides an opportunity for both Russia and America to find out what Nadya and John have already discovered for themselves: they may dress, eat, and sing slightly differently, but Americans and Russians are fundamentally alike.

The North Star, Days of Glory, and *Song of Russia* gave consistent messages. Sympathy for the Russians was to be grounded in their basic similarity to Americans. The slight differences displayed either served as instruction—the selfless way in which Russians worked together to fight off the Nazis—or provided local color—the singing and the Orthodox church services. Although focusing more on the military effort, *The Battle of Russia* also built sympathy for the Soviet Union by making the Russian people sympathetic. Neither the Hollywood films nor the *Why We Fight* series seriously addressed the Soviet state and the relationship of Communism to American democracy.

Most wartime American analyses of Russia, whether in books or magazine articles, could not so totally avoid discussing Soviet Communism. But Hollywood's wartime image of Russia forms a good starting point for our exploration of celebrations of the U.S.-Soviet alliance, because the movies distilled two major features of these celebrations. First, the Soviet people were, in some essential way, similar to Americans and thus deserved their sympathy. Second, pluralism and tolerance could bridge the differences that existed between Americans and Russians. In this way, the people of the USSR were fundamentally different from the Germans, who, with growing frequency over the course of the war, were represented as having national characteristics that made them so unlike Americans—and, by extension, the rest of humanity—that, absent some kind of psychological reconstruction, they were inassimilable into the community of nations.

Like wartime analyses of Germany, much American writing on Russia focused on the postwar world. By January 1942 it was apparent that the United States would be fighting a war alongside Russia. The future of this alliance, once Hitler was defeated, was less obvious and thus became the subject of much speculation. For the many cultural producers who thought that the U.S.-Soviet alliance could and would continue, at least three models existed to explain Soviet Communism and its relationship to American democracy and capitalism. Each could build on sympathy for the Russian nation to make the case for American-Soviet friendship after the war. The first model rested on the contention that the USSR was becoming increasingly like the United States. A number of different narratives were invoked to support it: the transformation of the Soviet Union into a country whose political and economic systems resembled those of the United States could represent the fulfillment of the Russian Revolution or its abandonment; such a transformation could come about as a result of Stalin's wishes or despite them; it could be hastened by war or delayed by it. But each of these scenarios ultimately provided the same rationale for American-Soviet friendship: soon the Russian political and economic systems would be basically like those of America.[25]

A second, somewhat more common model acknowledged that the Soviet system was decidedly different but ought to be tolerated much as Americans tolerated different religions in the United States. Rather than expecting the Russians to become pluralists, this view merely subjected them to a brand of international pluralism: as the Soviet Union wanted communism for itself and meant no harm to others, its political decisions should be respected and its regime should be treated as a normal member of the community of nations.[26] A third and much less frequently mentioned approach argued that both the United States and Russia could contribute to a better postwar world by forging a new political model for all nations that would draw on the positive aspects of both the Soviet and American social and political systems.[27]

These three positions were not mutually exclusive. Many who believed that the Russian regime was becoming a pluralistic democracy like America acknowledged that some differences would remain and would have to be accepted. Many who argued for friendly relations with a Russia that was politically very different from the United States also suggested that the USSR was less different than it had once been. And many who stopped well short of supporting the emergence of a single, better form of government based on both the U.S. and Soviet systems acknowledged that the two countries could learn from one another.

Nevertheless, a number of influential analysts advocated each of these models. Sociologist Pitirim Sorokin was the most forceful and thoroughgoing supporter of the view that the USSR was already like the United States and would become even more so after the war. The notion that the United States and the USSR, although different, should remain friendly had many proponents, including former Republican presidential candidate Wendell Willkie, *New York Times* Russian correspondent Walter Duranty, and Joseph E. Davies, FDR's special envoy to the Soviet Union in the late 1930s and author of the best-selling *Mission to Moscow* (1941). Finally, by far the most prominent believer in the theory that the United States and the Soviet Union would each contribute to a new, more democratic system of government was Vice President Henry Wallace. Each of these commentators invoked sympathy for the Russian people as a starting point for his argument.

Having grown up in tsarist Russia and having served as editor in chief of a metropolitan newspaper in his homeland and as a member of Aleksandr Kerensky's provisional government, Sorokin had impeccable credentials both as an interpreter of Russia and as a skeptic regarding communism. Arriving in the United States in 1923, he became a professor of sociology at Harvard University. In *Russia and the United States* (1944), a book written for the general public, Sorokin contended that the United States and the USSR were the most natural allies in the world. Russia was unique among nations in that uninterrupted peace had existed between it and the United States from 1776 to the present. Though he maintained that this claim was "undeniable," charting such a peace proved troublesome. It was necessary to explain, for example, that the fact that an American expeditionary force was sent to battle the Bolsheviks in 1918 did not constitute hostility between the two nations as "it was dispatched not *against* Russia but rather to *help* Russia."[28]

Most of *Russia and the United States* sets out to explain the extraordinary fact of the peace and goodwill that Sorokin believed had always existed between the two countries. As in Hollywood's Russian movies, the chief explanation lay in the similar national characteristics of Americans and Russians. The unchanging peace between Russia and America, claimed Sorokin, *"has been mainly due to the lack of any serious clash between the vital interests or basic values of the two countries, and it has been facilitated by the mutual mental, cultural, and social congeniality of the two nations."* Both countries occupied whole continents, expanded peacefully, and represented the principle of "unity in diversity." And both tolerated differences and cultivated freedom of thought.[29]

Unlike the makers of the Russian films, however, Sorokin could not ignore the Soviet state. Instead, he argued that what differences that once existed between the Russian and American systems of government were fast disappearing. The United States was no longer "purely capitalistic," and Russia was no longer "purely communistic." Sorokin did not clarify his views on U.S. capitalism, but nowhere in his book did he suggest that America would soon undergo a profound change. The Soviet Union, on the other hand, was experiencing such a transformation. The period immediately after the Russian Revolution, Sorokin declared, was a radical departure from the past. In the 1930s, however, Russia began to return to a course of development similar to that in the United States. Although the Communist Party and Stalin retained the same aspirations, the national characteristics of the Russian people—what Sorokin called "irresistible sociocultural forces"—compelled them to abandon their goals.[30]

According to Sorokin, in the years leading up to World War II, these irresistible forces pushed the Soviet regime to move "from the destruction of family to its rebuilding," "from the persecution of religion to its toleration," "from vilification to glorification of Russian culture," and "from the Communist Red Army to the Russian National Army." Stalin's purges of the CP leadership were a positive sign that the country was abandoning its revolutionary past. There was already *"scarcely any fundamental difference"* between the Russian and American economic systems.[31]

Even in the area of personal liberty, Sorokin argued, great progress had been made, pointing to the Stalin Constitution of 1936. Sorokin, like many other Americans who looked with hope to the 1936 Soviet constitution during the war, stated that the fact that the constitution had been primarily honored in the breach was due to the brief time between its enactment and the coming of war. The Soviet Union had moved "from [a] Communist Dictatorship to [a] National Democracy and then to [a] War Dictatorship."[32] Given the nature of Russian culture and prewar political trends, at the end of the war the USSR could be expected to continue to evolve in a way that would guarantee civil liberties. Because of the Russian people's purported similarity to the American people, their economic and political systems would inevitably become similar to those of America.

Few others were willing to go as far as Sorokin in predicting that the Soviet Union would soon have American-style political and economic systems. Many more observers built on sympathy for the Russian people to argue that the United States should fully accept the Soviet Union into the community of nations despite its disparate political and economic systems. In his *Round Trip to Russia* (1943), one of many similar political travelogues of the USSR published during the war, *Time* correspondent Walter Graebner puts forward such an argument. Primarily composed of a long series of vignettes on both the author's own experiences and those of more famous visitors such as Winston Churchill and Wendell Willkie, Graebner's book presents the Russian people, from simple peasants to Stalin himself, as characters to whom his readers can easily relate. Toward the end of the volume, the author is compelled to devote a chapter to analyzing what "socialism"—the term Graebner, echoing official Soviet usage, uses for the Soviet system—means for the USSR. He concludes that socialism is supported by most people primarily as an expedient, that it allows Russians to work together somewhat more cooperatively than Americans, and, most importantly, that Russians and the Soviet state have no interest in spreading their system to other countries. As Graebner heads home at the end of the book, his thoughts return to the Russian people. Though he does not find that their similarity to Americans will lead to the democratization of the Soviet Union, he does suggest that mutual sympathy between the Russian and American peoples must be the basis for a lasting peace. The keystone of a more democratic world, like the keystone of democracy at home, is toleration:

> In Russia I learned, above all, that the people of the Soviet Union are good people—brave and strong, and willing to make any sacrifices, not out of fear, but out of love for their country and out of hatred for Fascism. On my travels I learned, above all, that while people of the United Nations are fighting with all their might to win the war they have not yet achieved the spiritual unity to win the peace. Before that is possible, they must, I believe, think less about material things, forget their prejudices, and become more tolerant of one another.[33]

Wendell Willkie, the 1940 Republican presidential candidate, conveyed a similar message in *One World* (1943), his best-selling account of his 1942 trip around the world. In his chapter on "Our Ally, Russia," Willkie recounted his experiences among the Russian people and with Joseph Stalin. He depicted a people deeply dedicated to the war effort and thus worthy of American sympathy: "The phrase 'This is a people's war' has real meaning. It is the Russian people in the fullest sense who are resolved to destroy Hitlerism. What they have been through and what they face in the months ahead cannot fail to stir any American. . . . The Russian people—not just their leaders—the Russian people, I was convinced, had chosen victory or death. They talked only of victory."[34]

Though it does not provide a detailed look at Soviet Communism, *One World* makes clear that Russia was not a democracy in the American sense. Willkie challenged Stalin on the issue of personal liberty, and the Soviet leader failed to come up with an acceptable response. However, the Soviet people generally supported the regime. According to Willkie, neither the United States nor the Soviet Union desired the other's political system; nor did either nation fear that one would impose its way of life on the other: "Russia is neither going to eat us nor seduce us. . . . The best answer to Communism is a living vibrant, fearless democracy—economic, social, and political. All we need to do is to stand up and perform according to our professed ideals. Then those ideals will be safe." Like Graebner, Willkie argued that mutual respect and recognition of difference were the keys to postwar Soviet-American cooperation. At the heart of Willkie's argument for respect was American sympathy for the Russian people and their achievements in war and peace.[35]

Henry Wallace used American sympathy for the Russian people to put forward a very different vision of the relationship between American democracy and Soviet Communism. The vice president envisioned a postwar world in which the United States and the USSR would each contribute elements of its political and economic system to form a superior, new kind of democracy. Wallace expressed these ideas most clearly in an address to a Soviet Friendship Rally in Madison Square Garden on 8 November 1942. As Graebner, Willkie, and Sorokin would later do, Wallace took as the starting point of his argument the affinity that existed between the Russian and American peoples:

> It is no accident that Americans and Russians like each other when they get acquainted. Both peoples were molded by the vast sweep of a rich continent. Both peoples know that their future is greater than their past. Both hate sham. When the Russian people burst their shackles of Tsarist absolutism, they turned instinctively to the United States for engineering and agricultural guidance. Thanks to the hunger of the Russian people

for progress, they were able to learn in twenty-five years that which had taken us in the United States 100 years to develop.[36]

To the theme of mutual sympathy, Wallace added the notion that Russians and Americans had a history of working together and learning from one another. He thus was able to suggest that the affinity of the Russian and American peoples would lead them to combine the best aspects of their systems. Expanding on the theme that U.S. political democracy complemented Soviet economic democracy, he suggested to the Soviet Friendship Rally that the new, postwar democracy must also embrace "ethnic democracy," "educational democracy," and "democracy in the treatment of the sexes." In each of these areas, according to the vice president, the Soviet Union had outpaced the United States.[37]

Sorokin, Graebner, Willkie, and Wallace built their different ideas for Soviet-American postwar cooperation on the same foundation: the friendship and similarity of the Russian and American peoples. Of course, not all American writers who considered the relationship between the United States and the Soviet Union after the defeat of Germany placed such an emphasis on the sympathy between the people of the two nations. An older tradition of writing about foreign relations concerned itself only with states, national interests, and power relationships.[38] But suspicion of the Russian people per se was virtually absent from analyses of the future of U.S.-Soviet relations. In stark contrast to the Germans, who were so often represented as a dangerous people, the Russians were beyond criticism. Even those who were deeply critical of Soviet Communism avoided criticizing the Russian people during the war. Whereas American critics of Nazism focused more frequently on German national characteristics as the war progressed, those who censured Communism retreated from criticism of the Russian people.

This retreat occurred despite the slow but increasing disapproval of the Soviet Union in America after 1942. With the war against Hitler far from won, U.S. support for Russia continued to run high in 1943. By early 1943, when Russian forces had broken the siege of Stalingrad, the Nazi invasion of Russia had obviously failed. Although Leningrad's "900 Days" would not be over for another year, the Red Army had fractured the German blockade of the city in January 1943. Particularly in southern Russia, the front began to move westward, as Soviet troops recaptured territory that had been held by the Nazis. Although much celebrated in the United States, Russia's success began to reawaken old American suspicion of the Soviet Union among the more lukewarm supporters of the U.S.-Soviet alliance. Once the Germans had been expelled from Russian soil, would Stalin seek a separate peace, allowing Hitler to concentrate all of his forces in the West? Or would his troops continue marching into Europe to ensure Soviet domination of the continent after the war?[39]

The May 1943 news from Moscow that the Comintern had decided to dissolve itself buoyed many supporters of the Soviet alliance from across the American political spectrum. Writing in the *New Republic,* Malcolm Cowley, expressing the feelings of many former Communists and fellow travelers on the left, applauded Russia's apparent new role as a nation fighting fascism but not attempting to remake the world in its own image:

> All through the 1930's, the Soviet Union was a second fatherland for millions of people in other countries, including our own. It was the land where men and women were sacrificing themselves to create a new civilization, not for Russia alone but for the world. It was not so much a nation, in the eyes of Western radicals, as it was an ideal, a faith and an international hope of salvation. All these illusions have been shattered, as they deserved to be. Russia today is saving the democratic world because she wants to save Russia. If the Westerners are to have a new civilization they will have to create it for themselves; there will be no Russian messiah to lead them.[40]

The year 1944 brought more suspicion of the Soviet Union. Further Russian success in the East and the United Nations' successful invasion of Normandy in the West made German defeat seem close and focused American attention on the postwar world. Well before his sudden death later that year, Willkie was passed over in his bid for his party's presidential nomination. Instead, the Republicans nominated the more conservative New York governor, Thomas Dewey. With little else to run on, the GOP raised the specter of communism at home and questioned FDR's resolve to stand up to the Soviet Union abroad. The apparent intransigence of Stalin's territorial demands in Poland and the Baltic states strengthened the Republicans' hand. Although FDR won election to a fourth term, the 1944 race was the closest of his four campaigns for the presidency.[41] On 4 September 1944 *Life* magazine, which had strongly backed the U.S.-Soviet alliance and had printed an editorial expressing hope for continued collaboration between the two countries in July, published a long essay by William Bullitt, the Russophobic former U.S. ambassador to the Soviet Union. Written from Rome and apparently endorsing the Vatican's views on an inevitable struggle between Christianity and communism and the danger of a Soviet-dominated Europe, Bullitt's piece drew fire from many *Life* readers; the magazine's editors, however, defended his point of view.[42] Although support for U.S.-Soviet cooperation remained high in America in 1944, that support was definitely declining.

Despite the slow erosion in U.S. goodwill toward the Soviet Union, American cultural producers did not vilify the Russian people. Even those most mistrustful of Soviet Russia, who frequently wrote that both Soviet Communism and German Nazism were totalitarian, did not speak of the Russian people as the root cause of the evils of the Soviet system. Indeed, the American wartime celebration of the heroic Russian people had a significant effect on the writings of many cultural producers most hostile to the Soviet Union and communism. The remainder of this chapter will focus on changes in these writings and in American ideas about totalitarianism, a concept that remained a touchstone during the war among Americans hostile to the Soviet Union.

In wartime America, "totalitarian" and "totalitarianism" retained many of their associations before Pearl Harbor. Most importantly, the terms continued to refer to dictatorships of the right and the left, to both Nazism and Communism. Although many cultural producers casually called Nazi Germany totalitarian without necessarily implying any particular beliefs about the Soviet Union, totalitarian and totalitarianism were virtually never used to exclude communism explicitly.[43] Sigmund Neumann defined the scope of his *Permanent Revolution* (1942), the most thorough study of totalitarianism from early in the war, as "the totalitarian dictatorships in Europe"; Neumann clearly included Soviet Russia in that category. Although Frank Munk's *The Legacy of Nazism: The Economic and Social Consequences of Totalitarianism* (1943) spoke only of Nazi Germany, it was suspiciously silent about the USSR and communism. That this silence was largely a matter of wartime politics is born out by the fact that his earlier work, *The Economics of Force* (1940), also based on the concept of totalitarianism, states simply that "Communism, like Fascism, is totalitarian." In March 1944 Carl Friedrich, who would emerge after the war as one of the primary theorists of totalitarianism, wrote in passing of "the totalitarian dictatorship of the Soviet."[44]

During the war, the use of "totalitarianism" was common among those on both the left and the right who wanted to emphasize their anti-Stalinism. As the term applied equally to Nazism and had been important to interventionist rhetoric before the collapse of the Nazi-Soviet Pact, accusing the Soviet Union of totalitarianism was a powerful way to critique a U.S. ally while making clear that the writer had no sympathy for America's enemies. Socialist Party leader Norman Thomas repeatedly used the term to refer to the Soviet Union.[45] Like many on the right, he declared that those who uttered kind words for the Soviet system were, by extension, "totalitarian liberals," an expression coined before the war by Eugene Lyons. Other prominent left-of-center cultural producers who frequently declared that Soviet Communism was totalitarian were pacifist Dwight Macdonald and philosopher John Dewey.[46]

Further to the right, the charge that the Soviet Union was totalitarian was more common during the war. Religious moderates and conservatives, who had long seen in the totalitarian state an encroachment on areas of life that ought to be reserved for the church, regularly used "totalitarian" and "totalitarianism" to express their distress at the Soviet regime and, in particular, its attitudes toward religious freedom. On the secular right, William Chamberlin, Max Eastman, William Bullitt, and Lyons—all of whom were once sympathetic to Soviet Communism—regularly used the terms.[47]

Occasionally, "totalitarianism" showed up in Hollywood. In *Chicken Little* (RKO, 1943), an anti-Nazi cartoon short produced by Walt Disney, the traditional children's story is told with a twist. When Chicken Little convinces the animals to flee to a cave, the evil Foxey Loxey traps and eats them. "Wait a minute," the voice-over narrator intones. "That's not how it ends in my book!" Nevertheless, Foxey insists, "Dat's how it ends in *my* book." Animator Ward Kimball, who worked on the picture, told film historian Richard Shale that in the original version, Foxey Loxey used the word "fascism" to describe what he believed in. But Disney objected. The cartoon mogul was an inveterate anticommunist who had tried to start an official investigation of Hollywood radicalism before the war. Disney insisted that the fox say "totalitarianism," not "fascism." This was an expensive and time-consuming last-minute change, for it involved not only altering the soundtrack but also reanimating the entire sequence so that Foxey's mouth synchronized with the new word. Kimball objected both to the extra work and the reasoning behind the change. Although the Soviet Union and communism were never mentioned in *Chicken Little,* the implications of totalitarianism in 1943 were absolutely clear. "In other words," Kimball told Shale, "if we called him Fascist, we should also kind of make it sound like we're condemning Russia too."[48]

The identification of the Soviet Union as totalitarian was thus attractive to certain cultural producers on both the left and right of the political spectrum. In 1943 Dwight Macdonald organized an open letter to protest Warner Brothers' film version of Joseph Davies's *Mission to Moscow* (1943), a movie that quickly became infamous for distorting historical events, whitewashing the Moscow show trials of the late 1930s, and implying that most U.S. non-interventionists were fascist sympathizers. The letter, which called the film "the first full-dress example of the kind of propaganda movie hitherto confined to the totalitarian countries" and compared its techniques to those of "the Kremlin," attracted signatures that represented a wide range of American political opinion, including those of Norman Thomas, A. Philip Randolph, George S. Counts, Alfred Kazin, Sidney Hook, Edmund Wilson, and Max Eastman.[49]

As had been the case in the years leading up to Pearl Harbor, the term "totalitarianism" continued to evoke both an all-powerful state and the rigid, political faith that underlaid it. On the nature of the totalitarian state, some writers were more specific. "To call the Soviet régime totalitarian is not a matter of argument or polemics," wrote William Henry Chamberlin in September 1944:

> It is a mere statement of scientific fact. Totalitarianism is a new type of government which emerged during the interval between the two World Wars. It possesses a number of distinctive and easily identifiable features. Among these are a supposedly infallible leader and a single legal political party, a streamlined form of administration in which there is no effective legislative or judicial check on the executive authority, a complete absence of civil and personal liberties, and intensive propaganda carried on through all the agencies of an omnipotent terror state. No one familiar with the nature of Stalin's régime can doubt that it conforms to these essential conditions.[50]

Descriptions of totalitarian belief systems were more general. By linking the seemingly hostile doctrines of fascism and communism, the term "totalitarianism" drew the focus away from the specific content of belief systems to the structure of those belief systems. Totalitarian belief systems were held with a rigid intensity that could accept no opposition; they were the antithesis of tolerance and pluralism. Declaring that an "educational totalitarianism" was developing on all sides of the debate over education between neo-Thomists like Robert M. Hutchins and neo-pragmatists like Sidney Hook, William Dighton of the American Council of Learned Societies suggested any kind of belief could become totalitarian: "The war of the professors is an ideological war. As a result, the tendency is constantly increasing to evaluate all education as propaganda, that is, propaganda for one or another political faith, right, middle, or left. And as this tendency grows, it is invariably accompanied by an intolerance which often ends and will inevitably do so, in a demand for national uniformity of educational practice, in educational totalitarianism, in short. . . . Totalitarian thinking . . . characterizes both extremists and moderates."[51]

As had been thought before Pearl Harbor, totalitarian thinking, regardless of the particular belief system, was believed to easily lead to a totalitarian state. "The totalitarian liberal is a liberal at all not by any philosophical definition of the term 'liberal,' but by courtesy and custom," wrote Norman Thomas in January 1943:

> He is a liberal because he hates Hitler and thinks he hates Hitlerism. He is a liberal because he calls himself by that name and because regularly, or occasionally, he reads and applauds the *Nation,* the *New Republic, PM,* or the New York *Post.* He is in line with a genuine liberal tradition in supporting fair play and no discrimination in the treatment of Negroes. He is a liberal, in a sense of the word common in America in the last generation, because he is skeptical or vigorously critical of big business, Wall Street, or monopoly capitalism—call it what you will—and concerned for the rights of workers. He is a totalitarian because he has somehow persuaded himself that methods of propaganda and social controls, basically fascist in character, can be used for a good cause; that democracy can still be democracy and yet be led by a just and humane fuehrer who will use many of Hitler's methods, but without his cruelty and always for righteous ends; that is, ends which can be rationalized in the English but not the German language.[52]

But in one important way, thinking about totalitarianism changed profoundly over the course of the war. Before Pearl Harbor, most cultural producers had argued that totalitarian regimes were mass regimes; totalitarian belief systems were dangerous largely because most, if not all, of the general public might subscribe to them. Modern dictators were supported by a regimented crowd. President Roosevelt, Dorothy Thompson, and countless others wrote and spoke of Nazism and Communism as mass regimes, caused by misplaced popular dissatisfaction with the status quo. Erich Fromm wrote of modern man's collective attempt to "escape from freedom."

In the late 1930s, with America still trapped in the socioeconomic crisis of the Great Depression, Nazi Germany and Soviet Russia were, for many cultural producers, primarily negative object lessons in what might happen in the United States if American democracy was unable to right itself. The coming of war to America resolved the country's economic crises and brought a new sense of unity to U.S. culture. Social revolution suddenly seemed much further away. During the war, revolution even momentarily receded for the Communist Party: the 1944 program of the short-lived CPA was unprecedentedly accommodationist.

On the other hand, the American state grew to an unprecedented size. Millions of men and women serving in uniform experienced firsthand the alternately magnificent, infuriating, and depersonalizing operations of this state. Decisions made by a small number of military planners in Washington could have profound effects on thousands upon thousands of men. And though social revolution seemed a remote possibility, many Americans continued to advocate schemes—including wartime civilian conscription, peacetime economic planning, and federally enforced racial desegregation—that seemed to others, especially on the political right, to imply the powers claimed by totalitarian states. A mass social movement no longer seemed necessary for totalitarianism to triumph. Although the totalitarian state demanded total obedience from all of society, a small number of true believers might be enough to install it.

The celebration of the Russian people played an important role in decoupling the idea of totalitarianism from mass social movements. The universal acclaim granted the Russian people during the war altered assessments of the relationship between the people and the Soviet state. Even the conservative *American Mercury,* a journal unwavering in its denunciation of Soviet Communism as a form of totalitarianism, published two articles that argued that the character of the Russian war effort suggested that the Russian people were actively seeking their freedom.[53]

Chamberlin's wartime writings are a good example of the change in rhetoric about the Russian people even among those most hostile to Soviet Communism. As a prolific writer of journal articles and founder (in November 1941), editor, and regular contributor to the *Russian Review,* Chamberlin left a paper trail that is fascinating to follow. Along with Max Eastman, Eugene Lyons, and Edmund Wilson, Chamberlin was a member of the first American generation to be entranced by and then disenchanted with Soviet Communism. His support for the Soviet Union came early. In 1922, having already become sympathetic to the new Soviet government, Chamberlin set off for Russia. Appointed as Moscow correspondent for the *Christian Science Monitor,* he stayed twelve years and became one of America's most important voices on Russia. For the first decade of his stay, he remained very supportive of the Soviet government. But Stalin's abandonment of the New Economic Policy, the campaign against the kulaks, and the famine of 1932–33 caused the journalist to change his mind. In the middle and late 1930s, Chamberlin, having returned to America, became an noninterventionist and a vocal anticommunist. In his 1937 book, *Collectivism: A False Utopia,* he equated communism with fascism, declaring both to be totalitarian.[54]

During the war Chamberlin abandoned his noninterventionism and came to support, albeit cautiously, the U.S.-Soviet alliance. Throughout this period, he continued to label the Soviet Union totalitarian. But in his writings, the relationship between the Soviet form of government and the Russian people changed radically between 1941 and 1945. In July 1941 Chamberlin contributed to the *New York Times Magazine* a piece, entitled "Russia—The Sprawling Giant," that set out to explain the Soviet Union in terms of the social psychology and national characteristics of its peoples: "In judging the Russian national character and psychology it is important to remember that Russia missed the direct effect of three movements which greatly contributed to the liberation of the individual personality, namely, the Reformation, the Renaissance, and the French Revolution. Moreover, those elements which counterbalanced absolute sovereignty in other European States, such as the existence of a powerful nobility or free cities or a substantial class of yeomanry, were absent in Russia." Chamberlin assured his readers that "there are certain traits of Russian personality—even of soul—which persist throughout the greatest of external shocks." Singling out "perfectionism" and "abstract thinking," he suggested that communism was particularly suited for "the Russian mind," whereas liberalism and skepticism were totally foreign to it.[55]

In the first issue of the *Russian Review* in November 1941, Chamberlin repeated some of these themes. Once again, he noted that "skepticism and liberalism have never penetrated deeply into the Russian national consciousness." As the Russians had, by November 1941, put up significant resistance to the Nazi onslaught, Chamberlin took a stab at explaining their success. He cited the indoctrination of young Russians under the Soviet system and the "Russian national spirit" as important contributing factors.[56]

Four months later, in a February 1942 article in the *Atlantic Monthly* entitled "Russia: An American Problem," Chamberlin expressed doubts about the future of American-Soviet cooperation because of the two nations' different national characters. "If the typical figure in America's century of westward expansion and settlement was the pioneer frontiersman, going where he chose," he wrote, "Russia's settlers of new territory in the East often went under compulsion and sometimes literally in chains. . . . Contrasted national psychologies are the natural outgrowth of such strongly different political systems." As a result, he warned, "America and Russia have never understood each other well."[57]

Early in the Russo-German conflict, then, Chamberlin linked Russian national character to the Soviet political system he so despised and to Russia's success at war. The people and the system were one, a connection reinforced by Soviet indoctrination. These linkages continued in Chamberlin's writing through mid-1942. In the April 1942 issue of the *Russian Review,* he argued that Russia's victories on the battlefield were due in large part to its totalitarian system and its successful indoctrination of the younger generation. He devoted an August 1942 piece in the *Christian Century* to his argument that totalitarianism was the cause of Soviet success in war and that America should thus view Russian victories in a "cool-headed" fashion.[58]

But Chamberlin's equation of the Russian people and Russian military effort with the Soviet system began to loosen in the autumn of 1942. In the 14 November issue of the *Saturday Evening Post,* he once again noted that the "national temperaments" of the American and Russian people were formed under "utterly contrasting circumstances." Absent, however, was any suggestion that this difference in temperaments made the Russian people desire communism. Indeed, Chamberlin implied that the Russian people could not have desired the behavior of the Soviet state since the revolution. "The price which [the Soviet experiment] has exacted, in human lives and human liberty," he wrote, "is a heavy one, much heavier than any people would voluntarily pay." He concluded this essay with an unusually enthusiastic celebration of the Russian people at war: "At this historic anniversary we send to the Russian people our warmest hope for full success in the struggle against Nazi enslavement." In the Autumn 1942 issue of the *Russian Review,* he questioned the idea, which he had supported previously, that Russian military success could be attributed to the Soviet system.[59]

In 1943 the antithesis between the Soviet regime and the Russian people grew still stronger in Chamberlin's writings. "What should be recognized," he observed in the March 1943 issue of *Harper's,*

is that the Russian people as a whole have not been associated with the intrigues and killings that reflected the fierce struggle for power at the top, or with many acts of government ruthlessness. The explorer in the Arctic, the scientist in his laboratory, the worker, the farmer, the teacher had no concern with the trials and the purge. Such a mass atrocity as the "liquidation of the kulaks as a class" was abhorrent to most of the peasants, as I know from personal observation. But they could do nothing to prevent it, just as the decent German now can do nothing to prevent the Gestapo from liquidating the Jews as a race. Because of the appalling concentration of power in the totalitarian state there has perhaps never been an age in human history when so few could inflict so much suffering on so many.[60]

In an article and a book review in the Spring 1943 issue of the *Russian Review,* he paid tribute to "the heroic resistance" and "self-sacrificing devotion of the Russian people" and to the "successful and important contribution to the world struggle against Hitlerism" of a Russian army, "more national, less and less specifically 'Red.'"[61]

Through early 1942 Chamberlin had believed that the very different paths of national development taken by Russians and Americans had led to opposite national temperaments that prevented real understanding between the two peoples. By late 1943 he had amended this view. In the Autumn 1943 issue of the *Russian Review,* he suggested that "whatever suspicious restraints may be imposed by officialdom, the average Russian is friendly toward Americans and appreciative of the help which America has given to Russia in its struggle against invasion."[62] Although Chamberlin still argued that the differences between American and Russian political development had a negative effect on the two countries' relationship, the difficulty was now the Soviet state, not the Russian national temperament: "Certain problems of Russian-American relations are rooted in the differing historical traditions and political institutions of the two countries. The free give-and-take that is possible between unofficial groups of Americans and citizens of other democracies is not feasible with Russians as long as dictatorship remains."[63]

In February 1944, in a negative answer to the *American Mercury*'s question, "Can Stalin's Russia Go Democratic?," Chamberlin held out hope for a democratic Russia but maintained that such a land would no longer be Stalin's at all. Part of his argument was an invocation of the Russian past that was strikingly different from that of only two years earlier. "There is a tradition of freedom as well as a tradition of oppression and absolutism in the Russian past," he explained. "There was the wild Cossack freedom of the Russian frontier that finds expression in the stormy careers of chieftains like Razin and Pugachev and Khmelnitsky. There was the reasoned freedom of Russia's thinkers and humanists of the nineteenth century. There was the local political freedom of the *mir* and the *zemstvo* under the Tsars." What stood in the way of the triumph of this tradition was not the greater strength of the tradition of absolutism but the "more and more arbitrary personal dictatorship" of Stalin.[64] An April 1944 article in *Harper's,* "Information, *Please,* about Russia," further emphasized the positive aspects of

Russia's past. Contending that much that was written about Russia was inaccurate, Chamberlin spent as much space correcting exaggerations about the evils of tsarist Russia as he did criticizing excessive praise for the Soviet system.

In an article in the Spring 1944 issue of the *Russian Review,* Chamberlin continued to write of the Soviet state as an imposition on the Russian people. The great power of the state simply did not reflect the traditions of the Russian nation. It was one of the "curious paradoxes of Russia's future" that "the bitter misery of tens of millions of the Soviet peoples has been accompanied by an immense increase in the prospective power, prestige, and influence of the Soviet state."[65]

By 1944 the change in Chamberlin's representations of the Russian people was complete. Throughout the war he held fast to the view that Soviet Communism was a form of totalitarianism as antithetical to democracy as Nazism. But his sense of the relationship of the Soviet system to the Russian people changed profoundly. From 1941 through early 1942 Chamberlin had continued to link the Russian people, their national characteristics, and their struggle against Germany to the system he so hated. Two years later, however, he regarded the Soviet system as an imposition on the heroic Russian people.

Chamberlin's view at the end of the war that the Russian people fundamentally opposed the Soviet regime, though new for him, had long been held by others.[66] But U.S. representations of the Russian people at war made his prewar opinions much more difficult to maintain by 1945. Although American cultural producers had deep disagreements about the Soviet state, there was almost unanimity among them that the Russian people desired freedom and were willing to fight for it. This struggle of the Russian people reinforced the view of optimists like Sorokin that a more democratic Soviet Union would emerge after the war. For those who believed that Soviet Communism was as totalitarian as German Nazism, however, the apparent Russian desire for freedom contributed to the emerging idea that a nation could be enslaved by totalitarianism even without mass support for a totalitarian state.

9 A BOOT STAMPING ON A HUMAN FACE—FOREVER TOTALITARIANISM AS NIGHTMARE IN POSTWAR AMERICA

As World War II came to a close, William Henry Chamberlin looked back angrily on the Soviet alliance: "Here is a war that is supposedly fought against totalitarianism. But it has made the first of the totalitarian states, the Soviet Union, the strongest land power in Europe and in Asia. It has extended the realm of totalitarianism to include large areas of eastern and possibly central Europe and, in all likelihood, much of East Asia."[1] However, Chamberlin's indignation was misplaced. Whatever World War II had been fought against—and there were many different ideas of what the greater enemy beyond the armies of the Axis nations was—few U.S. observers had claimed, after the collapse of the Nazi-Soviet Pact, that it was waged against totalitarianism. Indeed, "totalitarian" could not have been used to describe the enemy in a war in which the United States was allied with Soviet Russia, because by 1941 "totalitarianism" was almost invariably used to link German Nazism and Soviet Communism.

The concept of totalitarianism was largely dormant during the war, but afterward it quickly came to even greater prominence in Cold War America, far exceeding the large role it had played during the years leading up to Pearl Harbor. After 1945, it became far and away the dominant foundation for American understandings of dictatorship. The association of totalitarianism with the Cold War became so great that all of the scholarly and public debates over the usefulness of the term that raged in the last four decades of the twentieth century were limned by Cold War politics.[2] Yet, as this study has shown, we misunderstand the origins of the idea of totalitarianism— and misread American political culture in the 1930s and early 1940s—if we make the common mistake of regarding it as a product of the Cold War.

Nevertheless, the idea of totalitarianism was extraordinarily useful for U.S. supporters of the Cold War. The revival of the concept could clearly link America's erstwhile ally, the Soviet Union, with its recently defeated foe, Nazi Germany. Not surprisingly, as relations between the United States and the USSR soured after World War II, "totalitarianism" developed ever greater currency in American public and academic discourse, a rise that culminated in the 1950s with the publication of the generally considered classic texts on totalitarianism, Hannah Arendt's *Origins of Totalitarianism* (1951) and Carl Friedrich and Zbigniew Brzezinski's *Totalitarian Dictatorship and Autocracy* (1956).

This final chapter will not attempt to paint a complete portrait of postwar American understandings of Soviet Communism and their meanings for democracy; whole volumes could be (and have been) written on that subject.[3] Instead, it will focus more narrowly on the postwar revival of the concept of totalitarianism. In particular, it traces the foundations of three texts whose enormous popularity with both American intellectuals and the general public during the late 1940s and early 1950s places them at the heart of any investigation of postwar views of totalitarianism: Arthur Schlesinger Jr.'s *The Vital Center: The Politics of Freedom* (1949), George Orwell's *Nineteen Eighty-Four* (1949), and Arendt's *Origins of Totalitarianism*.

These three books are generally considered to be monuments of the Cold War era. Indeed, they are often treated as the *beginning* of a cultural discussion of totalitarianism. Though it is certainly correct to regard them as products of the early Cold War, understanding them only as such has obscured the many ways in which they continued the long-standing cultural conversation about dictatorship that this study has considered. By placing them at the end of this book, I hope to highlight the ways in which they resembled—and the ways in which they differed from—earlier understandings of totalitarianism and dictatorship more generally. And though this chapter, with its more or less exclusive focus on the materials of intellectual history, looks somewhat different from the rest of the book, its foundation remains the complicated, multifaceted cultural conversation about dictatorship with which this study is concerned.

By 1945 the term "totalitarianism" had established a firm foothold in American political culture. Its meaning had become in some ways extremely clear, and yet in others it remained entirely protean. What was unambiguous about it was that it referred to Nazi Germany *and* the Soviet Union, and that it was highly pejorative. These now settled issues had, as we have seen, once been open to debate. As the term's near disappearance from official and semi-official U.S. World War II propaganda and its equally frequent use by opponents of the Soviet alliance attest, the core linkage of Nazism and Stalinism was firmly established by the mid-1940s. Those who denied the linkage avoided the term.

The protean quality of "totalitarianism" can be seen in virtually every other aspect of the term. Some argued that totalitarianism was the product of the masses; others that it was the creation of a small ruling oligarchy. Some saw it as an essentially foreign phenomenon, tied to other cultures and other lands; others believed that it was a universal phenomenon, as likely to happen in the United States as anywhere else. Some surmised that it was the product of modernity, others that it represented a revolt against modernity. Despite general acknowledgment that the term referred to Nazism and Stalinism, few agreed on the precise characteristics that linked these regimes or on what other regimes might also fall into the category. With the collapse of Fascist Italy, there was no longer any major nation or political movement that actually called itself totalitarian, although Arthur Koestler, George Orwell, and other authors of antitotalitarian fictions would continue to put the word in the mouths of its alleged proponents. The absence of explicit supporters of totalitarianism made the term fundamentally unlike fascism, communism, and even racism, and added to the concept's vagueness.

One meaningful trend in U.S. understandings of totalitarianism had taken place during World War II, a trend that was reflected in Chamberlin's growing acceptance of the goodness of the Russian people. Whereas the most important American views of totalitarianism before Pearl Harbor had tended to see the masses themselves as responsible for these regimes, during the war blame shifted to smaller leadership groups, albeit with some vagueness about how best to characterize them. Celebrations of the Russian people, the representation of the Germans as themselves victims of Nazism, and the experience of the wartime American state all led cultural producers to associate totalitarianism less with mass movements and more with a small leadership group in charge of an all-powerful state. Nevertheless, mass politics was still seen as an essential aspect of these regimes; there was no return to the dictator-centered views of the 1920s and early 1930s. After World War II a tension existed in most American understandings of totalitarianism between the role of whatever leadership groups were thought to be responsible for creating the regimes and the role of the masses, whose political support tended to be seen as an essential component of totalitarianism.

Analysts in the decade after World War II did not resolve the conundrums that lay at the heart of the concept of totalitarianism in American political culture. Despite the flurry of books and articles written on the subject, and the newly central place of totalitarianism in American thought, public culture, and government policy-making, no single paradigmatic understanding of the phenomenon would emerge until at least the 1956 publication of Friedrich and Brzezinski's *Totalitarian Dictatorship and Autocracy*, which established a clear, if controversial, series of empirical criteria for determining whether a regime was totalitarian.[4] From this perspective, Schlesinger, Orwell, and Arendt belonged to the earlier period of thinking about dictatorship.

Rather than a common understanding of the phenomenon itself, what united American thought about totalitarianism in the half decade or so after World War II was both shared political concerns and a shared mood. Although they evolved in subtle but important ways, the underlying concerns about totalitarianism remained relatively unchanged from the late 1930s: among them were fears about modernity, about the growth of the state, about newly emerging forms of mass politics, about the long-run ability of capitalism to avoid economic catastrophe, about the international intentions of dictatorial regimes (after 1945, chiefly the Soviet Union), and about the ability of democracy to respond to these challenges.

The shared concerns may have been rooted in prewar culture, but the common mood was new. A deep, and at times horrific, pessimism marks the works on totalitarianism that gained popularity in America during this period. Schlesinger, Orwell, and Arendt all saw totalitarianism as extraordinarily virulent: once a society succumbed to it, there might be no way for it to change, absent outside intervention. Moreover, all three authors seemed to suggest that democracy, at least as it was currently practiced in America, might not be capable of withstanding totalitarian pressures from within and without. Although Schlesinger, Orwell, and Arendt disagreed on many things, they each presented totalitarianism as a nightmarish iron trap that destroyed all vestiges of individuality in its subjects, a view most graphically captured in *Nineteen Eighty-Four*. As O'Brien, a member of the Inner Party, tortures the novel's protagonist Winston Smith, he explains the goals and methods of the regime. "If you want a picture of the future," he tells Winston, "imagine a boot stamping on a human face—forever."[5]

In the half century since the publication of *Nineteen Eighty-Four* and *Origins of Totalitarianism*, Americans have so strongly associated totalitarianism with this nightmarish pessimism that we tend to take it for granted as an essential aspect of its meaning. Yet this pessimistic mood differed markedly from the ultimate optimism expressed in most wartime and even depression-era conceptions of the European dictatorships. Official and semi-official views of Nazi Germany during the war tended to be optimistic both about the survival of "good Germans," resisting the regime no matter how ineffectually, and about the possibilities of postwar reform. Even an author like Richard Brickner, who believed the German nation to be clinically paranoid, felt strongly that it was curable. What underlaid this optimism about Germany's future was faith, or at least a stated faith, in democracy and ultimately in human nature.

Even in the depths of the Great Depression, warnings about dictatorship tended to conclude with affirmations of the strength and superiority of democracy. The most pessimistic works tended to find reasons for hope. Although Sinclair Lewis's *It Can't Happen Here* (1935) sees little prospect for political change once America has fallen victim to dictatorship, the author still finds solace in the continued existence of men such as its protagonist, the almost stereotypical New England curmudgeon, Doremus Jessup. The few public voices declaring that dictatorship might actually defeat democracy, such as Lawrence Dennis's prediction of a fascist America or Charles Lindbergh's prophecy of Germany's triumph over France and England, tended to suggest that such victory would be a good thing.

Although the dominant American discourse about democracy and dictatorship remained optimistic during World War II, a diverse series of deeply pessimistic analyses of the challenges of dictatorship appeared in print, including James Burnham's *The Managerial Revolution* (1941), Joseph Schumpeter's *Capitalism, Socialism, and Democracy* (1942), Bruno Bettelheim's "Individual and Mass Behavior in Extreme Situations" (1943), Reinhold Niebuhr's *The Children of Light and the Children of Darkness* (1944), and Friedrich Hayek's *Road to Serfdom* (1944). Each of these works cut against the grain of wartime optimism. In very different ways, each questioned the ability of American democracy to defeat modern dictatorship at home or abroad or to undo the social damage that it caused. Each also reflected the intellectual shift from seeing the masses themselves as responsible for dictatorship to viewing smaller leadership groups as playing a more pivotal role. None of these works was wildly original; each reproduced ideas that the author—or someone else—had previously published, though often they applied these ideas for the first time to the problem of modern dictatorship. Although these works enjoyed some popularity during the war, only after 1945 would each gain a kind of canonical status and prove enormously influential. By examining them closely, we can see the roots of many new aspects of postwar American visions of totalitarianism.

Pessimistic Precursors

After the war James Burnham would become, in the words of the historian of American conservatism George Nash, "the most influential right-wing critic of liberal foreign policy."[6] In the early 1940s, however, he was still nominally a man of the left. The son of a wealthy Chicago industrialist, he studied with T. S. Eliot and began his career as a decidedly apolitical literary theorist. Soon after joining the philosophy faculty at New York University (NYU) in 1930, Burnham developed an interest in Marxism, as he became politically and intellectually close to NYU colleague Sidney Hook, who was trying to create a non-Stalinist, but still revolutionary, Marxist political movement. While Hook began to abandon revolutionary Marxism in the mid-1930s, Burnham became a key figure on the ever-shifting ground of the sectarian left as a leading Trotskyist ideologue. A ferocious polemicist, his slashing argumentative style helped constitute the milieu of 1930s Trotskyism, a small, intellectually rigorous movement. Absolutely convinced of their singular correctness, Trotskyists spent endless energy excoriating everyone else on the left, whether CP members and fellow travelers for supporting the "degenerated workers' state" of Stalinism, or other anti-Stalinist leftists, whose suspicions of the Soviet Union extended to the entire Leninist legacy.[7]

Despite his prominence in American Trotskyism, Burnham's commitment to Marxism was always tinged with philosophical doubt. Many doctrines of Marxism—including dialectical materialism, the withering away of the state, and the ultimate achievement of a classless society—left him unconvinced. As John Diggins has observed, Burnham became a communist less out of philosophical conviction than out of a sense of desperation about modern capitalism. It is thus not surprising that in the late 1930s he became embroiled in a major theoretical debate with Trotsky himself. Subscribing to the Marxist-Leninist view that the only two possible structures for modern societies were capitalism or socialism, Trotsky had to account for the USSR under Stalin: Was this society heading toward socialism or back to capitalism? Trotsky's description of the Soviet Union as a "degenerated worker's state" suggested that it was an imperfect form of socialism. In 1937 Burnham was one of a number of American Trotskyists who suggested that the USSR properly belonged in a third category. Adapting 1920s anarchist criticisms of Bolshevism that posited that the Soviet Union had created a "new class" of bureaucrats, Burnham argued that the Soviet regime was neither a worker's state nor a bourgeois state, but rather a bureaucratic one. Reprimanding Burnham, Trotsky denied that such a third possibility existed.[8]

Like so many others in the revolutionary left, Burnham experienced a moment of crisis after the signing of the Nazi-Soviet Pact in the summer of 1939. The Trotskyists' hatred of Stalin and their hardheaded understanding of his foreign policy had prepared them for the pact, and they were less surprised by it than anyone else on the American left. Burnham and others, however, were shocked when Trotsky himself announced his support for the Soviet invasion of Poland in September. A degenerated workers' state was still a workers' state, he proclaimed, and thus all loyal Marxist-Leninists had to rise to the defense of the Soviet Union at war. In opposition to this view, Burnham, Max Shachtman, and others left the orthodox American Trotskyist party, the Socialist Workers Party, to found the Workers Party (WP). The WP argued that the USSR was an example of "bureaucratic collectivism," a view nearly identical to the one for which Trotsky had criticized Burnham a few years earlier. Burnham soon abandoned Trotskyism altogether and began to move away from Marxism and the left. The first major public step in this process was his publication of *The Managerial Revolution* in early 1941.[9]

Having reached the conclusion that Trotskyism could not explain the great events of the day, Burnham set out to report, in the words of his book's subtitle, "What Is Happening in the World." *The Managerial Revolution* describes a great social transformation that was taking place around the world. As Marxists had predicted, a worldwide revolution was unseating the bourgeoisie as the ruling class. However, the bourgeoisie was not being replaced by the proletariat, but rather by a new class of "managers," a term Burnham uses broadly to include both corporate executives and governmental administrators and bureaucrats. Like capitalism, but unlike the Marxist vision of communism that Burnham now dismissed as a pipe dream, the emerging managerial economy would be based on exploitation. But instead of individual capitalists exploiting the working class, the state would organize the means of production for control by the managers; the "private exploitation" of capitalism would be replaced by "corporate exploitation." The managerial revolution was inevitable in part because managerial economies could solve the contradictions that inevitably plagued capitalism, eliminating such perennial problems as mass unemployment.[10]

Although Burnham had rejected Trotskyism, the tone of his writing remained largely unchanged. Neither his struggles with Trotsky nor his rejection of his earlier worldview had increased his sense of humility or fallibility. Throughout *The Managerial Revolution,* Burnham claims that he is engaging in a rigorously scientific study, that he refuses to let sentiment or emotions get in the way of the cold, hard facts of the world. Like his earlier works, *The Managerial Revolution* combines a rhetoric of objectivity with blustering self-assurance and a fiercely polemical tone.

Burnham had arrived at his theory of the managerial revolution as an alternative understanding of Stalinism, now that he had come to see orthodox Trotskyism as a hopeless muddle. As might be expected, the Soviet Union was his prime example of a managerial economy, though it was far from his only example. Both Fascist Italy and Nazi Germany were managerial states. Like the idea of totalitarianism, Burnham's managerial revolution could explain the Nazi-Soviet Pact, which contradicted many conventional understandings of the ideological relationship between Nazism and communism. The managerial revolution not only made sense of the pact, it practically required the agreement as a means for managerial society to spread across the globe. Burnham's managerial revolution also shared with theories of totalitarianism the tendency to downplay the role of the dictator. For Burnham, economic forces, not great or terrible men, drove history. His analysis resembled theories of totalitarianism in another important way: just as few regimes identified as totalitarian actually lay claim to the title, none of Burnham's managerial states called themselves "managerial." This did not trouble Burnham, who retained from his days as a Trotskyist ideologue a deeply teleological sense of history. The playing out of the managerial revolution was a historical necessity; it would take place whether or not the managers were even aware of it.

But Burnham's managerial revolution was not just another theory of totalitarianism. Indeed, he carefully distinguished the two. Though acknowledging that the three most developed managerial societies—Germany, Italy, and the Soviet Union—were all totalitarian dictatorships, he felt that the term "totalitarian" was so full of "moral and emotional considerations" that it hindered "scientific understanding." Burnham even went so far as to argue that American objections to totalitarianism were really objections to foreignness: "It is not totalitarianism but Russian or German, in general 'foreign' totalitarianism that is being objected to; 100% American totalitarianism would not be objectionable." More importantly, dictatorship was only a necessary stage through which managerial society would move, just as bourgeois society had done under the absolute monarchies of early modern Europe.[11]

Although Burnham predicted that managerial totalitarianism would be replaced by managerial democracy, his view of the future was hardly optimistic. He rejected the equation of democracy with freedom, liberty, or majority rule—all of which, in his view, were too vague for clarity—and defined as democratic any system in which the majority defined policy and in

which those holding minority opinions had the freedom to express themselves and thus the possibility of becoming the majority. Such systems were,
from Burnham's perspective, largely a sham: the ruling class—the bourgeoisie under capitalism or the managers under managerial society—controlled the significant, economic aspects of social life. Democracy existed
because it was always useful for the ruling class to establish an outlet
for dissent once the economic system was firmly in place. Though confident that some type of democracy would eventually appear in managerial
society, Burnham hesitated to specify its form. Parliament, political parties,
and the other institutions of bourgeois democracy seemed to him ill-suited
to the managers' interests. For supporters of democracy, the only certainty
was that capitalist democracy was already doomed.[12]

Applying this analysis to the United States as well as to Europe, Burnham argued that the New Deal represented the beginning of the managerial revolution in America. It differed from Stalinism and Nazism chiefly
in being more primitive. But, like those regimes, it transferred power from
capitalists to public and private managers and "curbed" the masses by tying
them closer to the state. Even the labor movement came to rely more on
the state than it ever had before. Predictably, managers liked the New
Deal, whereas capitalists hated it. This was, of course, not the doing of
Roosevelt, a "brilliant and demogogic popular politician," but rather of
the impersonal "inner structural drives of modern society." The changes
wrought by the New Deal were, like all significant changes, inevitable.
The missing piece of the puzzle in the United States was a revolutionary
mass movement, like Nazism in Germany or Communism in the USSR, to
complete the managerial transformation. Burnham boldly claimed that old
slogans such as "liberty," "free enterprise," "the American way," and "opportunity" had forever lost their power for the American masses. The 1940
presidential election would be the last, or at best the penultimate, presidential election in American history. Although he left open the possibility
that the United States might achieve a managerial society without the brutality and purges experienced abroad, he suggested that in all likelihood
America's path to the society of the future would resemble Russia's and
Germany's.[13]

Once the revolution was complete around the world, a process hastened
by the war that had already begun in Europe and Asia, Burnham predicted
that the world would be ruled by three "super-states," centered around the
beneficiaries of the present war: Germany, the United States, and Japan.
Economic power dictated this much. Smaller sovereign states would simply
disappear. Future wars would be fought among the super-states over the

periphery. Great Britain, for instance, could end up being controlled by Germany or the United States.[14]

In *The Managerial Revolution,* Burnham carefully avoided stating his feelings about the changes he boldly forecast. He painted a grim picture but repeatedly argued that this was a scientific study that left no room for moralizing. Toward the end of the book, he noted in passing that "my personal interests, material as well as moral, and my hopes are in conflict with the conclusions of this theory." The truth of the managerial revolution was "a function not of belief, but of evidence." Nevertheless, his tone of predictive certainty and his rigidly teleological view of world history inevitably blurred the line between "is" and "ought." Despite his concluding protestations, Burnham often sounded a bit like a mad scientist in a Universal horror film, urging innocent, less sophisticated onlookers to accept their inevitable fate: "The world of tomorrow will be very different from yesterday's; but if we choose to accept it—and most will accept it, whether or not they choose—there will be some satisfaction in doing so in terms of realities, not illusions."[15]

The Managerial Revolution was a surprise best-seller in early 1941. It garnered enormous attention not only from scholars and politically active intellectuals, but also from a much broader audience. It received generally favorable notices in the popular press and apparently appealed to American businessmen. Burnham's publisher, John Day, proudly announced that managers were buying and reading the book. Economist Lincoln Gordon declared that "the volume is probably the most widely read essay in social theory and the philosophy of history to appear in recent years." Despite its popularity, readers had a hard time placing the book: some accepted Burnham's rhetoric of hard-nosed objectivity; others insisted that it represented a new form of Marxist analysis; still others suggested that Burnham was preaching a form of fascism.[16]

The initial success of *The Managerial Revolution* had much to do with the particular moment when it was published. During the period of the Nazi-Soviet Pact, unlike the years after Pearl Harbor, pessimistic assessments of the world scene were fairly common. However, with the German invasion of the USSR in June 1941, world events shifted. As the United States began to gear up for war, discursive space for Burnham's pessimism began to wane. As political scientist Peter Odegard noted on the eve of Pearl Harbor: "We need to be reminded again and again that 'democracy' and the 'democratic way of life' are not impoverished eighteenth-century symbols signifying nothing to a world in the throes of a managerial revolution. Democracy must restore, revive, or win anew faith in its purpose and its destiny; for if such faith is lacking we face inevitable defeat." Writing in 1942, Lincoln Gordon was more direct in his criticism of Burnham and suggested that the book was a dangerous passing fancy: "In the perspective of the world struggle to which we are now committed, the effect of any broad acceptance of Burnham's thesis among influential groups is clearly defeatist. It is perhaps not unreasonable to suppose that had this book been published after Pearl Harbor, the response would have been far less sympathetic." Indeed, after America entered the war Burnham's once fashionable thesis became a frequent punching bag for defenders of democracy and even for some dissenting pessimists.[17]

Like Burnham's book, Joseph Schumpeter's *Capitalism, Socialism, and Democracy* received surprising attention when it was published in 1942. Unlike Burnham, who was in the middle of his worklife and was just becoming a conservative, Schumpeter was reaching the end of a long, distinguished career in economics. Born in 1883 in Moravia, Schumpeter had spent his early life in Austria, teaching economics at the University of Graz in the 1910s, briefly serving as minister of finance of the postwar Austrian government in 1919, and engaging in private banking in the early 1920s. In 1925 he moved to Germany, where he accepted a post teaching economics at Bonn. Failing to get a more prestigious appointment at Berlin, Schumpeter left Germany in 1932 to take a position in the economics department at Harvard; he remained there until his death in 1950.[18]

Although by no means a public figure in the United States, Schumpeter—by the start of the 1940s—had developed a reputation in the field of economics as a brilliant, rigorous thinker and a fierce, conservative defender of free market capitalism against the rising tide of Keynesianism in economic thought and the New Deal in public policy. His highly technical writings seem to have been little read outside his own profession. That would change with the publication of *Capitalism, Socialism, and Democracy* in 1942.

Schumpeter had been working on the volume since 1939, though many of its principal concepts had appeared in his essays as early as 1918.[19] Like Burnham, Schumpeter wrote his most famous book during a period of personal and political despair. An Anglophile in his youth, Schumpeter had come to admire Germany in the interwar period. In the last two decades of his life, he described himself as a "cultivated conservative," which seems to have meant that he longed for Europe as it had existed before 1914. For all his brilliance, Schumpeter could be obtuse when analyzing quotidian politics. He seems to have had no inkling of the rise of Adolf Hitler as he left Germany in 1932. Throughout the 1930s Schumpeter had no particular ideological sympathy for Nazism. However, his hatred of the Soviet Union and the new European order created by the Versailles treaty, as well as his fear that U.S. participation in a war would accelerate the drift toward socialism that he saw in the New Deal, led him to embrace a form of noninterventionism that was at least akin to Nazi sympathy. Schumpeter was very open about his political views, which put him at odds with his colleagues at Harvard, and with the larger public mood, during the years in which he was writing *Capitalism, Socialism, and Democracy*.[20]

These political opinions are reflected only obliquely in his book. As nearly all reviewers noted at the time—and as later generations of students have since learned—its central argument can be summarized in three sentences: Capitalism, though wildly successful, will inevitably be replaced by socialism. Socialism is a workable economic system that can be as efficient as capitalism. Socialism and democracy are compatible. Schumpeter disagreed with all the standard positions about the relationship between the three subjects in the book's title. Though agreeing with Marx that capitalism was doomed, Schumpeter explicitly rejected nearly every other aspect of Marxism, including the theory of social classes, the labor theory of value, the growing impoverishment of the proletariat under capitalism, and the materialist conception of history. Unlike Marx, Schumpeter believed that under capitalism prosperity would continue to increase.[21]

Yet Schumpeter disagreed with the champions of capitalism. Although he regarded capitalism as an extraordinary and continuing economic success, he was convinced that it would be replaced by socialism. In a famous expression, he declared that the "essential fact" about capitalism was "Creative Destruction": capitalism "incessantly revolutionizes the economic structure *from within,* incessantly destroying the old one, incessantly creating a new one." This dynamism would prevent capitalism from stagnating, as many, including Schumpeter's Keynesian colleague Alvin Hansen, believed it would. What actually doomed capitalism was its success. Capitalism, according to Schumpeter, rationalizes social life, which had previously been dominated by various irrational beliefs, institutions, and practices. This process of rationalization is driven by entrepreneurial innovation. Eventually, small firms fall by the wayside and monopolies rise in their stead. Unlike most free market economists, Schumpeter argued that, economically speaking, monopolies are not bad for capitalism; they might even spur innovation and lower prices.[22]

As capitalism succeeds, however, entrepreneurship and innovation become increasingly mechanized and routine. In addition, capitalism, as a process of rationalization, destroys all the old, essentially irrational, political institutions of the feudal order. Unfortunately, these institutions are necessary to provide political protection for the bourgeoisie, which is essentially unheroic and incapable of real political leadership. Once these protecting institutions are destroyed, the bourgeoisie has neither the will nor the ability to defend the capitalist order. Private monopolies will prove politically unpopular and support for capitalism will drop, especially among intellectuals and the growing labor movement, which is largely in their thrall. This social atmosphere, itself created by capitalism, will inevitably result in the rise of socialism.[23]

Schumpeter next attempted to demonstrate that socialism can work. He defined socialism as "an institutional pattern in which the control over means of production and over production itself is vested with a central authority—or, as we may say, in which . . . the economic affairs of society belong to the public and not the private sphere." Schumpeter acknowledged that this definition excluded many accepted forms of socialism, among them guild socialism and syndicalism, and that, in asserting that socialism can work, he was not making any claims for the Soviet version of it. Indeed, the entire section on socialism is theoretical. Schumpeter carefully disproved standard objections to the efficiency of socialism—such as the need to determine prices without a market—but he did so without reference to any extant economic system.[24]

Finally, Schumpeter set out to prove the compatibility of socialism and democracy. To do so, he proposed a new definition of democracy. What he called the "classical doctrine of democracy" was grounded in notions of the common good or the will of the people. Objecting to these descriptions as hopelessly vague, he instead offered a characterization of democracy based completely on process: "The democratic method is that institutional arrangement for arriving at political decisions in which individuals acquire the power to decide by means of a competitive struggle for the people's vote." In this sense, he concluded, socialism and democracy are entirely compatible, especially if economic decision-making is removed from any political control. Although socialism and democracy are compatible, he argued, they do not have any particular affinity for one another. Schumpeter explained the limitations of his conclusions: "As a matter of practical necessity, socialist democracy may turn out to be more of a sham than capitalist democracy ever was. In any case, that democracy will not mean increased personal freedom. And . . . it will mean no closer approximation to the ideals enshrined in the classical doctrine."[25]

In many ways, the future worlds conjured up by Schumpeter and Burnham were similar. Both scholars recognized the growing power of large organizations. Broadly speaking, Schumpeter envisioned what Burnham would call "managers" replacing entrepreneurs as the guiding figures in the economy. Whereas Burnham disparaged democracy, Schumpeter suggested that it could continue, but only in a form barely recognizable to most Americans. Burnham, somewhat mercurially, never clarified his feelings about the managerial revolution, though he obviously admired its achievements and enjoyed playing the role of its prophet. Schumpeter, ever the scientist, tried to render an "objective" judgment about the future possibilities for capitalism, socialism, and democracy. Though one reviewer called him "a capitalistic Jeremiah," *Capitalism, Socialism, and Democracy* is, at least in tone, more an occasionally ironic thought experiment than a jeremiad.[26]

Schumpeter viewed *Capitalism, Socialism, and Democracy* as essentially speculative and popular; he consequently spent the last years of his life disappointed that it, rather than one of his more "scientific" works, had brought him fame. Nevertheless, the book was hardly a light read. It combined vast erudition with occasionally technical economic analysis and flashes of sardonic wit. One generally positive review began by declaring, "This is a provocative book written in a style which is likely to repel American readers." Though read outside of his discipline, Schumpeter's book, at least initially, did not attract the wide audience that Burnham's had. This was, in part, a matter of timing. If 1941 was the perfect year to paint a dark picture of the world's future, 1942, with the United States at war, was much less hospitable to such speculation. Nearly everyone who reviewed the first edition of *Capitalism, Socialism, and Democracy* expressed admiration for its erudition but disagreed on what it meant. "One begins to wonder whether the whole book is not a deep satire," observed one critic after describing its discussion of intellectuals and the labor movement. Virtually no one, even the book's many admirers, was convinced by its larger arguments. Only with the publication of the second edition in 1947 did the work receive wide acclaim; by the publication of the third and last edition in 1950, it had became an enormous success.[27] Like Burnham, Schumpeter would emerge as a major voice during the postwar period and an important influence on Cold War–era theories of totalitarianism in the United States.

Bruno Bettelheim's study of concentration camp inmates worked its way more quietly into public discourse. Bettelheim was born into an assimilated, upper-middle class Jewish family in Vienna in 1903. Employed for years in his father's lumber company, he completed his doctoral degree in philosophy in 1938. Only late in his studies did he begin to show an interest in psychoanalysis, with which he would later be so closely associated. Immediately after the Anschluss, Bettelheim and his wife attempted to leave Austria for Czechoslovakia or Hungary but were turned back at the border. Eventually, his wife was able to get out, but Bettelheim's passport was confiscated and he was ordered to return to Vienna. A series of arrests and police interrogations culminated, in May 1938, in three days in prison and then a transfer to the concentration camp at Dachau. Why Bettelheim was arrested is still unknown. Perhaps it was because he had been a member of the Austrian Social Democratic Party, which fought for Austrian independence, and had opposed Austria's own authoritarian government in the mid-1930s. The fact that his grandfather was apparently an officer with the Rothschild Bank may have been a factor. Or he may have simply fallen victim to a random street sweep or have been denounced by an associate. At any rate, he was not sent to Dachau solely on the basis of his Jewishness; the mass shipment of Jews to concentrations camps was still some years away.[28]

Bettelheim spent almost a year in the camps, first in Dachau and later in Buchenwald. Dachau and Buchenwald were not extermination camps—the first of these would not be constructed until 1942—but they were nonetheless horrific places. Prisoners had to endure meaningless hard labor, were regularly tortured both physically and psychologically, and could at any time be arbitrarily shot by Gestapo guards. To keep his mind busy and endure the brutal living conditions, Bettelheim began to study the psychological effects of camp life on his fellow prisoners, though, of course, he was unable to record his data or analyses.[29] He was released in April 1939. Bettelheim attributed his discharge to influential friends in the United States who had pressured the State Department to intercede. Although it was extremely difficult to gain release from the camps, Bettelheim's case is hardly unique. Before the war started, the Nazis haphazardly freed a steady trickle of prisoners, often from among those labeled "politicals." Bettelheim traveled to America and eventually received a short-term position at the University of Chicago. In 1941 he found a job teaching in the art department of Rockford College in northern Illinois.[30]

Although Bettelheim wrote down some impressions of camp life almost immediately after his release, it was several years before he decided to base a scholarly article on his data. After he completed the article in 1942, it was initially rejected by a number of psychological journals, which variously deemed its material unbelievable, impossible to confirm, unscientific due to a lack of field notes, or simply too harrowing for their readership.[31] "Individual and Mass Behavior in Extreme Situations"—Bettelheim's first single-author academic publication—finally appeared in the October 1943 issue of the *Journal of Abnormal and Social Psychology.*

Bettelheim painted a frightening portrait of life in the camps, graphically describing many physical and psychological tortures that the prisoners suffered at the hands of their Gestapo guards. The thrust of his article, however, concerned the psychological effects of this treatment on prisoners. Bettelheim's understanding of the social psychology of the camps would profoundly influence postwar theories of totalitarianism. He began by distinguishing between different groups of prisoners. Criminals, especially those who had already served time, and the "politically educated," who saw in their imprisonment a confirmation of their political commitments, adjusted most easily to conditions in the camps. Nonpolitical middle-class prisoners had the hardest time. By the end of the article, however, Bettelheim seemed to suggest that these distinctions waned with the passage of time. The most important distinction was ultimately between "old" prisoners, who had spent more than three years in camp, and "new" prisoners, who had been there less than a year.[32]

Bettelheim's portrayal of the old prisoners was arguably the most disturbing aspect of his study. The adult personalities of members of this group disintegrated. They eventually regressed to a state similar to infancy. They stopped caring about the outside world, even about family and friends. Rather than directing anger against their captors, they directed their anger against themselves. And like children, they lived only in the present. They were incapable of developing meaningful relationships with other inmates. In the "final stage of adjustment," these prisoners began to assume the values of the Gestapo as their own. They adopted the vocabulary of the Gestapo, accepted the Gestapo's brutal attitudes toward their fellow prisoners, and, when possible, dressed in old Gestapo uniforms.[33]

Bettelheim qualified his conclusions about the old prisoners. He noted that those who at times identified with the Gestapo, at other times resisted the guards heroically. He also tentatively suggested that the Gestapo appeared more interested in awakening fear in the prisoners than converting them to their values. But Bettelheim seems to have put aside these reservations, both about the effects of camp life and about the intent of the regime. He concluded that the camp served as "the Gestapo's laboratory." It was both a training ground for the young men who would police Germany and the conquered nations and a place in which "it develops methods for changing free and upright citizens not only into grumbling slaves, but into serfs who in many respects accept their masters' values." The camp ultimately appeared to be a microcosm of the entire regime: "*It seems that what happens in an extreme fashion to the prisoners who spend several years in the concentration camp happens in less exaggerated form to the inhabitants of the big concentration camp called greater Germany.*"[34]

Although Bettelheim was careful to present his findings as a scientific study, couched in the objective language of the psychologist, his account of the camps was also the first survivor testimony to be published in America and among the first to appear anywhere in English.[35] At the time of its publication in October 1943, both the concentration camps and the social psychology of Nazism were becoming important topics of discussion. Questions about German social psychology motivated the debate over such works as Richard Brickner's *Is Germany Incurable?* Concern over Germany's concentration camps, which had been expressed in the American press since their establishment back in 1933, began slowly to grow as the first reports of the extermination of European Jews began to filter across the Atlantic.

In the fall of 1943 Bettelheim's article was unique not only as survivor testimony but also as an account of the psychology of Nazism that placed the camps at its interpretive center. Bettelheim's explanation of the regime's ability to elicit support from the great mass of Germans and conquered peoples was especially grim. Although there was much disagreement among American observers about the nature of mass support for Nazism, Bettelheim's suggestion that the very process of repression created support for the regime was arguably more chilling than any other understanding of its popularity. Rather than indicating the inability of the government to fully stomp out opposition, the camps were, for Bettelheim, the engine of its peculiar form of social stability. He concluded on a positive note of postwar reconstruction: his findings might allow those nations that defeated Germany to devise methods to "resurrect within a short time as autonomous and self-reliant persons" those unfortunate souls trapped under Nazism.[36] But as the many rejections of his manuscript suggest, his analysis of the camps was inconsistent with the dominant wartime understandings of the Nazi enemy.

Because it appeared in a fairly small academic journal, Bettelheim's article did not receive the audience garnered by either Burnham or Schumpeter. But it almost immediately caught the attention of American intellectuals. Bettelheim took on some of the most pressing and intractable issues in the understanding of Nazism, and he brought to those issues both a new kind of authority, as a camp survivor, and new conclusions. His philosophical commitments also enhanced the study's reception. Although he did not cite a single work of psychology in his article, its intellectual foundations were clearly Freudian. Anyone familiar with psychoanalysis would likely have recognized concepts such as "infantile regression" and "magical thinking." Those well versed in Freudian thought might have recognized Anna Freud and Sándor Ferenczi's work on the identification of children with their aggressors in Bettelheim's description of the old prisoners' adop-tion of Gestapo values.[37] The 1940s were arguably the high-water mark of Freudianism in America, where psychoanalytic thought enjoyed enormous prestige. Its popularity doubtless added to the acceptance of Bettelheim's theories.[38]

Those who responded most positively to Bettelheim's conclusions about the Nazi concentration camps were often those most critical of America's prosecution of the war. Art historian and cultural critic Meyer Schapiro, an anti-Stalinist, left-wing critic of U.S. involvement in the war, so admired the article that he began sending it to his friends. Dwight Macdonald, whose brash opposition to the war had helped precipitate his departure from the *Partisan Review,* commended the essay in the first issue of his independent left-wing journal, *Politics,* in February 1944 and published a condensed ver-sion in the July 1944 issue. The article also drew the interest of Theodor Adorno, Max Horkheimer, and other members of the Frankfurt School, who built the final session of a 1944 lecture series on National Socialism around themes related to Bettelheim's work.[39]

In the postwar years, the article would become profoundly influential in shaping views of the workings of totalitarian regimes. With the liberation of the concentration camps in 1945, interest in the camps and their meaning, both within Nazism and for humanity at large, grew. As both the first camp survivor account published in the United States and an important analysis of that experience, "Individual and Mass Behavior in Extreme Situations" worked its way into social scientific, humanistic, and scientific research. It eventually achieved the status of a classic and was widely read by specialists and nonspecialists alike. Indeed, Bettelheim's notions about the psychologi-cal effects of concentration camps helped to shape Stanley Elkins's account of the effects of slavery on blacks in the antebellum South.[40] As interest in the Holocaust grew, Bettelheim began to write further about the camps and reactions to Nazi terror in general. In more recent decades, however, his reputation has collapsed.[41] But this decline should not lead us to underesti-mate the influence of his article on American thought in the years immedi-ately following World War II.

If Bettelheim's reputation has diminished, that of theologian Reinhold Niebuhr is largely intact. Niebuhr was one of the many intellectuals who traveled the path from radicalism in the 1930s, to New Deal liberalism in the early 1940s, and finally to Cold War liberalism. In the late 1920s and early 1930s Niebuhr was the leading advocate of "Christian socialism." In his most celebrated work of this period, *Moral Man and Immoral Society* (1932), he called for a combination of radical politics and conservative theology. Rejecting liberal Protestantism's belief in human perfectibility and its hopes for the peaceful inauguration of a kingdom of God on earth, Niebuhr praised Marxism both for its economic understanding of politics and its apocalyptic imagination. Liberal political theory was just a mask for the interests of the bourgeoisie. If Christians were to engage in politics, they would need to accept the use of force and occasionally violence.[42]

It is thus not surprising that Niebuhr would reject the pacifism that many liberal Protestants embraced as war erupted in Europe. In the winter of 1940–41, he founded the interventionist journal *Christianity and Crisis* as a rival to the still pacifist *Christian Century,* and he left the Socialist Party, which continued to oppose U.S. intervention in the war. By the time of Pearl Harbor, Niebuhr had emerged as the leading U.S. Protestant voice in favor of intervention.

Niebuhr had also abandoned his earlier radicalism for a brand of New Deal liberalism. Although he had held FDR in contempt in the early 1930s, he supported and voted for him in 1940. By the early 1940s Niebuhr began to defend liberalism along theological lines. The two-volume *The Nature and Destiny of Man* (1941–43), his theological magnum opus, suggested that the fundamental challenge facing humanity was not ignorance, but sin. In the words of Richard Wightman Fox, the mission of the book was "to justify Biblical religion as the only adequate foundation for self-understanding and political action in an age of lowered expectations and inexpressibly horrible disasters." Niebuhr had criticized liberalism as an ideological ruse in *Moral Man,* but in *Nature and Destiny,* liberalism appeared as "a realistic perspective that appreciated the potential for and limits upon human justice."[43]

Nature and Destiny attracted an enormous amount of attention. The book was hailed in theological circles, where Niebuhr came to be widely seen as the leading American Protestant theologian. Outside of the theological arena, the book received mixed reviews. Conservatives like Whittaker Chambers and Henry Luce endorsed it for its tough-minded emphasis on human limitations and the importance of traditional religious belief. Lewis Mumford, a friend of Niebuhr's and no conservative, was also delighted by the book. Its detractors, such as John Dewey and Sidney Hook, considered it an assault on the power of human reason. But for all the praise and criticism that it drew, *Nature and Destiny* did not reach a large audience. It was simply too difficult, and perhaps too discomfiting, to interest a popular readership, even within America's Protestant churches.[44]

Whereas *Nature and Destiny* cemented Niebuhr's reputation as a theologian, his next book, the much shorter and more directly political *The Children of Light and the Children of Darkness* (1944), established him, in the words of Campbell Craig, as "the archetypical American 'Cold War' intellectual." This work provided a crucial foundation for postwar thinking about totalitarianism. Originally delivered as the West Memorial Lectures at Stanford University in January 1944 and published late in the year, *Children of Light* was in many ways a political extension of some of the theological ideas that Niebuhr had developed in *Nature and Destiny*.[45]

As its subtitle indicates, *The Children of Light and the Children of Darkness* is "a vindication of democracy and a critique of its traditional defense." Niebuhr based its title on Luke 16:8: "The children of this world are in their generation wiser than the children of light." He argued that democratic civilization had been built by "children of light" who made positive assumptions about human nature and the ability of society to easily resolve conflict between the individual and the community. This civilization was threatened by "the children of this world" or, as he redesignated them, "the children of darkness," who were "moral cynics, who declare that a strong nation need acknowledge no law beyond its strength." The real threat to democracy, however, lay in the foolishness of the children of light, who, in their "fatuous and superficial view of man," set themselves up as victims of the scheming children of darkness, who better understood the darker side of human nature.[46]

In the category of the children of light, Niebuhr included an extraordinarily broad group of people, including "sentimentalists" of all political and religious stripes, from defenders of capitalism to Marxist idealists, from Catholics to American liberal Protestants. Indeed, most of the conflicts of the preceding two centuries—between aristocracy and the middle class, between scientists and priests, between proletarian revolutionaries and the bourgeoisie—were in fact conflicts among the children of light, not conflicts between children of light and children of darkness. Niebuhr even noted that German thinkers often accused of laying the foundation of Nazism—including Herder, Fichte, Hegel, and Nietzsche—were all, in their own way, children of light who assumed the perfectibility of human nature. The only group he clearly designated as "children of darkness" were the Nazis themselves, though he seemed to hint throughout his work that children of darkness may be lurking everywhere in modern society.[47]

The only way for democratic civilization to combat the children of darkness was to combine "the wisdom of the serpent with the harmlessness of the dove. The children of light must be armed with the wisdom of the children of darkness but remain free from their malice. They must know the power of self-interest in human society without giving it moral justification. They must have this wisdom in order that they beguile, deflect, harness and restrain self-interest, individual and collective, for the sake of the community." Niebuhr believed that democracy was necessary precisely because the children of darkness were correct about human nature. Since humanity and all it creates are open to sin and corruption, everything must be subject to criticism. This is only possible in a democracy. Echoing the pragmatism of William James, Niebuhr argued for religious, ethnic, and class pluralism based on the contingency of all theological, social, and political knowledge.[48]

Throughout *Children of Light* Niebuhr's pragmatic pluralism is in tension with his neo-orthodox theology. On the one hand, he repeatedly suggests that, although religion is necessary as the source of all transcendent truths, all believers must maintain a sense of humility and accept that any particular expression of religious faith is necessarily finite and flawed. On the other hand, most forms of Christian faith other than neo-orthodox Protestantism are examples of the foolish optimism of the children of light.

When Niebuhr turns to secularism, the very structure of his argument takes on a neo-orthodox cast. Secularism, he maintained, comes in two forms. The more mild, bourgeois form of secularism is a quasi-religious faith in progress. Democratic society thus becomes the end of human existence. To do this is "a less vicious version of the Nazi creed," for no society is "good enough to make itself the final end of human existence." The more "sophisticated" form of secularism found in modern Europe is a pervasive relativism. Faced with the social and political problems of modernity, but without Christianity's ability to give life tragic meaning, Europeans edged toward nihilism. The ultimate result was Nazism: "Since no one can live in despair, the primitive and demonic religion of Nazism and extravagant nationalism filled the vacuum."[49]

Rather subtly, Niebuhr edges away from his initial explanation of political evil. He began by dividing the world into foolish, but optimistic, children of light and wisely cynical, but evil, children of darkness. But in the second half of the book, no group—not even the Nazis—appear to be children of darkness. Having identified nearly every political and religious tendency other than Nazism as an example of the foolishness of the children of light, Niebuhr appears to provide an alternative explanation for Nazism itself in his discussion of secularism. Although his bourgeois secularists embrace a less vicious version of Nazism, they are almost classic children of light, foolishly assuming that humankind is perfectible. The despairing, sophisticated European secularists, though not exactly children of light, are hardly the manipulative, cynical children of darkness; yet, like the foolish children of light, sophisticated secularists are easy prey for the children of darkness.

Niebuhr makes the children of light all too human by giving countless examples of them. But although the children of darkness are frequently mentioned throughout the book, he seems to resist personifying them. Instead, they appear as a demonic, or more precisely satanic, force. Like the serpent in Eden, the children of darkness represent knowledge and evil. Ultimately, however, the responsibility for democracy's failure falls not on them, but on the weakness of the children of light. In *Children of Light,* Niebuhr is thus more concerned with the need for the children of light to acknowledge humanity's fallen nature than with the almost inhuman forces who can manipulate that nature to do political evil.

If these issues reflect Niebuhr's theological commitments, they also mirror a pronounced and more general tendency in some U.S. accounts of the European dictatorships. American understandings of dictatorship going back to the 1930s often showed more interest in "dupes" than in true believers. Many felt that the real danger, at least in America, was that well-intentioned people would be fooled into supporting a dictatorial movement. Moreover, such dupes, at home and abroad, often proved easier to explain than true believers in Nazism, Fascism, or Communism, whose power came in part from their absolute otherness. Dupe-centered accounts of totalitarianism tended to finesse the issue of totalitarianism's ultimate cause. Such accounts also become increasingly important during World War II, as the goodness of Americans' intentions could be emphasized even as their behavior could be criticized and corrected. Although Niebuhr found the ultimate responsibility for political evil in humanity's sinfulness, he did not entirely resolve the more concrete, and vexing, question of its social roots. He made clear how foolish optimism left the children of light vulnerable to cynical children of darkness, but the identity of these cynics remained strangely elusive.

In this survey of wartime pessimists, we finally turn briefly to Friedrich Hayek's *The Road to Serfdom* (1944), a book that became particularly influential in American conservative circles. Though less significant to Orwell, Schlesinger, and Arendt than the works thus far explored in this chapter, *The Road to Serfdom* is notable both for its salience in American political culture and for its many similarities to the books already discussed: its grim tone resembles that of all the other works; its understanding of totalitarianism as an often unintended consequence of the political decisions of modern elites closely resembles Burnham's and Schumpeter's views; and its sense of moral righteousness resembles Niebuhr's. None of these similarities should mask its profound differences with these other works. But the similarities are worth noting because the success of Hayek's book is very much the product of the same cultural moment as the success of Burnham's, Schumpeter's, Bettelheim's, and Niebuhr's. Like Burnham's *Managerial Revolution* in 1941, Hayek's *Road to Serfdom* was a surprise best-seller in America.[50] In April 1945 it appeared in condensed form in the *Reader's Digest*. Widely reviewed in the United States, it received accolades from conservatives and unfavorable commentaries from liberals and radicals. Like the other works examined in this chapter, then, it appealed initially to people who felt at odds with the dominant trends in American political life.

Hayek's book, which advanced an argument that the author had first made in a much shorter work, *Freedom and the Economic System* (1939), maintained that economic planning itself led to totalitarianism. Freedom could exist only in a free enterprise system. Whether in the name of Nazism, communism, or democratic socialism, planning led to the destruction of free enterprise, the eradication of individualism, and the triumph of totalitarianism. According to Hayek, planning did not merely limit property rights and greatly increase the coercive powers of the state. By imposing a plan, any plan, those in charge necessarily adopted a rigid system of priorities that inevitably destroyed moral freedom: "It is because successful planning requires the creation of a common view on the essential values that the restriction of our freedom with regard to material things touches so directly on our spiritual freedom."[51] Hayek thus linked two major concerns of American critics of totalitarianism—the totalitarian state and totalitarian belief systems—not by way of a mass movement, but by the desires of a small group of planners.

Hayek was another unlikely best-selling author. An academic economist, he was born in Austria and immigrated to England in 1931. Although *The Road to Serfdom* was broadly concerned with the western democracies, more narrowly Hayek's interests were British. The book also combined philosophy, economics, and politics in a way that many critics found vague, inaccurate, and heavy-handed.[52] Nevertheless, the book's weaknesses, its internal contradictions and vagaries, matched well the associations that the term "totalitarianism" had accumulated in the United States by the mid-1940s. Although U.S. reviewers focused primarily on the consequences of planning, many of Hayek's more oblique suggestions resonated on the American right. His genealogy of totalitarianism located its origins in Marxism, an argument that greatly pleased *Fortune*'s book reviewer, John Davenport, and that appealed to the conservative view that communism was a greater menace to America than fascism. And though Hayek's planners did not seem to require a mass movement to back them, *The Road to Serfdom* frequently offered negative invocations of social revolution that would have attracted American conservatives: "It was from the masses and not from the classes steeped in the Prussian tradition, and favored by it, that National Socialism arose."[53]

Although Hayek was anything but a cultural relativist, his association of the liberal tradition with the English-speaking countries and totalitarianism with Germany gave totalitarianism an added whiff of foreignness. The war over planning was also a war of East against West:

> For over two hundred years English ideas had been spreading eastward. The rule of freedom which had been achieved in England seemed destined to spread throughout the world. By about 1870 the reign of these ideas had probably reached its easternmost expansion. From then onward it began to retreat, and a different set of ideas, not really new but very old, began to advance from the East. England lost her intellectual leadership in the political and social sphere and became an importer of ideas. For the next sixty years Germany became the center from which ideas destined to govern the world in the twentieth century spread east and west. Whether it was Hegel or Marx, List or Schmoller, Sombart or Mannheim, whether it was socialism in its more radical form or merely "organization" or "planning" of a less radical kind, German ideas were everywhere readily imported and German institutions imitated.[54]

Despite his kind words for "the Prussian tradition" only a few pages earlier, Hayek seemed to condemn that tradition as the root of the current crisis.

Hayek thus combined a philosophical argument, linking planning whatever its goal other than "competition" to totalitarianism, with a historical argument, which variously blamed the existence of totalitarianism on the doctrines of socialism, the German intellectual tradition, and the masses themselves. All of these had been attacked by American cultural producers, particularly conservatives, before and during World War II. But though blaming Nazism on German-ness usually entailed denying that it could happen in America, Hayek's overdetermined and self-contradictory analysis, like John Roy Carlson's much less sophisticated picture of American fascism in *Under Cover* (1943), simultaneously saw totalitarianism as transnational and as essentially foreign. *The Road to Serfdom* would become enormously important for the libertarian strain of postwar American conservatism, which saw a slippery slope leading from any state intervention in the economy straight to totalitarianism.

For those who rejected this view, Burnham, Schumpeter, Bettelheim, and Niebuhr all provided foundations for understandings of totalitarianism. But those foundations were themselves grounded in over a decade of thought about the European dictatorships. For all the importance of *The Managerial Revolution, Capitalism, Socialism, and Democracy,* "Individual and Mass Behavior in Extreme Situations," and *The Children of Light and the Children of Darkness,* none of them offered strikingly original arguments. While a Trotskyist in the 1930s, Burnham had first suggested a "new class" explanation for the Soviet Union. His argument in *The Managerial Revolution* was close enough to that of other iconoclastic Trotskyists that some accused him of plagiarism. The most significant aspects of Schumpeter's argument had appeared in papers he had already published, some as far back as the 1920s. Bettelheim's reasoning drew heavily on the work of Anna Freud and Sándor Ferenczi and in some ways resembled the conclusions of Erich Fromm's *Escape from Freedom* (1941), which had provided an earlier, Freudian account of the rise of modern dictatorship. The theological conception of *Children of Light* was so firmly rooted in *The Nature and Destiny of Man* that one Niebuhr biographer has declared *Children of Light* to be little more than a codicil to the earlier work.[55]

More significantly, each of these thinkers was participating in a conversation about modern dictatorship that had been a crucial part of American political culture as far back as the 1920s. To the extent that these scholars reached a broad audience, they did so in large measure because Americans were already deeply interested in the problem of dictatorship and what it meant for the future of democracy. Despite full agreement on the importance of understanding dictatorship, the vibrancy of the public discourse in part depended on the lack of a consensus on the precise meaning of dictatorship for American democracy.

These works provided very different answers to the most vexing question about modern dictatorships: What could bring about such monstrous regimes? Burnham suggested that deep, historical forces would move the world inexorably toward the managerial state. Schumpeter argued that the success of capitalism would doom it and, along with it, bourgeois democracy. Bettelheim suggested that the most extreme forms of oppression practiced by these regimes actually created the conditions for their political success. And Niebuhr indicated that the greatest threat of dictatorship resulted from the foolish optimism of nearly everyone other than neo-orthodox Protestants.

But these four works shared at least two important qualities. First, each was extremely skeptical about American democracy as it was usually understood. Burnham had contempt for democracy. Schumpeter dismissed the usual understandings of it and offered a new, rather attenuated, definition.

Bettelheim seemed to question some of the core assumptions about human rationality that lay at the heart of much democratic thought. Niebuhr dedicated his book to a critique of the "traditional defense" of democracy. In rejecting common understandings of American democracy, the four works cut sharply against the grain of a wartime political culture that generally celebrated the American democratic tradition.

The second common aspect of these works is more subtle, but just as important. Each held elites essentially responsible for the creation of dictatorship, while reducing the great mass of the people to political pawns. Burnham's managers brought about his revolution. The central players in Schumpeter's drama were capitalists and, to a certain extent, intellectuals, who convince the working class to embrace socialism. In Bettelheim's story, action comes from the Gestapo guards: the prisoners are quickly turned into passive children. If we accept Bettelheim's characterization of the concentration camp as a microcosm of the German nation, most people end up in the position of the prisoners, not the Gestapo. Finally, Niebuhr places ideas, and more especially conceptions of human nature, at the heart of contemporary politics. At least implicitly, he holds intellectuals responsible for the great political developments of the day. Day-to-day political concerns, and with them most people's understanding of politics, seem ultimately unimportant in the world of *The Children of Light*. In understanding elites as largely responsible for modern dictatorship, these four authors echoed, if unintentionally, dominant wartime views that suggested that the people of the enemy nations were essentially good but had been led astray by evil leaders—we were at war with Nazis, not Germans. Although the beliefs of the wartime pessimists do not represent a return to the dictator-centered understandings of the early 1930s, they are also far from the crowd-based understandings of dictatorship that we saw in the late 1930s. The closest thing to a crowd in any of these works is Bettelheim's corps of infantilized prisoners, but they lack all political impetus beyond contributing to their own repression. Official and semi-official wartime views often found hope in the people, yet in the four works the people are either absent or pathetic. If the people had been the problem in many 1930s accounts of dictatorship, here they are rendered nearly irrelevant.

Postwar Visions of Totalitarianism

Each of the works just analyzed was written by, and initially appealed to, Americans critical either of participation in World War II or of the optimistic understandings of that participation surveyed earlier in this book. After the war, however, these four works would come to be seen as classics and would help form the foundation of postwar understandings of totalitarianism. They entered the mainstream of American thought at least in part because of significant changes in American life that took place as World War II drew to a close and America faced the postwar world.

In the 1930s most American thinking about dictatorship revolved around the possibility that it might happen in the United States. Such thinking was usually grounded in concerns about the social and political crisis of the Great Depression: whether or not the country's political and economic systems were irreparably broken, people might be convinced that they were and be moved to abandon democracy in favor of dictatorship. American writers from Hadley Cantril to Dorothy Thompson, from Robert and Helen Lynd to Sinclair Lewis, had suggested that the great mass of Americans might be on the verge of embracing some form of dictatorship. With the end of World War II, many people feared that the wartime economic boom might again be replaced by economic crisis. These fears were exacerbated by the postwar wave of labor strife, as workers who had largely honored wartime no-strike pledges began to demand their share of the economic growth that the country had experienced. But the postwar world did not bring renewed economic crisis. Instead, with economic prosperity came an easing of fears that the people themselves might abandon democracy.

If U.S. fears of antidemocratic mass movements eased after the war, fears of dictatorship, and more particularly of totalitarianism, increased. One marker of these continuing fears were public attitudes toward Nazi Germany after its defeat. Postwar public memory in victorious countries often softens the image of the enemy: exaggerated stories of atrocities are proven false, true crimes against humanity are gradually forgotten, and a sense of reconciliation begins to take hold. In the United States, Northern images of the South after 1877, interwar images of Germany, and post–World War II images of Japan are all examples of this phenomenon. The nation's images of Nazi Germany, however, did not follow this pattern. If anything, the horrors of Nazism came to play an increasingly central role in American memory as World War II receded into the past.

The growing sense of the horrors of Nazism was in part due to the liberation of the concentration camps and the wide dissemination of images of their prisoners. Fearing a repetition of the anti-German hysteria of World War I, the Roosevelt administration had been careful not to play up stories of German atrocities during the war itself. Bettelheim's difficulty in publishing his paper on the concentration camps in part reflected the extent to which American cultural producers had internalized this reluctance. Although during the war some Nazi crimes, such as the massacre at Lidice, were widely publicized, the events that later became known as the Holocaust received surprisingly little notice. This was due in part to a lack of information, as the death camps were located deep in Nazi-occupied Eastern Europe. But even what was known of the Nazi Judeocide was often downplayed in the United States. Despite the best efforts of activists like playwright Ben Hecht, many feared that focusing public attention on what was most often called the "refugee crisis" would encourage antisemitism at home by making the war in Europe appear to be a narrowly Jewish cause. Official and semi-official understandings of the Nazi enemy thus tended to focus on the more general political repressiveness of Nazism, as well as the horrors of the Blitzkrieg and Nazi rule in occupied territories. As the war in Europe wound to a close, the liberation of the camps made Nazism seem, if anything, more horrific as victory was finally achieved. In spite of the United Nations' triumph, the moral challenge posed by the regime increased.

Also contributing to continued worries about dictatorship was the state of the postwar world. By 1944 the U.S.-Soviet relationship had already begun to deteriorate. The concept of totalitarianism, largely kept alive during wartime by a diverse group of thinkers suspicious of the Soviet Union, became a convenient lens through which both to view America's erstwhile ally and to focus public concern. The idea of totalitarianism thus helped keep public interest in understanding Nazism alive; since totalitarianism suggested that Nazism and communism were essentially similar, understanding the former Nazi enemy became a way of grappling with the emerging Soviet foe. The creation of the atomic bomb also made the world appear to be more dangerous than it had been before the war. Despite the brief U.S. atomic monopoly, many Americans worried that a world with atomic weapons was a world on the brink of apocalypse, especially if such weapons ever fell into the hands of a totalitarian regime bent on world conquest.[56]

Given these new conditions, American fears of dictatorship in the postwar world were rather different from those of the 1930s. Dictatorial mass movements of domestic origin seemed increasingly unlikely. Instead, conquest and subversion, themes played up extensively during the war in describing both Nazi Germany's subjugation of Europe and its threat to the United States, became overriding concerns in U.S. postwar assessments of the dangers posed by totalitarianism. Official and semi-official wartime images of Germany had tended to conclude that, despite its many evils, Nazism would prove no match for American democracy and the power of the United Nations. Allied victory seemed to confirm this view. Many U.S. public intellectuals feared that the postwar world would bring a return to the complacency and isolationism that was widely understood to have seized America during the interwar period. The works of authors like Burnham, Schumpeter, Bettelheim, and Niebuhr, who had expressed skepticism about the vitality of American democracy, thus proved attractive to those who hoped to convince the reading public that despite the end of the Great Depression and the defeat of Nazism, the dangers of totalitarianism remained.

Even as postwar fears embodied the pessimism of these wartime works, they also built upon the rich discourse on dictatorship that had developed since the 1920s. By placing American postwar views of totalitarianism in this larger context, we gain a better understanding both of Cold War thought and of the complicated political legacies of the Great Depression and World War II. By analyzing Arthur Schlesinger Jr.'s *The Vital Center*, George Orwell's *Nineteen Eighty-Four*, and Hannah Arendt's *Origins of Totalitarianism* as the conclusion, rather than the beginning, of a cultural conversation about dictatorship, I hope to achieve a better sense of the positive and negative impacts that that conversation has had on American political culture.

Schlesinger's *Vital Center* has appropriately been called "the manifesto of postwar liberalism."[57] Its prescriptions of anticommunism and Cold War internationalism, its repudiation of the legacy of the Popular Front, and its attempt to nonetheless lay claim to the legacy of the New Deal both reflected and helped establish the tone of Cold War American political culture. In many ways, Schlesinger was perfectly situated to write such a book. The son of Harvard historian Arthur Schlesinger Sr., he was, intellectually speaking, to the manner born. Distinguishing himself at an early age, he graduated from Harvard before his twenty-first birthday. After college in the late 1930s, he became an active proponent of intervention in Europe and wrote articles for the *Boston Globe* arguing against pacifism and for conscription. In 1940, still in his early twenties, he was admitted to the Harvard Society of Fellows to study American history. During the war Schlesinger, who did not qualify for combat status, served in the Office of War Information and the Office of Strategic Services. In 1945 he published *The Age of Jackson*, his second book but the first to make a significant impact on American historiography. Indeed, *The Age of Jackson* set the principal issues in the study of Jacksonian democracy for years to come and established Schlesinger as a major young voice in American history.

But as Schlesinger began his career as a historian, he also played an important role in politics. In 1947 he became a founding member of Americans for Democratic Action (ADA). Established in the wake of the conservative gains in the 1946 midterm elections, the ADA was committed from the start to promoting liberalism while excluding not only CP members but also those whom it deemed "sympathizers with Communism," such as the Popular Fronters who supported the rival Progressive Citizens of America (PCA). In the next several years, the ADA emerged as the most prominent institutional face of liberal anticommunism. In 1948 the ADA and its supporters played a major role in Democrat Harry S Truman's surprisingly successful presidential campaign. In addition to being opposed by the Republican nominee Thomas E. Dewey and Dixiecrat Strom Thurmond, Truman faced a challenge on his left from former vice president Henry Wallace, the candidate of the PCA's successor organization, the Progressive Party. The Truman campaign decided to attack Wallace with a strategy devised by Truman's special counsel Clark Clifford. While Truman himself ignored Wallace, members of the Democratic Party's liberal wing would ceaselessly red-bait the former vice president. The plan worked like a charm: Wallace received only 2 percent of the national popular vote.[58] The leaders of the ADA, including Schlesinger himself, were among the chief participants in this strategy. *The Vital Center*, published in early 1949, was in part an extension of Schlesinger's anti-Wallace articles.

In its broadest outlines, *The Vital Center* is an attempt to separate the legacy of the New Deal from the legacy of the Popular Front. In the New Deal Schlesinger finds a future for an anticommunist liberalism that is simultaneously radical—in its pragmatism and manly commitment to action—and centrist. In the Popular Front, he sees feminized sentimentalism and at least latent totalitarianism. Although much of the book is about liberalism and, in the words of its subtitle, "The Politics of Freedom," *The Vital Center* also considers freedom's opposite, totalitarianism, a term Schlesinger uses in the already standard fashion to include both Nazism and communism. Indeed, much of his portrayal of totalitarianism, one that would become critical to the Cold War liberal consensus, should be very familiar as it is grounded in over a decade of American thought about the European dictatorships. His descriptions both of the origins of totalitarianism and of its unique qualities are like earlier analyses of these regimes. According to Schlesinger, totalitarianism arises when the "anxious man" of the twentieth century seeks to escape his anxiety. He cites Fromm's *Escape from Freedom* to support this view. Unlike previous dictatorships, which left much of the social structure intact, "totalitarianism . . . pulverizes the social structure, grinding all independent groups and diverse loyalties into a single amorphous mass."[59]

Schlesinger's discussion of totalitarianism partakes of the discourse about masculinity and authenticity that was also typical of American writings on dictatorship since the mid-1930s. Once "anxious man" escapes freedom, he becomes "totalitarian man." Having experienced "forlornness, impotence, and fear," he embraces "the losing of self in masochism or sadism." These "members of a totalitarian party *enjoy* the discipline." Man is remade as robot: "We know well the visages of these new men in the Gestapo or the MVD [Soviet Ministry of Internal Affairs, one of the predecessors of the KGB], in the Politburo or in the Assembly of the United Nations—the tight-lipped, cold-eyed, unfeeling, uncommunicative men, as if badly carved from wood, without humor, without tenderness, without spontaneity, without nerves." As they are devoid of all individuality and originality, totalitarian men are also incapable of truly creative activity. Echoing the critique of mass culture that had been developed in the *Partisan Review* beginning in the late 1930s, Schlesinger attacks Popular Front authors and Hollywood screenwriters for becoming "slick and false" under the influence of communism. The "betrayal of taste" represented by everything from the radio plays of Norman Corwin to the "Ballad for Americans" reflects the essential inauthenticity of Popular Front artists. The hint of sexual perversion lurks just beneath the surface of Schlesinger's text, whether in the masochism and sadism embraced by totalitarian men, the "half-concealed exercises in penetration and manipulation [that] represent . . . a part of the mission of the Communist party in the United States," or the practice of politics itself in totalitarian societies, which Schlesinger compares to "homosexuality in a boys' school." He goes so far as to suggest that Americans join the Communist Party for sexual fulfillment.[60]

Although some aspects of Schlesinger's portrait of totalitarianism conform to late 1930s and early 1940s American ideas about dictatorship, *The Vital Center* departs from these views in others. Most obviously, the book's chief concern is communism, not Nazism. Although this clearly reflects the realities of the late 1940s—Nazi Germany had been defeated, the Soviet Union still existed—Schlesinger goes out of his way to provide an intellectual ground on which to distinguish between the two regimes. He acknowledges that the legacy of Karl Marx, not himself a totalitarian in Schlesinger's estimation, gave communism "an appearance of existing within a framework of existing values." This appearance just made communism more dangerous. Indeed, he argues, communism, not Nazism, was the more complete expression of totalitarianism, largely because of its elimination of private property.[61]

The Vital Center exemplifies other, more subtle, changes in American views of dictatorship. Schlesinger's "anxious men" are rather different from

Fromm's modern men with "pseudo-selves." Fromm, still as much a Marxist as a Freudian at the time he wrote *Escape from Freedom,* saw the possibility of profound social transformation to rid people of their anxieties and unite social and individual desires. In a decade of depression, in which deep material social crisis gripped the United States, such a view was both plausible and attractive. Schlesinger, on the other hand, believed that the anxieties of modernity were, at their base, existential. Quotations from Kierkegaard, Sartre, and Dostoyevsky join those from Fromm in the pages of *The Vital Center.* The proper solution to modern humanity's anxiety is not the creation of a world free of such anxiety, but rather the individual's embrace of a tragic understanding of the human condition. Whereas Fromm offered hope for a future in which anxiety and alienation could be eliminated, Schlesinger accepts "alienation and fallibility . . . doubt and ambiguity." These are the "insights into man which strike democrats and Christians as the marrow of experience."[62]

This departure from Fromm is part of what makes *The Vital Center* such an archetypally postwar text. It reflects the newfound influence of existentialism among American intellectuals. Anxieties about dictatorship that, when expressed by a thinker like Fromm, had appealed to material concerns in a country wracked by depression, were now generalized into essential facts about the human condition, even as both American economic thought and the U.S. economy itself seemed to be leaving behind the world of crisis and secular stagnation that had characterized the 1930s.[63] Like Niebuhr, who is repeatedly cited in *The Vital Center* and whose influence is felt throughout, Schlesinger finds the deepest causes of totalitarianism not in peculiar changes that take place in modernity but rather in the essentially fallen nature of humanity.

The horrific extent of the bargain made by "totalitarian man" also reflects the pessimistic tendencies examined earlier in this chapter. Schlesinger's totalitarian man is so enthralled by discipline, sadism, and masochism that he may lose the will to preserve his physical being. Citing a July 1948 *Partisan Review* article by Hannah Arendt on the Nazi concentration camps—a piece that reflected both the moral enormity of the new task of grappling with the death camps proper and Bettelheim's earlier but still enormously influential account of Dachau and Buchenwald—Schlesinger suggests that "the ghastly, shambling anonymity, who shuffles obediently into the gas chamber is the end product of the totalitarian state."[64]

Like Niebuhr, who turned the battle against totalitarianism into only the latest chapter in a war against evil rooted in the Fall, Schlesinger projects America's battle against totalitarianism back into the past. According to him, all of American history is marked by a conflict between realistic pessimists, like Nathaniel Hawthorne and Reinhold Niebuhr, and sentimental progressives, who are at best liable to become the unwitting dupes of totalitarianism. Indeed, in Hawthorne's *The Blithedale Romance* (1852), Schlesinger finds "the essence of totalitarianism" in the utopia-seeking residents of the fictionalized version of Brook Farm.[65] Schlesinger also takes from the American past his term of abuse for progressives. He labels them "Doughfaces," after the antebellum northerners who refused to support the abolition of slavery despite their general commitment to social reform.[66] In projecting the battle against totalitarianism back into American history, Schlesinger is borrowing a trope from much World War II propaganda, which similarly cast that most recent war into a larger story of Americans fighting for freedom.

Schlesinger employs another wartime theme that we have also seen in Niebuhr: ultimately the biggest danger to America comes not from the "anxious men" who willingly embraced totalitarianism's destruction of individuality, but rather from the happy-go-lucky Doughfaces, whose optimism blinds them to the dangers of the world and sets them up as dupes for totalitarianism. Once again, masculinity is at issue; the language in which Schlesinger describes the Doughface is deeply gendered. If the communist is a dehumanized and regimented man, the progressive is a feminized one: "He must be distinguished, on the one hand, from the Communist; for the progressive is soft, not hard. . . . He must be distinguished, on the other hand, from the radical democrat; for the progressive, by refusing to make room in his philosophy for the discipline of responsibility . . . has cut himself off from the usable traditions of American democracy." The Doughface evinces a "weakness for impotence," a "weakness for rhetoric," and a "weakness for economic fetishism." Renouncing power, he "seeks compensation in emotion." His sentimentality, "soften[s] up the progressive for Communist permeation and conquest."[67]

Whereas Niebuhr mourned the naive foolishness of the "children of light," Schlesinger's Doughfaces are a good deal more villainous. Not merely a potential victim of totalitarianism, the Doughface is "an accessory before the fact." And he can be found among those with little or no direct connection to communism: "The type of progressive today is the fellow traveler or the fellow traveler of the fellow traveler." Despite his later consistent opposition to Joseph McCarthy, Schlesinger's brand of liberal anticommunism—like much of the antifascism of the 1930s and early 1940s—flowed in part from the rich and poisonous stream of the American countersubversive tradition. Indeed, his iconic example of the contemporary Doughface is Henry

Wallace, against whom the ADA had just finished waging a countersubversive battle.[68]

While Schlesinger depicts the general public as threatened by anxiety and Doughfaced optimism, he often portrays politics itself as dominated by elites. Once they have embraced totalitarianism, the masses become little more than political pawns of a system run by a small political class. Far from becoming the fervent, regimented crowds of the late 1930s, Schlesinger's totalitarian masses are "plunged into a profound and trancelike political apathy." Meanwhile, a new ruling class emerges that resembles both the image of totalitarianism as a vast conspiracy described previously in Carlson's *Under Cover* and Burnham's notion of a new, bureaucratic state. On the one hand, a "tight, disciplined élite, plotting in secrecy and mistrusting the world, impregnated Bolshevism with conspiratorial obsessions." On the other hand, the Russian Revolution "has brought into existence a new ruling class," whose interests are "at least as much opposed to those of the working class" as were those of the old capitalist ruling class. The best designation for this new society, Schlesinger argues, is "bureaucratic collectivism." Mass support remains a hallmark of totalitarian regimes, but their direction is determined not by mass psychology, but by the new bureaucratic elite.[69]

Not everyone is condemned in Schlesinger's analysis. A very different, older set of elites receives high political praise. His chapter on "The Failure of the Right" lauds Alexander Hamilton and the Federalists, whom Schlesinger regards as the original American conservatives for their realism about the inevitability of class conflict, their "intellectual candor and robustness," and their willingness to promote an active role for government. Later generations of the American right showed none of these virtues, largely because they were capitalists, not patricians. The Hamiltonians well understood that businessmen were out of place in politics. In his praise of the old aristocracy and his concerns about the political will of business, Schlesinger sounds much like his Harvard colleague Joseph Schumpeter, whom he cites on the declining élan of the capitalist class. With Schumpeter and Hamilton, Schlesinger believed that members of the business community were essentially incapable of political leadership.[70]

Schlesinger, however, was much more of an optimist than Schumpeter. Rather than the inevitable fall predicted in *Capitalism, Socialism, and Democracy, The Vital Center,* as its title suggests, sees strength in the opposition to totalitarianism. Schlesinger hoped to awaken a revived "radicalism" to combat the totalitarian political extremes of fascism and communism, and to create a mild, pragmatic form of social democracy in America. *The Vital*

Center has its share of positive prescriptions for a better political future, though these passages often lack the passion of its jeremiads. Toward the end of the book, Schlesinger suggests that democracy's greatest advantage over its enemies is "the long-run impossibility of totalitarianism." "Terror is the essence of totalitarianism," he asserts, "and normal man, in the long run, instinctively organizes himself against terror." Of course, as a professed Keynesian, Schlesinger would have been familiar with Keynes's dictum about long-run outcomes: in the long run, we are all dead. And few of the anxious, totalitarian, or Doughfaced men who inhabit *The Vital Center* could be described as "normal" in the psychological sense that the author intends. In fact, a Niebuhrian sense of humanity's propensity for evil lies at the heart of Schlesinger's new radicalism. Such a view of human nature necessarily clouds whatever optimism Schlesinger can muster. Totalitarianism, he declares, is not simply "an internal crisis for democratic society. It signifies an internal crisis for democratic man. There is a Hitler, a Stalin in every breast."[71]

Schlesinger's solution to this dilemma is a classic statement of the philosophy of postwar liberalism. In a world filled with irrationality, individuality must be carefully fostered: "We must somehow give the lonely masses a sense of individual human function, we must restore community to the industrial order." Schlesinger's separation of "we" from "the masses" is a crucial move that is indicative of changes in American liberalism that *The Vital Center* helped to chart. Echoing his early praise for Hamilton, it suggests a separation between those engaged in political life and the great mass of society. Indeed, in an admiring essay, John Morton Blum has plausibly described Schlesinger as a "Tory Democrat." Schlesinger's portrait of the democratic society that encourages individuation is a typical picture of postwar pluralism as a prophylactic against totalitarianism. Schlesinger focuses on the importance of independent groups and voluntary associations and the acknowledgment and acceptance of disagreement and social conflict. Unlike many Popular Front liberals of the 1930s, who saw political action, broadly understood, as deeply empowering, Schlesinger postulates that "there is an evident thinness in the texture of political democracy, a lack of appeal to those irrational sentiments once mobilized by religion and now by totalitarianism." Since democratic political life is necessarily "thin," the emotional energies of the citizens of a democracy must have some other outlet. Voluntary associations can give a sense of meaning to the lives of individuals who might otherwise feel powerless in modern society and are thus a bulwark against totalitarianism. Similarly, the acceptance of conflict as essentially irresolvable prevents the "schizophrenia or torpor" that feeds the totalitarian desire to transcend all social differences.[72]

The Vital Center's view of totalitarianism combines old and new elements of American thinking about dictatorship. The result is a synthesis that characterizes totalitarianism as the eternal Other to a postwar liberal conception of democracy. Much of Schlesinger's portrait of totalitarianism is familiar from American thinking about dictatorship before Pearl Harbor: the linking of left-wing and right-wing regimes, the masses' desire to escape freedom, the warped masculinity of totalitarians, and the brutal suppression of all other groups and forces in society on which the novelty of totalitarianism rests. But in *The Vital Center* this picture is marked by a new kind of pessimism about human nature, social psychology, and mass politics already shown in the works of Burnham, Schumpeter, Bettelheim, and Niebuhr. Rather than being a problem rooted in the particular, and potentially transient, inequities of modernity, the masses' flight from freedom to totalitarianism is caused by existential anxieties. All people will always have a little Hitler or Stalin inside of them. Totalitarianism is an eternal, nightmarish specter haunting humanity.[73] Moreover, the greatest danger to American society comes not from the outright supporters of totalitarianism, but from foolish, Doughfaced dupes. New, democratic forms of mass political life cannot address the threat posed by totalitarianism. The notion of popular, meaningful political life seems totally illusory in *The Vital Center*. In democracies, political life is unfulfilling. Although the masses may create totalitarianism, they are systematically shut out of political life by a small ruling cadre once that system has taken hold. A vital center that includes a rich associational life away from politics, societal acceptance of cultural differences, and wise political leadership that accepts human imperfectability can preserve democracy in America and spread it to countries abroad.

If *The Vital Center* made Schlesinger the leading intellectual voice of postwar liberalism, it was soon eclipsed as a popular portrait of totalitarianism. Later in 1949, George Orwell's *Nineteen Eighty-Four* became an instant critical and public success. American intellectuals—among them, Lionel Trilling, Rebecca West, Philip Rahv, Reinhold Niebuhr, and Schlesinger—heaped praise on the novel. It became a Book-of-the-Month Club selection in July 1949; the club's president confidently predicted that it would become "one of the most influential books of our generation." Indeed, the novel's popularity matched its critical reception. It rose to number three on the *New York Times* best-seller list in 1949, sold nearly 200,000 copies through the Book-of-the-Month Club, and returned to the U.S. best-seller lists in 1951, when it was issued in a paperback edition. *Nineteen Eighty-Four* was not Orwell's first success in America. Although he had written a regular column in *Partisan Review* during World War II, Orwell first came to the attention of a larger American reading public with his anti-Stalinist fable *Animal Farm* (1945), which had sold 460,000 copies through the Book-of-the-Month Club between 1946 and 1949.[74]

No other work of fiction or nonfiction has had as much influence on popular American conceptions of totalitarianism as *Nineteen Eighty-Four*. The terms "newspeak," "doublethink," and "Thought Police" (among others from the novel) have entered the language. The adjective "Orwellian" has also, for better or worse, become a common way of describing aspects of the real world that resemble the fictional Oceania. The nightmarish world of *Nineteen Eighty-Four,* an utterly dirty and bleak place characterized by want, war, and terror, in which the state pursues power for its own sake and all individual freedom, including even private freedom of thought, is systematically eradicated, is what the word "totalitarianism" conjures up for most Americans. Scholars, too, have credited the book with being the most vivid portrait of totalitarian life, the ultimate presentation of totalitarianism as liberalism's Other.[75]

Despite the nearly universal acknowledgment of *Nineteen Eighty-Four*'s significance, its author's politics have been a continual source of debate in the United States. The initial American reputation of the book was midwifed by that group of writers commonly called the "New York intellectuals," who were drawn to the novel largely because of its unequivocal anticommunism. In the next several decades, the members of this circle would begin to travel along wildly divergent paths, as some became neoconservatives while others remained liberals or social democrats. Each group has tried to claim Orwell as its own, a process facilitated by his death within a year of *Nineteen Eighty-Four*'s appearance, thus making his future political development entirely a matter of speculation.[76] Orwell was, if nothing else, an idiosyncratic and complicated character. It is apparent that he remained committed to socialism until his death, even as he maintained his longstanding aversion to communism and became extremely frustrated with both the follies of left-wing intellectuals in Britain and the limited achievements of the British Labour government. Certainly, American intellectuals' continued interest in the reputation of this very English author attests to the influence of his writings in the United States. For our purposes, however, resolving the endless search for the "real" George Orwell (or, perhaps one should say, the real Eric Blair) is less important than understanding the impact of *Nineteen Eighty-Four* in America at the time of its publication.[77]

The story of *Nineteen Eighty-Four* is well known. Protagonist Winston Smith is a member of the Outer Party in London, the principal city of Airstrip One (formerly Great Britain), a province of Oceania, one of three great superstates that control the world. Life in Oceania is dreary and oppressive. Three-quarters of the population—the "proles"—live in squalor and are fed a steady diet of mindless mass culture and pornography by the state. The remainder of Oceanians are Party members, but their lives are arguably even worse. As a member of the Outer Party, Winston's life is under constant surveillance by the Thought Police; even at home, his every action is monitored by a two-way telescreen. Everywhere, citizens of Oceania are confronted with the mustachioed image of Big Brother, their heroic leader. Oceanians must regularly participate in demonstrations against either Eastasia or Eurasia, the two other superstates, for Oceania is always at war with one of them. Party members are also encouraged to take part in Two-Minute Hates against Emmanuel Goldstein, the Trotsky-like figure who is presented as the chief internal enemy of the regime.

Winston works at the Ministry of Truth, where he falsifies the past by rewriting old articles from the *Times*. Longing to escape from this life, he begins to keep a journal on his doubts about life in Oceania. He starts an affair with Julia, a fellow Outer Party member and apparently avid supporter of the Junior Anti-Sex League, who turns out to harbor many of the same oppositional attitudes as Winston does. Soon Winston and Julia decide to seek out Goldstein's Brotherhood. O'Brien, a member of the shadowy Inner Party, initiates them into this group and gives them a copy of "the book," Goldstein's manifesto. Shortly after reading it, however, Julia and Winston are captured and taken to the Ministry of Love, the center for torture and reeducation. It turns out that the Brotherhood, the book, and perhaps Goldstein himself are all inventions of the regime. In a series of brutal torture sessions, O'Brien explains the true workings of Oceania and breaks Winston's will, forcing him both to internalize the hideous illogic of the Party's ideology and to turn against Julia. At novel's end, Winston has been reduced to a horrible shell of his former self. After his release from the Ministry of Love, he realizes that he truly loves Big Brother.

Although *Nineteen Eighty-Four* converts theories about totalitarianism into a dramatically realized fictional world, much of Orwell's vision should be familiar. The single most important intellectual influence on the book was James Burnham. Orwell was fascinated by *The Managerial Revolution* and by Burnham's follow-up volume, *The Machiavellians* (1943), which suggests that the primary purpose of any ruling elite is to maintain its own power. Orwell thought Burnham provided a brilliant analysis of the world situation but vehemently disagreed with him on a number of points. The first was Burnham's contempt for the common people. Second, Orwell rejected Burnham's claim that the drift of the world toward totalitarianism was more or less inevitable. Finally, though acknowledging the desire for power as one motivating force in politics, Orwell felt that Burnham exaggerated its importance. In a series of reviews and exchanges of letters in the British journal *Tribune,* Orwell argued with Burnham on these points.[78]

Despite these disagreements, Burnham's influence can be felt throughout *Nineteen Eighty-Four;* in fact, one critic has plausibly characterized the novel as kind of thought experiment in which Orwell imagines a world in which Burnham is right. As predicted in *The Managerial Revolution,* the world in *Nineteen Eighty-Four* is divided into three superstates: East Asia, Continental Europe, and the Western Hemisphere plus the English-speaking countries outside of it. Each of these superstates is ruled by a new elite class, the Party, which roughly conforms to Burnham's managers. Political life, such as it is, is entirely the realm of this elite. O'Brien and the Inner Party consider the proles to be utterly beneath contempt. "Perhaps you have returned to your old idea that the proletarians or the slaves will arise and overthrow us," O'Brien tells Winston in the Ministry of Love. "Put it out of your mind. They are helpless like the animals. Humanity is the Party. The others are outside—irrelevant."[79] Notwithstanding the frequent parades and demonstrations and the state's reliance on mass media, this is not a mass regime in any simple sense of the term. Oceania is controlled by a small elite that does not rely on mass support; rather, it views the great mass of the people as politically irrelevant. Like Burnham's political elites in *The Machiavellians,* the Party is motivated by the quest for pure power, as O'Brien explains to Winston in excruciating detail.

Yet *Nineteen Eighty-Four* is far more than just an imaginative rendition of the world according to James Burnham. Burnham suggests throughout *The Managerial Revolution* that the new, managerial economy is powerful and efficient. Oceania, on the other hand, is a world of squalor. Unlike previous dystopias, such as Eugene Zamyatin's *We* and Aldous Huxley's *Brave New World,* Orwell's is not a world in which the inhabitants have traded freedom or other higher values for material goods or sensual pleasures. Even on a strictly material level, life in Oceania is almost unbearable. In part, this reflects Orwell's deep belief that the great sacrifices demanded by dictatorial regimes needed to be motivated by more than mere creature comforts. Such states used the lack of creature comforts as evidence of the depth of sacrifice and the greatness of the cause.[80]

Even more horribly, the regime's most extreme repressive measures, the tortures of the Ministry of Love, are also its most effective way to build support among Party members. The use of torture and interrogation goes one critical step further than the closest literary predecessor of O'Brien's colloquy with Winston, Arthur Koestler's *Darkness at Noon* (1941). In Koestler's novel, a fictionalized exploration of why those wrongly accused in the Moscow show trials confessed to crimes they did not commit, the regime demands confession, but not the total destruction of the will of the accused. The aim of the interrogators is to get the prisoner Rubashov to say the right thing and to assent that doing so is for the good of the Party. Rubashov is left to struggle with his own conscience and the novel ends with his death, which seems to release him from the horrors of the regime. More insidiously, in *Nineteen Eighty-Four* O'Brien is centrally concerned with Winston's conscience. It is not enough for Winston to say "two plus two equals five," he has to believe it. The regime demands not just obedience but love. Winston must embrace the Party's beliefs of his own free will. The regime strives for the total destruction of the individual because only such destruction represents total power. Instead of the release of death, *Nineteen Eighty-Four* concludes with Winston's chilling realization that he loves Big Brother. In presenting the most horrible physical torture as the Party's method for building support among its members, Orwell ends up reaching conclusions similar to those of Bruno Bettelheim, though one should not take this comparison too far: Bettelheim's theory of regression is essentially Freudian, whereas Orwell's presentation of the characters in *Nineteen Eighty-Four* is largely nonpsychoanalytic.

Orwell departs from Burnham in another, more significant way. Although O'Brien describes the world as a nightmarish variation on Burnham's prophesies, there is no reason to believe that the author believes— or the reader should believe—what O'Brien has to say. O'Brien seems to be correct about the effectiveness of the regime's use of torture; Winston is successfully reeducated. But is O'Brien right about the proles? In fact, the proles are much more ambiguous figures than O'Brien's complete dismissal of them suggests. Orwell did not share Burnham's disdain for ordinary people; rather, he frequently celebrated them in his books and essays. Though the proles are almost certainly not the revolutionary force imagined by Goldstein's book, they live more free and pleasurable lives than do the members of the Party. Winston alternately views them romantically—as a potential revolutionary force—or with disdain, but neither of these attitudes seems to quite capture their lives. The most striking aspect of life in Oceania, the horrific world of the Ministry of Love, is experienced only by Party members. The possibility that the proles, the vast majority of Oceania's population, live a life of relative freedom and happiness exists precisely because of the regime's Burnham-like scorn. However, since readers of the novel experience Oceania entirely from the perspective of the elite, the proles remain shadowy figures. They seem just a step outside the comprehension of the novel and its Party member characters.

Although *Nineteen Eighty-Four* received extraordinary acclaim in the United States, reviewers interpreted the novel in ways that can help us understand both the cultural work done by Orwell's book in America and the broader place of totalitarianism in early Cold War American political culture. Most American reviews of *Nineteen Eighty-Four* assumed that the book was about the present or, at most, a near-future based closely on current trends. In particular, many commentators claimed that Orwell was really writing about life in the Soviet Union. In its 4 July 1949 issue, *Life* magazine featured a richly illustrated summary of the novel's plot in which Big Brother is drawn to look precisely like Joseph Stalin. Nearly all reviewers used "totalitarian" or "totalitarianism" to describe the state in Orwell's novel.[81] In fact, O'Brien goes out of his way to distinguish between the totalitarian regimes of the past and the regime he serves: "Later, in the twentieth century, there were the totalitarians, as they were called. There were the German Nazis and the Russian Communists. . . . The command of the old despotisms was 'Thou shalt not.' The command of the totalitarians was 'Thou shalt.' Our command is *'Thou art.'*"[82] In other words, Oceania is explicitly post-totalitarian.

Relatively few American reviewers seem to have taken much notice of the novel's English setting, most preferring to consider it a fable about Soviet communism. The few who did note the setting saw it as a warning that totalitarianism was far broader than Soviet Communism. Diana Trilling, writing in the *Nation,* and Lionel Trilling, in the *New Yorker,* both argued that by setting the novel in England, Orwell was suggesting that democratic ideologies could internally transform themselves into totalitarianism. Mark Schorer, in his piece for the *New York Times Book Review,* suggested that the setting indicated criticism of contemporary British socialism.[83] All observers took note of the nightmarish quality of the world Orwell imagined. With the single exception of Robert Hatch's unusually negative review in the *New Republic,* Orwell's depiction of the horrors of the Oceania regime was regarded as one of the book's most distinctive strengths.

Many reviewers treated Winston Smith, who as a member of the Outer Party is part of his society's elite, as a kind of Everyman. Some failed to recognize that the vast majority of the population are proles. Few mentioned that, unlike Winston, the proles are largely outside the regime's constant surveillance.[84] Many reviewers assumed that Orwell shared O'Brien's contempt for, or Winston's occasional disgust at, the proles.[85] Only Rahv, who saw the novel as a brilliant analysis of the workings of Soviet Communism, seems to have taken full measure of the possibility that O'Brien is wrong about the proles and that we are supposed to see in them a ray of hope. However, Rahv criticizes Orwell's hope in the proles as one of the book's few flaws.[86]

These American reviews of Orwell's novel help place *Nineteen Eighty-Four* in postwar U.S. political culture. Read as an only slightly fantastic dramatization of life under contemporary totalitarianism, the novel appealed directly to the pessimism about human nature that marked postwar thinking about dictatorship. Unlike Koestler's *Darkness at Noon,* in which Rubashov's humanity and individuality, which the character himself refers to as "the grammatical fiction," continually resurfaces despite his own disbelief in it, *Nineteen Eighty-Four* suggests that Winston's humanity can be completely, irreversibly destroyed despite his fondest desire to maintain it. O'Brien's sense of the proles as culturally debased and politically irrelevant was easily accepted by most American reviewers, as it accorded with the view of the masses in totalitarian regimes shown in Schlesinger's work. This perspective reflected the growing importance of elites in American understandings of dictatorship. Life in Oceania is horrific and squalid for all. Any sense that totalitarianism represented a trade of material comfort for spiritual freedom, an argument frequently made in the 1930s, is as absent from *Nineteen Eighty-Four* as it is from most postwar American accounts of dictatorship. The Party's reliance on war, its utter ruthlessness in its struggle to gain power for power's sake, its hostility to common sense, and even its attempt to remake the English language also corresponded to already familiar notions about totalitarian regimes: their constant need to expand their power, outward and inward; the irrelevance of their stated political intentions to their actual purposes; and the importance of illogical sloganeering and tortured ideological reasoning. Especially for that apparent majority of American reviewers who saw no hope in the proles, *Nineteen Eight-Four* also described a regime that, once established, would be impossible to end from within. A decade after its publication, Sir Isaac Deutscher famously attacked it as an "ideological superweapon in the Cold War."[87] Although this verdict is unfair to Orwell, it is an accurate reflection of the way his novel was read and understood in the United States.

Like Orwell's *Nineteen Eighty-Four,* Arendt's *The Origins of Totalitarianism* (1951) played an enormously important role in American conceptions of totalitarianism almost from the moment of its publication. Also like Orwell's novel, it was particularly significant for the New York intellectuals. Unlike *Nineteen Eighty-Four, Origins* is an exceedingly difficult book. One historian has described it as "brilliant, impassioned, loosely organized, and self-contradictory." Its language is challenging and at times abstruse; Dwight Macdonald, who greatly admired it, expressed disappointment that "too much of the book sounds as if it had been literally translated from the German." Its title and organization—three roughly chronological sections devoted respectively to antisemitism, imperialism, and totalitarianism—imply causation without putting forward a clearly causal argument. Its method seems historical, but its argument appears to be philosophical. No wonder, then, that despite the nearly universal acknowledgment of the book's importance, *Origins* has continued to provoke dissent about what it means. This debate has raged especially since Arendt's death in 1975, when an explosion of interest in her work began. Among the many points of contention have been: Is *Origins* a work of history or of political theory?[88] How do the book's three parts relate to one another? Are we to read antisemitism and imperialism as causes of totalitarianism, as the "Origins" referred to in the title?[89] Should the book's three parts be treated in toto, or should more attention be paid to certain sections than others?[90] What is the relationship of *Origins* to the rest of Arendt's oeuvre, particularly to *The Human Condition* (1959), often regarded as her most important work, and to *Eichmann in Jerusalem* (1965), her next book to deal directly with the Holocaust and her most widely read and controversial volume? Is *Origins* a brave, iconoclastic attempt to deal with a nearly unimaginably horrific subject, or is it a relic of Cold War ideology?[91] Both the book's complexity and Arendt's pointed refusal to connect herself with a particular school of thought, or even a particular academic discipline, promise to keep these questions alive.

Not surprisingly, *Origins* has never enjoyed the popular readership of *Nineteen Eight-Four.* However, despite its difficulty and the many disagreements about its meaning and even its ultimate value, from nearly the moment of its publication, *Origins* was granted canonical status both inside and outside the academy. Because it was one of the earliest—if not *the* earliest—major canonical works on totalitarianism, a number of misconceptions have arisen regarding its significance. Some scholars claim, and many more suggest, that Arendt's great achievement was linking Soviet Communism and German Nazism under the term "totalitarianism."[92] Others believe that among the book's most distinctive departures from conventional wisdom was Arendt's notion that the leaders of totalitarian regimes were not important to the course of totalitarianism.[93] Of course, neither of these ideas originated with Arendt; both had been commonplace in America since the mid-1930s. By seeing Arendt as the initiator of American thinking about totalitarianism, later scholars have largely misunderstood the place of her work in American thinking about dictatorship in the early years of the Cold War. Rather than offering a complete reading of *Origins,* I will instead attempt to evaluate its place in American political culture at the time of its original publication. In particular, why did this often brilliant, but idiosyncratic and difficult, text almost immediately become a classic and have such a profound impact on American understandings of dictatorship?

Hannah Arendt was born in 1906 to a well-to-do, nonreligious Jewish family in Königsberg, East Prussia. Early in life she developed an interest in philosophy. In the 1920s and early 1930s she studied with Martin Heidegger and Karl Jaspers, two of the most prominent existential philosophers, who would eventually end up in a bitter disagreement over the meaning of Nazism. Before the early thirties Arendt showed little interest in politics, but the Nazis' rise to power in 1933 opened her eyes to the horrific possibilities of modern dictatorship. Arendt fled to Paris, where she lived and worked until 1941, when she escaped to the United States and settled in New York. For the next decade she formulated the ideas that would appear in *Origins.*

By the late 1940s Arendt was moving in the world of the New York intellectuals and publishing articles in their journals, including *Politics, Commentary,* and the *Partisan Review.* Indeed, Alfred Kazin arranged to have Harcourt Brace publish *Origins* when its original publisher backed out.[94] But although Arendt was among the New York intellectuals, she was never entirely one of them. Like that group, she hoped to establish herself as a thinker outside of traditional disciplinary boundaries. But she had emerged from a very different intellectual milieu. Unlike most of the New Yorkers, Arendt had never gone through a Marxist-Leninist phase. Nor had the New York intellectuals had much direct exposure to Jaspers, Heidegger, and the kind of philosophical thought on which Arendt had cut her teeth.

Arendt's larger reputation was established by the publication of *The Origins of Totalitarianism,* which thrust her onto the public stage, where she stayed, often uncomfortably, for the rest of her life. The book received high praise from Kazin, Dwight Macdonald, Mary McCarthy, and other prominent New York intellectuals who had embraced her earlier essays. Not surprisingly, a number of reviewers in academic journals found fault with the book, largely because it seemed to be neither fish nor fowl: some found it not historical enough to be a work of history, others not carefully theorized enough to be a work of theory. However, despite the difficulty of the book, *Origins* received very positive reviews in the nonacademic press.[95]

What seems to have drawn many reviewers to *Origins* is its blending of eclectic intellectual brilliance with passion, a combination that many felt was well suited to the nightmarish subject at hand. *Origins* may be "unconventional history," wrote H. Stuart Hughes in the *Nation,* "but it is a magnificent effort of creative imagination." Hinting at Arendt's status as a refugee from Nazi Germany, E. H. Carr in the *New York Times Book Review* described *Origins* as "the work of one who has thought as well as suffered." Also noting Arendt's personal relationship to her subject, August Heckscher, writing in the *New York Herald Tribune Book Review,* declared that the book "will stand as the measure of one person's spiritual torment and victory." Reviewers believed that such intellectual creativity and passion was necessary to deal with a topic that, for many of them, seemed to elude careful explanation. "The monstrous absurdities and crimes of totalitarianism," wrote M. A. Fitzsimons in a glowing review of *Origins* for the *Chicago Sunday Tribune Magazine of Books,* "have rendered the serious study of it particularly difficult. Horror, indignation, and incredulous amusement distract the inquirer, and the terrible reality remains unexplained." Sociologist David Riesman began his review in *Commentary* by remarking that science fiction is the genre best suited for the representation of totalitarianism. "Hannah Arendt's extraordinarily penetrating book," he continued, "makes plain that totalitarianism, whether Nazi or Stalinist, cannot be understood so long as we continue to use the traditional categories of common sense."[96]

Due to the book's complexity and richness, reviewers disagreed about what constituted its central argument or greatest achievement. Whereas Macdonald, writing in the *New Leader,* praised its third section on totalitarianism as a magnificent work of political theory that did not really address the question of origins at all, Riesman saw the entire book as a powerful causal argument that found in antisemitism and imperialism the origins of totalitarianism. Oscar Handlin, in a positive but critical assessment of *Origins* in the *Partisan Review,* regarded the book's "careful delineation of the exact features that distinguish totalitarianism from other modes of political organization" as its primary contribution, whereas Carr, in a generally positive review, criticized the work for providing an insufficient historical context for its observations about Nazism and Communism.[97] Not a single reviewer cited Arendt's linking of Communism and Nazism as a principal achievement of *Origins.*[98] Although a few quibbled with her explicit exclusion of Fascist Italy from the category, "totalitarianism" was already overwhelmingly understood as chiefly describing Nazism and Stalinism. Hughes, Heckscher, and Carr all took Arendt to task for extrapolating from her knowledge of Nazi Germany to draw particular conclusions about the Soviet Union, but they did not dissent from her general argument that these two regimes were fundamentally similar and deserved to be called "totalitarian."

As the reviews suggest, far from starting a new public conversation about dictatorship and totalitarianism, Arendt's book made a positive impression in large part because it powerfully evoked a phenomenon of great interest to American readers while fitting into a long-standing public conversation. *Origins* confirmed many beliefs of much of the reading public. Like Orwell, Arendt emphasized the nightmarishness of totalitarianism. Although she acknowledged the importance of propaganda and party organization, the outstanding aspect of totalitarianism for Arendt was terror and its outstanding institutions were concentration and extermination camps.[99] In her discussion of the camps, Arendt drew extensively on Bettelheim's "Individual and Mass Behavior in Extreme Situations" in a number of places. Like Bettelheim, Arendt argued that the camps served as the "laboratories" of totalitarianism. Like Bettelheim, too, she focused on the psychological impact of the camp experience, which she compared to hell itself. Though her account was less obviously marked by Freudianism than Bettelheim's, the end result of life in the camps was the same: "Through the creation of conditions under which conscience ceases to be adequate and to do good becomes utterly impossible, the consciously organized complicity of all men in the crimes of totalitarian regimes is extended to the victims and thus made really total." Long before the inmates were actually killed, they were turned into "living corpses."[100]

Arendt's camps also bore a close resemblance to Orwell's Ministry of Love, whose ultimate goal was to create such living corpses. There were, of course, significant differences: Arendt explicitly rejected the desire for power for power's sake as the driving force of totalitarianism; Orwell imagined a more personalized form of torture, accompanied by a pseudorational argument, and reserved that treatment for the party elite. However, in one important aspect, Arendt agreed with O'Brien: "It is in the very nature of totalitarian regimes to demand unlimited power. Such power can only be secured if literally all men, without a single exception, are reliably dominated in every aspect of life." Only in the concentration camps was this truly possible. Thus, as in Bettelheim, the camps became a microcosm of the regime's ideal society. In making this argument about total domination, Arendt also joined Orwell in portraying totalitarianism as the horrific realization of a fantasy of total power, the boot stamping on a human face forever. To emphasize the otherworldly horror of the camps, Arendt peppered her discussion of the camps with the argument that it was impossible to accurately describe the camp experience, that even those who had lived through it could not truly report it. The camps were not only difficult to understand, they also defied common sense. They "stand outside of life and death" and thus "can never be fully embraced by the imagination."[101] Arendt's treatment of the camps suggests an even more horrific world than do Orwell's long torture scenes. Despite the horror of imagining a world governed by Orwell's Party, the rats faced by Winston in Room 101 are just rats. By claiming that the real horrors of the camps are ultimately ineffable, Arendt conjures up a horror so vast that it cannot be described. Totalitarianism is not merely the triumph of humanity's worst instincts, but something almost superhuman, "absolute evil."[102]

Origins also matched already dominant American notions about modern dictatorship in its emphasis on front organizations, which Arendt viewed as one of the distinctive features of totalitarian movements. Front organizations, according to her, performed a dual function: to the outside world, they put a relatively acceptable face on the totalitarian movement; to the inner ranks of that movement, they presented a picture of the outside world that corresponded to totalitarian ideology. Thus they shielded reality and totalitarianism from each other. Sympathizers, argued Arendt, were as crucial to totalitarianism's success as true believers.[103] Although her front organizations were a good deal different from Schlesinger's Doughfaces, both suggested that totalitarianism's dupes were as dangerous as its open supporters. This argument had a long history in American understandings of the European dictatorships and was especially important after 1945.

To say that *Origins* reflected much conventional wisdom about totalitarianism should not obscure the fact that it presented many new and thought-provoking ideas that would be debated in the United States for decades. Arendt's depth of knowledge, especially about Germany and Western Europe, and her brilliant, idiosyncratic mode of thought allowed her to draw new connections among seemingly disparate phenomena and to conceptualize many aspects of the problem of totalitarianism in original ways. It is hard even today not to agree with Macdonald's observation that "the mental texture of the book is almost *too* dense, *too* rich. A paragraph, or even a sentence, often presents so novel and at the same time persuasive a point of view that one feels compelled to think about it."[104] Yet this density of intellectual trees often makes it difficult for readers of *Origins* to see the forest.

In fact, the very complexity of the work, as well as its ambiguities and contradictions, made *Origins* fit particularly well into the American public discourse about the meaning of modern dictatorship. Rather than resolving the many paradoxes that lay at the heart of this public discussion, Arendt's book seemed to be built on them. It presented an image of totalitarianism that was nightmarish, yet, despite her careful and dense argumentation, ultimately elusive. This elusiveness mapped easily onto the protean qualities of American thinking about dictatorship in a variety of ways. These qualities represented, as I have already suggested, something other than a mere failure to resolve difficult issues. Instead, the perceived lability of totalitarianism added to a growing sense of its almost mystical power. Totalitarianism was seen as both a foreign phenomenon that was essentially "un-American" and a universal phenomenon that potentially threatened the United States, internally as well as externally. The question of the ultimate cause of these regimes was also murky. Totalitarian states were almost always perceived to be mass regimes, but, especially since World War II, a small elite was often blamed for their evils. Whether elites or masses were responsible, the question of motivation remained: What drove people to embrace these regimes? Arendt's book addresses each of these issues but does not resolve any of them.

Like Hayek's *Road to Serfdom* and many other serious accounts of totalitarianism that became popular in the United States, *Origins* fudges the question of the foreignness of totalitarianism. The only two regimes that Arendt considered totalitarian, Nazi Germany and the Soviet Union, were European. Moreover, the book's first two sections, on antisemitism and imperialism, in which Arendt located the elements that eventually crystallized into totalitarianism, contained essentially historical arguments about Europe. Yet the final section on totalitarianism, though taking its material from the experience of two European regimes, is more theoretical; by the book's end, totalitarianism appears to threaten all of humanity. Part of the explanation for this shift can be found in Arendt's rather intense Eurocentrism: to a great extent, European history appears here as human history. But whatever the explanation, the United States both is and is not covered by Arendt's grim assessment of the crisis of the twentieth century.

On the relationship between masses and elites under totalitarianism, Arendt is even more elusory. Quoting Carlton J. H. Hayes's paper from the 1939 American Philosophical Society symposium on the totalitarian state, she starts the book's third section by placing the masses front and center in her understanding of totalitarianism: "In view of the unparalleled misery which totalitarian regimes have meant to their people—horror to many and unhappiness to all—it is painful to realize that they are always preceded by mass movements and that they 'command and rest upon mass support' up to the end." Indeed, mass support for totalitarian regimes is so critical that native forms of totalitarianism cannot take root in countries with small populations. However, Arendt uses the word "masses" in a particularly limited way. Throughout *Origins,* she draws an absolute distinction between the mob and the masses. Both the mob and the masses consist of people who have been thrown to the margins of society and lie outside the class system that structures it. The similarity ends there. Well established as a social force by the nineteenth century, the mob orients itself, at least in a negative way, to the classes that exclude its members. The mob is fickle, but it has a distinct political will, usually supporting a "great leader" who promises revenge on the society that excludes it. The masses, on the other hand, are a twentieth-century phenomenon. Unlike the mob, they have no political will. And unlike the mob, they are not oriented to the society that excludes them, nor even toward the classes from which they individually fell. Instead, the masses are marked by the "radical loss of self-interest, the cynical or bored indifference in the face of death or other personal catastrophes, the passionate inclination toward the most abstract notions as guides for life, and the general contempt for even the most obvious rules of common sense." The masses are "philistines." They are the product of a society already atomized, so "the chief characteristic of the mass man is not his brutality and backwardness, but his isolation and lack of normal social relationships." Arendt's masses bear some resemblance to Schlesinger and Fromm's anxious modern men. Unlike Schlesinger's, or even Fromm's, modern men who lose their individuality by embracing totalitarianism, Arendt's masses have already lost their individuality, have already become human robots, long before the rise of the totalitarian movement.[105]

Of course, such people are singularly unlikely political actors. It is not surprising, then, that although Arendt sees the masses as the distinctive social base of totalitarianism, the movement itself is led by a combination of the elite, especially some intellectuals, and the mob. The intellectuals are eliminated as soon as the movement seizes power. The mob thus provides the leadership, structure, and early impetus of the movement. According to Arendt, both Hitler and Stalin emerged from the mob. The elite and the mob soon discover that the masses, whom the former groups see merely as a route to power, are much better at totalitarianism than either of these older groups, for whereas the mob and the elite are essentially goal-oriented and seek individual gain, the masses are completely without goals, scruples, or even individuality, thus freeing them to work toward "the total domination of man."[106]

In ascribing the initial impetus for totalitarianism to the elite and the leaders of the mob, Arendt still does not make the totally apathetic, isolated, and undifferentiated masses particularly plausible political actors—just plausible pawns. Though she initially places the masses at the center of totalitarianism, as her argument continues, human responsibility for totalitarianism begins to dissipate almost entirely. She writes as if *all* relevant social groups are being acted upon by totalitarianism from without: "Only the mob and the elite can be attracted by the momentum of totalitarianism itself; the masses have to be won by propaganda."[107] Indeed, for much of the last section of the book, Arendt attributes a host of political desires and actions to totalitarianism itself.[108] Her description of the structure of totalitarianism similarly seems to eliminate any sort of individual responsibility. Totalitarianism, according to Arendt, is structured in layers, with front groups on the outside and the leader buried within. Each layer has a function similar to that of the front group, blocking reality from having an impact on the next layer within while sufficiently filtering out the madness of totalitarian ideology for the next layer. Like an onion, to which Arendt later compared this structure, totalitarianism thus has no center. She calls this structure "planned shapelessness," though no person or group is in any position to plan it.[109]

Rather than resolving the ambiguities in American thinking about totalitarianism, *Origins* is, in many ways, their apotheosis. In its pages, the relationship between those ambiguities and the sense of horror caused by the regime is clearer than in any previous text, for it is precisely in its utter inhumanity and ineffability that Arendt finds totalitarianism's greatest horrors. In turning the phenomenon itself into her principal protagonist, she suggests that totalitarianism will always defy rational explanation; the paradoxes, the contradictions, the violations of common sense are the essence of totalitarianism. The result is a kind of secularized theodicy. Reflecting her grounding in European existentialism, Arendt repeatedly says that modern man can no longer believe in a divine purpose and, in fact, that inability increases the horrors of totalitarianism: the extermination camps are like the medieval conception of hell, but worse for their lacking any eschatological significance. But Arendt's view of totalitarianism is almost as theological as is Niebuhr's. Totalitarianism represents an absolute evil that ultimately stands outside of human desires and actions and that threatens humanity itself. Arendt concludes *Origins* by quoting Acts 16:28 ("Do thyself no harm; for we are all here") in a thoroughly humanist vein, but her choice of texts adds to the book's theological feel.

Taking her cue from the 1958 science fiction film, political theorist Hanna Fenichel Pitkin has described totalitarianism in *Origins* as a "Blob," an exogenous, horrific force that attacks humanity from without. Arendt, writes

Pitkin, "discern[s] an emerging pattern of events, giv[es] it a name, and then think[s] of that name as an intentional, active force, composed of humans who have lost their agency."[110] Pitkin argues that such Blobs play a central role in Arendt's thought. Like many of her intellectual idiosyncrasies, her penchant for Blobs happened to perfectly fit American anxieties about dictatorship. Although Pitkin is rather apologetic for finding her metaphor in a work of Hollywood fantasy, the choice is both telling and appropriate. Although *The Vital Center, Nineteen Eighty-Four,* and *The Origins of Totalitarianism* are all serious books that are rightly seen as playing an important role in the intellectual history of the late 1940s and early 1950s, their images of totalitarianism mirror much broader cultural anxieties about dictatorship. Many of the Hollywood science fiction films of the 1950s—among them, *The Day the Earth Stood Still* (1951), *Red Planet Mars* (1952), *Earth vs. the Flying Saucers* (1956), *Invasion of the Body Snatchers* (1956), and *The 27th Day* (1957)—played off of these anxieties. Such films, as well as later television series like *The Twilight Zone,* seem to bear out Riesman's comment that science fiction is the genre best suited to represent totalitarianism. We should, perhaps, amend that thought: science fiction was a particularly appropriate genre for conveying Cold War–era American understandings of totalitarianism. Although those understandings in many ways resembled earlier conceptions of dictatorship, they departed from them in their sheer horror. Both fictional and nonfictional American accounts of dictatorship in the 1930s and early 1940s tended to find hope in humanity, whether in the form of good Germans, pangs of regret felt by Nazis who came to their senses, or simply the common sense of Americans faced with propaganda. In the late 1940s and early 1950s humanity was either the problem, as in Schlesinger and Orwell, or, as in Arendt, an insufficient barrier to the complete triumph of absolute evil.

Shortly after Arendt's book appeared, the idea of totalitarianism reached new heights of academic respectability with the publication of Carl Friedrich and Zbigniew Brzezinski's *Totalitarian Dictatorship and Autocracy* (1956). The authors grounded their analysis in a more empirical understanding of totalitarianism than Arendt or her predecessors had attempted, a six-point description that seemed, at least at the time, to fit both Nazi Germany and the Soviet Union.[111] Although "totalitarianism" had been in common usage for nearly two decades, there was finally a paradigmatic account of the term, at least within the American academy. *Totalitarian Dictatorship and Democracy* would structure much research for about a decade. The triumph of the Friedrich and Brzezinski paradigm, however, proved short lived. By the mid-1960s, its six-point description seemed empirically inadequate. With awareness of the Holocaust on the rise, growing questions about the Vietnam War and, with it, many aspects of the Cold War itself, and a sense that the Soviet Union had changed much since the death of Stalin, empirical American social science began to move away from the idea of totalitarianism. Herbert J. Spiro's entry on "totalitarianism" in the *International Encyclopedia of the Social Sciences* (1968), the first such encyclopedia since the mid-1930s, consisted of a six-page attack on the utility of the term. "If [my] expectations are borne out," Spiro concluded, "then a third encyclopedia of the social sciences, like the first one, will not list 'totalitarianism.'"[112]

In fact, the idea of totalitarianism has survived in America, both in popular culture and, despite Spiro's prediction, among academics. The reasons for its survival are based less on its empirical utility, about which many still agree with Spiro, than on its extraordinary cultural force.[113] The image of dictatorship as the ultimate embodiment of evil, as democracy's demonic Other, deeply shaped American political identity in the mid- and late twentieth century. Later echoed in President Ronald Reagan's famous descriptions of the Soviet Union as "the evil empire" and "the focus of evil in the world," the visions of dictatorship produced by Schlesinger, Orwell, Arendt, and others have kept alive the idea of totalitarianism in American political culture, even as the intellectual fortunes of the term have waxed and waned over the years. This image of dictatorship did not spring to life fully formed as a result of the Cold War. Rather, it developed through a complex cultural discussion that took place from the 1920s through the 1940s. This conversation was, of course, powerfully influenced by America's glimpses of Nazi Germany, the Soviet Union, Fascist Italy, and other dictatorships. But the particular directions it took were also the result of domestic concerns and anxieties.

The centrality of dictatorship in American political culture has had many results. Ideas about dictatorship helped rally many Americans to support intervention in World War II, even before Pearl Harbor. But they also contributed to a wartime Brown Scare, in which those opposed to entering the war were accused of harboring Nazi sympathies, as well as to the more famous and vicious postwar Red Scare. The social scientific interest in dictatorship led to a diverse series of important studies—from Cantril's analysis of the *War of the Worlds* broadcast to Arendt's *Origins of Totalitarianism*—that grappled with the problem of the individual in modernity. But these concerns about threatened individuality also helped lead to generalized fears about all mass political movements and the vilification of a variety of suspect groups as dupes whose political choices were necessarily inauthentic.

The horrors of the European dictatorships were real enough. On its face, the notion that American democracy should strive first and foremost to avoid becoming like them seems, in retrospect, almost inevitable. But Schlesinger's and Niebuhr's idea that these regimes were the result of an insufficiently pessimistic understanding of human nature, Burnham's and O'Brien's (if not Orwell's) sense that the ultimate motivation of human political activity was the desire for raw power, and even Arendt's concerns about the political behavior of the masses all contributed to a generalized suspicion of popular political activity outside of the safe, normal acts of American representative democracy such as voting or attending a town meeting. If, as Schlesinger suggested, simply being a typical American progressive was not only mistaken but actually paved the way for totalitarianism, the slippery slope to dictatorship appeared very broad, indeed.

NOTES

ABBREVIATIONS

CJF   Carl J. Friedrich
DT   Dorothy Thompson
FDR   Franklin D. Roosevelt
Manual U.S. Office of War Information, Bureau of Motion Pictures,
           Government Information Manual for the Motion Picture Industry
NAC   National Americanism Commission
WHC   William Henry Chamberlin

INTRODUCTION

1. Quoted in Kazin, *Populist Persuasion,* 139.
2. In private political button collection of Stephen H. Amos, St. Johnsbury, Vt.
3. Boutwell et al., *America Prepares for Tomorrow,* 514.
4. Quoted in Denning, *Cultural Front,* 25.
5. For a good recent example of the refusal to see totalitarianism as anything but a rhetorical creature of the Cold War, see Novick, *Holocaust in American Life,* 86. Novick insists that the term was "coined in the interwar years, but [came] into wide usage after 1945." But the sources that Novick cites, most notably Abbott Gleason's *Totalitarianism,* indicate that the term was regularly used in the United States by the end of the 1930s. Similarly, a paper based on this manuscript was dismissed by a well-known American historian because it is common knowledge that totalitarianism was a product of the Cold War.
6. For the most thorough exploration of this tradition, see Kazin, *Populist Persuasion.*
7. Gleason, *Totalitarianism,* 109–10.
8. Lippmann, *Phantom Public;* Purcell, *Crisis of Democratic Theory,* 101–9.
9. Denning, *Cultural Front,* 362, 371, 391.

CHAPTER ONE

1. Cannon and Fox, *Studebaker,* 138; Bonsall, *More Than They Promised,* 137–38; Newspaper advertisement, 1 July 1927, from 1927 Scrapbook, Studebaker National

Museum, South Bend, Ind. Production figure courtesy of the Studebaker National Museum.

2. Cannon and Fox, *Studebaker,* 138 (quotation); Diggins, *Mussolini,* 33.

3. Large factions of the young party during the 1920s attempted to proclaim "American exceptionalism," which suggested that the U.S. path to communism would be significantly different from Russia's. The exceptionalists, however, repeatedly lost intraparty skirmishes in the 1920s both within the United States and, more importantly, in the Comintern, which decisively turned against them in 1928.

4. Purcell, *Crisis of Democratic Theory,* 119–24.

5. Diggins, *Mussolini,* 77–110; for a full discussion of Mussolini's positive reception in the United States, see pp. 5–283. See also Bean, "Fascism and Italian-American Identity," 101–19.

6. Purcell, *Crisis of Democratic Theory,* 122–23; Diggins, *Mussolini,* 169–72 (Gompers), 22 (Ludwig).

7. Purcell, *Crisis of Democratic Theory,* 117–18.

8. On the rise of individualism during this period, see Wiebe, *Self Rule,* 185–201.

9. Quoted in Purcell, *Crisis of Democratic Theory,* 117.

10. Mussolini, "Youth"; Diggins, *Mussolini,* 61; "Benito Amicare Andrea Mussolini," 106.

11. Brooks, *Deliver Us from Dictators!,* 108 (Mussolini);. "The State: Fascist and Total," 48–49; Diggins, *Mussolini,* 72.

12. Purcell, *Crisis of Democratic Theory,* 119 (USSR as dictatorship); Feuer, "American Travelers," 119–49 (esp. p. 139). For a critical account that praises accomplishments of the USSR, see, e.g., Tunney and Davenport, "So This Is Russia!"

13. Lyons, *Assignment in Utopia,* 390; Brooks, *Deliver Us from Dictators!,* 197.

14. "Vivid Russian Portrait of Russia's Strong Man." See also "Close-up of Russia's 'Big Boss'"; "Behind the Scenes in Moscow"; and "Stalin Tramples on His Enemies."

15. Essad Bey, "Red Czar" (Conclusion), 44.

16. Scheffer, "Stalin's Power," 552, 566.

17. Fischer, "Why Stalin Won."

18. Heale, *American Anticommunism,* 90–93; Klehr, *Heyday of American Communism,* 9.

19. *Publisher's Weekly,* 2 April 1932, 1537. Hitler was already linked with Stalin and Mussolini, even though this advertisement dates from well before his gaining the chancellorship (January 1933). In April 1932 Hitler was a presidential candidate against Hindenburg.

20. Brooks, *Deliver Us from Dictators!,* 169; Diggins, *Mussolini,* 53–57.

21. Anderson, "Moronic Conventions." Ironically, Senator Reed would go on to become one of the most indefatigable opponents of FDR's desire to increase the powers of the federal government and the executive branch.

22. Blanker, "What a Real Dictator Would Do."

23. "Semi-Dictator?"

24. FDR, "Inaugural Address, March 4, 1933."

25. Levine, "Hollywood's Washington," 176 (n. 15). Levine also gives other ex-

amples of major political figures—including Alf Landon and Al Smith—who suggested giving the president wartime powers. For an example of popular support for this rhetoric, see "Farm Group Maps 'Dictator' Measure."

26. During its initial week at the Palace, it grossed $12,500 at twenty-five to seventy-five cents a ticket. At the end of the two-week run, the Palace reported that 175,000 tickets had been sold. Nollen, "Mussolini Speaks," 337.

27. Ibid., 336–37 (first and last quotations); Review of *Mussolini Speaks, New York Times.*

28. Quoted in Nollen, "Mussolini Speaks," 337.

29. Useful accounts of the making of *Gabriel* include McConnell, "Genesis and Ideology"; Schindler, *Hollywood in Crisis,* 109–16; and Black, *Hollywood Censored,* 137–45. Years later *Gabriel* would be reworked as *Dave* (1993), a film that eliminated both the supernatural and the dictatorial aspects of the story.

30. Black, *Hollywood Censored,* 137.

31. Ibid., 140–41; "'Gabriel' Film Sent Back to Hollywood"; Mordaunt Hall, "Gabriel over the White House."

32. McConnell, "Genesis and Ideology," 220, 219; Mordaunt Hall, "Gabriel over the White House"; Review of *Gabriel over the White House, Time;* "Fascist Fantasy."

33. Unfortunately, this political moment occurred a few short years before George Gallup began to produce the first regular and reliable polling data; by 1935, when the Gallup poll began, the moment had long since passed.

34. For a good example of Stalin as the ultimate pragmatist, see "Leaders—Russian and American." Here, the "spirit of Stalin" is favorably compared to the "defeatism" of U.S. government and business leaders, who, unlike Stalin, were unwilling to discard received dogma to achieve results.

35. As Edward Purcell (*Crisis of Democratic Theory,* 127–38) suggests, the arrival of the Great Depression actually led Americans to question democracy less than they had in the previous decade.

36. Warren, *Liberals and Communism,* 77–79 (on sympathetic liberals' explanations of Soviet dictatorship). On particular objections to *contemporary* dictatorship, see Brooks, *Deliver Us from Dictators!,* 1–24, and Rogers, *Crisis Government,* 60–61.

37. DT, *I Saw Hitler!,* 108.

38. Klehr, *Heyday of American Communism,* 11, 97.

39. O. Hall, "Attitudes and Unemployment," 26. Engineers, who for decades had been told from various quarters that their profession held the key to social management, could be more expected to have held such views than other Americans.

40. FDR, "Survey of the Purposes." For a more extended example of this rhetoric, see FDR, "First 'Fireside Chat' of 1934."

41. President's Research Committee on Social Trends, *Recent Social Trends,* lxviii–lxix; Armstrong, *"We or They",* 1–25. Ironically, Armstrong relies heavily on Ortega y Gasset's *Revolt of the Masses* (1932) for his descriptions of modern European politics. Although his view of Europe echoes Ortega's, the conservative Spanish philosopher characterizes this reign of unreason as the "Americanization of Europe." See also Sigel, "Opinions on Nazi Germany." Hitler's rise was frequently

explained in American magazines in terms of phenomena peculiar to Germany: the harshness of the Versailles Treaty and the nature of German political culture.

42. For the most thorough account of the exaggeration of the fascist threat and its relationship to the exaggeration of the communist menace during the Cold War, see Smith, *To Save a Nation*. See also Radosh, *Prophets on the Right,* and Ribuffo, *Old Christian Right,* 178–224.

43. Diggins, *Mussolini,* 160–61, 164–66.

44. Krok, "Relation of Business to Government," 90.

45. Bell, *In Hitler's Shadow,* 15–16; Smith, *To Save a Nation,* 90; MacDonnell, *Insidious Foes,* 42–47.

46. Hoberman, *Bridge of Light,* 194–98. When Hoberman's book appeared in 1991, *Der Vandernder Yid* was considered lost. Since then it has been almost entirely restored; only the opening sections of the first reel are missing.

47. Purcell, *Crisis of Democratic Theory,* 130; Hoberman, *Bridge of Light,* 197.

48. Bell, *In Hitler's Shadow,* 14 (mock trial of Hitler); Wentz, "American Protestant Journals."

49. See, e.g., Diggins, *Mussolini,* 314.

50. Swanberg, *Citizen Hearst,* 523–26; Nasaw, *The Chief,* 488–99; Schlesinger, *Age of Roosevelt,* 84–85.

51. Hanfstaengl, "My Leader," 9; Tuttle, "American Higher Education and the Nazis," 54–59; "Supreme Eugenic Courts"; "Death to a Dutchman"; "Adolf and Ignatz"; "Kosher and Kultur!"; "Gentle Adolf"; "'Bless Me, Natzi.'"

52. Sigel, "Opinions on Nazi Germany"; Zalampas, *Hitler . . . in American Magazines.* John Diggins and a number of other historians rely on Sigel's unpublished dissertation to suggest that Americans were entirely uncritical of Hitler on his rise to power. Sigel's study, limited as it is to three conservative magazines that rarely focused on foreign affairs, simply does not suggest such a sweeping judgment. Cf. Zalampas, *Hitler . . . in American Magazines,* for a much broader study that indicates how swiftly American press response to the Nazis became negative, though Zalampas is too quick to conclude that magazines were totally objective observers and fully grasped the horrors of the regime. The impression that U.S. responses to Nazi Germany were *positive,* I believe, is the result of the much fairer analysis that America did not respond negatively enough to the Nazis. This historical argument has special poignancy given the refusal of the United States to admit large numbers of refugees who were later slaughtered in the Holocaust. Even Sigel is primarily concerned not with positive appraisals of Hitler, but with the lack of negative assessments of (specifically) the German people as a whole, whom she holds collectively responsible for the horrors of Nazi Germany.

53. Ribuffo, *Old Christian Right,* 80–127; Smith, *To Save a Nation,* 66–76; MacDonnell, *Insidious Foes.*

54. "Ban Urged on Film of Nazi Activities."

55. Diggins, *Mussolini,* 314. For the distinction between Nazism and Italian Fascism in early anti-Nazi writings, see, e.g., Wise, Introduction to Van Paassen and Wise, *Nazism,* xi.

56. DT, *I Saw Hitler!,* 13–14.

57. Josephson, *Nazi Culture*, 16–17. For similar references, see, e.g., Ludwig Lewisohn, "The Revolt against Civilization," in Van Paassen and Wise, *Nazism*, 150.

58. Cohen, *Making a New Deal*, 332.

59. Diggins, *Mussolini*, 62–63, 243; Mordaunt Hall, "Gabriel over the White House."

60. Cohen, *Making a New Deal*, 283–85.

61. Ibid., 246–48; Melosh, *Engendering Culture*, 1.

62. Herbert Hoover, "Responsibility of the Republican Party to the Nation," 43; Melosh, *Engendering Culture*, 2–5.

63. See, e.g., "Footnote"; "Germany's All-Nazi, Womanless Parliament"; Tolischus, "Woman's Place in the 'Manly' Nazi State"; Alice Hamilton, "The Enslavement of Women," in Van Paassen and Wise, *Nazism*, 76–87; Brooks, *Deliver Us from Dictators!*, 105–14.

64. *Fortune*, July 1934, 7.

65. Melosh, *Engendering Culture*, 2.

66. Steiner, "Fascism in America?," 821.

67. Cohen, *Making a New Deal*, 283.

68. *Little Man* was followed by *Three Comrades* (MGM, 1938) and *The Mortal Storm* (MGM, 1940).

69. Indeed, the studio inserted an opening title, signed by studio head Carl Laemmle, which made this claim explicit: "In presenting 'Little Man, What Now?' to the screen, I strove to render a social service. The story of LITTLE MAN is the story of EVERYMAN—and the question of WHAT NOW? is the WORLD'S DAILY PROBLEM, a problem that men can only hope to overcome by a courage born of great faith in the hearts of women. Against the tide of time and chance *all* men are little—but in the eyes of a woman in love, a man can become bigger than the whole world."

70. Williams, "Some Thoughts," 306–7.

71. Caspar, *Fallada-Studien*, 292; Hackett and Burke, *80 Years of Best Sellers*, 115; Hicks, Review of *Little Man, What Now?*, 703. *Commonweal* (Review of *Little Man, What Now?*) also chose to review the book as "a social document" and found it wanting due to the weakness of its protagonist. For examples of positive reviews, see Marsh, "Little Family Faces the World," and Ruhl, "Made to Be Trampled On."

72. Katz, *Film Encyclopedia*, 143–44. Borzage pioneered the use of soft focus and gauze shots in a series of films, including *Humoresque* (1920), *Seventh Heaven* (1927), and *Bad Girl* (1931), which featured idealized lovers struggling to survive in a cruel and cold world.

73. The filmmakers made a point of Germanizing *Little Man* as much as possible. Frau Pinneberg—"Bunny" in Eric Sutton's American translation of the novel —is once again "Lämmchen." Mordaunt Hall ("Little Man, What Now?"), in reviewing the film for the *New York Times*, noted the fine detail of the production and the great success of its German feel.

74. Ditzen, *Little Man, What Now?*, 194.

75. In the following analysis I am deeply indebted to Barbara Melosh's chapter on *It Can't Happen Here* in Melosh, *Engendering Culture*, 15–31.

76. Schorer, *Sinclair Lewis,* 501, 600–601, 608. Schorer expresses surprise that Lewis declined to comment on German politics in 1934 in light of events reported by Daniel Longwell. According to Longwell, he and Lewis were drinking at Lewis's farm in June 1934 when news of the "Night of the Long Knives" came over the radio. Lewis apparently became deeply upset, as DT was still in Germany. "The news agitated [Lewis] extremely," writes Schorer, "and he became nearly hysterical in his fear that her life was in danger, in his helplessness somehow to arrange for her protection. It required the whole evening to calm him down" (p. 601). In fact, this anecdote from the year before the appearance of *It Can't Happen Here,* far from making Lewis's refusal to comment on German politics two months later mysterious, as Schorer suggests, actually brings to light an understanding of politics similar to that in the novel. For Lewis, the news of Hitler's purge was reduced not merely to apprehensions about his wife's personal safety—an obvious concern—but to a drama about his own masculinity. Lewis was most upset by his own helplessness. The ability of "This Situation" to disturb his autonomy and power, by causing his wife to go to Europe, by turning her attentions from him, and ultimately by threatening her life in such a way that he could do nothing, contributed mightily both to Lewis's long attempt not to deal with "It" and to the eventual vision of "It" that he produced in his novel.

77. Lewis, *It Can't Happen Here,* 19.

78. See, e.g., Stone, "Ironical Tract."

79. Lewis, *It Can't Happen Here,* 51, 59, 69, 101, 108, 122–23, 251.

80. Schorer, *Sinclair Lewis,* 611.

81. Lewis, *It Can't Happen Here,* 331.

82. Ibid., 75, 233, 301, 309, 99, 150–51, 92.

83. Melosh, *Engendering Culture,* 17; Lewis, *It Can't Happen Here,* 15–24.

84. Lewis, *It Can't Happen Here,* 32, 61, 74.

85. Ibid., 119, 19, 327; Melosh, *Engendering Culture,* 20. This message was softened in the theatrical version of *It Can't Happen Here,* which was popularized through numerous Federal Theatre Project productions. The play resolved some of the book's temporizing by suggesting that the love of a woman could, in fact, form the basis of healthy masculinity. For an account of the play, see Melosh, *Engendering Culture,* 15–31.

86. Stein, *Everybody's Autobiography,* 133.

87. The magazine ran extensive coverage of each election campaign, starting no later than 1928. In addition, it printed numerous articles and editorials about disarmament and other issues presumably of interest to women.

CHAPTER TWO

1. *Fascist Dictatorship,* 72. In 1926 the sense that Stalin was Russia's *dictator* had not yet established itself in the United States.

2. Maddux, "Red Fascism, Brown Bolshevism." Thomas R. Maddux conducted a content analysis of thirty-five U.S. newspapers and twenty-three U.S. magazines

to trace the Communism-Nazism comparison in the early and late 1930s. Ten of the thirty-five papers had taken the occasion of the Kirov Purge to compare the two systems. According to Maddux, only *two* of the papers (the *Omaha Morning World-Herald* and the *Chicago Tribune,* both conservative) believed that Germany and Russia had "similar systems." But his one brief quotation to illustrate a "similar systems" argument (from the *World-Herald*) calls into question the conclusion that even these two organs saw *systems,* as opposed to *dictators.* The Omaha paper, according to Maddux, "when considering communism, found it 'difficult to distinguish between its absolutism, its cruelty, its terrorism and that practiced by a Hitler, a Dollfuss, or a Mussolini'" (p. 91).

3. Kutulas, *Long War,* 80–81 (Kallen); Herbert Hoover, "Constitution Day Address."

4. Among the significant works that explore this subject are Skotheim, *Totalitarianism and American Social Thought;* Adler and Patterson, "Red Fascism"; Maddux, "Red Fascism, Brown Bolshevism"; McClay, *The Masterless,* 189–225; and Gleason, *Totalitarianism.*

5. For a recent example of this problem in a generally excellent work of history, see Novick, *Holocaust in American Life,* 86.

6. Gleason, *Totalitarianism,* 14–15.

7. Ibid., 16–20.

8. Ibid., 20–23.

9. Jänicke, *Totalitäre Herrschaft,* 41 (Goebbels), 42–43; Schapiro, *Totalitarianism,* 13–14; Gleason, *Totalitarianism,* 27–30.

10. Rodgers, *Contested Truths,* 144–75, 177; Wolin, "Idea of the State," 43. For a good example of what an Oxford-trained political philosopher thought of the American political "scientists'" evasion of the concept of the state, see Elliott, *Pragmatic Revolt in Politics,* 217.

11. Discarding the idealist state becomes symbolic of CJF's passage from Europe. CJF (*Constitutional Government*) argued that the importance of the state to European political thought had to do with historical accidents of public law in his native Germany. "The political scientist," he wrote, "not only cannot accept these national vocabularies, but he must transcend them." This requirement was particularly important in this case, as "the word 'state' is itself a propaganda tool of the absolutist" (pp. 10–11, 212).

12. *Oxford English Dictionary,* 18:287; Sturzo, *Italy and Fascismo;* Schapiro, *Totalitarianism,* 14; Gentile, "Philosophic Basis of Fascism." For an example of an apologetic American use of "totalitarian," see Spencer, "Political Developments in Italy." For a description of the Italian state as "total," see "The State: Fascist and Total," 48–50.

13. Jänicke, *Totalitäre Herrschaft,* 35.

14. See, e.g., Bottai, "The Corporative State" (in the same collection an article by Italy's minister of justice, Alfredo Rocca ["Transformation of the State"], carted out much of the theory of the totalitarian state but never used either that or any other adjective to describe the result); Villari, "Economics of Fascism"; and Diggins, *Mussolini,* 258–59.

15. Diggins, *Mussolini,* 160–66, 225–27, 172. For a more idealist image of the corporative state, see Bottai, "Corporative State."

16. "Ordeal of German Protestantism"; "Totalitarian State Finally Achieved by Hitler"; Rice, *Judgment Day,* 15.

17. Wise, Introduction (p. xii), DT, "Record of Persecution" (p. 11), High, "War on Religious Freedom" (pp. 32, 37–38), Hegemann, "Debasement of the Professions" (p. 71), Lore, "Fate of the Worker" (p. 110), and Holmes, "Threat to Freedom" (p. 132)—all in Van Paassen and Wise, *Nazism.*

18. Gleason, *Totalitarianism,* 33–38.

19. For an example of a Protestant opponent of "German Christianity," see Tillich, "Totalitarian State." On American magazine coverage of Gleichschaltung, see Zalampas, *Hitler . . . in American Magazines,* 34.

20. Fred Eastman, "God or Caesar?" Eastman's one-act play dramatizes the repression of pacifists during the "next war" in the United States.

21. "Hitler's New Religion."

22. "Prussian Protestantism and the Political Reaction"; Homrighausen, "Hitler and German Religion"; "Hitler's New Religion"; Cavert, "Hitler and the German Churches"; "Has Hitler Cowed the Churches?"; Niebuhr, "Religion and the New Germany."

23. Cavert, "Hitler and the German Churches."

24. For explicit attacks on the totalitarian state, see "Ordeal of German Protestantism"; "Nazi Progress toward Totalitarianism"; Homrighausen, "Barth Resists Hitler"; Hutchinson, "Germany Welcomes the Messiah"; and "German Catholics Make Common Cause with Protestants." For other articles concerned with the growth of the German state, see "Hitler Attacks Autonomy of Protestant Churches"; "Is This Another Kulturkampf?"; "Churches Should Be Wooed, Not Clubbed"; "Relation of Church and State Must Be Studied"; and "Nazis Win German Church Elections."

25. "German nazism, apparently, intends to go the full length of the new theory. It describes its ruling conception as that of a 'totalitarian state.'" "Ordeal of German Protestantism," 902.

26. "Second Revolution?" See also "Totalitarian State Finally Achieved by Hitler."

27. "Ordeal of German Protestantism"; Strunsky, "Behind the Masks."

28. Wise, Introduction to Van Paassen and Wise, *Nazism,* xi–xii. See also Hegemann, "The Debasement of the Professions," ibid., 71. Hegemann suggests that the totalitarian state was supported even by the German left in the early twentieth century, though he does so by translating *reiner Verwaltundstaat* (lit. "pure administrative state") as "totalitarian administrative state."

29. Diggins, *Mussolini,* 209–10, 259–60, 139–40.

30. Ibid., 140–43 (Salvemini); "Meeting the Nazi Threat"; "Hail, Exiled Scholars!"; Coser, *Refugee Scholars,* 102–9; Tillich, "Totalitarian State."

31. Ogg, *European Governments and Politics,* 830, 782; Lorwin, "Social Aspects"; Mason, Review of *The New Church and the New Germany;* Kunz, Review of *Sicher-*

heit; Sandifer, "Comparative Study of Laws," 276; Bond, "The Curriculum and the Negro Child," 163.

32. Gleason, *Totalitarianism,* 38–39; Ford, *Dictatorship,* 10 (Lerner); Fay, "The Nazi 'Totalitarian' State'"; Loewenstein, "Autocracy versus Democracy"; Steiner, "Fascism in America?"

33. Rogers, *Crisis Government,* 160–62.

34. Bingham, *Insurgent America,* 150–54; Warren, *Liberals and Communism,* 94–95 (on Bingham); Bates, "Battlefield of Liberty"; "Christian Totalitarianism"; "The Church and Christian Totalitarianism." In August 1935 Professor Robert McElroy of Oxford University, at a conference sponsored by the National Conference of Christians and Jews, put forward a similar idea: "There is a form of totalitarianism which is not lawless, cruel or barbarous, that includes within its scope all states, all races and culture groups. The moral leadership of the world . . . awaits that great nation which first adopts this new totalitarian philosophy. America, more than any other nation is equipped by her very nature to think in terms of universal interests." Quoted in Baker, Hayes, and Straus, *American Way,* 82.

35. For another similar attempt, see Strunsky, "Behind the Masks." Strunsky used "totalitarian state" to refer only to Germany, but, like Lindsay Rogers, he felt that the same growth in the state's power could be attainable in a democracy. Strunsky argued that this had occurred in New Zealand: "Obligatory arbitration in New Zealand was only one feature in a wide-ranging program which reveals a startling resemblance to the ideas of Mussolini's Corporative State and Hitler's Totalitarian State. Statism without an adjective flourished in the Antipodes more than a decade before the war. New Zealand laid a restraining hand on capitalism in the form of an elaborate code of factory legislation" (p. 1).

36. Laski, "Government by Consent"; Brickell, "He Knows His History."

37. Gleason, *Totalitarianism,* 22, 33.

38. On these comparisons, see Adler and Patterson, "Red Fascism"; Maddux, "Red Fascism, Brown Bolshevism"; and Gleason, *Totalitarianism,* 39–45.

39. Calvin B. Hoover, *Economic Life of Soviet Russia, Germany Enters the Third Reich,* and "Dictators and Democracies," 161, 163–66, 173. For more on Hoover, see Gleason, *Totalitarianism,* 39–42.

40. Calvin B. Hoover, "Dictators and Democracies," 168, 172.

41. Calvin B. Hoover, *Dictators and Democracies,* 20, 55–56.

42. Ibid., 15–16.

CHAPTER THREE

1. Lynd and Lynd, *Middletown in Transition,* 487–510, 501.

2. Ibid., 501–9.

3. Guttmann, *The Games Must Go On,* 62–81; Cantril, *Public Opinion,* 810.

4. On 11 January 1937 the AIPO asked Americans whether their sympathies were with the Loyalists, the rebels, or neither side. Of those surveyed, 22 percent said that they sided with the Loyalists, 12 percent with the rebels, and 66 percent

with neither. In May 1937 an AIPO poll indicated that 79 percent of Americans had no sympathies for either side. Almost two years later, an AIPO poll taken on 16 December 1938 indicated that 76 percent of Americans supported the Loyalists and 24 percent supported Franco; even 42 percent of Catholics surveyed stated a preference for the Loyalists. Cantril, *Public Opinion,* 807–8.

5. In April 1940 only 2 percent of Americans polled in a national AIPO poll felt that a third term was the most important issue. Nobody mentioned the third term in a concurrent poll that asked what issue respondents "would most like to hear discussed." By the fall, however, polling results showed much concern among Willkie supporters about a third term for FDR. According to an AIPO poll of 30 October 1940, the third term was the single most decisive factor for prospective Willkie voters, cited by 36 percent as their reason for choosing the GOP nominee. These numbers almost held up: following the election, a mid-November poll asking why people had voted as they did showed the third term as the number one reason among Willkie voters at 21 percent. On the other hand, the more serious charge of dictatorship appears to have had little impact on the election: only 2 percent of respondents to the October poll even mentioned it; the November poll lists no separate number for it, which, given the data, suggests that it was mentioned by less than 1 percent. Cantril, *Public Opinion,* 617, 619–20. GOP campaign button in private collection of Stephen H. Amos, St. Johnsbury, Vt.

6. U.S. Congress, Senate Committee on the Judiciary, *Reorganization,* pt. 4, 858–84; Bailey, "Speech on Reorganization." The one national poll that sought public opinion on FDR's intentions was taken on 12 July 1937, in the heat of the controversy. It asked, "Why do you think President Roosevelt wants to enlarge the membership of the Supreme Court?" The most popular answer was "To complete his program" (13 percent). However, the next three most frequent responses, accounting for 23 percent of those polled, all suggested a desire to increase his personal power: "Wants more power" (11 percent); "To have more votes; his own way, pack it" (8 percent); "Wants to be a dictator; strengthen power" (5 percent). "For his own personal use" was suggested by 3 percent. Thus over one-quarter of those surveyed (26 percent) believed that FDR wanted to reorganize the Court to increase his power in one way or another. Cantril, *Public Opinion,* 150.

7. The numbers on the administration's tendency toward dictatorship held up in later AIPO polls: 37 percent surveyed in October 1937 believed that "the policies and acts of the Roosevelt administration may lead to dictatorship"; 34 percent thought so in April 1938. In August 1938, 50 percent of respondents felt that "the possibility of a dictatorship in this country has been increased . . . by Roosevelt's policies"; only 16 percent felt that the possibility had decreased. Cantril, *Public Opinion,* 868–69.

8. The greatest danger to democracy, DT suggested, was "that reforms, often very good and much needed reforms, should be rushed through at a rate in which they cannot be digested in society. It is the danger that eager and unchecked majorities should set up new instruments of power, before they are equipped properly to administer such instruments. It is that the will of powerful pressure groups, even when such groups embrace a majority of voters, should find expression in

total disregard of the feelings, apprehensions, and interests of large and important minorities. . . . Everywhere there is a demand for more efficient instruments of political power. And accompanying these demands is a growing tendency toward personal leadership and personal government, and for a very simple reason: Personal leadership and personal government are the quickest and easiest way to get the things that people want." U.S. Congress, Senate Judiciary Committee, *Reorganization,* pt. 4, 861. See also the testimony of Princeton University president H. W. Dodds: "I do not mean to charge [that] the conscious purpose of the present public policy is to establish authoritative government without popular or judicial restraint. But the consequences of the President's proposal, if adopted, will be a first step, and a long step, toward this result in its effect on the public mind." Ibid., pt. 3, 620–56. See also testimony of Edwin Borchard, Professor of Constitutional Law at Yale University, ibid., pt. 4, 823–58, esp. 856–57).

9. Guttmann, *Wound in the Heart,* 25, 33, 41, 57.

10. Charlie Chaplin is most famous for doing this in *The Great Dictator* (United Artists, 1940), but the Three Stooges also released two short films caricaturing Hitler: *You Nazty Spy* (Columbia, 1940)—which appeared before Chaplin's film— and *I'll Never Heil Again* (Columbia, 1941).

11. "Comedy Has Its Limits."

12. For the publishing history of *Mein Kampf* in the United States during the 1930s, see Barnes and Barnes, *Hitler's Mein Kampf,* 73–140.

13. Quoted in *Gagging the Dictators,* 8. This fifty-page magazine is a spectacular compendium of cartoons, jokes, and humorous commentary about Mussolini, Hitler, Stalin, and the Japanese culled from around the world. The collection does not represent any single point of view; it even includes Nazi cartoons about the Soviet Union and Soviet cartoons about Nazi Germany. Except where otherwise noted, I have only considered the jokes and cartoons of U.S. origin for this study.

14. "'Let's Be Friends!'" The following month, *Time* referred to Hitler as "this fuzzy-lipped little man" "Plan v. Plan v. Plan." See also *Gagging the Dictators,* 36.

15. *Gagging the Dictators,* 43; "Games at Garmisch"; "'Let's Be Friends!'"; Gunther, "Der Führer." The Riefenstahl quotation actually appears twice in the 9 March issue of *Time:* once in the text of "'Let's Be Friends!'" and once under a picture of Riefenstahl with movie stars Marlene Dietrich and Anna May Wong looking seductive.

16. *Hollywood NOW,* 1 May 1937.

17. Gunther, "Der Führer," 55; "Plan v. Plan v. Plan"; *Gagging the Dictators,* 7, 5; "'Let's Be Friends!'" Review of *My New Order* quoted in Sigel, "Opinions on Nazi Germany," 67; the review appeared on 11 October 1941.

18. "Business of Empire." Diggins, *Mussolini,* 318–19. Nevertheless, Il Duce remained more popular than either Hitler or Stalin. He easily won an October 1938 poll that asked Americans, "If you absolutely had to decide which dictator you liked best, Mussolini, Stalin, or Hitler, which would you choose?" Mussolini received 53 percent of the vote to Stalin's 34 percent and Hitler's 13 percent. No doubt Mussolini's victory was largely by default; despite the wording of the question, fully 21 percent declined to choose. Cantril, *Public Opinion,* 162.

19. "Red, Altogether"; "Comedy Has Its Limits"; "Hitlerism Unveiled."

20. MacEachen, "Paper Hanger Makes Good."

21. Grace, "Hitlerism"; Knickerbocker, "Why Doesn't Somebody Kill Hitler?"

22. Sigel, "Opinions on Nazi Germany," 167. For humorous versions of this theme, see *Gagging the Dictators,* 24, 35–36, 42.

23. See, e.g., the Austrian cartoon of Hitler as Chaplin in *Gagging the Dictators,* 18. The story that the two men had been born on the same day was untrue: Chaplin was four days older than the German dictator.

24. Maland, *Chaplin and American Culture,* 166–69, 178–79. Fritz Lang's *Man Hunt* (20th Century Fox, 1941) opens with a famous sequence in which a British hunter attempts to shoot Hitler, but neither the audience nor the protagonist ever gets any closer to the Führer than a view through the crosshairs.

25. Maland, *Chaplin and American Culture,* 166.

26. Although most reviews were mixed, a number of publications, among them *Christian Century, Commonweal,* and the *Saturday Review,* objected to making light of Hitler. The *New Republic* and the *Nation* criticized the film's blend of earnestness and humor. Ibid., 180, 185; "Comedy Has Its Limits."

27. Charles Maland (*Chaplin and American Culture,* 179–82) has suggested that these formal aspects of the ending are what make it unconvincing.

28. For an exploration of the politics of CP anti-interventionism in Hollywood, see Ceplair and Englund, *Inquisition in Hollywood,* 165–77.

29. Maland (*Chaplin and American Culture,* 181) argues that this reading is "tortuous," but Chaplin's film is as good a case for left noninterventionism as any other major cultural artifact of the time. Indeed, the film would easily fit into the worldview that social revolution was the only solution to fascism. Moreover, the *Daily Worker* was perfectly capable of writing negative reviews of would-be progressive movies if they did not fit the party line.

30. Denning, *Cultural Front,* 383.

31. MacLeish, *Fall of the City,* 7, 29, 32–33.

CHAPTER FOUR

1. "Background of War: III," 233–34, 212, 214–24.

2. Ibid., 95. The image on pp. 96–97 features another crowd, this one composed mainly of civilians giving the Hitler salute, photographed similarly from just above head level. This second crowd photograph has been cropped so the object of the crowd's attention is entirely absent.

3. Cantril, *Psychology of Social Movements,* 270.

4. See, e.g., FDR, "Extemporaneous Speech at the Subsistence Homes Exhibition," "First 'Fireside Chat' of 1934," 317–18, and "Extemporaneous Remarks at Tupelo, Miss." Cf. "Regimentation Is the Least of Our Dangers."

5. For portions of DT's and Dodds's testimony, see Chapter 3, n. 8.

6. Quoted in Thomas and Braley, *Stand Fast for Freedom,* 68.

7. Wilson, *The New Freedom,* 281–82.

8. Chase, *New Deal,* 189.

9. Mumford, *Technics and Civilization,* 9–59.

10. Guttmann, *Wound in the Heart,* 169–95, 178. For more on *Air Raid,* see Brady, *Citizen Welles,* 165–66.

11. Stuart Chase turned his back on his previous work, focusing instead on an effort to eliminate language that objectified abstract social concepts. In *The Tyranny of Words* (1938), his first example of such language in his appendix of "Horrible Examples" (p. 363) was taken from his own *New Deal.*

12. Ceplair and Englund, *Inquisition in Hollywood,* 310–11.

13. Not surprisingly, the German government and the Nazi Party were deeply hostile to *The Mortal Storm* and refused to grant copyright permission to use the lyrics to the "Horst Wessel Song." The filmmakers avoided this potential legal problem by having composer Edward Kane and lyricist Earl Kent pen a tune entitled "Close Up the Ranks," the music for which was essentially identical to the "Horst Wessel Song," and the lyrics for which were substantially similar. Although this nicety of copyright law was carefully recorded in the files of the Production Code Administration (PCA) and received some notice in the entertainment press at the time, "Close Up the Ranks" was clearly intended to be the "Horst Wessel Song," and, as the two sound identical, would have been identified as such by film audiences at the time. PCA file on *The Mortal Storm,* Academy of Motion Picture Arts and Sciences, Los Angeles.

14. A similarly seductive party-oriented woman draws German American Nazi Dr. Kassel away from his wife in *Confessions of a Nazi Spy.*

15. Sherwood, *There Shall Be No Night,* 169.

16. Cantril, *Invasion from Mars,* xii.

17. Strecker, *Beyond the Clinical Frontiers,* 54–55.

18. See, e.g., Herbert Hoover, *American Individualism,* 1–13.

19. For example, Walter Lippmann (*Good Society,* 379, 386) located the origin of the problem in the nineteenth century's "fury to explain men rationally," which "explained away their essence, which is their manhood." Man thus met a new kind of challenge: "Men have learned to defend themselves against personal sovereigns, against the doctrine that as slaves they belong to their lord, as subjects to their king. But in the presence of the anonymous master, the super-organism of the collectivists, they do not so easily discern its inhuman pretensions and brutalizing dominion." In Lippmann's view, the creation of the Good Society depended on an aggressive reassertion of the importance of the individual.

20. On Armstrong's relationship with FDR, see Lifka, *Concept of "Totalitarianism,"* 39.

21. Sigel, "Opinions on Nazi Germany," 39–40, 43–47.

22. NAC, *ISMS,* 14.

23. This was never more apparent than in March 1938, when, in response to allegations surrounding his proposed restructuring of the executive branch (nicknamed the "Dictator Bill" by his opponents), FDR circulated among reporters a letter explicitly denying his desire for dictatorship. The fact that the letter was distributed at midnight added symbolic weight to precisely the accusations he sought

to quell. For more on this incident and charges of dictatorship aimed at FDR during the 1936 campaign, see Lifka, *Concept of "Totalitarianism,"* 44–54.

24. For an example of this argument, see FDR, "'We in Turn Are Striving.'" See also his acceptance of the 1940 Democratic nomination, in which he justified his decision to run for an unprecedented third term by asserting that, if "called upon to do so by the people of my country," it was his duty to run. FDR, "The President Accepts the Nomination for a Third Term," 296. The entire speech was about the struggle between dictatorship and democracy and included a further elaboration along majoritarian lines: "My conscience will not let me turn my back upon a call to service. The right to make that call rests with the people through the American method of a free election. Only the people themselves can draft a President. If such a draft should be made upon me, I say to you, in the utmost simplicity, I will, with God's help, continue to serve with the best of my ability and the fullness of my strength."

25. See FDR, "Survey of the Purposes" and "First 'Fireside Chat' of 1934."

26. For poll results, see Chapter 3, n. 7.

27. FDR, "We in Turn Are Striving," 42.

28. FDR, "'Dictatorships Do Not Grow,'" 242.

29. FDR, "'We Are Not Only the Largest and Most Powerful Democracy,'" 619–20, and "Annual Message to Congress, January 4, 1939," 5, 7–8, 11.

30. FDR, "'I Have Every Right to Speak,'" 398–99.

31. For later examples of FDR equating majority rule with democracy, see fascism as excessive private power in FDR, "Recommendations to the Congress to Curb Monopolies," 305, and his argument that the principle of free choice in elections was the very basis of the U.S. Constitution in "'We Believe,'" 150–51. See also FDR, "'He Believed,'" 579.

32. Jay, *Dialectical Imagination,* 38–40.

33. Ibid., 86–90; McClay, *The Masterless,* 208.

34. Burston, *Legacy of Erich Fromm,* 18–22 (quotation, p. 20). One measure of the immediate impact of Fromm's book was that the February 1942 issue of *Psychiatry* devoted 24-pages to it: "*Escape from Freedom:* A Synoptic Series of Reviews" by eight scholars, including Ruth Benedict. Many of these reviewers responded enthusiastically to the work, especially its assessment of fascism. The incorporation of psychoanalytic concepts was one of the main points of contention among the reviewers.

35. Fromm, *Escape from Freedom,* 4–5, 80–81, 89, 94–95, 128–30, 193, 223.

36. Lewis B. Hill, in "*Escape from Freedom:* A Synoptic Series of Reviews," 117–18.

37. See, e.g., Macdonald, "New Dimension."

38. Mumford, *Men Must Act,* 58–59.

39. Mumford, *Faith for Living,* 37, 118–19.

40. Lerner, *Later Than You Think,* 71–72, 36, 57, 31.

41. Mumford, *Faith for Living,* 307. Such a language of preservation was striking coming from Mumford, who had offered a radical critique of capitalism and a vision of a postcapitalist future. Although he sometimes expressed the hope that

the challenge of fascism would force such a revolutionary turn, Mumford spent much of his time in the late 1930s attacking liberals for not living up to their principles. Allison, "Two Public Philosophers," 88.

42. For a thorough account of the making of *Confessions of a Nazi Spy,* see Birdwell, *Celluloid Soldiers,* 57–86.

43. Lerner, "The Pattern of Dictatorship," quoted in Ford, *Dictatorship,* 22–23.

44. Lederer, *The State of the Masses,* 232.

45. For a literary near equivalent, see Kressmann Taylor's popular epistolary novella *Address Unknown* (1939). This work consists of a series of letters between Max Eisenstein, a first-generation German American, and Martin Schulse, his business partner and fellow immigrant, who moved back to Germany in November 1932. Over the course of their correspondence, Schulse—to the horror of his friend —slips into Nazism, then becomes a victim of the new regime. Max's final letter of 3 March 1934 is returned bearing the stamp "Address Unknown" in German.

46. For studio responses to Nazism in the 1930s, see Birdwell, *Celluloid Soldiers,* and Colgan, "Warner Brothers' Crusade."

47. Quoted in McBride, *Capra,* 376–78.

48. Ibid., 256–61.

49. Capra, *The Name above the Title.*

50. Thorp, *America at the Movies,* 146–48.

51. See, e.g., Dudley Andrew, "Productive Discord in the System," in Charles Wolfe, *Meet John Doe,* 253–68.

52. Capra, "Just What Is the Capra Touch?"

53. Capra, "Mr. Capra (Humanist) Shares a Bow."

54. McBride, *Capra,* 438–39, 432.

55. In all three movies, the heroine is a reporter. In *Smith* and *Doe,* the protagonist is a media personality: Jefferson Smith comes from a journalistic family and runs a boys' newspaper before becoming a senator; "John Doe" is a media creation. Even Longfellow Deeds makes his money writing slogans for mass-marketed greeting cards. The press and radio are crucial to the plot of each film: they attack Deeds and announce his decision to give his money away; they run state politics in *Smith,* as well as provide the most important support and opposition that the new senator gets; they create John Doe and determine the shape of the John Doe movement.

56. Although the ruffians who beat up the children who are distributing their pro-Smith newspaper in *Smith*'s final montage sequence bear a certain resemblance to a regimented crowd, they are probably meant to be the hired thugs of the anti-Smith political machine and newspaper.

57. For the best account of the many endings considered, see Charles Wolfe, "*Meet John Doe:* Authors, Audiences, and Endings," in Wolfe, *Meet John Doe,* 3–29.

58. One of the endings that Capra considered for the film involved an additional scene in which Ann Mitchell, John Willoughby, and the Millville club set up a John Doe Club storefront, thus presumably operating without mass mediation.

59. McBride, *Capra,* 432, 436. A letter in Capra's files suggests the ending. However, it was addressed to Riskin, not Capra, and signed "EGF," not "John Doe."

60. McBride, *Capra,* 436.

61. It is in this way that the *War of the Worlds* broadcast figures in a sequence in *Radio Days* (1987), Woody Allen's atmospheric, comic evocation of the radio culture of the 1930s.

62. Cantril, *Invasion from Mars,* 47.

63. Quoted in Callow, *Welles,* 309.

64. Brady, *Citizen Welles,* 123, 159–60.

65. Callow, *Welles,* 398–407; Brady, *Citizen Welles,* 162–67, 178. Hadley Cantril credited Howard Koch with the script, while Welles insisted that he had authored it himself. This set off an argument between Welles, Koch, and Princeton University Press that continued for decades and eventually spread into other critical literature on the broadcast. It now appears that Koch wrote the script. Unfortunately, supporters of Koch's authorship have seemed quick to embrace the notion that *War of the Worlds* was intended to be nothing more than light entertainment (see, e.g., Callow, *Welles,* 399–408). In fact, Koch, like Welles and most of the rest of the Mercury troupe, was deeply committed politically; indeed, he later went to Hollywood and was eventually blacklisted in the late 1940s for his politically suspect screenplays, including *Mission to Moscow.* Though Welles was responsible for little more than directing *War of the Worlds,* it—like many Mercury programs—reflected commitments broadly shared by Welles and his collaborators.

66. Brady, *Citizen Welles,* 170–71.

67. Ibid., 173–74, 164. Cantril, despite calling for progressive social legislation to improve the lot—and thus the judgment—of most Americans, was deeply suspicious of social movements per se. In his *Psychology of Social Movements,* he considers participation in any such movement (he mentions both major American political parties, Nazism, nudism, and many others) a sign of irrationality. Although the category "social movement" was a very broad one for Cantril, every case study in the book was of a movement that he found either ridiculous or threatening: the lynch mob, the kingdom of Father Divine, the Oxford Group ("its individualism and refusal to consider the social context that gives rise to social problems makes it inevitably anti-democratic"—p. 168), the Townsend Plan, and Nazism.

68. Cantril notes that these so-called experts added to audience acceptance of the play as actual news but fails to mention that the experts are repeatedly proven wrong.

69. Cantril, *Invasion from Mars,* 43.

70. Welles's most magnificent rehearsal of this theme was *Citizen Kane* (1942), whose entire structure, as André Bazin and others have pointed out, is to turn the viewer into an investigator. The film never really answers its own questions about the identity of the title character. The on-screen investigating reporter ends up stumped; by seeing the sled at the film's end, the viewer is immediately aware that she knows more than any character did. Not only do the possible on-screen authorities fail, but the narrative falls short of offering a single right conclusion for the viewer. Instead, the film forces the viewer to puzzle over Kane for herself. Laura Mulvey (*Citizen Kane,* 18) has argued that it does all of this in the larger context of an antifascist, anti-isolationist argument.

71. Denning, *Cultural Front,* 391.

72. Cantril, *Invasion from Mars,* ix, 203–4.

73. Ibid., 114–18.

74. Ibid., 195. Other, smaller subsections of those who panicked, Cantril concluded, did so because (1) the broadcast fit into strong standards of judgment that they possessed (e.g., religious fundamentalists who interpreted the invasion as an act of God), (2) their standards of judgment were inadequate to determine a good from a bad source of information, or (3) they entirely lacked standards of judgment.

75. Ibid., 203–4. However, Cantril did warn that if educational levels exceeded economic attainment by too much, rising expectations would simply lead to greater disappointment and frustration (p. 156).

76. Ibid., 67–84, 3.

CHAPTER FIVE

1. Brooks, *Deliver Us from Dictators!,* 169.

2. Quitman and Allen, *Dictator Isms,* 4–5, 8–9.

3. Lifka, *Concept of "Totalitarianism,"* 66. Lifka estimates that between 1938 and 1939, the American reading public would have familiarized itself with the term used in this way.

4. Maddux, "Red Fascism, Brown Bolshevism," 85–103.

5. Ibid.

6. Examples of each of these groups include Sidney Hook, Calvin Hoover and DT, Eugene Lyons, and the editors of *Commonweal* and *Christian Century.*

7. Warren, *Liberals and Communism,* 105, 127–42.

8. For example, Max Lerner (*Later Than You Think,* 236–37) criticized the Soviet Union in 1938 for having an insufficiently democratic form of collectivism, while fully endorsing the Popular Front.

9. Warren, *Liberals and Communism,* 109–10, 116–17, 122–26.

10. Ibid., 163–92.

11. FDR, "'Do Not Seek or Expect Utopia Overnight,'" 93. For an earlier example of the same trope, see "Russian Tragedy."

12. Ceplair and Englund, *Inquisition in Hollywood,* esp. 80–81, 104–12.

13. CP members and fellow travelers in Hollywood were not absolutely silent. The 1937 version of *The Prisoner of Zenda* features an obvious pro-Soviet image. The story concerns the attempt of an evil prince to become king of a small central European country by kidnapping his brother, the good crown prince. Luckily for the forces of good, an English tourist happens to be a spitting image of the rightful heir and is convinced by the crown prince's advisers to stand in for the prince during the coronation. In one climactic scene, the courtly supporters of the crown prince face off against the evil prince's retinue. The former three, in tan uniform shirts, with small, rounded collars, are dressed like Soviet commissars. The attendants of the evil prince, all in black with riding boots, resemble Nazi SS officers.

To top off the image, the most senior of the men in commissar outfits has a bushy mustache and smokes a pipe reminiscent of Joseph Stalin's. It is unclear who was responsible for this symbolism. Ernst Dryden, who costumed the production, was a European refugee, but his politics are unknown. A number of Popular Front supporters did work on the film, including Donald Ogden Stewart, a fellow traveler and head of the Hollywood Anti-Nazi League, who is credited with "additional dialogue." All of this seems to have gone unnoticed by anticommunist watchdogs in Sacramento and Washington. *The Prisoner of Zenda* was never mentioned in the hearings on "propaganda" films before the war. I thank Professor Richard Stites for alerting me to this image.

14. Even before the Hays Code was enforced in 1934, Hollywood studios were able to stop such projects. Frank Capra spent four months of 1932 working on a film called *Soviet.* Capra, a generally conservative but apolitical figure in the early 1930s who later became a rabid anticommunist, was attracted to the project not by its politics, which were apparently fairly neutral, but by the Soviet Union as a setting for human drama. Nevertheless, due to political concerns MGM postponed production indefinitely. McBride, *Capra,* 282–84. After 1934, such projects were terminated even more quickly. When, in 1934, director Lewis Milestone wanted to make a sympathetic film about Soviet life entitled *Red Square,* Joseph Breen, the head of the Hays Office, rejected the idea. Koppes and Black, *Hollywood Goes to War,* 187.

15. In *Ninotchka* and *Comrade X,* the communist is a Russian woman. In *He Stayed for Breakfast,* he is a Frenchman (played by Melvyn Douglas—the capitalist converter of Garbo in *Ninotchka*).

16. Much of this role was created to play off of Garbo's screen image. In one of the first exchanges in which Ninotchka takes part, one of the commissars asks her if she would like to be left alone. "No," she snaps, in violation of the Garbo persona.

17. NAC, *ISMS,* 266.

18. One famous example of this is Dilling, *Red Network* (1936).

19. The infamous "Spider-Web Chart" purporting to show the links between prominent individuals and organizations in the communist conspiracy was apparently first produced by the Chemical Warfare Service of the War Department in 1923. Davis, *American Heroine,* 263–65.

20. Kurth, *American Cassandra,* 287 (DT); Ribuffo, *Old Christian Right,* 123; FDR, "A Message to the Foreign Policy Association" and "'We Americans Have Cleared Our Decks.'"

21. Cantril, *Public Opinion,* 809. To the question, "Do you believe that Germany has already started to organize a fifth column in this country?," the response was 71.0 percent, yes; 6.8 percent, no; and 22.2 percent, "Don't know." For the most thorough account of American concern about a Nazi fifth column, see MacDonnell, *Insidious Foes.*

22. Kurth, *American Cassandra,* 286–89; High, "Star-Spangled Fascists"; "The Nazis Are Here."

23. *Newsweek* noted that German Americans opposed to Hitler met in the Bronx

on the same night as the Bund rally. "America's 'Isms,'" 14. For a general account of isms in Western discourse, see Harro Höpfl, "Isms and Ideology."

24. High, "Star-Spangled Fascists," 5.

25. The term had been a pejorative for religious sects as far back as 1680. *Oxford English Dictionary,* 8:112.

26. For examples of rhetorically neutral surveys, see Wasserman, *Handbook of Political "Isms,"* and Americana Institute, *Isms.* For examples of more polemical works, see NAC, *ISMS;* Quitman and Allen, *Dictator Isms;* and "Guide to Isms" in DT, *Dorothy Thompson's Political Guide,* 11–32.

27. See, e.g., Coyle et al., *American Way;* Baker, Hayes, and Straus, *American Way,* esp. chap. 5; Thomas and Braley, *Stand Fast for Freedom,* esp. Introduction.

28. DT, *Dorothy Thompson's Political Guide,* 11–13, 25.

29. Ibid., 62, 58, 90.

30. Quitman and Allen, *Dictator Isms,* 11, 10–45.

31. Ibid., 26, 49, 51.

32. NAC, *ISMS.* Raoul E. Desvernine's right-wing critique of the New Deal, *Democratic Despotism,* contrasts "Americanism" with the "New Despotisms," which included all the various movements listed under isms in later works.

33. For more on Hoover and this essay, see Chapter 2.

34. Rahv, "Two Years of Progress" and "Crisis in France"; Hook, "Anatomy of the Popular Front"; Greenberg, "Avant-Garde and Kitsch," 34–49.

35. But the *Christian Century* editors felt that the Vatican and Catholics generally were too quick to see fascism as the lesser evil.

36. Cavert, "When Is the Church Free?"; Vann, "Jews, Reds, and Imbeciles," 17.

37. Lyons, "Our Totalitarian 'Liberals,'" 385–86, 387.

38. WHC, *Collectivism.* WHC uses "collectivism" exclusively to talk about fascism and communism together. See also Lippmann, *Good Society.* Lippmann's main concern is collectivism, although the totalitarian state (as the goal of collectivism) makes an occasional appearance. Other writers who also use "totalitarianism" mention that both communism and fascism are forms of collectivism. DT, *Dorothy Thompson's Political Guide,* 13–14.

39. See, e.g., Lerner, *Later Than You Think,* 159–66.

40. Drucker, *End of Economic Man.*

41. At least one academic suggested that we might have to coin terms such as "halfitarianism" to deal with compromise situations. Herbert Heaton, "Discussion of Totalitarianism," in "Symposium on the Totalitarian State," 89–90.

42. For example, DT (*Dorothy Thompson's Political Guide,* 14–15) answers her own question, "What is Totalitarianism?," with a discussion devoted to the totalitarian state and the relationship between the state and various aspects of society. Louis Wasserman's *Handbook of Political "Isms"* does not have a separate chapter on totalitarianism and uses the word "totalitarian" entirely in the context of the relationship between the state and the individual in Italy and Germany (pp. 106, 114–15).

43. Quoted in Lifka, *Concept of "Totalitarianism»,"* 178.

44. Warren, *Liberals and Communism,* 182–85. The Committee for Cultural Free-

dom, which apparently disappeared shortly after the publication of its manifesto, should not be confused with the Congress for Cultural Freedom, a Cold War–era, CIA-sponsored international organization.

45. "Manifesto." The statement of the Committee for Cultural Freedom, signed on 22 May 1939, was published in a variety of newspapers and magazines.

46. For the international dimension of this phenomenon, see Alexander, *Right Opposition;* Liebich, *From the Other Shore;* and Jones, *Lost Debate.*

47. Alexander, *Right Opposition,* 127–28; Myers, *Prophet's Army,* 143–71; Callinicos, *Trotskyism,* 55–61; Wohlforth, "Trotskyism." The WP broke from the Trotskyite Socialist Workers Party when Shachtman and his supporters rejected the orthodox Trotskyite line that the Soviet Union, though a degenerate workers' state, was still a workers' state, and thus worthy of some admiration. For more on Burnham, see the section on "Pessimistic Precursors" in Chapter 9.

48. Boutwell et al., *America Prepares for Tomorrow,* 514.

49. Lerner, "Lippmann Agonistes"; Kirchwey, "Red Totalitarianism."

50. Lifka, *Concept of "Totalitarianism,"* 185.

51. Boutwell et al., *America Prepares for Tomorrow,* 514–23.

52. DT, *Dorothy Thompson's Political Guide,* 114–20. The *Partisan Review,* for its part, was highly critical of such status quo–oriented invocations of totalitarianism. See, e.g., Macdonald, "War and the Intellectuals," and "War of the Neutrals."

53. MacIver, Bonn, and Perry, *Roots of Totalitarianism,* 20 (Perry); "Symposium on the Totalitarian State," 89 (Heaton).

54. MacIver, Bonn, and Perry, *Roots of Totalitarianism,* 9.

55. Calvin Hoover, *Dictators and Democracies,* 9–12. The essay that argues for the intentional distinction between the two kinds of regimes was originally published in the *Virginia Quarterly* in April 1934. See Chapter 2.

56. Ibid., 56, 39, 46.

57. "Symposium on the Totalitarian State," 4 (Marx); MacIver, Bonn, and Perry, *Roots of Totalitarianism,* 6 (MacIver); "Symposium on the Totalitarian State," 77, 87 (Bonn). See also MacIver, Bonn, and Perry, *Roots of Totalitarianism,* 19.

58. Perry characterized this factor as "uniformitarianism," one of the "tributary ideas" of totalitarianism. MacIver, Bonn, and Perry, *Roots of Totalitarianism,* 20–23. See also Hans Kohn in "Symposium on the Totalitarian State," 68.

59. "Symposium on the Totalitarian State," 28. See also Carlton J. H. Hayes on totalitarianism as a substitute for religion in "Symposium on the Totalitarian State," 95, and Robert MacIver on the totalitarian definition of the nation as a community of believers in a new cult in MacIver, Bonn, and Perry, *Roots of Totalitarianism,* 7.

60. "Symposium on the Totalitarian State," 98 (Hayes); MacIver, Bonn, and Perry, *Roots of Totalitarianism,* 8 (MacIver).

61. In addition to the instances of this quoted below, see Thomas Woody in "Symposium on the Totalitarian State," 55. Cf. Hans Kohn in ibid., esp. 59–60, where he discusses the ideational roots of the "totalitarian philosophy of war" but remains more or less silent about who bears these ideas.

62. "Symposium on the Totalitarian State," 98–99 (Hayes); MacIver, Bonn, and

Perry, *Roots of Totalitarianism,* 10, 12, 16 (Bonn); "Symposium on the Totalitarian State," 37 (Marx).

63. Ibid., 68 (Kohn), 61, 73 (Whittlesey); MacIver, Bonn, and Perry, *Roots of Totalitarianism,* 9 (Bonn).

64. "Symposium on the Totalitarian State," 37, 100, 70.

65. For example, in 1936 Calvin Hoover (*Dictators and Democracies,* 62) wrote: "Any group of capitalists who attempt to set up a politically totalitarian state as a sort of Prætorian Guard for capitalism would find that they had in effect set their feet on the surprisingly short road which leads to economic totalitarianism."

66. In fact, the original plan for the American Philosophical Society meeting included a proposed session on the totalitarian state and biology. In their initial memorandum, the organizers stated that they did not intend this to be a session on the state of the biological sciences in totalitarian regimes—as one of the invitees seemed to think in his letter of regret to the meeting's organizers—but rather an extension of the idea of totalitarianism to the animal kingdom: "The types of animal societies represented by ants and mammals. The former being especially totalitarian, the latter not." Dr. Walter B. Cannon to Dr. Edwin G. Conklin, 26 September 1939, and "Memorandum on the Proposed Symposium on the Totalitarian State," attached to Conklin to Dr. William E. Lingelbach, 7 June 1939, APS Secretary's Correspondence, 1938–39, American Philosophical Society Library.

67. CJF, *Constitutional Government,* 499–500 (quotation), 261–62, 482–84.

68. In the famous pro-Loyalist League of American Writers' *Writers Take Sides*—a collection of responses by a largely handpicked group of writers to a rather leading set of questions put by the Popular Front–aligned league on choosing sides in the Spanish Civil War—98 percent of the more than four hundred replies favored the Loyalists. *Writers Take Sides* reprinted over two hundred of these pro-Loyalist letters (although the sympathies of some of the responses are unclear); not a single pro-Loyalist respondent employed the words "totalitarian" or "totalitarianism." The concept does show up in the one response listed as pro-Franco: Gertrude Atherton asserted that "as far as totalitarianism goes there is not tuppence to choose between fascism [*sic*] and communism." Atherton went on to profess a slight preference for Franco because at least fascists were honest in their antidemocratic views.

69. Opinion on the Spanish Civil War, the most visible manifestation of the communist-fascist struggle in the late 1930s, is a good indication of this. Polls conducted by the American Institute for Public Opinion between January 1937 and February 1939 indicate that only a minority of Americans polled ever supported either side. Cantril, *Public Opinion,* 807–8.

70. Kurth, *American Cassandra,* 308–27; "War of the Neutrals"; Macdonald, "National Defense."

71. Lifka, *Concept of "Totalitarianism,"* 175–76, 121, 178–92. Lifka devotes an entire chapter (91–212) to an exhaustive run-through of uses of the totalitarian concept during the period between the invasion of Poland and the bombing of Pearl Harbor.

72. Pratt, *America and Total War.*

73. John F. Kennedy, *Why England Slept,* 183. For an interesting reading of this rather odd book—as well as a good account of who actually wrote which portions of it—see Wills, *Kennedy Imprisonment,* 72–83.

74. Lifka, *Concept of "Totalitarianism,"* 134. A less extreme version of the same argument was made by former Wisconsin governor Philip F. LaFollette in a debate with Upton Sinclair over intervention on 13 March 1941 in Pasadena, Calif. Sinclair, *Peace or War in America.*

75. Lifka, *Concept of "Totalitarianism,"* 192–94.

76. Ibid., 197.

77. Ibid., 203–4.

78. Ibid., 202.

79. An August 1941 *Fortune* poll by Elmo Roper showed a list of possible sacrifices that might have to be made if the United States entered the war and asked, "If we were actually in the war and the government put these things in effect, which would you do willingly, which would you do unwillingly, and which would you fight against?" Different questions were asked of men and women (depending on which each applied to). Of both men and women surveyed, 77.7 percent said they would willingly pay double luxury taxes, 74.5 percent would willingly pay an across-the-board sales tax, and 74.5 percent would also willingly cut gasoline consumption by one-third (although pluralities would willingly support national prohibition and lowering of the minimum rate for income taxes, these fell well short of majorities). A majority of men would willingly spend one day a week training for home defense (88.9 percent) and would willingly be drafted into the armed forces for possible service abroad (53.3 percent; only 18.8 percent said they would fight this). Most men and employed women would work sixty-hour weeks (78.6 percent); just under half (49.3 percent) would willingly change jobs to lower-paying, defense-related work in the same community. Women would willingly work one day a week in the Red Cross (88.9 percent) and give up aluminum pots and pans (79.2 percent). Narrow pluralities would willingly move their husbands to the lower-paying defense jobs (37.8 percent) or allow their son to be drafted into the armed forces (37.9 percent). Most unpopular of all was the suggestion of their husbands' being drafted: 26.7 percent were willing, 36.6 percent were unwilling, and 32.1 percent would fight such a proposal. Cantril, *Public Opinion,* 1171–73.

CHAPTER SIX

1. Wesley, *NEA,* 307–9.

2. Morgan, "Significance of Citizenship Recognition Day"; "Between Editor and Reader"; Schofield, "'I'm an American.'" "I Am an American Day" was also known as "Citizens Day."

3. Educational Policies Commission, *Purposes of Education,* 29–30. This pamphlet was written by Dr. William G. Carr. On the incompatibility of democracy

and modern war, see also Educational Policies Commission, *Education of Free Men,* 41–42, a pamphlet written by George S. Counts.

4. Throughout this text, "United Nations" refers to the twenty-six countries, including the United States, that fought the Axis powers. Following the attack on Pearl Harbor in December 1941, FDR decided not to ask Congress to declare the United States formally allied with its cobelligerents, in part because the idea of alliances could still send former noninterventionists scurrying for copies of George Washington's Farewell Address. When Roosevelt and Churchill met at the end of the month to draft a joint declaration by the countries fighting the Axis forces to express unity of purpose, FDR thus rejected the title "Joint Declaration of Allied Unity." Instead, he suggested "United Nations," and on 1 January 1942 the "Declaration of the United Nations" was issued. "United Nations," rather than "Allies," was thus the preferred official U.S. usage during the war. Dallek, *Roosevelt and American Foreign Policy,* 317–20.

5. FDR, *Fireside Chats,* 240.

6. Winkler, *Politics of Propaganda,* 8–31. These agencies had themselves replaced an even more chaotic alphabet soup of information offices in place before December 1941.

7. Ibid., 38–72. More liberal OWI officials, such as Archibald MacLeish and Robert Sherwood, felt that the agency should play a forceful role in forging a vision of America's future; more moderate officials, such as Milton Eisenhower and Gardner Cowles Jr., objected.

8. By far the most thorough account of the BMP is Koppes and Black, *Hollywood Goes to War.*

9. Ibid., 65.

10. For the history and work of the Research Branch, see Stouffer et al., *American Soldier,* 1:3–53.

11. For examples of this in film, see Capra's *War Comes to America* (1945), the short *Ring of Steel* (Office of Emergency Management Film Unit, 1942), and countless passing references to America's past wars in other films—e.g., the invocation of Lexington and Concord in *Song of Russia* (MGM, 1943). For a radio script, see Stephen Vincent Benét's "Dear Adolf: Letter from an American Soldier." Benét, *We Stand United.* The Civil War plays a pivotal role in this script.

12. David M. Kennedy, *Over Here,* 178–85.

13. On 3 May 1940 the American Institute of Public Opinion asked Americans, "Do you think the United States will go into the war in Europe or do you think we will stay out of the war?" A comparable sample was asked, "Do you think that before the war in Europe is over, the United States will get into it?" The combined results showed that 51 percent of the respondents believed that the United States would enter the war. Cantril, *Public Opinion,* 969.

14. In one of the most blatantly interventionist Hollywood films at the time of its November 1940 release, war interrupts a different comedy genre. Ray Milland plays an American pilot disenchanted with war after fighting on the losing side in Spain and getting captured by Franco's forces. A journalist (Claudette Colbert) arranges for his release from a Nationalist prison. She wants him to tell her about

his adventures for a magazine article; he simply wants to go home and, if possible, win the affections of Colbert. Despite the eruption of war in Europe, a fairly standard screwball comedy ensues. Their growing love and Milland's desire for a peaceful life in America compete with Colbert's desire to cover the growing conflict. Milland's noninterventionism eventually wins outs, but as the two sail back to America, their ship is torpedoed by a German U-boat in the Irish Sea. On shore, the authorities need a pilot to help rescue the survivors. Milland is thus thrust back into the war against fascism. At the end of the film, unable to participate in the war as a fighter pilot due to an injury, Milland again vows to return home. This time, however, he intends to contribute to military preparedness by training other Americans to fly warplanes. Colbert agrees to return with him in order to lecture the public on the need for intervention.

15. A few stalwart anti-interventionists, most notably members of the anti-Stalinist left such as Paul Goodman and Dwight Macdonald, continued to suggest even after Pearl Harbor that America's participation in the war would lead the country to totalitarianism. See Wreszin, *Rebel in Defense of Tradition,* 105–13.

16. Johnson, Pepper, Ellwood, *Christian Century,* and Holmes, reprinted in "Pro and Con Discussion," 13–14, 17, 21, 27, 31.

17. Waring, "Eternal Vigilance," 229. See also Ball, "Foes of Democracy."

18. On psychiatric screening, see Bérubé, *Coming Out under Fire,* 8–33; on the general task of social science during the war, see Samuel A. Stouffer, "Social Science and the Soldier," in Ogburn, *American Society in Wartime,* 105–17.

19. Grinker and Spiegel, *Men under Stress,* 450. Although apparently not an official War Department study, *Men under Stress* was produced within the Medical Corps with the full support of other military personnel (ix–x); it also was frequently cited in the final study of the U.S. Army Research Branch. Stouffer et al., *American Soldier,* 2:663.

20. Grinker and Spiegel, *Men under Stress,* 453–54.

21. Grinker and Spiegel (ibid., 455–60) went on to suggest that Americans might actually be predisposed to this effect of the combat experience due to the fact that their families made boys too dependent during adolescence. This view was elaborated the following year by Dr. Edward Strecker (who had earlier written *Beyond the Clinical Frontiers*), who blamed American mothers for preconditioning their sons to become psychological casualties. In *Their Mothers' Sons,* Strecker based much of his thinking on Philip Wylie, a magazine columnist, novelist, and would-be public intellectual whose rambling, misogynistic 1942 philosophical best-seller, *A Generation of Vipers,* introduced the concept of "momism." Wylie enjoyed a moment of popularity following the publication of *Generation* and then faded from public attention for a few years until Strecker and other social psychologists revived his ideas following the war. I am indebted to Rebecca Plante for information about Wylie's reception in the 1940s.

22. Van Creveld, *Fighting Power,* 69–71.

23. In 1942 Penguin published for the general public *The New Soldier's Handbook,* which included the entire text of *The Soldier's Handbook* along with some additional material. All succeeding references are to the Penguin edition.

24. *New Soldier's Handbook,* v, 1–2. The handbook deals with other matters in similar ways. The section on "Relationship with Noncommissioned Officers and Officers" begins, "For every business, every game, every group activity, and in every walk of life there is a leader, a 'boss,' an executive, or some directing agency" (p. 2). The section on "Military Courtesy" suggests that the military variety is no different from the courtesy taught "in your home and school," except that "the military man is so proud of his profession and has such high respect for the men who belong to it that in the Army courtesy is more carefully observed than in civil life" (pp. 11–12). Thus military courtesy—an aspect of the army experience so widely disliked by the troops that in its more extreme manifestations it earned the nickname "chickenshit" during the war—was explained as a product of individual soldiers' pride in the military.

25. Ibid., 10.

26. It also plays a role in other portions of *The New Soldier's Handbook.* See Foreword," vi, and "Military Obligations," 5–6.

27. "What Is Morale?," 1.

28. Benét, "Your Army," 198.

29. Fussell, *Wartime,* 73.

30. The individuality of U.S. soldiers was similarly emphasized in one of FDR's first wartime Fireside Chats, delivered on 28 April 1942. FDR, *Fireside Chats,* 229.

31. Quoted in Doherty, *Projections of War,* 123.

32. Ibid., 123–24.

33. Today Americans tend to associate the multiethnic combat unit with film, largely because the films of the World War II era are more readily available than the books, radio plays, and other cultural productions. For an example in a book, see Hargrove, *See Here, Private Hargrove,* especially the introduction by Maxwell Anderson. For a radio play, see Benét, "Dear Adolf," 49–58.

34. Basinger, *World War II Combat Film,* 101; Van Creveld, *Fighting Power,* 46; David M. Kennedy, *Over Here,* 158. Basinger provides a good history of the convention of the multiethnic combat unit in motion pictures but gives a purely internalist reading of its rise to generic prominence.

35. It lives on in American culture not so much as an image of the military but as a marker for a series of generic conventions associated with the World War II combat film outlined by Basinger. More recent examples include such science fiction action films as *Aliens* (1986) and *Predator* (1987), both of which open with the introduction of a multiethnic combat unit, thus indicating to the viewer the kind of film she is about to see.

36. For a rather different but interesting account of the significance of the multiethnic combat unit, see May, "Making the American Consensus."

37. Black-white relations were, however, clearly seen as a question of race. And the Japanese and Japanese Americans were frequently understood in racialist terms. See Dower, *War without Mercy;* cf. Robert Redfield, "The Japanese-Americans" in Ogburn, *American Society in Wartime,* 143–64. Redfield argues that the major problem with FDR's Japanese internment policy was its racialism.

38. This was the message of the Frank Sinatra short film, *The House I Live In*

(RKO, 1945), in which the crooner convinces a crowd of white children to stop harassing their Jewish schoolmate by telling them a heroic story of a multiethnic bomber crew taking revenge on "the Japs."

39. The work of the social scientists in the Research Branch was collected in the four-volume *Studies in Social Psychology in World War II*. In the first two, 600-page volumes on *The American Soldier* there is no attempt to break down the data by the ethnic background of the white soldiers under study. There is only one reference to attitudinal differences between Protestant and Catholic soldiers, and this is on the issue of military chaplains. Region of origin is seen as a slightly more important question, especially in the area of race relations. The study mentions differences between northerners and southerners in general attitude, attitudes toward blacks, health by climate, and job satisfaction. Stouffer et al., *American Soldier,* 1:174–75, 349–50, 400, 2:618.

40. See, e.g., Robert E. Park, "Racial Ideologies," in Ogburn, *American Society in Wartime,* 165–84.

41. See also the similar Army Signal Corps live action three-reeler *Don't Be a Sucker* (1945) and Frank Capra's *War Comes to America* (1945). The Capra film features a montage of ethnic groups "building" the United States. Each group is shown with an identifying close-up of a man from that group; some men have specific talents that they brought to America (i.e., the German has "his technical skill"). But in each case, his job in "building America" is allowed to overtake any ethnic particularity. Thus both Welshmen and Poles work mines dressed in identical mining outfits. Danes and Swedes plant seed side by side with coordinated motions.

42. Basinger, *World War II Combat Film,* 74–75.

43. Consideration of attitudinal differences between black and white soldiers and of soldiers' opinions on race appears throughout the work of the Research Branch. The most sustained treatment of race occurs in a long chapter on black soldiers in Stouffer et al., *American Soldier,* vol. 1, which compares northerners and southerners (white and black) by educational level, willingness for combat, and attitudes toward Military Police; white attitudes toward blacks and segregation, black attitudes toward northerners and southerners, and so forth (pp. 491, 560, 506, 512, 559, 580–82).

44. "The Question of Civilian Conscription for War."

45. "The Children's Army" (Fact Sheet No. 12, n.d.), in *Manual*. The *Manual* was distributed in a loose-leaf binder, allowing Fact Sheets and other addenda to be inserted in their proper place. As a result, however, the *Manual* is not paginated.

46. I have not had the opportunity to screen either *Mr. Lucky* or *Lucky Jordan* and have relied on Koppes and Black, *Hollywood Goes to War* (128–30) for synopses of the films.

47. *Army Life,* 139. The section on discipline goes on to invoke the team metaphor.

48. The Research Branch found Snafu to be the most popular part of the *Army-Navy Screen Magazine* when troops' reactions to the film were tested as they watched. In retrospect, however, the cartoon was rated lower. Although many men

liked the film's "moral" and its humorous presentation, others felt that its tone was not in keeping with the rest of the motion picture program; still others would have preferred comedy unrelated to the army. "Measuring the Effectiveness of Informational Motion Pictures," 100–101.

49. Smoodin, *Animating Culture,* 71–95. Smoodin's book provides the most thorough analysis of the Snafu cartoons, but it remains in some ways dissatisfying. It puts far too much emphasis on the notion that the "Pvt. Snafu" series was "perceived as harmless [presumably by the audience] because of its association with children's entertainment." I tend to think that its fairly safe semisubversions of the childish aspect of cartoons (e.g., the appearance of nudity) made the audience's relationship to the cartoon something more intense than harmless entertainment. Smoodin sees the cartoons as generally controlling discontent by making such discontent aberrant and wartime unity the norm.

50. In *Spies* (1943), Snafu's failure to keep a secret from ubiquitous Axis spies ends up with him blown literally to hell, where Hitler, in the form of the devil, reveals to him that he was responsible for his own fate.

51. FDR, *Fireside Chats,* 207–8, 213. This speech was delivered on 23 February 1942.

52. "The Framework of the Government Information Program," *Manual.*

53. Price, "Censorship an Evil of War," 159.

54. Roeder, "U.S. Photo Censorship in WW II"; FDR, *Fireside Chats,* 213–14, 214n.

55. Bohn, *Historical and Descriptive Analysis,* 92–93.

56. Quoted in Hovland, Lumsdaine, and Sheffield, *Experiments on Mass Communication,* 24.

57. Bohn, *Historical and Descriptive Analysis,* 95–96; McBride, *Capra,* 455–56.

58. McBride, *Capra,* 455–56.

59. Bohn, *Historical and Descriptive Analysis,* 98; "WW II: The Propaganda Battle"; Capra to Moyers, quoted in McBride, *Capra,* 465–66.

60. McBride, *Capra,* 466.

61. Ibid., 453–54, 459–65, 470, 474.

62. Hovland, Lumsdaine, and Sheffield, *Experiments on Mass Communication,* 22.

63. It was also, incidentally, a cost-cutting measure: enemy newsreel footage was absolutely free.

64. McBride, *Capra,* 479–81.

65. Marshall provided a comment to this effect at the beginning of *Prelude to War.*

66. Lowell Mellett to FDR, 9 November 1942, quoted in McBride, *Capra,* 473.

67. Frederick Osborn to Frank Capra and Capra to Osborn, 21 November 1944, quoted in McBride, *Capra,* 482.

68. James Agee, writing in the *Nation* (12 June 1943), provided the most famous contemporary evaluation of *Prelude to War.* He criticized the film for underestimating its audience, but to an extremely limited extent. He called the frequent references to "Mr. John Q. Public . . . an underestimation of the audience of which the picture as a whole is hearteningly free." Indeed, Agee, who was deeply critical

of the OWI and of Hollywood's efforts to capture the war, saw the *Why We Fight* films as "responsible, irreplaceable pieces of teaching" and bemoaned the fact that they did not receive broader circulation among the public, particularly as their presentation to the soldiers "serve[s] inadvertently to widen the abyss between fighters and . . . civilians" (*Nation*, 30 October 1943). See also *Nation*, 25 December 1943. All quotations reprinted in Agee, *Agee on Film*, 40–41, 56, 66.

69. When asked if they liked the film *The Battle of Britain*, 77 percent of the tested audience said "Yes, very much," and 16 percent responded "Yes, fairly well." Replies to the same question regarding *The Nazis Strike* and *Divide and Conquer* were only slightly less favorable, with 64 percent responding "Yes, very much" and 25 percent answering "Yes, fairly well." Hovland, Lumsdaine, and Sheffield, *Experiments on Mass Communication*, 85–86.

70. Ibid., 88–92, 255, 56, 74–75.

71. Ibid., 255–56.

72. Stouffer et al., *American Soldier*, 1:26, 484n.

73. Dollard, *Fear in Battle*, 40–42, 48.

74. Ibid., 60, 63.

75. Mauldin, *Up Front*, 50, 60.

76. Stouffer et al., *American Soldier*, 1:423. The Research Branch defined this as accepting the defensive nature of the war effort; rejecting both "cynical" explanations of the war—such as blaming it on big business or British imperialism—and the "superficial theory" that the war was yet another example of America straightening out Europe's messes; and understanding the Four Freedoms. Even without this last qualification, fewer than a fifth of the men surveyed measured up.

77. FDR, *Fireside Chats*, 217; Stouffer et al., *American Soldier*, 1:433. The ability to name more than two of the Four Freedoms was important as many of the troops apparently confused the Four Freedoms and the Bill of Rights. The troops who experienced such confusion could correctly name two of the Four Freedoms: freedom of speech and freedom of religion.

78. Stouffer et al., *American Soldier*, 1:485.

79. Price, "Censorship an Evil of War," 160.

80. Van Creveld, *Fighting Power*, 65–70; Adams, *Best War Ever*, 81.

81. Van Creveld, *Fighting Power*, 64; Adams, *Best War Ever*, 81.

82. Van Creveld, *Fighting Power*, 32, 38, 131, 33. A group of former Wehrmacht officers asked in 1953 by the U.S. Army to contribute to a revision of the *Field Service Regulations* that would incorporate lessons learned in World War II reached similar conclusions. Ibid., 39–40.

83. Ibid., 37.

84. For details on the systems in these countries, see "Compulsory Service in Other Countries."

85. Dower, *War without Mercy*.

86. When army education films had to deal with explaining more practical encounters with the workings of the Nazi German military, the picture could be quite different. *Resisting Enemy Interrogation*, an army information short subject directed by Irving Pichel (who before the war had directed *The Man I Married*),

presents Nazi officers who are engaged in a mental chess game with their captured American soldiers. There is nothing particularly ideological about the Germans' behavior in this film. What separates them from their captives is that they are on opposite sides of a war, not that their behavior is governed differently.

87. Limpus, *How the Army Fights*, 193.

CHAPTER SEVEN

1. Dallek, *Roosevelt*, 293.

2. Maslow, "Authoritarian Character Structure," 401.

3. Dower, *War without Mercy*. See also Doherty, *Projections of War*, 133–39, and Koppes and Black, *Hollywood Goes to War*, 248–77.

4. Dower, *War without Mercy*, 118–46.

5. One recent dissertation that explores this question is Hönicke, "'Know Your Enemy.'"

6. The only partial exception that I have found, and it is from before Pearl Harbor, is in Richard Wright's *Native Son* (1940), in which his African American protagonist, Bigger Thomas, admits: "He liked to hear of how Japan was conquering China; of how Hitler was running the Jews to the ground; of how Mussolini was invading Spain. He was not concerned with whether these acts were right or wrong; they simply appealed to him as possible avenues of escape. He felt that some day there would be a black man who would whip the black people into a tight band and together they would act and end fear and shame" (p. 130). Here Japan appears as only one example of fascism (and it is telling that its unusual appeal is to an American who has himself been identified as a racial Other). In his 1940 essay "How 'Bigger' Was Born," Wright insisted that Bigger was intended to be a portrait of the human roots of fascism or communism: "I was fascinated by the emotional tensions of Bigger in America and Bigger in Nazi Germany and Bigger in Old Russia." For Wright, such emotions "ignored racial and national lines of demarcation" (pp. 519–22). Although Wright does not mention Japan in "How 'Bigger Was Born," for a writer concerned with racism it was doubtless important to include Japan as one of the objects of Bigger's admiration.

7. Throughout this chapter, I use "good German" in the way in which it was used throughout the war: as a term to describe Germans who rejected Nazism and embraced, more or less, the Four Freedoms. I suspect that the ubiquity of the phrase "good German" to describe such people during the war led to its adoption after the war as an ironic description of those many Germans who went about their business in the Third Reich with a blind eye to the regime's horrors. The latter usage incorporates a stronger sense of the word "German" (i.e., to be a *good* German is to support the status quo), which was undoubtedly associated with the many wartime views of Nazism that stressed its connection to various German cultural traditions.

8. FDR, *Fireside Chats*, 180. The quotation is from the written text of FDR's remarks. In delivering them, he apparently misspoke, declaring, in part, "the mas-

ters of Germany—those, at least, who have not been assassinated or escaped to free soil—have marked these silenced people and their children's children for slavery."

9. For more on *There Shall Be No Night,* see Chapter 4.

10. On the 1943 London production, see Joki and Sell, "Sherwood and the Finnish Winter War."

11. "The Enemy: Whom We Fight: The Nature of Our Adversary," *Manual.*

12. Koppes and Black, *Hollywood Goes to War,* 280.

13. "The Enemy: Whom We Fight: The Nature of Our Adversary," *Manual.*

14. "Footprints of the Trojan Horse" (Fact Sheet No. 4, n.d.), ibid.

15. "The Enemy: Whom We Fight: The Nature of Our Adversary," ibid.; FDR, *Fireside Chats,* 23 February 1942, 208.

16. "'They' Got the Blame" (Fact Sheet No. 5, n.d.), *Manual.*

17. Koppes and Black, *Hollywood Goes to War,* 298–99.

18. Ziemer, *Education for Death,* 32.

19. Gow and d'Usseau, *Tomorrow the World.* The following discussion is based on the script of the play.

20. Ibid., 105.

21. Ibid., 160.

22. Winkler, *Politics of Propaganda,* 53–72.

23. Henry C. Wolfe, "Enemy Mind," 11, 21; Green, "Free Men or Slaves?," 28, 110.

24. See, e.g., Kittredge, "Anthropologist Looks at the War"; zu Loewenstein, "Christian World Revolution"; "In the Face of the World's Crisis"; Norman Thomas, "Totalitarian Liberals"; Lyons, "What Price 'Security'?"; Padover, "Jefferson vs. Totalitarianism."

25. Many U.S. industrialists "had succumbed to the false security of cartel agreements with totalitarian German concerns." Wallace, "Wallace Defines 'American Fascism,'" 7. One of the "essential ingredients" of fascism was that "the government acknowledges no restraint upon its powers—totalitarianism." Flynn, *As We Go Marching*

26. Militarism did not admit to much analysis. On pan-Germanism and other specifically national understandings of the Nazi threat, see below.

27. Isserman, *Which Side Were You On?,* 208, 132–33.

28. Seldes issued at least eight "editions" of *Facts and Fascism,* all in 1943. One, presumably the first, was marked "Subscriber's edition." Three through eight were numbered as such. Judging from the pagination, these so-called editions were identical.

29. Cathy Packer, "Seldes, George," 639–40. Packer mistakenly reports that *In Fact* was founded in 1949. Diggins, *Mussolini,* 53–55.

30. Seldes, *Facts and Fascism,* 12.

31. Seldes devotes an entire chapter to the press's partial suppression of Wallace's "Century of the Common Man" speech of May 1942, and he proudly reprints a piece of fan mail that he received from the vice president. Ibid., 242–51, 13.

32. Land, "Anatomy of Fascism," 501; "Does Wallace Know What Fascism Is?"; Wallace, "Price of Free World Victory."

33. Wallace, "Price of Free World Victory," 483.

34. Wallace, "Wallace Defines 'American Fascism,'" 7, 34–35.

35. Flynn, *As We Go Marching*, 161–62, 67.

36. Ibid., 172–89, 189–226, 257.

37. "Does Wallace Know What Fascism Is?"; Land, "Anatomy of Fascism," 498.

38. Cowley, "Who's Fascist Now?," 246, 248.

39. Flynn, *As We Go Marching*, 253.

40. Hutchinson, "Is a Planned Economy Slavery?"; Land, "Anatomy of Fascism," 502.

41. On Vansittart's own rejection of Vansittartism, see Benvenisti, "Two Germanies?," 531. For arguments against the purported racial militarism of Germans, see Warburg, "Can the Germans Cure Themselves?," 11; "You Can't Keep a Whole Nation in Chains"; Reves, "How to Civilize Germany," 549; and Adey, "German Problem," 461.

42. Coole and Potter, *Thus Speaks Germany*. For a favorable review, see Reinhold, Review of *Thus Speaks Germany*. For other examples of quotation-based assessments of German national character, see Weigert, "Freedom and the Germans," and W. W. Parker, "Frustratious Joins the Party." On *Germany: A Self-Portrait*, see Griswold, "Germans and Nazis." For a critique of explanations of Nazism based on German national character, see "Are Germans Incurable?"

43. Brickner, "Is Germany Incurable?: The Treatment" and "Some Observations on the Incurable Controversy"; "What Shall We Do with Germany?"; *Saturday Review of Literature* (all 1943), 19 June, 19; 31 July, 17; 18 September, 13–14; 2 October, 17–19; 9 October, 13–14; 26 October, 27–28; 23 October, 14–15; 30 October, 29; 27 November, 11 (At this point one correspondent aptly remarked: "The whole [debate] has the character of a discussion by engineers of a criticism by a biologist of a series of reviews by astronomers of a book on music written by a chemist").

44. Brickner, "Is Germany Incurable?," 84–85, and *Is Germany Incurable?*, 31–32, 41–42.

45. Brickner, "Is Germany Incurable?," 84–85, and *Is Germany Incurable?*, 100–101.

46. Brickner, "Is Germany Incurable?," 84, 86–87.

47. Brickner, *Is Germany Incurable?*, 305.

48. See Kubie et al., "Is Germany Incurable?"

49. Kallen, Review of *Is Germany Incurable?*

50. "What Shall We Do with Germany?"

51. Although he was overly conspiratorial in his thinking, Pol's suspicions of Strasser were on the mark. Strasser's brother, Gregor, had been a leading radical Nazi until he was killed in the Night of the Long Knives purge. Otto had been expelled from the party in 1930, unsuccessfully attempted to found an alternative revolutionary, national socialist party, the Black Front, and finally fled Germany in 1933 for Switzerland and Canada. After packaging himself as an anti-Nazi "good

German" for the American public, Strasser returned to Germany following the war and tried, unsuccessfully, to start another party along antisemitic and neo-Nazi lines. Taylor and Shaw, *Third Reich Almanac,* 319.

52. Hanc, "What to Do with Germany," 191; Fodor, Review of *Germany Will Try It Again;* Peters, Review of *What to Do with Germany* (Nizer).

53. See, e.g., de Sales, "What Makes a German?"; Motherwell, "Germany after Hitler"; Foerster, "After the Defeat of Naziism, What?"; Schwarzschild, "Six Delusions about Germany"; Glueck, "Punishing the War Criminals"; and Kohn, "The Mass-Man: Hitler."

54. Dower, *War without Mercy,* 118–21. Among the most influential practitioners of national character analysis was Margaret Mead, who contributed an introduction to Brickner's book.

55. See, e.g., "Germany's Secret Weapon"; "Symptoms and Diagnosis"; Glueck, "Punishing the War Criminals"; Fried, "German Militarism"; Axelson, "Goetterdaemmerung—By Hitler"; Warburg, "Can the Germans Cure Themselves?"; and "Germany in the Peace."

56. Reimann, "Inside Germany"; Paetel, "Crisis in Germany"; "Germany in the Peace"; Lerner, "Germany without Illusions"; "Sense about Germany"; DT, "Germany—Enigma of the Peace." DT's article received high praise from *Commonweal,* which printed a summary of her argument and commented that "rarely is an American magazine privileged to publish as profound an article." "Talk about Germany."

57. DT, "Germany—Enigma of the Peace," 69.

58. Gow and d'Usseau, *Tomorrow the World,* 136–37.

59. Carlson, *Under Cover,* 10.

60. Ibid., 16, 15–21.

61. Ibid., 512.

62. McBride, *Capra,* 495, 468, 473.

63. Ibid., 495–96. Ultimately this represented Rheinhardt's own point of view. When he took over the project in 1943, he asked Capra, "What's the official doctrine?" Capra told him to "make up your own doctrine."

64. Even at this late date, the bodies are not identified as Jewish. They are "murdered Poles, Italians, Belgians, American POWs . . . ," the voice-over tells us.

65. Cantril, *Public Opinion,* 500, 800. The first of the eight times it was presented, the third viewpoint was worded somewhat differently: "The German people are like any other people. If they could really choose the leaders they want, they would become good citizens of the world."

66. Smith, "Did War Service Produce International-Mindedness?"

CHAPTER EIGHT

1. The Soviet Union was by no means the country's only ideologically troublesome partner during World War II. Chiang Kai-shek's China also provided its inhabitants with little assurance of the Four Freedoms. But Nationalist China, cele-

brated most vigorously by Henry Luce, was arguably America's most popular ally immediately following Pearl Harbor. China was tainted by neither communism nor the monarchical imperialism that some Americans still associated with Great Britain. It was a major power whose involvement in the war seemed entirely that of victim. Dallek, *Roosevelt,* 328–29.

2. Levering, *American Opinion,* 36.

3. Churchill and *Post* quoted in ibid., 39–40.

4. Sirgiovanni, *Undercurrent of Suspicion,* 73–94, 121–46.

5. It is difficult to characterize these journals as simply liberal, moderate, or conservative (whatever value those inexact terms usually have as shorthand for complicated political beliefs). *Commonweal* and the *Christian Century* generally had liberal views on most social and economic issues, but both remained extremely cautious about U.S. involvement in the war for most of 1941. *Commonweal* and the *Christian Century,* due largely to their strong, theological anticommunism, were willing to publish the views of conservatives during the war. *Christianity and Crisis* was founded early in 1941 by Reinhold Niebuhr and other liberal Protestants to vigorously make the case against pacifism and for intervention in the war in Europe.

6. Criticism of communism, though common during the war in both of these journals, was by no means universal. Ralph Bates, Harold Laski, and a number of other contributors to the *Nation* and the *New Republic* continued to express sympathy for the achievements of Soviet communism throughout the conflict.

7. Isserman, *Which Side Were You On?,* 205; WHC, "Russia: An American Problem," 151 (Chamberlin); TRB, "The Communist Party" (Crawford); "Tovarich Hague" and "Hold That Line!" (Hague); "Red Flipflop"; "'Down with Us!'"; and Kirchwey, "Stalin's Choice" (Browder, CPA); Lerner, "Russia and the Future," 85; Isserman, *Which Side Were You On?,* 130 (Wallace).

8. Lerner, "Homage to a Fighting People," 643.

9. In a July 1941 Gallup poll, when asked the question, "In the present war between Germany and Russia, which side would you like to see win?," 72 percent of American adults said Russia, 4 percent answered Germany, 17 percent said it made no difference, and 7 percent did not respond. Levering, *American Opinion,* 43.

10. Dean, *Russia at War.*

11. Norman Thomas, "Thomas on Bates on Russia"; Burnham, "Russia as an Ally"; Wohl, "Passage to Freedom"; "As Long as the Comintern Rules"; Iswolsky, "Righting the Russian Balance"; Marta Wankowicz, "'In Russia . . . It's Colder.'"

12. "The United Nations and Peoples with Whom We Are Allied in Fighting: Our Brothers in Arms," *Manual.*

13. At various times, the production unit also worked on projects entitled *Know Your Ally: Russia* and, one assumes toward the end of the war, *Know Your Enemy: Russia.* McBride, *Capra,* 462, 487.

14. Ibid., 459–65. Leonard Spiegelgass, an anticommunist screenwriter and a member of Capra's unit throughout the war, told Joseph McBride, "If you said 'Hello' to Frank, you were a Communist."

15. Ibid., 463.

16. Ibid., 461.

17. Ibid., 476, 488–89; *Nation,* 30 October 1943 (Agee). Only two months after sounding this positive note, Agee, in comparing the war movies of various countries, referred to *The Battle of Russia*'s "sterile political equipment." *Agee on Film,* 57, 66.

18. Koppes and Black, *Hollywood Goes to War,* 186.

19. For the production history of *The North Star,* see ibid., 209–11.

20. Throughout my discussion of *The North Star,* I refer to the characters as Russians, for, despite living in a fictional Ukraine, in Hollywood's eyes the residents of *The North Star* were "Russians." The film never refers to the characters as "Ukrainians," and the audience is not supposed to think of them as such.

21. Koppes and Black, *Hollywood Goes to War,* 213.

22. See, e.g., WHC, "Russia—The Sprawling Giant"; Ralph Parker, "The Man Who Stopped Hitler"; "Peoples of the U.S.S.R."; "Republics of Russia"; and Sorokin, *Russia and the United States,* 33–47.

23. I was unable to locate a viewable copy of *Song of Russia.* What follows is based on a continuity script in the Library of Congress Motion Picture Section's copyright collection (LP12520).

24. As in other Hollywood Russian villages, it is a single, and hence collective, farm. In most Hollywood films on Russia, little is made of the collective character of the farm; in *Song of Russia* it is not even explicitly described as a collective.

25. Iswolsky, "Russia at War" and "Righting the Russian Balance"; Baldwin, "Question of Liberty"; Wohl, "Passage to Freedom"; Pares, "On the Fear of Russia"; Kerensky, "Russia Is Ripe for Freedom"; "'Greatest Democracy'"; Pope, "Can Stalin's Russia Go Democratic?"; Ellis, "Will Russia Communize Europe?"; Magidoff, "Americans and Russians are *So* Alike."

26. Bates, "Need We Fear Russia?" (Bates's argument here may be strategic: cf. Bates, "Russia, Reform, and Revolution"); Lindley, "Russia: Partner in War and in Peace"; "Russia in the Alliance"; Lerner, "Russia and the Future"; WHC, "Russia as a Partner"; Willkie, "We Must Work with Russia" and "'Don't Stir Distrust of Russia'"; Niebuhr, "Russia and the West" and "Russia and the Peace"; Kirchwey, "Red Star Rises"; Soule, "Russia, Germany"; Perry, "American-Soviet Friendship"; Cowley, "Russian Turnabout"; Moley, "You Can Do Business with Stalin"; Hromádka, "Soviet Enigma"; "Those Russians"; Duranty, "Is the Russian Revolution Over?"; Johnston, "Business View of Russia"; DeVoto, "Easy Chair."

27. Eddy, "Russia in the World Crisis"; Ward, "Is Russia Forsaking Communism?"; Wallace, "Beyond the Atlantic Charter."

28. Sorokin, *Russia and the United States,* 15–17 (quotation p. 17).

29. Ibid., 19, 25–47, 55.

30. Ibid., 178–81.

31. Ibid., 182–95, 206, 200.

32. Ibid., 195.

33. Graebner, *Round Trip to Russia,* 177–87, 216.

34. Willkie, *One World,* 58–59.

35. Ibid., 68, 53, 86.

36. Wallace, "Beyond the Atlantic Charter," 667. This article was a reprint of Wallace's 8 November 1942 speech.

37. Ibid., 667–69.

38. See, e.g., Fox, *Super-Powers.*

39. Levering, *American Opinion,* 97–145; Bess, "What Does Russia Want?"; "Meaning of It All." Stronger supporters of the alliance denounced such worries as dangerous to world peace. Kirchwey, "Red Star Rises"; Soule, "Russia, Germany."

40. Cowley, "Russian Turnabout," 801.

41. On communism, the Soviet Union, and the 1944 presidential campaign, see Levering, *American Opinion,* 169–75, and Sirgiovanni, *Undercurrent of Suspicion,* 56–69.

42. Bullitt, "World from Rome"; Letters to the Editor, *Life,* 25 September 1944, 2–10.

43. Robinson's "Universalism or Totalitarianism?" and McNeil's *American Peace* are two examples of wartime texts in which the author might have meant to exclude Soviet Communism from the category of totalitarianism, although in neither case is this exclusion clear.

44. Neumann, *Permanent Revolution,* e.g. 78–79; Munk, *Economics of Force,* 38–39; CJF, "Role . . . of the Common Man," 425.

45. See, e.g., Norman Thomas, Letter to the Editor.

46. Norman Thomas, "Totalitarian Liberals." On Dewey, see Byrns, "Dewey on Russia." Also on the left, see Hagen, "This Is No Maneuver!"

47. For religious moderates and conservatives, see, e.g., Iswolsky, "Russia at War" and "Righting the Russian Balance"; Strakhovsky, "America"; zu Loewenstein, "Christian World Revolution"; Burnham, "Russia as an Ally"; "In the Face of the World's Crisis"; and C. P. Thomas, "Prelude to Invasion." For the secular right, see, e.g., WHC, "Our Russian Ally"; Max Eastman, "Stalin's American Power" and "Gamblers with Liberty"; Bullitt, "World from Rome"; and Lyons, "Progress of Stalin Worship."

48. Shale, *Donald Duck Joins Up,* 65.

49. Culbert, *Mission To Moscow,* 257–59.

50. WHC, "Laski's Wave of the Future," 370–71.

51. Dighton, "Educational Totalitarianism," 20. On totalitarian belief systems, see also Beals, "Catholics and Communists," 702–3.

52. Norman Thomas, "Totalitarian Liberals," 342.

53. Alexandrova, "Russia Is Changing"; Kerensky, "Russia Is Ripe for Freedom."

54. Skotheim, *Totalitarianism,* 31–34, 40–44.

55. WHC, "Russia—The Sprawling Giant," 4–5.

56. WHC, Foreword, 3–4.

57. WHC, "Russia: An American Problem," 149.

58. WHC, "The Soviet-German War" (*Russian Review*) and "Our Russian Ally" (*Christian Century*).

59. WHC, "Russia as a Partner" (*Saturday Evening Post*) and "Russian Revolution" (*Russian Review*).

60. WHC, "Sources of Russia's Strength," 402.

61. WHC, "Russia's Role in the Postwar World," 9, and Review of *The Red Army*, 104.

62. WHC, "American-Russian Cooperation," 4–5. This is, in part, an oblique reference to a minor scandal caused by Admiral William Standley, U.S. ambassador to the USSR, who, in March 1943, had complained that Stalin was not sufficiently informing the Russian people of the extent of American Lend-Lease aid to Russia. For more on this incident, see Levering, *American Opinion*, 107–10.

63. WHC, "American-Russian Cooperation," 8.

64. WHC, "Can Stalin's Russia Go Democratic?," 146–47.

65. WHC, "Russia after the War," 9, 3.

66. See, e.g., Lyons, "Some Plain Talk."

CHAPTER NINE

1. WHC, *America*, 52.

2. Siegel, "Changing Popularity."

3. The many works that provide broader glimpses of postwar anticommunism or Cold War culture include Fousek, *To Lead the World;* Fried, *The Russians Are Coming!* and *Nightmare in Red;* May, *Recasting America;* Pells, *Liberal Mind;* Sayre, *Running Time;* Schrecker, *Many Are the Crimes;* and Whitfield, *Culture of the Cold War.*

4. CJF and Brzezinski explicitly tried to establish a paradigmatic understanding of totalitarianism. By designating as totalitarian any regime that had six "basic features"— (1) a totalist chiliastic ideology, (2) a single party with a strict, hierarchical structure, (3) a system of terroristic police control, (4) a communications monopoly, (5) a weapons monopoly, and (6) a centrally directed economy— they produced a straightforward, agreed-upon definition of the phenomenon that quickly came to dominate American political science and Russian studies. This dominance was, however, relatively short-lived. Within a decade of its appearance, CJF began to seriously revise their model in light of events in the USSR since its original publication. See, e.g., CJF, Curtis, and Barber, *Totalitarianism in Perspective.* At around the same time, the model (even in its revised form) came under heavy attack from scholars who rejected the concept of totalitarianism as a description of the Soviet regime. Siegel, "Changing Popularity," 17–23. Even Arendt's *Origins of Totalitarianism,* which rapidly achieved canonical status, did not really create a model that structured American thought on the subject, although the notion that it represented the beginning of a process of paradigm construction, which would conclude with CJF and Brzezinski, took hold soon after they brought out *Totalitarian Dictatorship and Autocracy.* Burrowes, "Totalitarianism: The Revised Standard Version."

5. Orwell, *Nineteen Eighty-Four,* 239.

6. Nash, *Conservative Intellectual Movement,* 81.

7. Dorrien, *Neoconservative Mind,* 21–29. Dorrien's study provides the most sat-

isfying account of Burnham's intellectual journey from left to right. Wohlforth, "Trotskyism."

8. Dorrien, *Neoconservative Mind,* 25, 30–33.

9. Ibid., 28–29; Wohlforth, "Trotskyism." On Shachtman and the Workers Party, see also Chapter 5, n. 47.

10. Burnham, *Managerial Revolution,* 77–82, 133–35.

11. Ibid., 152–53, 164–65.

12. Ibid., 161–62, 167–71.

13. Ibid., 257–60, 254, 261–62, 271–72.

14. Ibid., 172–84.

15. Ibid., 273–74, 138.

16. Gordon, "Managerial Revolution," 631; Tumin, "Managerial Revolution," 739; Gordon, "Managerial Revolution," 626. For Burnham as an objective analyst, see Walker, Review of *The Managerial Revolution;* for Burnham as "following the left-wing line," see Rosen, Review of *The Managerial Revolution,* 384; for Burnham as fascist, see Kingley and Petegorsky, *Strategy for Democracy,* 261.

17. Odegard, Review of *What Is Democracy?,* 1161; Gordon, "Managerial Revolution," 631. For some of the many optimistic detractors, see Gerth and Mills, "A Marx for the Managers"; Rosen, Review of *The Managerial Revolution;* Kingsley and Petegorsky, *Strategy for Democracy,* 350; Stead, "Democracy and Social Controls in Industry"; Gordon, "Managerial Revolution"; and Neumann, Review of *Peace by Power.* For a dissenting, pessimistic wartime criticism of Burnham, see "Koestler: Some Political Remarks," 4.

18. Swedberg, *Schumpeter,* 5–108.

19. Allen, *Opening Doors,* 115.

20. Swedberg, *Schumpeter,* 146–51; Semmel, "Schumpeter's Curious Politics." After the publication of the book and America's entry into the war, Schumpeter drifted into ever more reactionary and paranoiac understandings of the world situation. His diaries reveal that, by 1945, he believed that the war had been a "Jewish victory" and that it would bring about the Bolshevik domination of the world. His increasingly vocal defenses of Nazi Germany and Japan, and attacks on FDR and Churchill, professionally marginalized him during the war and led to his exclusion from the Bretton Woods talks.

21. Schumpeter, *Capitalism, Socialism, and Democracy,* 1–58.

22. Ibid., 83, 87–106.

23. Ibid., 131–63.

24. Ibid., 168, 167–231.

25. Ibid., 269, 235–302.

26. A. B. Wolfe, Review of *Capitalism, Socialism, and Democracy,* 266.

27. Allen, *Opening Doors,* 132, 131; Carpenter, Review of *Capitalism, Socialism, and Democracy,* 523 (first quotation); A. B. Wolfe, Review of *Capitalism, Socialism, and Democracy,* 267 (second quotation); Swedberg, *Schumpeter,* 151.

28. Fleck and Müller, "Bettelheim," 2–3.

29. Bettelheim, "Individual and Mass Behavior," 420–21. The exact nature of

this study is somewhat controversial. To say the least, conditions in the camps made social scientific work difficult. When Bettelheim attempted to publish his findings, many journals questioned his methodology: whereas today his status as a camp survivor might have improved his authority to write of life in the camps, at the time it raised questions about his objectivity. To get his paper published, he had to emphasize the "scientific" nature of his study, its large sample size, and so forth. Some have questioned the accuracy of this account. For more on this issue, see Fleck and Müller, "Bettelheim."

30. Fleck and Müller, "Bettelheim," 4–5; Pollak, *Creation of Dr. B,* 94–109.

31. Fleck and Müller, "Bettelheim," 5–6 (n. 45).

32. Bettelheim, "Individual and Mass Behavior," 424–29.

33. Ibid., 439–50.

34. Ibid., 451, 450, 451–52.

35. Pollak, *Creation of Dr. B,* 116. Two accounts of the camps written by survivors, Bruno Heilig's *Men Crucified* and Peter Wallner's *By Order of the Gestapo,* had been published in England in 1941 but received little readership there and even less in the United States.

36. Bettelheim, "Individual and Mass Behavior," 452.

37. Ernst Federn, brother of psychoanalyst Paul Federn, was in Buchenwald with Bettelheim. He recalled that both he and Bettelheim had noted the similarity between Freud and Ferenczi's conclusions and the behavior of the inmates. Pollak, *Creation of Dr. B,* 121.

38. One sign of the importance of psychoanalysis for the article's reception was Dwight Macdonald's mistaken identification of Bettelheim as a psychiatrist when Macdonald printed an abridged version of "Individual and Mass Behavior in Extreme Situations" in his journal *Politics* in July 1944. Pollak, *Creation of Dr. B,* 125. Bettelheim's Viennese origins no doubt also contributed to his authority as a psychoanalytic thinker.

39. Pollak, *Creation of Dr. B,* 124–25. Both Gordon Allport, editor of the *Journal of Abnormal and Social Psychology,* and Bettelheim often claimed that General Dwight Eisenhower had ordered the article distributed to all troops in occupied Germany following the war. There seems to be no evidence, however, that Eisenhower did any such thing.

40. Elkins, *Slavery.*

41. By the 1960s Bettelheim's views on the Holocaust had become mired in controversy, not least because of an essay in which he was highly critical of the behavior of Anne Frank's family and held it largely responsible for its fate. His authority as a survivor also began to wane as public interest shifted to the Nazi Judeocide itself. Although he would occasionally admit that his experiences at Dachau and Buchenwald in the late 1930s were fundamentally different from the experience of prisoners at Auschwitz and other death camps in the 1940s, he nevertheless insisted on viewing the experience of the Holocaust through the lens of his own time in the camps. In the 1970s, as more work was done on the Holocaust and more survivors wrote of their experiences, his notion of infantile regression was

deeply criticized. The declining influence of psychoanalysis in American culture and intellectual life also affected his reputation. By the 1990s Bettelheim himself became reviled in many circles for his alleged mistreatment of autistic children in his care at the University of Chicago's Orthogenic School. Although at least one recent study has tried to revive his argument in "Individual and Mass Behavior in Extreme Situations" (Marcus, *Autonomy in the Extreme Situation*), contemporary accounts of the Holocaust usually either quickly mention the article as a "classic" or attack it at length.

42. Richard Wightman Fox, *Niebuhr*, 136–41.

43. Merkley, *Niebuhr*, 148; Richard Wightman Fox, *Niebuhr*, 204, 214.

44. Richard Wightman Fox, *Niebuhr*, 201–2, 214–17.

45. Campbell Craig, "New Meaning of Modern War," 687; Richard Wightman Fox, *Niebuhr*, 219; Merkley, *Niebuhr*, 173.

46. Niebuhr, *Children of Light*, 9, 11.

47. Ibid., 31–41.

48. Ibid., 40–41, 68–71, 124–51. For an insightful discussion of the paradoxical relationship between Niebuhr's neo-orthodox theology and his Jamesian politics, see Purcell, *Crisis of Democratic Theory*, 243–47.

49. Niebuhr, *Children of Light*, 133–34.

50. Hayek, *Road to Serfdom*. For a good overview of the American reception of Hayek, see Rosenof, "Freedom, Planning."

51. Hayek, *Road to Serfdom*, 113.

52. See, e.g., Hansen, "New Crusade against Planning."

53. Davenport, "Books and Ideas"; Hayek, *Road to Serfdom*, 9.

54. Hayek, *Road to Serfdom*, 21.

55. Merkley, *Niebuhr*, 173.

56. See Boyer, *Bomb's Early Light*, esp. 179–240.

57. Matusow, "Kennedy and the Intellectuals," 142.

58. Culver and Hyde, *American Dreamer*, 465–67, 501.

59. Schlesinger, *Vital Center*, 51–53.

60. Ibid., 53–54, 56–57, 122–26, 161, 151, 104.

61. Ibid., 63–67 (quotation, p. 63).

62. Ibid., 51–57 (quotations, p. 57).

63. Rosenof, "Freedom, Planning," 87–93, 110–11.

64. Schlesinger, *Vital Center*, 87.

65. Ibid., 161–63.

66. This is interesting given that, at the time, much of the historiography of the antebellum period continued to portray abolitionists as utopian fanatics. Schlesinger's casting of abolitionists as realists and Doughfaces as utopians is thus more unusual than it may at first appear to the twenty-first-century reader. Elsewhere in *The Vital Center* (p. 87), George Fitzhugh, arguably the antebellum South's most intellectually significant defender of slavery, is cast as a Victorian communist (in fact, Fitzhugh did use the term "Communism" to describe the Southern plantation, but he was most certainly not thinking of state socialism).

67. Schlesinger, *Vital Center,* 36, 40–41, 37.

68. Ibid., 40, 37. On the countersubversive tradition in America, see Rogin, *Ronald Reagan, the Movie.*

69. Schlesinger, *Vital Center,* 59, 65, 74.

70. Ibid., 11–34.

71. Ibid., 247, 250.

72. Ibid., *Vital Center,* 247 (first quotation), 253–56; Blum, "Schlesinger, Jr."

73. In 1987, in a new introduction to the reprint edition of *The Vital Center,* Schlesinger reaffirmed his commitment to the book's ideas with one notable exception: "I would, however, retreat from the mystical theory of totalitarianism popularized by George Orwell and Hannah Arendt. This theory must have been much in the air in the late 1940s, because *The Vital Center* came out before *Nineteen Eighty-Four* and *The Origins of Totalitarianism.* . . . Totalitarian states, far from representing, as I thought in 1949, a change of phase in social organization, are hardly more than Tartar courts equipped with modern technology" (p. x).

74. Rodden, *Politics of Literary Reputation,* 44–46. Rodden's excellent book is the foremost account of the many George Orwells who have been imagined on both sides of the Atlantic and around the world.

75. Halberstam, *Totalitarianism,* 118–20.

76. Rodden, *Politics of Literary Reputation,* 336–62.

77. "George Orwell" was the pen name of Eric Arthur Blair.

78. Steinhoff, *Orwell,* 200, 43–54.

79. Ibid., 54; Orwell, *Nineteen Eight-Four,* 240.

80. Steinhoff, *Orwell,* 149.

81. "Strange World of 1984"; "Where the Rainbow Ends"; Rahv, "Unfuture of Utopia"; Diana Trilling, Review of *Nineteen Eighty-Four;* Lionel Trilling, "Orwell on the Future"; Schorer, "Indignant and Prophetic Novel"; Hilton, "Orwell's Nightmare"; Hatch, "Orwell's Paradise Lost." Of all these reviewers, Rahv argues most forcefully that the book is simply a fictionalized look at the contemporary Soviet Union. Both Lionel and Diana Trilling see the world of *Nineteen Eighty-Four* as that of the USSR, but suggest that Orwell is warning that the democratic world might end up in a similar situation of its own accord. Mark Schorer suggests that the book expresses Orwell's "moral and intellectual indignation before the concept of totalitarianism." Both James Hilton, in a positive review, and Robert Hatch, in one of the few negative reviews, view the book as a simple projection of current trends. Hatch, alone among reviewers, suggests that fascism, not communism, is Orwell's principal target. Of all these reviewers, only Lionel Trilling does not use the terms "totalitarian" or "totalitarianism" in connection with the Oceanian regime.

82. Orwell, *Nineteen Eighty-Four,* 226–28.

83. Diana Trilling, Review of *Nineteen Eighty-Four;* Lionel Trilling, "Orwell on the Future"; Schorer, "Indignant and Prophetic Novel."

84. Diana Trilling, Review of *Nineteen Eighty-Four;* Lionel Trilling, "Orwell on the Future"; and "Where the Rainbow Ends" all fail to note that the majority of the population are proles. Of the reviewers mentioned, only Hatch ("Orwell's Paradise

Lost") and Rahv ("Unfuture of Utopia") mention that the proles are beyond the regime's constant glare.

85. "Where the Rainbow Ends," Hilton's "Orwell's Nightmare," Schorer's "Indignant and Prophetic Novel," and Hatch's "Orwell's Paradise Lost" all assume that we are to accept O'Brien's sense of the proles as the truth. Only Hatch is critical of this attitude, which he believes is typical of Orwell's misanthropy!

86. Rahv, "Unfuture of Utopia." Hilton ("Orwell's Nightmare") briefly considers the possibility that Orwell finds hope in the proles but then seems to dismiss it.

87. Quoted in Steinhoff, *Orwell*, 193.

88. Zaretsky, "Arendt," 218 (first quotation); Macdonald, "New Theory of Totalitarianism," 19. Most Arendtians, who are themselves political theorists, see the book as a work of political theory (e.g., Halberstam, *Totalitarianism,* and O'Sullivan, "Politics, Totalitarianism," 191). For an intellectual historian who shares this view, see Zaretsky, "Arendt," 214–15. A smaller number of sympathetic political theorists, among them Agnes Heller, have suggested that the book is basically historical (Hansen, *Arendt*, 132.) Many historians have tended to regard it as a work of history and have often criticized it as such (e.g., Van Duzer, Review of *The Origins of Totalitarianism,* and Krieger, "The Historical Hannah Arendt"; cf. Whitfield, *Into the Dark,* whose generally favorable assessment is based on an understanding of the book as a history). Arendt ("Reply to Eric Voegelin," 77–78) herself seems to have wanted it both ways, arguing in 1953 that the work was both historical in its approach yet, essentially because of its subject matter, not a work of history.

89. In opposition, some point out that the book was originally titled *The Burden of Our Times.*

90. Most scholars see the three parts as interrelated but not entirely integrated. For instance, Lewis and Sandra Hinchman (*Arendt,* 1) refer to the book as "a trilogy." However, in an early, positive review, Macdonald ("New Theory of Totalitarianism," 17) argued that the book's three sections are essentially separable and saw the greatest value in the third section on totalitarianism. Zaretsky ("Arendt," 215) has asserted that the third section was an afterthought and that the main argument in the book comes in the first two sections. On whether or not the book's chronological organization should be seen as implying causation, Arendt's famous clarification that the first two sections describe "'elements' which eventually crystallize into totalitarianism" ("Reply to Eric Voegelin," 81), while evocative and frequently cited, seems to raise as many questions as it answers.

91. Hinchman and Hinchman, *Arendt,* 2. In fact, as in the case of Orwell and *Nineteen Eighty-Four,* it is probably best to acknowledge both the author's opposition to the Cold War and the book's appropriation by Cold Warriors. Bittman, "Totalitarianism," 56.

92. See, e.g., Wald, *New York Intellectuals,* 269, and Bittman, "Totalitarianism." Bittman cites Stephen Whitfield to support this claim. Though Whitfield (*Into the Dark*) does not make the mistake of claiming that Arendt was the first to link communism and Nazism, he obviously feels that this was the book's principal achievement. In fact, correspondence between Arendt and her publisher make clear that

the book's final section as originally planned was much shorter and would not have included any reference to Stalinism. What changed was not Arendt's evaluation of the Soviet regime (which she had already declared to be totalitarian in an earlier essay) but rather her growing interest in it. Canovan, *Arendt,* 18–19.

93. Hansen, *Arendt,* 129–30, 145.

94. Wald, *New York Intellectuals,* 269.

95. Ibid.; Van Duzer, Review of *The Origins of Totalitarianism;* Baer, Review of *The Origins of Totalitarianism;* Dunham, Review of *The Origins of Totalitarianism* and of *The Open Society and Its Enemies;* Cook, Review of *The Origins of Totalitarianism.* Among the major newspapers and journals giving positive notices were the *Chicago Tribune, Commonweal, Commentary, Nation, New Leader, New York Herald Tribune, New York Times, New Yorker, Partisan Review,* and *Saturday Review.* Although most of them asked academics to review the book, in these more popular publications, the reviewers seemed inclined to look more kindly on the book's eclecticism than did the reviewers for strictly academic journals.

96. Hughes, "Historical Sources of Totalitarianism," 281; Carr, "Ultimate Denial," 24; Heckscher, "Forces of Disaster"; Fitzsimons, "Totalitarian Absurdities"; Riesman, "Path to Total Terror," 392.

97. Macdonald, "New Theory of Totalitarianism"; Riesman, "Path to Total Terror"; Handlin, "Dictators and Mobs"; Carr, "Ultimate Denial."

98. Indeed, the only review I found that prominently mentions this linkage was J. F. Brown's admiring but ultimately negative review in the *Annals of the American Academy of Political and Social Sciences.* Noting that the book was widely seen in the popular press as confirming the view that communism was as bad as Nazism, Brown wrote (Review of *Origins of Totalitarianism,* 273): "I know this viewpoint is increasingly popular in our current world political climate. But I still dissent vehemently. I think the movements differ radically in background and in purpose. Further, I feel that failure to recognize these differences is bound to increase rather than decrease the current threat to the autonomy of American democracy. Finally, although I know that today most social scientists will agree with Dr. Arendt, I feel that in the future they will agree with my criticism."

99. We see in *Origins* the beginnings of a growing awareness of the distinction between "normal" Nazi concentration camps and death camps set up in the early 1940s for the express purpose of extermination. Arendt talks of both concentration camps and extermination camps. But in *Origins,* the two function similarly and tend to be lumped together. This was in part based on her judgment that even Nazi concentration camps were fundamentally different from their historical predecessors.

100. Arendt, *Origins* (1951), 414, 424, 419. Arendt later substantially revised the work on a number of occasions.

101. Ibid., 416. For better or for worse, this notion of the ultimate ineffability of the camps has, since Arendt, become one of the most prominent tropes in writing about the Holocaust.

102. Ibid., 433. This formulation was supplemented in later editions (*Origins* [1973], 459) by the notion of "radical evil," a stronger and even more abstract for-

mulation, borrowed from Kant, that has become associated with Arendt's view of totalitarianism.

103. Arendt, *Origins* (1951), 353–63.

104. Macdonald, "New Theory of Totalitarianism," 19.

105. Arendt, *Origins* (1951), 301, 107, 310. On people as robots in Arendt's view of totalitarianism, see Canovan, "Arendt on Ideology," 158, and Pitkin, *Attack of the Blob,* 93.

106. Arendt, *Origins* (1951), 319–32.

107. Ibid., 333.

108. For example, "Totalitarianism will not be satisfied to assert . . . that unemployment does not exist." Ibid.

109. Pitkin, *Attack of the Blob,* 90.

110. Ibid., 93. Most of Pitkin's study is concerned with a later "Blob" in Arendt's thought, the concept of "the social."

111. See n. 4 above.

112. Spiro, "Totalitarianism," 112.

113. Although linking Stalinism and Nazism under "totalitarianism" has enjoyed spurts of academic popularity in the last three decades, especially since the end of the Cold War in the former Soviet Union and former bloc countries, many careful students of Nazi Germany and the Soviet Union continue to see enormous differences between Stalinism and Nazism. See Kershaw, "Totalitarianism Revisited," and Kershaw and Lewin, *Stalinism and Nazism.*

BIBLIOGRAPHY

PRIMARY SOURCES

Archives and Museums
Cambridge, Mass.
    Houghton Library, Harvard University, Robert Sherwood Papers
College Park, Md.
    National Archives
        Motion Picture, Sound, and Video Branch
Los Angeles, Calif.
    Margaret Herrick Library, Academy of Motion Picture Arts and Sciences
Philadelphia, Pa.
    American Philosophical Society Library
South Bend, Ind.
    Studebaker National Museum
Washington, D.C.
    Library of Congress
        Motion Picture Section

Books and Pamphlets
Agee, James. *Agee on Film.* Drawings by Toni Ungerer. Vol. 1. 1958. Reprint, New
    York: Grossett and Dunlap, 1972.
Americana Institute. *Isms.* New York: Americana Institute, 1939.
Arendt, Hannah. *The Origins of Totalitarianism.* 1st ed. New York: Harcourt
    Brace, 1951.
————. *The Origins of Totalitarianism.* New Edition with Added Prefaces. New
    York: Harcourt Brace Jovanovich, 1973.
Armstrong, Hamilton Fish. *"We or They": Two Worlds in Conflict.* New York:
    Macmillan, 1937.
Army Life. War Department Pamphlet 21–13. Washington, D.C.: GPO, 1944.
Arnold, Thurman Wesley. *The Folklore of Capitalism.* New Haven: Yale University
    Press, 1937.
Baker, Newton Diehl, Carlton J. H. Hayes, and Roger Williams Straus, ed. *The
    American Way: A Study of Human Relations among Protestants, Catholics, and
    Jews.* New York: Willett, Clark, 1936.
Benét, Stephen Vincent, with a foreword by Norman Rosten; decorated by Ernest
    Stock. *We Stand United and Other Radio Scripts.* New York: Farrar and
    Rinehart, 1945.

Bernays, Edward L. *Speak Up for Democracy: What You Can Do—A Practical Plan of Action for Every American Citizen.* New York: Viking, 1940.

Bettelheim, Bruno. *The Informed Heart: Autonomy in a Mass Age.* Glencoe, Ill.: Free Press, 1960.

Bingham, Alfred Mitchell. *Insurgent America: Revolt of the Middle Classes.* New York: Harper, 1935.

Boutwell, William Dow, B. P. Brodinsky, Pauline Frederick, Joseph Harris, Glenn Nixon, and Archie Robertson. *America Prepares for Tomorrow: The Story of Our Total Defense Effort.* New York: Harper, 1941.

Brickner, Richard M., with introductions by Margaret Mead and Edward A. Strecker. *Is Germany Incurable?* Philadelphia: Lippincott, 1943.

Brooks, Robert Clarkson. *Deliver Us from Dictators!* Philadelphia: University of Pennsylvania Press, 1935.

Burnham, James. *The Machiavellians: Defenders of Freedom.* New York: John Day, 1943.

———. *The Managerial Revolution: What Is Happening in the World.* New York: John Day, 1941.

Cantril, Hadley, with the assistance of Hazel Gaudet and Herta Herzog. *The Invasion from Mars: A Study in the Psychology of Panic. With the Complete Script of the Famous Orson Welles Broadcast.* Princeton: Princeton University Press, 1940.

———. *The Psychology of Social Movements.* New York: John Wiley and Sons, 1941.

———, ed. Prepared by Mildred Strunk. *Public Opinion, 1935–1946.* Princeton: Princeton University Press, 1951.

Capra, Frank. *The Name above the Title: An Autobiography.* New York: Macmillan, 1971.

Carlson, John Roy. *Under Cover: My Four Years in the Nazi Underworld of America.* New York: Dutton, 1943.

Chamberlin, William Henry. *America: Partner in World Rule.* New York: Vanguard, 1945.

———. *Collectivism: A False Utopia.* New York: Macmillan, 1937.

Chase, Stuart. *A New Deal.* New York: Macmillan, 1932.

———. *The Tyranny of Words.* New York: Harcourt, Brace, 1938.

Coole, W. W., and M. F. Potter, eds. Foreword by Hamilton Fish Armstrong. *Thus Speaks Germany.* New York: Harper, 1941.

Coyle, David Cushman. Together with three additional discussions by Carl Dreher, Carl Landauer, and Gerald W. Johnson. *The American Way.* New York: Harper, 1938.

Crossman, Richard, ed. *The God That Failed.* New York: Harper and Brothers, 1949.

Crippen, Harlan R., ed. *Germany: A Self-Portrait: A Collection of German Writings from 1914 to 1943.* New York: Oxford University Press, 1944.

Dean, Vera Micheles. *Russia at War: Twenty Key Questions and Answers.* New York: Foreign Policy Association, 1942.

Desvernine, Raoul E. *Democratic Despotism.* New York: Dodd, Mead, 1936.

Dilling, Elizabeth. *The Red Network: A "Who's Who" and Handbook of Radicalism for Patriots.* 1934. Reprint, New York: Arno, 1977.

Ditzen, Rudolf [Hans Fallada, pseud.]. *Little Man, What Now?* Translated by Eric Sutton. New York: Simon and Schuster, 1933.

Dollard, John, with the assistance of Donald Horton. *Fear in Battle.* Washington, D.C.: The Infantry Journal, 1944.

Drucker, Peter. *The End of Economic Man: A Study of the New Totalitarianism.* New York: John Day, 1939.

Educational Policies Commission. *The Education of Free Men in American Democracy.* Washington, D.C.: Educational Policies Commission, 1940.

———. *The Purposes of Education in American Democracy.* Washington, D.C.: Educational Policies Commission, 1938.

Elkins, Stanley. *Slavery: A Problem in American Institutional and Intellectual Life.* Chicago: University of Chicago Press, 1959.

Elliott, William Yandell. *The Pragmatic Revolt in Politics: Syndicalism, Fascism, and the Constitutional State..* New York: Macmillan, 1928.

The Fascist Dictatorship, Including an Essay by Professor Gaetano Salvemini, an Address by Professor W. J. Elliott of Harvard University, Reprints of Articles from Various American Magazines on Fascism, with Expressions of American Liberal Opinion. New York: International Committee for Political Prisoners, 1926.

Flynn, John T. *As We Go Marching.* Garden City, N.Y.: Doubleday, Doran, 1944.

Fodor, Marcel William. *The Revolution Is On.* Boston: Houghton Mifflin, 1940.

Ford, Guy Stanton, ed. *Dictatorship in the Modern World.* Minneapolis: University of Minnesota Press, 1935.

Fox, William T. R. *The Super-Powers: The United States, Britain, and the Soviet Union — Their Responsibility for Peace.* New York: Harcourt, Brace, 1944.

Friedrich, Carl Joachim. *Constitutional Government and Politics: Nature and Development.* New York: Harper, 1937.

Friedrich, Carl J., and Zbigniew K. Brzezinski. *Totalitarian Dictatorship and Autocracy.* Cambridge: Harvard University Press, 1956.

Friedrich, Carl J., Michael Curtis, and Benjamin R. Barber. *Totalitarianism in Perspective: Three Views.* New York: Praeger, 1969.

Fromm, Erich. *Escape from Freedom.* New York: Farrar and Rinehart, 1941.

Gagging the Dictators: The Comedy of Terrors. New York: Ace Magazines, 1938.

Gow, James, and Arnoud d'Usseau. *Tomorrow the World.* New York: Scribner, 1943.

Graebner, Walter. *Round Trip to Russia.* Philadelphia: Lippincott, 1943.

Grinker, Roy R., and John P. Spiegel. *Men under Stress.* Philadelphia: Blackiston, 1945.

Hargrove, Marion. Foreword by Maxwell Anderson. *See Here, Private Hargrove.* New York: H. Holt, 1942.

Hayek, Friedrich A. von. *Freedom and the Economic System.* Chicago: University of Chicago Press, 1939.

―――. Foreword by John Chamberlain. *The Road to Serfdom*. Chicago: University of Chicago Press, 1944.

Hoover, Calvin B. *Dictators and Democracies*. New York: Macmillan, 1937.

―――. *The Economic Life of Soviet Russia*. New York: Macmillan, 1931.

―――. *Germany Enters the Third Reich*. New York: Macmillan, 1933.

Hoover, Herbert. *Addresses upon the American Road, 1933–1938*. New York: Scribner, 1938.

―――. *American Individualism*. New York: Doubleday, Doran, 1922.

―――. *Further Addresses upon the American Road, 1938–1940*. New York: Scribner, 1940.

Hovland, Carl I., Arthur A. Lumsdaine, and Fred D. Sheffield. *Experiments on Mass Communication*. Vol. 3 of *Studies in Social Psychology in World War II*. Princeton: Princeton University Press, 1949.

Josephson, Matthew. *Nazi Culture: The Brown Darkness over Germany*. John Day Pamphlets no. 37. New York: John Day, 1933.

Kennedy, John F. *Why England Slept*. New York: W. Funk, 1940.

Kingsley, J. Donald, and David W. Petegorsky, with chapters by Pierre Cot, Max Werner, Albert Guérard, Oscar I. Janowsky, [and] Mordecai Ezekiel. *Strategy for Democracy*. New York: Longmans, Green, 1942.

Koestler, Arthur. *Darkness at Noon*. 1941. Reprint, New York: Signet, 1961.

Laurents, Arthur. Foreword by Robert Garland. *Home of the Brave*. New York: Random House, 1946.

League of American Writers. *Writers Take Sides: Letters about the War in Spain from 418 American Authors*. New York: League of American Writers, 1938.

Lederer, Emil. *The State of the Masses: The Threat of the Classless Society*. New York: Norton, 1940.

Lerner, Max. *It Is Later Than You Think: The Need for a Militant Democracy*. New York: Viking, 1938.

Lewis, Sinclair. *It Can't Happen Here*. 1935. Reprint, New York: Signet, 1970.

Limpus, Lowell M. *How the Army Fights: A Clear Expression of Modern High-Power Warfare*. New York: Appleton-Century, 1943.

Lippmann, Walter. *An Inquiry into the Principles of the Good Society*. Boston: Little, Brown, 1937.

―――. *The Phantom Public*. New York: Harcourt, Brace, 1925.

Lynd, Robert S., and Helen Merrell Lynd. *Middletown in Transition: A Study in Cultural Conflicts*. New York: Harcourt, Brace, 1937.

Lyons, Eugene. *Assignment in Utopia*. New York: Harcourt, Brace, 1937.

MacIver, Robert M., Moritz J. Bonn, and Ralph Barton Perry. *The Roots of Totalitarianism: Addresses Delivered at a Meeting of the American Academy of Political and Social Science, November 18, 1939*. Philadelphia: American Academy of Political and Social Science, 1940.

MacLeish, Archibald. *The Fall of the City: A Verse Play for Radio*. New York: Farrar and Rinehart, 1937.

Mailer, Norman. *The Naked and the Dead*. New York: Rinehart, 1948.

Mauldin, Bill. *Up Front*. New York: H. Holt, 1945.

McGovern, William Montgomery. *From Luther to Hitler: The History of Fascist-Nazi Political Philosophy.* Cambridge, Mass.: Riverside Press, 1941.

McNeil, Neil. *An American Peace.* New York: Scribner, 1944.

Mumford, Lewis. *Faith for Living.* New York: Harcourt, Brace, 1940.

———. *Men Must Act.* New York: Harcourt, Brace, 1939.

———. *Technics and Civilization.* New York: Harcourt, Brace, 1934.

Munk, Frank. *The Economics of Force.* New York: George W. Stewart, 1940.

———. *The Legacy of Nazism: The Economic and Social Consequences of Totalitarianism.* New York: Macmillan, 1943.

National Americanism Commission of the American Legion, ed. *ISMS: A Review of Alien Isms, Revolutionary Communism, and Their Active Sympathizers in the United States.* 2d ed. Indianapolis: National Americanism Commission of the American Legion, 1937.

Neumann, Sigmund. *Permanent Revolution: The Total State in a World at War.* New York: Harper, 1942.

The New Soldier's Handbook. New York: Penguin, 1942.

Niebuhr, Reinhold. *The Children of Light and the Children of Darkness: A Vindication of Democracy and a Critique of Its Traditional Defense.* New York: Scribner, 1944.

Ogburn, William Fielding, ed. *American Society in Wartime.* Chicago: University of Chicago Press, 1943.

Ogg, Frederic A. *European Governments and Politics.* New York: Macmillan, 1934.

Orwell, George. *Nineteen Eighty-Four.* 1949. Reprint, New York: Plume, 1983.

Pettengill, Samuel B. *Smoke-Screen.* New York: Southern Publishers, 1940.

Pol, Heinz. *The Hidden Enemy: The German Threat to Post-War Peace.* New York: J. Messner, 1943.

Pratt, Fletcher. *America and Total War.* New York: Smith and Durrell, 1941.

President's Research Committee on Social Trends. *Recent Social Trends in the United States.* Vol. 1. New York: McGraw-Hill, 1933.

Quitman, Gertrude, and William H. Allen. *Dictator Isms and Our Democracy: Nazism, Fascism, Communism: "Made in America" Brands.* New York: Institute for Public Service, 1940.

Rice, Elmer. *Judgment Day: A Melodrama in Three Acts.* New York: Coward-McCann, 1934.

Rogers, Lindsay. *Crisis Government.* New York: Norton, 1934.

Roosevelt, Franklin D. *FDR's Fireside Chats.* Edited by Russell D. Buhite and David W. Levy. New York: Penguin, 1993.

Schlesinger, Arthur M., Jr. *The Vital Center: The Politics of Freedom.* Boston: Houghton Mifflin, 1949. Reprint, New York: Da Capo, 1988.

Schumpeter, Joseph Alois. *Capitalism, Socialism, and Democracy.* 1942. 3d ed., New York: Harper and Brothers, 1950.

Seldes, George, assisted by Helen Seldes. *Facts and Fascism.* New York: In Fact, 1943.

Sherwood, Robert E. *The Petrified Forest.* New York: Scribner, 1935.

———. *There Shall Be No Night.* New York: Scribner, 1940.

Sinclair, Upton Beall. *Peace or War in America: A Debate between Upton Sinclair and the Hon. Philip F. LaFollette*. Girard, Kans.: Haldeman-Julius Publications, 1941.

The Soldier's Handbook. Field Manual 21–100. Washington, D.C.: GPO, 1940.

Sorokin, Pitirim A. *Russia and the United States*. New York: Dutton, 1944.

Stein, Gertrude. *Everybody's Autobiography*. New York: Random House, 1937.

Stouffer, Samuel A., Arthur A. Lumsdaine, Marion Harper Lumsdaine, et al. *The American Soldier: Combat and Its Aftermath*. Vol. 2 of *Studies in Social Psychology in World War II*. Princeton: Princeton University Press, 1949.

Stouffer, Samuel A., Edward A. Suchman, Leland C. DeVinney, Shirley A. Star, and Robin M. Williams Jr. *The American Soldier: Adjustment during Army Life*. Vol. 1 of *Studies in Social Psychology in World War II*. Princeton: Princeton University Press, 1949.

Strecker, Edward. *Beyond the Clinical Frontiers: A Psychiatrist Views Crowd Behavior*. New York: Norton, 1940.

———. *Their Mothers' Sons: The Psychiatrist Examines an American Problem*. Philadelphia: Lippincott, 1946.

Sturzo, Luigi. *Italy and Fascismo*. Translated by Barbara Barclay Carter. With a preface by Gilbert Murray. New York: Harcourt, Brace, 1926.

Taylor, Kressmann. *Address Unknown*. New York: Simon and Schuster, 1939.

Thomas, Lowell, and Berton Braley. *Stand Fast for Freedom: A Call for the Emancipation of the Generous Energies of a People*. Philadelphia: John C. Winston, 1940.

Thompson, Dorothy. *Dorothy Thompson's Political Guide: A Study of American Liberalism and Its Relationship to Modern Totalitarian States*. New York: Stackpole, 1938.

———. *I Saw Hitler!* New York: Farrar and Rinehart, 1932.

U.S. Congress. Senate Committee on the Judiciary. *Reorganization of the Federal Judiciary*. Parts 3 and 4. Washington, D.C.: GPO, 1937.

U.S. Office of War Information. Bureau of Motion Pictures. *Government Information Manual for the Motion Picture Industry*. Hollywood, Calif.: Bureau of Motion Pictures, 1942.

Vansittart, Robert. *Black Record: Germans Past and Present*. London: Hamish Hamilton, 1941.

Wasserman, Louis. *Handbook of Political "Isms."* New York: Association Press, 1941.

West, Nathanael. *Novels and Other Writings*. New York: Library of America, 1997.

Willkie, Wendell L., with an introduction by Donald Bruce Johnson. *One World*. 1943. Reprint, Urbana: University of Illinois Press, 1966.

Wilson, Woodrow. *The New Freedom: A Call for the Emancipation of the Generous Energies of a People*. 1913. Reprint, New York: Doubleday, Page, 1919.

Wise, James Waterman, and Pierre Van Paassen, eds. *Nazism: An Assault on Civilization*. New York: Harrison Smith and Robert Haas, 1934.

Wright, Richard. *Native Son and How "Bigger" Was Born*. 1940. Reprint, New York: HarperPerennial, 1993.

Wylie, Philip. *A Generation of Vipers*. New York: Rinehart, 1942.

Ziemer, Gregor. *Education for Death: The Making of the Nazi*. New York: Oxford University Press, 1941.

Articles, Speeches, and Advertisements

Adey, Alvin. "The German Problem." *Current History* (August 1942): 461–65.

"Adolf and Ignatz." *Time*, 1 January 1934, 13–14.

Advertisement for *Romance of a Dictator*. *Publisher's Weekly*, 2 April 1932, 1537.

Advertisement for *Woman's Home Companion*. *Fortune*, July 1934, 7.

Alexandrova, Vera. "Russia Is Changing." *American Mercury* (March 1943): 311–18.

Alsop, Stewart. "Wanted: A Faith to Fight For." *Atlantic Monthly*, May 1941, 594–97.

"America's 'Isms.'" *Newsweek*, 6 March 1939, 14–15.

Amory, Cleveland. "What We Fight For." *Atlantic Monthly*, June 1941, 687–89.

Anderson, Paul Y. "The Moronic Conventions." *Nation* (22 June 1932): 698.

———. "Wanted: A Mussolini." *Nation* (6 July 1932): 9–10.

"Are Germans Incurable?" *Christian Century* (6 October 1943): 1128–29.

Arendt, Hannah. "A Reply to Eric Voegelin." *Review of Politics* 15 (1953): 76–84.

"As Long as the Comintern Rules." *Catholic World* (April 1942): 102–3.

Axelson, George. "Goetterdaemmerung—By Hitler." *New York Times Magazine*, 30 July 1944.

"Background of War: III, 'We Thank Our Führer.'" *Fortune*, May 1937, 95–101.

Baer, Werner. Review of *The Origins of Totalitarianism*, by Hannah Arendt. *American Economic Review* 42, no. 3 (1952): 437–38.

Bailey, Josiah W. Speech on Reorganization of Federal Judiciary. *Vital Speeches of the Day* (1 August 1937): 618–21.

Baldwin, Roger N. "The Question of Liberty." *New Republic* (17 November 1941): 649–51.

Ball, Max W. "Foes of Democracy." *Vital Speeches of the Day* (15 September 1944): 728–31.

"Ban Urged on Film of Nazi Activities." *New York Times*, 29 April 1934.

Barnes, Harry Elmer. "'Is Germany Incurable.'" *Saturday Review of Literature* (18 September 1943): 13–14.

Bates, Ralph. "The Battlefield of Liberty." *Christian Century* (13 December 1933): 1566–68.

———. "Need We Fear Russia?" *Nation* (17 January 1942): 60–62.

———. "Russia, Reform, and Revolution." *Nation* (3 April 1943): 502–3.

Beals, Lawrence W. "Catholics and Communists." *New Republic* (24 May 1943): 702–3.

"Behind the Scenes in Moscow." *Literary Digest* (24 January 1931): 13.

Benét, Stephen Vincent. "Dear Adolf." In *We Stand United and Other Radio Scripts*, 9–67. New York: Farrar and Rinehart, 1945.

———. "Your Army." In *We Stand United and Other Radio Scripts*, 183–202. New York: Farrar and Rinehart, 1945.

"Benito Amicare Andrea Mussolini." *Fortune,* July 1934, 102–17.

Benvenisti, J. L. "Two Germanies?" *Commonweal* (17 September 1943): 530–33.

Bess, Demaree. "What Does Russia Want?" *Saturday Evening Post,* 20 March 1943, 19, 91–92, 94.

Bettelheim, Bruno. "Individual and Mass Behavior in Extreme Situations." *Journal of Abnormal and Social Psychology* 38 (1943): 417–52.

"Between Editor and Reader." *Journal of the National Education Association* 29 (May 1940): A-87.

Blanker, Fredericka. "What a Real Dictator Would Do." *North American Review* (December 1932): 484–92.

"'Bless Me, Natzi.'" *Time,* 8 January 1934, 21.

Bond, Horace Mann. "The Curriculum and the Negro Child." *Journal of Negro Education* 4, no. 2 (April 1935): 159–68.

Bottai, Giuseppe. "The Corporative State." In *What Is Fascism and Why?,* edited by Tomaso Sillani, 30–39. New York: Macmillan, 1931.

Brickell, Herschel. "He Knows His History." *North American Review* (July 1934): 91–92.

Brickner, Richard M. "Is Germany Incurable?" *Atlantic Monthly,* March 1943, 84–93.

———. "Is Germany Incurable? The Treatment." *Atlantic Monthly,* April 1943, 94–98.

———. "Some Observations on the Incurable Controversy." *Saturday Review of Literature* (29 January 1944): 15–17.

Brown, J. F. Review of *The Origins of Totalitarianism,* by Hannah Arendt. *Annals of the American Academy of Political and Social Sciences* 277 (1951): 272–73.

Bullitt, William C. "The World from Rome." *Life,* 4 September 1944, 94–109.

Burnham, Philip. "Russia as an Ally." *Commonweal* (6 February 1942): 381–83.

Burrowes, Robert. "Totalitarianism: The Revised Standard Version." *World Politics* 21, no. 2 (1969): 272–94.

"Business of Empire." *Time,* 20 July 1936, 25–30.

Byrns, Ruth. "John Dewey on Russia." *Commonweal* (18 September 1942): 511–13.

Capra, Frank. "Just What Is the Capra Touch? Its Possessor Attempts to Explain." *New York Herald Tribune,* 5 November 1939.

———. "Mr. Capra (Humanist) Shares a Bow." *New York Times,* 19 April 1936.

Carey Jones, N. S. "Democracy, Dictatorships, and Totalitarianism." *Political Studies* 17, no. 1 (1969): 79–86.

Carpenter, William S. Review of *Capitalism, Socialism, and Democracy,* by Joseph Schumpeter. *American Political Science Review* 37, no. 3 (1943): 523–24.

Carr, E. H. "The Ultimate Denial." Review of *The Origins of Totalitarianism,* by Hannah Arendt. *New York Times Book Review,* 25 March 1951.

Cavert, Samuel McCrea. "Hitler and the German Churches." *Christian Century* (24 May 1933): 683–85.

———. "When Is the Church Free?" *Christian Century* (26 March 1937): 675–76.

Chamberlin, William Henry. "American-Russian Cooperation." *Russian Review* 3 (Autumn 1943): 3–9.

———. "Can Stalin's Russia Go Democratic? No." *American Mercury* (February 1944): 142–48.

———. Foreword. *Russian Review* 1 (November 1941): 1–5.

———. "Information, *Please,* about Russia." *Harper's Magazine,* April 1944, 405–12.

———. "Laski's Wave of the Future." *American Mercury* (September 1944): 370–76.

———. "Our Russian Ally." *Christian Century* (21 August 1942): 976–78.

———. Review of *The Red Army. Russian Review* 3 (Spring 1943): 102–4.

———. "Russia after the War." *Russian Review* 3 (Spring 1944): 3–9.

———. "Russia: An American Problem." *Atlantic Monthly,* February 1942, 148–56.

———. "Russia as a Partner in War and Peace." *Saturday Evening Post,* 14 November 1942, 124.

———. "Russia's Role in the Postwar World." *Russian Review* 2 (Spring 1943): 3–9.

———. "Russia—The Sprawling Giant." *New York Times Magazine,* 6 July 1941.

———. "The Russian Revolution, 1917–1942." *Russian Review* 2 (Autumn 1942): 3–9.

———. "The Sources of Russia's Strength." *Harper's Magazine,* March 1943, 396–403.

———. "The Soviet-German War: Results and Prospects." *Russian Review* 1 (April 1942): 3–9.

"Christian Totalitarianism." *Christian Century* (7 February 1934): 174–76.

"The Church and Christian Totalitarianism." *Christian Century* (14 February 1934): 214–16.

"Churches Should Be Wooed, Not Clubbed." *Christian Century* (5 July 1933): 867–68.

"A Close-up of Russia's 'Big Boss.'" *Literary Digest* (7 December 1929): 17.

"Comedy Has Its Limits." *Christian Century* (26 June 1940): 816.

"Communism and Fascism Are Not Opposites." *Christian Century* (13 January 1937): 38.

"Compulsory Service in Other Countries." *Congressional Digest* (April 1944): 107.

Cook, Thomas I. Review of *The Origins of Totalitarianism,* by Hannah Arendt. *Political Science Quarterly* 66, no. 2 (June 1951): 290–93.

Couch, W. T. "Is America Incurable?" *Saturday Review of Literature* (19 June 1943): 19.

Cowley, Malcolm. "Russian Turnabout." *New Republic* (14 June 1943): 800–801.

———. "Who's Fascist Now?" *New Republic* (21 February 1944): 246, 248.

Davenport, John. "Books and Ideas." *Fortune,* November 1944, 218–22.

"Death to a Dutchman." *Time,* 1 January 1934, 13.

de Sales, Raoul de Roussy. "What Makes a German." *Atlantic Monthly,* March 1942, 335–44.

DeVoto, Bernard. "The Easy Chair." *Harper's Magazine,* October 1944, 426–29.

Dighton, William. "Educational Totalitarianism." *Current History* (July 1944): 19–23.

"Does Wallace Know What Fascism Is?" *Saturday Evening Post,* 11 March 1944, 112.

"'Down with Us!'" *Time,* 17 January 1944, 13.

Dunham, Aileen. Review of *The Origins of Totalitarianism,* by Hannah Arendt, and *The Open Society and Its Enemies,* by Karl Popper. *Journal of Modern History* 24, no. 2 (1952): 184–86.

Duranty, Walter. "Is the Russian Revolution Over?" *New York Times Magazine,* 30 July 1944.

Eastman, Fred. "God or Caesar?" *Christian Century* (12 October 1932): 1240–43.

Eastman, Max. "The Gamblers with Liberty." *American Mercury* (July 1944): 42–49.

———. "Stalin's American Power." *American Mercury* (December 1941): 671–80. (Also appeared in *Reader's Digest,* December 1941, 39–48.)

Eddy, Sherwood. "Russia in the World Crisis." *Christianity and Crisis* (18 July 1941): 2–6.

Editorial Statement. *Partisan Review* (December 1937): 3–4.

Ellis, Ray C. "Will Russia Communize Europe?" *American Magazine,* November 1944, 24–25, 111–12, 114–16.

"*Escape from Freedom:* A Synoptic Series of Reviews." *Psychiatry* 5 (February 1942): 109–34.

Essad Bey. "The Red Czar." *Collier's,* 23 January 1932, 18–19, 44.

"Farm Group Maps 'Dictator' Measure." *New York Times,* 13 March 1933.

"Fascist Fantasy." *Time,* 13 February 1933, 51–52.

Fay, Sidney B. "The Nazi 'Totalitarian' State." *Current History* 38 (August 1933): 610–18.

Fischer, Louis. "Why Stalin Won." *Nation* (13 August 1930): 174–76.

Fitzsimons, M. A. "Totalitarian Absurdities: Their Origin." Review of *The Origins of Totalitarianism,* by Hannah Arendt. *Chicago Sunday Tribune Magazine of Books,* 25 March 1951.

Fodor, M. W. Review of *Germany Will Try It Again. Saturday Review of Literature* (5 February 1944): 8–9.

Foerster, F. W. "After the Defeat of Naziism, What?" *Christian Science Monitor Magazine,* 31 July 1943.

"Footnote." *North American Review* (December 1932): 483.

"The Future of Norman Thomas." *Christian Century* (23 November 1932): 1431.

Fried, Hans. "German Militarism: A Substitute for Revolution." *Political Science Quarterly* 58 (December 1943): 481–513.

Friedrich, Carl J. "The Role and the Position of the Common Man." *American Journal of Sociology* 49 (March 1944): 421–29.

———. "The Unique Character of Totalitarian Society." *Totalitarianism: Proceedings of a Conference Held at the American Academy of Arts and Sciences, March 1953.* Edited by Carl J. Friedrich. Cambridge: Harvard University Press, 1954.

"'Gabriel' Film Sent Back to Hollywood." *New York Times,* 17 March 1933.

"Gabriel over the White House." *Time,* 10 April 1933, 27.

"Games at Garmisch." *Time,* 17 February 1936, 37–40, 42.

Gentile, Giovanni. "The Philosophic Basis of Fascism." *Foreign Affairs* 6 (January 1928): 290–304.

"Gentle Adolf." *Time,* 8 January 1934, 21.

"German Catholics Make Common Cause with Protestants." *Christian Century* (29 November 1933): 1491–92.

"Germany in the Peace." *New Republic* (30 October 1944): 551–52.

"Germany's All-Nazi, Womanless Parliament." *Literary Digest* (30 December 1933): 15.

"Germany's Secret Weapon." *Saturday Evening Post,* 31 January 1942, 26.

Gerth, H. H., and C. Wright Mills. "A Marx for the Managers." *Ethics* 52, no. 2 (1942): 200–215.

Glueck, Sheldon. "Punishing the War Criminals." *New Republic* (22 November 1943): 706–9.

Gordon, Lincoln. "The Managerial Revolution." Review of *The Managerial Revolution,* by James Burnham. *American Economic Review* 32, no. 3 (1942): 626–31.

Grace, William J. "Hitlerism." *Commonweal* (13 October 1939): 560.

"'Greatest Democracy.'" *Time,* 30 August 1943, 26.

Green, William. "Free Men or Slaves?" *American Magazine,* April 1942, 28, 110.

Greenberg, Clement. "Avant-Garde and Kitsch." *Partisan Review* (September 1939): 34–49.

Griswold, A. Whitney. "Germans and Nazis." *Virginia Quarterly Review* (September 1944): 605–9.

Gunther, John. "Der Führer." *Reader's Digest,* May 1936, 54–57.

Hagen, Paul. "This Is No Maneuver!" *Nation* (12 June 1943): 837.

"Hail, Exiled Scholars!" *Nation* (11 December 1933): 398.

Hall, Mordaunt. "Gabriel over the White House." *New York Times,* 17 March 1933.

———. "Little Man, What Now?" *New York Times,* 1 June 1934.

Hall, O. Milton. "Attitudes and Unemployment: A Comparison of the Opinions and Attitudes of Employed and Unemployed Men." *Archives of Psychology* 165 (1934): 1–66.

Hanc, Josef. "What To Do with Germany." *Virginia Quarterly Review* (March 1944): 285–92.

Handlin, Oscar. "Dictators and Mobs." Review of *The Origins of Totalitarianism,* by Hannah Arendt. *Partisan Review* 51 (1951): 721–23.

Hanfstaengl, Ernst. "My Leader." *Collier's,* 4 August 1934, 7–9.

Hansen, Alvin. "The New Crusade against Planning." *New Republic* (1 January 1945): 9–12.

"Has Hitler Cowed the Churches?" *Christian Century* (14 June 1933): 775–77.

Hatch, Robert. "George Orwell's Paradise Lost." Review of *Nineteen Eighty-Four,* by George Orwell. *New Republic* 121 (1949): 23–24.

Heckscher, August. "The Forces of Disaster." Review of *The Origins of Totalitarianism,* by Hannah Arendt. *New York Herald Tribune Weekly Book Review,* 8 April 1951.

Hicks, Granville. Review of *Little Man, What Now? Nation* (21 June 1933): 703.

High, Stanley. "Star-Spangled Fascists." *Saturday Evening Post,* 27 May 1939, 5–7, 70–73.

Hilton, James. "Mr. Orwell's Nightmare of Totalitarianism." Review of *Nineteen Eighty-Four,* by George Orwell. *New York Herald Tribune Weekly Book Review,* 12 June 1949.

"Hitler Attacks Autonomy of Protestant Churches." *Christian Century* (5 July 1933): 867.

"Hitlerism Unveiled." *Christian Century* (29 March 1939): 417–18.

"Hitler's New Religion." *Christian Century* (26 April 1933): 550–52.

"Hold That Line!" *Time,* 19 July 1943, 44.

Homrighausen, E. G. "Barth Resists Hitler." *Christian Century* (26 July 1933): 954–55.

———. "Hitler and German Religion." *Christian Century* (29 March 1933): 418–20.

Hook, Sidney. "The Anatomy of the Popular Front." *Partisan Review* (March 1939): 29–45.

Hoover, Calvin B. "Dictators and Democracies." *Virginia Quarterly Review* 10 (April 1934): 161–76.

Hoover, Herbert. "Constitution Day Address, San Diego, California [September 17, 1935]," *Addresses upon the American Road, 1933–1938,* 58–62. New York: Scribner, 1938.

———. "Responsibility of the Republican Party to the Nation, Sacramento, California [March 22, 1935]," *Addresses upon the American Road, 1933–1938,* 40–44. New York: Scribner, 1938.

Hromádka, Joseph L. "The Soviet Enigma." *Christianity and Crisis* (24 January 1944): 2–5.

Hughes, H. Stuart. "Historical Sources of Totalitarianism." Review of *The Origins of Totalitarianism,* Hannah Arendt. *Nation* 172 (1951): 280–81.

Hutchinson, Paul. "Germany Welcomes the Messiah." *Christian Century* (16 August 1933): 1031–33.

———. "Is a Planned Economy Slavery?" *Christian Century* (3 January 1945): 18–19.

"'I.G.I.?'—Cont." *Saturday Review of Literature* (16 October 1943): 27–28.

"In the Face of the World's Crisis: A Manifesto by European Catholics Sojourning in America." *Commonweal* (21 August 1942): 415–21.

"The Incurable Controversy." *Saturday Review of Literature* (30 October 1943): 29.

"The Incurable Controversy." *Saturday Review of Literature* (27 November 1943): 11.

"'Is Germany Incurable?'—Cont." *Saturday Review of Literature* (2 October 1943): 17–19.

"Is Germany Incurable?—Cont." *Saturday Review of Literature* (9 October 1943): 13–14.

"Is This Another Kulturkampf?" *Christian Century* (5 July 1933): 867.

Iswolsky, Helen. "Righting the Russian Balance." *Commonweal* (19 June 1942): 198–201.

———. "Russia at War." *Commonweal* (25 July 1941): 318–20.

Johnston, Eric. "A Business View of Russia." *Nation's Business* (October 1944): 21–22.

Kallen, Horace M. Review of *Is Germany Incurable? Saturday Review of Literature* (29 May 1943): 4.

Kerensky, Alexander. "Russia Is Ripe for Freedom." *American Mercury* (August 1943): 158–65.

Kirchwey, Freda. "The Red Star Rises." *Nation* (27 February 1943): 293–94.

———. "Red Totalitarianism." *Nation* (27 May 1939): 605–6.

———. "Stalin's Choice." *Nation* (22 January 1944): 89.

Kittredge, Eleanor. "An Anthropologist Looks at the War." *New York Times Magazine,* 12 October 1941.

Knickerbocker, H. R. "Why Doesn't Somebody Kill Hitler?" *American Magazine,* October 1941, 9, 112–13.

"Koestler: Some Political Remarks." *Politics* 1, no. 1 (1944): 4–5.

Kohn, Hans. "The Mass-Man: Hitler." *Atlantic Monthly,* April 1944, 101–4.

"Kosher and Kultur!" *Time,* 8 January 1934, 20.

Krok, Arthur. "The Relation of Business to Government." *Vital Speeches of the Day* (5 November 1934): 89–91.

Kubie, Lawrence, Edward A. Strecker, Arthur H. Ruggles, Smith Ely Jelliffe, David Levy, and Lawson G. Lowrey. "'Is Germany Incurable?'" *Saturday Review of Literature* (31 July 1943): 17.

Kunz, Josef L. Review of *Sicherheit und Gerechtigkeit: Eine Gemeinverständliche Einführung in die Hauptprobleme der Volkerrechtspolitik. American Journal of International Law* 29, no. 2 (April 1935): 350.

Land, John. "The Anatomy of Fascism." *American Mercury* (April 1944): 497–502.

Laski, Harold J. "Government by Consent." *New Republic* (20 June 1934): 162–63.

"Leaders—Russian and American." *New Republic* (12 August 1931): 327–29.

Lerner, Max. "Germany without Illusions." *New Republic* (30 October 1944): 553–56.

———. "Homage to a Fighting People." *New Republic* (17 November 1941): 643–44.

———. "Lippmann Agonistes." *Nation* (27 November 1937): 590.

———. "Russia and the Future." *Atlantic Monthly,* November 1942, 79–87.

"'Let's Be Friends!'" *Time,* 9 March 1936, 21–22.

Letters to the Editor. *Life,* 25 September 1944, 2–10.

"The Light of the Torch." *New York Times,* 1 August 1936.

Lindley, Ernest K. "Russia: Partner in War and in Peace." *Newsweek,* 8 June 1942, 31.

Loewenstein, Karl. "Autocracy versus Democracy in Contemporary Europe, I." *American Political Science Review* 29, no. 4 (August 1935): 571–93.

Lorwin, Lewis. "Social Aspects of the Planning State." *American Political Science Review* 28, no. 1 (February 1934): 16–22.

Lyons, Eugene. "Our Totalitarian 'Liberals.'" *American Mercury* (April 1939): 385–87.
———. "The Progress of Stalin Worship." *American Mercury* (June 1943): 693–97.
———. "Some Plain Talk about Russia." *American Mercury* (November 1941): 583–89.
———. "What Price 'Security'?" *American Mercury* (April 1943): 416–20.
Macdonald, Dwight. "National Defense: The Case for Socialism." *Partisan Review* (July 1940): 250–66.
———. "A New Dimension." *Common Sense* (January 1942): 29.
———. "A New Theory of Totalitarianism." *New Leader* 34, no. 20 (1951): 17–19.
———. "War and the Intellectuals: Act Two." *Partisan Review* (March 1939): 3–4.
MacEachan, Roderick. "Paper Hanger Makes Good." *Commonweal* (8 April 1938): 652.
Magidoff, Nila. "Americans and Russians Are *So* Alike." *American Magazine* (December 1944): 17, 118–20.
"Manifesto." *Nation* (27 May 1939): 626.
Marsh, Fred T. "A Little Family Faces the World." *New York Times,* 4 June 1944.
Maslow, A. H. "The Authoritarian Character Structure." *Journal of Social Psychology* 18 (1943): 401–11.
Mason, John Brown. Review of *The New Church and the New Germany,* by Charles MacFarland. *Political Science Quarterly* 50, issue 1 (March 1935): 159–60.
"The Meaning of It All." *Commonweal* (4 June 1943): 159–60.
"Measuring the Effectiveness of Informational Motion Pictures." *What the Soldier Thinks* (August 1943): 87–104.
"Meeting the Nazi Threat." *Nation* (26 July 1933): 89–90.
"Men Who Never Grew Up." *Woman's Home Companion,* May 1935, 2.
Moley, Raymond. "You Can Do Business with Stalin." *Newsweek,* 18 October 1943, 112.
Morgan, Joy Elmer. "The Significance of Citizenship Recognition Day." *Journal of the National Education Association* 28 (December 1939): 257.
Motherwell, Hiram. "Germany after Hitler." *Nation* (30 January 1943): 152–55.
"Mr. Barnes Replies." *Saturday Review of Literature* (23 October 1943): 14–15.
Mussolini, Benito. "Youth." *Saturday Evening Post,* 5 May 1928, 3–5, 117–18, 121.
"Mussolini Speaks." *New York Times.* 13 March 1933.
"Nazi Progress toward Totalitarianism." *Christian Century* (19 July 1933): 924.
"The Nazis Are Here." *Nation* (4 March 1939): 253.
"Nazis Win German Church Elections." *Christian Century* (2 August 1933): 971–72.
Neumann, Sigmund. Review of *Peace by Power,* by Lionel Gelber, and *Strategy for Democracy,* edited by J. Donald Kingsley and David W. Petegorsky. *American Political Science Review* 37, no. 2 (1943): 348–50.
"Nickel Word Needed." *New York Times,* 6 June 1938.

Niebuhr, Reinhold. "Religion and the New Germany." *Christian Century* (28 June 1933): 843–45.

———. "Russia and the Peace." *Christianity and Crisis* (13 November 1944): 2–4.

———. "Russia and the West." *Nation* (16 January 1943): 82–84.

Odegard, Peter H. Review of *What Is Democracy?*, by Charles E. Merriam, *Democracy in American Life,* by Avery Craven, and *Aspects of Democracy,* by R. B. Huliman. *American Political Science Review* 35, no. 6 (1941): 1161–62.

"The Ordeal of German Protestantism." *Christian Century* (12 July 1933): 901–3.

Padover, Saul. "Jefferson vs. Totalitarianism." *American Mercury* (September 1943): 318–19.

Paetel, Karl O. "The Crisis in Germany." *New Republic* (7 August 1944): 154–55.

Pares, Bernard. "On the Fear of Russia." *New Republic* (19 April 1943): 498–503.

Parker, Ralph. "The Man Who Stopped Hitler." *New York Times Magazine,* 8 March 1942.

Parker, W. W. "Frustratious Joins the Party." *School and Society* (29 April 1944): 311–12.

"The Peoples of the U.S.S.R." *Life,* 23 March 1943, 23–26.

Perry, Ralph Barton. "American-Soviet Friendship." *New Republic* (5 April 943): 433–37.

Peters, Capt. C. Brooks. Review of *What to Do with Germany. Saturday Review of Literature* (5 February 1944): 10.

"Plan v. Plan v. Plan." *Time,* 13 April 1936, 24–26.

Pope, Arthur Upham. "Can Stalin's Russia Go Democratic? Yes." *American Mercury* (February 1944): 135–42.

Price, Byron. "Censorship an Evil of War." *Vital Speeches of the Day* (15 December 1942): 158–60.

"The Pro and Con Discussion: Should the United States Adopt Compulsory Peacetime Training?" *Congressional Digest* (January 1945): 12–31.

"Prussian Protestantism and the Political Reaction." *Christian Century* (15 February 1933): 212–13.

"The Question of Civilian Conscription for War." *Congressional Digest* (April 1944): 101.

Rahv, Philip. "The Crisis in France." *Partisan Review* (December 1939): 3–4.

———. "Two Years of Progress—From Waldo Frank to Donald Ogden Stuart." *Partisan Review* (February 1938): 22–30.

———. "The Unfuture of Utopia." *Partisan Review* 16, no. 7 (1949): 743–49.

"Red, Altogether." *Commonweal* (13 October 1939): 561.

"Red Flipflop." *Newsweek,* 17 January 1944, 46.

"Regimentation Is the Least of Our Dangers." *Christian Century* (24 August 1932): 1019.

Reimann, Guenther. "Inside Germany." *New Republic* (10 August 1942): 182.

Reinhold, H. A. Review of *Thus Speaks Germany. Commonweal* (3 April 1942): 594–95.

"Relation of Church and State Must Be Studied." *Christian Century* (5 July 1933): 868.

"The Republics of Russia." *Time,* 14 February 1944, 34–35.

Reves, Emery. "How to Civilize Germany." *American Mercury* (November 1944): 549–58.

Review of *Gabriel over the White House. Time,* 10 April 1933, 27.

Review of *Little Man, What Now? Commonweal* (4 August 1933): 354.

Review of *Mussolini Speaks. New York Times,* 13 March 1933.

Richardson, A. S. "Outstanding Campaign Issues." *Woman's Home Companion,* February 1932, 33.

Riesman, David. "The Path to Total Terror." Review of *The Origins of Totalitarianism,* by Hannah Arendt. *Commentary* 11 (1951): 392–98.

Robinson, Elmo A. "Universalism or Totalitarianism?" *Christian Century* (12 August 1942): 978–80.

Rocca, Alfredo. "The Transformation of the State." *What Is Fascism and Why?,* edited by Tomaso Sillani. New York: Macmillan, 1931.

Roosevelt, Franklin D. "Annual Message to Congress, January 4, 1939." In *The Public Papers and Addresses of Franklin D. Roosevelt,* edited by Samuel I. Rosenman, 8:1–12. New York: Macmillan, 1941.

———. "'Dictatorships Do Not Grow Out of Strong and Successful Governments, but Out of Weak and Helpless Ones': Fireside Chat on Present Economic Conditions and Measures Being Taken to Improve Them, April 14, 1938." In *The Public Papers and Addresses of Franklin D. Roosevelt,* edited by Samuel I. Rosenman, 7:236–48. New York: Macmillan, 1941.

———. "'Do Not Seek or Expect Utopia Overnight: Do Not Seek or Expect a Panacea. . . .': Address to the Delegates of the American Youth Congress, Washington, D.C., February 10, 1940." In *The Public Papers and Addresses of Franklin D. Roosevelt,* edited by Samuel I. Rosenman, 9:85–94. New York: Macmillan, 1941.

———. "Extemporaneous Remarks at Tupelo, Miss., November 18, 1934." In *The Public Papers and Addresses of Franklin D. Roosevelt,* edited by Samuel I. Rosenman, 3:460–63. New York: Random House, 1938.

———. "Extemporaneous Speech at the Subsistence Homes Exhibition, April 24, 1934." In *The Public Papers and Addresses of Franklin D. Roosevelt,* edited by Samuel I. Rosenman, 3:193–200. New York: Random House, 1938.

———. "First 'Fireside Chat' of 1934: 'Are You Better Off Than You Were Last Year?,' June 28, 1934." In *The Public Papers and Addresses of Franklin D. Roosevelt,* edited by Samuel I. Rosenman, 3:312–18. New York: Random House, 1938.

———. "'He Believed, as We Do, That the Average Opinion of Mankind Is in the Long Run Superior to the Dictates of the Self-Chosen': Address at the Cornerstone Laying of the Jefferson Memorial, Washington, D.C., November 15, 1939." In *The Public Papers and Addresses of Franklin D. Roosevelt,* edited by Samuel I. Rosenman, 8:577–79. New York: Macmillan, 1941.

———. "'I Have Every Right to Speak. . . .': Fireside Chat, June 24, 1938." In *The*

Public Papers and Addresses of Franklin D. Roosevelt, edited by Samuel I.
Rosenman, 7:391–400. New York: Macmillan, 1941.

———. "Inaugural Address, March 4, 1933." In *The Public Papers and Addresses of
Franklin D. Roosevelt,* edited by Samuel I. Rosenman, 2:11–16. New York:
Random House, 1938.

———. "A Message to the Foreign Policy Association, October 25, 1941." In *The
Public Papers and Addresses of Franklin D. Roosevelt,* edited by Samuel I.
Rosenman, 10:434–35. New York: Harper, 1950.

———. "The President Accepts the Nomination for a Third Term: Radio Address
to the Democratic National Convention in Chicago, Illinois, from the White
House, Washington, D.C., July 19, 1940, at 12:25 A.M." In *The Public Papers and
Addresses of Franklin D. Roosevelt,* edited by Samuel I. Rosenman, 9:293–303.
New York: Macmillan, 1941.

———. "Recommendations to the Congress to Curb Monopolies and the
Concentration of Economic Power, April 29, 1938." In *The Public Papers and
Addresses of Franklin D. Roosevelt,* edited by Samuel I. Rosenman, 7:305–32.
New York: Macmillan, 1941.

———. "A Survey of the Purposes, Accomplishments, and Failings of NRA:
Extemporaneous Address before the Code Authorities of Six Hundred
Industries, March 5, 1934." In *The Public Papers and Addresses of Franklin D.
Roosevelt,* edited by Samuel I. Rosenman, 3;123–32. New York: Random
House, 1938.

———. "'We Americans Have Cleared Our Decks and Taken Our Battle Stations':
Navy and Total Defense Day Address, October 27, 1941." In *The Public Papers
and Addresses of Franklin D. Roosevelt,* edited by Samuel I. Rosenman,
10:438–45. New York: Harper, 1950.

———. "'We Are Not Only the Largest and Most Powerful Democracy in the
Whole World, but Many Other Democracies Look to Us for Leadership That
World Democracy May Survive': Address at University of North Carolina,
Chapel Hill, North Carolina, December 5, 1938." In *The Public Papers and
Addresses of Franklin D. Roosevelt,* edited by Samuel I. Rosenman, 7:613–21.
New York: Macmillan, 1941.

———. "'We Believe in the . . . Freedoms That Are Inherent in the Right of Free
Choice by Free Men and Women': Address on the Occasion of the One
Hundred and Fiftieth Anniversary of Congress, March 4, 1939." In *The Public
Papers and Addresses of Franklin D. Roosevelt,* edited by Samuel I. Rosenman,
8:147–53. New York: Macmillan, 1941.

———. "'We in Turn Are Striving to Uphold the Integrity of the Morals of Our
Democracy': Address at the Jackson Day Dinner, Washington, D.C.,
January 8, 1938." In *The Public Papers and Addresses of Franklin D. Roosevelt,*
edited by Samuel I. Rosenman, 7:37–45. New York: Macmillan, 1941.

Rosen, S. McKee. Review of *The Managerial Revolution,* by James Burnham.
Ethics 52, no. 3 (1942): 383–85.

Ruhl, Arthur. "Made to Be Trampled On." *Saturday Review of Literature* (3 June
1933): 629.

"Russia in the Alliance." *New Republic* (22 June 1942): 843–44.

"The Russian Tragedy." *Christian Century* (30 June 1940): 830–31.

Sandifer, Durward V. "A Comparative Study of Laws Relating to Nationality at Birth and to Loss of Nationality." *American Journal of International Law* 29, no. 2 (April 1935): 248–79.

Scheffer, Paul. "Stalin's Power." *Foreign Affairs* 8 (July 1930): 549–68.

Schofield, Lemuel B. "'I'm an American.'" *Christian Science Monitor Magazine,* 5 May 1941, 3.

Schorer, Mark. "An Indignant and Prophetic Novel." Review of *Nineteen Eighty-Four,* by George Orwell. *New York Times Book Review,* 12 June 1949.

Schwarzschild, Leopold. "Six Delusions about Germany." *New York Times Magazine,* 1 October 1944.

"Second Revolution?" *Time,* 2 July 1934, 16.

"Semi-Dictator?" *Barron's,* 13 February 1933, 12.

"Sense about Germany." *New Republic* (25 December 1944): 854–55.

"Shirley Temple and the Big Bad Wolf." *Saturday Evening Post,* 18 March 1939, 22.

"Should the United States Adopt Compulsory Peacetime Military Training?" *Congressional Digest* (January 1945): 3–32.

"Should the U.S. Adopt Civilian Conscription for War?" *Congressional Digest* (April 1944): 101–27.

Smith, M. B. "Did War Service Produce International-Mindedness?" *Harvard Educational Review* 15 (October 1945): 250–57.

Soule, George. "Russia, Germany, and the Peace." *New Republic* (22 March 1943): 372–75.

Spencer, Henry R. "Political Developments in Italy." *American Political Science Review* 23, issue 1 (February 1929): 139–49.

Spiro, Herbert J. "Totalitarianism." In *International Encyclopedia of the Social Sciences,* edited by David L. Sills, 106–12. New York: Macmillan, 1968.

"The Stakes in the Election." *Christian Century* (26 October 1932): 1294–98.

"Stalin Tramples on His Enemies." *Literary Digest* (29 January 1932): 12–13.

"The State: Fascist and Total." *Fortune,* July 1937, 47–56.

Stead, W. H. "Democracy and Social Controls in Industry." *American Sociological Review* 7, no. 2 (1942): 176–84.

Steiner, H. Arthur. "Fascism in America?" *American Political Science Review* 29 (October 1935): 821–30.

Stone, Geoffrey. "An Ironical Tract." *Commonweal* (22 November 1935): 107–8.

Strakhovsky, Leonid I. "America: The Savior of Red Tyranny?" *Catholic World* (November 1941): 140–44.

"The Strange World of 1984." *Life* 27, no. 1 (1949): 78–85.

Strunsky, Simeon. "Behind the Masks of Dictators." *New York Times Magazine,* 21 January 1934.

"Supreme Eugenic Courts." *Time,* 1 January 1934, 12.

"Symposium on the Totalitarian State from the Standpoints of History, Political Science, Economics, and Sociology." *Proceedings of the American Philosophical Society* 82 (23 February 1940): 1–102.

"Symptoms and Diagnosis." *Time,* 8 November 1943, 20.

"Talk about Germany." *Commonweal* (17 December 1943): 220.

Thomas, C. P. "Prelude to Invasion." *Catholic World* (May 1943): 149–54.

Thomas, Norman. Letter to the Editor. *Nation* (31 January 1942): 129.

———. "Thomas on Bates on Russia." *Nation* (31 January 1942): 124.

———. "Totalitarian Liberals." *Commonweal* (22 January 1943): 342–44.

Thompson, Dorothy. "Germany—Enigma of the Peace." *Life,* 6 December 1943, 60–62, 64, 69–70, 72, 74.

Thompson, Dorothy, M. W. Fodor, Hans Kohn, and Captain C. Brooks Peters. "The Enemy and His Future." *Saturday Review of Literature* (5 February 1944): 5–10, 33.

"Those Russians." *Life,* 17 July 1944, 26.

Tillich, Paul. "The Totalitarian State and the Claims of the Church." *Social Research* 1 (November 1934): 405–33.

Tolischus, Otto D. "Woman's Place in the 'Manly' Nazi State." *New York Times Magazine,* 10 September 1933.

"'Totalitarian' Idea Spreads." *New York Times,* 22 March 1936.

"Totalitarian State Finally Achieved by Hitler." *Newsweek,* 9 December 1933, 14.

"Tovarich Hague." *Newsweek,* 19 July 1943, 48.

TRB [Kenneth Crawford]. "The Communist Party." *New Republic* (2 June 1942): 859.

Trilling, Diana. Review of *Nineteen Eighty-Four,* by George Orwell. *Nation* 168 (1949): 716–17.

Trilling, Lionel. "Orwell on the Future." Review of *Nineteen Eighty-Four,* by George Orwell. *New Yorker* 26 (1949): 78–83.

Tumin, Melvin M. "The Managerial Revolution." Review of *The Managerial Revolution,* by James Burnham. *American Sociological Review* 6, no. 5 (1941): 737–39.

Tunney, Gene, and Walter Davenport. "So This Is Russia!" *Collier's,* 3 October 1931, 7–9, 48, 50–51.

Van Duzer, C. H. Review of *The Origins of Totalitarianism,* by Hannah Arendt. *American Historical Review* 57, no. 4 (1952): 933–35.

Vann, Gerald. "Jews, Reds, and Imbeciles." *Catholic World* (April 1939): 10–18.

Villari, Luigi. "The Economics of Fascism." *Bolshevism, Fascism, and Capitalism.* Edited by George S. Counts, Luigi Villari, Malcolm C. Rorty, and Newton Baker, 55–113. New Haven: Yale University Press, 1932.

"A Vivid Russian Portrait of Russia's Strong Man." *Literary Digest* (5 January 1929): 15–16.

Voegelin, Eric. "The Origins of Totalitarianism." Review of *The Origins of Totalitarianism,* by Hannah Arendt. *Review of Politics* 15 (1953): 68–76.

Walker, Charles R. Review of *The Managerial Revolution,* by James Burnham. *Atlantic Monthly* 168, no. 2 (1941): 128.

Wallace, Henry A. "Beyond the Atlantic Charter." *New Republic* (23 November 1942): 667–69.

———. "The Price of Free World Victory: The Century of the Common Man."
   Vital Speeches of the Day (1 June 1942): 482–85.
———. "Wallace Defines 'American Fascism.'" *New York Times Magazine,* 9 April
   1944.
Wankowicz, Marta. "'In Russia . . . It's Colder.'" *Commonweal* (4 September
   1942): 461–63.
"The War of the Neutrals." *Partisan Review* (September 1939): 3–15.
Warburg, James P. "Can the Germans Cure Themselves?" *New York Times
   Magazine,* 20 August 1944.
Ward, Harry F. "Is Russia Forsaking Communism?" *Christian Century* (28 October
   1942): 1314–16.
Waring, Roane. "Eternal Vigilance Is the Price of Liberty." *Vital Speeches of the
   Day* (1 February 1942): 228–30.
"We Highly Resolve." *Woman's Home Companion,* January 1930, 4.
Weigert, W. W. "Freedom and the Germans." *Christian Century* (21 January
   1942): 80–82.
"What Is Morale?" *What the Soldier Thinks* (December 1943): 1–6.
"What Shall We Do with Germany? A Panel Discussion of 'Is Germany
   Incurable?'" *Saturday Review of Literature* (29 May 1943): 4–10.
"Where the Rainbow Ends." Review of *Nineteen Eighty-Four,* by George Orwell.
   Time 53 (1949): 91–96.
Willkie, Wendell L. "Don't Stir Distrust of Russia." *New York Times Magazine,*
   2 January 1944.
———. "We Must Work with Russia—Willkie." *New York Times Magazine,*
   17 January 1943.
Wohl, Paul. "Passage to Freedom." *Commonweal* (6 February 1942): 383–87.
Wolfe, A. B. Review of *Capitalism, Socialism, and Democracy,* by Joseph
   Schumpeter. *Political Science Quarterly* 58, no. 2 (1943): 265–67.
Wolfe, Henry C. "The Enemy Mind." *New York Times Magazine,* 21 December
   1941.
"You Can't Keep a Whole Nation in Chains." *Saturday Evening Post,* 2 October
   1943, 112.
zu Loewenstein, Prince Hubertus. "Christian World Revolution." *Atlantic
   Monthly,* January 1942, 104–11.

Motion Pictures and Television Shows
American Madness. Producer-Director: Frank Capra. Columbia, 1932. Screenplay:
   Robert Riskin. Cast: Walter Huston, Pat O'Brien, Kay Johnson, Constance
   Cummings, Gavin Gordon.
Blockade. Director: William Dieterly. Producer: Walter Wanger. United Artists,
   1938. Screenplay: John Howard Lawson. Cast: Henry Fonda, Madeleine
   Carroll, Leo Carillo, Vladimir Sokoloff.
Cat People. Director: Jacques Tourneur. Producer: Val Lewton. RKO, 1942. Cast:
   Jane Randolph, Elizabeth Russell, Jack Holt, Alan Napier, Simone Simon,
   Kent Smith, Tom Conway.

Censored. A Private Snafu film. Director: Frank Tashlin. War Department, 1944.

Chicken Little. Director: Gerry Geronimi. Producer: Walt Disney. RKO, 1943. Animators: Ward Kimball, Norman Tate, Milt Kahl, Ed Aardal, Ollie Johnston, George Rowley, Andy Engman, John Lounsbery.

Comrade X. Director: King Vidor. Producer: Gottfried Reinhardt. MGM, 1940. Screenplay: Ben Hecht, Charles Lederer. Cast: Clark Gable, Hedy Lamarr, Felix Bressart, Oscar Homolka, Eve Arden, Sig Ruman.

Confessions of a Nazi Spy. Director: Anatole Litvak. Warner Brothers, 1939. Screenplay: Milton Krims, John Wexley. Cast: Edward G. Robinson, George Sanders, Paul Lukas, Francis Lederer.

The Dark Horse. Director: Alfred A. Green. Producer: Raymond Griffith. Warner Brothers, 1932. Screenplay: Joseph Jackson, Wilson Mizner. Story: Melville Crossman [Darryl F. Zanuck]. Cast: Warren William, Bette Davis, Guy Kibbee.

The Day the Earth Stood Still. Director: Robert Wise. Producer: Julian Blaustein. 20th Century Fox, 1951. Screenplay: Harry Bates, Edmund H. North. Cast: Michael Rennie, Patricia Neal, Hugh Marlowe, Sam Jaffe.

Days of Glory. Director: Jacques Tourneur. Producer: Casey Robinson. RKO, 1944. Cast: Gregory Peck, Alan Reed, Maria Palmer, Lowell Gilmore, Tamara Toumanova.

Don't Be a Sucker. Produced by the Army Signal Corps. 1945.

Duck Soup. Director: Leo McCarey. Paramount, 1933. Screenplay: Bert Kalmar, Holly Ruby. Cast: Groucho Marx, Chico Marx, Harpo Marx, Zeppo Marx, Louis Calhern, Margaret Dumont, Edgar Kennedy.

Earth vs. the Flying Saucers. Director: Fred F. Sears. Producer: Charles H. Schneer. Columbia, 1956. Screenplay: Donald Keyhoe, Curt Siodmak, George Worthing Yates, Bernard Gordon (credited as "Raymont T. Marcus"). Cast: Hugh Marlowe, Joan Taylor, Donald Curtis, Morris Ankrum.

Foreign Correspondent. Director: Alfred Hitchcock. Producer: Walter Wanger. United Artists, 1940. Screenplay: Charles Bennett, Joan Harrison. Cast: Joel McCrea, Laraine Day, Herbert Marshall, George Sanders.

Gabriel over the White House. Director: Gregory La Cava. Producer: Walter Wanger. Cosmopolitan, 1933. Screenplay: Carey Wilson, Bertram Block. Cast: Walter Huston, Karen Morley, Franchot Tone, David Landau, Mischa Auer, C. Henry Gordon.

The Great Dictator. Producer-Director-Writer: Charlie Chaplin. United Artists, 1940. Cast: Charlie Chaplin, Paulette Goddard, Jack Oakie, Billy Gilbert, Reginald Gardiner, Henry Daniell.

Here Is Germany. Director: Gottfried Reinhardt. Supervisor: Frank Capra. Army Pictorial Service, Signal Corps, U.S. War Department, 1945. Script: Gottfried Reinhardt, Anthony Veiller, William L. Shirer, Ernst Lubitsch (originally scripted by Bruno Frank and Ernst Lubitsch). Narrators: John Beal, Anthony Veiller. Note: The films produced by Capra's unit during the war—which in this filmography include *Here Is Germany, Know Your Enemy—Japan, The Negro Soldier,* and the films in the *Why We Fight* series—are uncredited. Over the years, researchers have established a list of contributors for each film. The official name of Capra's unit changed a number of times during the war. The information in this filmography is from Wolfe, *Frank Capra*.

He Stayed for Breakfast. Director: Alexander Hall. MGM, 1940. Cast: Loretta Young, Melvyn Douglas, Una O'Connor, Eugene Pallette, Alan Marshall.

Hitler's Children. Director: Edward Dmytryk. Producer: Edward A. Golden. RKO, 1943. Screenplay: Emmet Lavery. Cast: Tim Holt, Bonita Granville, Kent Smith, Otto Kruger.

Hitler's Reign of Terror. Director: Michael Mindlin. Jewel Productions, 1934.

The House I Live In. Director: Mervyn LeRoy (uncredited). Producers: Mervyn LeRoy, Frank Ross. RKO, 1945. Screenplay: Albert Maltz. Cast: Frank Sinatra.

Invasion of the Body Snatchers. Director: Don Siegel. Producer: Walter Wanger. Walter Wanger Productions, 1956. Screenplay: Richard Collins (uncredited), Jack Finney, Daniel Mainwaring, Sam Peckinpah (uncredited). Cast: Kevin McCarthy, Dana Wynter, Larry Gates, King Donovan.

It Happened One Night. Producer-Director: Frank Capra. Columbia, 1934. Screenplay: Robert Riskin. Cast: Clark Gable, Claudette Colbert, Walter Connolly, Jameson Thomas, Roscoe Karns.

Keeper of the Flame. Director: George Cukor. Producer: Victor Saville. MGM, 1942. Screenplay: Donald Ogden Stewart. Cast: Spencer Tracy, Katharine Hepburn, Richard Whorf, Margaret Wycherly, Forrest Tucker, Frank Craven, Horace McNally, Percy Kilbride.

Know Your Enemy—Japan. Directors: Frank Capra, Edgar Peterson, Leonard Spigelgass, Joris Ivens. Supervisor: Frank Capra. Army Pictorial Service, Signal Corps, U.S. War Department, 1945. Script: Irving Wallace, Edgar Peterson, Carl Foreman, Frances Goodrich, Albert Hackett, John Huston, Joris Ivens, Howard Duff, Frank Capra. Narrators: Walter Huston, Jean Beal, Anthony Veiller.

Little Man, What Now? Director: Frank Borzage. Producer: Carl Laemmle Jr. Universal, 1934. Screenplay: William Anthony McGuire. Cast: Margaret Sullavan, Douglass Montgomery, Alan Hale, Alan Mowbray.

Lucky Jordan. Director Frank Tuttle. Paramount, 1942. Cast: Alan Ladd, Helen Walker, Marie McDonald, Mabel Paige, Sheldon Leonard, Lloyd Corrigan.

Man Hunt. Director: Fritz Lang. 20th Century Fox, 1940. Screenplay: Dudley Nichols. Cast: Walter Pidgeon, Joan Bennett, George Sanders, John Carradine, Roddy McDowall.

The Man I Married. Director: Irving Pichel. Producer: Darryl F. Zanuck. Fox, 1940. Screenplay: Oliver H. P. Garrett. Cast: Joan Bennett, Francis Lederer.

Meet John Doe. Director: Frank Capra. Producers: Frank Capra, Robert Riskin. Warner Brothers, 1941. Screenplay: Robert Riskin, Myles Connoly (uncredited). Cast: Gary Cooper, Barbara Stanwyck, Edward Arnold, Walter Brennan, James Gleason.

Mission to Moscow. Director: Michael Curtiz. Producer: Robert Buckner. Warner Brothers, 1943. Screenplay: Howard Koch. Cast: Walter Huston, Ann Harding, Oscar Homolka, George Tobias, Gene Lockhart, Eleanor Parker, Richard Travis, Frieda Inescort.

Modern Times. Director: Charlie Chaplin. Producer: Charlie Chaplin (uncredited). United Artists, 1936. Screenplay: Charlie Chaplin. Cast: Charlie Chaplin, Paulette Goddard, Henry Bergman, Tiny Sandford, Chester Conklin, Hank Mann, Stanley Blystone, Allan Garcia, Dick Alexander.

The Mortal Storm. Director: Frank Borzage. MGM, 1940. Screenplay: Claudine West, Anderson Ellis, George Froeschel. Cast: Margaret Sullavan, James Stewart, Robert Young, Frank Morgan, Robert Stack.

Mr. Deeds Goes to Town. Producer-Director: Frank Capra. Columbia, 1936. Screenplay: Robert Riskin, Myles Connolly (uncredited). Cast: Gary Cooper, Jean Arthur, George Bancroft, Leionel Stander, Douglas Dumbrille.

Mr. Lucky. Director: H. C. Potter. RKO, 1943. Cast: Cary Grant, Laraine Day, Charles Bickford, Gladys Cooper, Alan Carney, Henry Stephenson, Paul Stewart, Kay Johnson, Florence Bates.

Mr. Smith Goes to Washington. Producer-Director: Frank Capra. Columbia, 1939. Screenplay: Sidney Buchman, Myles Connolly (uncredited). Cast: James Stewart, Jean Arthur, Claude Rains, Edward Arnold, Thomas Mitchell.

Mussolini Speaks. Edited and compiled by Jack Cohn. Columbia, 1933. Described and interpreted by Lowell Thomas.

The Negro Soldier. Director: Stuart Heisler. Supervisor: Frank Capra. Special Services Division, Army Services Forces, U.S. War Department, 1944. Script: Carlton Moss. Cast: Carlton Moss, Bertha Wolford.

Ninotchka. Producer-Director: Ernst Lubitsch. MGM, 1939. Screenplay: Charles Brackett, Billy Wilder, Walter Reisch. Story: Melchior Lengyel. Cast: Greta Garbo, Melvyn Douglas.

The North Star. Director: Lewis Milestone. Producer: Samuel Goldwyn. Samuel Goldwyn, 1943. Screenplay: Lillian Hellman. Cast: Anne Baxter, Dana Andrews, Walter Huston, Ann Harding, Erich von Stroheim, Jane Withers, Farley Granger, Walter Brennan.

Our Daily Bread. Producer-Director-Story: King Vidor. United Artists, 1934. Adaptation: Elizabeth Hill. Cast: Tom Keene, Karen Morley, John Qualen, Barbara Pepper.

The Phantom President. Director: Norman Taurog. Paramount, 1932. Screenplay: Walter de Leon, Harlan Thompson. Cast: George M. Cohan, Claudette Colbert, Jimmy Durante.

The President Vanishes. Director: William Wellman. Producer: Walter Wanger. Paramount, 1934. Screenplay: Carey Wilson, Cedric Worth. Cast: Arthur Byron, Janet Beecher, Osgood Perkins, Andy Devine, Edward Arnold, Rosalind Russell, Edward Ellis.

Prisoner of Zenda. Director: John Cromwell. MGM, 1937. Screenplay: Donald Ogden Stewart, John Balderston, Willis Root. Cast: Ronald Colman, Douglas Fairbanks Jr., Madeleine Carroll, David Niven, Raymond Massey, Mary Astor, C. Aubrey Smith, Montagu Love, Byron Foulger, Alexander D'Arcy.

The Ramparts We Watch. Producer-Director: Louis de Rochemont. RKO, 1940. Story: Robert L. Richards, Cedric R. Worth. Commentator: Westbrook Van

Voorhis. Cast: John Adair, John Sommers, Julia Kent, Ellen Prescott, C. W. Stowell, Ethel Hudson, Frank McCabe.

Sergeant York. Director: Howard Hawks. Producers: Hal Wallis, Jesse Lasky. Warner Brothers, 1941. Screenplay: Abem Finkel, Harry Chandler, Howard Koch, John Huston. Cast: Gary Cooper, Walter Brennan, George Tobias.

Song of Russia. Director: Gregory Ratoff. Producer: Joseph Pasternak. MGM, 1943. Screenplay: Paul Jarrico, Richard Collins. Cast: Robert Taylor, Susan Peters, John Hodiak, Robert Benchley, Felix Bressart, Joan Lorring, Darryl Hickman.

Spies. A Private Snafu film. Director: Chuck Jones. War Department, 1943.

This Day and Age. Producer-Director: Cecil B. DeMille. Paramount, 1933. Screenplay: Bartlett Cormack. Cast: Charles Bickford, Richard Cromwell.

This Is the Army. Director: Michael Curtiz. Warner Brothers, 1943. Cast: George Murphy, John Leslie, Ronald Reagan, Alan Hale Jr., Kate Smith, George Tobias, Irving Berlin, Joe Louis.

Three Comrades. Director: Frank Borzage. Producer: Joseph L. Mankiewicz. MGM, 1938. Screenplay: F. Scott Fitzgerald, Edward Paramore. Cast: Margaret Sullavan, Robert Taylor, Robert Young, Franchot Tone, Lionel Atwell, Henry Hull.

Tomorrow the World. Director: Leslie Fenton. Producers: Lester Cowan and David Hall. United Artists, 1944. Screenplay: Leopold Atlas, James Gow, Ring Lardner Jr., and Armand d'Usseau. Cast: Fredric March, Betty Field, Agnes Moorehead, Skippy Homeier, Joan Carroll, Edit Angold, Rudy Wissler, Boots Brown, Marvin Davis, Patsy Ann Thompson, Mary Newton, Tom Fadden.

The 27th Day. Director: William Asher. Producer: Helen Ainsworth. Romson, 1957. Screenplay: John Mantley. Cast: Gene Barry, Valerie French, George Voskovec, Stefan Schnabel, Azemat Janti, Frederick Ledebur, Ralph Clanton.

Wake Island. Director: John Farrow. Paramount, 1942. Screenplay: W. R. Burnett, Frank Butler. Cast: Brian Donlevy, Robert Preston, Macdonald Carey, William Bendix, Albert Dekker, Walter Abel.

The Wandering Jew. Director: George Roland. Producer: Herman Ross. Jewish American Film Arts, 1933. Screenplay: Jacob Mestel. Cast: Ben Adler, Jacob Ben-Ami, Natalie Browning, William Epstein, Jacob Mestel.

Washington Masquerade. Director: Charles Brabin. MGM, 1932. Screenplay: John Meehan, Samuel Blythe. Cast: Lionel Barrymore, Karen Morley, C. Henry Gordon.

Washington Merry-Go-Round. Director: James Cruze. Producer: Walter Wanger. Columbia, 1932. Screenplay: Jo Swerling. Story: Maxwell Anderson. Cast: Lee Tracy, Alan Dinehart.

Weapon of War. Produced by Army Pictorial Service for *Army-Navy Screen Magazine.* 1944.

Why We Fight: The Battle of Britain. Director: Anthony Vieller. Supervisor: Frank Capra. Special Services Division, Army Service Forces, U.S. War Department, 1943. Script: Anthony Veiller. Narrators: Walter Huston, Anthony Veiller.

Why We Fight: The Battle of China. Directors: Frank Capra, Anatole Litvak.

Supervisor: Frank Capra. Army Pictorial Service, Signal Corps, U.S. War Department, 1944. Script: Eric Knight, Anthony Veiller, Robert Heller. Narrators: Anthony Veiller, Walter Huston.

Why We Fight: The Battle of Russia. Director: Anatole Litvak. Supervisor: Frank Capra. Special Services Division, Army Service Forces, U.S. War Department, 1943. Script: Anatole Litvak, Anthony Veiller, Robert Heller (original script by John Sanford). Narrators: Walter Huston, Anthony Veiller.

Why We Fight: Divide and Conquer. Directors: Frank Capra, Anatole Litvak. Supervisor: Frank Capra. Special Services Division, Army Service Forces, U.S. War Department, 1943. Script: Anthony Veiller, Robert Heller. Narrators: Walter Huston, Anthony Veiller.

Why We Fight: Prelude to War. Director: Frank Capra. Supervisor: Frank Capra. Producer: Frank Capra. Special Services Division, Army Service Forces, U.S. War Department, 1942. Script: Eric Knight, Anthony Veiller. Narrator: Walter Huston.

Why We Fight: The Nazis Strike. Directors: Frank Capra, Anatole Litvak. Supervisor: Frank Capra. Special Services Division, Army Service Forces, U.S. War Department, 1943. Script: Eric Knight, Anthony Veiller, Robert Heller. Narrators: Walter Huston, Anthony Veiller.

Why We Fight: War Comes to America. Director: Anatole Litvak. Supervisor: Frank Capra. Army Pictorial Service, Signal Corps, U.S. War Department, 1945. Script: Anatole Litvak, Anthony Veiller. Narrators: Walter Huston, Lloyd Nolan.

The Wizard of Oz. Director: Victor Fleming. Producer: Mervyn LeRoy. MGM, 1939. Screenplay: Noel Langley, Florence Ryerson, Edgar Allan Woolf. Cast: Judy Garland, Frank Morgan, Ray Bolger, Bert Lahr, Jack Haley, Billie Burke, Margaret Hamilton.

A World at War. Producer: Samuel Spewack. Office of War Information, Bureau of Motion Pictures, 1942. Narrated by Paul Stewart.

"WW II: The Propaganda Battle." *Bill Moyers' Walk through the Twentieth Century.* PBS, 13 March 1984.

You Can't Take It with You. Producer-Director: Frank Capra. Columbia, 1938. Screenplay: Robert Riskin. Cast: Jean Arthur, Lionel Barrymore, James Stewart, Edward Arnold, Ann Miller.

SECONDARY SOURCES

Books

Adams, Michael C. C. *The Best War Ever: America and World War II.* Baltimore: Johns Hopkins University Press, 1994.

Alexander, Robert J. *The Right Opposition: The Lovestoneites and the International Communist Opposition in the 1930s.* Westport, Conn.: Greenwood Press, 1981.

Allen, Robert Loring. *Opening Doors: The Life and Work of Joseph Schumpeter.* Vol. 2, *America.* New Brunswick, N.J.: Transaction, 1991.

Balio, Tino. *Grand Design: Hollywood as a Modern Business Enterprise, 1930–1939.* Berkeley: University of California Press, 1993.

Barnes, James J., and Patience P. Barnes. *Hitler's Mein Kampf in Britain and America: A Publishing History, 1930–1939.* Cambridge: Cambridge University Press, 1980.

Basinger, Jeanine. *The World War II Combat Film: Anatomy of a Genre.* New York: Columbia University Press, 1986.

Bell, Leland V. *In Hitler's Shadow: The Anatomy of American Nazism.* Port Washington, N.Y.: Kennikat Press, 1973.

Bérubé, Allan. *Coming Out under Fire: The History of Gay Men and Women in World War II.* New York: Free Press, 1990.

Birdwell, Michael E. *Celluloid Soldiers: The Warner Bros. Campaign against Nazism.* New York: New York University Press, 1999.

Black, Gregory D. *Hollywood Censored: Morality Codes, Catholics, and the Movies.* New York: Cambridge University Press, 1994.

Bohn, Thomas W. *An Historical and Descriptive Analysis of the 'Why We Fight' Series.* New York: Arno, 1977.

Bonsall, Thomas E. *More Than They Promised: The Studebaker Story.* Stanford, Calif.: Stanford University Press, 2000.

Boyer, Paul. *By the Bomb's Early Light: American Thought and Culture at the Dawn of the Atomic Age.* Chapel Hill: University of North Carolina Press, 1994.

Boyers, Robert, ed. *The Legacy of the German Refugee Intellectuals.* New York: Schocken, 1972.

Brady, Frank. *Citizen Welles: A Biography of Orson Welles.* New York: Doubleday, 1989.

Brinkley, Alan. *The End of Reform: New Deal Liberalism in Recession and War.* New York: Vintage, 1995.

———. *Voices of Protest: Huey Long, Father Coughlin, and the Great Depression.* New York: Knopf, 1982.

Buhle, Mari Jo, Paul Buhle, and Dan Georgakas. In *Encyclopedia of the American Left.* New York: Garland, 1990.

Burston, Daniel. *The Legacy of Erich Fromm.* Cambridge: Harvard University Press, 1991.

Callinicos, Alex. *Trotskyism.* Minneapolis: University of Minnesota Press, 1990.

Callow, Simon. *Orson Welles: The Road to Xanadu.* New York: Penguin, 1997.

Cannon, William A., and Fred K. Fox. *Studebaker: The Complete Story.* Blue Ridge Summit, Pa.: TAB Books, 1981.

Canovan, Margaret. *Hannah Arendt: A Reinterpretation of Her Political Thought.* Cambridge: Cambridge University Press, 1992.

Caspar, Günter. *Fallada-Studien.* Berlin: Aufbau-Verlag, 1988.

Ceplair, Larry, and Steven Englund. *The Inquisition in Hollywood: Politics in the Film Community.* Berkeley: University of California Press, 1983.

Cohen, Lizabeth. *Making a New Deal: Industrial Workers in Chicago, 1919–1939.* New York: Cambridge University Press, 1990.

Coser, Lewis A. *Refugee Scholars in America: Their Impact and Their Experiences.* New Haven: Yale University Press, 1984.

Culbert, David, ed. *Mission to Moscow.* Madison: University of Wisconsin Press, 1980.

Culver, John C., and John Hyde. *American Dreamer: The Life and Times of Henry A. Wallace.* New York: Norton, 2000.

Dallek, Robert. *Franklin D. Roosevelt and American Foreign Policy, 1932–1945.* New York: Oxford University Press, 1979.

Davis, Allen F. *American Heroine: The Life and Legend of Jane Addams.* New York: Oxford University Press, 1973.

Denning, Michael. *The Cultural Front: The Laboring of American Culture in the Twentieth Century.* New York: Verso, 1996.

Depoe, Stephen P. *Arthur M. Schlesinger Jr. and the Ideological History of American Liberalism.* Tuscaloosa: University of Alabama Press, 1994.

Diggins, John P. *Mussolini and Fascism: The View from America.* Princeton: Princeton University Press, 1972.

Doherty, Thomas. *Projections of War: Hollywood, American Culture, and World War II.* New York: Columbia University Press, 1993.

Dorrien, Gary J. *The Neoconservative Mind: Politics, Culture, and the War of Ideology.* Philadelphia: Temple University Press, 1993.

Dower, John. *War without Mercy: Race and Power in the Pacific War.* New York: Pantheon, 1986.

Fousek, John. *To Lead the World: American Nationalism and the Cultural Roots of the Cold War.* Chapel Hill: University of North Carolina Press, 2000.

Fox, Richard Wightman. *Reinhold Niebuhr: A Biography.* New York: Pantheon, 1985.

Fraser, Steve, and Gary Gerstle, eds. *The Rise and Fall of the New Deal Order, 1930–1980.* Princeton: Princeton University Press, 1989.

Fried, Richard M. *Nightmare in Red: The McCarthy Era in Perspective.* New York: Oxford University Press, 1990.

———. *The Russians Are Coming! The Russians Are Coming!: Pageantry and Patriotism in Cold-War America.* New York: Oxford University Press, 1998.

Fussell, Paul. *Wartime: Understanding and Behavior in the Second World War.* New York: Oxford University Press, 1989.

Gleason, Abbott. *Totalitarianism: The Inner History of the Cold War.* New York: Oxford University Press, 1995.

Guttmann, Allen. *The Games Must Go On: Avery Brundage and the Olympic Movement.* New York: Columbia University Press, 1984.

———. *The Wound in the Heart: America and the Spanish Civil War.* New York: Free Press of Glencoe, 1962.

Hackett, Alice Payne, and James Henry Burke. *80 Years of Best Sellers, 1895–1975.* New York: R. R. Bowker, 1977.

Halberstam, Michael. *Totalitarianism and the Modern Conception of Politics.* New Haven: Yale University Press, 1999.

Hansen, Phillip. *Hannah Arendt: Politics, History, and Citizenship*. Stanford, Calif.: Stanford University Press, 1993.

Harper, John Lamberton. *American Visions of Europe: Franklin D. Roosevelt, George F. Kennan, and Dean G. Acheson*. New York: Cambridge University Press, 1994.

Heale, M. J. *American Anticommunism: Combating the Enemy Within, 1830–1970*. Baltimore: Johns Hopkins University Press, 1990.

Hinchman, Lewis P., and Sandra K. Hinchman, eds. *Hannah Arendt: Critical Essays*. Albany: State University of New York Press, 1994.

Hoberman, J. *Bridge of Light: Yiddish Film between Two Worlds*. New York: Schocken, 1991.

Hofstadter, Richard. *The Age of Reform: From Bryan to F.D.R.*. New York: Vintage, 1955.

Isserman, Maurice. *Which Side Were You On? The American Communist Party during the Second World War*. Middletown, Conn.: Wesleyan University Press, 1982.

Jänicke, Martin. *Totalitäre Herrschaft: Anatomie eines politischen Begriffes*. Berlin: Dunker and Humbolt, 1971.

Jay, Martin. *The Dialectical Imagination: A History of the Frankfurt School and the Institute of Social Research, 1923–1950*. Boston: Little, Brown, 1973.

Jones, William David. *The Lost Debate: German Socialist Intellectuals and Totalitarianism*. Urbana: University of Illinois Press, 1999.

Katz, Ephraim. *The Film Encyclopedia*. New York: Crowell, 1979.

Kazin, Michael. *The Populist Persuasion: An American History*. New York: Basic Books, 1995.

Kennedy, David M. *Over Here: The First World War and American Society*. New York: Oxford University Press, 1980.

Kershaw, Ian, and Moshe Lewin, eds. *Stalinism and Nazism: Dictatorships in Comparison*. New York: Cambridge University Press, 1997.

Klehr, Harvey. *The Heyday of American Communism: The Depression Decade*. New York: Basic Books, 1984.

Kleinman, Mark L. *A World of Hope, a World of Fear: Henry A. Wallace, Reinhold Niebuhr, and American Liberalism*. Columbus: Ohio State University Press, 2000.

Koppes, Clayton R., and Gregory D. Black. *Hollywood Goes to War: How Politics, Profits, and Propaganda Shaped World War II Movies*. Berkeley: University of California Press, 1990.

Kurth, Peter. *American Cassandra: The Life of Dorothy Thompson*. Boston: Little, Brown, 1990.

Kutulas, Judy. *The Long War: The Intellectual People's Front and Anti-Stalinism, 1930–1940*. Durham, N.C.: Duke University Press, 1995.

Levering, Ralph B. *American Opinion and the Russian Alliance, 1939–1945*. Chapel Hill: University of North Carolina Press, 1976.

Liebich, André. *From the Other Shore: Russian Social Democracy after 1921*. Cambridge: Harvard University Press, 1997.

Lifka, Thomas E. *The Concept of "Totalitarianism" and American Foreign Policy, 1933–1949.* New York: Garland, 1988.

MacDonnell, Francis. *Insidious Foes: The Axis Fifth Column and the American Home Front.* New York: Oxford University Press, 1995.

Maland, Charles J. *Chaplin and American Culture: The Evolution of a Star Image.* Princeton: Princeton University Press, 1989.

Marcus, Paul. *Autonomy in the Extreme Situation: Bruno Bettelheim, the Nazi Concentration Camps, and Mass Society.* Westport, Conn.: Praeger, 1999.

May, Lary, ed. *Recasting America: Culture and Politics in the Age of Cold War.* Chicago: University of Chicago Press, 1989.

———. *Screening Out the Past: The Birth of Mass Culture and the Motion Picture Industry.* Chicago: University of Chicago Press, 1980.

McBride, Joseph. *Frank Capra: The Catastrophe of Success.* New York: Simon and Schuster, 1992.

McClay, Wilfred M. *The Masterless: Self and Society in Modern America.* Chapel Hill: University of North Carolina Press, 1994.

Melosh, Barbara. *Engendering Culture: Manhood and Womanhood in New Deal Public Art and Theater.* Washington, D.C.: Smithsonian Institution Press, 1991.

Merkley, Paul. *Reinhold Niebuhr: A Political Account.* Montreal: McGill-Queen's University, 1975.

Mulvey, Laura. *Citizen Kane.* London: BFI Publishing, 1992.

Myers, Constance Ashton. *The Prophet's Army: Trotskyists in America, 1928–1941.* Westport, Conn.: Greenwood Press, 1977.

Nasaw, David. *The Chief: The Life of William Randolph Hearst.* Boston: Houghton Mifflin, 2000.

Nash, George H. *The Conservative Intellectual Movement in America since 1945.* Wilmington, Del.: Intercollegiate Studies Institute, 1998.

Novick, Peter. *The Holocaust in American Life.* Boston: Houghton Mifflin, 1999.

The Oxford English Dictionary. 2d ed. Oxford: Clarendon Press, 1989.

Pells, Richard H. *The Liberal Mind in a Conservative Age: American Intellectuals in the 1940s and 1950s.* New York: Harper and Row, 1985.

———. *Radical Visions and American Dreams: Culture and Thought in the Depressions Years.* New York: Harper and Row, 1973.

Pitkin, Hanna Fenichel. *The Attack of the Blob: Hannah Arendt's Concept of the Social.* Chicago: University of Chicago Press, 1998.

Pollak, Richard. *The Creation of Dr. B: A Biography of Bruno Bettelheim.* New York: Simon and Schuster, 1997.

Powers, Richard Gid. *G-men: Hoover's FBI in American Public Culture.* Carbondale: Southern Illinois University Press, 1983.

Purcell, Edward. *The Crisis of Democratic Theory: Scientific Naturalism and the Problem of Value.* Lexington: University Press of Kentucky, 1973.

Radosh, Ronald. *Prophets on the Right: Profiles of Conservative Critics of American Globalism.* New York: Simon and Schuster, 1975.

Ribuffo, Leo P. *The Old Christian Right: The Protestant Far Right from the Great Depression to the Cold War.* Philadelphia: Temple University Press, 1983.

Rodden, John. *The Politics of Literary Reputation: The Making and Claiming of "St. George" Orwell.* New York: Oxford University Press, 1989.

Rodgers, Daniel T. *Contested Truths: Keywords in American Politics since Independence.* New York: Basic Books, 1987.

Rogin, Michael Paul. *Ronald Reagan, the Movie, and Other Episodes in Political Demonology.* Berkeley: University of California Press, 1987.

Rosenof, Theodore. *Economics in the Long Run: New Deal Theorists and Their Legacies, 1933–1993.* Chapel Hill: University of North Carolina Press, 1997.

Savage, Robert L., James Combs, and Dan Nimmo, eds. *The Orwellian Moment: Hindsight and Foresight in the Post-1984 World.* Fayetteville: University of Arkansas Press, 1989.

Sayre, Nora. *Running Time: Films of the Cold War.* New York: Dial Press, 1982.

Schapiro, Leonard B. *Totalitarianism.* New York: Praeger, 1972.

Schatz, Thomas. *Boom and Bust: American Cinema in the 1940s.* Berkeley: University of California Press, 1999.

Schindler, Colin. *Hollywood in Crisis: Cinema and American Society, 1929–1939.* London: Routledge, 1996.

Schlesinger, Arthur M., Jr. *The Politics of Upheaval.* Vol. 3 of *The Age of Roosevelt.* Boston: Houghton Mifflin, 1960.

Schorer, Mark. *Sinclair Lewis: An American Life.* New York: McGraw-Hill, 1961.

Schrecker, Ellen. *Many Are the Crimes: McCarthyism in America.* Princeton: Princeton University Press, 1999.

Shale, Richard. *Donald Duck Joins Up: The Walt Disney Studio during World War II.* Ann Arbor: UMI Research Press, 1982.

Sherry, Michael S. *In the Shadow of War: The United States since the 1930s.* New Haven: Yale University Press, 1995.

Sirgiovanni, George. *An Undercurrent of Suspicion: Anti-communism in America during World War II.* New Brunswick, N.J.: Transaction, 1990.

Skotheim, Robert Allen. *Totalitarianism and American Social Thought.* New York: Holt, Rinehart, and Winston, 1971.

Smith, Geoffrey S. *To Save a Nation: American Extremism, the New Deal, and the Coming of World War II.* Rev. ed. Chicago: Elephant Paperbacks, 1992.

Smoodin, Eric Loren. *Animating Culture: Hollywood Cartoons from the Sound Era.* New Brunswick, N.J.: Rutgers University Press, 1993.

Steinhoff, William. *George Orwell and the Origins of 1984.* Ann Arbor: University of Michigan Press, 1975.

Swanberg, W. A. *Citizen Hearst.* New York: Scribner, 1961.

Swedberg, Richard. *Schumpeter: A Biography.* Princeton: Princeton University Press, 1991.

Taylor, James, and Warren Shaw. *The Third Reich Almanac.* New York: World Almanac, 1987.

Thorp, Margaret. *America at the Movies.* New York: Arno, 1970.

Van Creveld, Martin. *Fighting Power: German and U.S. Army Performance, 1939–1945.* Westport, Conn.: Greenwood Press, 1982.

Wald, Alan M. *The New York Intellectuals: The Rise and Decline of the Anti-Stalinist*

Left from the 1930s to the 1980s. Chapel Hill: University of North Carolina Press, 1987.

Warren, Frank A. *Liberals and Communism: The "Red Decade" Revisited.* New York: Columbia University Press, 1993.

Wesley, Edgar Bruce. *NEA: The First Hundred Years: The Building of the Teaching Profession.* New York: Harper, 1957.

Whitfield, Stephen J. *The Culture of the Cold War.* Baltimore: Johns Hopkins University Press, 1991.

—. *Into the Dark: Hannah Arendt and Totalitarianism.* Philadelphia: Temple University Press, 1980.

Wiebe, Robert H. *Self-Rule: A Cultural History of American Democracy.* Chicago: University of Chicago Press, 1995.

Wills, Garry. *The Kennedy Imprisonment: A Meditation on Power.* Boston: Little, Brown, 1982.

Winkler, Allan M. *The Politics of Propaganda: The Office of War Information, 1942–1945.* New Haven: Yale University Press, 1978.

Wolfe, Charles. *Frank Capra: A Guide to References and Resources.* Boston: G. K. Hall, 1987.

—, ed. *Meet John Doe: Frank Capra: Director.* New Brunswick, N.J.: Rutgers University Press, 1989.

Wreszin, Michael. *A Rebel in Defense of Tradition: The Life and Politics of Dwight Macdonald.* New York: Basic Books, 1994.

Zalampas, Michael. *Adolf Hitler and the Third Reich in American Magazines, 1923–1939.* Bowling Green, Ohio: Bowling Green State University Press, 1989.

Articles

Adams, Carole E. "Hannah Arendt and the Historian: Nazism and the New Order." In *Hannah Arendt: Thinking, Judging, Freedom,* edited by Gisela T. Kaplan and Clive S. Kessler, 31–41. Sydney: Allen and Unwin, 1989.

Adler, Les K., and Thomas G. Patterson. "Red Fascism: The Merger of Nazi Germany and Soviet Russia in the American Image of Totalitarianism." *American Historical Review* 75 (April 1970): 1046–64.

Bean, Philip A. "Fascism and Italian-American Identity: A Case Study: Utica, New York." *Journal of Ethnic Studies* 17 (June 1989): 101–19.

Bittman, Michael. "Totalitarianism: The Career of a Concept." In *Hannah Arendt: Thinking, Judging, Freedom,* edited by Gisela T. Kaplan and Clive S. Kessler, 56–68. Sidney: Allen and Unwin, 1989.

Blum, John Morton. "Arthur Schlesinger, Jr.: Tory Democrat." In *The Liberal Persuasion: Arthur Schlesinger Jr. and the Challenge of the American Past,* edited by John Patrick Diggins, 67–72. Princeton: Princeton University, 1997.

Canovan, Margaret. "Hannah Arendt on Ideology in Totalitarianism." In *The Structure of Modern Ideology: Critical Perspectives on Social and Political Theory,* edited by Noel O'Sullivan, 151–71. Brookfield, Vt.: Gower Publishing, 1989.

Carter, Bill. "Him Alone." *New York Times Magazine,* 4 August 1991.

Castoriadis, Cornelius. "The Destinies of Totalitarianism." *Salmagundi* 60 (1983): 107–22.

Craig, Campbell. "The New Meaning of Modern War in the Thought of Reinhold Niebuhr." *Journal of the History of Ideas* 53, no. 4 (1992): 687–701.

Craig, Gordon. "The True Believer." *New York Review of Books,* 24 March 1994.

Dranos, Stan. "The Totalitarian Theme in Horkheimer and Arendt." *Salmagundi* 56 (1982): 155–69.

Feuer, Lewis S. "American Travelers to the Soviet Union 1917–1932: The Formation of a Component of New Deal Ideology." *American Quarterly* 14 (June 1962): 119–49.

Fleck, Christian, and Albert Müller. "Bruno Bettelheim and the Concentration Camps." *Journal of the History of the Behavioral Sciences* 33, no. 1 (1997): 1–37.

Gregor, James A. "Totalitarianism." In *Historical Dictionary of Fascist Italy,* edited by Philip V. Cannistaro. Westport, Conn.: Greenwood Press, 1982.

Höpfl, Harro. "Isms and Ideology." In *The Structure of Ideology: Critical Perspectives on Social and Political Theory,* edited by Noel O'Sullivan, 3–26. Brookfield, Vt.: Gower Publishing, 1989.

Joki, Illka, and Roger D. Sell. "Robert E. Sherwood and the Finnish Winter War: Drama, Propaganda, and Context 50 Years Ago." *American Studies in Scandinavia* 21 (1989): 51–69.

Kershaw, Ian. "Totalitarianism Revisited: Nazism and Stalinism in Comparative Perspective." *Tel-Aviver Jahrbuch für deutsche Geschichte* 23 (1994): 23–40.

Krieger, Leonard. "The Historical Hannah Arendt." *Journal of Modern History* 48 (1976): 672–84.

Levine, Lawrence. "Hollywood's Washington: Film Images of National Politics during the Depression." *Prospects* 10 (1985): 169–95.

Maddux, Thomas R. "Red Fascism, Brown Bolshevism: The American Image of Totalitarianism in the 1930s." *Historian* 40 (November 1977): 85–103.

Matusow, Allen J. "John F. Kennedy and the Intellectuals." *Wilson Quarterly* 7, no. 4 (1983): 140–53.

May, Lary. "Making the American Consensus: The Narrative of Conversion and Subversion in World War II Films." In *The War in American Culture: Society and Consciousness during World War II,* edited by Lewis Erenbert and Susan E. Hirsch, 71–102. Chicago: University of Chicago Press, 1996.

McConnell, Robert L. "The Genesis and Ideology of *Gabriel over the White House.*" In *Cinema Examined,* edited by Richard Dyer MacCann and Jack C. Elis, 202–21. New York: Dutton, 1982.

Nollen, Scott Allen. "Mussolini Speaks." *Films in Review* 40 (June 1989): 334–38.

O'Sullivan, Noel. "Politics, Totalitarianism, and Freedom: The Political Thought of Hannah Arendt." *Political Studies* 21, no. 2 (1973): 183–98.

Packer, Cathy. "Seldes, George Henry." In *Biographical Dictionary of American Journalism,* edited by Joseph P. McKerns. Westport, Conn.: Greenwood Press, 1989. 639–40.

Roeder, George H., Jr. "A Note on U.S. Photo Censorship in WW II." *Historical Journal of Film, Radio, and Television* 5 (1985): 191–98.

Rosenof, Theodore. "Freedom, Planning, and Totalitarianism: The Reception of F. A. Hayek's *Road to Serfdom.*" *Canadian Review of American Studies* 5 (September 1974): 149–65.

Semmel, Bernard. "Schumpeter's Curious Politics." *Public Interest,* no. 106 (1992): 3–16.

Siegel, Achim. "The Changing Popularity of the Totalitarian Paradigm in Communist Studies." In *The Totalitarian Paradigm after the End of Communism,* edited by Achim Siegel, 9–24. Vol. 65, *Poznan Studies in the Philosophy of the Sciences and the Humanities.* Amsterdam: Rodopi, 1998.

Tuttle, William M., Jr. "American Higher Education and the Nazis: The Case of James B. Conant and Harvard University's 'Diplomatic Relations' with Germany." *American Studies* 22 (March 1979): 49–70.

Wentz, Frederick K. "American Protestant Journals and the Nazi Religious Assault." *Church History* 23 (December 1954): 321–38.

Williams, Jennifer. "Some Thoughts on the Success of Hans Fallada's *Kleiner Mann—Was Nun?*" *German Life and Letters* 40 (July 1987): 305–18.

Wohlforth, Tim. "Trotskyism." In *Encyclopedia of the American Left,* edited by Mari Jo Buhle, Paul Buhle, and Dan Georgakas, 782–86. Chicago: St. James, 1990.

Wolin, Sheldon. "The Idea of the State in America." In *The Problem of Authority in America,* edited by John P. Diggins, and Mark E. Kann, 41–58. Philadelphia: Temple University Press, 1981.

Zaretsky, Eli. "Hannah Arendt and the Meaning of the Public/Private Distinction." In *Hannah Arendt and the Meaning of Politics,* edited by Craig Calhoun and John McGowan, 207–31. Minneapolis: University of Minnesota Press, 1997.

Dissertations

Allison, Rebecca P. "Two Public Philosophers: Lewis Mumford, Walter Lippmann, and the Challenge of Totalitarianism." Ph.D. diss., Arizona State University, 1989.

Colgan, Christine Ann. "Warner Brothers' Crusade against the Third Reich: A Study of Anti-Nazi Activism and Film Production, 1933–1941." Ph.D. diss., University of Southern California, 1985.

Hönicke, Michaela. "'Know Your Enemy': American Interpretations of National Socialism, 1933–1945." Ph.D. diss., University of North Carolina, 1998.

Scovronick, Nathan B. "Broadcasting 'In The Public Interest': The N.B.C. Advisory Council, 1927–1941." Ph.D. diss., Rutgers University, 1973.

Sigel, Roberta S. "Opinions on Nazi Germany: A Study of Three Popular American Magazines, 1933–1941." Ph.D. diss., Clark University, 1950.

INDEX

among Germans, 104, 113. *See also*
Antifascism
Antisemitism, 195, 213, 333–34 (n. 51);
of Adolf Hitler, 38, 84, 88; in U.S.,
39, 168, 207, 215, 277; in Italy, 84,
86; Arendt on, 292, 294, 297
Anti-Stalinism: and U.S. left, 4, 5, 6,
9, 11, 12, 76, 109, 131, 135, 139; and
concept of totalitarianism, 12, 145,
241–42, 326 (n. 15); and Nazi-Soviet
Pact, 223
Arendt, Hannah, 70; and totalitarian-
ism, 9; and *Origins of Totalitarian-
ism,* 13, 251, 253, 278, 291–300, 301,
302, 338 (n. 4), 342 (n. 73), 343–
44 (nn. 90–92), 344 (nn. 98, 99),
344–45 (n. 102); on concentration
camps, 281, 344 (n. 99)
Arise My Love, 161, 325–26 (n. 14)
Armenian Americans, 215–16
Armstrong, Hamilton Fish, 35, 103,
209
Army. *See* Military; U.S. Army
Army Life (pamphlet), 172
Army-Navy Screen Magazine, 169, 172,
196
Arnold, Edward, 10, 98, 116
Associationalism, 65
As We Go Marching (Flynn), 205–8
Atherton, Gertrude, 323 (n. 68)
Atlantic Charter, 158, 182, 189
Atlantic Monthly, 176, 209, 246
Atomic bomb, 277
Audiences, 94, 112–13, 124, 126,
167. *See also* Dictatorship: crowd-
centered views of
Authoritarianism, 62, 72
Authoritarian personality, 189
Authority, 17, 41–58, 82, 92, 119–20,
159, 201
Autocratic state, 68. *See also* Corpora-
tive state; Totalitarian state
Automatons, individuals as, 96, 99,
103, 105, 108, 280, 298
Axis powers (World War II): U.S.

understandings of, 158, 189, 194–95,
203–8, 216, 223

Bailey, Josiah, 79–80
Baker, Newton, 132
Barron's, 3, 26, 32
Barth, Karl, 66, 67
Bates, Ralph, 335 (n. 6)
Battle of Britain, 193
Baxter, Anne, 228
Bazin, André, 318 (n. 70)
Beard, Charles, 16, 132
Beard, Mary, 37
Benchley, Robert, 232
Benét, Stephen Vincent, 165
Bennett, Joan, 100
Berlin, Irving, 166
Bettelheim, Bruno, 254, 272, 285; early
life and work of, 263–64; on con-
centration camps, 264–66, 273–74,
276, 281; U.S. reception of, 267,
339–40 (n. 29), 340 (n. 39), 340–41
(n. 41); on democracy, 274–75, 278;
influence on Arendt of, 295
Beyond the Clinical Frontiers
(Strecker), 326 (n. 21)
Bingham, Alfred, 72, 132
Birth of a Nation, 228
Black, Gregory, 159
Black Record (Vansittart), 208, 213
Blackshirts, 19, 20, 29. *See also* Fas-
cism, Italian
Blair, Eric (pseud. George Orwell).
See Orwell, George
Blanker, Fredericka, 26
Blithedale Romance (Hawthorne), 282
Blitzkrieg, 101, 193, 272
Blockade, 97
Blood Purge. *See* Röhm Purge
Blum, John Morton, 284
Bolshevism. *See* Communism, Soviet
Bonaparte, Napoleon, 85, 227
Bonn, Mauritz, 148, 150
Bonus Expeditionary Force (BEF),
24–25

China, 334–35 (n. 1). See also *Why We Fight: Battle of China*

Christian Century, 40, 222, 268, 335 (n. 5); on totalitarian state, 65, 66–67, 68; on Nazism and religion, 66–67, 86–87; on totalitarianism, 72, 141, 207–8; on comedic portrayals of dictators, 86; on military training, 161; on USSR, 247

Christianity and Crisis, 222, 268, 335 (n. 5)

Christian Science Monitor, 65, 245

Churchill, Winston, 91, 220–21, 237

Citizen Kane, 10, 91, 318 (n. 70)

Citizenship education, 157–58

Civil War, U.S., 1, 160, 216, 276

Clifford, Clark, 279

Clinton, William J., 1

Clouch, Shepard B., 69

Cohn, Jack, 28

Colbert, Claudette, 325–26 (n. 14)

Colby, Bainbridge, 37

Collective farms, 336 (n. 24)

Collectivism, 4, 60, 75, 142, 143, 145, 246, 256

Collectivism: A False Utopia (Chamberlin), 246

Collier's, 22, 38, 39, 85

Columbia Pictures, 228

Comintern, 33, 80, 135, 240

Commentary, 293, 294

Committee for Cultural Freedom, 12, 144–45, 146, 147, 321–22 (n. 44)

Committee on Public Information, 36, 209

Committee to Defend America, 153

Common Sense, 59, 72

Commonweal, 32, 86–87, 141, 155, 222, 335 (n. 5)

Communism (general phenomenon), 45, 82, 83, 103, 106; as example of totalitarianism, 8, 60, 76; as threat to family, 48–51, 54; as distinct from fascism, 59, 79, 131–34, 207–8; and regimented crowd, 95; as vast conspiracy, 102, 320 (n. 19); Hollywood images of, 111, 132–34; image of, converges with image of fascism, 134–39; internal threat of, to U.S., 207, 272; as more totalitarian than Nazism, 280; universal attraction of, 331 (n. 6). *See also* Communism, Soviet

Communism, Soviet, 2, 22, 32, 82, 251, 335 (n. 6); Bukharinite critique of, 8; as mass movement, 11, 12, 17, 244; equated with Nazism, 12, 59, 63, 68, 69, 73, 74–75; as form of anarchy, 18, 21, 95; equated with fascism, 35, 53, 59, 68, 69, 109, 137–39, 143, 189; as form of minority rule, 59, 249; similar to but distinct from fascism, 73–74, 75, 130–31; as international movement, 134; avoidance of, in U.S. wartime representations of USSR, 229, 233, 238; U.S. wartime understandings of, 234–39, 240, 249. *See also* Communism (general phenomenon); Moscow show trials; Russian Revolution (1917); Soviet Union (USSR)

Communist Party, USA (CP), 5–6, 53, 135, 226, 240; during "Third Period," 3, 11, 16, 23, 33, 59, 81; and Popular Front, 3–4, 78, 80–81, 132; and U.S. intervention in Europe, 7, 78–79, 90–91, 131, 189; membership figures for, 23, 223; and FDR, 33, 81; fellow travelers of, 33, 91, 282; antifascism of, 41, 81, 90, 203; criticism of, 132, 136, 223, 280; former members of, and idea of totalitarianism, 140–41, 142, 145; anti-German publications of, 203; and American exceptionalism, 304 (n. 3). *See also* Communist Political Association (CPA)

Communist Political Association (CPA), 203, 223, 245

Communists, Italian, 20, 36

alism, 103; as system of majority rule, 105; need for faith in, 106, 176, 259–60; and media, 112, 115–16, 120; importance of education for, 125–27, 157–58; as pluralism, 130, 146–47; limited political life in, 153, 284, 285; and voluntarism, 157, 171–73; problems of, at war, 158–59, 160–63, 183; importance of truth to, 173–75, 179, 183; understandings of relationship of, to Communism, 224, 234–39; optimism about, 254, 275, 305 (n. 35); and managerial revolution, 257–58; must learn from moral cynics, 269–70, 281

Democratic Party, 7, 79, 81, 105, 106, 278–79

Denning, Michael, 11, 124

Dennis, Lawrence, 7, 254

Derounian, Arthur A. (pseud. John Roy Carlson), 215–16, 273, 283

Der Vandernder Yid (*The Wandering Jew*), 37

Deutscher, Isaac, 291

Dewey, John, 132, 242, 268

Dewey, Thomas, 240, 279

Dictator Isms and Our Democracy (Quitman and Allen), 129–30, 138–39

Dictators, 53, 106; as personally responsible for nature of their regimes, 11, 17, 24, 32, 58, 76, 78, 81, 82, 83; U.S. fascination with, 15–17, 23–24, 57–58, 81–82; sexuality of, 17, 24, 41, 42; as Great Men, 23, 40, 81–82; fictional U.S., 30–33, 34, 41, 42, 52–56, 98, 100, 117; as not personally responsible for nature of their regimes, 82, 91–93, 292–93; as madmen or buffoons, 83–90, 112. *See also* Dictatorship; Dictatorships, European; Franco, Francisco; Hitler, Adolf; Mussolini, Benito; Roosevelt, Franklin Delano (FDR); Stalin, Josef; Studebaker "Dictator"

Dictators and Democracies, 74–75

Dictatorship, 3, 4, 6, 54, 56, 71–72, 89, 257; as temporary measure, 1, 32; modern, as new phenomenon, 1, 33, 60; relationship to democracy of, 1–2, 3–4, 16, 27, 30, 32–33, 34–35, 80–82, 105; Marxist views of, 2, 3, 16, 82; attraction to, in U.S., 3, 16, 17, 25–34, 36, 41, 77, 192; crowd-centered views of, 11, 12, 17, 52, 76, 82, 93, 94–95, 96, 103–28, 129, 139, 192, 275; dictator-centered views of, 11, 17, 24, 32, 58, 76, 78, 81, 82, 92–93, 94–95, 129, 139, 275; condemnation of, in U.S., 11, 34–41, 77–78, 80–82, 107, 192; and social disorder, 35, 41, 45, 80, 83; Hitler's effect on reputation of, in U.S., 36–41; and gender, 56–57; all forms of, said to be similar, 59–60, 75, 142–43; fear of U.S., 77–78, 79–80, 81, 105, 107, 120–21, 276, 277–78; media-based explanations of rise of, 90, 104, 112–27; military as metaphor for, 97; as system of minority rule, 102, 105; as system with mass support, 102, 105–6, 107; explained in terms of national character, 103–4, 210; social psychological explanations of rise of, 104, 107–12, 125, 193; socio-economic explanations of rise of, 104–7, 109, 112, 126, 193; propaganda under, 105, 111–12, 125. *See also* Dictators; "Semi-dictatorship"

Dictatorships, European, 2, 17, 32, 33, 65, 87, 94, 95, 156; differences between U.S. and, 80, 86, 111; fictional representations of, 83–84; as object lessons for U.S., 104, 127, 129, 191, 192, 244; as direct threat to U.S., 128, 129. *See also* Dictators; Dictatorship

Dies, Martin, 222

Dies Committee, 135

Diggins, John, 255

Dighton, William, 243–44
Directors, motion picture, 83, 114, 115–16
Discipline: need for, in U.S., 27, 55; in fascism, 29, 110; and totalitarianism, 74, 75, 161, 280, 281; military, 161, 165, 172, 173. *See also* Regimentation
Disney, Walt, 242
Ditzen, Rudolph (pseud. Hans Fallada), 46, 47, 54, 84, 94
Divide and conquer, 186, 195–97, 201–2
Dodds, H. W., 96, 312–13 (n. 8)
Dolgoruki, Igor, 230
Dollard, John, 181–82
Donlevy, Brian, 165
Don't Be a Sucker, 196–97, 202
Dorothy Thompson's Political Guide (Thompson), 137–38, 147
Doucet, Catherine, 48
Doughfaces, 282–83, 284, 285, 296, 341 (n. 66)
Douglas, Melvyn, 133
Drucker, Peter, 143
Dryden, Ernst, 319–20 (n. 13)
Duck Soup, 83
Dumont, Margaret, 83
Dupes, 35, 285, 302; of Nazism, 135, 191, 196–97, 202, 217; of totalitarianism, 271, 282–83, 296
Duranty, Walter, 235
Durst, Edward, 230
D'Usseau, Arnaud, 200

Eastman, Max, 142, 144, 242, 243, 245
Economics of Force (Munk), 241
Education, 125–27, 157–58, 243–44
Education for Death (Ziemer), 13–14, 197–98, 199. See also *Hitler's Children*
Eichmann in Jerusalem (Arendt), 292
Eisenhower, Dwight, 340 (n. 39)
Eisenstein, Sergei, 225
Elections, U.S.: of 1940, 4, 105, 258,

312 (n. 5); of 1932, 25; of 1936, 77, 81, 104, 105; of 1938, 135; of 1944, 240; of 1946, 278–79; of 1948, 279
Elkins, Stanley, 267
Ellis, Edward, 44–45
Ellwood, Charles A., 161
Encyclopedia of the Social Sciences, 148
End Poverty in California (EPIC), 8
Engineers, 21, 33–34, 96
England, 56, 154, 272, 273, 290
Escape from Freedom (Fromm), 107–9, 274, 279, 281, 316 (n. 34)
Essad Bey, 22
Ethical Culture movement, 59
Ethiopia, 78, 80, 129, 131
Ethnicity, 167–72, 213, 215
Europe, 2, 78, 240; U.S. concerns about war in, 7, 39, 44, 79, 81, 89–90, 97, 104, 122, 125; as essentially different from U.S., 35, 95, 103, 111, 191, 213–16, 219; Hollywood images of, during World War II, 213–14
Everybody's Autobiography, 56
Evil, 205, 296, 299, 300, 301, 344–45 (n. 102)
Existentialism, 281, 285, 293, 299
Expansionism, 74, 131, 151, 217, 253, 291

Facts and Fascism (Seldes), 204
Faith for Living (Mumford), 110
Fallada, Hans. *See* Ditzen, Rudolph (pseud. Hans Fallada)
Fall of the City (radio play; Macleish), 91–93
Family: as bulwark against dictatorship, 17, 42–51, 56–57; Mussolini's policies toward, 20; Hitler's policies toward, 85; as metaphor for military life, 164–65; destruction of, under Nazism, 197–202, 229
Fascism (general phenomenon), 3, 32, 41, 82, 113, 259; struggle with democracy of, 4, 46, 88, 111; Popu-

lar Front opposition to, 5, 81; in U.S., 7, 44–46, 52–56, 98, 162–63, 204–8, 215–16; as elite movement, 11, 95, 110; as mass movement, 11–12, 95, 106, 109–10; social, 23, 33, 53, 81; relationship to communism of, 35, 59, 76, 79, 131–49, 207–8; Hollywood images of, 87–91, 92–93, 97–103, 203; USSR said to be example of, 109, 143, 189; universal attraction of, 110, 331 (n. 6); idea of, used to link left- and right-wing dictatorships, 142, 143; as U.S. description of enemy in World War II, 189, 203–8; social hatred basis of, 204, 205, 206–7, 215

Fascism, Italian, 2, 15–16, 17, 28–29, 44, 64, 82, 134; positive U.S. assessments of, 16, 18, 26, 59, 63, 69, 73–75, 130–31; U.S. disenchantment with, 35–36; compared to Nazism and Stalinism, 40, 59, 66, 68, 69; and word "totalitarian," 61–62, 65, 252; and corporative state, 64. *See also* Anti-Fascism (opposition to Italian regime); Italy; Mussolini, Benito

Fay, Sidney B., 71

Fear in Battle (Dollard), 181–82

Federal Bureau of Investigation (FBI), 102, 135

Federalists, 283

Federal Theatre Project, 10

Federn, Ernst, 340 (n. 37)

Federn, Paul, 340 (n. 37)

Femininity, 55, 101, 279

Feminism, 43

Ferenczi, Sándor, 266–67, 274, 340 (n. 37)

Feuerstaufe (Baptism by Fire), 177

Field Service Regulations, 185

Fighting 69th, 168

Film industry, U.S. *See* Hollywood

Finland, 12, 100, 132, 155, 189, 193–94, 220

Fireside Chats. *See* Roosevelt, Franklin Delano (FDR): use of radio by

Fischer, Louis, 22–23

Fitzhugh, George, 341 (n. 66)

Fitzsimmons, M. A., 294

Five-Year Plans, Soviet, 3, 21, 22

Flynn, John T., 205–8

Ford, Henry, 96

Foreign Affairs, 22, 64

Foreign correspondents, 3, 13, 65, 66, 81, 84, 112

Foreignness, 144, 252, 257, 273, 297

Fortune, 20, 35, 82, 94, 101, 108, 222, 272

Four Freedoms, 158, 182, 189, 330 (n. 77)

Fox, Richard Wightman, 268

Fox Movietone News, 28

France, 86, 98

Franco, Francisco, 56, 78, 79, 82–83, 97, 114, 323 (n. 68)

Frank, Anne, 340–41 (n. 41)

Frank, Bruno, 217

Frank Capra Productions, 114, 115

Frankfurt School, 70, 107, 267

Freedom and the Economic System (Hayek), 272

French Revolution, 2, 5

Freud, Anna, 266–67, 274, 340 (n. 37)

Freud, Sigmund, 108

Freudianism: popularity of, in U.S., 54, 340–41 (n. 41); and Fromm, 107, 112, 274, 281; as one root of fascism, 110; and reconstruction of Germany, 211; and Bettelheim, 263, 266–67, 295, 340 (nn. 37, 38)

Friedrich, Carl, 63–64, 152–53, 241, 251, 253, 300–301, 309 (n. 11), 338 (n. 4)

Friends of the New Germany, 36–37. *See also* German American Bund

Fromm, Erich, 70, 104, 110, 112, 120, 244, 316 (n. 34); Freudianism of, 107, 112, 274; and skepticism, 127; and need for radical social transformation, 128, 280–81; use of word "totalitarian" by, 146, 148; on *Is Germany Incurable?*, 209, 211; and *Vital Center*, 279; and *Origins of Totalitarianism*, 298

Front organizations, 296, 299

Fussell, Paul, 166

Gabriel over the White House (film), 3, 30–33, 34, 41, 42, 44, 45, 83

Gabriel over the White House (novel; Tweed), 31, 32

Gagging the Dictators, 86, 313 (n. 13)

Garbo, Greta, 98, 133, 320 (n. 16)

Geisel, Theodor (pseud. Dr. Seuss), 172

Gender, 43, 45, 46, 54, 55. *See also* Femininity; Masculinity; Women

Generation of Vipers (Wylie), 326 (n. 21)

Gentile, Giovanni, 62, 64

German American Bund, 37, 113, 135, 136–37, 214. *See also* Friends of the New Germany

German Americans, 36, 39–40, 113, 200–201, 214–15, 217

German Christianity, 37, 66, 67

Germans, 71; distinguished from Nazis, 12, 87, 182, 190–91, 193–94, 198–99, 208, 214–15; as collectively responsible for Nazism, 94, 101, 208–13; "good," 190, 191, 198–99, 211, 247, 300, 331 (n. 7), 333–34 (n. 51); U.S. images of, during World War I, 190, 276; U.S. representations of, during World War II, 190–91, 216–18, 219, 220; as victims of Nazism, 193, 252; U.S. at war with, not just Nazis, 208–13; as utterly unlike Americans, 214–15, 234. *See also* Germany; Nazism

Germany, 2, 4, 17, 44, 78, 79, 80, 86, 91, 94, 100, 199, 257; invasion of USSR by, 7, 12, 91, 155–56, 224, 227, 229, 230, 232, 233, 239; invasion of

Poland by, 7, 87, 91; expansion of Nazi, before World War II, 7, 88, 131; rise of Nazism in, 11, 41, 65, 73, 96, 110; Nazi, as example of totalitarianism, 12, 70, 241; U.S. visitors to, 33, 38, 51, 73; during Weimar period, 33, 44, 46–51, 58, 62, 73, 74, 196; image of, in U.S., 36, 46, 47–51, 104, 105, 109, 276–77; religion in Nazi, 37, 65, 66–67, 86–87; Nazi Machtergreifung (seizure of power) in, 39, 46, 98; Nazi, as only example of totalitarian state, 61, 65–71; influence of idea of "total state" in, 62–63; Nazi, as one of many regimes with totalitarian state, 72–76, 150; military of Nazi, 97, 99, 101; invasion of Greece by, 172, 193–94; postwar reconstruction of, 191–92, 201, 209, 211–13, 218, 234, 266; predisposed to Nazism, 208–13, 217–18; Nazi, as huge concentration camp, 265, 275. *See also* Germans; Nazism; Nazi-Soviet Pact

Germany: A Self-Portrait (Crippen), 209

Germany Will Try It Again (Schulz), 212

Gershwin, Ira, 228

Gestapo, 40, 247, 264, 265, 275, 280

Gilmore, Lowell, 230

"Giovinezza" (Fascist anthem), 28

Gleason, Abbott, 61

Gleason, James, 117

Gleichschaltung (coordination), 66, 73, 95

Goebbels, Josef, 40–41, 62–63, 190

Gompers, Samuel, 18, 23, 36

Goodman, Paul, 326 (n. 15)

Good Society (Lippmann), 146

Gordon, Lincoln, 259, 260

Göring, Hermann, 40, 85, 190

Government Information Manual for the Motion Picture Industry, 159, 171, 175, 194–96, 225, 228

Gow, James, 200
Graebner, Walter, 237, 238, 239
Granger, Farley, 228
Grant, Cary, 171–72
Granville, Bonita, 198
Great Depression, 5, 7, 58, 65, 71, 192–93; and U.S. views of dictatorship, 3, 16, 17, 18, 24, 61, 95, 276; effect on U.S. families of, 43; optimism about democracy and human nature during, 254, 275, 305 (n. 35); political legacies of, 278
Great Dictator, The, 87–91, 92–93
Green, William, 23
Gregory, Horace, 53
Grinker, Roy R., 162–63, 181, 326 (nn. 19, 21)
Gunther, John, 85
Guttmann, Allen, 97

Haas, Hugo, 230
Hague, Frank, 223
Halfitarianism, 321 (n. 41)
Hall, Mordaunt, 31
Hamilton, Alexander, 283, 284
Handlin, Oscar, 294
Hanfstaengl, Ernst "Putzi," 38
Hansen, Alvin, 261
Harcourt Brace, 293
Harding, Warren G., 31
Harper's, 248–49
Hart, Henry, 53
Hatch, Robert, 290, 342 (n. 81), 342–43 (nn. 84, 85)
Hawthorne, Nathaniel, 281–82
Hayek, Friedrich, 254, 271–73
Hayes, Carlton J. H., 69, 150, 151, 152, 297
Hays, Will, 31, 42
Hays Office, 31, 133, 134
Hearst, William Randolph, 31, 32, 38, 222
Heaton, Herbert, 148
Hecht, Ben, 277
Heckscher, August, 294–95

Hegel, G. W. F., 63, 191, 269, 273
Hegelianism, 62, 63, 70
Hegemann, Werner, 65
Heidegger, Martin, 293
Hell, 299
Hellman, Geoffrey, 116
Hellman, Lillian, 228, 229
Hemingway, Ernest, 97
Here Is Germany, 217–18
Herrmann, Bernard, 91
He Stayed for Breakfast, 133
Heydrich, Reinhard, 190
Hidden Enemy: The German Threat to Post-War Peace (Pol), 212
High, Stanley, 65, 136–37
Hilton, James, 342 (n. 81), 343 (n. 86)
Hinchman, Lewis and Sandra, 343 (n. 90)
Hindenburg, Paul von, 11
Hitler, Adolf, 24, 29, 33, 54, 68, 91, 98, 114, 153, 181, 190, 199, 201, 203, 222, 232, 240, 244, 284, 313 (n. 18); and changing views of dictatorship in U.S., 17, 40, 58; compared to Stalin, 21, 59, 308–9 (n. 2); compared to Mussolini, 36, 39, 40, 68; initial responses to, in U.S., 36–41, 69; religious policies of, 37, 65, 66; anticommunism of, 38, 39; antisemitism of, 38, 40, 84, 88; purported U.S. sympathy for, 38–39, 306 (n. 52); purported sexual deviance of, 40, 42, 54, 84–85, 89; as "Little Man," 40, 84, 89; purported insanity of, 40, 85, 86–87; and women, 44, 85; rise to power of, 51, 61, 62, 65, 66, 79, 96, 107, 195, 212; and idea of totalitarian state, 63, 65, 66, 67, 69; comedic portrayals of, 84–91; as not personally responsible for Nazism, 94, 108, 129–30; and propaganda, 101, 108, 112, 116; as leader of international movement, 135; in U.S. propaganda films, 178, 180, 217, 218; said to emerge

from mob, 298. *See also* Germany; Nazism

Hitler's Children, 14, 197–200, 201–2

Hitler's Reign of Terror, 39–40

Hofstadter, Richard, 8

Hollywood, 42, 89, 114, 115, 133, 159, 160–61, 198; and dictatorial desires, 28–33; and images of Germany, 46, 47–49, 87, 118; and gender, 46, 51, 56; and European markets, 47, 87, 97–98, 222; antifascist filmmaking in, 83, 87–88, 97–102, 104, 110–11, 113–20, 134, 203; and images of USSR, 132–34, 228–33, 235–36, 242–43; and images of communism, 132–34, 319–20 (nn. 13, 14); and totalitarianism and science fiction, 300. *See also* Hays Office; Office of War Information (OWI)

Hollywood Anti-Nazi League, 85, 133, 203, 319–20 (n. 13)

Hollywood NOW, 85

Holmes, John Haynes, 65, 161

Holocaust, 84, 247, 266, 267, 276–77, 292, 301, 340–41 (n. 41)

Holt, Tim, 198

Homeier, Skip, 200

Home of the Brave (play; Laurents), 169

Homosexuality, 40–41, 54, 85, 187, 280

Hook, Sidney, 6, 144–45, 146, 153, 243, 255, 268

Hoover, Calvin B., 73–75, 76, 139, 149, 323 (n. 65)

Hoover, Herbert: after presidency, 7, 43, 59, 60; as president, 25, 31, 32, 35, 42, 64–65; as engineer, 96

Hoover, J. Edgar, 102

Hopkins, Harry, 228

Horkheimer, Max, 267

"Horst Wessel Song," 99, 113, 315 (n. 13)

Houseman, John, 121, 122

How the Army Fights (Limpus), 186

How to Treat the Germans (Ludwig), 212

Hughes, H. Stuart, 294–95

Human Condition (Arendt), 292

Human nature, 138–39, 254, 269–71, 275, 284, 285, 291, 300, 302

Huntley, G. P., Jr., 49

Huston, John, 217

Huston, Walter, 30, 228

Hutchins, Robert M., 243

Hutchinson, Paul, 207–8

Huxley, Aldous, 288

"I Am an American Day," 157

Ideology, 75, 128, 149–50

I'm an American! (radio show), 115–16

Immigration, 18, 104, 168

Imperialism, 292, 294, 297

Individualism, 18, 54, 73, 143, 167, 272

Individuality, 96, 102, 112–27, 159, 166–68, 170–71, 253, 280, 298

In Fact, 203

Inside Europe (Gunther), 85

In Stalin's Secret Service (Krivitsky), 153

Institute for Public Service, 129

Institut für Sozialforschung. *See* Frankfurt School

International Encyclopedia of the Social Sciences, 301

International Olympic Committee (IOC), 78

Interventionism, 4, 87, 178; of liberals and the left, 7, 81; and concept of totalitarianism, 12, 130, 153–56, 188, 301; and nature of dictatorial threat, 128, 193; among Protestants, 268

Invasion from Mars (Cantril), 125–27

I Saw Hitler!, 33, 40

Is Germany Incurable? (Brickner), 209–11, 213, 266

Isms, 129–30, 137–39, 144, 176

ISMS (American Legion), 139

Isolationism. *See* Noninterventionism

Italian Americans, 18, 36, 216

Italians: as victims of Fascism, 193

and mob, 297–99. *See also* Crowd, chaotic; Crowd, regimented; Crowd mind; Mob; Political movements, mass

Mass movements. *See* Political movements, mass

Mass psychology. *See* Psychology, social

Matteotti, Giacomo, 16

Mauldin, Bill, 182, 208, 219

Mayer, Louis B., 31

McBride, Joseph, 114, 177–78, 335 (n. 14)

McCarthy, Frank, 176–77

McCarthy, Joseph, 282

McCarthy, Mary, 293

McCormick, Robert, 7, 222

McElroy, Robert, 311 (n. 34)

Mead, Margaret, 209

Mechanization, social, 96, 98, 109. *See also* Machine

Media, 9–11, 90, 101, 104, 112–27

Meet John Doe, 9, 10, 98, 100, 114, 115–20, 124, 317 (nn. 55, 58). *See also* Capra, Frank

Mein Kampf (Hitler), 52, 84, 86, 108

Mellett, Lowell, 159, 179

Melosh, Barbara, 54

Men Must Act (Mumford), 109

Men under Stress (Grinker and Spiegel), 162–63, 181, 326 (nn. 19, 21)

Mercury Theatre, 10, 121–24, 126, 318 (n. 65)

Meredith, Burgess, 91

Metro-Goldwyn-Mayer (MGM), 31, 228, 320 (n. 14)

Mickey Mouse, 13

Middletown (Lynd and Lynd), 77

Middletown in Transition (Lynd and Lynd), 77

Militarism: of Nazism, 68, 88; of totalitarianism, 74, 151, 153, 154, 157, 161; of European dictatorships, 128; of Axis powers, 158, 206, 208, 216, 217, 223; in democracy at war, 158–59, 161, 206; as enemy in World War II, 194, 223

Military: as metaphor for nation, 27; German, 97, 99, 101, 184–85, 191, 193, 221; Soviet, 97, 221, 225, 227, 248; under totalitarianism, 151, 157, 168; in democracy, 158–59, 160–87. *See also* U.S. Army; U.S. War Department

Milland, Ray, 325–26 (n. 14)

Mission to Moscow (book; Davies), 235

Mission to Moscow (film), 228, 242–43, 318 (n. 65)

Mob, 19, 83, 215, 297–99

Modernity: problems of, 96, 104, 107, 109, 252, 253, 281

Modern Times, 87

Montgomery, Douglass, 48

Morale, combat, 181–82

Morale programs, military, 159–60, 175–83

Moral Man and Immoral Society (Niebuhr), 267–68

Mortal Storm, 98–99, 100, 101, 113, 133, 315 (n. 13)

Moscow show trials, 95, 130–31, 132, 242–43, 289

Motherhood, 54, 57, 326 (n. 21)

Moyers, Bill, 177

Mr. Deeds Goes to Town, 9, 114, 116, 317 (n. 55)

Mr. Lucky, 171–72

Mr. Smith Goes to Washington, 9–10, 114, 115–16, 317 (nn. 55, 56)

Multiethnic combat unit, 167–71, 215, 228, 230, 231, 327 (n. 35)

Mulvey, Laura, 318 (n. 70)

Mumford, Lewis, 11, 96, 109–10, 112, 138, 143, 189, 268, 316–17 (n. 41)

Mundelein, Cardinal George, 86

Munich Crisis, 122, 125

Munk, Frank, 241

Murphy, George, 166–67, 170

Mussolini, Benito, 11, 23, 32, 35, 56,

Ortega y Gasset, José, 305 (n. 41)
Orwell, George: and *Nineteen Eighty-Four*, 13, 251, 252, 253, 278, 285–92, 300, 301, 302, 342 (n. 73), 343 (n. 91); Burnham's influence on, 287–88, 289–90; and Arendt's *Origins*, 295–96
Osborn, Frederick, 180
Oumansky, Constantine, 155
Overmothering, 54, 326 (n. 21)

Pacifism, 66, 74, 91, 193, 278, 355 (n. 5)
Palmer, Maria, 230
Pan-Germanism, 191, 212
Papan, Franz von, 68
Paranoia, 41, 209–11
Parents' Magazine, 161
Parsons, Wilfrid, 141
Partisan Review, 9, 76, 267, 280, 281, 286, 293, 294; and idea of totalitarianism, 140–41, 142
Pearl Harbor, 156, 160–61, 175, 192
Peck, Gregory, 230
Pelley, William Dudley, 204
Penn, Dena, 230
People's War in Russia. See *Why We Fight: Battle of Russia*
Pepper, Claude, 161
Permanent Revolution (Neumann), 241
Perry, Ralph Barton, 148, 152
Pessimism, political, 253–75, 278, 281–82, 285, 291, 302
Peters, Susan, 231
Peterson, Edgar, 177
Petrified Forest (play; Sherwood), 100
Phantom Public (Lippmann), 19
Phelps, William Lyon, 69
Pichel, Irving, 330–31 (n. 86)
Pitkin, Hanna Fenichel, 299–300
Pius XI, 142
Pluralism: as foundation of democracy, 130, 138, 139, 146–47, 270, 284, 285; in wartime, 170–71, 183–84, 196–97, 234

PM, 244
Pol, Heinz, 212, 333–34 (n. 51)
Political movements, mass: suspicion of, 12, 54, 76, 117, 118, 130, 152–53, 301–2, 318 (n. 67); and idea of totalitarianism, 76, 253; and managerial revolution, 258
Politics, 267, 293, 340 (n. 38)
Polls, 305 (n. 33); on U.S. participation in 1936 Olympics, 78; on dictatorship in U.S., 80; on existence of Nazi "Fifth Column" in U.S., 136, 320 (n. 21); on U.S. entering World War II, 156, 160, 324 (n. 79), 325 (n. 13); in *War Comes to America*, 179; on U.S. views of Germans, 219; on U.S. views of Russo-German war, 224, 335 (n. 9); on Spanish Civil War, 311–12 (n. 4); on FDR's third term, 312 (n. 5); on court packing, 312 (n. 6); on FDR's policies leading to dictatorship, 312 (n. 7); on U.S. preference among Mussolini, Hitler, and Stalin, 313 (n. 18)
Popular Front, 4–5, 10, 13, 76, 80–81, 103, 133; antifascism of, 3–4, 6, 11–12, 80, 109, 203; populism of, 8, 11; shattered by Nazi-Soviet Pact, 90, 132, 189; and isms, 139; and collectivism, 143; and idea of totalitarianism, 146, 153; legacy of, 278, 279; latent totalitarianism in, 279, 280, 318 (n. 67). *See also* Communist Party, USA (CP)
Populism, 8–11, 114
Potter, M. F., 209
Poynter, Nelson, 159
Pratt, Fletcher, 153–54
President Vanishes, 44–46, 58
Price, Byron, 175, 183–84
Princeton Radio Project, 101–2. *See also* Cantril, Hadley
Prisoner of Zenda, 319–20 (n. 13)
Private Snafu films, 172–73, 328–29 (nn. 48–50)

Production Code Administration. *See* Hays Office

Progressive Citizens of America (PCA), 279

Progressive Party (1920s), 23

Progressive Party (1948), 279

Propaganda, 74, 243, 300; U.S., for intervention in Europe, 89, 90; U.S., during World War II, 91, 116, 173, 176, 179, 216–18, 330–31 (n. 86); under dictatorship, 105, 111–12, 125; Axis, during World War II, 177, 178–79, 195; images of USSR in U.S., during World War II, 225–28; under totalitarianism, 295, 299. *See also* Office of War Information (OWI)

Protestantism, 37, 66–68, 72, 78, 82, 84, 108–9, 222, 267–69. See also *Christian Century; Christianity and Crisis;* Confessional Church (Germany); German Christianity; Germany: religion in Nazi; Niebuhr, Reinhold

Prussianism, 209, 213, 273

Pseudo-self, 108, 109

Psychiatrists, 162–63, 209–11, 212

Psychoanalysis. *See* Freudianism

Psychology, social, 57; of dictatorship, 17, 95, 101, 125; of military, 159–60, 162–63, 187; of democracy, 181; of Germany, 209–12; of Nazism, 264–67; of concentration camps, 264–67, 295

Psychology of Social Movements (Cantril), 318 (n. 67)

Public Opinion (Lippmann), 19

Pudovkin, Vsevelod, 228

Quisling, Vidkun, 215

Quitman, Gertrude, 129–30, 138–39

Race: in U.S. during World War II, 168–71, 215, 328 (n. 43)

Radio, 36; use of, by FDR, 41–42, 116, 158, 174, 175, 193; in representations of dictatorship, 88, 101–2, 198, 232; plays, 91–93, 97, 121–27, 165; in Capra films, 115–16, 117, 118, 119

Rahv, Philip, 140, 285, 291, 342 (n. 81), 342–43 (n. 84)

Raines, Claude, 9, 116

Ramparts We Watch, 177

Randolph, A. Philip, 243

Rationality, 159, 186

Rauschning, Herman, 153, 212

Razin, Stenka, 225, 248

Reader's Digest, 14, 85, 198, 272

Reagan, Ronald, 167, 301

Reconstruction, post–World War II: and Germany, 191–92, 201, 209, 211, 212, 213, 218, 234, 266; and USSR, 223–24, 234, 240

Red Army, 97, 221, 225, 227, 248

Red Army Oath, 227, 229, 230–31

Red Scare, First (1919), 18, 95

Red Scare, Second (post–World War II), 301

Reed, Alan, 230

Reed, Dave, 25, 304 (n. 21)

Refugee intellectuals, 3, 13, 18, 28, 65, 66, 69–70, 112, 212, 294

Regimentation, 36; in dictatorships, 69, 105, 106, 110, 157, 171, 205–6; fears of, in U.S., 95, 96, 132, 154; and sexuality, 99–101; in regimented crowd, 102; in modern societies, 109–10; in democracy at war, 158–59, 161–64, 185–86. *See also* Discipline

Reichstag: burning of, 38

Republican Party, 4, 6, 7, 79, 80, 105, 114, 159, 240

Research Committee on Social Trends, 35

Resisting Enemy Interrogation, 330–31 (n. 86)

Revolt of the Masses (Ortega y Gasset), 305 (n. 41)

Revolution of Nihilism (Rauschning), 153

to be tolerated despite differences from U.S., 234–35, 237–38; and U.S. could learn politically from each other, 234–35, 238–39; negative U.S. assessments of, during World War II, 239–41, 246–47; assessments of, during Cold War, 253, 290, 301; James Burnham's views of, 255–57. *See also* Communism, Soviet; Moscow show trials; Nazi-Soviet Pact; Russia; Russian Revolution (1917); U.S.-Soviet alliance (World War II)

Spain, 78–79, 80, 81, 82, 86, 97, 100, 129

Spanish Civil War, 7, 80, 99, 132, 204; debates over, in U.S., 78–79, 82, 97, 311–12 (n. 4), 323 (n. 68); Abraham Lincoln Brigade in, 181–82

Spewack, Samuel, 177

Spiegel, John P., 162–63, 181, 326 (nn. 19, 21)

Spiegelgass, Leonard, 335 (n. 14)

Spiro, Herbert J., 301

SS (Schutzstaffel), 90, 94, 98

Stalin, Josef, 3, 6, 29, 53, 56, 57, 68, 144, 245, 284, 313 (n. 18), 319–20 (n. 13); personal qualities of, 21–23, 24, 42; as similar to Hitler, 59, 308–9 (n. 2); in political cartoons, 86; as not personally responsible for Communism, 130; and World War II, 155, 224, 228, 232, 234, 237–38, 240, 248, 338 (n. 62); Trotskyist views of, 255; during Cold War, 290, 298, 301. *See also* Communism, Soviet; Soviet Union (USSR)

Stalinism. *See* Communism, Soviet

Standley, William, 338 (n. 62)

Stanwyck, Barbara, 10, 116

State, 62, 88, 95, 253, 255, 256; involvement in economy of, 35, 36, 64, 206; concept of, in U.S. political science, 63–64, 70, 71; relationship between democratic and totalitar-

ian, 74, 75, 311 (n. 35); growth of, in U.S., 79, 106. *See also* Corporative state; Totalitarian state

Stato corporativo. See Corporative state

Stato totalitario. See Totalitarian state

Stein, Gertrude, 56, 57

Steiner, Arthur, 71

Sten, Anna, 100

Steuben Society of America, 39–40

Stewart, Donald Ogden, 203, 319–20 (n. 13)

Stewart, James, 9, 98, 116

Stimson, Henry, 175–76, 226

Stites, Richard, 319–20 (n. 13)

Strasser, Gregor, 333–34 (n. 51)

Strasser, Otto, 212, 333–34 (n. 51)

Strecker, Edward, 102–3, 209, 326 (n. 21)

Streit, Clarence, 20

Stroheim, Erich von, 229

Strunsky, Simeon, 68, 311 (n. 35)

Studebaker "Dictator," 15–17, 24

Studies in Social Psychology in World War II, 160, 328 (nn. 39, 43), 330 (nn. 69, 76)

Sturzo, Luigi, 64

Sullavan, Margaret, 48, 98–99

Suvarov, Alexander, 225

Taft, Robert, 155–56

Taggard, Genevieve, 53

Taylor, Frederick W., 96

Taylor, Kressmann, 317 (n. 45)

Taylor, Robert, 231

Tchaikovsky, Peter, 227, 231–32

Team: as metaphor for U.S. military, 165–67

Technics and Civilization (Mumford), 96

Their Mothers' Sons (Strecker), 326 (n. 21)

There Shall Be No Night (play; Sherwood), 100, 113, 193–94

of, to U.S., 63, 65–66, 76; concept of, used to mean state's claim of competence in all aspects of life, 67, 68, 69, 71, 73, 76, 139, 149. *See also* State; Totalitarian (word); Totalitarianism

Totalitarian system (*sistema totalitaria*), 61. *See also* Totalitarian (word); Totalitarianism; Totalitarian state; Total state (*totaler Staat*)

Total state (*totaler Staat*), 62–63. *See also* State; Totalitarian (word); Totalitarianism; Totalitarian state; Totalitarian system

Toumanova, Tamara, 230

Tourian, Leon, 215–16

Tribune, 288

Trilling, Diana, 290, 342 (n. 81)

Trilling, Lionel, 285, 290, 342 (n. 81)

Triumph of the Will, 177

Trotsky, Leon, 23, 255–56, 287

Trotskyism, 6, 140, 145, 255–57, 274

Truman, Harry S, 279

Truppenführung, 184–85

Truth, 124–27, 173–76, 178–86, 195

Tweed, Thomas F., 31, 32

Twilight Zone, 300

Tydings, Millard, 37

Tyranny of Words (Chase), 315 (n. 11)

Under Cover (Carlson), 215–16, 273, 283

Undset, Sigrid, 209, 211

United Mine Workers, 7

United Nations (World War II), 158, 182, 189, 225, 227, 231, 240, 277, 325 (n. 4)

U.S. Army: training manuals, 18–19, 164–65, 172, 184–85; Information and Education Division, 159–60, 170–71, 176, 178, 180–83, 330–31 (n. 86); Air Force Medical Corps, 162–63; Signal Corps, 172, 177, 196. *See also* Military; U.S. War Department

U.S. Congress, 25, 26, 27, 28, 104. *See also* U.S. House of Representatives; U.S. Senate

U.S. Department of Justice, 115–16

U.S. House of Representatives: Committee on Un-American Activities, 135

U.S. Office of Education, 4, 145

U.S. Olympic Committee, 78

U.S. Senate, 79, 82, 90, 135

U.S.-Soviet alliance (World War II), 12, 192, 220, 232; Red Army and Russian people as central images of, in U.S., 221, 224–34, 235; anticommunist support for, 222–23; continuation of, after World War II, 234, 239–40; criticism of, 239, 241–43; collapse of, after World War II, 251, 277

U.S. Supreme Court, 80, 81. *See also* Court packing

U.S. War Department, 19, 159–60, 162–63, 172, 186. *See also* Military; U.S. Army

Van Creveld, Martin, 185

Vanderbilt, Cornelius, 39

Vandenberg, Arthur, 154

Van Doren, Carl, 53

Vann, Gerald, 142

Vansittart, Robert, 208, 213

Vansittartism, 208, 213

Vatican, 20, 240

Vernon, Glenn, 230

Versailles Treaty, 191, 213

Veterans, 162–63

Victor Emanuel II, King (of Italy), 11

Virginia Quarterly, 73, 75, 139

Vital Center (Schlesinger), 13, 251, 253, 278, 279–85, 300, 341 (n. 66), 342 (n. 73)

Voluntarism, 157, 171–73